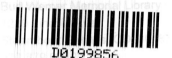

Panama

THIS EDITION WRITTEN AND RESEARCHED BY
Carolyn McCarthy, Steve Fallon

PLAN YOUR TRIP

MACDUFF EVERTON / GETTY IMAGES ©

CAYOS ZAPATILLAS P200

DAVID TIPLING / GETTY IMAGES ©

HUMMINGBIRD, PARQUE NACIONAL SOBERANÍA P78

ON THE ROAD

Contents

UNDERSTAND

SURVIVAL GUIDE

SPECIAL FEATURES

Welcome to Panama

From clear turquoise seas to the coffee farms and cloud forests of Chiriquí, Panama can be as chilled out or as thrilling as you wish.

Endless Summer

With a spate of deserted islands, chilled Caribbean vibes on one side and monster Pacific swells on the other, Panama sits poised to deliver the best of beach life. And a whole other world begins at the water's edge. Seize it by scuba diving with whale sharks in the Pacific, snorkeling the rainbow reefs of Bocas del Toro or setting sail in the indigenous territory of Guna Yala, where virgin isles sport nary a footprint. Meanwhile surfers will be psyched to have world-class breaks all to themselves. Hello, paradise.

Cosmopolitan Panama

The dazzling blue coastline and shimmering skyscrapers say Miami, though many joke that you hear more English spoken in Panama. Panama City is culturally diverse and driven, rough-edged yet sophisticated. There's much that's new or improved. Central America's first subway is ready, the historic Casco district is renovated and a massive canal expansion nears completion. Take in the city's funky particulars. Pedal the coastal green space, explore the Casco or attend an avant-garde performance and you will realize this tropical capital isn't just about salsa: that's just the backbeat.

The Great Outdoors

In Panama, nature is all about discovery. Explore the ruins of Spanish forts on the Caribbean coast or boat deep into indigenous territories in a dugout canoe. Wildlife is incidental: a resplendent quetzal on the highland trail, an unruly troupe of screeching howler monkeys outside your cabin or a breaching whale that turns your ferry ride into an adrenaline-filled event. Adventure tourism means zipping through rainforest canopies, swimming alongside sea turtles or trekking to sublime cloud-forest vistas. One small tropical country with two long coasts makes for a pretty big playground.

Lost-World Adventure

You don't have to make it all the way to the Darién to get off the beaten path – though if you do, you've hit one of the most biodiverse spots on the planet. Go where the wild things are. Soak in the spray of towering waterfalls near highland Santa Fé. Visit one of Panama's seven indigenous groups through community tourism. Live out your castaway fantasies in the Guna Yala or idle on a wilderness beach in Península de Azuero. Howl back at the creatures sharing the canopy. Panama is as wild as you want it to be.

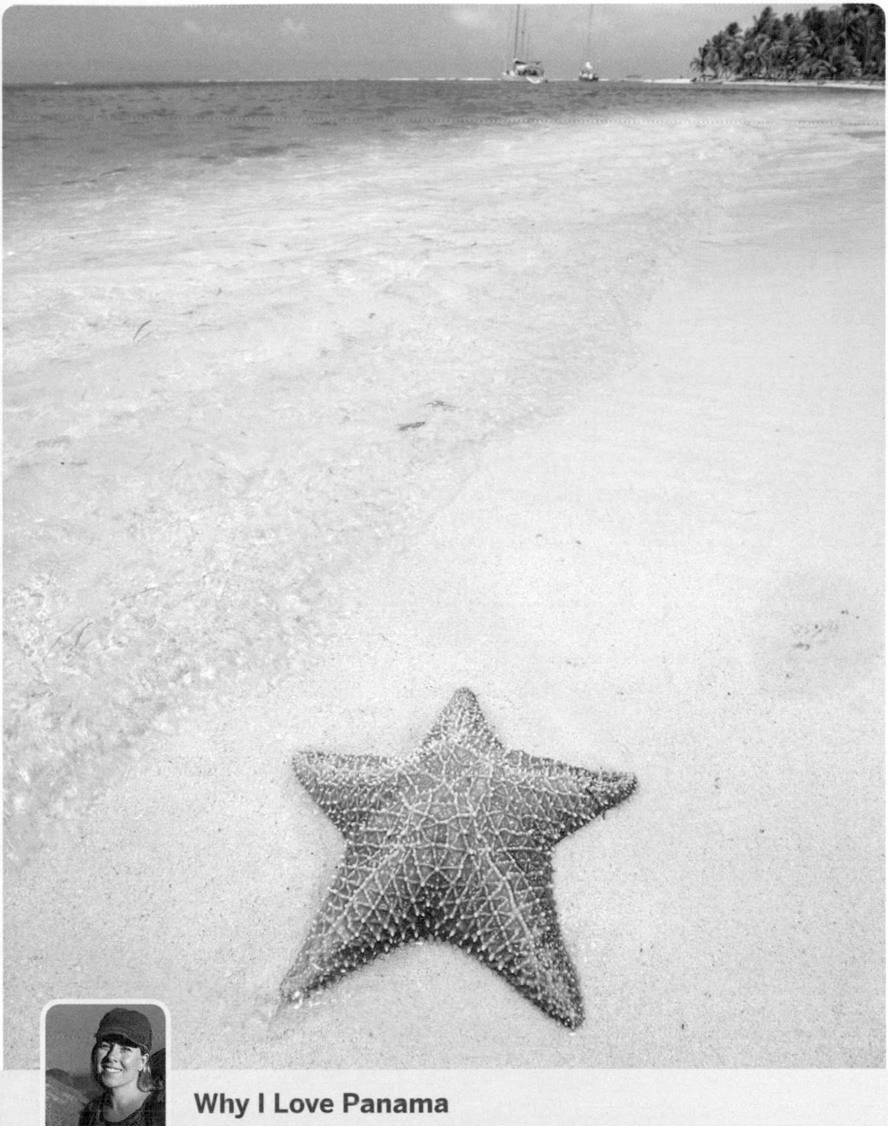

Why I Love Panama

By Carolyn McCarthy, Writer

In a world where wilderness and native cultures are disappearing, Panama – against all odds – continues with its essence intact. Trekking through rainforests, watching Congo drumming and sailing between pristine tropical islands offer wonder and delight. The wildlife viewing is astounding both in expected places, like the waters of Isla de Coiba, and in patches of preserved forest just outside the capital. For me Panama is a confluence – an explosion of nature, cultures and beliefs in that messy, musical arrangement that's everyday life in Latin America. All that energy feeds you, and you see the world in new ways.

For more about our writers, see p320

Above: Beach, Archipiélago de San Blás p236

Panama

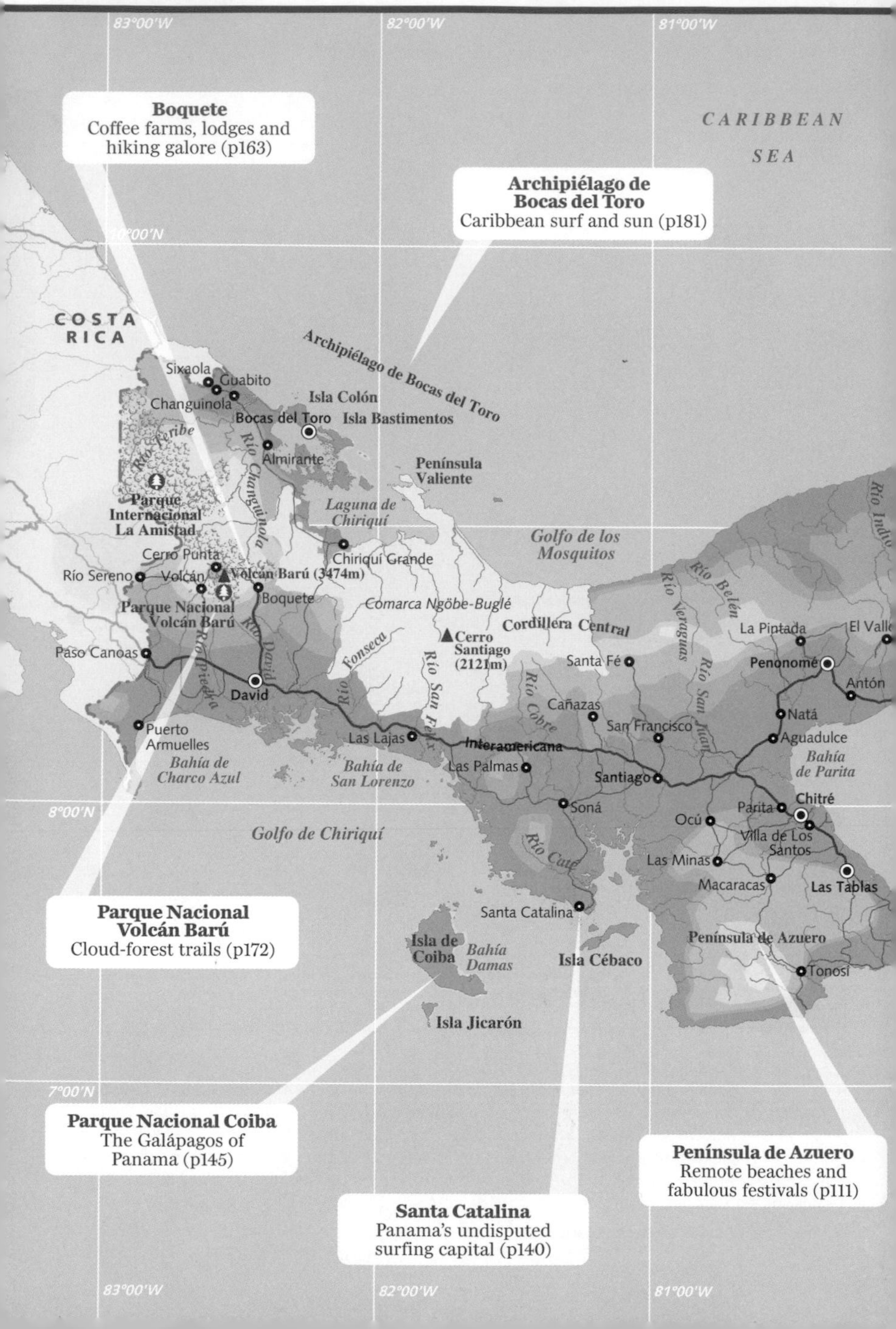
Boquete
Coffee farms, lodges and hiking galore (p163)
Archipiélago de Bocas del Toro
Caribbean surf and sun (p181)
Parque Nacional Volcán Barú
Cloud-forest trails (p172)
Parque Nacional Coiba
The Galápagos of Panama (p145)
Santa Catalina
Panama's undisputed surfing capital (p140)
Península de Azuero
Remote beaches and fabulous festivals (p111)
CARIBBEAN SEA
COSTA RICA
Archipiélago de Bocas del Toro
Sixaola
Guabito
Changuinola
Isla Colón
Bocas del Toro
Isla Bastimentos
Almirante
Península Valiente
Laguna de Chiriquí
Parque Internacional La Amistad
Río Teribe
Río Changuinola
Chiriquí Grande
Golfo de los Mosquitos
Cerro Punta
Río Sereno
Volcán
Volcán Barú (3474m)
Boquete
Parque Nacional Volcán Barú
Comarca Ngöbe-Buglé
Cerro Santiago (2121m)
Cordillera Central
Paso Canoas
David
Río David
Río Piedra
Río Fonseca
Río San Félix
Santa Fé
Río Cobre
Cañazas
San Francisco
Río Belén
Río Veraguas
Río San Juan
La Pintada
El Valle
Penonomé
Antón
Natá
Aguadulce
Bahía de Parita
Río Indio
Puerto Armuelles
Bahía de Charco Azul
Las Lajas
Bahía de San Lorenzo
Interamericana
Las Palmas
Santiago
Soná
Golfo de Chiriquí
Río Cate
Parita
Chitré
Ocú
Villa de Los Santos
Las Minas
Macaracas
Las Tablas
Santa Catalina
Isla de Coiba
Bahía Damas
Isla Cébaco
Península de Azuero
Tonosí
Isla Jicarón
83°00'W
82°00'W
81°00'W
10°00'N
8°00'N
7°00'N

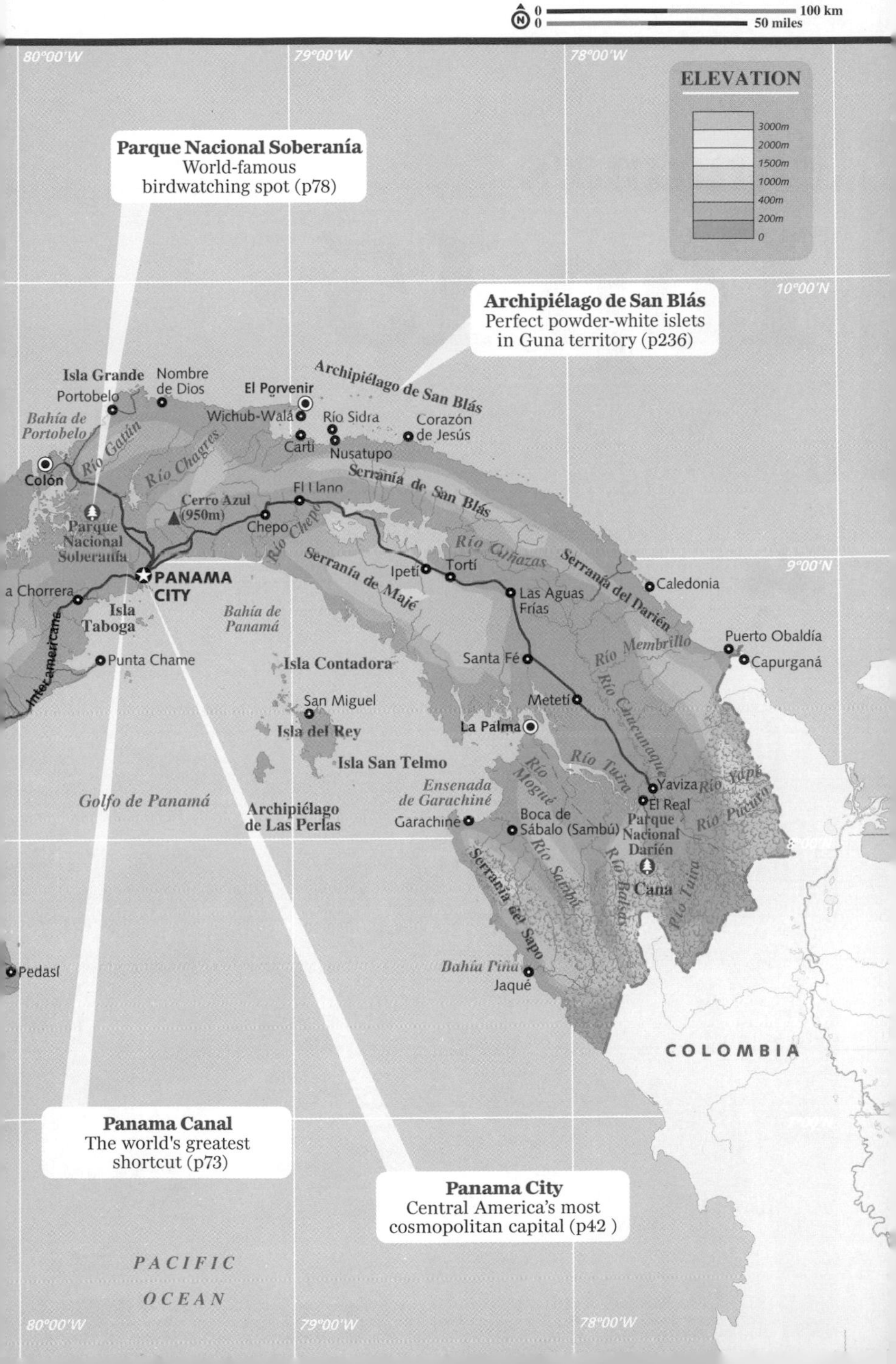

0
100 km
0
50 miles
ELEVATION
3000m
2000m
1500m
1000m
400m
200m
0
80°00'W
79°00'W
78°00'W
10°00'N
9°00'N
Parque Nacional Soberanía
World-famous birdwatching spot (p78)
Archipiélago de San Blás
Perfect powder-white islets in Guna territory (p236)
Isla Grande
Nombre de Dios
Portobelo
Bahía de Portobelo
El Porvenir
Archipiélago de San Blás
Wichub-Walá
Río Sidra
Corazón de Jesús
Cartí
Nusatupo
Río Gatún
Río Chagres
Colón
Serranía de San Blás
El Llano
Cerro Azul (950m)
Chepo
Río Chepo
Parque Nacional Soberanía
Río Cañazas
Serranía del Darién
Serranía de Majé
Ipetí
Tortí
PANAMA CITY
a Chorrera
Las Aguas Frías
Caledonia
Isla Taboga
Bahía de Panamá
Interamericana
Punta Chame
Isla Contadora
Santa Fé
Río Membrillo
Puerto Obaldía
Capurganá
Río Chucunaque
Metetí
San Miguel
Isla del Rey
La Palma
Isla San Telmo
Río Tuira
Río Mogué
Ensenada de Garachiné
Yaviza
El Real
Golfo de Panamá
Archipiélago de Las Perlas
Garachiné
Boca de Sábalo (Sambú)
Parque Nacional Darién
Río Pucuro
Río Sabalo
Río Balsas
Serranía del Sapo
Cana
Río Tuira
Pedasí
Bahía Piña
Jaqué
COLOMBIA
Panama Canal
The world's greatest shortcut (p73)
Panama City
Central America's most cosmopolitan capital (p42)
PACIFIC
OCEAN
80°00'W
79°00'W
78°00'W

Panama's Top 15

1

Panama City

1 Panama City (below left; p42) is high-octane Latin America: think *ceviche* (marinated seafood), casinos and a stacked skyline. For this sparkling city of nearly a million, transformation is afoot: coastal green space, a biodiversity museum, colonial restoration in Casco Viejo and Central America's first subway system. Sure, the traffic resembles a boa constrictor digesting one megalithic meal, but its appeal persists. People are real here and nature is never very far away. Beauty lives in the skewed rhythms, incongruous visions and fiery sunsets.

Panama Canal

2 One of the world's greatest shortcuts, the canal (below; p73) cuts right through the Continental Divide, linking the Atlantic and the Pacific. And it's worth marveling at. Just as stunning as the hulking steel container ships passing through the locks are the legions of creatures watching from the jungle fringes. Two visitors centers offer viewing platforms and museums that lay bare the construction and its expansion. There are also worthwhile boat and kayak trips on the waterway. Or you can book a partial transit and squeeze through the locks yourself.

GTS PRODUCTIONS / SHUTTERSTOCK ©

FOTOS593 / SHUTTERSTOCK ©

Casco Viejo

3 Don't miss Panama City's historical neighborhood of Casco Viejo (below; p45), full of crumbling convents and cobblestones. The colonial architecture may hark back to Havana, but this is not a spot where time stands still. It's as much about today's urban mix as the eclectic, easygoing vibe. The Cinta Costera, a recently completed green space, takes walkers and bikers from downtown past Casco Viejo. On sticky evenings artists' booths line the promenade, couples dine under parasols and live music fills the plazas.

Wildlife-Watching

4 Bring your binoculars. With 220 mammal and 978 bird species, Panama is crack for naturalists. Scarlet macaws (bottom), toucans, sloths and squirrel monkeys are just a few of the local stars. As a spectator sport, wildlife-watching is nothing short of thrilling, but it's the calls, cries and rumbles of the rainforest that will stamp your memory forever. Serious birdwatchers might head to the highlands (p163) to spot a quetzal or brave the Darién (p251) for a glimpse of the legendary harpy eagle.

ALFREDO MAIQUEZ / GETTY IMAGES ©

KATE / LONELY PLANET ©

Archipiélago de Bocas del Toro

5 No wonder this Caribbean island chain is Panama's number-one vacation spot (above; p181). 'It's all good,' say the locals. Pedal to the beach on a cruiser bike, hum to improvised calypso on Isla Bastimentos and laze over dinner in a thatched hut on the waterfront. Lodgings range from cheap backpacker digs to stunning jungle lodges and luxury resorts located on outer islands. Surfers hit the breaks, but there's also snorkeling with varied sea life or volunteering opportunities to help nesting sea turtles.

Boquete

6 A window into the country's wilder side, Panama's many festivals (p22) also reveal the breadth of cultures packed into this small nation. From Caribbean Congo celebrations in Portobelo to the vibrant folkloric traditions of the Península de Azuero, the three-day Guna stomp that is Nogapope or Panama City's open-air jazz festival, all of Panama loves a good rum-soaked time. When it's all over, a replenishing bowl of 'Get Up Lazarus' (a potent seafood soup) at Mercado de Mariscos (p63) in Panama City is in order.

Top: Festival de Diablos y Congos (p110)

Festiivals

7 Equal parts adventure hub and mountain retreat, Boquete (p163) is a magnet for expats, retirees and travelers of all stripes. Birdwatchers come for a glimpse of the resplendent quetzal, while adventurers come to climb a mountain, ride a zip line or raft white water. But what really moves this small town is the one of the world's most important export crops: coffee. Coffee farms (above) dot the countryside, with tours showing the process from leaf to cup. Fuel up, and you're ready for the next adventure.

8

LOGAN MOCK-BUNTING / GETTY IMAGES ©

9

10

Parque Nacional Coiba

8 Often compared to the Galápagos, this marine park (p145) is a veritable lost world of pristine ecosystems and unique fauna. Spy flocks of scarlet macaws, enormous schools of fish, migrating humpback whales with calves, and manta rays (pictured above) scuffing the ocean floor. Scuba divers might glimpse a hammerhead or a whale shark. Most importantly, it's still wild, with few visitors and little infrastructure. Not long ago an infamous prison isolated all on the main island, but now everyone comes here by choice.

Archipiélago de San Blás

9 With little to do but negotiate the price of a coconut, sway in a hammock or snorkel turquoise waters, many find the Archipiélago de San Blás (top right; p236) to be paradise here. Locally known as Guna Yala, this 400-plus-island archipelago in the Caribbean is an independent indigenous territory steeped in tradition. Get around by speedboat, sailboat or dugout canoe. Most guest lodges are remote palm-fringed islets surrounded by clear waters. The Guna residents mostly live on community islands teeming with livestock, commerce, and thatched or concrete homes.

The Highlands

10 In the tropics, the highlands (p163) are the equivalent of a breath of fresh air. Panama's highlands range from lush forest with tiny golden frogs to mist-covered coffee plantations. From Panama City, weekenders take to El Valle (pictured bottom; p95) and El Copé (p108). Boquete (p163) is the classic mountain town, but if you are looking to get off the beaten path, the hamlet of Santa Fé (p137) has true mountain tranquility, with local-led horse rides and hikes to waterfalls with swimming holes. Paradise is not lost.

Water Sports

11 Dive with a rare whale shark, ocean kayak around uninhabited islands or get soaked while rafting in the highlands. For many, it's fantasy enough to swim in warm waters teeming with tropical fish. Clear and colder, the Pacific is the best place to spot a wide variety of marine mammals, including whales, in spots such as Parque Nacional Coiba and the Golfo de Chiriquí, while the Caribbean is known for its colorful corals and starfish around Bocas del Toro and the powdery white-sand beaches of the Archipiélago de San Blás (p32).

Península de Azuero

12 Sweet landscapes of sculpted hills, lonely beaches and crashing surf feed the growing buzz: this rural peninsula (p111) has become today's hot getaway. Yet the strongest impression is one of tradition. Spanish culture has deep roots here, evident in the charm of tiled colonials, country hospitality, religious festivals and elaborate *polleras* (embroidered lace dresses). Playa Venao has emerged as a major surf destination, while to the west the delightfully untrammeled Sunset Coast has quiet beaches, great surfing and community turtle tours. Bottom: Fiesta de la Pollera (p123), Las Tablas

11

12

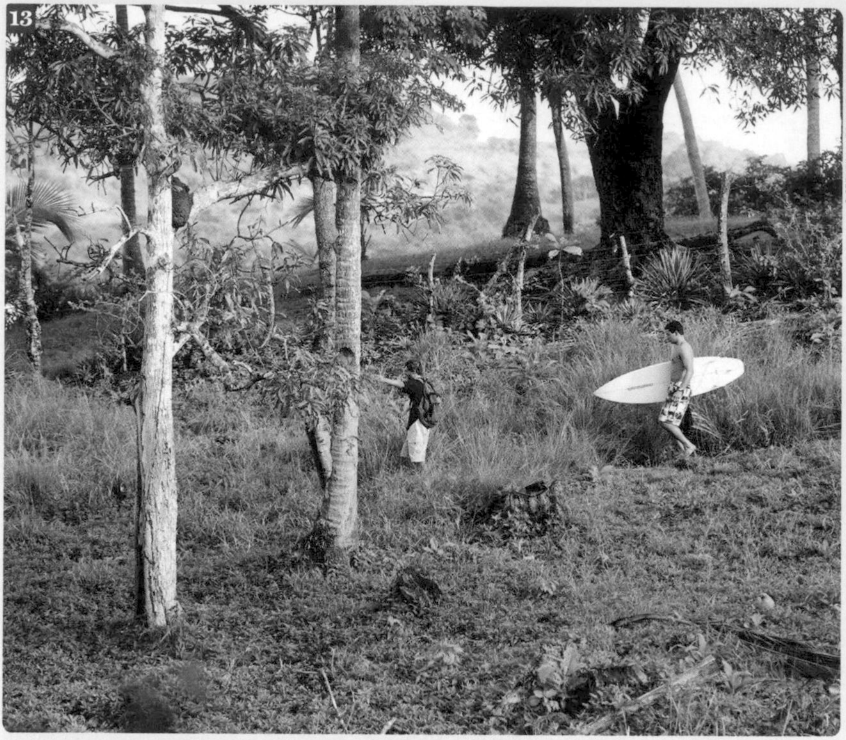

PAUL KENNEDY / GETTY IMAGES ©

Santa Catalina

13 This surf village (p140) is all small town, with wave-front *hotelitos* and hostels far off the one paved road. Here, nature is a delight and 'resort' is still a foreign word. The biggest draws are the world-class waves that roll in year-round but peak in February and March. The town is also the launching pad for excursions and diving trips into the wildlife-rich Parque Nacional Coiba, an island where nature and marine life flourish. Day trips here are now easier than ever.

Parque Nacional Volcán Barú

14 Panama's only volcano (top right; p173) dominates the landscape of the misty Chiriquí highlands. At 3474m it's also the highest point in the country. Enthusiasts can make the predawn climb, steep and usually muddy, for the reward of viewing the Atlantic and Pacific Oceans at the same time – *if* it's clear. Another, perhaps saner, option is the Sendero Los Quetzales, a stunning trail that traverses the park, crossing over the Caldera River, with the possibility of seeing exotic orchids, tapirs and resplendent quetzals.

Parque Nacional Soberanía

15 A day trip from the glass towers of Panama City and you're in one of the premier birdwatching sites in the world. Parque Nacional Soberanía (p78) has one of the most accessible tropical rainforests in Panama. While on the trail look for sloths, howler monkeys or white-faced capuchins. On Pipeline Rd more than 500 bird species – from toucans to tanagers (right) – have been sighted. For an alternative view of the canopy, climb the towers at Rainforest Discovery Center or visit the neighboring Emberá and Wounaan communities.

CHRISTIAN KOBER / GETTY IMAGES ©

ALFREDO MAIQUEZ / NTCO / GETTY IMAGES ©

Need to Know

For more information, see Survival Guide (p287)

Currency
US dollar ('Balboa'; $)

Language
Spanish

Visas
Visas are generally not required for stays of up to 90 days.

Money
ATMs are readily available except in the most isolated places. Credit cards are widely accepted at restaurants and upscale hotels, but may be problematic elsewhere.

Cell Phones
Local SIM cards can be used in unlocked phones. Choose your carrier carefully, as only certain operators have coverage in the San Blás Islands and Darién Province.

Time
During daylight-saving time (end of October to early April) Panama is on New York City/East Coast time. The rest of the year it is one hour behind New York.

When to Go

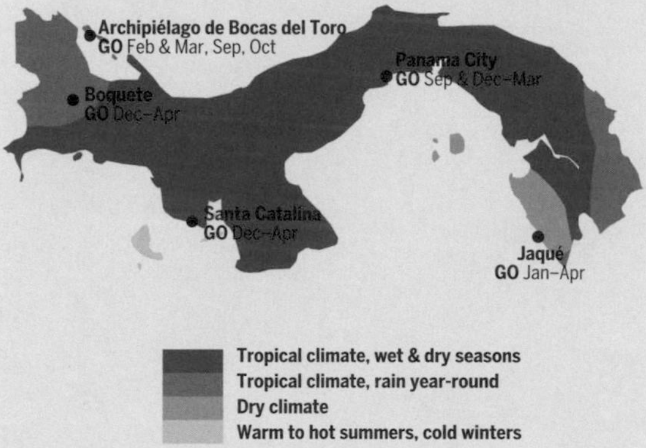

High Season (mid-Dec–mid-Apr)

- Corresponds with the Pacific-side dry season.
- Little rain in Panama City and elsewhere south of the Continental Divide.

High-Season Peak (holidays)

- Includes November festivals, Christmas and New Year, plus Easter.
- Hotel rates may be up to double that of normal rates.
- Resorts, festival towns and beaches are crowded with Panamanian vacationers.

Low Season (mid-Apr–early Dec)

- Corresponds with rainy season in most of the country.
- Rain is sporadic: check regional climate guides, as many destinations can still be enjoyed.
- Lodging rates and resorts are better priced.

Useful Websites

Visit Panama (www.visitpanama.com) The English-language official national tourism website.

The Panama News (www.thepanamanews.com) English newspaper useful for culture and local politics.

Lonely Planet (www.lonelyplanet.com/panama) The Thorn Tree forum, travel news and links to other useful sites.

Panama Info (www.panamainfo.com) Good travel resource.

Backpacking & Hacking Panama (www.backpackingandhackingpanama.com) Fun instructional videos

Important Numbers

Panama has no regional dialing codes.

Panama country code	☎507
International access code	☎106
Directory assistance	☎102
National tourist information	☎526-7000
Police	☎104

Exchange Rates

Australia	A$1	US$0.73
Canada	C$1	US$0.77
Euro zone	€1	US$1.13
Japan	¥100	US$0.92
New Zealand	NZ$1	US$0.68
UK	£1	US$1.44

For current exchange rates, see www.xe.com.

Daily Costs

Budget: Less than US$35

- Dorm bed: US$13
- Dine on *comida corriente* (set meals), visit markets and street stalls
- Plan sightseeing via bus, DIY visits to beaches and waterfall hikes

Midrange: US$70 to US$150

- Double room at a midrange hotel: US$60 to US$130
- Some fine dining, activities (snorkel rental or surf lessons) and regional flights

Top End: More than US$150

- Double room at a high-end hotel, resort or lodge: from US$130
- Guided trips with bilingual naturalist guides
- Internal flights and car rental

Opening Hours

Opening hours vary throughout the year. The following are high-season hours.

Banks 8:30am to 1pm or 3pm; some open Saturday morning

Bars and clubs Bars from 9pm; clubs from 11pm to 3am or 4am

Government offices 8am to 4pm Monday to Friday

Malls and shops 10am to 9pm or 10pm

Offices 8am to noon and 1:30pm to 5pm Monday to Friday

Restaurants 7am to 10am, noon to 3pm and 6pm to 10pm; later in Panama City; often closed Sunday

Supermarkets 8am to 9pm; some open 24 hours

Arriving in Panama

Tocumen International Airport (p299; Panama City) Most international flights arrive here. Hire taxis (from US$30) at the transport desk near baggage claim. A 40-minute ride to downtown. In daylight hours local buses (US$1.25) depart every 15 minutes for Albrook Bus Terminal (one hour), and other destinations.

Aeropuerto Enrique Malek (p299) David's airport frequently handles flights to and from San José (Costa Rica). It's about 5km from town; take a taxi (US$5).

See p299 for more information on airports and airlines servicing Panama.

Getting Around

As most Panamanians use public transportation, it's reasonably priced and connections are frequent.

Bus Most cities have a bus terminal with frequent regional departures and connections to Panama City and Costa Rica.

Car Rentals are not cheap, but roads are generally in good condition. Some areas, including Panama City and many rural parts of the country, are very poorly signposted.

Train Mostly a novelty, a rail service runs between Panama City and Colón.

Air Domestic flights depart Panama City's Albrook Airport to destinations throughout the country.

For much more on **getting around**, see p301.

First Time Panama

For more information, see Survival Guide (p287)

Checklist

- Valid passport.
- Check the visa situation and government travel advisories.
- Organize travel insurance.
- Check luggage restrictions.
- Check your immunization history.
- Contact your credit-card provider to see if there's car-rental insurance coverage.

What to Pack

- Passport.
- Phrasebook.
- Swimsuit.
- Camera and battery charger.
- Flip-flops.
- Sun protection.
- Poncho or rain jacket.
- Binoculars.
- Strong insect repellent (30% to 50% DEET).
- Refillable water bottle.
- Driver's license, if you plan to rent a car.
- Field guide.
- Flashlight or headlamp.

Top Tips for Your Trip

- Don't flag a taxi in front of a high-end hotel if you don't want to be charged tourist rates off the bat; taxis aren't metered, so walk a block – it pays!
- Outside the cities, many perfectly good lodgings don't have a handle on email and websites. Don't get frustrated if no one sees your reservation – the hotel email might have been created by a precocious nephew who never checks it. If you have even basic Spanish, call ahead.
- Panamanians are used to foreigners dissing local idiosyncrasies, such as drivers not using signals, or crowds that can't form lines. But, instead, if you ask *why* it is the way it is you'll have a lively conversation.

What to Wear

Locals rarely wear shorts if not at the beach. Bring lightweight pants or skirts and short-sleeved shirts or tops. Dining and nightlife can be formal in the capital: bring proper dress shoes or sandals and a skirt or dress for women, and pants and a dress shirt for men. Pack a light sweater for over-air-conditioned restaurants and bus rides. A fleece and lightweight shell are necessary for the highlands. For hiking, long sleeves and (quick-drying) pants help keep the bugs away.

Sleeping

Book two to six months ahead for the week preceding Easter, the November festivals and between Christmas and New Year. Accommodations usually require reservations in high season.

- **Hotels** Abound in midrange and high-end categories.
- **B&Bs** A midrange phenomenon most common in the capital, Boquete and Bocas.
- **Hostels** Cheap and spreading in Panama, ranging from quiet digs to party central.
- **Lodges** From rustic to high end, found mostly in the highlands.

Etiquette

➡ **Asking for help** Say *disculpe* to get someone's attention; *perdón* to say excuse me.

➡ **Personal space** Don't be surprised if locals have fewer boundaries about personal space than what's customary in North America and Europe.

➡ **Visiting indigenous communities** Ask permission to take photos, particularly of children, and dress more modestly than beachwear; bargaining may be appropriate for buying crafts but not for lodging and food; the best gifts for children are those that are useful (pens, paper, notebooks, creative games or books).

➡ **Surfing** Novice surfers should be aware of 'dropping in' on more experienced surfers and of swimmers in their path.

➡ **Hitchhiking** Picking up hitchhikers in rural areas is common. If you get a ride from a local, offer a small tip.

Money

ATMs are readily available except in the most isolated places. Credit cards are widely accepted at restaurants and upscale hotels, but may be problematic elsewhere.

For more information see p294.

Bargaining

It's OK to bargain at markets and street stalls, but educate yourself first by asking around to get an idea of the pricing of different items and the specific factors that contribute to the quality.

IVAN_SABO / SHUTTERSTOCK ©

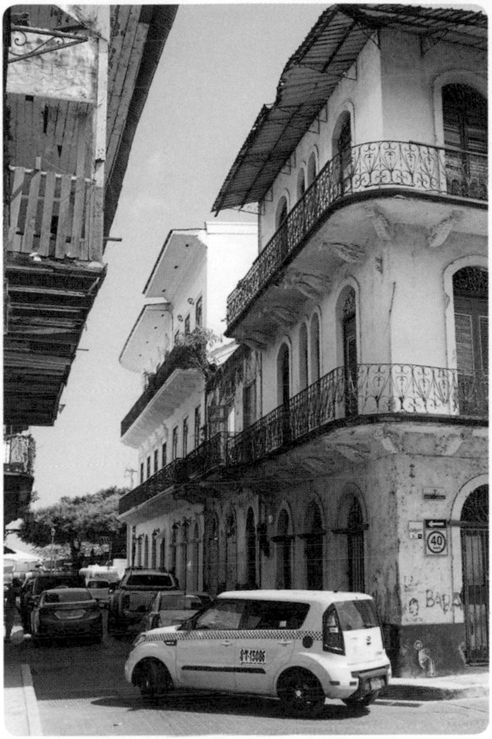

Casco Viejo (p45), Panama City

Tipping

➡ **Restaurants** Tipping should be 10%; check to see if it's included in the bill.

➡ **Taxis** Tipping is optional, but you can round up a dollar or two, especially at night.

➡ **Guides** It is customary to tip US$7 to US$10 per person for day tours; tip on the high end for naturalist guides.

Language

Spanish is the national language of Panama, and knowing some very basic phrases (see p303) is not only courteous but often essential, particularly when navigating through rural areas, interacting with park rangers and shopping at local markets. That said, English speakers are easier to find here than in other parts of Latin America. Not only did the US occupation leave its stamp, but many Panamanians have lived abroad. Some restaurants feature English menus and it's certainly the standard for guides. If you visit Guna Yala, learning a few words of Guna (see p232) beforehand is a great way to warm relations.

If You Like...

Beaches

Guna Yala Known for perfect – and plentiful – postage stamp–size islets with turquoise waters. (p226)

Isla Contadora Vacation like a high roller on this island of mansions and gorgeous beaches with a good dose of privacy. (p84)

Golfo de Chiriquí The national marine park boasts islands of monkeys, nesting turtles and plenty of patches of sand for you only. (p160)

Farallón Within reach of the capital, this wide, brilliantly white resort beach is a natural beauty perfect for long strolls. (p103)

Nightlife

Casco Viejo Dart across the cobblestones between underground bars, brewpubs, wine bars and live-music venues. (p66)

Bocas del Toro With Aqua Lounge's deckside swings and La Iguana and Selina partying hard, it's the scene of the young and the restless. (p184)

Tántalo Bar The best exotic cocktails and rooftop bar rolled into one – you could only do better booking its dominatrix-themed suite. (p66)

Boquete Offering comfort and *cervezas* to expats and locals alike are places like Mike's Global Grill and Boquete Brewing Company, with 10 originals on tap. (p163)

Romantic Getaways

Los Quetzales Cabins Cabins tucked into the rainforest canopy, with fireplaces and the mountain air buzzing with hummingbirds. (p177)

Casco Viejo B&Bs A hefty dose of pampering with this vibrant old-world neighborhood right out the door. (p57)

Archipiélago de Bocas del Toro From secluded ecolodges to thatched beach huts, these resorts can erase the world beyond. (p181)

Playa Los Destiladeros This tiny cove seduces with achingly blue skies, a secluded beach of pounding surf and candlelit dinners for two. (p129)

Villa Távida Lodge Luxury summit villas surrounded by a waterfall, gardens and shrouded peaks. (p108)

Outdoor Adventures

Nivida Bat Cave Trek to this massive Caribbean cavern rife with nectar bats; perfect for a subterranean swim. (p201)

Parque Internacional La Amistad True wilderness hiking without the drama of the Darién; access via the highlands or the Caribbean coast. (p178, p207)

Sunset Coast Sportfishing Good-value guided trips that take in Isla de Coiba, the Tuna Coast and fish-rich Banco Hannibal. (p150)

Volcán Barú Terribly steep, hard, and invariably foggy and muddy, but how else can you view Atlantic and Pacific at once? (p173)

Surfing

Santa Catalina It's all about world-class waves here, and hostels boast front-row seats. (p141)

Playa Venao Gorgeous stretches of dark volcanic sand and consistent waves for all abilities. (p131)

Playa Bluff Powerful barrels rush this wilderness beach; avoid May to September, when turtles nest. (p196)

Playa El Palmar A Panama City weekend break with two surf schools and a white-sand beach as your campus. (p91)

Playa Morillo The latest hot spot south of Torio to attract

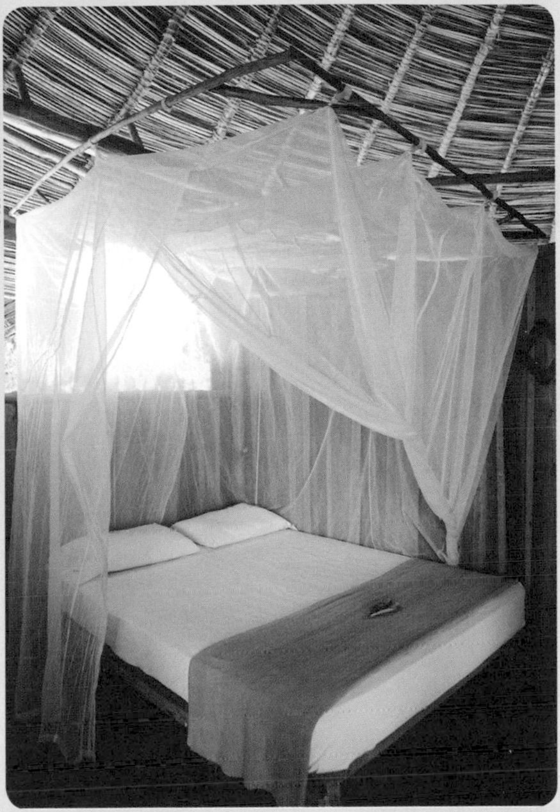

MACDUFF EVERTON / GETTY IMAGES ©

FEEL4NATURE / GETTYIMAGES ©

Top: Al Natural Resort (p204), Isla Bastimentos, Bocas del Toro Province

Bottom: Fan coral, Isla de Coiba (p145), Veraguas Province

surfers to the Sunset Coast. (p149)

Off-the-Beaten-Track Destinations

Soposo Rainforest Adventures Step off the gringo trail to sleep in stilted huts and explore remote Naso villages. (p210)

Sante Fé Dancing butterflies, swimming holes and giant waterfalls grace this humble mountain town. (p137)

The Darién Steeped in indigenous culture and exotic wildlife; with permits required, checkpoints and delays, the real trouble is arriving. (p240)

Isla Cébaco Seldom-visited island offering a crowd-free retreat with comfortable lodgings. (p148)

Wildlife

Isla Barro Colorado Nature geeks shouldn't miss this rainforest, the most intensely studied area in the neotropics. (p80)

Parque Nacional Coiba Dive with a whale shark, spy scarlet macaws or search for endemic howlers. Wildlife is epic here. (p145)

San San Pond Sak Sloths, river otters and the occasional manatee inhabit this little-known Caribbean wetland near Changuinola. (p207)

Isla Bastimentos From July to August, loggerhead, hawksbill, green and leatherback turtles hatch on the north shore. (p201)

Parque Natural Metropolitano A patch of rainforest amid Panama City. Don't mind the titi monkeys on the trail! (p49)

Month by Month

TOP EVENTS

Panama Jazz Festival, January

Carnaval, February–March

Festival de Diablos y Congos, February–March

Festival of Nogagope, October

January

With dry season and tourist season at their peaks, this is a big month for travel in Panama. It's prime time for kitesurfing and swimming, since Pacific Ocean temperatures are at their warmest, but the wind is up.

Panama Jazz Festival

The weeklong jazz festival (www.panamajazzfestival.com) is one of the biggest musical events in Panama, drawing top-caliber international musicians from jazz, blues, salsa and other genres. Held all over the city, the open-air events are usually free. (p57)

Fiesta del Mar

Held at the end of the month on tiny Isla Taboga, a boat ride away from Panama City, this new tradition seeks to revive island culture with a weekend festival (www.fiestadelmarpanama.com) of calypso music, dancing and food events. (p82)

March

It's prime time for surfing on both Pacific and Caribbean swells. High season is winding down. Events related to the religious calendar may take place in February or March.

Carnaval

On the four days preceding Ash Wednesday, general merriment prevails in Panama City and on the Península de Azuero. This anything-goes, multi-event period features street parades, water fights, costumes and live music till the wee hours. (p56)

Festival de Diablos y Congos

Held every other year, this Congo festival celebrates rebellious slave ancestors with spirited public dancing featuring beautiful masks and costumes. Participants assume the role of escaped slaves and take captives on the street. (p220)

Semana Santa

During Holy Week (the week before Easter), the country hosts many special events, including a re-enactment of the crucifixion and resurrection of Christ. On Good Friday, religious processions are held across the country.

May

With sporadic, refreshing rain showers, the weather is generally pleasant throughout the country. May begins a five- to six-month nesting season for both loggerhead and green sea turtles on the Caribbean coast.

Fiesta de Corpus Christi

Forty days after Easter, this religious holiday features colorful celebrations in Villa de Los Santos. Masked and costumed dancers representing angels, devils, imps and other mythological figures perform dances, acrobatics and dramas. Held in May or June. (p120)

July

Though it's the middle of rainy season, the weather is relatively dry on the Caribbean side. It's also off-peak for visitors and hotels offer better rates.

Nuestra Señora del Carmen

Celebrating the patron saint of Isla Taboga, this event on July 16 starts with a procession parading the Virgin statue, followed by fire breathing, games and dance. (p83)

Fiesta de Santa Librada

Celebrating the patron saint of Las Tablas and incorporating the Festival de la Pollera, this July 19 event lasts four days, with huge street celebrations, music and dance, in addition to solemn religious services and processions in Península de Azuero. (p123)

August

Breeding humpback whales can be observed in the Archipiélago de Las Perlas. Mid-month Panama City celebrates its founding in 1519 with a stream of events. Rainy season continues.

Festival del Manito Ocueño

Among the country's best folkloric events, this three-day bash features traditional music and dancing, and culminates in a country wedding. Held the third week of August in the rural village of Ocú.

September

The rain usually lets up a little, particularly around Panama City. Still low season, it's a good time to travel around the country, with no need of reservations.

Festival de la Mejorana

In late September, Panama's largest folkloric festival draws musicians and traditional dancers from all over the country to tiny Guararé on the Península de Azuero. With oxcart parades and *seco* cocktails, it's a fun time to soak up tradition. (p122)

October

October 12 is Día de la Raza (Colombus Day); a dubious legacy nonetheless celebrated by every high-school brass band letting loose. Throughout Panama, some very different yet excellent festivals are well worth attending.

Festival of Nogagope

Guna converge on Isla Tigre for three days of tireless traditional dancing. It's visually engaging and fully authentic. Held from October 10 to 12, it's followed by a four-day fair with art shows and canoe races. (p231)

Festival of the Black Christ

On October 21, thousands honor the black Christ in Portobelo. Many make the pilgrimage on foot from the capital. Miracles aplenty have been attributed to the black Christ. After a nighttime procession there's dancing and drinking till late. (p220)

Toro Guapo

One of the best street parties in the country, the 'Handsome Bull' festival takes place in the Coclé town of Antón for three days during the second week of October. (p104)

November

Don't come to Panama for business between November and December, as the whole country takes off to celebrate multiple independence-related holidays in November, and then there's the Christmas holiday. Panama City empties out and beaches are full.

Día de Independencia

On November 28 Panama celebrates its independence from Spain with parties and revelry throughout the country. Most locals head to the beach and enjoy a drink or 10. Book any travel well ahead.

Plan Your Trip
Itineraries

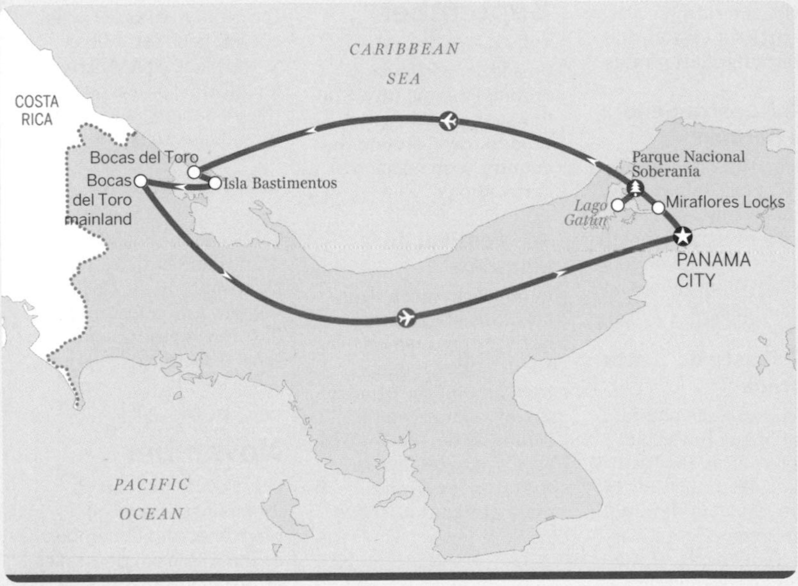

1 WEEK

Essential Panama

For a taste of tropical Panama, start with hyper-charged capital. Explore the city and see colonial ruins and landmarks such as the famous Panama Canal while getting a dose of rainforest adventure. Top it off with a chilled Caribbean getaway.

Start by imbibing the rush of **Panama City**, the country's vibrant capital.

In Panamá Viejo, take time to visit Spain's first Pacific settlement, which was laid waste in a massive pirate raid during the 17th century. After admiring the ruins, take a walk or pedal along the coastal beltway of the Cinta Costera to historic Casco Viejo, with its hip plaza restaurants, rooftop bars, galleries and 18th-century cathedrals.

Take a day trip to **Miraflores Locks**, to watch mammoth ships slip through the Panama Canal, followed by a visit to a nearby rainforest in the wildlife-rich **Parque Nacional Soberanía**, a favorite of birdwatchers. Alteranatively paddle a kayak on **Lago Gatún** alongside howler monkeys and sunbathing crocodiles.

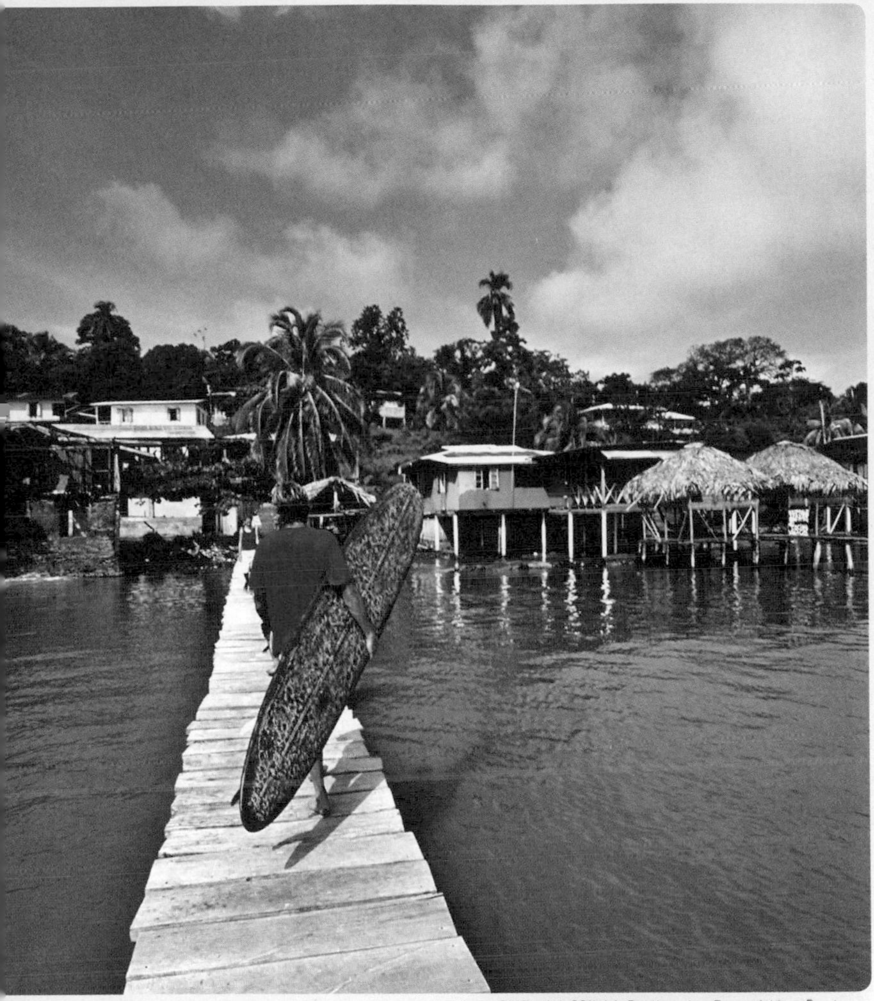

Above: Old Bank (p201), Isla Bastimentos, Bocas del Toro Province
Below: Beachside, Bocas del Toro Province

From Panama City, fly to **Bocas del Toro** for four days of Caribbean relaxation and snorkeling in colorful coral reefs. Explore Isla Colón by cruiser bike and enjoy a pub crawl in quirky Bocas Town.

From here, boat out to the thatched resorts at **Isla Bastimentos**, take a chocolate tour on the Bocas del Toro **mainland** or alternatively visit some of the indigenous groups on other islands with a community-tourism initiative.

Fly back to the capital for a final call in the city's many open-air restaurants, sleek bars and salsa clubs.

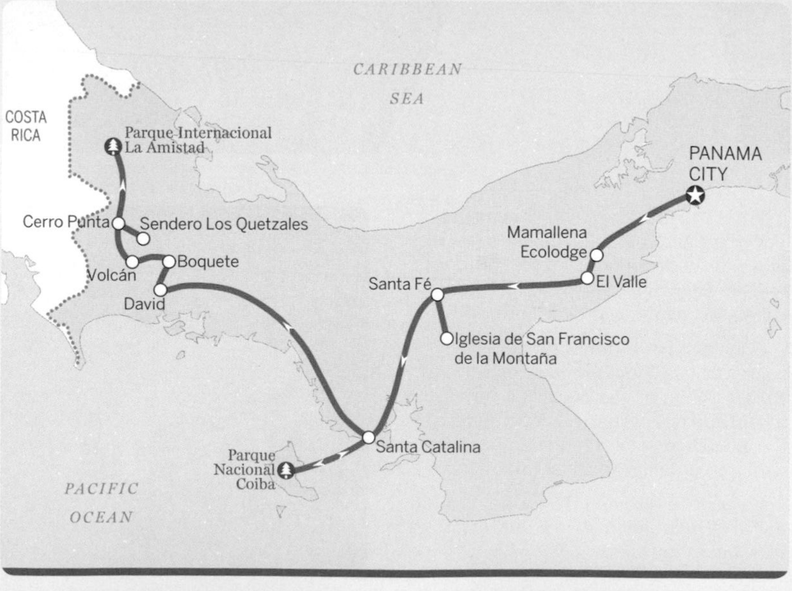
CARIBBEAN SEA
COSTA RICA
Parque Internacional La Amistad
Cerro Punta
Sendero Los Quetzales
Volcán
Boquete
David
Santa Fé
Iglesia de San Francisco de la Montaña
El Valle
Mamallena Ecolodge
PANAMA CITY
Santa Catalina
Parque Nacional Coiba
PACIFIC OCEAN

RIEGER BERTRAND / HEMIS.FR / GETTY IMAGES ©

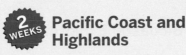

NANCY NEHRING / GETTY IMAGES ©

Top: Finca Lérida (p170), Chiriquí Province

Bottom: Common black hawk, Parque Nacional Coiba (p145), Veraguas Province

2 WEEKS

Pacific Coast and Highlands

Whether you're traveling on buses or with your own wheels, hit the Interamericana for a route that alternates between scenic beaches and highland cloud forests.

Spend your first days exploring **Panama City**, then head west along the Interamericana where you can stop for a leisurely seafood lunch and explore the string of beaches along the Pacific coast. Overnight at **Mamallena Ecolodge** in the cool, sculpted foothills. The next stop is **El Valle**, a mountain retreat surrounded by lush cloud forests and green peaks. Returning to the Interamericana, visit Coclé's roadside attractions, then detour for **Santa Fé**, a highland town amid rivers and waterfalls. On your way out, browse gorgeous **Iglesia de San Francisco de la Montaña** outside Santa Fé.

For surf time, backtrack to the Interamericana and detour to **Santa Catalina**. Soak up the laid-back vibe at thatched restaurants and join the local surfing kids nailing the waves on the town beach. Another very good reason to stop here is to connect to **Parque Nacional Coiba**, a far-flung, yet pristine, island in a vast marine park. Snorkeling, diving and hiking are all top notch; although there's minimal infrastructure, it's worth staying a few days.

Head via **David** to the popular highland retreat of **Boquete** in Chiriquí. Go hiking or rafting or take a canopy tour and fill up on mountain-grown coffee. Birdwatchers can stalk the resplendent quetzal. Choose from among fine dining options and sleep soundly in clean mountain air.

If you have your own wheels, take the new road to **Volcán**, a very scenic shortcut. Those without wheels can bus via David to **Cerro Punta**. Retreat to a charming rainforest cabin before hitting the trail to hike the **Sendero Los Quetzales**, a stunning trail through wildlife-rich cloud forest. If traveling by bus, you can loop back to Boquete on this hike. If adventure *still* calls, from Cerro Punta you can access the trails of **Parque Internacional La Amistad**. Take a guide – the Panamanian side of this international park is virtually undeveloped and largely unexplored.

To save time, you can fly back to Panama City from David.

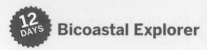

12 DAYS Bicoastal Explorer

IIf you're itching to get off the beaten path, this seafarer route will bring you to the less-touristed Península de Azuero on the Pacific coast, and on to the Afro-Caribbean heartland and the furthest reaches of Guna Yala (and possibly even Colombia).

Start in the capital of **Panama City**. From there, take a ride in the luxury train along the historical Panama Railroad through the Canal Zone to **Colón** to admire the Unesco World Heritage Site of **Fuerte San Lorenzo**. While in the area, check out the Panama Canal expansion at the nearby **Agua Clara Visitor Center**. Using **Portobelo** as your base, explore 16th-century Spanish forts, boat out to deserted island beaches, scuba dive or attend a festival.

Return to Panama City to travel to the **Península de Azuero** by bus. From time to time traditional festivals take over the streets of these tiny colonial towns. If your visit coincides, join the revelers! Otherwise, check out workshops where regional artisans craft Panama hats, lace dresses and colorful *diablo* (devil) masks. Make your base **Pedasí** for leisurely trips to the beach and a friendly village atmosphere. Move on to the more remote **Playa Venao** to enjoy a pretty half-moon bay, meet other travelers and ride some waves without the crowds. If turtles are hatching, it's worth making the pilgrimage to **Isla Cañas**.

When you're ready, return to the capital and take a 4WD or flight to **Guna Yala**, a string of hundreds of pristine islands ruled by Guna. Thatched huts on dozens of islands run the gamut from bare bones to creature comforts, with meals and excursions always included. Snorkel and swim to your heart's content, or charter a sailboat for the grand tour. Highlights include snorkeling the reefs and wrecks of the **Cayos Holandeses** and meeting the locals on the tiny community islands. If you are heading on to South America – and bent on adventure – consider a three- to four-day sailing or boat trip to Colombia.

Otherwise, end your trip by returning to Panama City, where you can check out the world-class BioMuseo and have a night out in Casco Viejo.

DANNY LEHMAN / GETTY IMAGES ©

ALFREDO MAIQUEZ / GETTY IMAGES ©

Top: Panama Railroad (p302), Panama Canal
Bottom: Festival de Diablos y Congos, Portobelo (p220), Colón Province

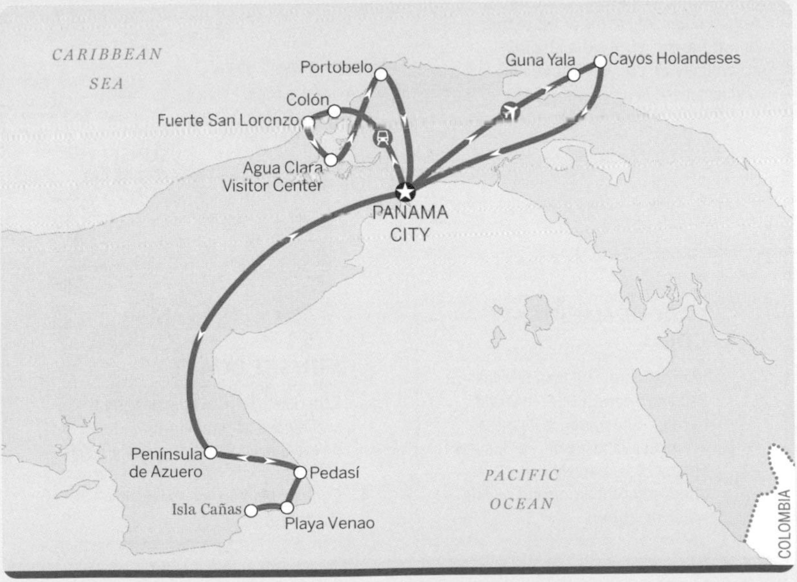
CARIBBEAN
SEA
Portobelo
Guna Yala
Cayos Holandeses
Colón
Fuerte San Lorenzo
Agua Clara
Visitor Center
PANAMA
CITY
Península
de Azuero
Pedasí
Isla Cañas
Playa Venao
PACIFIC
OCEAN
COLOMBIA

Off the Beaten Track: Panama

BOCAS DEL TORO MAINLAND

Tour a chocolate farm, search for endangered manatees or travel by dugout canoe to little-known Naso villages. Alternatively trek through the rugged but beautiful Parque Internacional La Amistad. (p205)

SANTA FÉ

A highland gem, this cowboy town is all about mountain panoramas. Go tubing in the cool river, hike to lush waterfalls and swimming holes or jump in the saddle to explore. (p137)

ISLA GOBERNADORA

Sun, surf and art are the draws of this out-of-the-way Pacific island with community-art projects inspired by resident installation artists. (p149)

PARQUE NACIONAL COIBA

With extraordinary marine wildlife, Panama's newest Unesco World Heritage Site was once its most infamous island prison. Far flung yet pristine, this sparsely visited park offers excellent diving and wildlife watching. (p145)

SUNSET COAST

Experience remote beaches, great surfing and community-turtle tours on the Sunset Coast: the western side of Península de Azuero facing the Golfo de Montijo and the Pacific Ocean. (p149)

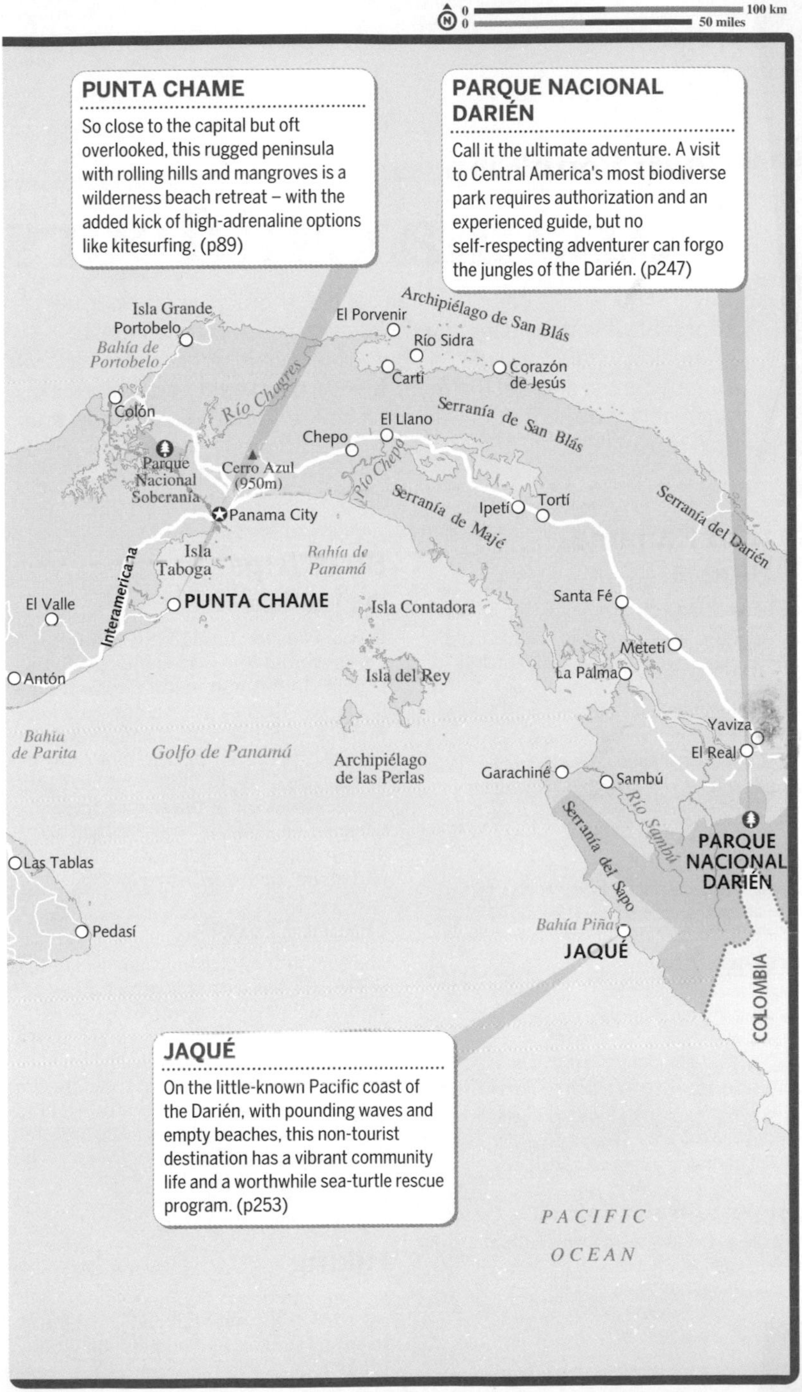

PUNTA CHAME

So close to the capital but oft overlooked, this rugged peninsula with rolling hills and mangroves is a wilderness beach retreat – with the added kick of high-adrenaline options like kitesurfing. (p89)

PARQUE NACIONAL DARIÉN

Call it the ultimate adventure. A visit to Central America's most biodiverse park requires authorization and an experienced guide, but no self-respecting adventurer can forgo the jungles of the Darién. (p247)

JAQUÉ

On the little-known Pacific coast of the Darién, with pounding waves and empty beaches, this non-tourist destination has a vibrant community life and a worthwhile sea-turtle rescue program. (p253)

Plan Your Trip

Panama Outdoors

Beyond Panama's cosmopolitan capital, there's big appeal outdoors. Start with wildlife that ranges from curious primates to breaching whales and darting butterflies. Visit jungle waterways via dugout canoe, snorkel the reefs, trek through misty cloud forest or surf Pacific tubes. Refuel with fresh coffee from the highlands, and then repeat.

Best of Panama Outdoors

Best Surf Beach

Laid-back vibes, access to Parque Nacional Coiba and world-class waves: it's all at Santa Catalina (p140).

Best Hike

Sendero Los Quetzales (p172) is a beautiful 8km route, running between Cerro Punta and Boquete in Chiriquí Province.

Best Sportfishing

If you want to break a sportfishing world record, your chances are high at Bahía Piña (p253).

Best Dive Site

Parque Nacional Coiba (p145) has extraordinary marine wildlife; you might spot hammerheads or a whale shark.

Best Accessible Wildlife-Watching

More than 500 bird spices have been sighted along Pipeline Rd (p78) in Parque Nacional Soberanía – hit the trail and start counting!

Best White-Water Rafting

Tackle the white water of Río Chiriquí (p165) from May until December.

Boat Trips

On the River

Partial transits through the Miraflores Locks are the best way to appreciate the Panama Canal, and one of the highlights of any trip to Panama. Another great option is to wildlife-watch from a kayak on Lago Gatún. In the Darién, tours cruise up Río Mogué to an Emberá village. In the Wekso sector of the Parque Internacional La Amistad, travelers can explore indigenous villages while heading upriver on motorized dugouts.

Ocean Travel

The 226km-long Archipiélago de San Blás is a thrill for ocean explorers. Run as an autonomous region by the Guna people, it features hundreds of coconut-fringed islands and islets surrounded by turquoise waters. Independent travelers can travel by small boat between the islands, or charter sailboats through the area and even on to Colombia.

Hiking

Panama offers everything from dry tropical rainforests and highland cloud forests to humid jungles and blistery mountain peaks.

THE TRANSPANAMA TRAIL

This cross-country circuit (www.transpanama.org) runs from the border of Costa Rica toward Panama City, but you can hike any three-day stretch for a good taste of Panama's rugged backcountry. More information is available on the website, where you can also download GPS tracks for free.

Starting near the capital on the shores of the canal, Parque Nacional Soberanía contains a section of the historic Sendero Las Cruces. Closer to Panama City, Parque Natural Metropolitano boasts a number of short but rewarding hikes in plush rainforest that skirts the capital.

Popular highland retreats include Boquete; El Valle, nestled into the extinct volcano now known as Valle de Antón; and Santa Fé, surrounded by rivers, waterfalls and cloud forests. All feature hikes in a pristine mountain setting.

Chiriquí is home to two of Panama's most famous hikes: Volcán Barú and Sendero Los Quetzales in Parque Nacional Volcán Barú. While Los Quetzales is more scenic in poor weather, ascents up Barú, which is Panama's highest peak, can offer views of both oceans on a clear day.

Recommended remote destinations include the Las Nubes sector of the Parque Internacional La Amistad. With trails only accessible with a guide, it is as rugged and uncharted as Central America gets.

Diving & Snorkeling

Panama's underwater world spans two great oceans, and abounds with colorful coral gardens, towering rock shelves, sunken wrecks and a rich diversity of marine life. Fans of multicolored reef fish and bathtub-warm water should head for the Caribbean, while more advanced divers in search of enormous pelagic animals and remote dive sites should head to the Pacific. Three major spots in Panama that have a deserved reputation for fine scuba diving are the Archipiélago de Bocas del Toro, the Caribbean town of Portobelo and the Pacific-coast Isla de Coiba.

The Caribbean islands of Bocas del Toro have a thriving dive community. During the rainy season (mid-April to mid-December) underwater visibility is extremely poor – nearly 40 rivers deposit silt into the seas around the islands, which turns the water a murky green.

Near historic Portobelo, 16 major dive sites feature underwater attractions including a 110ft cargo ship, a C-45 twin-engine plane, soft-coral-laden walls, off-shore reefs and rock gardens.

The best diving in Panama is around Isla de Coiba, the centerpiece of a national marine park accessed via Santa Catalina. Divers here scout for enormous sharks including schools of hammerheads, blacktips and whitetips as well as the occasional tiger or whale shark.

The Guna prohibit dive operators from working in the Comarca de Guna Yala, but the snorkeling is some of the best in Panama.

Surfing

Although the joy of Panama is riding some of the lesser-known surf breaks – or even discovering your own – the country

DIVING RESPONSIBLY

- Never anchor on the reef and take care not to ground boats on coral.
- Avoid touching or standing on living marine organisms. Polyps can be damaged by even the most gentle contact. If you must hold on, only touch exposed rock or dead coral.
- Watch your fins. The surge from fin strokes can damage delicate reef organisms and clouds of sand can smother organisms.
- Make visits quick to underwater caves, as trapped air bubbles damage organisms.
- Resist the temptation to collect or buy corals or shells or to loot marine archaeological sites.
- Do not feed fish and never ride on the backs of turtles.

has two world-class spots in Santa Catalina and the Archipiélago de Bocas del Toro. Even these are significantly less crowded than similar places in neighboring Costa Rica.

The face of a typical wave at Santa Catalina is 2m, though during February and March, 4m waves are fairly common. Waves are at their best during medium to high tide, when rides approaching 150m are possible. On the Caribbean side, the islands of Bocas del Toro offer some of the best and most varied surfing in Panama, especially from December to March.

Surfing spots are also found in the provinces of Panamá, Veraguas (Playa Morillo), Los Santos, Colón and Chiriquí.

Fishing

Panamá means 'abundance of fish,' and with 2988km of coastline, there's no problem finding a fishing spot. Freshwater anglers usually set their sights on trout and bass, while serious sportfishers ply the seas for trophy fish including tarpon, sailfish and marlin. Freshwater angling can be pursued independently, especially in the highland rivers of Chiriquí and Veraguas. In the Canal Zone you can fish for peacock bass in Lago Gatún and the Río Chagres.

For deep-sea fishing, Panama offers three world-class areas – Bahía Piña, the Archipiélago de Las Perlas and Isla de Coiba – all served by extremely professional fishing outfits. In the Darién's Bahía Piña, more International Game Fish Association world records have been broken than anywhere else on the planet. This top spot is served exclusively by Tropic Star Lodge. The seas around Isla de Coiba are home to several species of sport fish including yellowfin tuna, wahoo, dolphinfish, Spanish mackerel, jacks and rooster fish. The Veraguas coast is another good option.

Cycling

Owing to its compact size and modern infrastructure, Panama is the perfect country to unleash a little pedal power. As with all long-distance cycling, you need to prepare yourself both physically and mentally for the rigors of the road. The major factor when considering a lengthy bike ride is the weather. With

SURVIVING A RIPTIDE

Rip currents are formed when excess water brought to shore by waves returns to the sea in a rapidly moving depression in the ocean floor. They are comprised of three parts: the feeder current, the neck and the head.

The feeder current consists of rapidly moving water that parallels the shore but isn't always visible from the beach. When this water reaches a channel, it switches direction and flows out to sea, forming the neck of the rip. This is the fastest-moving part of the riptide, moving with a speed of up to 10km/h. The head of the riptide current occurs past the breakers where the current quickly dissipates.

If caught in a riptide, immediately call or signal for help. Conserve your energy and do not fight the current – this is the principal cause of drownings as it's almost impossible to swim directly back to shore. Instead, try one of two methods. The first is to float or tread water and let yourself be swept out past the breakers; once you're in the head of the rip, you can swim out of the channel and ride the waves back to shore. Alternatively you can swim parallel to shore until the current weakens.

Rip currents usually occur on beaches with strong surf, but temporary rips can occur anywhere, especially when there is an offshore storm or during low tide. Indicators include a brownish color to the surface of the water caused by swept-up sand and debris. Also look for surface flattening, which occurs when the water enters a depression in the ocean floor and rushes back out to sea. If you're ever in doubt, it's best to inquire locally about swimming conditions. And never ever swim alone.

Top: Surfing in Bocas del Toro Province (p180)

Right: Waterfall on Río Chiriquí Viejo (p165), Chiriquí Province

heat a serious factor, riding in the early morning and resting in the heat of the day is a good strategy. Also, it's not entirely safe to ride in the rain. Throughout much of the country, the rains come from mid-April to mid-December, though the Caribbean has rain virtually year-round. Beyond the capital, you're essentially on your own, but never underestimate the prowess of the village mechanic.

Wildlife-Watching

Unlike in the savannahs of Africa, wildlife-watching in the neotropical rainforest is an exercise in patience and stealth – a little luck doesn't hurt, either. Although it's unlikely you'll come across top predators such as jaguars and pumas, primates and lesser mammals are commonly sighted. Top national parks for watching wildlife include La Amistad, Volcán Barú and the Darién. Closer to the capital, Parque Natural Metropolitano and Parque Nacional Soberanía are easily accessible and quite good.

Highlights

Nowhere else in the world are rainforests as easily accessible as they are in this tiny sliver of a country. To make the most of your wildlife-watching experience, pick up a good field guide. Some highlights include:

- **Two- and three-toed sloths** Found only in neotropical rainforests, these ancient mammals came into being when South America was isolated. Curled up high on a branch, they are hard to spot. They spend 16 hours a day asleep or inactive but busy with digestion.
- **Mantled howlers** Greeting sunrise and sunset with booming calls that resonate for kilometers, howlers are incredibly vocal. Their antics are also good storm indicators.
- **Jaguars** The largest cat in the Americas, jaguars are extremely rare and elusive, though their evidence is all around, from dried spoor to fresh tracks.
- **Parrots and macaws** Panama has more than 20 species, including five macaws. Big macaws can be identified by their huge bills, bare facial patch and long, tapered tails.
- **Toucans** The spectacular multicolored bill is a giveaway. This powerful tool is full of air cavities and quite lightweight. A serrated upper mandible helps grip slippery fruits and intimidate other birds.

Birdwatching

With more than 900 bird species in Panama, all you need to do to spot feathered friends is get a good pair of binoculars and hit the trails. Two popular spots include Pipeline Rd in Parque Nacional Soberanía and Burbayar Lodge in Panamá Province. Panama Audubon Society (p55), located in Panama City, organizes the annual Christmas bird count on Pipeline Rd, and runs birdwatching expeditions throughout the country.

White-Water Sports

Whether you take to the water by raft or kayak, Panama boasts some excellent opportunities for river running. The best-known white-water runs are on the ríos Chiriquí and Chiriquí Viejo, with Class III-plus rapids. The unofficial river-running capital of Panama is the highland town of Boquete. Sea-kayaking centers are Bocas del Toro and Chiriquí Provinces.

Regions at a Glance

Located at the heart of the Americas, Panama is the narrow but crucial link between Central and South America. The Panama Canal joins the Atlantic to the Pacific, wedding east to west in global commerce. In the last century, the canal defined Panama, but it's what lies just beyond that may define it next. Pristine beaches, lush rainforest and big-city nightlife are major assets. English is widely spoken, yet the lost world of rainforests and dugout canoes is never too far off. The canal expansion will translate to further growth and glitz. But, for now, you can still pick an empty islet and play survivor for a day.

Panama City

History
Cuisine
Nightlife

Colonial Echoes

Wander the cobblestone streets of the Casco Viejo, admire the 16th-century ruins of Panamá Viejo or pedal the greenbelt Cinta Costera for the long view. Admire the treasures privateers forgot. History's most notorious explorers, pirates and marauders came before you.

Tastes Go Tropical

Panama chefs are reinventing traditional ingredients and refining tropical tastes, and the capital's lively dining scene is finally reflecting its cultural plurality, with more options than ever reflecting its global citizenship. *Provecho*!

La Rumba

From rooftop cocktails with city views to live salsa bands and open-air bars under crumbling colonial walls, Panama City nightlife is dynamic, daring and ever hip. While anything goes, locals usually dress to the nines.

p42

Panamá Province

Human-Made Marvels
Rainforests
Island Getaways

Panama Canal

The expansion of this 80km cross-continental shortcut is even more reason to set your sights on the impressive Panama Canal. Yet few know that, off the shipping lanes, there are also fishing, kayaking and wildlife-watching in these tropical waterways.

Wildlife-Watching

Rainforest adventures and some of the best wildlife-watching in Central America sit just outside Panama City. For nature on steroids, reserve ahead for the exclusive Smithsonian Tropical Research Institute tour, or explore the leafy stillness of Parque Nacional Soberania.

Beaches

Isla Contadora makes a great city escape, with pristine beaches and deserted shores on this underpopulated island – for a price. On a budget? Flee to lively Isla Taboga for the day for beach time. Both now have frequent ferry services.

p72

Coclé Province

Highlands
Culture
Beaches

Mountain Time

Coclé's highland retreats are prime weekend getaways. El Valle is an established resort town with boutique hotels and charming waterfall walks. For something wilder, seek replenishment in the deep forests of Reserva Privada Távida or Parque Nacional Omar Torrijos.

Latin Tradition

Pick up the signature product of Coclé: a Panama hat (a striped sombrero woven from natural fibers) at a street-side stand, or take an up-close look at the production of fine cigars and cane sugar on a factory tour.

Resorts

Wide, pearly beaches are a Coclé signature. With an airport at Río Hato near Farallón and resorts popping up, the area is poised to boom. Day trippers can stop in Farallón or Santa Clara to kick back for a couple days.

p93

Península de Azuero

Festivals
Beaches
Turtles

Street Parties

If the peninsula is the heart and soul of Panama, then festivals are its pulse. Villa de Los Santos, Las Tablas and Guararé are the best places to get your groove on; Panama's biggest festival, La Mejorana, happens here in September.

Deserted Beaches

With access improving, the rugged Azuero coast may not remain solitary for long. Yet today its essence is still wild, especially further down, towards the end of the fabulous Sunset Coast in Veraguas Province.

The Moonlight Hatch

Late August through November, thousands of olive ridley turtles land on remote Isla Cañas in the wee hours to lay their eggs, which hatch later in the season; visitors come to bear witness to the stirring nighttime spectacles, accompanied by guides.

p111

Veraguas Province

Surfing
Diving
Country Roads

Ride a Wave

With some of the biggest breaks in Central America, Santa Catalina surfing is deliriously good. Big tubes and long rides attract the experts (especially December through April); beginners have their own sandy-bottom spot at Playa El Estero, a 15-minute walk away.

Marine Life

Pure delight for divers and snorkelers, Parque Nacional Coiba hosts amazing biodiversity. With whale sharks and sea horses, it's not your average plunge. Though out of the way, it's very worthwhile, especially if you overnight and double your time underwater.

Off the Beaten Track

Brave the winding lanes to the rugged and relatively undiscovered landscapes of the highlands. The village of Santa Fé makes an ideal base for waterfall hikes with swimming holes, river tubing, horseback riding and hiking Santa Fé National Park.

p134

Chiriquí Province

Rafting & Kayaking
Hiking
Highland Lodges

White Water

Adrenaline addicts head to Boquete, the highland coffee-farm town that has become a major hub for rafting and kayaking. You can paddle year-round on the Río Chiriquí (though it's best from May to December) or on Chiriquí Viejo.

Highland Trails

The iconic Quetzal Trail weaves through gorgeous highland forest in search of its exquisite namesake. Brave Volcán Barú or set out expedition-style to Parque Internacional La Amistad from Las Nubes, located just 10km northwest of highland village Cerro Punta.

Coffee with a View

A delicious treat in high country, cabin lodges in the coffee farms of Boquete and the cloud forests of Cerro Punta and Buena Vista take the chill off with fireplaces, bottles of wine and hot tubs, with porch views of dancing hummingbirds.

p152

Bocas del Toro Province

Beaches
Surfing
Culture

Idyllic Shores

Many an idyllic palm-fringed crescent is a bicycle or boat-taxi ride away from Bocas town. Take care of the many starfish on its namesake beach as well as on Red Frog Beach and its neighbors, Playas Wizard, Polo and Larga.

Waves for All

While second to Santa Catalina, Bocas offers the most varied waves in Panama, with plenty of options to get beginners on board, especially at Old Man's and Black Rock on Isla Carenero. Then a cool Caribbean vibe reels you in.

Community Tourism

Connect with local and indigenous culture through the popular Oreba chocolate-farm tour, a visit to the Ngöbe community on Isla San Cristóbal, or a real adventure to little-known Naso country, where three ecotourism projects are up and running.

p180

Colón Province

History
Diving
Culture

Essential Sites

Old Spanish fortresses, the Panama Railroad and the canal expansion seen from Agua Clara Visitor Center: the tumultuous history of Colón is Panama's most compelling. Visit on a day tour from Panama City or spend a few days around Portobelo.

Underwater Treasures

While it doesn't quite rival the clear waters of the Pacific, there's enjoyable diving to soft coral walls, offshore reefs and Atlantic wrecks replete with storied pasts. Keep an eye out for eagle rays, nurse sharks and reef sharks.

Caribbean Culture

The Caribbean province of Colón marches to its own beat. To get a sense of this vibrant Congo culture, it's worth checking out the artist workshop in Portobelo, attending a lively, color-spattered festival and wandering the forts.

p211

Comarca de Guna Yala

Islands
Culture
Arts

Back to Basics

With hundreds of idyllic islands and waters of turquoise, you could indeed do much worse. Resort islands consist of little more than thatched huts with sandy floors and a few hammocks, but what more do you need in paradise?

Guna Culture

With the world of the strong, self-governing Guna very different from mainland Panama, it's well worth engaging a local guide or host to learn about their crafts and everyday lives. Community islands further your cultural understanding, especially at festival time.

Molas

Beautiful and often exquisitely crafted, *molas* (colorful panels of intricate embroidery) are the signature of Guna culture and Panama's most beloved craft. Designs range from abstract, with traditional maroon, white and black, to modern, adorned with cats or Santa.

p226

Darién Province

Nature
Culture
Fishing

Remote Wilderness

Beyond the last kilometer of the fabled Interamericana, the lush rainforest of Parque Nacional Darién is the most ecologically diverse park in Central America. Search for jaguars and harpy eagles and bathe in chilly waterfalls. Just arriving is an adventure.

Indigenous Culture

Remote pockets of Emberá and Wounaan peoples have inhabited the Darién's ancient forests and paddled its labyrinthine waterways for centuries. With a guided expedition to several villages promoting community tourism, the most intrepid of travelers can learn about real jungle survival.

Sportfishing

Bahía Piña is the granddaddy of sportfishing destinations, reeling in mammoth marlin and sailfish. More world records have been set here than anywhere. An exclusive fishing lodge is fitted with all the trimmings on this windswept Pacific coast.

p240

On the Road

Comarca de Guna Yala
p226
Bocas del Toro Province
p180
Colón Province
p211
Panamá Province
p72
Panama City
p42
Coclé Province
p93
Chiriquí Province
p152
Veraguas Province
p134
Darién Province
p240
Península de Azuero
p111

Panama City

POP 880,700 / AREA 275 SQ KM / ELEV SEA LEVEL

Includes ➡

Best Places to Eat

- ➡ Donde José (p63)
- ➡ Mercado de Mariscos (p62)
- ➡ Madrigal (p64)
- ➡ Avatar (p64)
- ➡ Super Gourmet (p63)

Best Places to Sleep

- ➡ Las Clementinas (p58)
- ➡ Magnolia Inn (p58)
- ➡ Luna's Castle (p57)
- ➡ American Trade Hotel (p58)
- ➡ Panama Hat Hostel (p60)

Why Go?

The most cosmopolitan capital in Central America, Panama City is both vibrant metropolis and gateway to tropical escapes. Many worlds coexist here. Welcoming both east and west, Panama is a regional hub of trade and immigration. The resulting cultural cocktail forges a refreshing 'anything goes' attitude, more dynamic and fluid than its neighbors.

Unflinchingly urban, the capital rides the rails of chaos, with traffic jams, wayward taxis and casinos stacked between chic clubs and construction sites. A center of international banking and trade, the sultry skyline of shimmering glass and steel towers is reminiscent of Miami. In contrast, the peninsula of Casco Viejo has become a thriving colonial neighborhood where cobblestones link boutique hotels with underground bars and crumbled ruins with pirate lore.

Escape is never far. Day-trip to sandy beaches (Pacific or Caribbean), admire the canal, or explore lush rainforests of howler monkeys, toucans and sloths.

When to Go

➡ **Jan** In the peak of high season, the weeklong Panama Jazz Festival features open-air concerts and events held mostly in the historic neighborhood of Casco Viejo.

➡ **Dec–mid-Mar** High season is dry season, with sunnier weather for outdoor cafe dining and day trips to the beach; hotel rates are up and travelers should book ahead.

➡ **Apr–Nov** Low-season prices and occasional showers, though a rain reprieve usually comes in October. A slew of public holidays in November means ubiquitous parades, party events and closures.

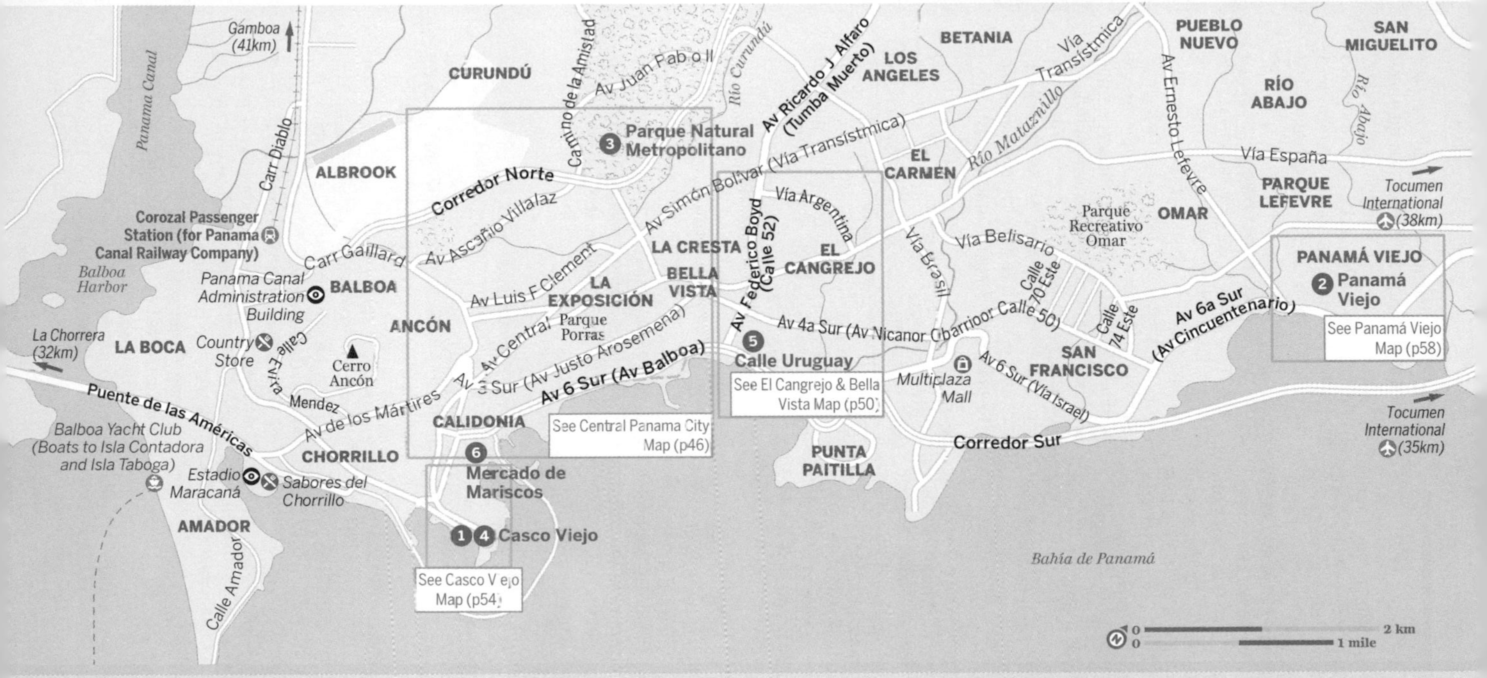

Panama City Highlights

1 Casco Viejo (p45) Exploring a history-filled, gentrifying neighborhood of crumbling colonials, soaring churches and grand plazas.

2 Panamá Viejo (p52) Reconnecting with the past at the ruins of Panamá Viejo, the original Panama City.

3 Parque Natural Metropolitano (p49) Hiking through rainforest, just 10 minutes from downtown.

4 Casco Viejo (p62) Feasting on tropical fusion cuisine in Casco Viejo's fine assortment of restaurants.

5 Calle Uruguay (p66) Partying like a rock star on Calle Uruguay, home to the city's most sophisticated nightlife.

6 Mercado de Mariscos (p62) Pedaling along the Cinta Costera for cheap *ceviche* (citrus-cured seafood) and the freshest fish around.

History

Panama City was founded in 1519 by the Spanish governor Pedro Arias de Ávila (Pedrarias), not long after conquistador Vasco Núñez de Balboa first saw the Pacific. Although the Spanish settlement quickly became an important center of government and church authority, the city was ransacked and destroyed in 1671 by the English pirate Captain Henry Morgan, leaving only the stone ruins of Panamá Viejo.

Three years later, the city was reestablished about 8km to the southwest in the area now known as Casco Viejo. Although the peninsular location was well defended, the Spanish overland trade route faded upon the destruction of the Caribbean port at Portobelo in 1746.

Panama gained independence from Spain in 1821 and became part of Gran Colombia; a decade later the regional confederation dissolved and Panama belonged to Colombia. Panama City subsequently declined in importance, though it would return to prominence in the 1850s when the Panama Railroad was completed, and gold seekers on their way to California flooded across the isthmus by train.

Panama declared its independence from Colombia on November 3, 1903, and Panama City was firmly established as the capital. Since the Panama Canal was completed in 1914, the city has emerged as a center for international business and trade.

The city's greatest modern setback occurred in 1989, when the USA invaded to oust dictator (and former US collaborator) Manuel Noriega from power. The capital suffered damage both from the invasion itself and from the subsequent looting, with residential blocks of Chorrillo destroyed by combat-ignited fire.

Following the handover of the Panama Canal from the USA to Panama in 1999, and the subsequent closure of American military bases in the country, Panama City has taken charge of its own destiny. Today Panama City is by far the wealthiest city in Central America. With an influx of foreign investment and the Panama Canal expansion, the city is poised to continue its transformation.

Sights

Panama City stretches about 20km along the Pacific coast, from the Panama Canal at its western end to the ruins of Panamá Viejo to the east.

Near the canal are Albrook airport, the Causeway and the wealthy Balboa and Ancón suburbs, first built for US canal and military workers. The colonial part of the city, Casco Viejo, juts into the sea on the southwestern side of town. In the south, the Causeway has numerous restaurants, bars and fine vantage points on the edge of the ocean.

The main drag is Av Central, which runs through Casco Viejo to Parque Santa Ana and Plaza Cinco de Mayo; between these two plazas, the avenue is a pedestrian-only shopping street. At a fork further east, the avenue becomes Av Central España; the section that traverses the El Cangrejo business and financial district is called Vía España. The other part of the fork becomes Av Simón Bolívar and, finally, Vía Transístmica as it heads out of town and across the isthmus toward Colón.

★ Museo de Arte Contemporáneo — MUSEUM

(Map p46; ☎262-3380; www.macpanama.org; Av de los Mártires, Ancón; adult/child US$5/1.50; ⏱9am-4pm Mon-Fri, to noon Sat, to 3pm Sun) This wonderful privately owned museum features the best collection of Panamanian art anywhere, an excellent collection of works on paper by Latin American artists, and the occasional temporary exhibition by a foreign or national artist.

Estadio Maracaná — STADIUM

(Chorrillo) Inaugurated in April 2014, this is the home stadium of Chorrillo FC and Club Deportivo Plaza Amador. It was named after the legendary Maracanã Stadium in Rio de Janeiro, Brazil.

Parque Recreativo Omar — PARK

The biggest park in the city is filled with children, joggers and the occasional salsa class. It's located in Omar, behind the San Francisco neighborhood. Access is from Vía Belisario.

Panama Canal Murals — PUBLIC ART

(Balboa; ⏱7:30am-4:15pm Mon-Fri) FREE The story of the monumental effort to build the Panama Canal is powerfully depicted in murals by notable artist William B Van Ingen of New York. The murals are mounted in the rotunda of the Panama Canal Administration Building. The paintings have the distinction of being the largest group of murals by an American artist on display outside the USA.

The murals tell the story of the canal's construction through four main scenes: the digging of Gaillard Cut at Gold Hill, where the canal passes through the Continental

Divide; the building of the spillway of the Gatún Dam, which dammed the Río Chagres and created Lago Gatún; the construction of one of the giant lock gates (the canal uses some 80 of these gates); and the construction of the Miraflores Locks near the Pacific entrance to the canal. A frieze located immediately below the murals presents a panorama of the excavation of Gaillard Cut.

Van Ingen is also known for his murals in the Library of Congress and the US Mint. These he produced for US$25 per sq ft; the finished murals cover about 1000 sq ft.

It's closed on weekends, but guards may allow visits between 10am and 2:30pm if you ask politely.

Balboa Statue LANDMARK
(Map p46) Sculpted by Miguel Blan and Mariano Benlliure, the statue overlooks the Bahía de Panamá and was inaugurated in 1924, a gift from Spain.

Museo Afro-Antilleano MUSEUM
(Map p46; ☎501-4130; cnr Av Justo Arosemena & Calle 24 Este, Ancón; admission US$1; ⏲9am-4pm Tue-Sat) The small Afro-Antillean museum has exhibits on the history of Panama's West Indian community, particularly their work building the railroad and later the canal.

Baha'i House of Worship TEMPLE
(☎231-1137; ⏲10am-6pm) On the northeastern outskirts of Panama City, the white-domed Baha'i House of Worship is the mother temple for all of Latin America. It looms like a giant egg atop the crest of a hill, with a beautiful, breezy interior.

Readings from the Baha'i writings (in English and Spanish) are held Sunday morning at 10am. Any bus to Colón can let you off on the highway, but it's a long walk up the hill. It's 11km from the city center on Vía Transístmica.

World Trade Center LANDMARK
(Map p50) Located within the financial district, these two towers were built in 1996.

Museo de Ciencias Naturales MUSEUM
(Map p46; ☎info 225-0645; Av Cuba btwn Calles 29 Este & 30 Este, Calidonia; admission US$1; ⏲9am-3:45pm Tue-Sat) Museo de Ciencias Naturales has sections on geology, paleontology, entomology and marine biology, as well as an impressive display of taxidermy.

Casco Viejo

Following the destruction of the old city by Captain Henry Morgan in 1671, the Spanish moved their city 8km southwest to a rocky peninsula at the foot of Cerro Ancón. The new location was easier to defend as the reefs prevented ships from approaching the city except at high tide. The new city was also easy to defend, as a massive wall surrounded it, which is how Casco Viejo (Old Compound) got its name.

In 1904, when construction began on the Panama Canal, all of Panama City existed where Casco Viejo stands today. However, as population growth and urban expansion pushed the boundaries of Panama City further east, the city's elite abandoned Casco Viejo and the neighborhood rapidly deteriorated into a slum.

CAPTAIN HENRY MORGAN

After sacking the original Panama City settlement (now known as Panamá Viejo) in 1671, Captain Henry Morgan burnt the place to the ground, massacred its inhabitants and made off with the richest booty in the Americas. Because his actions violated a peace treaty between England and Spain, Morgan was arrested and conducted to England the following year, but he was acquitted because he supposedly had no prior knowledge of the treaty. In 1674 Morgan was knighted before departing for Jamaica to take up the post of lieutenant governor.

Although Captain Morgan is best remembered for his nefarious exploits at sea, the last several years of his life in Port Royal (the 'Sodom of the New World') are the stuff of legend. Here, he lived out his life spending the riches of Panama.

The events surrounding his death remain a mystery. He died in 1688, at the age of 53, leaving behind an immense personal fortune. Although his death has been attributed to tuberculosis and dropsy (edema), local lore has it that the world's most infamous pirate simply drank himself to death. Now his name lives on in the form of spiced rum.

To see the legacy left by Captain Morgan, visit the ruins of Panamá Viejo, or check out Casco Viejo's Iglesia de San José, which houses a golden altar – the only item salvaged after Morgan's raid.

Central Panama City

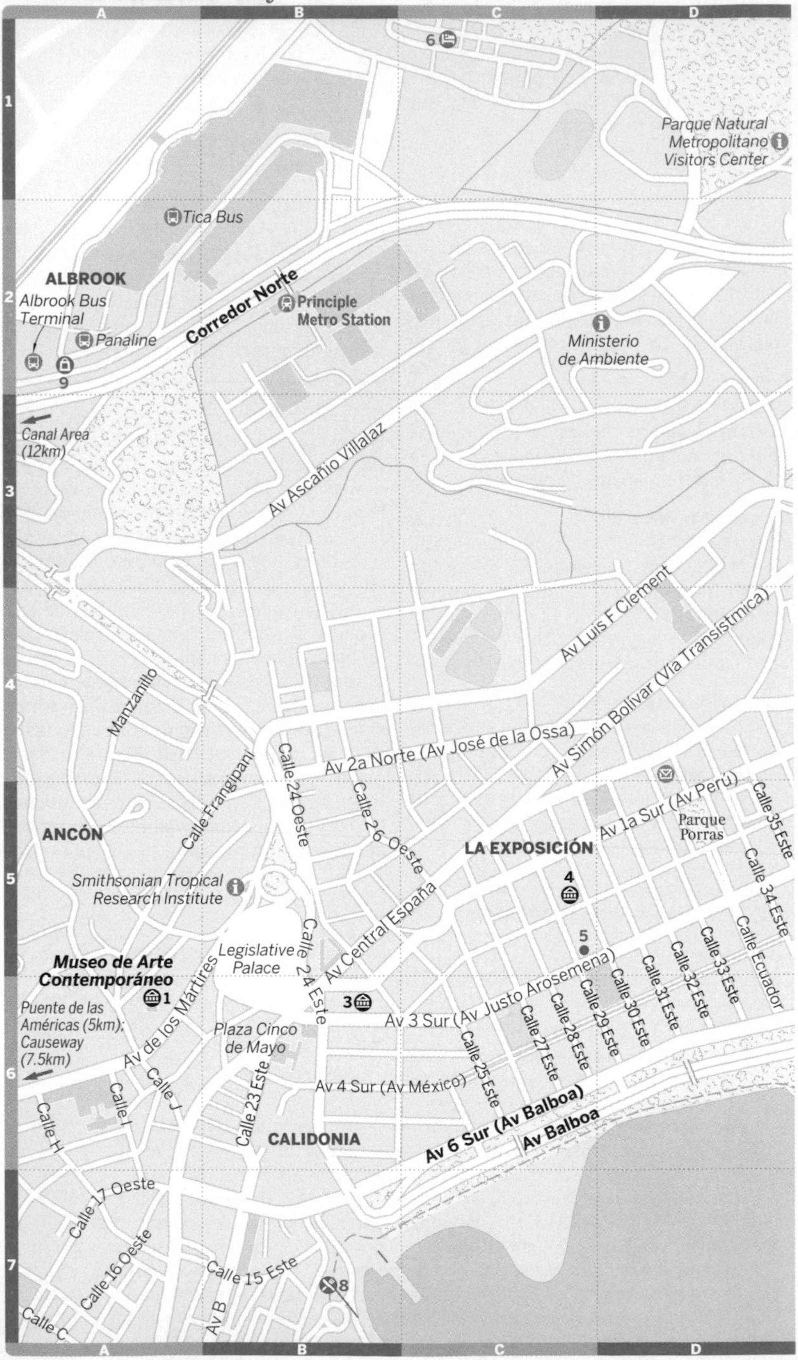
ALBROOK
Albrook Bus Terminal
9
Panaline
Tica Bus
Corredor Norte
Principle Metro Station
6
Parque Natural Metropolitano Visitors Center
Ministerio de Ambiente
Canal Area (12km)
Av Ascanio Villalaz
Av Luis F Clement
Av Simón Bolívar (Vía Transístmica)
Manzanillo
Av 2a Norte (Av José de la Ossa)
Calle Frangipani
Calle 24 Oeste
Calle 26 Oeste
ANCÓN
LA EXPOSICIÓN
Av 1a Sur (Av Perú)
Parque Porras
Calle 35 Este
Calle 34 Este
Calle Ecuador
Calle 33 Este
Calle 32 Este
Calle 31 Este
Calle 30 Este
Calle 29 Este
Calle 28 Este
Calle 27 Este
Calle 25 Este
4
5
Smithsonian Tropical Research Institute
Legislative Palace
Calle 24 Este
Av Central España
Museo de Arte Contemporáneo
1
3
Av 3 Sur (Av Justo Arosemena)
Puente de las Américas (5km); Causeway (7.5km)
Av de los Mártires
Plaza Cinco de Mayo
Calle J
Calle I
Calle H
Calle 23 Este
Av 4 Sur (Av México)
Av 6 Sur (Av Balboa)
Av Balboa
CALIDONIA
Calle 17 Oeste
Calle 16 Oeste
Calle 15 Este
Calle C
Av B
8

Central Panama City

Top Sights

1 Museo de Arte Contemporáneo A6

Sights

2 Balboa Statue E6
3 Museo Afro-Antilleano B6
4 Museo de Ciencias Naturales C5

Activities, Courses & Tours

5 City Sightseeing Panama C5
Panama Travel Unlimited .... (see 7)

Sleeping

6 Albrook Inn C1
7 Mamallena E4

Eating

8 Mercado de Mariscos B7

Entertainment

Albrook Cinemark .... (see 9)

Shopping

9 Albrook Mall A2

Today Casco Viejo's crumbling facades have been mostly replaced by immaculate renovations. Declared a Unesco World Heritage Site in 2003, the area is getting international recognition. The newly restored architecture gives a sense of how magnificent the neighborhood must have looked in past years. Some developers, committed to mitigating the effects of gentrification here, are creating one affordable unit for each high-end one constructed, and working on interesting local cultural initiatives. Yet the consensus is that most of the neighborhood's former occupants have already been relegated to the periphery.

Change continues to prove tricky for the Casco. The expansion of the Cinta Costera, a coastal beltway, has ringed the peninsula with an elevated highway built some 8m above the sea and 200m offshore. With little regard for environmental concerns, the project threatened the area's World Heritage status. Worst of all, the US$189 million project, created to fix city traffic problems by providing an alternative route, has not been effective as it does not bypass the worst bottleneck areas.

Museo del Canal Interoceánico MUSEUM
(Canal Museum; Map p54; ☎211-1649; www.museodelcanal.com; Calle 6a Oeste, Casco Viejo; admission US$2; ⏲9am-5pm Tue-Sun) This impressive museum is housed in a beautifully restored building that once served as the headquarters for the original French canal company.

The Panama Canal Museum (as it's more commonly known) presents excellent exhibits on the famous waterway, framed in their historical and political context. Signs are in Spanish, but English-speaking guides and audiotours (US$5) are available.

Iglesia de San José CHURCH

(Map p54; Av A) This Casco Viejo church protects the famous Altar de Oro (Golden Altar), the sole relic salvaged after privateer Henry Morgan sacked Panamá Viejo.

According to local legend, when word came of Morgan's impending attack, a priest attempted to disguise the altar by painting it black. The priest told Morgan that the famous altar had been stolen by another pirate, and even convinced Morgan to donate handsomely for its replacement. Morgan is said to have told the priest, 'I don't know why, but I think you are more of a pirate than I am.' Whatever the truth, the baroque altar was later moved from the old city to the present site.

Plaza de Francia PLAZA

(Map p54) At the tip of the southern point of Casco Viejo, this beautiful plaza pays homage to the French role in the construction of the canal. Its large stone tablets and statues are dedicated to the memory of the 22,000 workers who died trying to create the canal.

Most of the workers died from yellow fever and malaria. Among the busts is a monument to Cuban doctor Carlos J Finlay, whose discovery of how mosquitoes transmit yellow fever led to the eradication of the disease.

On one side of the plaza are nine restored dungeons that were used by the Spaniards and later by the Colombians. Although they're now home to some rather upscale art galleries and shops, you can still see the original stonework. Also on the plaza are the Teatro Anita Villalaz and the Instituto Nacional de Cultura.

Teatro Nacional THEATER

(Map p54; ☎262-3525; Av B) Built in 1907, the interior of this ornate Casco Viejo theater has been completely restored. It boasts red and gold decorations, a once-magnificent ceiling mural by Roberto Lewis (one of Panama's finest painters) and an impressive crystal chandelier. Performances are still held here. For information visit the office at the side of the building.

Iglesia y Convento de Santo Domingo CHURCH

(Map p54) Built in 1678, these gorgeous ruins in Casco Viejo are what remain after two major fires brought down the church's tower and interior areas. Left are the walls and arches, including a notable flat arch meant to aid in the acoustics of the choir.

Iglesia de La Merced CHURCH

(Map p54) An example of the baroque style in Panama, this Casco Viejo church was built in 1673 with a facade transferred from Panamá Viejo.

Diablo Rosso GALLERY

(Map p54; ☎209-9380; www.diablorosso.com; Calle José de Obaldía s/n, Casco Viejo; ⏲1-7pm Tue-Sat) This gallery with biting social commentary and quirky folk art would be perfectly at home in Buenos Aires' Palermo neighborhood. Check for art openings.

Iglesia y Convento de la Compañía de Jesús CHURCH

(Map p54) This 1741 convent and church in Casco Viejo has numerous seashell niches that represent the marine riches of Panama.

Catedral Metropolitana CATHEDRAL

(Map p54; Plaza de la Independencia, Casco Viejo) The headquarters of the Panama archdiocese. Construction started on this 1796 cathedral in 1688.

Paseo las Bóvedas WATERFRONT

(Map p54) This esplanade runs along the top of the sea wall built by the Spanish to protect the city. From here, you can see the Puente de las Américas arching over the waterway and the ships lining up to enter the canal.

Parque Bolívar PLAZA

(Map p54) In 1826, in a schoolroom opposite this Casco Viejo park, Simón Bolívar held a meeting urging the union of the Latin American countries. Bolívar eventually succeeded in liberating Bolivia, Colombia, Ecuador, Peru and Venezuela from Spanish rule and uniting them as Gran Colombia. Although he was unable to keep Gran Colombia together, he is venerated as a hero throughout Latin America.

Museo de Arte Religioso Colonial MUSEUM

(Museum of Colonial Religious Art; Map p54; ☎228-2897; www.inac.gob.pa/museos; cnr Av A & Calle 3a Este, Casco Viejo; admission US$1; ⏲9:20am-4pm Tue-Sat) Housed beside the ruins of the Iglesia y Convento de Santo Domingo, the Museo de Arte Religioso Colonial has a collection of colonial-era religious artifacts, some dating from the 16th century.

Just inside the ruins' doorway, the Arco Chato is a long arch that stood here unsupported for centuries. It even played a part in the selection of Panama over Nicaragua as the site for the canal since its survival was taken as proof that the area was not subject to earthquakes. It collapsed in 2003 but has since been rebuilt.

Museo de Historia de Panamá MUSEUM
(Map p54; ☎501-4128; www.inac.gob.pa/museos; Palacio Municipal, Calle 6a Oeste, Casco Viejo; adult/child US$1/0.50; ⏰9am-4pm Mon-Fri) FREE The modest Museo de Historia de Panamá has a small selection of exhibits covering Panamanian history from the colonial period to the modern era.

Plaza de la Independencia PLAZA
(Map p54) In this plaza, in the heart of Casco Viejo, Panama declared its independence from Colombia on November 3, 1903.

Palacio de las Garzas HISTORIC BUILDING
(Presidential Palace; Map p54; Av Alfaro) The Palacio de las Garzas is named after the great white herons *(garzas blancas)* that reside here. The president of Panama lives on the upper floor.

Casa de la Municipalidad LANDMARK
(Map p54) This 1881 neoclassical townhouse in Casco Viejo was built on top of the castle gatehouse of the city.

Palacio Municipal HISTORIC BUILDING
(Map p54) This neoclassical Casco Viejo building, dating to 1910, houses the modest Museo de Historia de Panamá (p49).

Iglesia de San Francisco CHURCH
(Map p54) This Casco Viejo church exhibits Gothic, Romantic and Renaissance architectural influences.

Instituto Nacional de Cultura GALLERY
(INAC; Map p54; ☎211-4034; Plaza de Francia, Casco Viejo; ⏰8:30am-4pm Mon-Fri) INAC is responsible for maintaining the country's museums and other cultural institutions. There is a small gallery on the 1st floor that displays works by Panamanian artists.

Parque Natural Metropolitano

On a hill north of downtown, the 265-hectare **Parque Natural Metropolitano** (☎info 232-5516; www.parquemetropolitano.org; Av Juan Pablo II; admission US$5; ⏰8am-5pm Mon-Fri, to 1pm Sat) protects vast expanses of tropical semideciduous forest within the city limits.

PANAMA CITY FOR CHILDREN

Panama City has a variety of attractions to enthrall and entertain kids. The city's Cinta Costera has waterfront paths and a playground. The setting also hosts sporting events and occasional fairs. Another park option is Parque Recreativo Omar, the local answer to New York City's Central Park, with greens that were once a golf course.

A perfect reward for a day well spent is ice cream, and Casco Viejo's Granclement is a parlor that even mom and dad would beg to visit.

Great rainforest excursions abound. At the Rainforest Discovery Center, kids can walk short paths and check out the wildlife from the top of a 32m tower. Alongside huge canal boats, jungle boats cruise along Lago Gatún, fishing for peacock bass or just spotting troupes of monkeys, birds and other animals.

Isla Taboga is another interesting day trip, with plenty of sand to play in and a cool ferry ride that's a blast for small travelers.

For more adventure, families can visit an Emberá village in the Parque Nacional Soberanía, tour the old cannon-lined forts in Portobelo, or take a moderate hike through Parque Nacional Soberanía or even just in town at Parque Natural Metropolitano, where the chances of spotting a monkey or toucan are pretty good.

The Panama Canal Railway Company, which links the two oceans, provides a lovely journey along the canal and through rainforest. Kids might also enjoy a visit to the Miraflores Locks, especially since the new museum there has lots of eye-catching multimedia exhibitions and is hands-on in parts.

If you need a respite from the heat (or the rain), head to Centro Natural Punta Culebra to get close to Panama's amazing underwater world. Or if all else fails, stroll down to Multicentro Mall, which has dozens of shops and restaurants, a movie theater and an internet cafe.

El Cangrejo & Bella Vista

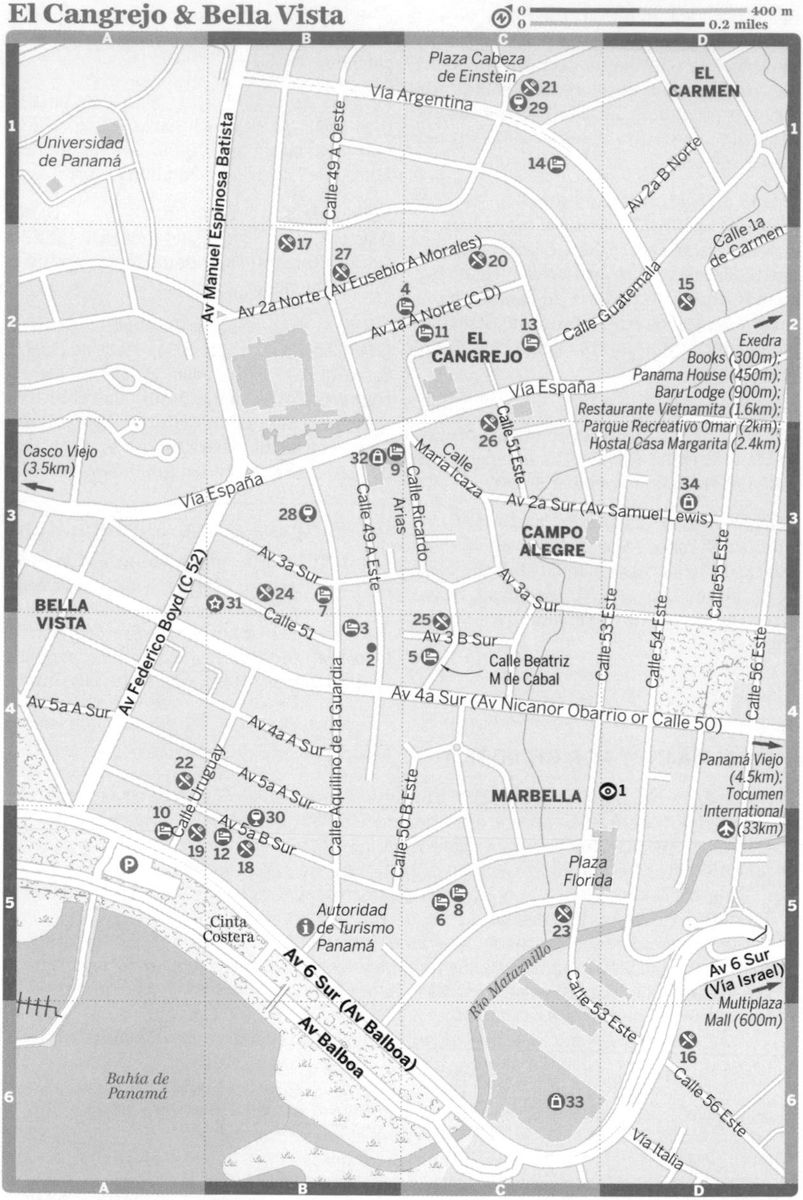

It serves as an incredible wilderness escape from the trappings of the capital. Two main walking trails, the Nature Trail and the Tití Monkey Trail, join to form one long loop, with a 150m-high *mirador* (lookout) offering panoramic views of Panama City, the bay and the canal, all the way to the Miraflores Locks.

Mammals in the park include *tití* monkeys, anteaters, sloths and white-tailed deer, while reptiles include iguanas, turtles and tortoises.

El Cangrejo & Bella Vista

Sights

1	World Trade Center	D4

Activities, Courses & Tours

2	Ancon Expeditions	B4

Sleeping

3	Bristol Panama	B4
4	Coral Suites Aparthotel	C2
5	DeVille Hotel	C4
6	El Machico	C5
7	Executive Hotel	B3
8	Hostel Villa Vento Surf	C5
9	Hotel Continental	B3
10	Le Meridien	A5
11	Metro Hotel	C2
12	Panama Hat Hostel	B5
13	Riande Granada Hotel	C2
14	Saba Hotel	C1

Eating

15	Avatar	D2
16	Caminito de la Empanada	D6
17	Chez Titi	B2
18	Crêpes & Waffles	B5
19	La Posta	A5
20	Martín Fierro	C2
21	New York Bagel Café	C1
	Niko's Café	(see 26)
22	Ozone	A4
23	Petit Paris	C5
24	Sabores de la India	B3
25	Sukhi	C4
26	Supermercado Rey	C3
27	Wine Bar	B2

Drinking & Nightlife

28	Club Moat	B3
29	La Rana Dorada	C1
30	Starlight	B5

Entertainment

	Multicentro Cinemark	(see 33)
31	Restaurante-Bar Tinajas	B3

Shopping

32	Joyería La Huaca	B3
33	Multicentro Mall	C6
34	Reprosa	D3

More than 250 bird species have been spotted here. Fish and shrimp inhabit the Río Curundú along the eastern side of the park.

The park was the site of an important battle during the US invasion to oust Noriega. Also of historical significance, concrete structures just past the park entrance were used during WWII as a testing and assembly plant for aircraft engines.

The park is bordered to the west and north by Camino de la Amistad and to the south and east by Corredor Norte; Av Juan Pablo II runs right through the park.

Pick up a pamphlet for a self-guided tour in Spanish and English at the **visitors center** (Map p46; 232-5516; 8am-5pm Mon-Fri, to 1pm Sat), 40m north of the park entrance.

Canopy Crane TOWER

(232-5552; www.parquemetropolitano.org) Scientists set up this research crane to study the Parque Metropolitano forest canopy, a complete ecosystem 30m to 50m up from the ground. It was off-limits to the public, but now tour operators take tourists up to the treetops. It provides an entirely different view of the rainforest. Book ahead.

Panamá Viejo

Founded on August 15, 1519, by Spanish conquistador Pedro Arias de Ávila, the city of Panamá was the first European settlement along the Pacific. For the next 150 years it profited mainly from Spain's famed bullion pipeline, which ran from Peru's gold and silver mines to Europe via Panamá. Because of the amount of wealth that passed through the city, the Spaniards kept many soldiers here, and their presence kept the buccaneers away.

In 1671, 1200 pirates led by Captain Henry Morgan (see p45) ascended the Río Chagres and proceeded overland to Panamá. Although the city was not fortified, it was protected on three sides by the sea and marshes, and on the land side was a causeway with a bridge to allow tidal water to pass underneath. But to the bewilderment of historians, when Morgan and his men neared the city, the Spanish soldiers left this natural stronghold and confronted the buccaneers in a hilly area outside town.

It was the first of many mistakes in battle. After the Spanish force fell to pieces nearly everything of value was either plundered and divvied up or destroyed by fire.

For the next three centuries, the abandoned city served as a convenient source of building materials. By the time the government declared the ruins a protected site in 1976 (Unesco followed suit in 1997), most of the old city had already been dismantled and overrun.

So little of the original city remains that its size, layout and appearance are the subject of much conjecture. Today much of Panamá Viejo lies buried under a poor residential neighborhood, though the **ruins** (Map p58; ☎226-8915; www.panamaviejo.org; adult/child US$12/5; ⏰8:30am-4:30pm Tue-Sun) are a must-see, even if only to stand on the grounds of one of Central America's greatest cities.

For safety reasons it's best to explore the area during daylight hours.

Panamá Viejo buses will drop you off at the Mercado Nacional de Artesanías (p68) behind the first remnants of the old city as you approach from Panama City.

Catedral de Nuestra Señora de la Asunción CATHEDRAL

(Map p58) Built between 1619 and 1626, this cathedral is the best-preserved building of the Panamá Viejo ruins. In traditional fashion, it was designed so that its two side chapels gave the cathedral a cross-like shape when viewed from the heavens. The bell tower at the back of the church may have served double duty as a watchtower for the Casas Reales (Royal Houses). The main facade, which faced the Plaza Mayor, is gone – only the walls remain.

Puente del Rey BRIDGE

(Map p58) Built in 1617, this Panamà Viejo landmark may be the oldest standing bridge in the Americas.

Iglesia y Convento de Santo Domingo CHURCH

(Map p58) Iglesia y Convento de Santo Domingo is the best-preserved church of the ruins of Panamá Viejo. The convent dates from the 1570s, though the church was built 20 or more years later.

Iglesia y Convento de San Francisco CHURCH

(Map p58) Like other Panamá Viejo churches, this is among the settlement's most outstanding structures: rectangular, with stone outer walls, timber roofs, internal wooden supports and a lack of towers. The adjoining convent had inner courts surrounded by wooden galleries, and the larger ones had enclosed gardens and orchards.

Iglesia y Convento de la Compañía de Jesús CHURCH

(Map p58) In Panamá Viejo, the Jesuits arrived a decade or so after Dominican friars and built Iglesia y Convento de la Compañía de Jesús, whose stone ruins are visible today. These spacious ruins of a church and convent were erected by the nuns of Nuestra Señora de la Concepción. Most of the ruins, which cover the better part of two blocks, were part of the church – little remains of the convent.

Iglesia y Convento de la Concepción CHURCH

(Map p58) In Panamá Viejo, Iglesia y Convento de la Concepción was erected by the nuns of Nuestra Señora de la Concepción. Most of the ruins, which cover the better part of two blocks, were part of the church – little remains of the convent.

Iglesia de San José CHURCH

(Map p58) In Panamá Viejo, Iglesia de San José belonged to the Augustine order. Of special interest here are the building's vaulted side chapels, an architectural feature seldom seen in Panama.

Casa Alarcón HISTORIC BUILDING

(Map p58) The massive ruins of Casa Alarcón represent Panamá Viejo's best-preserved and largest known private residence, which dates from the 1640s.

Casas Reales HISTORIC BUILDING

(Map p58) Panamá Viejo's center of power resided at Casas Reales (Royal Houses), a complex ringed by timber ramparts and separated from the city proper by a moat. Within the complex were the customs house, the royal treasury, a prison and the governor's house. Despite the obvious historical importance of the site, past governments have allowed sections of the property to be used as a landfill and for horse stables. Only scattered walls remain of the once impressive structures.

Iglesia y Convento de La Merced CHURCH

(Map p58) Erected by the Mercedarian friars in the early 17th century, these Panamá Viejo buildings survived the fire that swept the city following privateer Henry Morgan's assault. However, the church's facade was dismantled by friars and moved to Casco Viejo, where it can be seen today.

Casas de Terrín HISTORIC BUILDING

(Map p58) Facing the Plaza Mayor in Panamá Viejo, these houses were built by Francisco Terrín. The better houses were usually built from timber and placed wall to wall, with small inner courts, open-air kitchens and separate wings for the servants. Some had ground-floor galleries and balconies, and most had plain exterior walls. The ruins of a few of the fancier stone homes remain.

The poor had far simpler dwellings, usually thatched huts built with inexpensive materials such as reeds.

Cabildo de la Ciudad HISTORIC BUILDING
(Map p58) Facing the Plaza Mayor in Panamá Viejo, the Cabildo de la Ciudad (City Hall) was built by one of the city's wealthiest citizens, Francisco Terrín.

Museo de Sitio Panamá Viejo MUSEUM
(Map p58; ☎226-8915; www.panamaviejo.org; Av 6 Sur, Panamá Viejo; adult/child US$12/5; ruins only adult/child US$8/free; ⏰8:30am-4:30pm Tue-Sun) In the original settlement, this museum hosts an impressive scale model of Panamá Viejo prior to 1671 as well as a few colonial artifacts. Signs are in Spanish, though a brochure and tape recording recount the site's history in English. An optional extra is climbing Mirador de la Torre, the lookout tower, though note that children under eight are not allowed.

Puente del Matadero BRIDGE
(Map p58) This awkwardly over-restored stone bridge in Panamà Viejo took its name from a nearby slaughterhouse. It marked the beginning of the Camino Real to Portobelo.

Hospital de San Juan de Dios RUIN
(Map p58) There's not much left of Panamá Viejo's sole hospital, Hospital de San Juan de Dios. Much of the remains were scattered when Av Cincuentenario and a side road were put in.

The Causeway

At the Pacific entrance to the Panama Canal, a 2km palm tree–lined *calzada* (causeway) connects the four small islands of Naos, Culebra, Perico and Flamenco to the mainland. The Causeway is popular in the early morning and late afternoon, when residents walk, jog, skate and cycle its narrow length.

The Causeway also offers sweeping views of the skyline and the old city, with flocks of brown pelicans diving into the sea. Some people come here simply to savor the pleasant breeze at one of the many restaurants and bars.

If you don't have your own vehicle, it's most convenient to take a taxi to the Causeway (US$4 to US$8). Any of the restaurants or bars can call one for you.

★**BioMuseo** MUSEUM
(Museum of Biodiversity; www.biomuseopanama.org; Causeway; adult/child US$22/11; ⏰10am-4pm Tue-Fri, to 5pm Sat & Sun) Celebrating Panama as the land bridge that has permitted astonishing biodiversity in the region, this museum is a visual feast. World-renowned architect Frank Gehry, who created the Guggenheim Museum in Bilbao (Spain), designed this landmark museum of crumpled multicolor forms.

THE SECRET LIFE OF THE CAUSEWAY

All four of the Causeway islands once comprised Fort Grant, which was established in 1913 to guard the southern entrance to the canal. Between 1913 and WWII, the USA made Fort Grant the most powerful defense complex in the world.

In 1928 two 14in guns with ranges up to 44km were brought to Panama. Mounted on railway carriages, they could be moved across the isthmus via the Panama Railroad to defend either entrance to the canal (the Pacific-side emplacement for the railroad guns was on Culebra). You can still see the tracks on the driveway leading up to the Centro de Exhibiciones Marinas. The concrete rooms nearby, now used by marine-center staff, once housed the guns' ammunition.

In 1941 the Japanese assault on Pearl Harbor showed that carrier-based aircraft could attack successfully far beyond the range of artillery. Suddenly obsolete, many of the big guns were retired from service even before the end of WWII. However, in 1942 the US military was still determined to bulk up its defenses and paid the enormous cost of US$400,000 to build a command post on Isla Flamenco.

The Causeway, its four islands and a chunk of the peninsula leading to the Causeway were turned over to Panama in October 1979 in compliance with the Torrijos–Carter Treaty of 1977. Today part of the Fuerte Amador shopping center is built on a massively protected bombproof structure that was needed 'for use in case of emergency and vital to the security of important data,' according to the US general who ordered its construction. Even today the US military will not disclose what data was so important that it needed to be stored at the center of a rock island.

Casco Viejo

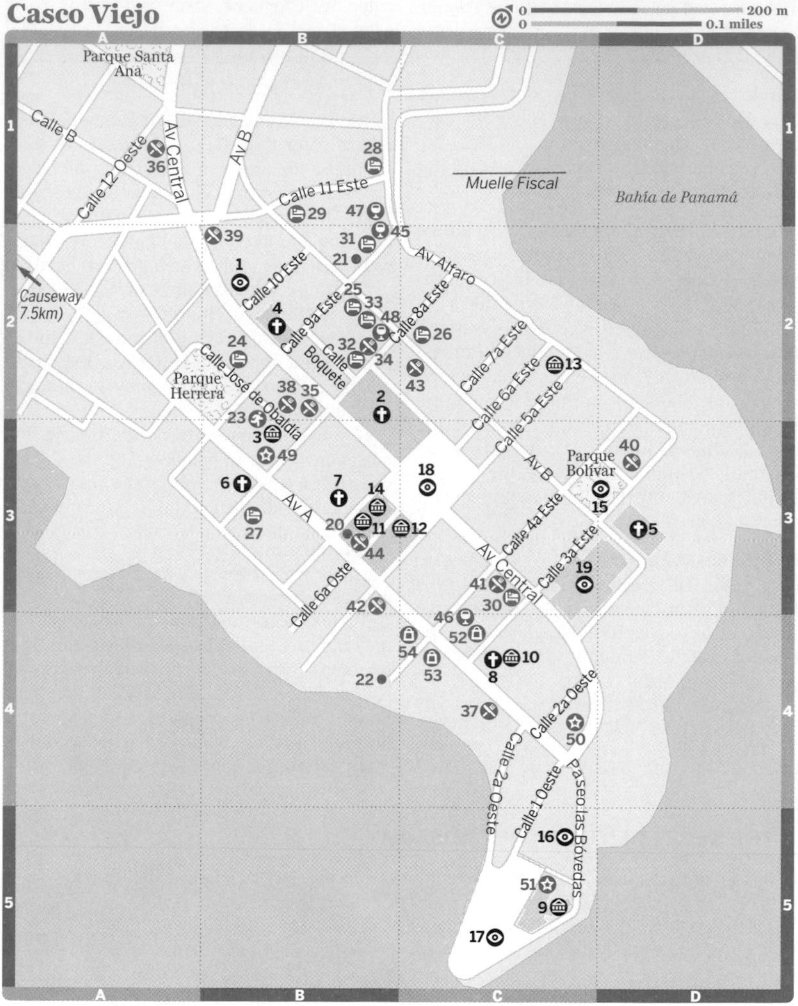

Exhibits are world class, with botanical gardens in the works. Audio guides come in five languages. It's located on the Causeway.

Centro Natural Punta Culebra MUSEUM
(CEM; ☎212-8000; Amador Causeway, Punta Culebra; adult/child US$5/1; ⊙1-5pm Tue-Fri, 10am-6pm Sat & Sun) Ideal for families, CEM is operated by the Smithsonian Tropical Research Institute (STRI). This informative marine museum features two small aquariums and a nature trail through a patch of dry forest containing sloths and iguanas. Signs are in English and Spanish.

Separate aquariums contain fish from the Pacific and the Caribbean, allowing you to compare the two. Staff can explain to you the reasons for the differences. Exhibits examine the role that Panama's marine resources play in the country's economy, and the destructive effects of harvesting fish and shrimp by net.

Exhibits include a small six-sided building with sweeping views of the Bahía de Panamá, built by Manuel Noriega for intimate gatherings. Today it has exhibits on the history of Panama's indigenous cultures.

Outside, large, intelligent illustrations of vessels allow visitors to glance out at the

Casco Viejo

Sights

1	Casa de la Municipalidad	B2
2	Catedral Metropolitana	B2
3	Diablo Rosso	B3
4	Iglesia de La Merced	B2
5	Iglesia de San Francisco	D3
6	Iglesia de San José	B3
7	Iglesia y Convento de la Compañía de Jesús	B3
8	Iglesia y Convento de Santo Domingo	C4
9	Instituto Nacional de Cultura	C5
10	Museo de Arte Religioso Colonial	C4
11	Museo de Historia de Panamá	B3
12	Museo del Canal Interoceánico	C3
13	Palacio de las Garzas	C2
14	Palacio Municipal	B3
15	Parque Bolívar	D3
16	Paseo las Bóvedas	C5
17	Plaza de Francia	C5
18	Plaza de la Independencia	C3
19	Teatro Nacional	C3

Activities, Courses & Tours

20	Barefoot Panama	B3
21	Cacique Cruiser	B2
22	Casco Antiguo Spanish School	B4
23	Casco Yoga	B2

Sleeping

24	American Trade Hotel	B2
25	Casa Nurrati	B2
26	Casa Sucre	C2
27	Hospedaje Casco Viejo	B3
28	Hotel Casa Panama	B1
29	Las Clementinas	B1
30	Los Cuatro Tulipanes	C3
31	Luna's Castle	B2
32	Magnolia Inn	B2
33	Tántalo	B2

Eating

34	Aki	B2
35	Barrio Pizza	B2
36	Café Coca Cola	A1
37	Café Per Due	C4
38	Crave	B2
39	Donde José	B2
40	Ego y Narciso	D3
41	Granclement	C3
42	Madrigal	B3
43	Restaurante L'Osteria	C2
44	Super Gourmet	B3

Drinking & Nightlife

45	Bar Relic	B2
46	Duke's Bar	C4
47	La Rana Dorada	B1
48	Tántalo Bar	B2

Entertainment

49	Fundación Danilo Perez	B3
50	Platea	C4
51	Teatro Anita Villalaz	C5
	Teatro Nacional	(see 19)

Shopping

52	Karavan	C4
53	No Me Olvides	C4
54	Papiro y Yo	C4

ocean and identify the types of ships waiting to transit the canal, aided by a telescope.

Just south of the Puente de las Américas is a surviving patch of dry forest, which once lined Central America's Pacific coast. Keep your eyes open for three-toed sloths as well as other wildlife.

Fuerte Amador Resort & Marina MARINA
(☎314-1980; Isla Flamenco s/n) At the end of Isla Flamenco, this complex contains a two-story shopping center, a marina, a cruise-ship terminal and a number of restaurants and bars. At night, these open-air spots are a big draw, providing a fine setting for cocktails or a decent meal. At the marina, daily boats leave for the nearby resort island of Isla Taboga.

Activities

Panama Audubon Society OUTDOORS
(☎232-5977; www.audubonpanama.org) Holds bird-watching walks and monthly meetings with interesting speakers at Parque Natural Metropolitano visitors center. It's a good opportunity to get to know some Panamanian birdwatchers and to learn more about tropical bird species. Both English and Spanish are spoken.

Casco Yoga YOGA
(Map p54; ☎6265-5588; www.cascoyogapanama.com; Calle José de Obaldía, Casco Viejo) Offers a variety of yoga classes in a 2nd-floor studio, with English-speaking instruction.

Casco Charters BOATING
(☎6058-4386; http://cascocharters.com; charters from US$450; ⏲Dec-May) Great for groups, these charters can take you to Isla Taboga, the Pearl Islands or out for a fine day of fishing (several area restaurants will cook your catch). The captain is a friendly American. Boats are well equipped and fully licensed and the company promotes responsible

fishing practices. Trips leave from the American Trade Hotel.

Bicicletas Moses BICYCLE RENTAL
(☎211-2718; Amador Causeway; per hour from US$4; ⏰9am-7pm Sat & Sun) This bike tent has mountain bikes as well as reclining bikes, tandems, bicycle carts and options for kids. Has a Facebook page.

Scubapanama DIVING
(☎261-3841; www.scubapanama.com; Calle 52c Oeste, Vista Hermosa) Panama's oldest dive operator, offering a variety of trips throughout the country.

Courses

Casco Antiguo Spanish School LANGUAGE COURSE
(Map p54; ☎228-3258; www.cascospanish.com; Calle 4a Oeste; 1-week 20hr intensive US$249) This reader-recommended Spanish school sits in the heart of Casco Viejo. In addition to private and group lessons, it also offers accommodations and activities.

Institute for Spanish Language Studies LANGUAGE COURSE
(ILERI; ☎260-4424; www.isls.com/panama; Camino de la Amistad, El Dorado; per week from US$255) Located in the suburban El Dorado neighborhood, this language school offers four hours of one-on-one instruction per day, five days a week. Also has homestay options.

Tours

Panama Road Trips TOUR
(☎6800-7727; www.panamaroadtrips.com; tours from US$25) This small enterprise runs affordable day trips to Portobelo or an Emberá village in addition to popular canal and city tours. Also works with interesting rural tourism options throughout Panama.

Ancon Expeditions BOAT TOUR
(Map p50; ☎269-9415; www.anconexpeditions.com; Edificio Dorado, No 3, Calle 49 A Este, El Cangrejo) Ancon Expeditions offers regularly scheduled canal transits. It's a good idea to book in advance as this is one of the company's most popular offerings.

Barefoot Panama TOUR
(Map p54; ☎6780-3010; www.barefootpanama.com; Av A s/n; city tour per person US$85) Prompt and professional, this tiny American-run agency based in Casco Viejo does a great tour of Panama City that takes in everything from the history to the flora and fauna. There are also day trips to San Lorenzo and Gamboa, with visits to a Wounaan indigenous village.

City Sightseeing Panama BUS TOUR
(Map p46; ☎392-6000; www.city-sightseeing.com; Av Justo Arosemena & Calle 29 Este, Calidonia; 24hr ticket adult/child US$29/15) A good way to get your bearings, these red double-deckers loop the city. Stops include Multicentro Mall, Calle Uruguay, Casco Viejo and the Amador Causeway. Service is hop on, hop off, so you can explore the sights all you want with hourly pickups. Departures run between 9am and 4pm, except for the night tour. Tickets are good for 24 or 48 hours.

The outfit also offers a tour of the canal zone.

Festivals & Events

Panama City goes wild for holidays, with public events, parades and concerts. Festivals – both traditional and modern – are well worth attending.

Carnaval CULTURAL
(⏰Feb/Mar) Carnaval in Panama City is celebrated with merriment and wild abandon in the days preceding Ash Wednesday, between February and March. From Saturday until the following Tuesday, work is put away and masks, costumes and confetti come out, and for 96 hours almost anything goes.

Festivities begin with the coronation of the Carnaval queen on Friday, followed by a small Saturday parade with the queen and her court. Vía España fills with people, music pours from all directions and spontaneous dancing breaks out. Masqueraded characters cavort among the crowd. Colorful street vendors wander through the throngs of people, and improvised entertainment abounds. The party moves indoors at night – into *cantinas*, private clubs and hotels – where combos play Afro-Cuban and typical Panamanian music, and the dancing and drinking continue till dawn.

On Sunday folk-dance groups decked out in Panama's national costumes join the queen and her attendants in the afternoon parade down Vía España, traveling from near Vía Brasil to near Av Federico Boyd (the exact beginning and ending points vary from year to year). To cool the sunbaked masses, fire and garden hoses are turned on the crowd. The amount of water sprayed on partygoers during Carnaval during these four festive days equals the amount the city uses during the previous four months.

The madness peaks on Shrove Tuesday with the biggest parade of all. Floats of all sizes rule the avenue, not the least conspicuous of which is the traditional entourage of transvestites. Most of them carry a razor in each hand as a warning to macho types that a punch thrown at them will not go unanswered.

Carnaval officially closes with the first rays of sunlight on Wednesday morning, when the hardiest celebrants appear on the beach of the Bahía de Panamá to bury a sardine in the sand – a symbolic gesture intended to convey the end of worldly pleasures for the Lenten season.

Panama Jazz Festival MUSIC
(www.panamajazzfestival.com; ⊙mid-Jan) A blast, the Panama Jazz Festival is gaining momentum as one of the biggest musical events in Panama, drawing hundreds of thousands of spectators for a week in mid-January. It's held all over the city. Open-air events are usually free, while big-draw theater spectacles require tickets.

🛌 Sleeping

Panama City offers every kind of accommodation. A glut of options means that many high-end hotels offer deals that bring them into the midrange.

Boutique lodgings are on the rise. Post urban renewal, old-world charmer Casco Viejo is an excellent place to stay, with many restaurants and cafes within walking distance.

Fast-paced modern Panama is best experienced in the overlapping neighborhoods of Bella Vista, Marbella and El Cangrejo. For those who prefer the quiet life, outlying neighborhoods have excellent B&B options. These include the former US-occupied neighborhoods of Albrook, Ancón and Amador, located in the Canal Zone.

🛏 Casco Viejo

★**Luna's Castle** HOSTEL $
(Map p54; ☑262-1540; www.lunascastlehostel.com; Calle 9a Este, Casco Viejo; dm/d/tr incl breakfast US$16/34/51; @🛜) Housed in a creaky, colonial mansion, Luna's masterfully blends Spanish-colonial architecture with funky, laid-back backpacker vibes and great service. Shell out the extra dollar for a dorm with air-conditioning. A bit loony and very friendly, it's the kind of hostel people keep talking about long after their trip.

Perks include free bikes, laundry service, an activities concierge and a basement movie house showing popular flicks.

Hospedaje Casco Viejo HOSTEL $
(Map p54; ☑211-2027; www.hospedajecascoviejo.com; Calle 8a Oeste, Casco Viejo; dm/d incl breakfast with shared bathroom US$14/28, d US$33; 🅿@🛜) This renovated hostel offers triple-decker

THE JAZZ SOLUTION

Once a down-and-out section of the city with crumbling architecture and serious poverty, Casco Viejo is coming into a new chapter. Making a strong push towards revitalization, the neighborhood is home to dozens of new restaurants, cafes, shops and renovated historical buildings. In the midst of this architectural revival, another less tangible one struggles to take place: that of the Panamanian music community.

Jazz great and native Panamanian Danilo Perez returned here to the musical conservatory where he learned his first notes to establish **Fundación Danilo Perez** (Map p54; ☑211-0272; www.fundaciondaniloperez.com; 1069 Av A, Casco Viejo), a musical foundation that has generated over US$1 million in youth scholarships. It also sponsors the Panama Jazz Festival, a wildly popular citywide event featuring artists from all over the world.

In an interview with *El Casqueño* Perez says, 'Through the discipline of music we can create relevant leaders and good citizens. We can solve many of society's problems.' Youth are chosen from inner-city Panama and all parts of the country, including Colón and the Comarca de Guna Yala. Some grants take students as far as the Berklee College of Music and the New England Conservatory. Many come back to the music conservatory to teach others and complete the cycle of community participation.

The Panama Jazz Festival is held every January, with a week of events in theaters around the city, culminating in a free Saturday concert in the Casco's Plaza de la Independencia. The foundation in Casco Viejo also houses a library and music museum and is open to the public (admission is free).

Panamá Viejo

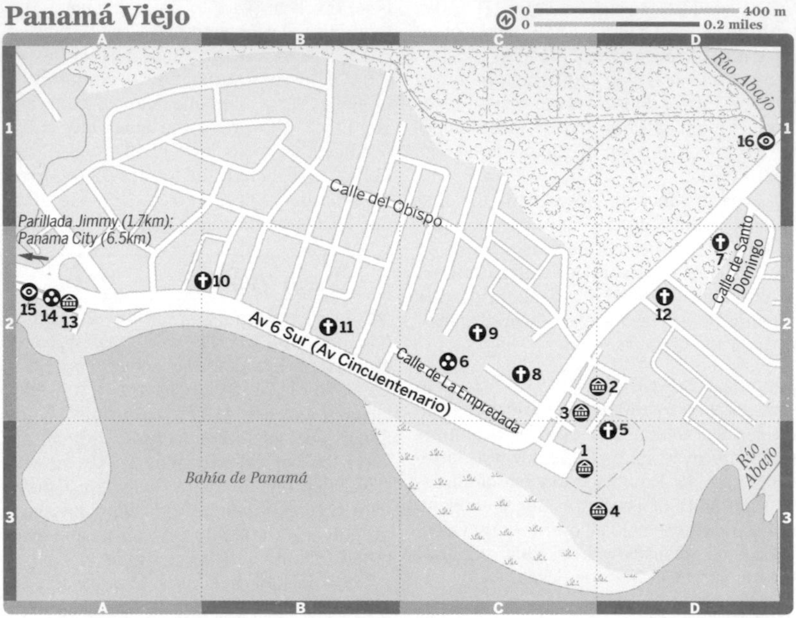

bunks and plain, pleasant rooms at great prices. Showers are temperate. There's a lovely rooftop with city views, a communal kitchen and an open-air courtyard. It's on a quiet side street near the Iglesia de San José.

★ Magnolia Inn INN $$

(Map p54; ☎202-0872, in USA 1-786-375-9633; www.magnoliapanama.com; cnr Calle Boquete & Calle 8a Este, Casco Viejo; dm US$15, r US$88-135; ❄📶) Every detail speaks to the thoughtfulness of this cool inn, a restored three-story colonial run by American expats. Air-conditioned dorms are grown-up friendly, with orthopedic mattresses, quality bedding, individual lamps and numerous power plug-ins. Shared bathrooms are immaculate and service is top-notch. Ample doubles with city views come stocked with minifridges, flat-screen TVs and coffee makers. There's also a kitchen.

Offers good travel advice and an English-speaking taxi service.

Casa Nurrati BOUTIQUE HOTEL $$

(Map p54; ☎262-2315; http://casanuratti.com; Av B, Casco Viejo; d/tr incl breakfast US$80/120; ❄📶) A minimally boutique offering above an Italian restaurant, this small lodging features 12 white rooms, many of them small, accessed via elevator. It's low-lit and simply decorated, with recycled palettes, themed photography and polished-concrete floors. For a bit more (US$20) the balcony rooms are brighter and more cheerful. Has rooftop views. Near Calle 8a Este.

★ Las Clementinas BOUTIQUE HOTEL $$$

(Map p54; ☎228-7613; www.lasclementinas.com; cnr Calle 11 Este & Av B, Casco Viejo; d incl breakfast from US$180; ❄@📶) 🍃 All happy families may be alike, but great hotels have their particularities. This one, with its antique regional maps, recycled hardwood floors from the canal, and unusual relics from the original house, feels like authentic Panama. The restored colonial has six airy suites, a leafy courtyard and a wonderful restaurant.

Guests have the opportunity to locally engage, with free cruising bikes and house-made pocket guides that include listings of the best neighborhood dives. Original tours visit marginal areas where tradespeople like traditional tailors work, to show the many complex issues of the city.

★ American Trade Hotel HISTORIC HOTEL $$$

(Map p54; ☎211-2000; www.acehotel.com/panama; Plaza Herrera s/n, Casco Viejo; d US$251-386; P❄📶🏊) Evoking old-time tropical grandeur, the refurbished trade hotel reinvests Plaza Herrera with a prosperous feel. With recycled floors from the canal expansion, a pool

Panamá Viejo

Sights

1 Cabildo de la Ciudad ... C3
2 Casa Alarcón ... D2
3 Casas de Terrín ... C2
4 Casas Reales ... D3
5 Catedral de Nuestra Señora de la Asunción ... D3
6 Hospital de San Juan de Dios ... C2
7 Iglesia de San José ... D2
8 Iglesia y Convento de la Compañía de Jesús ... C2
9 Iglesia y Convento de la Concepción ... C2
10 Iglesia y Convento de La Merced ... B2
11 Iglesia y Convento de San Francisco ... B2
12 Iglesia y Convento de Santo Domingo ... D2
13 Museo de Sitio Panamá Viejo ... A2
14 Panamá Viejo ... A2
15 Puente del Matadero ... A2
16 Puente del Rey ... D1

Shopping

Mercado Nacional de Artesanías ... (see 14)

and a library, it has many pleasant nooks to explore. It's hard to believe that it long sat abandoned and trolled by gangs (though their graffiti decorates an interior staircase). Upper floors offer views of the Causeway.

Also has a restaurant, a fairtrade cafe and a jazz club.

Los Cuatro Tulipanes APARTMENT **$$$**
(Map p54; ☎211-0877; www.loscuatrotulipanes.com; office Av Central btwn Calles 3 & 4, Casco Viejo; apt from US$175; P❄☜) Ideal for travelers yearning for a little independence and privacy, the 'four tulips' are a set of luxury apartments in distinct Casco Viejo locations. While each is unique, all are elegant, restored spaces with features like handpainted tiles, hardwood details, high ceilings and private terraces. Some have a concierge.

Kitchens are fully equipped, and maid service, wi-fi, cable TV, and coffee and tea are included.

Tántalo BOUTIQUE HOTEL **$$$**
(Map p54; ☎262-4030; www.tantalohotel.com; cnr Calle 8a Este & Av B, Casco Viejo; d incl breakfast from US$148) Industrial chic has hit Casco hard. Various artists were commissioned to create the 12 rooms of this boutique hotel. Do oversized spikes on the ceilings work for you? With oversized murals, stenciled Bukowski quotes and stripped-down decor, none of the rooms are shy – or too serious. A brick lobby with a vegetation wall at the bar says, 'Welcome, what's your story?'

Casa Sucre B&B **$$$**
(Map p54; ☎393-6130, 6982-2504; http://casasucreboutiquehotel.com; cnr Calle 8a Este & Av B, Casco Viejo; d incl breakfast US$160, 2-/3-person apt US$170/185; ❄☜) Set in an 1873 convent, this American-run B&B features plush lodgings amid family heirlooms and period furniture. The setting is serene, with a wraparound balcony overlooking the action of Casco Viejo. Watch for the friendly ghost rumored to dwell on the entrance staircase. There's also a downstairs cafe with great coffee, run by California natives Alyce and Rich.

Hotel Casa Panama BOUTIQUE HOTEL **$$$**
(Map p54; ☎303-0992; www.hotelcasapanama.com; cnr Av Alfaro & Calle 11 Este, Casco Viejo; d US$121-203; ❄☜≋) With a good location and dark, modern rooms featuring polished concrete and tropical decor, this new boutique offering has appeal. However, service seems a bit indifferent, especially given the price tag. Still, some will come for the rooftop pool alone. Some rooms are tiny – ask to see a few. Those with sea views are considerably more expensive.

Calidonia

Calidonia is central to city highlights but is a very working-class area not frequented by outsiders. Given that foot traffic dwindles in the evening, it's best to take taxis at night.

Mamallena HOSTEL **$**
(Map p46; ☎6676-6163, 393-6611; www.mamallena.com; Calle Primera Perejil, Calidonia; dm/d incl breakfast US$13/33; ❄@☜) On a residential street that's somehow survived the wrecking ball, this small, homey hostel nails the mark on service. Amenities include 24-hour desk service, pancake breakfasts and DVD library. High-ceilinged dorms have air-con at night and the cute motel-style doubles offer considerable privacy. The on-site travel agency offers sailing to San Blás and popular day trips.

Renovations with more doubles and a swimming pool are coming. If you want to be close to trendy restaurants and bars, the location is a downside.

🛏 El Cangrejo, Marbella & Bella Vista

As central as it gets, these neighborhoods have no lack of restaurants or bars within walking distance. However, this area is one of the noisier spots in town, with snaking traffic and honking horns dominating the daytime hours.

★ Panama Hat Hostel HOSTEL $

(Map p50; ☑ 269-3315; www.thepanamahathostel. com; Av 5a B Sur s/n, Bella Vista; dm/d incl breakfast US$25/50; ❄ 🛜 🏊) Let's start with the downer: there's no kitchen use. However, this small retro-adorable hostel delivers with sparkling rooms, air-conditioning and fresh decor. There's also a backyard pool and hot tub. The affordable cafe (lunch US$5) serves healthy daily specials with vegetarian options, and breakfast with eggs is included in room rates.

Hostel Villa Vento Surf HOSTEL $

(Map p50; ☑ 6101-4841, 397-6002; http:// hostelvillaventosurf.com; Calle 47 No 7, Marbella; dm/d/tr incl breakfast US$17/35/45; ❄ @ 🛜 🏊) This relaxed hostel with pleasant staff sits in a suburban-style home around the corner from the nightlife hot spot of Calle Uruguay. Young internationals come for the swimming pool or the easy-access partying, though it's relatively calm (all laptops engaged). Bunks crowd larger dorms, but air-con keeps them cool. Breakfast is pancakes and coffee.

Panama House B&B $

(☑ 263-4366; www.panamahousebb.com; Calle 1a de Carmen 32, El Carmen; dm/d with shared bathroom incl breakfast US$15/45, d/tr incl breakfast US$55/65; 🅿 ❄ @ 🛜) In a cozy colonial near Vía Brasil, this congenial home is lovely and sought-after. Fresh rooms have safe boxes, high ceilings, warm light and tiled bathrooms with scalloped sinks. Mattresses are a bit slim. Guests of all ages congregate in the communal kitchen or lounge area or on the lush hammock patio.

El Machico HOSTEL $

(Map p50; ☑ 6473-5905, 203-9430; www.el machicohostel.com; Calle 47 Este No 2, Marbella; dm with shared/private bathroom US$15/16; ❄ 🛜 🏊) In a suburban-style home, this Italian-run hostel indulges your inner kid with projected movies in the swimming pool, a PlayStation and cruiser bikes for rent. It also arranges cheap tours. Rooms house six to 12 people. Sheets and towels are a little chintzy, but blessed air-conditioning runs in rooms at night.

Riande Granada Hotel DESIGN HOTEL $$

(Map p50; ☑ 204-4444; http://riandehoteles. com; Av Eusebio A Morales, El Cangrejo; d US$110; 🅿 ❄ @ 🛜 🏊) Remodeled for a chic look and feel, Riande is good value. Spare and modern, it's clad in dripping foliage and a curtain of cascading water. There's a reputable restaurant and an enormous wooden lounge deck around the outdoor pool. Rooms feature minifridges and flat-screen TVs.

Baru Lodge B&B $$

(☑ 393-2340; www.barulodge.com; Calle 2a Norte H-7, El Carmen; s/d incl breakfast US$60/75; ❄ @ 🛜) Tasteful and cordial, this inn sits on a residential street central to the action. Rooms are sleek and modern, with subdued colors and soft lighting. The English-speaking owner makes guests right at home. Cable TV, fast wi-fi and air purifiers are among the perks. The garden patio has wicker seating, where continental breakfasts are served.

Getting here is a challenge, as streets are unmarked, but you can tell the taxi it's located behind Exedra Books.

Executive Hotel HOTEL $$

(Map p50; ☑ 265-8011; www.executivehotel-panama.com; cnr Calles 52 & Aquilino de la Guardia, El Cangrejo; s/d/tr incl breakfast US$85/95/105; 🅿 ❄ @ 🛜 🏊) Bustling and efficient, this business hotel (remodeled and expanding) is centrally located in El Cangrejo and has an array of prim white rooms with tropical accents. Service is friendly and caring. There are flat-screen TVs, in-room coffee and safe boxes. The 24-hour cafe is the secret spot in the city for outstanding American breakfasts.

Saba Hotel HOTEL $$

(Map p50; ☑ 201-6100; www.thesabahotel. com; Vía Argentina s/n, Bella Vista; s/d US$63/68; ❄ @ 🛜) Modern and cheerful, the Saba is great value in Bella Vista. With lots of glass and bamboo, there's a sustainable theme that's probably more stylish than substantial. You can get a carrot juice at the detox bar or just order room service while watching your flat-screen TV. Service is great and there's a restaurant.

Metro Hotel HOTEL $$

(Map p50; ☑ 202-5050; www.metrohotelpanama. com; Calle D, El Cangrejo; d/tr US$66/88; ❄ @ 🛜) Cute and convenient in a busy part of town, Metro feels like a chain hotel with an extra ounce of cool. Rooms feature tile floors, safe boxes, flat-screen TVs and minifridges. Those with two beds have better decor. Staff is willing but on the slow side.

Coral Suites Aparthotel APARTMENT $$

(Map p50; ☎269-3898; www.coralsuites.net; Calle D, El Cangrejo; s/d/tr US$88/99/110; P ❄ @ ≋) This all-suites hotel is serviceable for traveling executives wanting amenities, or long-term visitors in need of more than a hotel room. Suites are unremarkable yet functional, with spacious bathrooms, bouncy mattresses and fully equipped kitchens. Staff is pleasant and guests have use of a full gym, business center and 24-hour rooftop pool.

DeVille Hotel BOUTIQUE HOTEL $$$

(Map p50; ☎206-3100; www.devillehotel.com.pa; Calle Beatriz M de Cabal, Bella Vista; d/ste incl breakfast US$137/220; P ❄ @ ≋) Overshadowed by newer, bigger hotels, the sleepy DeVille remains a sweetheart option with 33 classy, tasteful rooms and sterling service. Rooms feature antique Thai dressers, glistening with inlaid mother-of-pearl, and marble-topped antique tables set with Louis XV chairs. Guests sleep on the finest quality US-made mattresses, dressed with custom Egyptian-cotton bed linen and goose-feather pillows. Located near Calle 50a Este.

Bristol Panama HOTEL $$$

(Map p50; ☎265-7844; www.thebristol.com; Calle Aquilino de la Guardia, Bella Vista; d incl breakfast from US$219; P ❄ @ ≋) The elegant Bristol features oriental carpets, flamboyant orchids and precious woods, and that's just the lobby. Rooms are refined and lovely. No more do-not-disturb tags here: heat sensors determine if rooms are occupied. Other five-star amenities include a spa, 24-hour butler service and free cell-phone loan. The restaurant, run by an award-winning Panamanian chef, is currently getting an update.

Le Meridien HOTEL $$$

(Map p50; ☎297-3200; www.starwoodhotels.com; cnr Calle Uruguay & Av Balboa, Bella Vista; d from US$190; P ❄ @ ≋) Created by 100 artists, Le Meridien features cool digital art and even birdsong in the elevator. Yet, while it's daring and innovative, some details are simply off. Rooms have laminated-wood walls and the furniture seems a bit cheap given the all-out setting. The effect is a little Le Mediocre. But the rooftop pool offers a delicious city-skyline view.

There's also a Clarins spa and a swish fusion restaurant.

Hotel Continental HOTEL $$$

(Map p50; ☎265-5114; www.continentalhotel.com; cnr Calle Ricardo Arias & Vía España, El Cangrejo; d incl breakfast from US$144; P ❄ @ ≋) This well-located casino hotel has a swinging, tropical style more associated with Havana than Panama, thanks to the open architecture, cool breezes and abundance of fresh-cut flowers. Service is often praised and recently remodeled rooms are tasteful and spacious. With online discounts that sometimes halve the rate, it can be a steal.

Suites feature eye-popping skyline views from the sitting area, the bed and even the walk-in closet. Of course, the real action happens poolside, grab a cocktail and watch it all swirl by.

San Francisco & Punta Paitilla

Similar to Bella Vista, San Francisco is a central, busy location with the added perk of having the biggest green space in this part of the city – Parque Recreativo Omar. Punta Paitilla is a peninsula of modern high-rises that juts into Bahía di Panamà.

Hostal Casa Margarita B&B $$

(☎394-5557; www.hostalcasamargarita.com; Casa 97, Calle Los Claveles, San Francisco; s/d/tr incl breakfast US$70/80/95; P ❄ @) Irresistibly cozy and chic, this stucco house features seven smart, impeccable but simple rooms with colorful touches, flat-screen TVs and minifridges. A huge garden and breakfast patio provide ample space to lounge or dally over a complete

DAY TRIPS FROM PANAMA CITY

Looking to get out of the city for the day? Take our author-tested suggestions:

- Lay eyes on the awe-inspiring Panama Canal.
- Spot feathered friends along Pipeline Rd in Parque Nacional Soberanía.
- Visit the world-famous tropical biology center on Isla Barro Colorado.
- Escap to the flower-dotted island of Isla Taboga.
- Surf gnarly breaks along the Pacific coast.

breakfast that includes fresh fruit. Guests also have access to the kitchen, but the real treasures here are the warm hosts.

Canal Zone

Hostal Amador Familiar INN $
(☎314-1251; www.hostalamadorfamiliar.com; Casa 1519, Calle Akee, Balboa; dm incl breakfast US$17, d with fan/air-con US$33/39; P ❄ @ ☎) If you like quiet, this big, red canal house offers cheap accommodations. Tiled high-ceilinged rooms with rod-iron beds are worn out but clean. Dorms are dark and less appealing and service is, sadly, lax. Highlights are the pleasant dining patio and open-air kitchen. Guests must take a taxi to the center (US$7); it's just off the Causeway.

Dos Palmitos B&B $$
(☎391-0994, 6051-4723; www.panamabedandbreakfast.com; Calle Victor Hugo 0532B, Cerro Ancón; s/d incl breakfast US$75/88; ❄ @ ☎) If your attraction to Panama is more about wildlife than wild life, check out this tucked-away French B&B. There are just four rooms, decorated with retro posters and vintage newsclips and featuring immaculate wooden floors, king-size beds and wicker furniture. The backyard terrace offers birdwatching and abundant breakfasts featuring homemade bread and fresh juice. Also offers transportation and tours.

It's on the quiet Cerro Ancón – it's a good place to take a walk, but for everything else you'll need a taxi.

La Estancia B&B $$
(☎314-1417; www.bedandbreakfastpanama.com; Casa 35, Quarry Heights, Cerro Ancón; d incl breakfast US$125; P ❄ @ ☎) Perched atop Cerro Ancón and surrounded by tropical flora and fauna, La Estancia is a small concrete apartment building that's been converted into a tranquil and friendly B&B. For the price it's pretty plain, with uncluttered rooms and notable breakfasts, best enjoyed on the patio while gazing upon the Puente de las Américas.

Albrook Inn INN $$
(Map p46; ☎315-1789; www.albrookinn.com; Calle Hazelhurst 14, Albrook; d/ste incl breakfast US$66/99; P ❄ ≋) Set amid lush greenery and removed from city chaos, this lodging near Albrook airport aspires to country inn but feels a bit lackluster and impersonal. Motel-style rooms have modern decor and flat-screen TVs but could be roomier. A small kidney-shaped pool spruces up the garden. Ideal for an early-morning domestic flight.

Country Inn & Suites HOTEL $$
(☎211-4500; www.countryinns.com/panamacanalpan; cnr Avs Amador & Pelicano, Amador; d US$66; P ❄ ≋) They say there are only two lodgings overlooking the canal: one is the prison holding Noriega, the other is this chain hotel. Though reminiscent of a retirement community in Panama City, Florida, it's well run and good value, with causeway access and a huge swimming pool. Rooms boast private balconies overlooking the Puente de las Américas.

Eating

Boasting the most innovative contemporary cuisine of Central America, Panama City is a fun place to dine out. There are literally hundreds of places to eat and – thanks to a big immigrant population – cuisine from every corner of the globe.

Casco Viejo is home to a number of boutique eateries and European-inspired cafes. Bella Vista, the self-proclaimed restaurant district, is the best spot in the city for lightening the wallet and satisfying the taste buds.

With so many salaried earners on their lunch break, the banking district of El Cangrejo is home to a number of pricey eateries. These tend to be slightly more conservative and less trendy.

Owing to the wealth of city denizens and the popularity of dining out, reservations are a good idea. Although you can probably get a table most days of the week, don't even think about just showing up on Friday or Saturday night without phoning ahead.

For groceries and self-catering, stop by the 24-hour Supermercado Rey, which has several locations throughout the city, including one in **El Cangrejo** (Map p50; Plaza Concordia, Via España s/n, El Cangrejo), and another inside the El Dorado Mall (p68).

Street vendors sell everything from shaved ice to grilled chicken or *empanadas* (turnovers stuffed with meat, cheese or veggie mixes). In the evening, sausage, *papas rellenas* (stuffed potatoes) and *arepa* (savory corn cake) stands on Vía España do brisk business and the food is cheap and good.

Casco Viejo

★ **Mercado de Mariscos** MARKET $
(Map p46; Av Balboa, Casco Viejo; mains US$3-14; ⏲ from 6am) Above a bustling fish market,

this unassuming restaurant is *the* place to get your seafood fix. Come early as service at peak time is painfully slow. Gems include whole fried fish and cavernous bowls of 'Get Up Lazarus' soup (a sure hangover cure).

Outside, stands ladle out delicious US$3 plastic cups of *ceviche* (citrus-cured seafood), including classic concoctions, Mediterranean style (with olives) and curry.

★ Super Gourmet
DELI $

(Map p54; Av A, Casco Viejo; mains US$3-9; ⊙8am-5pm Mon-Sat, 10am-4pm Sun; 🏛) Stocking gourmet goods that range from wine to wasabi peas, this is the perfect pre-picnic stop. You can also grab soup, natural juices or a baguette deli sandwich with roasted chicken and peppers, pastrami or three cheeses. For breakfast, eggs on English muffins or *arepas* (savory corn cakes) hit the spot.

Café Per Due
ITALIAN $

(Map p54; ☑228-0547; Av A, Casco Viejo; mains US$5-12; ⊙9am-10pm Tue-Sun, closed Dec; 🖋) Our pick for a quick bite, this casual Italian-run eatery serves scrumptious thin-crust pizzas. Check out the bacon and blue cheese or the fresh tomato, basil and garlic. Mozzarella is not skimped on. For privacy, try the tiny brick courtyard with a couple of tables.

Granclement
GELATERIA $

(Map p54; Av Central, Casco Viejo; gelato US$3.50-5; ⊙11:30am-8pm Mon-Thu, to 11pm Fri, to 9pm Sat, 12:30-8pm Sun) Pure pleasure defines these intense tropical-fruit gelatos and rich, creamy flavors such as coffee, orange-chocolate and ginger. A few scoops of these fussy French creations will sweeten a leisurely stroll through the Casco.

Aki
JAPANESE $

(Map p54; ☑6938-8473; Calle 8a Este s/n, Casco Viejo; mains US$9-12; ⊙noon-midnight Sun-Fri, 3pm-midnight Sat) Duck into this dark nook for delicious fusion-style sushi. Spicy tuna on crispy rice squares hits the spot. Cocktails are innovative and well prepared. For a bargain, check out the weekday lunch special (US$6).

Barrio Pizza
PIZZA $

(Map p54; ☑399-3521; www.barriopizza.com; Av Central s/n, Casco Viejo; mains US$8-12; ⊙11am-11pm; 🏛🏶) Happiness is blistering wood-fired pizza baked to order and topped with truffle oil, roasted eggplant or meatballs. The simple menu also has Caesar salads, wine and beer. Come early for a seat.

Crave
CAFE $

(Map p54; ☑209-0094; Calle José de Obaldía s/n, Casco Viejo; mains US$8-13; ⊙11:30am-11:30pm Mon-Sat, 10am-4pm Sun) A refreshing casual option serving fresh cafe fare that's artfully prepared. Think handcut fries, fish tacos and burgers served with crispy Brussels sprouts or pots of delicious pickled vegetables. There's a range of boutique beers, and cocktails are prepared with house-made infusions and sugarcane. Also does Sunday brunch.

Café Coca Cola
PANAMANIAN $

(Map p54; Av Central, Casco Viejo; plates US$3-8; ⊙7:30am-11pm; 🏶) A neighborhood institution, this old-school diner comes complete with chess-playing señoras and no-nonsense waitresses. TVs broadcasting soccer matches seal its status as working-class hangout. Of course, the real reason you're here is to eat out on hearty platefuls of rice, beans and the featured meat of the day without breaking the bank.

Ego y Narciso
FUSION $$

(Map p54; ☑262-2045; Plaza Bolívar, Calle 3a Este, Casco Viejo; mains US$8-20; ⊙noon-3pm Mon-Fri, 6-11pm Mon-Sun) With cosmopolitan flash, this tiny restaurant is perfect for appetizers and drinks. Outdoor tables on Plaza Bolívar offer romantic ambience. Graze on quality *ceviche* (citrus-cured seafood), octopus toasts with balsamic reduction and tender kebabs.

Restaurante L'Osteria
ITALIAN $$

(Map p54; ☑212-0809; Av B, Casco Viejo; mains US$9-18; ⊙noon-3:30pm & 6-11pm) This Italian-run brick bistro is a dependable option. Crusted-cheese rice balls and leafy green salads make a nice starter. Gnocchi with fresh ricotta and percorino cheese, unusual pastas and well-priced arugula pizzas are highlights.

★ Donde José
PANAMANIAN $$$

(Map p54; ☑262-1682; www.dondejose.com; Av Central s/n, Casco Viejo; 8-course meal US$73; ⊙7pm-late Tue-Sat) Elevating humble Panamanian staples to haute cuisine, this four-table eatery is Panama's hottest reservation, though overpriced. Chef Jose prepares *ñandu* beans (native black beans), crisp, tender pork and *ñame* (an indigenous tuber) in playful fashion. Servers have an intimate, casual rapport, though with a cascade of eight courses, they sometimes neglect to describe the dishes, which is key to enjoying the innovation.

Reservations are hard to come by – try stopping by before it opens. Drinks are extra.

★Madrigal SPANISH $$$

(Map p54; ☎211-1956; www.andresmadrigal.com; Av A, Casco Viejo; mains US$26-30; ⏲noon-2:30pm Mon-Fri, 6:30-10:30pm Mon-Sat) Pure delight, this upscale eatery from Michelin-starred chef Andrés Madrigal has a fetish for details. Start with sea-bass *ceviche* (citrus-cured seafood) with coconut foam, slivers of hot pepper and passionfruit mousse and you'll wonder if anything has ever tasted this good. *Ropa vieja* (shredded beef) is done to perfection and the seafood soup is earthy and satisfying. Great service.

El Cangrejo, Marbella & Bella Vista

New York Bagel Café CAFE $

(Map p50; Plaza Cabeza de Einstein, El Cangrejo; mains US$3-9; ⏲7am-8pm Mon-Fri, 8am-8pm Sat, 8am-3pm Sun; ❄📶) More San Francisco than Brooklyn, this fully American creation near Vía Argentina nonetheless packs in expats with freshly baked bagels, lox and oversized breakfasts. It also serves handsome burgers. The setting offers jazz, soft sofas and an assortment of laptop geeks.

Sukhi THAI $

(Map p50; ☎395-6081; Calle Beatriz M de Cabal, Bella Vista; mains US$8-13; ⏲11:30am-10pm Mon-Sat) A casual and cheerful cafe offering lovely, though not the most authentic, Southeast Asian food. Portions run small. Start with the fried calamari with ginger-cilantro dipping sauce. Flavors pop in the green-bean green curry, while ladna (noodles in gravy) comes in fragrant beef broth with broccoli rabe. Service is good and the price is right.

Crêpes & Waffles CREPERIE $

(Map p50; ☎269-1574; Av 5a B Sur, Bella Vista; mains US$5-10; ⏲noon-10pm Mon-Sat, 9am-10pm Sun; 🌿) Ideal for an afternoon pick-me-up or a quick bite before clubbing, this salad bar and crêpe factory has something for everyone. Spinach, ricotta and tomato is a good standby, but the sweet crêpes, with fillings such as cheese, apples, chocolate and caramel, are delectable. There's also a salad bar.

Petit Paris BAKERY $

(Map p50; ☎391-8778; Galeria Marbella, Marbella; ⏲6:30am-8:30pm) Get your fresh croissants and baguettes at this tiny bakery.

Niko's Café CAFETERIA $

(Map p50; Calle 51 Este, El Cangrejo; mains US$3-8; ⏲24hr) The creation of a Greek immigrant who once sold food from a cart, Niko's has become one of Panama City's most successful chains with locations throughout the city (this one's near Vía España). These 24-hour cafeterias serve hearty portions of inexpensive food ranging from made-to-order breakfasts to Panamanian dishes and desserts.

Sabores de la India INDIAN $

(Map p50; Calle 51, Bella Vista; mains US$5-10; ⏲noon-10:30pm; 🌿) With Bollywood on the telly and staff and cooks from the subcontinent, this unassuming spot is a fast track to your spicy-food fix. We only wish it were a little less dusty. Vegetarian options (with tofu) are plentiful. Big appetites should check out the lunch buffet.

★Avatar INDIAN $$

(Map p50; ☎393-9006; www.avatarindiancuisine.com; cnr Vías Argentina & España, El Cangrejo; mains US$9-16) Serving rich kormas, fragrant rice and complex curries in a swanky piano bar, Avatar is sheer delight for spice enthusiasts. Southern Indian cuisine is the house specialty, though if you want it really hot you will have to insist. On weekdays, lunch is 25% off.

Ozone INTERNATIONAL $$

(Map p50; Calle Uruguay, Bella Vista; mains US$10-22; ⏲11am-3pm & 6-11pm) Packed with worker bees at midday, Ozone is a local fixture serving enormous, fragrant portions of good food from 110 countries. There are even kosher and halal options. It's too bad the ambience is wanting – the dark location was once a garage. It's also hard to find – look closely for the sign.

Lung Fung CHINESE $$

(Av Periodista & Vía Transístmica, Los Angeles; mains US$5-15) Locals swear by this longtime Chinese restaurant, one of the best in a city with good Chinese fare. Stop by on the weekend for dim sum.

Wine Bar ITALIAN $$

(Map p50; Av Eusebio A Morales, El Cangrejo; mains US$7-17; ⏲5pm-1am) Some say this Italian bistro with an encyclopedic wine list is the best dinner value in town. It's certainly popular among the local cognoscenti. You can order off two menus: Wine Bar for a bite with wine, or Pomodoro (open for lunch) for pizza and satisfying pasta. Or grab a plate of soft and hard cheeses and enjoy the patio.

Chez Titi CAFE $$$

(Map p50; ☎390-5018; www.cheztitipanama.com; Calle 49 Oeste, El Cangrejo; mains US$22-27;

⊕ 11am-9pm Tue-Fri, 9am-8pm Sat, 9am-5pm Sun) With a look that says French countryside, this European tea house focuses on food that's organic and homemade. The Cordon Bleu–trained chef prepares only fresh, unprocessed foods. While set menus are expensive, they are also delicious. Try the organic wine or a house specialty: Champagne infused with raspberry tea. Also does weekend brunch.

Martín Fierro
STEAK $$$

(Map p50; ☑ 264-1927; Av Eusebio A Morales, El Cangrejo; steak US$14-25; ⊕ noon-3pm & 6-11pm Mon-Sat, noon-9:30pm Sun) For serious steaks, there is only one name in Panama City, and it's Martín Fierro. Top selections include the best in US-imported New York rib steaks, grass-fed Argentine fillets and locally raised Panamanian cuts. The salad bar (included) and a selection of Chilean wines round out your meal.

La Posta
ITALIAN $$$

(Map p50; ☑ 269-1076; www.lapostapanama. com; Calle Uruguay, Bella Vista; mains US$16-38; ⊕ noon-2:30pm & 7-10pm Mon-Fri, to 11pm Sat) A bistro with seasonal menus, La Posta usually dishes up beautifully presented food – though recent offerings don't always make the grade. Organic and local foods are used when possible. The tropical setting says hacienda, with a breezy dining room decked out with white linens and big wicker chairs.

✗ San Francisco & Punta Paitilla

Restaurante Vietnamita
VIETNAMESE $

(☑ 394-6923; Casa 7A, Calle 68 Este, San Francisco; mains US$7-9; ⊕ 11am-10pm) Fragrant *pho* (broth with noodles) with brisket, garlicky sea bass with gangalal and barbecued pork over rice noodles are some of the mouthwatering specialties at this authentic eatery with friendly owners from Hanoi. A cold beer or avocado smoothie and you are all set.

Caminito de la Empanada
ARGENTINE $

(Map p50; ☑ 215-2101; Paitilla; mains US$2; ⊕ 7:30am-7:30pm Mon-Sat) Cheap and tasty, with a selection of tiny savory Argentine *empanadas* (turnovers filled with meat, cheese or veggie mixes) and *medialunas* (crescent rolls). Near Av 6a Sur.

Parillada Jimmy
PARRILLA $$

(☑ 226-1096; Av Cincuentenario, San Francisco; mains US$9-18; ⊕ 11:30am-11:30pm) The long, open porch with high ceilings and wrought-iron chandeliers lend a farmhouse feel to this Panama City institution. An open grill sears some serious cuts of beef, chicken and country-style sausage. Located in the San Francisco district just east of the Multiplaza Mall, Parillada Jimmy packs in lunchtime diners and an after-work crowd.

★ Maito
PANAMANIAN $$$

(☑ 391-4657; www.maitopanama.com; Av 3m Sur, San Francisco; mains US$8-27; ⊕ noon-3pm Mon-Fri, 7-11pm Mon-Sat) With style and pedigree, Maito toys with the classics, folding in everyday Caribbean, Latin and Chinese influences. While results are mixed, it's still worthwhile. Start with a watermelon Waldorf salad. Ribs glazed in passion fruit are tender but lack the crispness of the duck chow mein. Seafood risotto in squid ink proves divine. There's garden seating and impeccable service.

✗ Canal Zone & Around

Sabores del Chorrillo
SEAFOOD $

(Av de los Poetas s/n; mains US$5-15; ⊕ noon-10pm Tue-Sun) This new waterfront market contains a number of seafood stands, with miniature kitchens occupied by residents of Chorillos, an edgy neighborhood famous for its fried fish. Whole parga, squid, *ceviche* (citrus-cured seafood) and *patacones* (fried plantains) are served at shady outdoor tables.

Alongside the Cinta Costera, it's easiest to access heading toward downtown from the Amador area.

Country Store
CAFE $$

(☑ 203-5824; 2362 Calle C, Ancón; dishes US$10-18; ⊕ 7am-11pm Tue-Fri, 8:30am-11pm Sat, 8:30am-9pm

BEST TAKE-OUT

Panama City is not big on take-out, but any of these goodies could satisfy an urge to brown-bag a picnic to the Cinta Costera, Parque Recreativo Omar or Casco Antiguo, for US$5 to US$10:

Petit Paris (p64) Baguettes and croissants at this bakery and cafe.

Lung Fung (p64) Shrimp chow mein at this place in Chinatown.

Caminito de la Empanada (p65) Argentine-style snacks such as spinach or spicy beef *empanadas* (turnovers).

Super Gourmet (p63) Wine, cheese and deli goods.

Sun) Come for country breakfasts, fresh salads, pizza and baked goods with organic coffee roasted in-house or craft beer. A highlight is the live music (guitar, rock and jazz) Wednesday through Sunday. It also sells goods from a nearby farm. A little hard to find, it's basically behind Banistmo bank.

Drinking & Nightlife

Bars and clubs open and close with alarming frequency in Panama City, though generally speaking, nightlife is stylish, sophisticated and fairly pricey. The well-to-do denizens of the capital love a good scene, so it's worth scrubbing up, donning some nice threads and parting with a bit of dough. You might regret blowing your budget the next morning, but that's the price you pay to party with the beautiful people.

Big areas for nightlife include Casco Viejo, San Francisco and Bella Vista's Calle Uruguay. The current boom in craft beer has people hitting small breweries, a novelty for Panama.

Doors usually open at 11pm. Bars and clubs close between 2am and 3am, except for casinos, which now can't serve alcohol. Remember to bring ID. Most clubs have a cover charge of US$10 to US$25; this varies greatly depending on the place, the date and the time. For the latest on what's happening in the city, La Prensa (www.prensa.com) has weekend listings in the Thursday and Friday editions or on its website; look for the 'De Noche' section.

Casco Viejo

La Rana Dorada MICROBREWERY
(Map p54; Av Alfaro, Casco Viejo; ⌚noon-12:30am Sun-Wed, to 3am Thu-Sat) Replete with shiny brass fixings and wooden stools, this is a wonderful, award-winning brewpub of small craft beers, served alongside tasty thin-crust pizzas or bratwursts (mains US$3 to US$9). After-work happy hour is just catching on, but it goes gangbusters here. A second location is on Vía Argentina.

Bar Relic BAR
(Map p54; www.relicbar.com; Calle 9a Este, Casco Viejo; ⌚9pm-2am Tue-Sat) Wildly popular with travelers and hip young Panamanians, this cavernous hostel bar is a hit. Service is friendly and patrons easily mingle in the ample courtyard with shared picnic tables. Not only are you partying outside (a rarity in Panama City) but you're also next to the historical wall of the city.

Upstairs in the hostel there's a calmer, more grown-up option for cocktails.

Tántalo Bar COCKTAIL BAR
(Map p54; cnr Calle 8a Este & Av B, Casco Viejo; cover US$5-10; ⌚rooftop deck 5pm-2am) Though it serves casual lunches, this ultra-hip cafe-bar is best known for sunset happy hours on its rooftop deck. Pair your cocktail with good, fusion-style tapas. Cover is charged after 10pm, but to get a spot on the tiny roof deck, show up around 7pm. Wednesday is salsa night.

Around the City

The district of Bella Vista is home to Calle Uruguay, a strip of trendy bars and clubs reminiscent of Miami's South Beach. DJs usually pull from a broad repertoire, from salsa and merengue to UK and US '80s classics, with electronic music (house, drum 'n' bass) liberally added to the mix. The scene is young and you can expect to pay to play here. Moreover, clubs change hands quickly in this neighborhood, so its best to ask locals about the latest and greatest additions.

La Rana Dorada PUB
(Map p50; ☎269-2989; Vía Argentina 20, El Cangrejo; ⌚noon-2am) The sister outlet to a Casco Viejo microbrewery, with decent pub food and a congenial, relaxed atmosphere.

Lum's PUB
(☎317-6303; Bldg 340, Corozal Oeste, Ancón; ⌚from 11am Mon-Sat) Occupying a cavernous hangar that once housed machinery for the Panama Canal, Lum's is an expat hangout of choice. Satellite TV, pool table, foosball and tap beers pack in the crowds on weekends. The menu is heavy on ribs, steak and other grilled mains (dishes US$6 to US$12). It's located off Carretera Diablo on the edge of the canal.

Cayucos CAFE
(Causeway) This open-air resto-bar sits on the water with excellent views of the city. While not exactly a bar, it has the perfect ambience for the first cold beer of the evening or a leisurely drink on the weekend.

Starlight LOUNGE
(Map p50; ☎269-4626; Av 5a B Sur, Bella Vista; ⌚9pm-1am) The lion's den of karaoke, this older club has no cover; you just have to consume a drink and muster the courage to croon under the disco rays.

LGBT Venues

In addition to a few gay venues, the scene in Panama City takes place in the city's hippest bars and clubs.

Club Moat GAY & LESBIAN
(Map p50; ☎6747-2544; Calle Aquilino de la Guardia 12, El Cangrejo; ⊙10pm-3am) The hot spot of the moment is this multistory club with *musica electronica*, dancing and drinks. All-you-can-drink specials (US$12) are dangerous. Ideal for late at night.

Duke's Bar GAY & LESBIAN
(Map p54; ☎6597-6200; Edificio Cuatro Casas 3, Calle 4a Oeste, Casco Viejo; ⊙6:30pm-1am Tue-Sat) A new edition to Casco Viejo, this elegant, low-lit bar caters to the gay and lesbian crowd, late 20s and up, though it's friendly to all.

☆ Entertainment

If you're not looking to get blotto, there are numerous ways to spend a moonlit (or rainy) evening in the city. A good place to start is the arts section in the Sunday edition of *La Prensa* or the back pages of the *Panama News*.

Cinemas

Panamanians have a love affair with Hollywood and there are many air-conditioned cinemas in and around the city. Panamanians also love to gamble, and there are a few flashy casinos where you can get in on the action. There are also opportunities in the capital to see traditional folk dancing and live performances of music and theater.

Panama City's modern movie houses show mostly Hollywood films (with Spanish subtitles); tickets cost from US$4.50. VIP showings, with comfortable leather seats and alcoholic drinks on offer, cost US$15. Most theaters offer half-price regular tickets on Wednesday. For listings and show times, pick up a copy of *La Prensa* or go to www.prensa.com and click on 'cine.'

Multicentro Cinemark CINEMA
(Map p50; Multicentro Mall) Mainstream cinema with some dubbed films and some with subtitles. Near Punta Paitilla.

Albrook Cinemark CINEMA
(Map p46; Albrook Mall) Next to the Albrook bus terminal. There's also a Cinemark in the Multiplaza Mall.

Casinos

None of the casinos in Panama City are competition for Las Vegas, but there are three attractive and popular houses of chance in the capital. Most casinos in the city are located inside top hotels including the Sheraton, Miramar InterContinental and Hotel Continental (p61). By Panamanian law casinos do not serve alcohol.

Live Music

Platea JAZZ
(Map p54; ☎228-4010; Calle 1 Oeste) A tiny jazz club on the tip of the peninsula.

Traditional Dance

Restaurante-Bar Tinajas DANCE
(Map p50; ☎263-7890; www.tinajaspanama.com; Av 3a A Sur, Bella Vista; entry US$5; ⊙Mon-Sat) A good place to see traditional Panamanian folk dancing, this dinner show is a classic. Sure, it's touristy, but it's nicely done just the same. Shows are held Wednesday to Saturday at 9pm with a US$12 minimum per person for drinks and food. Reservations recommended. It's near Av Frederico Boyd.

Theater

For current listings of plays and shows, check out www.teatrodepanama.com.

Teatro Nacional THEATER
(Map p54; ☎262-3525; Av B, Casco Viejo) Casco Viejo's lovely 19th-century playhouse stages ballets, concerts and plays.

Teatro Anita Villalaz THEATER
(Map p54; ☎501-4020; Plaza de Francia, Paseo las Bóvedas, Casco Viejo) A historical spot in Casco Viejo to see live performances.

Teatro En Círculo THEATER
(☎261-5375; www.teatroencirculo.com; Av 6 C Norte, El Carmen) Plays and musicals are scheduled regularly at this theater near Vía Transístmica.

Shopping

The city has a number of markets where you can purchase handicrafts native to regions throughout the country. Here you'll find a range of handmade goods, from baskets made in Emberá villages to *molas* (colorful hand-stitched appliqué textiles) from Guna Yala.

A number of shopping malls, some quite luxe, highlight the increasing love of Americana in Panama. Consumerism aside, these air-conditioned spots can be a good place to escape the heat.

★ Karavan ARTS
(Map p54; ☎228-7177; www.karavan-gallery.com; Calle 3a Oeste, Casco Viejo; ⊙10am-6pm

Mon-Sat, 11am-3:30pm Sun) An excellent place to find original Guna embroidery with modern designs and Congo art from Portobelo, with artisans working on site. Karavan commissions local artists and works closely to develop new talent. Reduced hours in low season.

Papiro y Yo FASHION
(Map p54; ☎211-3830; info@papiroyyo.com; cnr Calle 4a Oeste & Av A, Casco Viejo; ⏰10am-7pm Mon-Sat) An innovative boutique selling *mola* (traditional Guna embroidery) designs reimagined on gorgeous Italian silk. It also sells stylish jewelry and baskets crafted from recycled materials.

No Me Olvides CLOTHING
(Map p54; ☎211-1209; cnr Calle 4a Oeste & Av A, Casco Viejo; ⏰10am-6pm Mon-Fri, 9am-5pm Sat) Featuring the classic Panamanian-made *guayaberas* (tropical dress shirts) made popular in the 1950s, in all colors and patterns, with a few selections for women as well.

Multiplaza Mall MALL
(cnr Vía Israel & Vía Brasil, Punta Pacifica; ⏰10am-9pm) The biggest downtown mall, with designer shops, restaurants and a cinema. It's east of downtown, on the way to Panamá Viejo.

Reprosa JEWELRY
(Map p50; ☎269-0457; www.reprosa.com; cnr Av 2 Sur & Calle 54 Este, Campo Alegre; ⏰9am-7pm Mon-Sat) Sells quality *huacas* (replicas of pre-Columbian gold pendants) and necklaces made of black onyx and other gemstones.

Multicentro Mall MALL
(Map p50; www.multicentropanama.com.pa; Av Balboa, Paitilla; ⏰10am-9pm) Has a cinema and shops, along with many outdoor restaurants.

Joyería La Huaca JEWELRY
(Map p50; ☎269-7254; www.joyerialahuaca.com; cnr Calle Ricardo Arias & Vía España, Campo Alegre) A reputable jewelry store in front of Hotel Continental.

Exedra Books BOOKS
(☎264-4252; cnr Vías España & Brasil, El Carmen; ⏰9:30am-9:30pm Mon-Sat, 11am-8:30pm Sun) Easily one of Central America's best bookstores.

Albrook Mall MALL
(Map p46; Albrook; ⏰10am-9pm Mon-Sat, 11am-8pm Sun) Next to the bus terminal, this mall has a cinema, a supermarket and dozens of stores, including American and European chains. If you need it, there's also an upscale chain hotel here.

Mercado Nacional de Artesanías MARKET
(National Artisans Market; Map p58; Panamá Viejo; ⏰9am-4pm Mon-Sat, to 1pm Sun) A great place to shop for memorable souvenirs.

El Dorado Mall MALL
(Av Ricardo J Alfaro, El Dorado; ⏰10am-9pm Mon-Sat, 11am-8pm Sun) Near one of Panama City's newer Chinatowns, El Dorado also has restaurants, shops and a cinema. It's located near Corredor Norte and Parque Natural Metropolitano.

Information

DANGERS & ANNOYANCES

Casco Viejo is the focus of an ambitious urban-renewal program. Always exercise caution, though, and stay where it's well lit and where there are plenty of people around. Generally speaking, the tip of the peninsula southeast of Calle 10 Este and Calle 11 Este is safe for tourists and patrolled by police officers. Inland (north of Parque Herrera and Parque Santa Ana), there are high-density slums. Other high-crime areas include Curundú, Chorrillo, Santa Ana, San Miguelito and Río Abajo.

Calle Uruguay, the clubbing hub of the city, also attracts opportunists. Don't take your full wallet out at night. We have heard reports of women approaching male travelers for a hug and taking their wallets.

Taxis generally allow unrelated passengers to share the cab, but robberies do occasionally occur. It's best not to get into a taxi that already has a passenger. If you speak Spanish, you can offer a slightly higher fare to keep your taxi to yourself. Evaluate any taxi you hail before getting in (check for door handles and taxi licensing numbers). It's very common for taxi drivers to refuse fares to destinations simply for their own convenience.

There are occasional reports of robbery near the ruins of Panamá Viejo – don't go after sunset, and always keep an eye out.

Panama has become stringent about drug control, which sometimes means roadblock checks of drivers and their passengers. Always have your passport with you.

When walking the streets of Panama City, be aware that drivers do not yield to pedestrians. Sometimes it's best to approach intersections like Panamanians – look both ways, then run like hell.

EMERGENCY

Police ☎104

INTERNET ACCESS

Most lodgings and restaurants have wi-fi, as do some public places.

MAPS

Instituto Geográfico Nacional (Tommy Guardia; Map p46; ☎236 2444; La Cresta; ⏰8am-4pm Mon-Fri) Has an excellent collection of maps for sale. Just off Av Simón Bolívar near Av Arturo del Valle, opposite the Universidad de Panamá.

MEDICAL SERVICES

Medical care in Panama, especially in Panama City, is of a high standard.

Centro Médico Paitilla (☎265-8800, 265-8883; cnr Calle 53 Este & Av Balboa, Paitilla) This medical center has well-trained physicians who speak both Spanish and English.

Centro Metropolitano de Salud (☎512-6600; Calle Principal 237, Los Ríos; ⏰7:30am-noon & 1-3pm Mon-Fri) Offers yellow-fever vaccinations with international certificate (required for travel to Colombia if returning) for a minimal charge. In the Canal Zone.

MONEY

ATMs are abundant throughout the city. The Banco Nacional de Panamá counter at Tocumen International Airport is one of the few places in Panama City that exchanges foreign currency.

Panacambios (☎223-1800; ground fl, Plaza Regency Bldg, Vía España, El Cangrejo; ⏰8am-5pm Mon-Fri) Buys and sells international currencies.

POST

Many hotels sell stamps and some will mail guests' letters.

Post Office (Map p46; ☎512-7657; www.correospanama.gob.pa; Av Central s/n, Calidonia; ⏰7am-5:45pm Mon-Fri, to 4:45pm Sat) Full postal services and express mail.

TELEPHONE

Purchase SIM cards at any cell-phone shop or kiosk. They come with minimal credit that can be topped up at the same shop.

TOURIST INFORMATION

Autoridad de Turismo Panamá (ATP; Panama Tourism Authority; Map p50; ☎526-7000; www.visitpanama.com; 29th fl, Edificio Bisca, cnr Av Balboa & Aquilino de la Guardia, Bella Vista; ⏰8:30am-3pm Mon-Fri) Panama's tourism bureau is headquartered in a high-rise next to the Hilton hotel. Help is limited here; it's mostly geared toward high-end tourism. There's also an ATP booth in Casco Viejo.

Ministerio de Ambiente (Map p46; ☎500-0855, 315-0855; www.miambiente.gob.pa; Calle Broberg 804, Cerro Ancón, Albrook; ⏰8am-4pm) Formerly known as ANAM, the Ministry of the Environment can occasionally provide maps and information on national parks. However, it is not set up to provide much assistance to tourists.

Getting There & Away

AIR

International flights arrive at and depart from **Tocumen International Airport** (Map p74; ☎238-2700; www.tocumenpanama.aero; Av Domingo Díaz), 35km northeast of the city center. From Albrook Bus Terminal (p70), airport buses (US$1.25, one to 1½ hours) marked 'Tocumen Corredor' depart every 15 minutes to Tocumen airport.

Domestic flights depart from **Albrook Airport** (Aeropuerto Marcos A Gelabert; ☎315-0403), in the former Albrook Air Force Station near the canal.

Air Panama (☎316-9000; www.airpanama.com; Albrook Airport) covers domestic routes and has its own travel agency. International carrier **Copa Airlines** (☎217-2672; www.copaair.com; Av Central s/n, Casco Viejo; ⏰8am-5pm Mon-Fri, 9am-1pm Sat) now flies to domestic destinations.

Flights within Panama are inexpensive and short – few are longer than an hour. However, if traveling to Darién Province, Isla Contadora or the Comarca de Guna Yala, it's quite possible that the plane may make multiple stops. Prices vary according to season and availability.

Fares listed below are one way.

DESTINATION	COST (US$)	FREQUENCY
Achutupu (San Blás)	74	daily
Bocas del Toro	100	multiple daily
Changuinola	112	multiple daily
David	88	multiple daily
Isla Contadora	45	daily
Jaqué (Darién)	84	2 weekly
Ogobuscum (San Blás)	74	4 weekly
Playón Chico (San Blás)	73	daily

BOAT

There are regular ferries to Islas Taboga and Contadora, leaving from Panama City's Causeway, the Trump Tower and the Balboa Yacht Club.

Barcos Calypso (☎314-1730; Balboa Yacht Club, Amador Causeway; round-trip US$14) Departures to Isla Taboga at 8:30am weekdays, plus 3pm Friday, and at 8am, 10:30am and 4pm weekends.

Sea Las Perlas (☎391-1424; www.sealasperlas.com; Balboa Yacht Club, Amador Causeway; adult/child one way US$45/35) This catamaran ferry service departs for Isla Contadora daily at 7am, returning at 3:30pm. There's an 11am departure on Sunday. The journey takes one hour and 40 minutes.

Taboga Express (☎6234-8989; www.tabogaexpress.com; Balboa Yacht Club, Amador Causeway; adult/child round-trip US$16/8) This new catamaran is your fastest option to Taboga (30 minutes one way). Departs daily from Panama City's Balboa Yacht Club on the Causeway at 8am, 9:30am, 11am, 3pm and 4:30pm. With four returns daily.

BUS

Albrook Bus Terminal (Gran Terminal; Map p46; ☎303-3030, 303-6255; www.grantnt.com), near Albrook Airport, is a convenient and modern one-stop location for most buses leaving Panama City. The terminal includes a food court, banks, shops, a sports bar, a storage room, bathrooms and showers. A mall, complete with supermarket and cinema, is next door.

Passengers must buy a *tarjeta* (a rechargeable, multi-use card for US$2, from a special kiosk in Albrook terminal or at designated locations such as supermarkets or main bus stops) to pay the US$0.10 terminal tax at the entry turnstile. You can try offering another passenger cash to swipe their card for you. The *tarjeta* also allows access to the bus-station bathrooms.

For assistance, go to the information booth.

All local buses are on the new **Metrobus** (www.elmetrodepanama.com; US$0.35-1.35; ⏲5am-10pm) system with designated bus stops and clean, new buses. Cash is not accepted, passengers must use their *tarjetas*.

Both **Panaline** (Map p46; ☎227-8648; www.viajeros.com/panaline; Albrook Bus Terminal) and **Tica Bus** (Map p46; ☎314-6385; www.ticabus.com; Albrook Bus Terminal) serve San José (Costa Rica); see their websites for hours.

Canal Zone buses depart from the Albrook terminal for Balboa and Clayton, Miraflores Locks, and Gamboa, leaving every 45 minutes. In transition, these buses will soon be run by Metrobus with the same card system.

DESTINATION	COST (US$)	DURATION (HR)	FREQUENCY
Aguadulce	6.35	3	33 daily
Antón	4.70	2	every 20min
Cañita	3	2½	11 daily
Chame	2.60	1¼	37 daily
Changuinola	29	10	8pm daily
Chitré	10	4	hourly
Colón	3.50	2	every 20min
David	15-19	7-8	15 daily
El Copé	6.50	4	9 daily
El Valle	4.25	2½	hourly
Las Tablas	10	4½	hourly
Macaracas	10	5	5 daily
Paso Canoas	17-22	8	5 daily
Penonomé	5.25	2½	48 daily
Pesé	9.65	4½	6 daily
San Carlos	3.25	1½	25 daily
San José (Costa Rica)	60	16	2 daily
Santiago	9	4	20 daily
Soná	10	6	6 daily
Villa de Los Santos	9	4	18 daily
Yaviza	16	6-8	8 daily

CAR

Rental rates start at US$20 per day for the most economical cars, including unlimited kilometers. Insurance is extra.

Tolls are your responsibility and carry heavy fines if unpaid. Make sure your dashboard toll sticker has credit before using it: use the ID number to refill the account in any supermarket.

Budget (☎263-8777; www.budgetpanama.com; Tocumen International Airport)

Hertz (☎301-2611; www.hertzpanama.com.pa; Tocumen International Airport)

National (☎275-7100; www.nationalpanama.com; Tocumen International Airport)

TRAIN

The **Panama Canal Railway Company** (PCRC; ☎317-6070; www.panarail.com; Carretera Gaillard, Corozal; one way adult/child US$25/15) operates a glass-domed train that takes passengers on a lovely ride from Panama City to Colón on weekdays, departing at 7:15am and returning at 5:15pm. The train follows the canal, at times engulfed by dense vine-strewn jungle. If you want to relive the heyday of luxury train travel for an hour or two, this is definitely the way to do it.

Note that Panama City's terminus is actually located in the town of Corozal, a 15-minute cab ride from the capital.

ℹ Getting Around

GETTING INTO TOWN

From the Airports

Tocumen International Airport (p69) is 35km northeast of the city center. The cheapest way to get into the city is to exit the terminal, cross the street (to the bus shelter) and catch a bus to the city. The 10-minute walk might seem longer with luggage. Taxis (around US$30) can be hired at the Transportes Turísticos desk at the airport exit; they're much faster than the bus. Beside the desk is a taxi stand with posted prices. Don't be distracted by touts offering rides at ridiculously high prices; they take their cut from the taxis.

Albrook Airport (p69), north of Cerro Ancón, handles domestic flights. The easiest way to get from the airport to downtown is by taxi; the ride should cost between US$5 and US$8.

From the Bus Terminal

All long-distance buses arrive at Albrook Bus Terminal (p70); from here there are connections throughout the city. Routes (such as Vía España and Panamá Viejo) are displayed in the front window; fares are US$0.35. If you arrive after dark, it is recommended that you take a taxi (US$3 to US$7) to your destination.

BICYCLE

You can rent bicycles in some hostels and at the Causeway. Bicicletas Moses (p56) operates a booth with rentals starting at US$4 per hour for mountain bikes. You can also rent tandems and rickshaw bikes.

BUS

Panama City has almost finished phasing out its *diablos rojos* (red devils) for modern, safe, air-conditioned Metrobus buses (p70). Rides cost US$0.35 to $1.25, with the higher cost for *corredor* (highway) routes.

Buses run along the three major west–east routes: Av Central–Vía España, Av Balboa–Vía Israel and Av Simón Bolívar–Vía Transístmica. The Av Central–Vía España streets are one way going west for much of the route; eastbound buses use Av Perú and Av 4 Sur – these buses will take you into the banking district of El Cangrejo. Buses also run along Av Ricardo J Alfaro (known as Tumba Muerto).

Metrobuses stop at official bus stops and Albrook Bus Terminal near Albrook Airport.

SUBWAY

El Metro (www.elmetrodepanama.com; fare US$0.35-1.35; ⏲5am-10pm) Panama City's new subway, El Metro is a fast and convenient way to get around town, though destinations are currently limited. Passengers must buy *tarjetas* at a kiosk in Albrook terminal or at designated locations (all listed on the website). The main subway route goes from Albrook Bus Terminal through downtown.

TAXI

Taxis are plentiful but problematic. Some drivers do not travel (or even know) the whole city, so don't be surprised if they leave you standing on the sidewalk upon hearing your destination.

Taxis are not metered, but there is a list of standard fares that drivers are supposed to charge, measured by zones. One zone runs a minimum of US$2; Canal Zone destinations run up to US$6. An average ride, crossing a couple of zones, would cost US$3 to US$6, and more for additional passengers or if it's late. Always agree on a fare before you get into the cab, or better yet, ask your hotel to estimate the fare to your destination and then simply hand the driver the money upon arriving. Taxis can also be rented by the hour.

Watch out for unmarked large-model US cars serving hotels as cabs. Their prices are up to four times that of regular street taxis.

America Libre (☎221-1932)

Radio Taxi America (☎221-1932)

Taxi Unico Cooperativa (☎221-3611)

Panamá Province

POP 1.7 MILLION / AREA 11,887 SQ KM / ELEV SEA LEVEL TO 100M

Includes ➡

Best Spots to Explore

- Parque Nacional Soberanía (p78)
- Miraflores Locks (p76)
- Lago Bayano (p82)
- Archipiélago de Las Perlas (p84)
- Pacific beaches (p90)

Best Places to Sleep

- Canopy B&B (p80)
- Mamallena Ecolodge (p89)
- Canopy Tower Ecolodge (p78)
- La Casa Amarilla (p89)
- Gamboa Rainforest Resort (p80)

Why Go?

Panamá Province has a rich history of pirates, plunder and pearls. Although it's the most populated province in the country, Panamá can be as big or as small as you want it to be. Tranquil rainforests and sizzling beach scenes are yours to explore, and the comforts of the capital are never more than an hour away.

The principal attraction remains the world's most daring engineering marvel. Explore the Panama Canal and its expansion by visiting its locks, boating through its watery recesses or hiking along its jungle-clad shore. It is also the unlikely host of one of the most accessible and best-studied tropical rainforests on the planet.

Day trips from Panama City abound, ranging from beaches and surf breaks to ferry trips to the island village of Taboga. Farther flung is the Archipiélago de Las Perlas, which attracts everyone from the moneyed elite to the occasional *Survivor* TV series.

When to Go

- **Dec–Apr** High season at the Pacific coast beaches when trade winds and dry weather translate to the perfect time to windsurf or kitesurf; beaches are usually full and hotels charge high season rates.
- **May–Nov** For huge savings, hit the resorts in the low season. Calmer conditions favor wakeboarders.
- **Aug–Oct** A visit to Isla Taboga or Archipiélago de Las Perlas is pleasant year-round, but if you want to see migrating humpback whales come when they put on spectacular displays. It's even possible to spot them on your ferry ride out to the island.

HISTORY

Throughout the 16th and 17th centuries, the Spanish used the isthmus as a transit point for shipping plundered gold between Peru and Spain. The main route was the famous cobblestoned Camino Real (King's Hwy), linking Panamá to Portobelo and serving as the only road across the isthmus for hundreds of years. In the 1700s, the route was abandoned in favor of shipping gold around Cape Horn, due to repeated pirate attacks, the most famous of which was Captain Henry Morgan's 1671 sacking of Panamá Viejo (p45).

As early as 1524, King Charles V of Spain had ordered a survey to determine the feasibility of constructing a trans-isthmian water route. But it wasn't until the 1880s that any country dared to undertake the momentous project of carving a trench through these dense jungles and mountains. The first canal attempt came from a French team led by Ferdinand-Marie de Lesseps, bolstered by his prior success building the Suez Canal.

Sadly, the French team grossly underestimated the difficulties and some 22,000 workers died during the construction attempt. Most lives were lost to yellow fever and malaria, which led to the establishment of an enormous quarantine on Isla Taboga. It was not yet known that mosquitoes were the disease vector. Several decades later, the USA learned from the mistakes of the French and succeeded in completing the canal in 1914.

Today the waterway rests firmly in the hands of the Panamanian government, and the face of the canal is rapidly changing as an ambitious expansion is completed.

AROUND PANAMA CITY

Panama Canal

One of the world's greatest human-made marvels, the Panama Canal stretches 80km from Panama City on the Pacific side to Colón

EXPANDING THE CANAL

In 2006 Panamanians, betting on burgeoning international shipping needs, voted to expand the canal. The plan was to widen and deepen existing navigation channels as well as constructing of two new locks. One of the biggest transportation projects in the world, this mega-project was planned at a projected cost of US$5.25 billion; it has now surpassed the US$17 billion mark as it nears completion and works have stretched more than a decade. Originally planned for inauguration at the canal's 100-year anniversary in 2014, the expansion is now expected to open in mid-2016. The resulting new locks will be 60% wider and 40% longer. Container traffic is expected to triple. But will it meet increased world shipping needs?

As container ships get bigger the need to accommodate them is plain. The increased traffic and volume through the canal will inject a huge boost into the Panamanian economy. The country will maintain its current role as the maritime logistics center in the Americas, and everything from the Free Trade Zone of Colón to the international financial hub of Panama City is likely to boom. It may increase tourism, since the new locks will be able to accommodate large cruise ships.

The rationale for the expansion is that the demands of the international maritime shipping community have changed. Although as much as 5% of the world's total sea commerce traverses the Panama Canal, the Suez Canal in Egypt, capable of handling larger vessels, serves more than 6%. Furthermore, the Panama Canal is already operating at more than 90% of its maximum capacity and will reach its saturation point in less than five years.

The biggest challenge the Panama Canal faces is luring in the enormous post-Panamax vessels, which currently depend on either the US Trans-continental Railway or the Suez Canal. Those in favor of canal expansion are hoping that this lucrative market will adopt the Panama route, especially as trade between Asia and the continental east coast increases.

Critics from all sectors of Panamanian society have serious concern that the expansion will not offset its construction costs, which have more than tripled from original estimates. Financing requires billions in loans from various foreign government-owned banks, in addition to funding by the Panamanian government and the Panama Canal Authority. Since tolls will increase significantly over the next 20 years, the hope is that the expected flow of post-Panamax vessels through the canal will eventually pick up the tab.

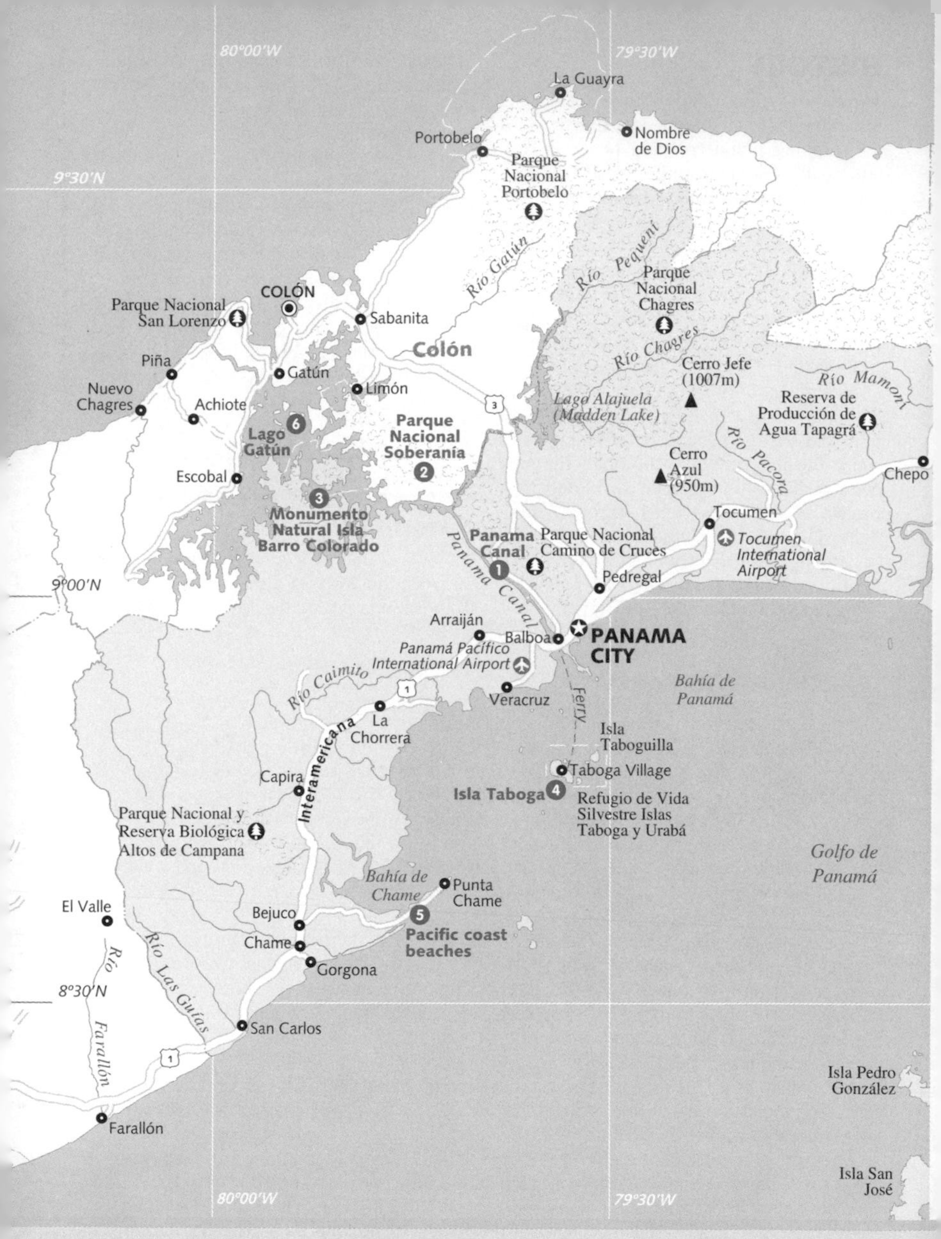

Panamá Province Highlights

1 Panama Canal (p73) Laying eyes on this awe-inspiring engineering marvel, which is in the midst of an expansion.

2 Parque Nacional Soberanía (p78) Spotting feathered friends along Pipeline Rd, one of the world's premier birdwatching sites.

3 Monumento Natural Isla Barro Colorado (p80) Visiting the world-famous tropical biology center at the most studied patch of rainforest in the world.

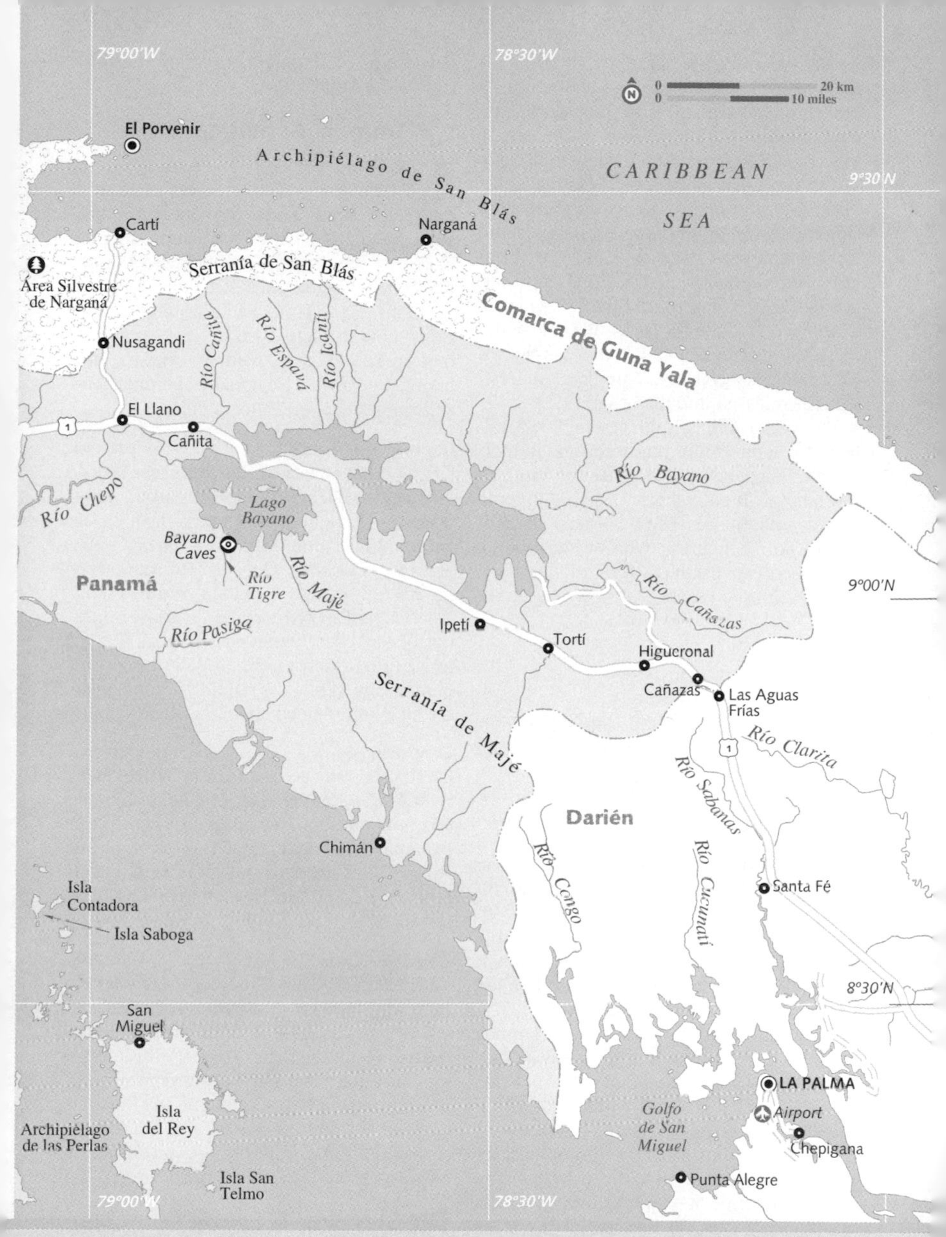

4 Isla Taboga (p81)
Escaping the urban grind of the capital on a day trip to this flower-dotted island.

5 Pacific coast beaches (p90) Soaking up the sun, surfing gnarly breaks and making the most of the romantic hideaways along the coastline.

6 Lago Gatún (p73)
Paddling a kayak or fishing for peacock bass on the lake, while spotting howler monkeys up above in the canopy.

on the Atlantic side, cutting right through the continental divide. Around 14,000 vessels pass through each year, and ships worldwide are built with the dimensions of the canal's locks (305m long and 33.5m wide) in mind.

The canal has three sets of double locks: Miraflores and Pedro Miguel on the Pacific side and Gatún on the Atlantic. Between the locks, ships pass through a huge artificial lake, Lago Gatún, created by the Gatún Dam across the Río Chagres, and the Culebra Cut, a 14km cut through the rock and shale of the isthmian mountains. With the passage of each ship, a staggering 197 million L of fresh water is released into the ocean.

The canal annually brings in US$2 billion in revenue. Ships pay according to their weight. The highest toll currently paid by the largest ships reaches US$450,000; the lowest amount was US$0.36, paid in 1928 by Richard Halliburton, who swam through. A planned expansion (p73) that's surpassed the US$17 billion mark is due to open mid-2016.

Sights

Miraflores Visitors Center MUSEUM

(Map p77; ☎276-8325; http://visitcanaldepanama.com; adult/child US$15/10; ⏲9am-5pm) The easiest and best way to visit the Panama Canal is to head to the Miraflores Visitors Center, located just outside Panama City. This modern visitors center features a large four-floor interactive museum, several viewing platforms and an excellent restaurant serving sumptuous buffet spreads with panorama views of canal transit. Tip: the best time to view big liners passing through is from 9am to 11am and from 3pm to 5pm, when they are more frequent.

To get there, take any Paraíso or Gamboa bus from the Albrook Bus Terminal in Panama City. Buses pass along the canal-side highway to Gamboa and will let you off at the 'Miraflores Locks' sign (US$0.35) on the highway, 12km from the city center. It's about a 15-minute walk to the locks from the sign. Otherwise you can take a taxi; drivers will typically wait 30 minutes at the locks and then drive you back to the capital. Expect to pay no more than US$30 round-trip; agree on the price beforehand.

Pedro Miguel Locks CANAL

(Map p77) FREE North past the Miraflores Locks, the Pedro Miguel Locks can be seen from the highway to Gamboa. One hundred meters beyond the locks there's a parking strip from where onlookers can watch ships transit the canal.

Tours & Activities

★Yala Tours ADVENTURE TOUR

(☎232-0215, 6641-6676; www.yalatourspanama.com) This small Swiss-run operation provides specialized trips throughout Panama, including day trips to Gamboa and the Canal Zone. A highlight is kayaking Río Chagres and Lago Gatún while watching canal ships mow through. Also offers a canal boat tour in Lago Gatún, wildlife-watching and hiking in Parque Nacional Soberanía, and cultural visits to an Embera village.

Canal & Bay Tours BOAT TOUR

(☎209-2002; www.canalandbaytours.com; partial/full transit US$125/170) Offers partial canal transits (4½ hours), which pass through the Pedro Miguel and Miraflores Locks, every Saturday morning. On one Saturday every month full transits (10 hours) run from Balboa on the Pacific Coast to Cristóbal on the Caribbean coast, passing all three sets of locks. Check the website for dates of upcoming transits. While the guiding is good, readers have complained about logistical snafus.

EcoCircuitos ADVENTURE TOUR

(☎315-1488; www.ecocircuitos.com; Albrook Plaza, 2nd fl, No 31, Ancón) A reputable, sustainable operator offering conventional tours to the Panama Canal and canal transits, tours of Parque Nacional Soberania, birdwatching on Pipeline Rd and fun kayaking trips on Lago Gatún.

Panama Canal Fishing FISHING

(☎315-1905, 6678-2653; www.panamacanalfishing.com; day trips per 2 anglers all-inclusive from US$495) If you have dreamed of reeling in the big one in the Canal Zone, try this outfit's signature tour that will have you fishing for peacock bass in Lago Gatún and the Río Chagres. An introduced species, the fish is now considered a plague; by fishing, you do a great favor to the lake. Canal tours also offered.

Sleeping & Eating

Jungle Land Panama HOUSE BOAT $$$

(☎213-1172; www.junglelandpanama.com; adult/child all-inclusive US$175/150) This overnight houseboat offers the novelty of a jungle retreat with canal ships passing by. Captain Carl hosts guests on a charmi ng wooden three-story houseboat on Lago Gatún, from where fishing, kayaking and nocturnal safaris are at your fingertips. Day trips also available. Leaves from the Gamboa public boat ramp.

Atlantic & Pacific Co. LATIN AMERICAN **$$$**

(☎ 232-3120; www.atlanticpacificrestaurant.com; 2nd fl Miraflores Visitors Center; buffet US$55; ⏲11:30am-4:30pm Mon-Sun, 5-10:30pm Tues-Sat; ❄) Finally; a restaurant worthy of the canal, though prices reflect the exclusive setting. Serving new Panamanian cuisine and using local produce, this upscale eatery offers distinctive choices, and plenty of them, at the lunch buffet. Seafood is a highlight, as well as rich Panamanian coffee and desserts. Ask for balcony seating and watch boats pass the locks.

Canal Zone

The Canal Zone is home to a number of impressive attractions, especially if you're into wildlife-watching, hiking and birdwatching. On a day trip from Panama City, you could visit the Miraflores Locks and finish at the Parque Nacional Soberanía and the Panama Rainforest Discovery Center. With prior arrangements, you could also take an organized tour of Isla Barro Colorado, one of the world's most famous tropical research

Panama Canal

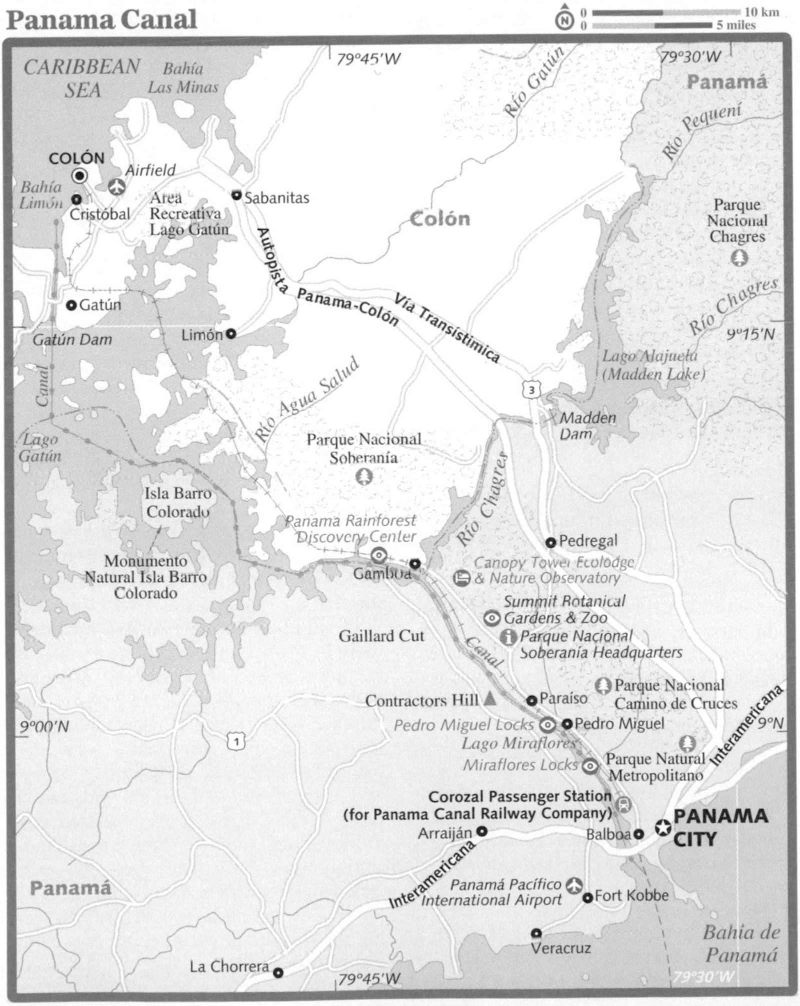

stations, or an Emberá or Wounaan indigenous village on the shores of the Río Chagres.

Parque Nacional Soberanía

Just 30 minutes from Panama City and a few kilometers into Colón Province, the 22,104-hectare **Parque Nacional Soberanía** (Map p77; www.miambiente.gob.pa; admission US$5) is one of the most accessible tropical rainforests in Panama. It extends much of the way across the isthmus, from Limón on Lago Gatún to north of Paraíso, and boasts hiking trails that brim with a remarkable variety of wildlife.

Leaflets and information about the park, including a brochure for self-guided walks along the nature trail, are available from the **park headquarters** (Map p77; ☎500-0906; ⏲8am-4pm) near Gamboa.

Hiking trails in the park include a section of the old Sendero Las Cruces (Las Cruces Trail) and the 17km Pipeline Rd, providing access to Río Agua Salud, where you can walk upriver for a swim under a waterfall.

Known residents include 105 species of mammal, 525 species of bird, 55 species of amphibian, 79 species of reptile and 36 of freshwater fish. In order to fully appreciate the wildlife here, it's wise to hire a guide.

Activities

Hiking

If you plan on hiking, note that the trailheads are quite far from the park headquarters.

Sendero el Charco HIKING

A very easy 800m trail, the Sendero El Charco is signposted from Carretera Omar Torrijos, 3km past the Summit Botanical Gardens & Zoo.

Sendero Las Cruces HIKING

The park has a short 10km section of the old Sendero Las Cruces (Las Cruces Trail), which was famously used by the Spanish to transport gold by mule train between Panama City and Nombre de Dios.

Birdwatching

Most visitors to the park come for birdwatching on **Pipeline Road**, one of the world's premier birdwatching sites. Unsurprisingly, it is intensely popular with birdwatchers, especially in the early morning hours.

More than 500 different species of birds have been spotted on the trail A healthy cluster of golden-collared manakins is usually found at the end of the first 100m of the road, on the left-hand side. Other typical sounds along the first 2km of the road come from white-bellied antbirds, black-bellied wrens, collared aracaris, keel-billed toucans and buff-throated woodcreepers. Also keep an eye out for rarities such as the tiny hawk, the hook-billed kite, the great jacamar and the black-tailed trogon. Also known as the Camino del Oleoducto, the 24km Pipeline Rd also provides access to Río Agua Salud, where you can walk upriver for a swim under a waterfall.

It's wise to hire a guide; you're in one of the world's premier birdwatching sites. It would be a shame to give it short shrift.

Fishing

Fishing is permitted on Río Chagres and Lago Gatún. To arrange a private tour, contact Panama Canal Fishing (p76).

Sleeping

★**Canopy Tower Ecolodge & Nature Observatory** LODGE $$$

(Map p77; ☎264-5720; www.canopytower.com; per person incl tours & meals US$185-303; P) Located in Parque Nacional Soberanía, this former US Air Force radar station now serves a very different function, namely ecotourism. Open only to guests, the Canopy Tower is an ecologically minded three-story, cylindrical lodge and observatory that offers a full immersion in the sights and sounds of the rainforest.

The birdwatching in the surrounding area is top-notch and there's no shortage of other tropical wildlife, including howler monkeys, sloths and a slew of frogs and lizards. From the 3rd and rooftop levels, you have a 360-degree view over the national park and you can even see ships passing through the Panam Canal, a mere 2km away.

In addition to the viewing platforms, there is also a small ground-floor museum, a tropical biology library, a cozy sitting area and a handful of attractive guest rooms, ranging from quaint singles to luxurious four-person suites. Each room is awash in tropical hues, natural hardwoods, firm beds and a few hammocks to help you pass the time. Some lodgings feature shared bathrooms. Rates include three meals and a complimentary tour with each three-night stay. Even if you're not spending the night, a day visit will allow you to visit the viewing platforms and partake in a few guided walks through the park.

EMBERÁ AND WOUNAAN COMMUNITIES

The Río Chagres, which flows through the Parque Nacional Soberanía and supplies most of the water for the Panama Canal, is home to several Emberá and Wounaan communities. Although the Darién is the ancestral home of these two indigenous groups, a wave of migration to the shores of the Río Chagres commenced in the 1950s. Following the establishment of the national park in the 1980s, however, the government culled the practice of slash-and-burn agriculture, which has severely affected their livelihood. Today several villages are turning to tourism for survival.

Before visiting these communities, it's important to realize that during the past 50 years both the Emberá and the Wounaan communities have had a turbulent history of land grabs, legal battles and political misrepresentation. Both groups have been forced to modernize, though the Emberá and the Wounaan still maintain their incredibly rich cultural heritage. If you arrive expecting to see villagers living traditional lifestyles in harmony with the land, then you will be disappointed. However, the Emberá and the Wounaan still have a lot to show to visitors, especially their traditional dances, music, handicrafts and the surrounding national park that has become their de facto home.

The Emberá community of **Ella Puru** (☎6537-7223, 6704-0380; http://ellapuruembera.weebly.com; tours per person US$25, entry $5) and Wounaan community of **San Antonio** (☎6637-9503; tours per person $30) regularly receive tourists. With prior notice you can arrange a pick up from the docks in Gamboa. Tour prices depend on the activities you arrange. There is no shortage of possible excursions, ranging from guided rainforest walks to watching traditional dances. Communities also sell traditional handicrafts.

Visitors praise **Embera Village Tours** (☎848-4072, 6758-7600; www.emberavillagetours.com), the agency of Anne Gordon de Barrigón, a former animal trainer who married into this warm Emberá community. The tour is well done and provides loads of cultural insight.

To reach the Canopy Tower, pass the entrance to Summit Botanical Gardens & Zoo on your way to Gamboa, and take the second road to the right; the turnoff is marked with a Canopy Tower sign. Follow the road for 1.6km until you reach the top of Semaphore Hill and the entrance to the hotel.

Getting There & Away

From Panama City take any Gamboa-bound bus from Albrook Bus Terminal (US$0.65) or a taxi (US$20 to US$30). If arriving by taxi, have the driver wait for you to pay the fee and then take you to the trailheads, as they are quite far from the entrance station and park headquarters.

Panama Rainforest Discovery Center

Geared towards ecotourism and environmental education, this excellent **park** (Map p77; ☎306-3133, 6450-6630; www.pipelineroad.org; adult/child US$30/4, night walk donation US$35; ⊙6am-4pm), attracts birdwatchers and nature-lovers. Since you are probably here to watch wildlife, it's worth making an effort to roll out of bed early. You will be rewarded for the effort. In fact, those arriving after 10am pay US$10 less in admission, a sure sign that you're getting less bang for your buck. During premium hours, just 25 visitors are admitted at one time to minimize the impact on wildlife.

A 32m-high observation tower is great for spotting blue cotinga and toucans. The sustainably built visitors center provides information and has 13 species of hummingbirds feeding nearby. Guides at the visitors center and tower can point out wildlife. Currently, a 1.2km circuit of forest trails offers options that range from easy to difficult. Lake-side you can view aquatic birds such as wattled jacanas, least grebes, herons and snail kites. Other animals around include monkeys, crocodiles, coatis and butterflies.

With advance reservations, groups can set up special night tours.

Contact the center if you'd like to participate in bird migration counts. These are run by the **Fundación Avifauna Eugene Eisenmann** (☎306-3133; www.avifauna.org.pa), a nonprofit organization working to promote the preservation of Panama's bird fauna and rainforest habitat. Within the center, scientific research includes studies of migratory birds, green macaws and raptors, as well as investigations into carbon capture.

There's no bus access to the park. It's best to negotiate a taxi, rent a car or go with an organized tour. The center is located 1.6km from the entrance to Pipeline Rd. You must pass the town of Gamboa, at the end of Gaillard Rd, and follow the signs.

Getting There & Away

Julio (☎6509-1731) Offers responsible boat transfers from the Gamboa dock to indigenous communities.

Monumento Natural Isla Barro Colorado

This lush island in the middle of Lago Gatún is the most intensively studied area in the neotropics. Formed by the damming of the Río Chagres and the creation of the lake, in 1923 Isla Barro Colorado (BCI) became one of the first biological reserves in the New World. Home to 1316 recorded plant species, 381 bird species and 120 mammal species, the island also contains a 59km network of marked and protected trails. It is managed by the Smithsonian Tropical Research Institute (STRI), which administers a world-renowned research facility here. The island is open to a limited number of visitors on guided tours.

Tours

Isla Barro Colorado Tour ECOTOUR
(www.stri.org; tour per adult/child incl lunch US$80/50) Once restricted to scientists, this 1500-hectare tropical research island is now open to a limited number of visitors on guided tours. The trip includes a boat ride down an attractive part of the canal, from Gamboa across the lake to the island. Hikes are demanding and last two to three hours. The entire trip lasts four to six hours, depending on the size of the group and on the weather. Reservations are essential; book as far in advance as possible.

Information

There are no public visits on certain holidays. For reservations and detailed visitor information, visit the **Smithsonian Tropical Research Institute** (STRI; Map p46; ☎212-8000; www.stri.org; Tupper Bldg, Av Roosevelt, Ancón; ⏲8:30am-4:30pm Mon-Fri) website.

Gamboa

A pleasant community of broad, curving streets, old wooden canal houses and leafy walks, Gamboa is an ideal base for wildlife-watchers who also want some quiet. The small town is the base for many foreign scientists working for STRI. Unfortunately, for groceries or interesting dining options you will have to backtrack toward the Panama City.

Sleeping & Eating

Mateo B&B CABIN $
(☎6690-9664; www.gamboabedandbreakfast.com; Calle Humberto Zárate 131A; s/d incl breakfast US$35/40) Hidden in a leafy suburban neighborhood, these two basic cabins offer respite and hospitality. Host Mateo is attentive and helpful. The bathroom is in the main house.

★**Canopy B&B** B&B $$$
(☎833-5929, reservations 264-5720; www.canopytower.com; Av Jadwin 114; s/d incl breakfast from US$95/140; ❄📶) In an old canal house, this lovely B&B has a clean design of classic features mixed with bold patterns. Heated towel racks and hair dryers add a nice touch. Upstairs rooms are a significant upgrade. In the morning, pancakes, eggs and wheat toast are served at a huge breakfast table. Rent bikes here to cruise the pleasant, shady neighborhood. Dinner (US$22) is an optional extra.

Gamboa Rainforest Resort RESORT $$$
(☎340-9889; www.gamboaresort.com; d from US$250; P❄@📶🏊) Near the junction of the Panama Canal and the Río Chagres, 9km past the turnoff for Canopy Tower on the road to Colón, is this US$30 million spot. It's not an ecolodge but a resort located in a rainforest; nevertheless, it's hard to deny its grandeur. All 110 luxurious guest rooms offer sweeping vistas of the jungle-flanked Río Chagres.

There are echoes of Disneyland, with an on-site golf course, spa, gym, marina, swimming pool and bar-restaurant. There's even an aerial tram that brings you up into the canopy, as well as guided nature walks and birdwatching trips (at extra cost). The website offers special package deals, which often include activities, meals and transfers.

Getting There & Away

Gamboa is 35km from Panama City. Take a taxi (US$20 to US$30), or the Gamboa-bound bus (US$0.65) from the Albrook Bus Terminal.

PACIFIC ISLANDS

Isla Taboga

POP 1600

A tropical island with just one road and no traffic, Isla Taboga is a pleasant escape from the rush of Panama City, only 20km offshore. With the addition of an annual festival and boutique lodgings, it's growing as a destination. Named the 'Island of Flowers,' it is covered with sweet-smelling blossoms much of the year. First settled by the Spanish in 1515, the quaint village is also home to the second-oldest church in the western hemisphere. While there are better beaches elsewhere, this quick getaway is a salve for city living.

History

Taboga is part of a chain of islands that were inhabited by indigenous peoples who resided in thatched huts and lived off the bounty of the sea. In 1515 Spanish soldiers announced their arrival by killing or enslaving the islanders and establishing a small colony. It then became a favorite haunt for English pirates.

On August 22, 1686, the ship of English buccaneer Captain Townley was in front of Taboga when attacked by three Spanish ships armed with cannons. During the ensuing battle, Townley destroyed one of the ships and took captive the two other vessels as well as a fourth ship that had arrived as reinforcement. Townley sent a messenger to the president of Panama demanding supplies, the release of five pirates being held prisoner and ransom for the Spanish captives. When the president refused, a standoff ensued, with Townley sending the president a canoe with the heads of 20 Spaniards. With that, the pirate's demands were soon met.

For years, peace eluded the little island that lay in such a strategic location. During the 1880s, when the French attempted to build a canal, Taboga became the site of an enormous sanatorium for workers who had contracted malaria or yellow fever.

The US Navy used the broad hill facing the town for artillery practice during WWII and even installed a number of anti-aircraft guns and machine-gun bunkers atop the island. Though abandoned in 1960, these ruins can still be visited today.

Sights

Fine sand beaches lie in either direction from the ferry dock. Walk left from the pier along the island's narrow main road to the village. After a fork, a high road leads to the church and a simple square. Further down the road, a beautiful public garden displays the statue of the island's patroness, Nuestra Señora del

PIRATES IN THE BAY

From the late 17th century Golfo de Panamá (Panama Bay) was the scene of pirate exploits unsurpassed anywhere in the New World. It served as both hideout and attack springboard. After Captain Henry Morgan's successful 1671 sacking of Panama City, other buccaneers flooded in to pillage and plunder along the Pacific coast.

In May 1685 the largest number of fighters ever assembled under a buccaneer flag in the Pacific played cat and mouse with a Spanish armada of 18 ships. English captain Edward Blake's French and English pirate fleet was deficient in cannons but sufficient in muskets, so avoided long range fighting. Despite inferior numbers, Blake itched for a close encounter with the Spaniards.

When the two great forces crossed paths on May 28, Blake ordered two of his principal ships to attack the Spanish fleet. Fearing the cannons, both refused to obey. The forces exchanged fire, but with odds stacked against Blake he ordered the slower ships to flee while his and another fast vessel delayed the conquistadors.

The pirates managed some risky evasive maneuvers between rocky islets and anchored that night, expecting the Spanish armada to engage them the next day. Instead the Spanish fleet fled to Panamá. Soon dissent arose among the buccaneers and the short-lived, French–English pirate confederacy dissolved.

Today almost the only evidence of pirates in the Archipiélago de Las Perlas are distant descendants of the Spaniards and their slaves. Forests once felled to build ships have grown back. Storms, termites and wood worms have destroyed the old Spanish structures, though a church and a stone dam on Isla Taboga testify to the Spaniards' presence.

WORTH A TRIP

NORTHEAST PANAMÁ PROVINCE

Heading toward the Darién and the Comarca de Guna Yala, there are some excellent attractions within an easy day trip from Panama City.

Created when the Río Bayano was dammed in 1976, the human-made Lago Bayano is a great destination for boating, birdwatching and caving. The lake takes its name from Bayano, the man who led the largest slave revolt in 16th-century Panama. The area, with little development and lots of waterbirds, is home to Emberá, Wounaan and Guna indigenous communities.

On the south side of the lake, the Bayano Caves are a fun adventure. Cavers wade up Río Tigre though a sculpted paleolithic cave that's 850m long, and full of bats and amphibians. At times it's necessary to swim, depending on water levels. Exploring the cave requires round-trip boat transportation, a guide, headlamps and helmets. It's located 1½ hours east of Panama City via the Interamericana.

With excellent birdwatching and good rainforest trails, the **Área Silvestre de Narganá** (www.miambiente.gob.pa; admission US$20) wildlife reserve was created by the Guna indigenous community, primarily to try to keep away squatters. The 96,000 hectares of species-rich primary forest are ideal to explore with a naturalist guide. This is the best place in Panama to spot the speckled antshrike, the black-headed ant thrush and the black-crowned antpitta. Access the reserve via the Interamericana, going via Chepo, and turning onto the rough El Llano–Cartí road. Go by sturdy 4WD with plenty of clearance.

Guided tours for the caves and reserve are available through Panama City tour agencies and Guna guide **Igua Jiménez** (☎6700-3512; iguat28@yahoo.com); tours may include a visit to nearby indigenous communities as well.

Carmen. The road meanders a total of 5.2km, ending at the old US military installation atop the island's highest hill, Cerro El Vigia.

Refugio de Vida Silvestre Islas Taboga y Urabá WILDLIFE RESERVE

This wildlife reserve was established to protect key avian habitat. Taboga and nearby Urabá are home to one of the world's largest breeding colonies of brown pelicans, with up to 100,000 individuals – about half of the world population of this species. The reserve covers about a third of Taboga as well as the entire island of Urabá, just off Taboga's southeast coast. May is the height of nesting season, but pelicans are seen from January to June.

La Restinga BEACH

Right of the pier as you arrive by boat, the main beach links to the tiny Isla El Morro at low tide by a sandbar.

Iglesia de San Pedro CHURCH

Founded in 1550, La Iglesia de San Pedro is the second-oldest church in the western hemisphere; inside is a handsome altar and lovely artwork.

Activities

Snorkeling

On weekends, fishers at the pier take visitors around the island to good snorkeling spots and caves on the western side, which are rumored to hold pirate treasure. During the week you can snorkel around Isla El Morro, which doesn't have coral but attracts some large fish.

Diving

The Pacific-style diving here has rocky formations, schools of fish and a wide variety of marine life. On a good dive you can see jack, snapper, jewfish, eels, rays, lobsters and octopuses. With a little luck, you may also come across old bottles, spent WWII-era shells and artifacts from pirate days (look, but don't take). Dive outfitters in Panama City occasionally make the trip.

Whale-Watching

Keep an eye out for whales while on the ferry over to the island. From August to October migrating humpback and sei whales can be seen leaping from the water near Taboga in spectacular displays.

Festivals & Events

Fiesta del Mar FIESTA

(www.fiestadelmarpanama.com; ⌚Jan) Only in its second year, this festival highlights local culture, with live Panamanian calypso music, dancing, a pageant and food events. It draws 4000 guests to the tiny island.

Nuestra Señora del Carmen FIESTA
(☉16 Jul) Island patroness Nuestra Señora del Carmen is honored with a seafaring procession each year. Seemingly everyone partakes in games, fire-breathing or dancing.

🛏 Sleeping

Zoraida's Cool GUESTHOUSE $
(☑6471-1123; d/tr US$40/45) Overlooking the bay, this turquoise house is run by Rafael, the widower of Zoraida. Rooms are small and mattresses plastic-wrapped, but it's the cheapest digs around. The clincher is a hammock deck that's ideal for a snooze with Pacific views. Turn left as you exit the dock and walk for a few minutes until you see a sign leading you up the hill.

Cerrito Tropical B&B $$
(☑390-8999, 6489-0074; www.cerritotropical-panama.com; d incl breakfast US$88, 2-person apt US$95-130; ✳☏) This smart Canadian and Dutch-owned B&B occupies a quiet nook atop a steep road. Rooms are stylish, but some are more spacious than others and not all have TVs. Management can arrange tours such as fishing, hiking and whale-watching, and daytime packages including lunch and showers for nonguests. Taxi from the pier, or make the steep walk, going right uphill at the end of Calle Francisco Pizarro.

Vereda Tropical Hotel HOTEL $$
(☑250-2154; www.hotelveredatropical.com; d with fan/air-con incl breakfast US$65/80; ✳☏) Atop a hill with commanding views, this boutique hotel charms with tropical tones, mosaic tiles and rod-iron railings. The dining patio (mains US$9 to US$17) has sweeping views and Julio Iglesias serenading from the speakers. Service may be a little slow. It's about 100m up a winding path off the main road.

★ Villa Caprichosa VILLA $$$
(☑6632-1725; www.villacaprichosa.com; r US$155-1750; ✳☏☒) This reincarnation of a classic Tuscan villa has fountains, a neutral palette and marvelous *trompe l'oeil* effects. Owner Diane specializes in Italian design and her work here, featured in *Architectural Digest*, is flawless. With canal sea views and decks to catch the breeze, this cliffside property says 'seize the day'. Options include studios, suites and a two-bedroom house, all with kitchenettes. If you can, book the suite with the small-scale infinity pool on the deck. Weekday rates are lower. There's a two-night preference for bookings.

✖ Eating

★ Calaloo SEAFOOD $
(☑6000-5172; mains $7-10; ☉9am-5pm Mon-Thu, to 8pm Fri-Sun, by reservation if closed; ☑) This cute, colorful eatery offers the standard fare of fish and chips in addition to veggie options. It's a great place to have a beer and watch the village hubbub. Service is notably slow, and crazy weekend crowds way outnumber the cooks. Just be patient. It's run by the folks from Cerrito Tropical B&B.

Donde Pope Si Hay PANAMANIAN $
(mains US$4-9; ☉8am-8pm) A simple concrete eatery serving fresh fish, cold green coconut water and *patacones* (fried plantains); there is nothing mysterious about Pope beyond its name.

ℹ Information
There are no ATMS on the island, so bring cash.
For more information, visit the excellent English-language site www.taboga.panamanow.com.

ℹ Getting There & Away
The scenic boat trip to Isla Taboga is part of the island's attraction. Ferries land at a pier near the north end of the island. Schedules can change, so check online for updates. Note that the police check ferry passengers for drugs upon arrival.

Barcos Calypso (☑314-1730; round-trip US$14) ferries depart from Isla Naos on the Causeway in Panama City. The easiest way to reach the dock is by taxi (US$7). Trips take 45 minutes and depart Panama City at the following times:

DAY	TIME
Mon & Fri	8:30am, 3pm
Tue, Wed & Thu	8am, 10:30am
Sat & Sun	4pm

Round-trip ferries from Isla Taboga:

DAY	TIME
Mon–Thu	4pm
Fri	9:30am, 4:30pm
Sat & Sun	9am, 3pm, 5pm

The new **Taboga Express** (☑6234-8989; www.tabogaexpress.com; adult/child round-trip US$16/8; ☏) catamaran takes 30 minutes and is killing the competition with good reason: it's fast. It leaves daily from Panama City's Balboa Yacht Club on the Causeway at 8am, 9:30am, 11am, 3pm and 4:30pm.
Round-trip catamarans depart Isla Taboga at 8:45am, 10:15 am, 2:30pm, 4pm and 5pm.

Archipiélago de Las Perlas

Named for the large pearls found in its waters, the Archipiélago de Las Perlas comprises 90 named islands and more than 100 unnamed islets, each surrounded by travel magazine–worthy white-sand beaches and turquoise waters. Home to the palatial mansions of the rich and powerful, Isla Contadora is the best known. Popular US TV show *Survivor* filmed its 2003 season on several islands in the chain. Real-estate developments, which would add luxury homes and resorts to areas with poor longtime settlements, are increasingly under fire.

Visitors mostly head to four islands: Isla Contadora, the most accessible, developed and touristed; Isla San José, the site of an exclusive resort; and neighboring Islas Casaya and Casayeta, frequented by pearl shoppers. Uninhabited isles offer ample opportunity for independent exploration, especially if you have a sense of adventure and the help of a local guide. But there's no ATM, so bring sufficient cash.

History

Pearls brought the archipelago to the Old World's attention. Vasco Núñez de Balboa, within days of discovering the Pacific Ocean, learned from a local guide of nearby islands rich with pearls. Balboa was anxious to visit, but he was told that a hostile chief ruled them and cautiously decided to postpone. Nonetheless, Balboa named the archipelago 'Islas de Las Perlas,' and declared it and all its undiscovered riches Spanish property. The year was 1513, and Balboa vowed to return one day to kill the chief and claim his pearls for the king of Spain.

Before he could fulfill his vow, Spanish governor Pedro Arias de Ávila dispatched his cousin Gaspar de Morales to the islands for the pearls. Morales captured 20 chieftains and gave them to his dogs. The purportedly hostile chief, a man named Dites, saw the futility of resisting so instead presented Morales with a basket of large and lustrous pearls. With their appetite unsated, however, the Spanish took just two years to exterminate the indigenous population.

In 1517, the same year that Morales raided Las Perlas, Pedrarias (as the governor was often called) falsely charged Balboa with treason, and had him and four of his closest friends beheaded.

In the years that followed, the Spaniards harvested the islands' oyster beds. Having slain the entire native population, they imported slaves from Africa to pearl dive. Their descendants live on the islands today.

Isla Contadora

POP 115

Isla Contadora (Counting House Island) was once the accounting center for pearls before they were shipped to Spain. In more recent times, multimillionaires have made the island their refuge; when Shah Mohammed Reza Pahlavi was ousted from Iran in 1979, he removed his large fortune to Isla Contadora. However, a government crackdown on tax evasion is embittering the previously sweet deal. Many empty mansions are now rented to vacationers.

With frequent air and sea connections to Panama City, Isla Contadora is the only island in the archipelago with a developed tourist infrastructure. A prestigious destination, it caters to its wealthy residents and moneyed visitors from the mainland. In low season it's more accessible for all. Beaches are spectacular; the snorkeling is world class; and the island is a great jumping-off

LA PEREGRINA

Archipiélago de Las Perlas has produced some of the world's finest pearls. However, none is as celebrated or well documented as the La Peregrina (the Pilgrim Pearl). Enormous and pear-shaped, this white pearl weighs 203.84 grains or 31 carats. Four hundred years ago, it earned the slave who discovered it his freedom.

In the mid-16th century, the pearl was given to King Phillip II of Spain, who later presented it as a wedding gift to his wife, Queen Mary I of England. Later the British Marquis of Abercorn acquired it from the son of French emperor Napoleon III.

In 1969 actor Richard Burton purchased it for US$37,000 for his wife, Elizabeth Taylor. La Peregrina was briefly lost when Taylor's dog scampered away with the pearl in its mouth. In 2011 the pearl was auctioned at Christie's as part of her estate, and fetched US$11 million.

point for independent exploration of the archipelago.

Sights

The island's 12 gold-sand beaches are virtually abandoned except during major holidays. Four are particularly lovely: Playa de las Suecas, Playa Cacique, Playa Ejecutiva and Playa Galeón. Although spread around the island, all can be visited in as little as 20 minutes in a rented ATV (all-terrain vehicle).

Playa Larga (Long Beach) occupies a long stretch, with an abandoned hotel that has an unfortunate sewage contamination issue – it's probably best not to swim here. Around the corner to the south is Playa de las Suecas (Swedish Women's Beach), where you can sunbathe in the buff legally. Continuing west 400m, you'll find Playa Cacique, a fairly large and unvisited beach ideal for a little peace and quiet. On the northern side of the island, Playa Ejecutiva (Executive Beach) is another intimate escape – the large house on the bluff to the east is where the Shah of Iran once lived. Playa Galeón (Galleon Beach), to the northeast, is another good spot for snorkeling when the surf is small.

Activities

Snorkeling & Diving

The snorkeling and diving around Contadora is fantastic. In five nearby coral fields you can see schools of angelfish, damselfish, moray eels, parrot fish, puffer fish, butterfly fish, white-tip reef sharks and much more. Even off Playa Larga, the most popular of Isla Contadora's beaches, you can often spot sea turtles and manta rays.

The coral fields are found offshore from the eastern end of Playa de las Suecas; Punta Verde, near the southern end of Playa Larga; both ends of Playa Galeón; and the western end of Playa Ejecutiva. There is also a lot of marine life among the rocks in front and east of Playa Roca.

Coral Dreams DIVING
(☎6536-1776; www.coral-dreams.com; 1hr dive $95, 3hr snorkeling $65) This small PADI-certified outfit with experienced instructors is located in front of the Contadora airport. Snorkeling tours go to Isla Mogo (Survivor Island). It also runs whale-watching trips (July to October) with a hydrophone to hear whale calls, and rents snorkel equipment.

Sailing & Boating

One of the best ways to appreciate the beauty and isolation of the Archipiélago de Las Perlas is to explore it on a chartered sailboat.

If you want to go island-hopping, you can contract a fishing-boat captain. Ask for recommendations at your hotel. Bring cash because they definitively do not take credit.

Las Perlas Sailing BOATING
(☎6413-7128; www.lasperlassailing.es.tl) Day charters on an 11.5m catamaran with snorkel equipment, lunch and drinks (US$100 per adult), in addition to cheaper sunset cruises and other excursions. Experienced sailors can rent one- and two-person sailboats as well as a range of motorboats. Sportfishing excursions are a high-end affair. Some guests have complained that reservations are not always honored; double and triple confirm.

Whale-Watching

Migrating humpback whales can be seen from July to October. Fishers take tourists out on their boats (and you might see whales while out on another excursion), but it's worth going with a naturalist guide.

Tours

Survivor Las Perlas ADVENTURE TOUR
(☎6738-1708; http://ecotourspanama.net/survivor lasperlas; 3-day camping tours per person US$249) Explore uninhabited islands in the archipelago, snorkel reefs and camp in hammocks on desolate beaches on a guided group trip. Scavenger hunts are part of the fun. The trip visits Mogo Mogo and Chapera islands, featured in the *Survivor* TV series. Meals and local boat transportation included. The tour is run by Panama Travel Unlimited (www.panamatravelunlimited.com) in Panama City.

Whale Watching Panama TOUR
(☎6758-7600; www.whalewatchingpanama.com; ⊙Jul-Oct) To see humpback whales and dolphin pods in the Islas de Las Perlas, these day trips ($225 for five passengers) and multiday trips are led by expert biologist guides. Some trips have a spiritual focus (ie animal communication or shamanic whale-watching with yoga). The company adheres to international guidelines for whale-watching.

Sleeping

Many accommodations will meet you at the airport and provide transportation (via golf cart) to the resort or hotel.

Isla Contadora

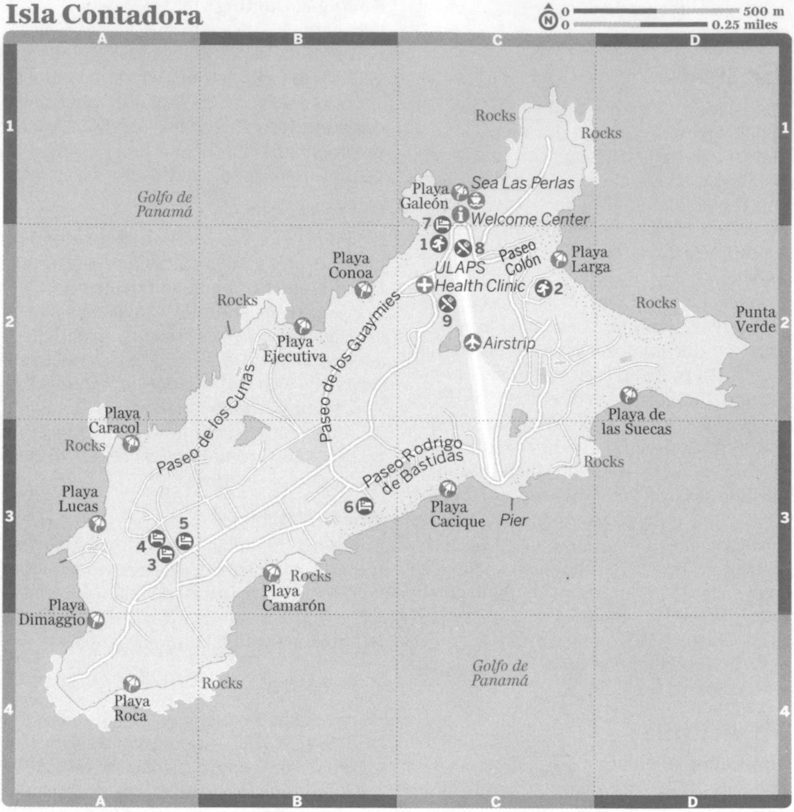

★**B&B Gerald's Place** B&B **$$**
(☎250-4159; www.island-contadora.com; d incl breakfast US$96; ❄📶) With a good location near the ferry landing, Gerald's is central and comfortable, with good service. Rooms may lack views, but are modern and well equipped, with flat-screen TVs and air-con.

★**Perla Real by the Sea** INN **$$**
(Hotel Playa Cacique; ☎6513-9064; www.perlareal.com; Playa Cacique No 50; d garden/sea view incl breakfast US$96/114, ste US$156; ❄📶) Overlooking lovely Playa Cacique, this small inn run by the inland Perla Real (p86) caters to romantic escapes. If you want to be right on the beach, it's your best option. Rooms have flat-screen TVs, lock boxes and minifridges, and suites feature full kitchens. A good on-site restaurant means you don't have to cross town to satisfy your hunger.

The hotel can also arrange tours, as well as provide water-sports rentals and golf carts.

Casa del Sol INN **$$**
(☎6518-8284, 250-4212; www.panama-islacontadora.com; s/d incl breakfast US$100/110; ❄📶) Located in a residential neighborhood, this pleasant inn features small rooms where you will be served a continental breakfast. The grounds are lovely but there is no living-room space, making it a little cramped if you are spending time inside. Also rents houses and has good ATV rental prices.

Perla Real B&B **$$$**
(☎250-4095, 6513-9064; www.perlareal.com; d/tr/ste incl breakfast US$127/145/165; ❄📶) Looking more Santa Fé than tropical, this comfortable inn is one of the best options on the island. Spacious rooms have French doors and prim decor, with painted ceramic sinks, stenciled walls and soft bedding. Ideal for long stays, suites come with an equipped kitchen and living space. The quiet residential area is a 10-minute walk from the beaches. Friendly

Isla Contadora

Activities, Courses & Tours

Sleeping

Eating

and well managed, the B&B loans kayaks and snorkel gear, and rents golf carts.

Contadora Island Inn B&B $$$
(6699-4614; www.contadoraislandinn.com; d incl breakfast US$110-140;) In a pleasant, large home with wooden decks, this B&B is relaxing and personalized. Modern rooms are ample and lovely, with tile floors, brocade bedspreads and French doors that you can fling open to catch the breeze. Some rooms have balconies and all have hot-water showers. Management also rents private homes.

Point HOTEL $$$
(836-5434; www.hotelthepoint.com; d US$144;) On a dramatic cliff above Playa Galeón, this is the island's only 'resort.' The 48 rooms are, however, small for the price tag. A wooden boardwalk leads to the swimming pool, a spa and bar and restaurants. Food quality may depend on how recently the supply ship has visited.

Eating

Isla Contadora's poor reputation for dining is due to sporadic food shipments from the mainland, which results in poor variety. Even fresh fish can be hard to come by. Three small supermarkets serve the island.

La Fonda de Clarita PANAMANIAN $
(6518-5396; mains US$5-12; 6:45am-2pm & 6-8:30pm) This outdoor eatery has good plain food that's popular with locals. Fish and chips is on the menu, but lunch specials such as chicken with rice and lentils are bountiful.

Gerald's Place INTERNATIONAL $$
(mains US$8-24; 7:30-10am, noon-3pm & 6-11pm;) This thatched restaurant attached to the hotel of the same name has the best food on the island. It's certainly where you would go for a little ambience, though it's still casual. Options include good pizza and seafood with vegetable sides, all cooked by a friendly German.

Information

Welcome Center (6544-8962, 250-4081; www.contadorapanama.com; boat tours per hr $40, kayak & golf cart rentals per hr $25; 8am-5pm) This privately run organization is the only place for general info. It also books boat tours, rents kayaks and golf carts, and brews espresso drinks.

ULAPS Health Clinic (250-4209; 24hr) A short walk from the airstrip. If closed, visit the house out the back for emergencies.

Getting There & Away

All flights arrive to the small airstrip, which has no on-site services available. Always schedule an extra day or two around your international flight in case of delays or cancellations.

Air Panama (316-9000; www.airpanama.com) Direct flights from Panama City to Isla Contadora. Has two daily departures on weekdays and multiple departures on weekends.

Sea Las Perlas (391-1424; www.sealasperlas.com; adult/child one way US$45/35) Cataman ferries leave from Balboa Yacht Club on the Panama City Causeway daily at 7am (11am departure on Sunday), returning from Isla Contadora at 3:30pm. The journey takes one hour and 40 minutes.

Getting Around

Because the island is only about 1 sq km in size, there are no taxis. It's easy to walk everywhere, but it's hilly. Most tourist facilities are on the northern side of the island, within walking distance of the airstrip. Hotels shuttle guests to and from the airport via golf cart. These and ATVs can be rented at hotels for getting around the island.

Isla San José

Home to the most exclusive resort in the Pearl Islands, Isla San José has a sinister history as a US chemical-weapons testing ground. During a 2001 inspection, the entire island was placed under temporary quarantine following the recovery of unexploded ordnance, which led to a tiff between Panama and the USA over who should pick up the cleaning bill.

Most of the 45.3-sq-km island is covered in a bank of rainforest networked by all-weather roads installed by the US military decades ago. Beyond the roads, the only development on the island is the cliffside resort.

Sleeping

Hacienda del Mar LUXURY HOTEL $$$
(☎832-5439, Panama City 269-6634; www.haciendadelmar.net; cabins from US$375; ❄) If you want to really get away, Hacienda del Mar has 37 tan-sand beaches, nine year-round rivers and seven accessible waterfalls all to itself. Each stand-alone luxury cabin overflows with amenities, and offers views to a picture-perfect sweep of beach. Plunge into the laundry list of tours or just soak up your exclusive slice of paradise. Prices fall to roughly half in low season.

Getting There & Away

Flights between Panama City and Isla San José (US$135 round-trip) are arranged through Hacienda del Mar. Leave a few days between your visit and international flights, as there can be weather delays.

Islas Casaya & Casayeta

Oysters are still harvested throughout the archipelago, and their pearls are just as legendary as they were when Spanish explorer Vasco Núñez de Balboa first arrived in the 16th century. Although pearls are sometimes offered for sale on other islands, the best places to shop for them are Isla Casaya and neighboring Isla Casayeta, which lie about 12km to the south of Contadora.

When you're looking at pearls, you should know that pearl sellers tend to keep their goods in oil, so that they'll have a lovely shine when presented – always dry the pearl that intrigues you before you buy. Prices are generally very reasonable, and there's always room for bargaining.

Accommodations on either Isla Contadora or San José can arrange transportation to the pearl shops on Islas Casaya and Casayeta.

WORTH A TRIP

QUESOS CHELA

In the nondescript town of Capira, 57km from Panama City, the famous **Quesos Chela** (☎223-7835; Interamericana; snacks $3; ⏲7:30am-9pm Mon-Sat) cheese shop is an institution that few Panamanian drivers can pass up. The simple shop serves piping-hot fresh cheese (string, mozzarella, farmers, ricotta) and homemade meat empanadas (turnovers). It is right next door to a gas station and a supermarket on the right-hand side of the road if you're heading west from the city.

PACIFIC COAST

La Chorrera

POP 60,000

One of the first major towns you hit along the Interamericana, La Chorrera is famous throughout Panama for its *chicheme* (a sweet nonalcoholic drink made from milk, mashed corn, cinnamon and vanilla).

Festivals & Events

La Feria de La Chorrera FERIA
(⏲late Jan/early Feb) La Feria de La Chorrera includes parades, a rodeo, the odd cockfight or two, and drum dances, which have their origin in African music brought by slaves.

Eating

El Chichemito PANAMANIAN $
(cnr Calles L Oeste & 26 Norte; chicheme drinks US$0.50; ⏲9am-3pm) Join what looks like a Friday bank line at El Chichemito to sample the homemade *chicheme*. It goes nicely with a *boyo chorrenano* (tamale filled with marinated chicken and spice).

Getting There & Away

East- and west-bound buses stop at the gas station on the Interamericana. Buses for Panama City (US$2, one hour) leave every 15 minutes; take the express to avoid frequent stops.

Parque Nacional y Reserva Biológica Altos de Campana

This obscure and relatively unknown **national park** (admission US$5) is a favorite of both local and international birdwatchers. Common sightings include the scale-crested

DON'T MISS

MAMALLENA ECOLODGE

Ever dreamed of crafting your own personal utopia but haven't got the time? Trek out to the mellow **Mamallena Ecolodge** (☎6673-0752, 6781-7545; http://mamallenaecolodge.com; Camino a La Laguna; dm/d without bathroom US$13/40, 2-person cabins with/without bathroom US$60/45, all incl breakfast), where folks are living off the land, making kombucha health drinks and spreading general good will. Get your kicks hiking, and swimming in a pleasing river pool. Lodgings are in a comfortable Swiss-style home and riverfront cabins, all in a stunning highland setting.

For sustainable living, this is the real deal. The Welsh and US hosts recycle and use organic permaculture to revitalize once-abandoned fruit orchards on the sprawling 174-hectare farm. Guests can cook for themselves or sign up for good-value shared dinners (with vegetarian options). There's a full bar that's enhanced with local herbs and chili peppers. Pancake breakfasts are included.

Mamallena Ecolodge is a 1½-hour drive from Panama City and 30 minutes from El Valle in Coclé Province. From Panama City, coordinate a transfer or bus to Coronado where you can catch the La Laguna *collectivo* (US$1.20, 30 minutes) to a crossroads 3km from the lodge. Arrange ahead for pickups from here.

pygmy-tyrant, orange-bellied trogon and chestnut-capped brush-finch; rare avians including the slaty antwren, the white-tipped sicklebill and the purplish-backed quail-dove are occasionally spotted here.

This park is best viewed on foot and requires at least several hours to be appreciated. Starting at the road's end, beyond the microwave tower, trails will take you into some lovely forest, which is on the much greener Atlantic slope. Nowhere else is the difference between the deforested Pacific and the lush Atlantic slopes more evident than here.

Visitors can camp at the **ranger station and campground** (☎254-2848; www.miambiente.gob.pa; campsite per night US$5), where there's access to water but no facilities.

Information

Pay entrance and camping fees at the ranger station at the entrance to the park.

Getting There & Away

The park is 75km (1½ hours) from Panama City. To reach the park it's best to go with your own vehicle or contract a guide. Buses along the Interamericana can drop you at the turnoff, but it's a very long hike into the park.

The easy-to-miss turnoff is 25km southwest of La Chorrera, on the western side of the Interamericana, at the top of a steep and windy section known locally as the Loma Campana. From the turnoff, a rocky road winds 4.6km to a ranger station at the entrance to the park, which is located on Cerro Campana.

Punta Chame

POP 440

Just before the Interamericana reaches the coastline, a turnoff immediately east of Bejuco leads to the tiny sliver of peninsula known as Punta Chame. The road out to the sea winds past rolling hills before opening up to flat land that consists mainly of shrimp farms and mangroves. The brackish water makes farming near impossible, though the environment here is unique to this region, and well worth the diversion.

Punta Chame is receiving more vacation homes and weekenders since the single road in to the long, 300m-wide peninsula was paved. To the north of the peninsula, a scenic but muddy bay is popular with windsurfers and kitesurfers from December to April, during trade-wind season. Outside of those months wakeboarding and stand-up paddling takes over.

Sights

Beaches at Playa Chame on the east coast of the peninsula have lovely tan sand and a wilderness backdrop. The area is notorious for stingrays, so swim with caution and shuffle your feet while walking out.

Sleeping & Eating

Punta Chame lodgings provide meals, and on-site restaurants are open to the public.

★**La Casa Amarilla** B&B **$$**
(☎6138-6738, 345-3679; www.hostalcasaamarilla.com; d US$75-110, s/d cabins without bathroom

US$25/35; mid-Oct–mid-Apr;) Guests adore La Casa Amarilla, a French-run B&B with manicured gardens and a sparkling pool. Rooms vary and include cute yellow cabins with immaculate shared bathrooms. There's also a pool table and hammocks. Enjoy exquisite Mediterranean cuisine (not to mention homemade pastries, salads and quiche) in an open-air restaurant (two-course meals US$16) that draws people from around the region.

Nitro City RESORT **$$$**
(223-1747, 202-6875; www.nitrocityresort.com; d/ste incl breakfast from US$129/325; adult/child day passes US$30/20;) Panama's first extreme-sports resort, Nitro City comes alive on weekends. It's pretty much what you would expect in a beach haven bankrolled by energy drinks and Jägermeister. Stylish lodgings have sleek decor, stone sinks and bamboo ceilings; pro suites boast their own outdoor hot-tub. On weekdays, lodging prices fall by almost half.

The real draw is a circus of adrenaline offerings also open to day-trippers, from a skate park to mountain and motorbike courses, wakeboarding, stand-up paddling and kitesurfing (lessons available). Tamer offerings include volleyball and soccer areas, games and video rooms, as well as a stunning pool replete with island. Hyperactive teens do well here, and young Panama City weekenders don't seem to mind the US$18-dollar burgers backed by live rasta-rock. Management is attentive and there's really nothing else of its kind around.

Getting There & Away

From Panama City, take any bus heading west on the Interamericana to the Plaza Imperial Bejuco (US$3, one hour), slightly past the crossroads. From here, buses to the Punta Chame (US$2) leave hourly from 6:30am to 5:30pm daily.

Taxis from Panama City cost US$110.

Pacific Coast Beaches

Starting just south of the town of Chame and continuing along the Pacific coast for the next 40km are dozens of beautiful beaches that are popular weekend retreats for Panama City residents. About half of these beaches are in Panamá Province, while the remainder are in Coclé Province.

Gorgona

This small oceanside community fronts a curving beach of mostly black sand. Bring your sandals – the beach gets very hot.

For a leisurely bite, **La Ruina** (345-3734, 6527-8462; www.laruinatavern.com; mains US$5-16; noon-midnight Thu-Sun) serves stem glasses of *ceviche* (citrus-cured seafood) and authentic chicken curried with coconut rice *bocatoreño*-style. Sit outside at the leatherette booths and pass the time by chatting with the owners, a friendly US Army retiree and his Panamanian wife, or tapping along to the country tunes and live rock on weekend nights.

Getting There & Away

Best accessed by car, Gorgona is 110km from Panama City via the Interamericana. The turnoff is 6km south of the turnoff for Punta Chame.

Playa Coronado

International retirees flock to this affluent beachside community, which is also a haven for water-sports lovers. A newly built mall, US chain restaurants and a hospital confirms its growing status. The salt-and-pepper beach here is one of the most developed strips of sand along the coast, and is extremely popular with Panama City denizens on the up and up. For something more chilled, check out the birdwatching trail near the village gate.

Sleeping & Eating

El Litoral B&B B&B **$$**
(6658-1143; www.litoralpanama.com; d incl breakfast from US$85;) El Litoral B&B is a cute yellow house with smart air-conditioned rooms. The kicker is a sumptuous patio breakfast with choices such as cappuccino, crêpes, waffles and juice. The lovely French-speaking owner offers yoga sessions and can arrange Spanish classes or kitesurfing. It's located in front of Blue Bay resort hotel.

Blue Bay HOTEL **$$$**
(Coronado Golf & Beach Resort; 240-4444; www.bluebayresorts.com; Av Punta Prieta 4381; d from US$156;) If you're keen to live it up in unchecked luxury, look no further than the Blue Bay. With 78 amenity-laden rooms, a top-notch beachside golf course, swimming pools, tennis courts, equestrian

SURFING IN PANAMÁ PROVINCE

The beaches to the southwest of Panama City are a popular destination for Panamanian surfers, especially since they're easy to access and offer relatively consistent surf year-round. The following list will help you get started, though don't be afraid to ask local surfers to let you in on their hidden spots.

Playa Malibú Near Gorgona. Sand-bottom right and left break. Best during medium to low tide. Consistent, good tubes and long rides when there is a strong swell.

Playa Serena In Coronado, past the security gate. Right point break with good tubes. Long rides when the there is a strong swell.

Frente de Teta Rock- and sand-bottom break at the mouth of the Río Teta. Long lefts at low tide, and rights and lefts at medium to high tide.

Punta Teta Point break over rocks to the south of the Río Teta mouth. Lefts and rights with good tubes, especially at medium tide going up.

Rinconcito Rock-bottom point south of Punta Teta with a long, right break on a good swell. Named after California's famous Rincón break.

Frente Palmar South of San Carlos. Beach break, partial rock bottom that is popular with beginners.

Punta El Palmar South of San Carlos. Rock-bottom point break. Right peeling waves at medium to high tide when there is a good swell.

Hawaiisito South of San Carlos. Rock-bottom point break. Lefts at full high tide. Closes out if there is a strong swell.

Frente Río Mar Somewhat rocky beach break in front of Río Mar. Rights and lefts at medium to high tide.

Punta Río Mar South of the Río Mar, near jutting rocks. Walk and paddle at low tide. Rights best. Breaks only at low tide.

center, casino, day spa, gym, marina and a whole slew of bars and restaurants, you may not actually be able to find the time to visit the beach.

Kids get their own miniclub with games. Even if you're not a guest here, the town's nightlife revolves around the hotel, so dress smartly and stop by the attached nightclub.

El Rincón del Chef INTERNATIONAL **$$**
(☎345-2072; cheffernando@elrincondelchefpanama.com; mains $7-16; ⏲1-9pm Mon, 8am-9pm Tue-Thu, to 10pm Fri & Sat, to 9pm Sun) A good bet for lunch and dinner, chef-run El Rincon del Chef serves grilled meats, pastas and Panamanian classics. It's located 300m from the Interamericana on the right.

Getting There & Away

The turnoff for Playa Coronado is 85km from Panama City and 4km southwest of the turnoff for Gorgona. Access is easiest by private vehicle.

Buses to/from Panama City (US$3.25, 1½ hours) run along the Interamericana, stopping at the turnoff; look for taxis at the intersection to take you into town.

Playa El Palmar

The lovely white-sand beach of Playa El Palmar lies 16km west of Playa Coronado, near the village of San Carlos. Although much less developed than Coronado, El Palmar is popular with weekending families from the capital, but the atmosphere remains low-key.

The **Panama Surf School** (☎6673 0820; www.panamasurfschool.com; Calle 4ta Sur s/n; 2hr lessons US$40), run by a well known local surfer, gives group and private ($10 extra) lessons, plus rents stand-up paddleboards and bodyboards. Some English is spoken.

Sleeping & Eating

★**Manglar Lodge** INN **$$**
(☎345-4014, 240-8970; d US$88-99; ❄📶) The area's most stylish digs, Manglar Lodge is professionally run by surfer Ivan, who can also share some tips. Outdoor showers will help you rinse off the sand. Manglar has pleasant manicured grounds, a good on-site restaurant serving burgers and craft beer, and ample rooms with contemporary styles.

Pacific Coast Beaches

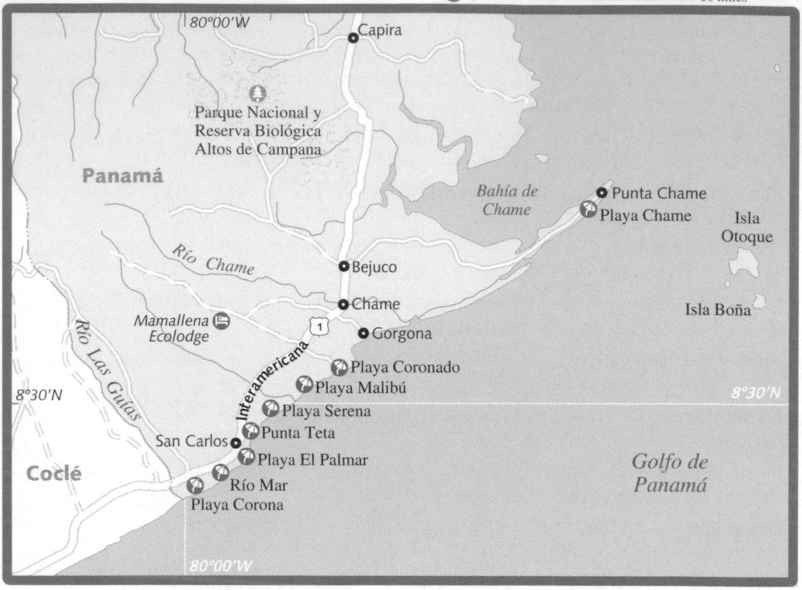

It's at the end of the road at the mouth of the river.

Palmar Surf Camp HOTEL **$$**
(☎240-8004; www.palmarsurfschool.com; campsites per person US$10, d/q US$65/88; P ❄ 📶) The wave-front Palmar Surf Camp aims at surfers or those who want to learn the ropes. Motel-style rooms feature cool murals, cable TV and free coffee. Campers can stake their tents under a thatched roof. Check for midweek discounts. An open-air restaurant serves simple preparations of fresh seafood. Surf lessons are US$40 for three hours; you can also rent kayaks.

Carlitos INTERNATIONAL **$**
(☎240-8526; www.carlitospizzas.com; Interamericana; pizza US$4-12; ⏲11am-9pm Thu-Tue) Found at the turnoff for El Palmar, Carlitos cooks delicious Argentine-style empanadas (turnovers stuffed with meat, cheese or veggie mixes) and thin-crust pizzas with a great selection of toppings, and the option of whole-wheat crust.

ℹ Getting There & Away

The turnoff for El Palmar is 96km from Panama City and 10km from the turnoff for Playa Coronado along the Interamericana. Buses (US$3.50, 1½ hours) stop at the turnoff, from where the beach is a US$3 taxi ride.

Río Mar

Río Mar is a small, rocky inlet where a few high-rises cast a shadow. A right turn on the road in from the Interamericana, **PSA RioMar** (☎345-4010, 6212-0707; http://panamasurfing.academy; s/d/tr US$30/55/70; ❄ 📶 🏊) at the Panama Surfing Academy offers pleasant bargain-rate rooms that sit on immaculate green grounds with a pea-sized pool. There are basic offerings from the on-site restaurant.

The attached surfing academy offers surf lessons and advanced coaching. Lessons are US$45 for 1½ hours. There are also boards for rent. Call ahead to reserve; weekends are busier.

ℹ Getting There & Away

Río Mar is five minutes along the road from Playa El Palmar. Frequent buses along the Interamericana go east to Panama City (US$3.50, 1½ hours) and west up the coast. It's a 10-minute walk from the Interamericana to the surf academy.

Coclé Province

POP 257,000 / AREA 4947 SQ KM / ELEV SEA LEVEL TO 1626M

Includes ➡

Best Places to Eat

- ➡ Mesón de Santa Cruz (p106)
- ➡ Xoko (p102)
- ➡ La Casa de Lourdes (p101)
- ➡ Pipa's Beach Restaurant (p104)
- ➡ Da Vinci Deli Pastas Gourmet (p101)

Best Places to Sleep

- ➡ Togo Bed & Breakfast (p103)
- ➡ Golden Frog Inn (p99)
- ➡ Park Eden (p99)
- ➡ Villa Távida Lodge (p108)
- ➡ La Casa de Lourdes (p100)

Why Go?

Coclé is known to Panamanians as the land of salt, sugar and presidents. More salt has been reclaimed from the sea, more sugar refined and more Panamanian presidents have been born here than in any other province. These facts are the source of great civic pride, but Coclé offers a lot more than table condiments and political legacies.

Coclé counts a wide variety of landscapes, from all-but-abandoned coastline to towering cloud forests, with vast agricultural land in between. With its southern side stretching along the Pacific Ocean for more than 100km, the province claims some of the country's most beautiful beaches, which are a magnet at the weekend for day-trippers from nearby Panama City. Up in the highlands, the magnificently situated mountain town of El Valle is another popular retreat. And shoppers take note: the sprawling provincial capital of Penonomé is the best place to pick up a 'real' Panama hat.

When to Go

➡ **Dec–Apr** High season on the Pacific coast is a party scene, with Panamanians arriving in droves after Christmas. A wild pre-Lenten carnival takes place around Mardi Gras (February or March) in Penonomé.

➡ **Jul–Oct** Rain means muddy trails but highland waterfalls are in full flow. It's the only season to see Panama's national flower, the ghost orchid, in bloom.

➡ **Oct–Dec** Bring on the noise: the city of Antón's rowdy Toro Guapo festival in October is followed by at least four days of *fiestas patrias* (national holidays) in November and celebrations of Penonomé's patron in early December.

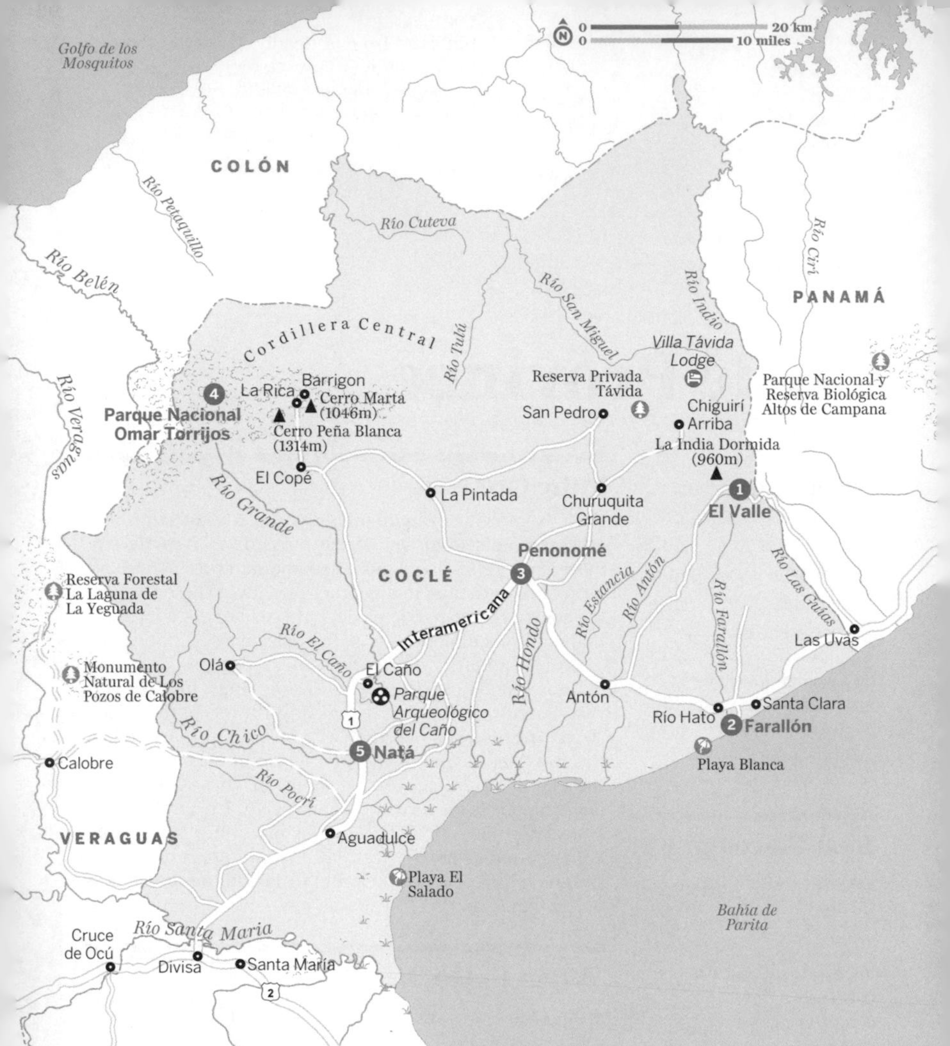

Coclé Province Highlights

1 **El Valle** (p95) Hiking to waterfalls, paying a call on the golden frog and browsing the handicrafts market in this lovely highland town.

2 **Farallón** (p103) Feasting on fresh fish with *patacones* (fried plantains), and strolling along the endless sands.

3 **Penonomé** (p104) Shopping for an authentic Panama hat and getting caught up in one of the regional capital's festivals.

4 **Parque Nacional Omar Torrijos** (p108) Hiking through dense rainforest and camping overnight in utter solitude.

5 **Natá** (p109) Enjoying the historic town's tranquility and visiting the splendid altar carvings at Panama's oldest church.

El Valle

POP 7600

Officially known as El Valle de Antón, this picturesque town is nestled in the crater of a huge extinct volcano, and ringed by verdant forests and jagged peaks. El Valle is a popular weekend getaway for urban dwellers in need of fresh air and scenery, and is also a North American retirement community. With an extensive network of trails, this is a superb place for walking, hiking or horseback riding. Nearby forests offer excellent birdwatching, and the valleys of El Valle are home to an impressive set of waterfalls as well as the increasingly rare golden frog.

History

Three million years ago, the volcano below where El Valle now sits erupted with such force that it blew off its top, creating a crater 5km across – one of the largest in the Americas. In the aeons that followed, the crater gradually filled with rainwater to create a large lake. However, through erosion or collapse, a breach opened at the present site of Chorro de Las Mozas and the entire lake drained. The resulting flood created an extensive network of waterways, which attracted indigenous populations to the valley. Early petroglyphs attesting to their arrival can still be seen throughout the valley.

Sights

Butterfly Haven WILDLIFE RESERVE

(El Mariposario; ☎6062-3131; www.butterflyhavenpanama.com; adult/child US$5/3; 9am-3:30pm) El Valle's latest attraction allows you to walk among up to 250 butterflies as they flutter by in a screened 'flight house.' Learn more about these ephemeral creatures, which live for just a couple of weeks maximum, through a 15-minute video, life-cycle exhibits and a rearing lab, where you'll see lepidoptera in various stages of development.

The enthusiastic owner from the USA will gladly tour you around the enclosure, pointing out fabulous specimens such as the giant blue morpho and the owl butterfly, whose wings mimic that bird's eyes.

El Valle Amphibian Conservation Center WILDLIFE RESERVE

(EVACC; http://amphibianrescue.org/evacc; 9am-5pm Wed-Mon) FREE This conservation center was created in 2007 with the support of Houston Zoo to help save amphibians from a deadly virus threatening their numbers around the world. Run by a dedicated team of conservationists, the center exhibits native Panamanian species, in particular the golden frog. The research area is private and devoted to quarantine, treatment and captive breeding efforts. It is located in the grounds of El Níspero zoo; entry is included in the zoo admission price. EVACC features educational exhibits and houses some 40 species.

El Níspero ZOO

(☎983-6142; adult/child US$5/2; 7am-5pm) About 1km north of Av Central, El Níspero is a zoo set in the forest. It is home to everything from tapirs and capuchin monkeys to jaguars and more than 50 species of bird. It is also the best place to see Panama's endangered *ranas doradas* (golden frogs); the strikingly colored, very photogenic amphibians are housed in the El Valle Amphibian Conservation Center on site.

Chorro El Macho WATERFALL

(Manly Falls; admission US$5; 8am-5pm) The most famous waterfall in the El Valle area is 35m-high Chorro El Macho, which is located about 2km north of town; it's a 10-minute walk from the road and the entrance to the Canopy Adventure (p97) tour. Below the falls you'll find a large rocky swimming pool surrounded by rainforest and fed by river water. There is also a series of short hiking trails that wend their way into the surrounding forest.

Aprovaca Orquídeas GARDENS

(☎983-6472; http://aprovaca.com; adult/child US$2/0.75; 9am-4pm) For the best selection of *orquídeas* (orchids) in the region, visit this idyllic not-for-profit garden run by the local association of orchid growers at the eastern end of town. Volunteers work to maintain the lovely flowers inside the greenhouse and the grounds, and they welcome visitors to show off the more than 100 species of orchids cultivated here. Orchids are temperamental bloomers; check out the display room near the entrance to see what's flowering at the moment.

Chorro Las Mozas WATERFALL

(Girls Waterfall; admission US$1; 10am-4pm Mon-Fri, 8am-noon Sat & Sun) The most accessible of the waterfalls around El Valle is Chorro Las Mozas, located about 2km southwest of town; you can reach it on foot from the center in about 25 minutes. This is the original site

El Valle

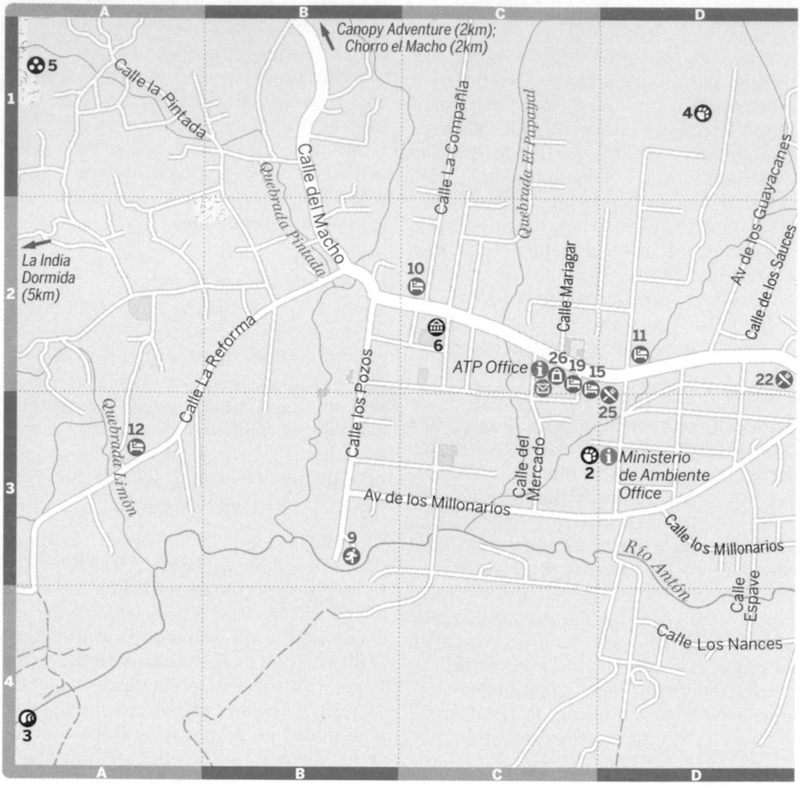

El Valle

Sights

1 Aprovaca Orquídeas......E3
2 Butterfly Haven......C3
3 Chorro Las Mozas......A4
4 El Níspero......D1
El Valle Amphibian Conservation Center......(see 4)
5 La Piedra Pintada......A1
6 Museo de Padre José Noto......C2
Square-Trunked Trees......(see 14)

Activities, Courses & Tours

7 Alquiler de Caballos......F2
8 Panama Explorer Tours......F3
9 Pozos Termales......B3

Sleeping

10 Anton Valley Hotel......C2
11 Bodhi Hostel......D2
12 Cabañas Potosí......A3
Crater Valley Boutique Hotel......(see 8)
13 Golden Frog Inn......F1
Hostal Orquídea......(see 1)
14 Hotel Campestre......F1
15 Hotel Don Pepe......C2
16 Hotel Valle Verde......E2
La Casa de Lourdes......(see 23)
17 Los Mandarinos Boutique Spa & Hotel......E1
18 Park Eden......E4
19 Residencial El Valle......C2

Eating

20 Da Vinci Deli Pastas Gourmet......E3
21 El Quijote......E2
22 El Valle Gourmet & Coffee Shop......D2
23 La Casa de Lourdes......E1
24 L'Italiano......E2
25 Los Hermanos......D3
Restaurante Bruschetta......(see 10)
Restaurante Valle Verde......(see 16)

Shopping

26 Mercado de Artesanía......C2

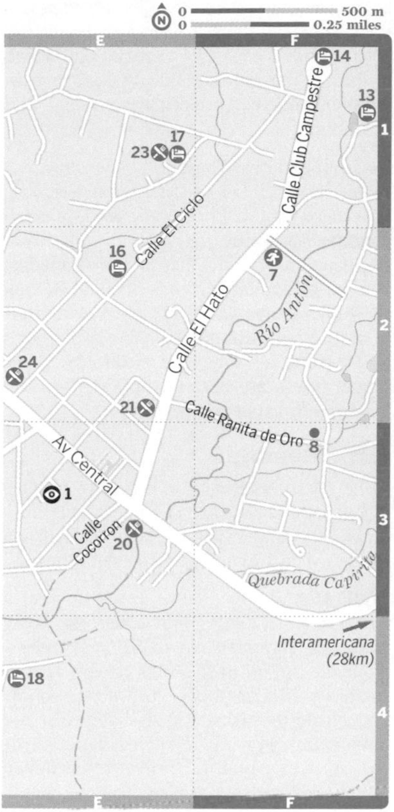

where the prehistoric lake breached its banks to form the area's scenic cascades and deep pools. It's popular with locals enjoying year-round, near-perfect spring weather.

Square-Trunked Trees FOREST
(Calle Club Campestre; admission US$2) El Valle's peculiar *arboles cuadrados* (square-trunked trees) are located behind the Hotel Campestre. After a 20-minute hike through the forest and climbing over two footbridges (including a scary suspension one), you'll reach a grove of trees that are certainly a lot closer to being square than round. These geometric formations are the source of much local pride, so dissing is not allowed.

La Piedra Pintada ARCHAEOLOGICAL SITE
(Colored Stone; Calle La Pintada; admission US$3) Located in the northwestern corner of the valley, La Piedra Pintada is a huge boulder adorned with pre-Columbian carvings. Locals often fill the grooves of the petroglyphs with chalk to facilitate their viewing. However, the meaning of the petroglyphs isn't clear; some think it is an early map of the area. That doesn't prevent children from giving their interpretation of the petroglyphs for US$2 (in Spanish only). The trail to the rock takes just a few minutes from the main road.

La Piedra Pintada can be reached by a white bus with 'Pintada' above the windshield. It passes along Av Central every 30 minutes or so from 6am to 6pm (US$0.25 one way).

Museo de Padre José Noto MUSEUM
(Museo de El Valle de Antón; ☎6592-5572; Av Central; adult/child US$1/0.50; ⏰10am-5pm Thu-Sat, to 2pm Sun) The most interesting exhibits in this small museum that's divided into five sections are the ones focusing on petroglyphs and ceramics left by indigenous peoples who lived in the area hundreds of years ago. There is also some religious art – the museum is run by the church next door – as well as historical and geological information on El Valle's extinct volcano.

Activities

Canopy Adventure ADVENTURE SPORTS
(☎6613-7220, 264-5720; www.canopytower.com/canopy-adventure; canopy rides US$65; ⏰8am-4pm) Canopy Adventure uses cable zip lines to send harnessed riders whizzing through the rainforest high above the jungle floor. You'll ride from one platform to another (there are four in all), at times gliding over 35m-high waterfall Chorro El Macho (p95).

Pozos Termales HOT SPRING
(Calle Los Pozos; admission US$3; ⏰8am-4:30pm) Pozos Termales thermal baths complex features a series of pools of varying temperatures and alleged curative properties. Post-soak, there are buckets for applying healing mud to your skin. The next step is to take a requisite photo and head to the showers. The baths are a 10-minute walk southwest of the center at the end of Calle Los Pozos, near Río Antón.

Alquiler de Caballos HORSEBACK RIDING
(☎6646-5813; Calle El Hato; per hr US$15) This stable northeast of the center of town rents out its two dozen horses, which provide an excellent way to explore the nearby mountains. Guides speak limited English only. Call ahead for free transport from your hotel.

Hiking

Surrounded by humid cloud forest and peaks that rise more than 1000m, El Valle is a hiker's paradise. From the town center, an extensive network of trails radiates out into the valley and up the hills, and there are possibilities for anything from short day hikes to excursions of several days.

Serious trekkers should consider excursions to the tops of Cerro Cara Coral, Cerro Gaital and Cerro Pajita to the north, Cerro Guacamayo to the south and Cerro Tagua to the east.

It's also possible to make an ascent to the top of La India Dormida, where there are well-defined, safe trails. According to local mythology, the 'Sleeping Indian' was a local maiden who fell in love with a conquistador. After her father refused to allow the marriage she took her own life and was buried in the hills. The mountains have taken on her shape as they rise over the valley; the outline of her forehead, nose, chin and breast is easily discernible. Legend has it that she is awaiting the day when her forbidden love can be pursued.

For the most part, the valley floor has been cleared for human habitation while the peaks remain covered in dense forest. Although it is possible to hike independently, trails are not always clearly marked, and it is highly recommended that you hire a guide – or at least seek out local advice.

Birdwatching

The forests around El Valle offer numerous opportunities for birdwatching, with some 300 species spotted. The area is especially rich in hummingbirds – commonly spotted species include the green hermit, the violet-headed hummingbird and the white-tailed emerald. Rates for a bilingual naturalist guide are around US$50 per person per day.

Tours

Manakin Adventures Panama ADVENTURE TOUR
(6384-4466; www.manakinadventures.com; per day from US$60) Juan José Calvache, one of the finest naturalist guides in Panama, will show you El Valle and surrounds like few others can; everything from jungle trekking and birdwatching to river-rafting is on offer. He knows the Parque Nacional Omar Torrijos like the back of his hand.

Mario Bernal BIRDWATCHING
(6693-8213; mariobernalg@gmail.com) Mario is an English- and Spanish-speaking birdwatching guide from El Valle who has a very high reputation internationally.

Mario Urriola ADVENTURE TOUR
(6569-2676; serpentariomaravillastropicales@hotmail.com) Mario is a reputable, locally based naturalist guide specializing in wildlife-watching, especially reptiles, and birdwatching.

Panama Explorer Tours ADVENTURE TOUR
(983-6942; www.panamaexplorertours.com; Calle Ranita de Oro, Crater Valley Boutique Hotel) Panama Explorer Tours is an adventure tourism outfit that offers a wide range of activities. Available tours include hiking La India Dormida (US$35, three to four hours), tree climbing (US$35, two hours) and mountain-biking tours (from US$25 per hour); prices are per person. There's also a kid-friendly ropes course.

Sleeping

Although reservations are generally not necessary, be advised that El Valle can get busy on weekends and national holidays as urban dwellers flee the capital and head for the hills.

Bodhi Hostel HOSTEL $
(908-7120, 6429-4143; http://bodhihostels.com; Av Central; dm/d incl breakfast US$15/35; @ wi-fi) A welcome arrival to El Valle's budget accommodations scene, this central hostel counts six private rooms with shared showers, and a massive, bright and airy dorm with 27 beds in triple-deck bunks. Dorms are curtained and have lockers; the artwork is by volunteers. The Buddha theme, bafflingly prevalent in Panama, is present here.

The Shisha loft lounge above the lobby is full of books and very cool, as is the 'tree' of Polaroids, which features everyone who's ever stayed here. Bicycle rentals available for US$2/8/12 per hour/half-day/full day.

Residencial El Valle HOTEL $
(6615-9616, 983-6536; www.hotelresidencialelvalle.com; Av Central; d/tr/q US$55/65/85; P wi-fi) Visitors become loyalists, given the high level of service offered at this motel-style lodging. The long-standing hotel offers 16 clean and airy rooms, and has an enormous veranda facing Av Central on the top floor with views to the hills. Room 4 has lovely wooden floors.

Hostal Orquídea HOSTEL $
(983-6472; http://aprovaca.com/l_en/hostal.php; dm US$12, s/d from US$25/50; wi-fi) How often do you get to spend the night in an orchid garden? This rather simple hostelry, with two private rooms for up to four people and another two with five bunk beds,

is on the edge of the Aprovaca Orquídeas (p95) orchid garden and a stay overnight includes a free tour. Rooms have fans and there is a communal kitchen.

★Golden Frog Inn INN $$
(Villa Rana Dorada; ☎6565-8307, 983-6117; www.goldenfroginn.com; d/ste incl breakfast from US$77/150; P ❄ 📶 ≋) Attentive and relaxing, this deluxe Canadian-Panamanian-owned lodge with six very different rooms and suites is the perfect place to laze after a long day of play. Start with the swimming pool and migrate to the open-air living spaces and large library. The expansive grounds include orchids and fruit trees; adjoining trails mean you can hike from right out the door.

The three suites have their own kitchens, stocked with fresh tropical fruit, coffee and coffee machines; the three rooms share a common kitchen. Reconfiguration and new additions will soon see three more rooms added, but our favorites are suites 1 and 2 by the pool for their lovely terraces and hammocks.

★Cabañas Potosí CABIN $$
(☎6946-6148, 983-6181; www.elvallepotosi.com; Calle La Reforma No 84; campsites US$15, d/tr US$59/69; P 📶) A very welcoming place and good for a peaceful sleep, Cabañas Potosí is situated just over 1km southwest of the town center. The park-like grounds offer lovely views of the peaks that ring the valley, including La India Dormida. The four concrete cabins each have three beds, a fridge and use of one of two outdoor communal kitchens.

We love the multiple bird houses and feeders (20 at last count), the *rancho* roof made of recycled plastic bottles and the handcrafted Adirondack chairs on the front porch. Campers have level ground and a rushing stream nearby. To get here, follow Av Central west to Calle La Reforma and turn left. Cabañas Potosí is 800m to the southwest.

★Park Eden B&B $$
(☎938-6167, 6695-6190; www.parkeden.com; Calle Espave No 7; d/ste incl breakfast from US$90/140, 2-person cabins incl breakfast US$135, 4-person house US$260; P ❄ 📶) A beautiful country retreat run by an North American–trained Panamanian designer and his Ecuadorian wife, this gorgeous property counts four rooms and suites, plus a separate cottage and two-story house. Decor is a bit over the top, with lots of powder blue, lace doilies and quilting, but the friendly couple and their gardens are simply a delight. Bikes are available for rent.

Hotel Campestre HOTEL $$
(☎983-6460, 983-6146; www.hotelcampestre.com; Calle Club Campestre; s/d incl breakfast US$76/89; P ❄ 📶) Dating back to 1939, El Valle's oldest hotel features enormous grounds, forested walking paths, and a large and comfortable restaurant and bar. Its 30 large, tastefully decorated rooms include heavy wooden 'sleigh' beds and stone-faced bathrooms. The staff is keen to please, and day trips to the beach at Farallón are offered.

Anton Valley Hotel HOTEL $$
(☎6804-2011, 983-6097; www.antonvalleyhotel.com; Av Central; d US$60-83, ste US$75-91; P ❄ 📶 ≋) Popular with groups, this small hotel packs in 16 renovated rooms that feature high-quality linens, orthopedic mattresses, fridges, and original details such as bamboo beds and stonework. Some really are on the small side, and service can be a bit cavalier, considering the category. Don't get too excited about the pool – it's not Olympic-sized.

GOLDEN FROG REFUGE

A symbol of good fortune since pre-Columbian times, the golden frog *(Atelopus zeteki)*, or *rana dorada* in Spanish, is also a symbol of Panama's incredibly varied wildlife. In the 1990s, a deadly fungus called chytrid began decimating the golden frogs, and spread, soon reaching epidemic levels on five continents, killing not just frogs but toads and salamanders too. The chytrid fungus, which infects amphibians' skin cells, kills more than 90% of the creatures that it comes into contact with. Scientists have found that, while it cannot be prevented in the wild, the fungus is effectively treated in captivity.

In 2006, with support from the Houston Zoo, the El Valle Amphibian Conservation Center (p95) set about collecting all the frogs they could find in the El Valle area, on order to protect those that weren't already infected and to treat the ones in captivity. At one stage, while the conservation center was being built, a room at the Hotel Campestre was used to house the frogs. It was the biggest amphibian rescue mission in history and helped to bring the golden frog back from the brink of extinction.

Hotel Don Pepe HOTEL $$
(☎983-6425; www.hoteldonpepe.com.pa; Av Central; s/d/tr US$55/65/75; P 📶) The very central Don Pepe offers 19 bright rooms (those on the 3rd floor – the floor 'for couples' – are best) with tiled baths, firm mattresses and craft touches. A sprawling open deck on the 3rd floor has hammocks and is great for a siesta or stargazing. There's a good Panamanian restaurant called Los Hermanos on the ground floor.

Hotel Valle Verde HOTEL $$
(☎6471-8250, 983-6080; www.hotel-valleverde.com; Calle La Cooperativa; s/d/tr from US$48/76/90; P ❄ 📶) This spick-and-span property with lovely grounds and excellent valley views boasts 18 quite different (and somewhat dated) rooms with firm mattresses on the beds, leather-work tables and spacious bathrooms. Amenities include a capacious terrace in the main building, a wading pool for the little ones and a good Peruvian restaurant (p101) that demands a visit in its own right.

★**La Casa de Lourdes** BOUTIQUE HOTEL $$$
(☎983-6450, 6114-0117; www.lacasadelourdes.com; d US$175-250; P ❄ 📶) Probably the most luxurious place to stay in El Valle, this secluded and quiet villa counts just four rooms in total. Two of them sit above the hotel's much-acclaimed restaurant (p101), while a larger pair occupy a cottage with a tower in the garden. The decor is country, with flower-print bedspreads and large carved-wood wardrobes. Bathrooms feature bathtubs. Book ahead.

Los Mandarinos Boutique Spa & Hotel HOTEL $$$
(☎983-6645; www.losmandarinos.com; d incl breakfast from US$176, ste US$256; P ❄ 📶 🏊) In El Valle's lush countryside, this 70-room fortress-like property contained in four stone 'towers' is way too big to be boutique but it is sumptuous nevertheless. Winding walkways link imposing Spanish-style tile lodgings, which look slightly better at a distance. Large modern rooms are decked in finery, some with king-sized beds, oversized tiles and stone baths. There are two pools.

Many rooms in buildings 3 and 4 have balconies; from the roof terrace you can view the peaks of Gaital and La India Dormida. The fountain-of-youth concept dominates the ritzy 'anti-aging' spa, which offers sauna, steam, massage and treatments (including 'chocotherapy'). Guests are split between those making the health pilgrimage and well-heeled couples and families on vacation from Panama City.

Crater Valley Boutique Hotel RESORT $$$
(☎6620-5818, 983-6942; www.crater-valley.com; Calles Capirita & Ranita de Oro; d incl breakfast from US$209; P ❄ 📶 🏊) Surrounded by beautifully tended grounds, Crater Valley's eight guest rooms are all different and executed with varying degrees of care. All feature stone floors, glass-brick showers and patios with hammocks. The honeymoon suite has a private garden and is a delight. You won't have to travel far to view wildlife; the fish and frog ponds are teeming.

Prices fluctuate depending on the time of year, the day of the week and the size of the room, so it's best to book ahead.

Eating

Los Hermanos PANAMANIAN $
(☎983-6425; Av Central; mains US$6-13; ⏰7am-10pm) One of just a pair of Panamanian restaurants left in cosmopolitan El Valle, 'The Brothers' serves up the usual favorites (chicken with rice, *ropa vieja* with beans etc) but ventures a bit further afield with a few Creole, Peruvian and even Chinese dishes. There are sandwiches (US$3.50 to US$6) too if you're peckish but not famished.

El Valle Gourmet & Coffee Shop CAFE $
(Av Central; sandwiches US$4-6.50; ⏰9am-4pm Tue-Thu, 8am-9pm Sat, to 6pm Sun) Selling gourmet sandwiches and smoothies, this decade-old cafe is a good place to stock up on picnic fare before heading for the trails. You can also find a decent selection of cheeses, cured meats and olives here. Lovely garden seating, too.

L'Italiano PIZZA $$
(☎6682-9398, 908-7378; www.facebook.com/L-italiano-660035177397679; Av Central; mains US$11-14; ⏰11am-9pm Wed-Sun) They say that this restaurant and pizzeria with just 40 covers inside and out has the best pizza in El Valle. With an Italian owner and chef at the oven it certainly tastes like the real thing. Along with some 15 different pizzas (US$6.50 to US$13), there are a number of pasta dishes (US$11 to US$13) and more complex mains on offer.

El Quijote SPANISH $$
(☎983-6210, 6095-0124; Calle El Hato No 1; mains US$5-9; ⏰8am-10pm Tue-Sun) This 'spit' (ie grill) restaurant is a local favorite, noted for its well-prepared Spanish dishes such as *pulpo a la plancha* (grilled octopus), pael-

THE HOLY GHOST ORCHID

While hiking though the forests around El Valle, be sure to keep an eye out for a terrestrial orchid known as *la flor del espíritu santo*, or the 'holy ghost orchid' *(Peristeria elata)*, which just happens to be Panama's national flower. Named by Spanish missionaries during the colonial period, it is shaped like a red-spotted dove emerging from ivory petals.

The flower is most commonly found along the forest floor beside trails, but it also grows on the branches of large trees. The orchid blooms from July to October and has an unforgettable aroma. The orchids are under threat from overharvesting and should not be picked.

la and the unusual *migas*, a dish of herbed breadcrumbs often served with ribs. El Quijote is a simple affair, almost like a *fonda*, with an incongruous little fountain in the center adding a dash of color.

Restaurante Bruschetta CAFE **$$**
(☎6518-4416, 983-5118; www.facebook.com/pages/Restaurante-Bruschetta-El-Valle-de-Anton/237616059663192; Av Central; mains US$6-13; ⏰11am-8:45pm Wed-Mon) Bruschetta features generous versions of its namesake (US$6.50 to US$8) as well as salads, sandwiches and tacos. Unusual treats include the carrot-and-orange juice. It's one of the more ambient cafe-restaurants around and always packed.

★ **Da Vinci Deli Pastas Gourmet** ITALIAN **$$$**
(☎983-6685; www.facebook.com/Da-Vinci-Deli-Pastas-Gourmet-509330165758426; Plaza Paseo El Valle, Av Central; mains US$13-19; ⏰noon-9pm Sun-Thu, to 10pm Fri & Sat) OK, its location in the spanking-new Plaza Paseo El Valle mall east of the center may not be the sexiest, but it's a nice mall and this place has its very own pasta machine. Feast on the trio of pastas – ravioli, tagliatelle and gnocchi (US$18.75) – or one of the pizzas cooked in Da Vinci's wood-fired oven (US$12.75 to US$15.75).

La Casa de Lourdes INTERNATIONAL **$$$**
(☎6114-0117, 983-6450; www.lacasadelourdes.com; mains US$11-20; ⏰noon-3:30pm & 6:30-9:30pm) Lourdes has a nationwide reputation that can seem overblown when many diners appear to be eating its version of the 21 Club hamburger. Still, it's hard to beat it for sheer elegance, with a setting around a garden patio in a lovely country villa and a menu that includes salmon in soy butter, Cajun chicken with tamarind and a tart of strawberries and passion fruit.

Restaurante Valle Verde PERUVIAN **$$$**
(☎983-6080, 6471-8250; www.hotel-valleverde.com/restaurante; Calle La Cooperativa; mains US$12-18; ⏰8am-9pm) From German to Peruvian, this upmarket eatery in the Hotel Valle Verde has made quite a journey in the recent past. Feast on Inca-inspired favorites such as *lomo saltado* (stir-fried beef with vegetables and potatoes) or *jalea de mariscos* (fried seafood platter) preceded, of course, by Peruvian *ceviche* (citrus-cured seafood) and a requisite pisco sour (US$4.50)

Shopping

Mercado de Artesanía MARKET
(Av Central; ⏰7am-5pm) El Valle is home to one of Panama's largest handicrafts market. Indigenous Ngöbe-Buglé people, and also some Emberá and Wounaan, bring a variety of handicrafts to sell to tourists (most of whom are Panamanians from the capital). If you're self-catering, the market also stocks a good selection of fresh produce from around the country. Sunday is the busiest day.

Information

ATP Office (☎983-6474; cocle@atp.gob.pa; Av Central; ⏰8am-4pm Wed-Sun) This small information booth next to the handicrafts market keeps bank hours but is among the most helpful in Panama. Can help with information on bicycle rentals and local guides, too.

Banco Nacional de Panama (Av Central; ⏰8am-3pm Mon-Fri, 9am-noon Sat) In the center; has an ATM.

Centro de Salud de El Valle (El Valle Health Center; ☎983-6112; Av Central; ⏰24hr) For your health needs, turn to this clinic near the western end of Av Central.

Ministerio de Ambiente Office (☎997-7538, 997-9805; off Av Central; ⏰8:30am-3:30pm Mon-Fri) Can answer questions about national parks and protected areas.

Post Office (Calle del Mercado; ⏰7am-3pm Mon-Fri, 8am-noon Sat) Behind the handicrafts market.

Getting There & Away

To leave El Valle, hop aboard a bus traveling along Av Central; on average, buses depart every 30 minutes. Final destinations are painted on windshields of the bus. If your next destination isn't posted, catch a bus going in the same direction and transfer.

To reach El Valle from the Interamericana, disembark from any bus at San Carlos, about 3km beyond the turning for El Valle. Minibuses collect passengers at the station here and travel to El Valle (US$1.50, one hour, every 30 minutes). Last departure is 4pm weekdays and 7pm at weekends. From Panama City the trip to El Valle takes 2½ hours (US$4.50).

Getting Around

Despite El Valle's small size, taxis ply Av Central all day long (though are hard to find after 7pm). You can go anywhere in town for US$2 or US$3, or US$10 per hour.

Many hotels offer bike rentals (US$2/10 per hour/day).

Santa Clara

POP 2140

With a long white-sand beach and towering coconut palms, Santa Clara, the first of three settlements on the so-called Costa Blanca (White Coast), is a great destination if you want to lounge about for a few days without having to worry about someone stealing your stretch of sand.

Santa Clara itself was once little more than a sparsely populated fishing village edged between patches of dry tropical rainforest and the vast blue expanse of the Pacific, though the opening of a US military base nearby during WWII to protect the canal probably livened things up a bit. These days upscale beach villas and apartment blocks dot the landscape, but there's still plenty of local flavor here to soak up in between beach sessions, which makes a nice change from some of the country's more popular destinations.

Sleeping

A short distance from the Interamericana you'll come to a fork in the road. Go left for about 1km and you'll see signs directing you to Cabañas Las Sirenas. Going to the right for the same distance leads to Cabañas Las Veraneras.

Cabañas Las Veraneras CABIN **$$**

(☎993-3313; http://veraneraspanama.com; 2- /5-person cabins from US$88/100; P ❄ ≋) The *cabañas* here come in three styles. A total of 20 cabins – some concrete, some thatched huts on two levels – cling to a slope set back from the beach. The loveliest are the five built on stilts, which overlook the crashing waves. Cabins 00 and 01 have the best views. There's a pool.

XS Memories MOTEL **$$**

(☎6729-1201, 993-3096; www.xsmemories.com; campsites per person US$7, RV hookups from US$20, d US$55; P ❄ ☰ ≋) You won't find many RV resorts with sports bars in Panama, so this friendly outfit from the USA definitely has the market cornered. Three spacious guest rooms – ask for the one with a kitchen in a separate cottage – feature air-con, platform beds and fridges. There are also more than 20 hookups for motor homes, providing water, sewers and electricity.

Campers can pitch their tents and all can enjoy the small round swimming pool smack in front of the sports bar. The gardens are lovely, home to a large collection of caged toucans, parrots and macaws. The cluttered bar is a kind of tropical TGI Friday, serving juicy cheeseburgers, grilled steaks and chicken to the drone of football. Follow the billboard to get here; it's just north of the turnoff for Santa Clara, 150m from the Interamericana.

Cabañas Las Sirenas RESORT **$$**

(☎6550-2500, 236-1385; www.lassirenasdesantaclara.com; 2-/4-person cottages from US$99/150; P ☰ ≋) A resort with a lot of history, Cabañas Las Sirenas is set over a terraced garden, with concrete structures from the 1950s at the top of the hill and a half-dozen newer huts set at an angle right on the beach. Fully equipped with kitchens and patios with barbecue and hammocks, but they could use an upgrade.

Eating

Santa Clara Beach Bar & Grill INTERNATIONAL **$**

(☎6711-9975; mains US$6-12; ⊙8am-7pm) Serving groomed fast-food dishes such as burgers, deep-fried shrimp and chicken with rice or *patacones* (fried plantains), this beachside eatery is a very convenient (and picturesque) spot for lunch. The *pipa fría* (cold coconut water) goes down a treat.

★**Xoko** SPANISH **$$**

(☎908-8090; www.facebook.com/pages/Restaurante-xoko/427120730652157; Interamericana s/n; dishes US$3.50-14; ⊙noon-9pm Mon-Thu, to 10pm Fri, to 10:30pm Sat, to 9:30pm Sun) With its oddly shaped columns and mustard-yellow exterior, this hangar-like eatery (it was once a US military social club) offers an excellent selection of tapas, paella, delicious clams in white wine and a catch of the day cooked Basque-style (with tomatoes and sweet or hot red peppers). It's on the Interamericana at the turnoff for Playa Santa Clara. Warm welcome.

Restaurante Las Veraneras SEAFOOD **$$**
(993-3313; http://veraneraspanama.com; mains US$5-18) This small thatched restaurant-bar fronts the beach. It's the perfect setting for fresh *ceviche* (citrus-cured seafood) or *patacones* (fried plantains) topped with baby octopus, accompanied by a sundowner, but service can be slow when the place is full.

Getting There & Around

Santa Clara is well serviced by buses.

DESTINATION	COST (US$)	DURATION (HR)	FREQUENCY
Antón	1	30min	every 30min
Chame	1.75	45min	every 20min
David	12	5½	hourly
Panama City	3.95	1¾	every 20min
Penonomé	1.25	1	every 30min
San Carlos	1.50	30min	every 20min

Except for late at night, there are always taxis parked beside the turnoff on the Interamericana for Santa Clara. You can take one for US$1 to get to any Santa Clara destination. The beach is 1.8km from the Interamericana.

Farallón & Playa Blanca

The village of Farallón lies on a picture-perfect stretch of powder-white sand called Playa Blanca (White Beach), one of the most beautiful Pacific-coast beaches, about 3km west of the Santa Clara turnoff. The main part of Playa Blanca is another 3km further on near the gated community of Buenaventura.

A decade ago, Farallón was a fishing village with the ruins of the Panamanian military base that was destroyed during the US invasion to oust Noriega. However, resort fever has recast it and the entire stretch of Playa Blanca as one of the hottest beach destinations in Panama. Indeed, a controversial international airport opened at nearby Río Hato in late 2013. Visitors are urged to go beyond the resorts. Much of the original village charm is still here, especially along Farallón's beach, 4km south of the highway, though it is apparent that apartments, condos and gated communities have created an alternate reality.

Activities

If you're just visiting for the day, and you don't have the cash to blow on a night of hedonistic luxury, Royal Decameron Beach Resort & Casino offers day passes (from US$75) that give you full access to the facilities. Of course, beaches are public land in Panama; so as long as you don't get into trouble, no one is going to stop you from lying out on the sand in front and working on your tan.

Sleeping

★**Togo Bed & Breakfast** B&B **$$**
(6804-2551, 993-3393; www.togopanama.com; d incl breakfast US$99-121, with kitchenette US$132-143, extra person US$25;) The perfect seaside destination, Togo occupies a renovated beach house and outbuildings where recycled materials are used to create a sleek and stylish design. The four rooms are spacious and airy, with cool pebble-tile bathrooms, gorgeous original artworks and private terraces. The centerpiece is the lush garden – a controlled jungle, with a tiny fountain and raked sand – strewn with hammocks.

A private passageway crosses the street to the beach. The B&B is adults-only and gay-friendly. To reach Togo, turn left at the National Car Rental and taxi stand. It's another 400m down the road.

Royal Decameron Beach Resort & Casino RESORT **$$$**
(993-2255; www.decameron.com; d 2-night all-inclusive from US$460;) Panama's answer to Vegas, Royal Decameron Beach Resort & Casino is a whopper, with 600 rooms and enough pools, bars, clubs and restaurants to count on both hands. Strolling a gated compound affixed with a bracelet ID may not be your idea of travel, but if you like buffet food and Latino nightlife, you'll be *en tu salsa*, as they say.

Families find plenty to do, including a daily kids show at 8:30pm. If you're planning on staying at the Decameron, check out the discounted all-inclusive packages (including all alcoholic drinks) online. Transportation to and from Panama City is included.

JW Marriott Golf & Beach Resort RESORT **$$$**
(908-3333; www.marriott.com/hotels/travel/ptyjw-jw-marriott-panama-golf-and-beach-resort; 340 Calle 3ra, Buenaventura; d from US$275;) More exclusive then heaven itself, the Marriott complex on Playa Blanca in Buenaventura counts 115 luxury rooms and four villas dotted around trails, open spaces and artificial lagoons. Five separate restaurants will keep you on site, with menus designed by an award-winning Panamanian

chef; and there are tennis courts, a world-class spa and a 36-hole golf course.

Eating

★Pipa's Beach Restaurant SEAFOOD **$$**
(☎6252-8430, 6844-0373; http://pipasbeach.com; mains US$10-20; ⏲10am-6pm) Love, love, love this mostly outdoor bar and restaurant hard by the beach and serving seafood with gourmet touches (think Thai mussels and crab claws in three sauces). One of the delights of dining here is enjoying a cold beer or cocktail while looking out to sea, feet buried in the sand and sometimes washed by the surf.

The service is friendly and those taking advantage of the beach can shower and rent thatched beach shelters (US$20 to US$30, depending on size) to escape the sun. Pipa's is at the very end of the road through Farallón, about 4km from the Interamericana.

Woody's INTERNATIONAL **$$**
(☎6597-1719; www.woodysbeachbarpanama.com; mains US$8-18; ⏲11am-11pm Tue-Sun) It's gringo city at this Canadian-owned bar-restaurant on the beach, festooned with football shirts. Among the menu choices is a mean poutine, a Quebec dish of French fries, cheese curds and gravy. Saner selections include clam linguini, whole sea bass and burgers ($10). Hosts Theresa and Debbie keep the punters in line. There's live music at 6pm Tuesdays and Saturdays.

Cosa Nostra ITALIAN **$$**
(☎6711-7424; mains US$8.50-17; ⏲noon-9:30pm Thu-Tue) This little Italian-owned restaurant and pizzeria serves some of the most authentic Italian fare on the Panamanian Pacific coast, with excellent pastas such as penne and gnocchi, and pizza. Owner Luka is the perennial host.

La Fogata PANAMANIAN **$$$**
(☎6688-2240, 908-3975; www.lafogatapanama.com; mains US$12-20; ⏲noon-3pm & 6-10pm Tue-Sun) This colorful and quirky little place run by an affable Panamanian–German couple serves up scrumptious Panamanian food à la Caribbean – meaning lots of seafood and coconut flavors. There are a couple of meat dishes to choose from but we'd go back for the three-course Sexy Lobster Special (US$35). The outside garden seating is coveted.

Getting There & Away

Buses generally drop you off at the Farallón exit on the Interamericana. There's a taxi stand about 2km along the main road to the beach, beyond the police station and National Car Rental office.

Antón

POP 9790

The town of Antón lies 15km northwest of Farallón and 18km southeast of Penomé, in the center of a lush valley dotted with rice fields and cattle ranches. Although it has little to offer visitors beyond its natural beauty, its annual patron's day festival and three-day folkloric festival **Toro Guapo** (Handsome Bull; www.festivaltoroguapo.org; ⏲Oct) are the best in the province. It's worth stopping by to partake in the festivities if you find yourself in the area.

Peach-colored, motel-like **Hotel Rivera** (☎6127-7216, 987-2245; www.hotelriviera-panama.com; d from US$58; P❄📶🏊) has 12 rooms with sparse furnishings but the air-con works and there's plenty hot water. It's hard to complain at this price, and the inviting pool is a nice amenity, especially when the summer sun is beating down.

Getting There & Away

Westbound buses, including those heading to Penonomé, will stop in Antón if you ask the driver in advance.

Penonomé

POP 21,750

The capital of Coclé Province is a bustling crossroads city with a rich history. Founded in 1581, Penonomé blossomed so quickly that it served as the temporary capital of the isthmus in 1671 after the destruction of the first Panama City (now known as Panamá Viejo)

Penonomé

Sights
1 Basilica Mayor San Juan Bautista A1
2 Museo de Penonomé Historia y Tradición Panameña A2

Sleeping
3 Hotel Dos Continentes D3

Eating
4 El Paisa A1
5 Mercado Público B2
6 Mesón de Santa Cruz A2
7 Pits Burgers & Grill D3

Shopping
8 Mercado de Artesanías Coclé D4

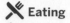

and until Nueva Panamá (today's Casco Viejo) was founded a few years later.

Today the lifeline of the city is the Interamericana, which bisects Penonomé and ensures a steady stream of goods flowing in and out. If you're heading west, it's likely that you will pass through here at some point, though it's worth hopping off the bus for the city's two principal attractions: its annual festivals and its traditional hats. Penonomé also serves as a good jumping-off point for the nearby artisan town of La Pintada.

Sights

Museo de Penonomé Historia y Tradición Panameña MUSEUM
(997-8490; www.inac.gob.pa/museos/107-museo-de-penonome; Calle San Antonio; adult/child US$1/0.25; 9am-4pm Tue-Sun) This small museum housed in a beautiful blue-and-white colonial building examines the history and traditions of Coclé and, by extension, Panama, with a surprisingly good collection of pre-Columbian pottery, religious art and historical furniture.

Basilica Mayor San Juan Bautista CATHEDRAL
(Plaza Bolívar) Dominating the central plaza, this 'major basilica' (a title bestowed on certain Catholic cathedrals) stands on the site of an original 16th-century church. Most of what you see today, however, including the lovely stained-glass windows in the clerestory, dates from a major rebuilding in 1948.

Festivals & Events

Carnaval FESTIVAL
Held during the four days preceding Ash Wednesday, Carnaval is Penonomé's red-letter event. In addition to traditional festivities such as dancing, dressing up in costumes and masks, and a queen's coronation, floats here are literally floated down a tributary of the Río Zaratí. The plaza and streets for three blocks around it are packed with people.

Penonomé

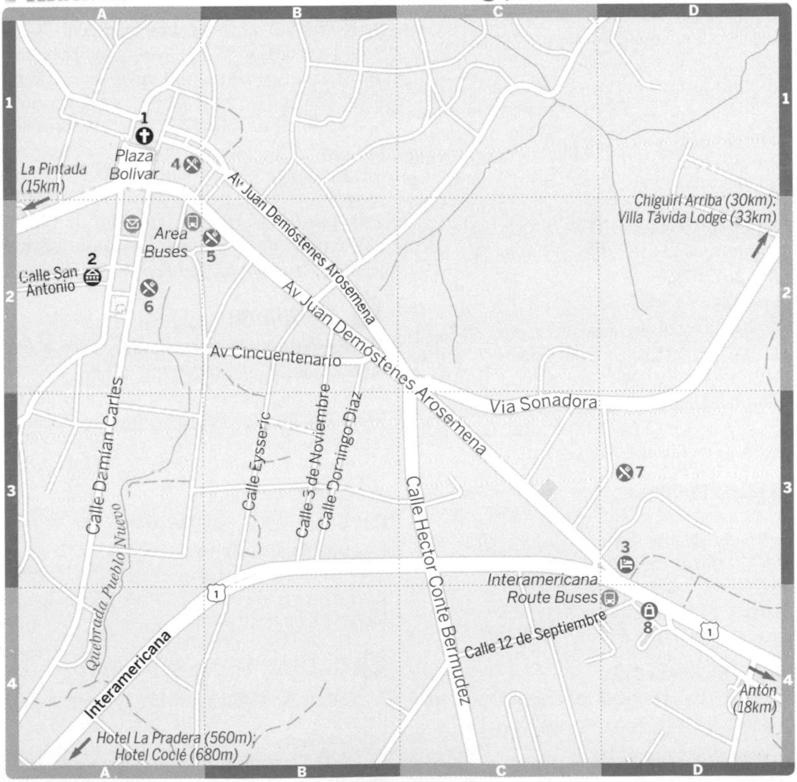

Sleeping

Hotel La Pradera HOTEL $
(☎991-0106; www.facebook.com/pages/Hotel-la-pradera-Penonome/321061187994025; Interamericana; d/tw US$55/66; P ❄ ☏) This hotel with terracotta roof tiles feels ritzy for Penonomé and is excellent value for the price. Smart earth-tone rooms include built-in cabinets, cable TV, a lounge chair and a desk. Choose a room overlooking the garden and swimming pool out the back.

Hotel Dos Continentes HOTEL $
(☎997-9326; www.hoteldoscontinentes.net; Av Juan Demóstenes Arosemena; d/tr US$30/44; P ❄ @ ☏) Near a fork in the Interamericana, this sprawling hotel is secure, spacious and relatively central. The 61 rooms are worn but serviceable, with ironed sheets. Ask for a room in the back for considerably less street noise. The on-site restaurant is popular for cheap and cheerful *comida típico* (regional specialties); locals swear its fried chicken (US$7.50) is the best in Panama.

Hotel Coclé HOTEL $$
(☎6418-6901, 908-5039; www.hotelcocle.com; Interamericana; s/d/ste incl breakfast from US$67/73/110; P ❄ ☏ ≋) This large new hotel, conveniently located next to the Iguana Mall, has 110 rooms and suites in a low-rise building recalling a Spanish hacienda. The 110 rooms and suites are tastefully done in blond wood and shades of blue. There's a fully equipped gym, and in the gardens you'll find an interestingly shaped pool.

Eating

El Paisa BAKERY $
(Av Juan Demóstenes Arosemena; pizza US$4.75-5.50; ⊙6am-9.30pm) At the northern end of Av Juan Demóstenes Arosemena this bakery sells wonderful cakes and sweet breads (US$1.75 to US$2.75) and has started baking pizzas in its ovens.

Mercado Público MARKET $
(Av Juan Demóstenes Arosemena; mains US$2.50; ⊙7am-5pm Mon-Fri, 8am-3pm Sat & Sun) Penonomé's central market serves hearty breakfasts on weekends, with *hojaldras* (fried dough), *bistec encebollado* (steak with onions and spices) and eggs.

Mesón de Santa Cruz SPANISH $$
(☎908-5311; www.facebook.com/pages/Restaurante-El-Meson-De-Santa-Cruz/104764689696534; Paseo Andaluz, off Calle Damían Carles; mains US$12-18; ⊙11am-9pm) The 'House of the Holy Cross' south of the central square has to be seen to be believed. It's housed in a sprawling one-time private residence crammed with religious statues and icons. The food is a mix of Panamanian, Spanish and Basque; try the unusual fried chicken *ceviche* (citrus-cured seafood) and the delicious sea bass cooked with tomatoes and green peppers.

In fine weather there's secular seating outside in the large back courtyard.

Pits Burgers & Grill BURGERS $$
(☎908-6330; www.facebook.com/pages/Pits-Burguer-Grill/962816170409142; mains US$8-28; ⊙noon-midnight Mon-Sat, to 10pm Sun) This place in Harinos Mall near the start of the main drag has a comfortable, well-stocked sports bar with pool table on the ground floor, and a rooftop grill and burger restaurant with open veranda above. There's a large selection of steaks, which tends to push prices up, but burgers and pasta dishes come in at US$8 to US$12.50.

Icacos INTERNATIONAL $$
(☎6873-3290; www.icacosadventure.com; Via El Coco s/n; mains US$7-20; ⊙noon-10pm Mon-Sat; 👪) A country restaurant in a recreational area, Icacos also has fishing, a playground and a small adventure park. It's ideal for families. The breezy, open-air restaurant serves standards like club sandwiches and local fare such as *pernil* (thinly sliced pork) with *patacones* (fried plantains) or tilapia fish farmed on site. Service is attentive and friendly. It's 4km south of town.

Shopping

Mercado de Artesanías Coclé MARKET
(Interamericana; ⊙8am-4pm) This market stocks both everyday and high-quality hats from Panama as well as other locally produced handicrafts.

Information

BBVA (Interamericana) Bank with ATM

Hospital Aquilino Tejeira (☎997-9386; Interamericana; ⊙24hr)

Post Office (Calle Damían Carles; ⊙7am-3pm Mon-Fri, 8am-noon Sat)

Getting There & Around

Area buses use a station two blocks southeast of Plaza Bolívar.

DESTINATION	COST (US$)	DURATION (MIN)	FREQUENCY
Aguadulce	2	45	every 20min
Chiguiri Arriba	3	80	hourly
Churuquita Grande	1	45	every 30min
El Copé	2.50	60	hourly
La Pintada	0.80	20	every 30min

Interamericana route buses use a small parking lot on the south side of the highway as a passenger pickup and drop-off point. Buses pass both directions every 15 minutes or so. From Penonomé there are frequent buses to Panama City (US$5.25, 2½ hours, every 20 minutes) and David (US$18, 4½ hours, every 35 minutes).

The best places to hail a taxi is by the station, near the entrance to town and Plaza Bolívar. The fare for any destination in town is not usually more than US$2.

La Pintada

POP 3880

This small foothill town, 15km northwest of Penonomé, attracts visitors with its natural beauty, its famous artisans' market selling Panama's very own *sombreros pintados* (painted hats) and its cigar factory. Be warned though: the world's largest copper deposit has been discovered in the hills just 30km north of La Pintada. Visit this delightfully sleepy town before large-scale mining and new money changes it beyond recognition.

Sights

Artesanías Reinaldo Quirós WORKSHOP
(☎6963-0945; ⏰8:30am-5pm) The workshop and residence of one of La Pintada's most famous hatmakers is in the center of the town on the left side of the soccer field. He'll gladly show you around his workshop. Hats for sale range in price from US$20 to US$150, but can reach as high as US$1000 for a multi-ring hat.

Cigarros Joyas de Panama FACTORY
(Joyas de Panama Cigars; ☎tours 6660-8935; www.facebook.com/joyasde.panama; ⏰8am-4pm Mon-Sat) Pay a visit to this local cigar factory, which enjoys quite a reputation internationally for its unique hand-rolled Cuban-seed *puros* (cigars). Depending on the time of year, up to 20 workers roll as many as 600 cigars a day. Owner Miriam Padilla, who set up the factory in 1982, will be glad to show you around. Five different vitolas (the measurement of a cigar) are for sale, starting at US$15 for a box of Coronitas and reaching US$100 for the #1 Especial.

The cigars are made in an assembly process that begins at one end of the building with leaf separation from stem. Employees roll the cigars at rows of desks in a long concrete-sided, aluminum-roofed building. Once finished they are placed in molds for 30 minutes, then cut and packaged before being shipped, primarily to the USA, France and Spain.

To get to the factory from the center of La Pintada, drive southeast toward Penonomé. After about 1km you'll come to a police station on your right. Turn right onto the well-maintained road just beyond it and drive for 400m. The factory is up on the hill to the right.

Mercado de Artesanías La Pintada MARKET
(☎983-0313; ⏰9am 4pm) La Pintada's famous artisans' market specializes in *sombreros pintados,* the 'painted hats' unique to Panama and especially famous in Penonomé and surrounds. The material used in these Panamas occasionally varies from one town to the next, but here hats are made of *bellota* (palm fiber), coarser *junco* dyed black and *pita,* a fiber related to cactus, used to sew it all together. These plants are growing in front of the market, so you can see what they look like. Other items on sale include dolls wearing handmade folkloric costumes, the local firewater called *seco* (distilled from sugarcane), bottle covers made from palm fiber and handmade brooms. The market is in the Casa Comunal on the far side of a very large soccer field on the left side of the road as you drive in from Penonomé.

Sleeping & Eating

La Pintada River Inn B&B **$$**
(☎6519-7848, 983-0384; www.lapintadainn.com/#inn; s/d/ste incl breakfast US$60/75/100; P ❄ 📶 🏊) This delightful inn set in lovely gardens lies just 4km north of La Pintada. Each of the eight spick-and-span rooms has its own bathroom, cable TV and fridge. There are lovely walks and trails in the area, including one down to the eponymous river. Swim here or in the lovely pool with grand views into the hills.

Dinner (US$12.50 per person) under the *bohío* (thatched hut) overlooking the pool is available with advance notice.

Getting There & Away

Buses costing less than US$1 link La Pintada with Penonomé at least every half-hour. The trip takes about 20 minutes.

Reserva Privida Távida

The Reserva Privada Távida is a private mountain reserve that forms part of the Mesoamerican corridor. Once used for livestock, the area is now undergoing reforestation and offers ample trails for hiking or horseback riding and a spectacular waterfall.

Activities

Guided hiking tours (US$20 to US$30 per person) from the Villa Távida Lodge range from easy nature walks to arduous treks, taking in river, forest scenes and the awesome 30m-high Cascada Távida. Wildlife to spot includes three-toed sloths, night monkeys, deer and armadillos. Four species of toucan and many species of hummingbird and butterflies also live here, and can occasionally be seen from the comfort of the creek-fed swimming pool.

Sleeping & Eating

★**Villa Távida Lodge** LODGE **$$$**
(6485-0505, 838-6114; www.villatavida.com; Chiriquí Arriba; d incl breakfast US$220, extra person US$27.50;) This mountain lodge sits inside the Reserva Privada Távida atop a summit surrounded by gardens, green valleys and shrouded peaks. Guests have their pick of four rooms in the main lodge, set by the stunning Cascada Távida.

The waterfall villa, some seven minutes away by foot, luxuriates in privacy. The site has an alfresco dining area and hammock terrace where you'll want to laze the hours away, great views, and walks available right out the door. Rooms have cable TV and hot-water showers. There is a swimming hole under Cascada Távida, so bring your suit.

The lodge restaurant offers quality dining, using produce fresh from local organic gardens. Massage (from US$50) and reflexology (US$30) services also available.

Getting There & Away

To reach Chiriquí Arriba and the Reserva Privada Távida from central Penonomé, follow the Caimito road to the well-marked turnoff for Churuquita Grande, several hundred meters northwest of the fork in the Interamericana near the landmark Hotel Dos Continentes. Proceed past Churuquita Grande and Caimito and follow the signs to Chiriquí Arriba.

Buses leave for Chiriquí Arriba (US$3, 80 minutes) from Penonomé's market every hour between 5:30am and 6:30pm.

Parque Nacional Omar Torrijos

Truly one of Panama's hidden gems through its difficulty of access, this 252-sq-km **park** (park admission US$5; 6am-8pm) encompasses some of the most beautiful forests in Panama, with montane forest on the Pacific side of the continental divide and humid tropical forest on the Caribbean.

El Copé – a short name for the park taken from a nearby village – is also home to the full complement of Panama's wildlife, including rare bird species such as the golden-olive woodpecker, red-fronted parrotlet, immaculate antbird and white-throated shrike-tanager, as well as all four species of felines, Baird's tapirs and peccaries.

Two great surprises await visitors to El Copé: the condition of the park's trail system is excellent; and the park offers the easiest and surest point from which to see both the Pacific and Atlantic Oceans, from the lookout above the park cabin.

Activities

Next to the ranger station just inside the entrance to the park you'll find two side-by-side trails. The left-hand trail follows the ridgeline and summits a nearby mountain in about an hour. From the top, you'll be rewarded with panoramic views of both oceans and the surrounding canopy.

The right-hand trail follows the Caribbean slope of the continental divide. Be advised that this trail does not end and it should under no circumstances be attempted without a guide organized through the ranger station. It's a fantastic trail that passes several rivers, winds up and down several mountain peaks and penetrates deep into the heart of the forest.

Behind the ranger station, just inside the park entrance and where where visitors pay for accommodations, camping permits and admission fees, you'll find a visitors center and a 500m-long interpretative trail that points out local species of trees and plants.

There are poisonous snakes in the park including the infamous fer-de-lance; as a precaution, inform others of your intentions, always hike in boots and stick to the trails.

Sleeping

Park Cabin CABIN $

(☎997-7538; campsites US$5, dm per person US$15) About 200m up the road from the ranger, station a small cabin run by Ministerio de Ambiente has four bunks, a kitchen with simple cooking facilities, a basic toilet and cold-water shower. It also has a loft and a lounge, allowing 10 people to sleep comfortably if you have your own gear. You'll need a sleeping bag and warm clothing – it gets cool at night in the mountains.

Navas Family House HOMESTAY $$

(Casa Navas; ☎983-9130; Barrigon; r per person incl 3 meals & tour guide US$45) The friendly Navas family rents rooms in their house in Barrigon. Accommodations are rustic, but very well maintained and inexpensive, with all meals included. The family – Santo and Anna Navas and their sons – work as guides and help to maintain the park and its trails. Their knowledge and love of the area is quite apparent.

Barrigon can be reached by car or public transportation from El Copé. From Barrigon it's a two- to three-hour hike or a horseback ride to La Rica.

Albergue Navas CABIN $$

(☎983-9130; La Rica; r per person incl 3 meals & tour guide US$45) The Navas family also rents rooms in their *cabaña* Albergue Navas in La Rica, a beautiful community inside the park. From here you can take day hikes to the summits of Cerros Marta and Peña Blanca, visit the impressive waterfalls of Chorros de Tife and even hike to the ruins of the plane that crashed, killing president Omar Torrijos, in 1981.

La Rica is remote (no phone, electricity or road) and the hiking is strenuous, but it is a nature-lover's dream and comes highly recommended. All the arrangements can be made through Santo and Anna Navas (Spanish only). Call ahead, or ask around for the Navas family when you reach Barrigon.

Getting There & Away

The turnoff to the national park is on the Interamericana, 18km southwest of Penonomé. From the turnoff, it's another 33km to the park entrance. The road, paved for the first 30km or so, winds through rolling countryside dotted with farms and small cattle ranches. The paved road ends at the village of Barrigon. The remaining 3km of the drive to the park is on a dirt road that requires a 4WD. Follow the signs directing you to the park entrance (to the right); the ones to the left indicate the park's Sede Administrativa (administrative office).

To reach here by public transportation, catch a bus from Panama City (US$6.50, three hours) or Penonomé (US$2.50, one hour) to El Copé and transfer onto a minibus to Barrigon (US$0.30, 15 minutes), the closest village to the park. From there it's a 3km hike into the park.

Parque Arqueológico del Caño

Although rather underwhelming and infested with mosquitoes in the rainy season, the **Parque Arqueológico del Caño** (☎228-6231; www.inac.gob.pa/museos/108-el-cano; adult/child US$1/0.50; ⏲8am-4pm Tue-Sun) will help you get a better idea of Panama's indigenous traditions.

This archaeological site contains three pre-Columbian mounds dating from between AD 500 and 1200. The larger of the two under excavation contains five skeletons in the same position as when they were unearthed at 4m below. One is believed to be the grave of a chieftain, as it contained a number of gold and emerald objects. A small museum displaying pieces of pottery, arrowheads and carved stones found at the site was under renovation at the time of research.

Also here are rows of stone pedestals, all that remains of the so-called Temple of a Thousand Idols, removed by an American adventurer in the 1920s and sent to a museum in New York.

Getting There & Away

The turnoff for the town of El Caño is 6.5km north of Natá; any bus plying the Interamericana will drop you here. But it's another 3km down an occasionally mud-slicked road to the site. Your best bet is to take a taxi (US$7) from Natá.

Natá

POP 6000

Natá is the oldest surviving town in Panama; it was founded in 1522 by conquistadors in search of gold. The 60 *caballeros* (knights) who took up residence here subdued the local indigenous population and put them to the task of building what is thought to be the oldest church still in use in the Americas: the **Basílica Menor Santiago Apóstol** (Minor Basilica of St James the Apostle; Plaza 19 de Octubre).

Indigenous artisans did all the woodcarving in the church, including the six side altars and the remarkable pulpit. A close look at the altar dedicated to the Virgin Mary shows the culture's influence in the sculpted fruit, leaves and feathered serpents on its two columns.

The columns in the nave are made of *níspero*, a hardwood found in Bocas del Toro Province.

The entire ceiling has been replaced with pine and cedar. The four bells in the belfry are from the 20th century. The originals, made of gold, were stolen years ago.

Ecuadorian artist José Samaniego created the Holy Trinity painting to the right of the altar in 1758. For many years it was kept hidden from public view, as it portrays three separate but equal Christ-like individuals, a considerable breach of Roman Catholic dogma and almost heretical. During a 1995 restoration, three skeletons were discovered under the floor beneath the painting. Their identities remain a mystery.

ℹ Getting There & Away

Natá can be reached by buses along the Interamericana; they pass in both directions every 15 minutes or so. Natá is 45 minutes from Penonomé (US$1.25) and 15 minutes from Aguadulce (US$0.75).

Aguadulce

POP 8700

Hot and flat, the town of Aguadulce is surrounded by fields and fields of sugarcane and is Panama's sugar capital. Oddly enough it is also known for the salt it still claims from the sea. Fans of industrial tourism will think they died and went to heaven, for both industries can be viewed up close.

⊙ Sights

Playa El Salado BEACH
(Salty Beach) Located 9km from central Aguadulce, this one-time salt works now serves as a crucial habitat for marsh and shore birds. The area draws local and international birdwatchers to view roseate spoonbills, wood storks and black-necked stilts. When the tide is out, you can walk nearly 2km before reaching the water. But be careful; once the tide turns, it rises quickly.

**Azucarera Nacional
Ingenio Santa Rosa** REFINERY
(Santa Rosa National Sugar Refinery; ☑ 987-8101; www.azunal.com; ⊙ 7am-4pm Mon-Fri, 7-11:30am Sat) FREE From mid-January to mid-March this sugar refinery 15km west of Aguadulce processes more than 6500 tons of raw sugarcane daily. The process involves thousands of workers in round-the-clock production. It's a fascinating time to visit the refinery, but requires 24 hours' notice. For tours in English, ask for Gonzalo Peréz. A taxi costs about US$18 round-trip; otherwise take any bus headed west and tell the driver to drop you at the Ingenio de Azúcar Santa Rosa (US$1, 20 minutes, every 15 minutes).

Museo de la Sal y Azúcar MUSEUM
(☑ 997-4280; www.inac.gob.pa/museos/110-sal-y-azucar; Av Rodolfo Chiari, off Plaza 19 de Octubre; ⊙ 8:30am-3:30pm Tue-Sat) FREE Officially called the Museo Regional de Aguadulce Stella Sierra, but better known by its former title, Museo de la Sal y Azúcar, this museum in the former post office facing the central plaza in Aguadulce documents the history of the sea-salt and sugar industries in Aguadulce. It also displays a number of pre-Columbian artifacts, mostly ceramics and tools found in the cane fields nearby

ℹ Getting There & Around

Aguadulce can be accessed from Penonomé (US$2, 45 minutes, every 20 minutes), Chitré (US$3, one hour, every 20 minutes) and Panama City (US$6.35, 2½ hours, every 20 minutes). Taxis are the best way to get around Aguadulce in the hot weather. Fares rarely exceed US$3, although you can expect to pay a little more at night.

Península de Azuero

POP 213,300 / AREA 9000 SQ KM / ELEV SEA LEVEL TO 3478M

Includes ➡

Best Places to Eat

- ➡ El Sitio Restaurant (p132)
- ➡ Bienvenidush (p128)
- ➡ Mare Bonita (p128)
- ➡ Colcos Cafe (p132)
- ➡ El Mirador (p117)

Best Places to Sleep

- ➡ Casa de Campo (p126)
- ➡ Eco Venao (p131)
- ➡ El Sitio Hotel (p132)
- ➡ Posada Los Destiladeros (p129)
- ➡ La Casa del Puerto (p122)

Why Go?

Cherished as Panama's cultural heart and soul, Península de Azuero is a farming and ranching hub, and the strongest bastion of Spanish colonial influence extant in the country. The area's rolling hills are matched by a long and lovely coastline. Over time the peninsula has seen stark transformations – from verdant rainforest to cattle country, from indigenous land to Spanish stronghold and, finally, from sleepy backwater to surf central and one of Panama's travel hot spots.

The passage of time here is a countdown to the next festival, be it Carnaval, La Mejorana or Corpus Christi. Costumes range from swirling devils and dragons to curtsying *reinas* (queens) turned dolls in traditional lace finery. Joining the throngs on sticky rum-soaked streets for these celebrations is a first-rate introduction to the real Panama.

Península de Azuero consists of three provinces: Herrera, Los Santos and a slice of Veraguas.

When to Go

➡ **Jul–Sep** Azuero is ground zero for Panama's best traditional festivals, with major celebrations all over the peninsula featuring oxcart parades, *seco* (alcoholic drink made from sugarcane) and live bands.

➡ **Aug–Nov** Thousands of endangered olive ridley sea turtles come ashore to nest on the broad beach of Isla Cañas; visitors come with guides to watch the nighttime hatchings.

➡ **Dec–Mar** Dry season is the best time to surf Pacific swells, and options from wilderness beaches to surf villages abound. Also hit Las Tablas' Carnaval – the country's best – in February or March.

Península de Azuero Highlights

❶ **Playa Venao** (p131) Riding the waves and staying in cool lodgings at this surf destination that is managing to evade the mainstream.

❷ **Pedasí** (p125) Enjoying the down-home ambience of a small town with lovely boutique lodgings, a few good eateries and long bike rides to the beach.

❸ **Isla Cañas** (p133) Spotting sea turtles as they arrive by the thousands during their annual nesting.

❹ **Las Tablas** (p123) Squeezing through the multitudes of revelers dancing in the streets during Carnaval.

❺ **Parita** (p117) Visiting a mask-maker's studio and strolling the colonial center of this historic town.

❻ **Playa El Aguillito** (p119) Heading out for birdwatching at a tidal mudflat that attracts migratory seabirds.

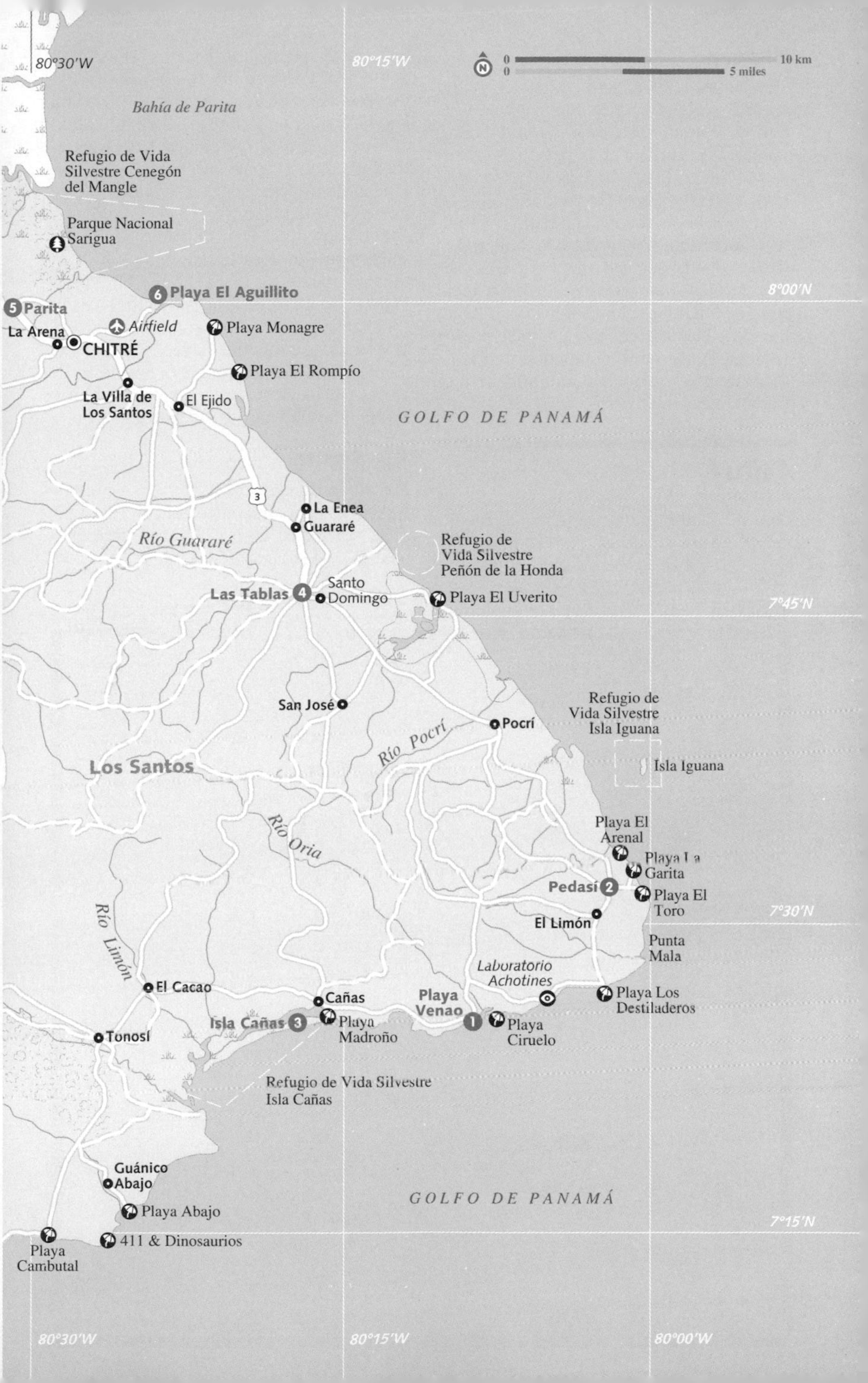
80°30'W
80°15'W
10 km
5 miles
Bahía de Parita
Refugio de Vida Silvestre Cenegón del Mangle
Parque Nacional Sarigua
8°00'N
6 Playa El Aguillito
5 Parita
Airfield
La Arena
CHITRÉ
Playa Monagre
Playa El Rompío
La Villa de Los Santos
El Ejido
GOLFO DE PANAMÁ
3
La Enea
Guararé
Río Guararé
Refugio de Vida Silvestre Peñón de la Honda
Santo Domingo
Las Tablas 4
Playa El Uverito
7°45'N
San José
Refugio de Vida Silvestre Isla Iguana
Pocrí
Río Pocrí
Isla Iguana
Los Santos
Río Oria
Playa El Arenal
Playa La Garita
Pedasí 2
Playa El Toro
7°30'N
El Limón
Río Limón
Punta Mala
Laboratorio Achotines
El Cacao
Cañas
Playa Venao
Playa Los Destiladeros
Isla Cañas 3
Playa Madroño
1
Playa Ciruelo
Tonosí
Refugio de Vida Silvestre Isla Cañas
Guánico Abajo
GOLFO DE PANAMÁ
Playa Abajo
7°15'N
Playa Cambutal
411 & Dinosaurios
80°30'W
80°15'W
80°00'W

History

The Península de Azuero region was one of the first parts of what is now Panama to be settled. Indeed, shell mounds and pottery fragments unearthed at Sarigua in the northeast of the peninsula have been dated as far back as 11,000 years. The peninsula likes to refer to itself as the *cuna* (cradle) of Panamanian culture and traditions, and rightly so: the colonial Spanish legacy is perhaps felt more strongly here than anywhere else in the country. But there's a dark side to that legacy, too. So efficient were the conquistadors in wiping out the native population that today there are no indigenous communities left on the Península de Azuero.

Chitré

POP 48,480

One of Panama's oldest settlements, the hot city of Chitré is hardly geared up for travelers, but it's an agreeable stop on the way down to the peninsula's beaches. The capital of Herrera Province, it's the largest city on the Península de Azuero, and the cultural and historic capital of the region. A handful of ornate red-tiled row homes hark back to the early days of Spanish settlement. Colonial records indicate that there was a village here as early as 1558.

For most travelers Chitré serves as a springboard for nearby attractions such as the ceramic shops in La Arena, birdlife at Playa El Aguillito, historic Parita, the *seco* (alcoholic drink made from sugarcane) factory at Pesé and the wildlife refuge at Cenegón del Mangle. Some of the country's best festivals are just a quick bus ride away, and Chitré hosts a few wild parties of its own.

Sights

Museo de Herrera MUSEUM

(996-0077; www.inac.gob.pa/museos/111-museo-de-herrera; Paseo Enrique Geenzier; adult/child US$1/0.25; 8am-4pm Mon-Sat, to noon Sun)

Chitré

This anthropology and natural history museum, housed in a lovely colonial building, contains many well-preserved pieces of pottery dating from 5000 BC until the Spanish conquest, some of which were found at excavation sites outside Parita. There are also replicas of *huacas* (golden objects placed with indigenous peoples at the time of burial) found on the peninsula, as well as a recreated chieftain's tomb.

Catedral San Juan Bautista CATHEDRAL
(Parque Union; ⊙6am-8pm) Unlike many cathedrals that impress through ostentation, this 18th-century number is striking for its elegant simplicity and fine balance of gold and wood. The pitched ceiling is polished mahogany, and figures of saints, teak crosses and vivid stained-glass windows adorn the walls. It was substantially remodeled in 1988.

Festivals & Events

Carnaval FESTIVAL
Chitré's Carnaval festivities, held each year on the four days before Ash Wednesday, are second only to the famed celebrations Las Tablas, and feature parades, folkloric dancing, water fights and lots of drinking.

Fiesta de San Juan Bautista FESTIVAL
(⊙24 Jun) Chitré's patron-saint festival starts with a religious service followed by bullfights (the animals are teased but not harmed), cockfights (the birds fight violently to the death) and other popular activities.

Foundation of Chitré Day FESTIVAL
(⊙19 Oct) Festivities celebrate the 1848 founding of Chitré, with parades, historical costumes and much merrymaking.

Sleeping

Hotel Versalles HOTEL $
(☎996-4422; www.hotelversalles.com; Paseo Enrique Geenzier; d/ste US$50/85; P ❄ 📶 🏊) Some 78 spacious rooms feature comfortable beds and tile floors, and the on-site restaurant-bar is good for an evening meal and a nightcap. The price tag is mostly justified by the swimming pool, ideal for those hot Azuero days, but it's located a bit away from whatever action there is in Chitré.

Hotel Rex HOTEL $
(☎996-4310, 996-2408; www.facebook.com/Hotel-Rex-Chitre-Panama-121877944544889; Calle Melitón Martín s/n; d/tr US$44/66; ❄ 📶) With a prime location on Parque Union and good dining downstairs, Rex is a solid choice. Its 33 clean tiled rooms have brick walls, cable TV, fresh towels and water thermoses. Ask for a room on the 2nd floor where there's a large communal veranda overlooking the cathedral and main square.

Hotel Santa Rita HOTEL $
(☎996-4610; cnr Calle Manuel Maria Correa & Av Herrera; d with/without air-con US$29/23; ❄ 📶) One of the city's first hotels, Santa Rita is economical but basic. The 19 high-ceilinged rooms are rough around the edges, but thoroughly clean. Perks include some rooms with private balconies, cable TV and very friendly service.

Hotel Los Guayacanes HOTEL $$$
(☎996-8969; www.losguayacanes.com; Vía Circunvalación; d/ste US$138/160; P ❄ 📶 🏊) Billed as a resort, Los Guayacanes' ample space is particularly good for families. Built around an artificial lake about 1.5km southwest of the center, it features a swimming pool, casino, weekend disco, tennis courts and a spa and gym connected by walkways. Its 64 rooms are tasteful and bright.

Eating

Pizzeria Ebenezer PIZZA $
(☎996-8831; Calle Julio Botello s/n; mains US$6-12; ⊙11:30am-9:30pm Mon-Thu, to 10:30pm Fri & Sat, 4-10pm Sun) In addition to pizza, this popular pizzeria a short distance from the main square does a good range of pasta, as well as tacos and burritos. It's a good choice when local food starts to grind you down.

Restaurante Aire Libre PANAMANIAN $
(☎996-3639; Av Obaldía; mains US$3.50-8; ⊙6am-9pm) Get your greasy-spoon fix at breakfast, lunch or dinner at this open-air plaza-cafe overlooking Parque Union. It offers two kinds

Chitré

Sights
1 Catedral San Juan Bautista C2
2 Museo de Herrera C1

Sleeping
3 Hotel Rex C2
4 Hotel Santa Rita C1
5 Hotel Versalles A1

Eating
6 Ceviches Tio Caimán B1
7 Pizzeria Ebenezer C2
8 Restaurante Aire Libre C2
9 Restaurante El Meson C2
10 Salsa y Carbon C2

of fried chicken and seafood such as *camarones al ajillo* (shrimp with garlic), served with crisp, thick-cut fries. Fresh fish dishes (US$6.50) are excellent value.

★Salsa y Carbon PARRILLA **$$**
(☎996-6022; www.salsaycarbon.com; cnr Calles Julio Botello & Francisco Corro; mains US$8-14; ⊙11am-10pm) This open-air Colombian thatched BBQ house grills some of the best steak and ribs in the region. Meat and chicken are exceptionally tender and served with salad and *arepas* (maize flatbreads). The covered outside seating catches cool breezes and is a delight.

Ceviches Tio Caimán SEAFOOD **$$**
(☎996-8040, 6615-0905; www.facebook.com/pages/Ceviches-Tio-Caiman/388581517910976; Calle Independencia; mains US$9-15; ⊙8am-midnight Mon-Sat, noon-11pm Sun) Chitré's favorite seafood restaurant specializes in *ceviche* (citrus-cured seafood) but has many more inventive dishes on offer, including those with a Caribbean slant. It's just north of the center, next to the public swimming pool.

Restaurante El Meson PANAMANIAN **$$**
(☎996-4310; www.facebook.com/Hotel-Rex-Chitre-Panama-121877944544889; Calle Melitón Martín s/n; mains US$5-13; ⊙7:15am-10pm; 📶) This plaza restaurant with long hours has a longlist of offerings, from sandwiches to steak and seafood. The chicken tacos will fully satisfy small appetites. Full breakfasts include fried yucca or *tortillas de maiz* (thick, fried cornmeal tortillas) with eggs and coffee. The ambience is muted; decor includes tall wooden chairs and fake vines cascading from overhead.

ℹ Information

ATP Kiosk (☎974-4532; azuero@atp.gob.pa; Parque Union; ⊙9am-4pm Mon-Fri) Tourist information in a kiosk at the northeast corner of the main square.

Banco Nacional de Panamá (☎970-3300; Paseo Enrique Geenzier; ⊙8am-3pm Mon-Fri, 9am-noon Sat) Has an ATM.

ℹ Getting There & Away

Chitré is a center for regional bus transportation from **Terminal de Transportes de Herrera** (☎996-6426), 1km south of downtown, near Vía Circunvalación. The terminal has a 24-hour restaurant and car rental agency. To get there, **Radio Taxi** (☎996-4442) charges US$2. The 'Terminal' bus (US$0.30) leaves from the intersection of Calle Aminta Burgos de Amado and Av Herrera.

Tuasa (☎996-2661) and **Transportes Inazun** (☎996-4177) buses depart from Chitré's Terminal de Transportes de Herrera for Panama City (US$9.10, four hours, every 40 minutes from 6am to 11pm). Other buses departing from Chitré operate from sunrise to sunset.

To get to David (US$9.50), take a bus to Santiago (US$3.25, every half-hour) and then catch a *directo* (direct bus). Buses leave from the gas station at the intersection of the Interamericana and the Carretera Nacional. Other services:

DESTINATION	COST (US$)	DURATION (HR)	FREQUENCY
Aguadulce	3	1	every 20min
Divisa	1.25	30min	every 15min
La Arena	0.30	15min	every 15min
La Villa de Los Santos	0.50	5min	every 10min
Las Minas	3	45min	every 30min
Las Tablas	1.50	35min	every 15min
Macaracas	2.50	1	hourly
Ocú	2.50	1	every 25min
Panama City	9.10	4	every 40min
Parita	0.65	15min	every 30min
Pedasí	3.25	1	hourly
Pesé	1.10	20min	every 20min
Playa El Aguillito	0.50	12min	every 20min
Playas Monagre & El Rompío	1.25	30min	every 20min
Santiago	3.25	1	every 30min
Tonosí	5.20	2	every 40min

ℹ Getting Around

When the Carretera Nacional reaches Chitré, it becomes Paseo Enrique Geenzier, changing its name again a dozen blocks further east to Calle Manuel Maria Correa. The Carretera Nacional re-emerges at the southern end of town. If you need to travel by car, a taxi is the best way to go. Most fares in town are between US$2 and US$3.

Around Chitré

La Arena

POP 7590

The tiny village of La Arena, about 4km west of Chitré, produces some of the highest-quality pottery in the country and is a great place to watch artisans working their trade. The pottery mimics the pre-Columbian designs of the indigenous Ngöbe-Buglé people who once lived nearby. Another product for which the village is noted is bread; *el pan de la Arena* is celebrated (and consumed) nationwide. You can buy traditional painted ceramics at wholesale prices at **Ceramica Hermanos Calderón** (☎910-4076; www.facebook.com/Ceramicas-Hermanos-calder%C3%B3n-835501223198677; near Calle del Río Parita & Carretera Nacional). Pieces are made in a workshop directly behind the roadside showroom. All pottery is handmade with the help of a foot-powered potter's wheel. Be sure to take a look at the impressive ovens out back.

Atop a hill in La Arena and next to the TV tower **El Mirador** (☎974-4647; mains US$6.50-10; ⊙noon-10pm) is a popular spot where visitors from around Panama congregate to take in the views of the city and the surrounding plains. The food is standard at best, but the twinkling lights of Chitré make for an atmospheric night out.

To find El Mirador from downtown Chitré, head west on Paseo Enrique Geenzier for about 2.5km and turn left onto the road that begins just past the large 'Corotú Disco' sign. At the fork, turn right and continue for another 400m until you reach the top of the hill.

Getting There & Away

La Arena can be reached by frequent bus (US$0.30) from Chitré. A taxi ride from Parque Union in central Chitré to La Arena shouldn't cost more than US$2 or US$3.

Parque Nacional Sarigua

Just 10km north of central Chitré, **Parque Nacional Sarigua** (☎park office 996-8216; admission US$5; ⊙8am-4pm) is arguably the most important pre-Columbian site in Panama.

This archaeological site has been dated back 11,000 years based on shell mounds and pottery fragments, although much of it is yet to be excavated. Created in 1984, the park consists of 80 sq km of wasteland that was once dry tropical rainforest and coastal mangrove patches. Sarigua is the end product of slash-and-burn agriculture; because the forest that had held the thin topsoil in place was removed, the heavy rainfalls that occur each year have carried the topsoil away.

A visit to Sarigua is a sober reminder of the earth's fragility, and the rapid speed in which humans can alter the environment. From the *mirador* (lookout) behind the ranger station, you can gaze out at the dry, cracked earth and swirling dust storms that used to be a living, breathing ecosystem. If you have your own transportation, you can drive a few kilometers into the park, but much of Sarigua is off-limits to the public. The coastal edges of the park are also home to privately owned commercial shrimp farms, which stand as testament to the rapid destruction of Panama's wetland habitat.

Getting There & Away

To get here from the Carretera Nacional, take the turnoff opposite the Super Candy convenience store just before you reach Parita. After going 2.5km, you'll reach a fork with a green-and-yellow sign indicating the park. The ranger's station is another five minutes further.

Buses do not go all the way to the park. A taxi ride to the park office from Parita costs about US$3 and from Chitré about US$10.

Parita

POP 3730

Just 7km northwest of downtown Chitré, the colonial town of Parita is one of those gems that travelers love to stumble across. Founded in 1558 and named after the departed Ngöbe-Buglé chief, Parita is full of 18th-century colonial structures. Buildings have thick walls and solid beams, red-tiled roofs and sweeping arcades. Despite its historic core, Parita is known to few outside the Península de Azuero, so it's unlikely that you will see any tourists here, Panamanian or otherwise.

Sights

★**Dario López** WORKSHOP

(☎6534-1958) One of Panama's top artisans, Dario López has been making colorful masks for folkloric dancers since the 1960s. While he continues to create masks and satin costumes worn by dirty-devil dancers, these days most are exported to the USA and Europe. Masks typically cost between US$20 and US$100, with some small masks under US$10. To visit his home workshop, look for the gas station near the Parita turnoff on Carretera Nacional. His house is green and on the opposite side about 100m north of the station.

Taller de Restauración WORKSHOP

(☎974-2136) This workshop specializing in the restoration of altars is the only such workshop in Panama. Macario José Rodriguez has been restoring the altars of Panama's colonial churches since the early 1980s and will be happy to show you his work. You'll find the workshop diagonally opposite Parita's church on the main square and just behind the Servicios Médicos building.

Iglesia de Santo Domingo de Guzmán CHURCH

This 18th-century church has some lovely carvings; check out the pulpit and the *retablo* (altarpiece). It is the only church in Panama that has its steeple located directly over its entrance rather than over a corner of the structure. This is very unusual as bell towers are always extremely heavy, and therefore are generally built on pillars that rest upon a massive foundation.

Getting There & Away

Parita is about 500m from Carretera Nacional and signposted to the left. Buses (US$0.60, 15 minutes) run every half-hour between Chitré and Parita. A taxi ride from Parque Union in central Chitré to Parita shouldn't cost more than US$5.

Interior Azuero

POP 2565 (PESÉ); 7010 (OCÚ)

Interior Azuero towns **Pesé** and **Ocú** west of Chitré offer a glimpse of rural life, with worthwhile traditional festivals, artisans' workshops and liquor production from the endless sea of sugarcane plantation.

Pesé, 21km southwest of Chitré, is home to the country's largest *seco* (alcoholic drink made from sugarcane) distillery. **Varela Hermanos** (917-0300; www.varelahermanos.com/en; 9am-5pm Mon-Sat Jan-Apr) FREE has been making the nation's favorite tipple, Seco Herrerano, since 1936. During harvest time from January to April, travelers can visit for free tours and taste samples of this liquor. Pesé is also famous for its annual Good Friday reenactment of the Passion of Christ.

About 20km west of Pesé, sleepy Ocú produces its own version of the Panama-style hat called *sombreros ocueños,* the best examples of which cost up to US$100. Ocu's festivals also have wide notoriety, including Festival del Manito Ocueño, held during the third week in August, and the late-January Feria de San Sebastián, celebrating Ocu's patron saint. Both Pesé and Ocú feature folklore programs and an agricultural fair.

Shopping

Ezequela Maure CRAFTS

(6033-4026; Ocú) Visitors are welcome at the Ocú workshop of this nationally known maker of Panama-style hats. Drive or walk north about 1km on Av Central; if you come to a fork in the road, you've gone too far. Ezequela's house is the blue one on the left side of the street, about four houses south of the fork.

Elena Montilla CRAFTS

(974-1365; Ocú) Elena Montilla is a nationally known maker of Panama-style hats based in Ocú; she also makes traditional *pollera* (traditional dress from the Península de Azuero). To visit her workshop, drive or walk north about 1km on Av Central; if you come

INSIDE AZUERO'S INTRIGUING PAST

Spanish settlements were so effective in wiping out the indigenous populations of Azuero that little is known about these communities. During the 1940s, a major tomb excavation just 10km outside Parita yielded some of the finest pre-Columbian objects ever discovered in Panama.

Artifacts included painted pots in the form of bird and batons shaped like stylized alligators exquisitely carved from manatee bone. Perhaps the most amazing find was a necklace made of more than 800 human teeth.

In the colonial era, the peninsula was covered by dry tropical rainforest and thick mangroves. Early communities subsisted on hunting and fishing, with small-scale agriculture included rice, beans and manioc. Several tribes shared the peninsula, though the region was controlled by a powerful Ngöbe-Buglé chief named Parita.

For decades, Parita and his fierce warriors held off Spanish settlement. Yet when Gaspar de Espinosa raided in the early 16th century, Parita was found lying dead, surrounded by his slaughtered wives, attendants and more than 160kg of gold ornaments. They were presumably killed by another tribe on the peninsula. Also found were 20 native captives lashed to house posts by cords around their necks – about to be buried alive with the great chieftain.

Following this episode, the Spanish rapidly colonized the Península de Azuero and exterminated its residents. A few Ngöbe-Buglé communities fled to the rainforested mountains in present-day Chiriquí Province. These same communities were so fearful of further attacks that they placed deadly traps along trails until only a few decades ago.

WORTH A TRIP

PLAYA EL AGUILLITO

Playa El Aguillito is a mudflat created by silt deposited by the Río Parita and the Río La Villa, 7km from Chitré. At low tide, it stretches more than 2km from the high-water mark to the surf, supplying a bounty of plankton and small shrimp to thousands of migrating birds.

Regulars include roseate spoonbills, sandpipers, warblers, black-necked stilts, white-winged doves, black-bellied plovers, yellow-crowned amazons, yellowlegs and ospreys. The beach is also home to common ground-doves, which are found only in this one spot in Panama. At high tide, birds congregate around salt ponds to the immediate east of Playa El Aguillito. The artificial beach is a failed attempt to create a sunbathing beach by destroying a mangrove forest back in the 1960s.

Playa El Aguillito is reached from Chitré via Av Herrera just past the airport. A bus (US$0.50, 45 minutes) leaves the Chitré station for the beach every 15 minutes or so during daylight hours. A taxi ride from town costs US$3 one way.

to a fork in the road, you've gone too far. Elena's house is the green one south of the fork.

Artesanías Ocueñas CRAFTS
(☎6392-3585, 6577-6338; Plaza Sebastián Ocú, Ocú; ⌚9am-4pm) Overlooking the central plaza in Ocú is this outlet of the internationally renowned women's co-op Artesanía Ocueña. The group sells intricate *montunos* (men's folkloric outfits), *polleras* (traditional dresses from the Península de Azuero) and handmade items such as tablecloths and place mats with exquisite embroidery.

Getting There & Away

From Chitré, frequent buses go to Pesé (US$1.10, 20 minutes) and to Ocú (US$2.50, one hour). The last bus returns sometime around 6pm.

Macaracas

POP 2890

The town of Macaracas, 40km southwest of Chitré and 50km northwest of Tonosí, is the site of the annual **Fiesta de los Reyes Magos** (⌚5-10 Jan), highlighted by dramatic theater performances. The festival, more than two centuries old, celebrates the Epiphany (on January 6) with a two-hour dramatization of the story of the Three Kings.

There is also a secluded, though popular on weekends, river just outside town, ideal for swimming. To get here, take a right off the main road at the San Juan gas station. Continue for 750m until you pass over a bridge, then turn right into the gravel lot.

Food stands and kiosks on the main square sell grilled pork sausages, for which the Península de Azuero is justifiably famous, while above the Farmacia Pinzón on the main road through town, **Pensión Lorena** (☎995-4181; Calle El Comercio s/n; d with/without bathroom US$15/25; P ❄) has eight spartan rooms with cold-water showers, that will do in a pinch. The friendly *refresquería* next door serves up hot meals, but don't expect anything beyond Panamanian staples.

Getting There & Away

Buses run between Macaracas and Chitré (US$2.50, one hour, hourly) and Macaracas and Tonosí (US$3, one hour, hourly) from 7am to 4pm.

La Villa de Los Santos

POP 7990

A quintessential Azuero town, La Villa de Los Santos is where Panama's first move toward independence from Spain began on November 10, 1821. Residents now honor their freedom-fighting forebears by holding truly wild parties on the anniversary of that date. In fact, the local calendar does not skimp on celebrations, making it a very entertaining destination.

Aside from its festivals, Los Santos (as it's usually called) boasts colonial structures dating back to the early days of the Spanish settlement. It is also home to a noteworthy museum dedicated to Panamanian independence as well as one of the country's most magnificent churches.

Sights

Iglesia San Atanasio CHURCH
(Plaza Simón Bolívar) On the east side of Plaza Simón Bolívar, this national treasure was consecrated in 1782, although the foundation stone had been laid more than two centuries earlier. It's a wonderful example of the baroque style, with lots of intricately carved and gilded wood depicting cherubs, saints,

FIESTA DE CORPUS CHRISTI

One of the most riotous events in Panama, Fiesta de Corpus Christi has been celebrated ever since Pope Urban IV sanctioned the festival in 1264. Yet the local version coolly incorporates animistic traditions passed down through generations in the Península de Azuero. As a means of converting the indigenous peoples of the region, Spanish missionaries used the festival to highlight the concept of good versus evil. At the core of the festival is a series of dances including the famous *baile de los diablos sucios* (dance of the dirty devils), which emphasizes the Christian belief in the Apocalypse.

Though God, heaven and the angels predictably win in the end, it doesn't prevent local artisans from creating some truly mind-blowing masks and costumes. Running from Thursday through Sunday 40 days after Easter, the festival attracts hundreds of performers, ranging from singers and dancers to theater troops and magicians.

plants and flowers. Almost everything is original, including the six side altars; some objects predate the church itself.

The 12m arch in front of the main altar, for example, bears the date 1733. The altar is made of mahogany and rosewood and is covered nearly from base to top in gold leaf. In a glass case to the left is an almost life-sized wooden statue of Christ that gets carried through the streets of Los Santos in a candlelit procession on Good Friday. The bier used to transport it is at the left as you enter the church.

Carlos Ivan de Leon WORKSHOP
(☎6938-1330; Calle Tomas Herrera; ⏰noon-1pm & 6-10pm) Master mask-maker Carlos Ivan de Leon creates the most elaborate and frightening masks in Panama at his house near Calle Segundo Villareal. He specializes in devil masks for the famous *baile de los diablos sucios* (dance of the dirty devils).

Masks are sold to professional dancers and international collectors. Look for the house with a black front door and a nameplate with 'De Leon' on it. Carlos speaks Spanish only.

Museo de la Nacionalidad MUSEUM
(☎966-8192; www.inac.gob.pa/museos/112-los-santos; Calle José Vallarino; adult/child US$1/0.25; ⏰9:30am-4pm Tue-Sat, 9am-noon Sun) This modest museum, on the north side of Plaza Simón Bolívar, occupies the former house where Panama's Declaration of Independence was signed in 1821. Pre-Columbian ceramics and colonial-era religious art comprise most of the exhibits, though obviously there's a fair amount on Los Santos' role in the independence movement. In an outbuilding in the lovely garden courtyard out the back is a restored *cocina típica* (traditional kitchen).

Festivals & Events

In addition to Los Santos' major celebrations of Fiesta de Corpus Christi, Feria Internacional de Azuero and El Grito de La Villa, notable festivals include Carnaval, celebrated over the four days before Ash Wednesday in February or March, and Semana Santa, the 'Holy Week' before Easter in March or April.

Fiesta de Corpus Christi FESTIVAL
Los Santos' biggest festival, the Fiesta de Corpus Christi plays out over four days some 40 days after Easter in May or June.

El Grito de La Villa FESTIVAL
(Cry of the Village; ⏰10 Nov) Also known as El Primer Grito de la Independencia, the anniversary of the historic *grito* (cry) of independence is celebrated in Los Santos in November. This patriotic occasion is usually overseen by the president of Panama and is highlighted by a parade, musical and dance performances and a healthy amount of drinking in the streets.

Feria Internacional de Azuero FAIR
(http://atp.gob.pa/eventos/feria-internacional-de-azuero; ⏰late Apr) This five-day mainly agricultural fair also features folkloric dancing and competitions among local singers performing regional songs.

Sleeping

Los Santos gets packed to the brim during its many festivals, but with plenty of options in Chitré, just 4km to the north, you need not panic.

La Saloma Hostal GUESTHOUSE $
(☎6782-3438, 923-1399; http://lasalomahostal.wix.com/hostal; Calle Segundo de Villarreal; dm/d US$15/30; 📶) Recently opened on the south side of the main square and opposite the

church, this colorful guesthouse counts a dozen rooms. Five of them are in a building dating from the 1870s and the rest are in a newer addition in the back courtyard. The rooms are pretty bare-bones, with no added comforts, and only one has its own bathroom, but the location is great.

Hotel La Villa HOTEL **$**
(966-8201; www.hotellavillapanama.com; d US$50-55; P❄📶≋) About 1.5km off the Carretera Nacional, this 34-room resort-like property is spread over a large garden and boasts a swimming pool that beckons like a beacon in the dry and dusty Azuero summer. Rooms of varying sizes and shapes have a folkloric theme, incorporating artisan crafts from Los Santos festivals. The attached bar-restaurant serves up Panamanian favorites.

Hotel Restaurante Kevin HOTEL **$**
(966-8276; kevinmoreno@hotmail.com; Vía Dr Belisario Porras; d US$35-45; P❄📶≋) Set back from the Carretera Nacional, this renovated 20-room hotel features a wide range of nearly identical-looking coral-colored rooms in an L-shaped structure behind the main building. The price is right, with private hot-water bathrooms and satellite TV available for just a few extra dollars extra, and guests get to use the owner's swimming pool behind the hotel.

Sol de Luna HOTEL **$$**
(923-0630; www.soldelunahotel.com; Carretera Nacional; s/d incl breakfast US$55/66; P❄📶≋) This bright-yellow hotel on the main road makes good with 22 deluxe motel-style rooms. It offers a beautiful pool, has solar panels and recycles the pool water for plant watering. It's very family-friendly and service is attentive. An on-site restaurant serves fresh juices, burgers and seafood.

JUNTA DE EMBARRE

The Spanish cultural heritage of Azuero lives on in various forms, including some bizarre and ancient traditions. One is *junta de embarre,* which literally translates to 'meeting of mud covering.' Following a local wedding, villagers will gather to build a crude mud hut for the newlyweds. This practice symbolizes the joining together of two households as well as the beginning of a new family. Although this custom is dying out in larger towns and cities, it continues on in some of the more traditional areas of the peninsula.

Information

Banco Nacional de Panamá (cnr Av 10 de Noviembre & Calle Tomas Herrera; 8am-3pm Mon-Fri, 9am-noon Sat) This BNP branch facing the main square has an ATM.

Getting There & Around

Buses between Chitré and Las Tablas stop at Los Santos on the Carretera Nacional; buses running from Chitré to Los Santos stop on Calle José Vallarino, half a block from the highway. Fares to these destinations are between US$0.50 and US$2.

Buses to Panama City (US$10, 3½ hours) depart hourly from Calle José Vallarino at Av 10 de Noviembre, and also from Calle Segundo Villarreal, one-and-a-half blocks northeast of Plaza Simón Bolívar.

Taxis are a quick way to get around Los Santos and to/from Chitré. The fare won't exceed US$2. Taxis can usually be found near the bus stop on the Carretera Nacional and northwest of Plaza Simón Bolívar.

Road to Las Tablas

The Carretera Nacional from La Villa de Los Santos to Las Tablas runs mostly past small farms and cattle ranches, with almost no remaining forest in sight – indeed, the province is the most heavily deforested in the country. However, the drive is still scenic.

About 3km southeast of Los Santos along the Carretera Nacional you'll see a rustic truck stop, **Kiosco El Ciruelo** (dishes from US$2.50; 6am-10pm Fri-Sun), where everything is cooked on a wood-fire grill. Among the offerings is a traditional specialty of Los Santos Province: tamales made with corn, pork and various spices, wrapped in plantain leaves.

About 9km from Los Santos you'll pass a small hut with a huge pile of coconut husks in front of it. This is Casa de las Pipas (House of Coconut Juices), which sells fresh, ice-cold coconut water. Nearby stands sell seasonal fruit, from strawberries to watermelons.

Getting There & Away

Buses from Los Santos to Las Tablas (US$1.90) are frequent throughout the day. A taxi between the two should cost you about US$13.

Guararé

POP 4520

Tiny Guararé, located on the Carretera Nacional between Los Santos and Las Tablas, is just another sleepy Azuero town until late

September, when the town explodes to life with Festival de la Mejorana, Panama's largest folkloric festival.

Founded by Manuel F Zárate in 1949 to stimulate interest and participation in traditional practices, the festival is the best place to see Panama's folklore in all its manifestations. Guararé is also the birthplace of Roberto Durán (1951–), widely regarded as one of the greatest boxers of all time and probably the world's most famous Panamanian.

Sights

Academia de Costumbres y Tradiciones Gabriel Villarreal ARTS CENTER
(6949-6885, 994-4581; www.facebook.com/Academia-De-Costumbres-Y-Tradiciones-141422649291981; Edificio Melo; 3-7pm Mon-Fri, 9am-noon Sat) A local training ground for young festival artists, the Academy of Customs & Traditions Gabriel Villarreal offers classes in dancing, *mejorana* (a kind of small guitar), accordion, violin and *cantaderas* (folk songs). Visitors are always welcome to watch; contact coordinator Pastor Falconett. It is in the Melo building opposite the Euromax minimarket, just west of the church.

Museo Manuel F Zárate MUSEUM
(994-5644; www.inac.gob.pa/museos/114-museo-zarate; Calle 21 de Enero; 8am-4pm Mon-Sat, noon-4pm Sun) FREE Set in the former home of Manuel F Zárate, the folklorist devoted to conserving the traditions of the Azuero region, this museum is a good introduction to Guararé's festivities. It contains *polleras* (traditional costume), masks, *diablito* (little devil) costumes and other folkloric items. Cultural performances happen on Monday and Friday afternoons. The museum is two blocks north of the church and about six short blocks from the main road (turn off at the Delta gas station).

Festivals & Events

Festival de la Mejorana FIESTA
(late Sep) Dance groups from all over the country – and even from other Latin American countries – attend this important annual event in late September. Festivities include a colorful procession in which decorated floats parade through the streets in oxcarts.

Folkloric dances that were once part of other celebrations in other places are today sometimes seen only at this event. For example, this is the only festival in which a dance known as La Pajarita (Paper Bird) is performed. In contrast to the various exuberant devil dances, a calm, religious quality pervades La Pajarita.

Sleeping

★**La Casa del Puerto** APARTMENT $
(6772-2863, 994-4982; www.panamacasadelpuerto.com; Playa El Puerto; apt US$50; P) An excellent beachfront option, La Casa del Puerto is located 10km east of Guararé at Playa El Puerto. It counts five apartments in two houses that sleep up to three people. Host Bonnie, a former Peace Corps volunteer, can arrange local excursions and will pick up guests in Guararé or Chitré, with advance notice.

Residencial La Mejorana HOTEL $
(994-5794;www.facebook.com/Hotel-Residencial-La-Mejorana-Guarar%C3%A9-135376686524135; Via Nacional; d US$44; P) Just off the Carretera Nacional, this nondescript hotel has 23 fairly cramped but clean rooms with good storage space, decent bathrooms and chunky carved wooden furniture. It's the only central place to stay; if there's a festival on, you'll need to book well advance.

Getting There & Away

Guararé is beside the Carretera Nacional, 16km south of Los Santos and 6km north of Las Tablas. You can hop on any bus that travels the highway in the direction of Guararé; from Los Santos the fare is US$1.50 and from Las Tables US$1.20. Call ahead for a local taxi (994-5600, 994-5410); they can be hard to hail during the Festival de la Mejorana.

La Enea

POP 1185

This small village 2km northeast of Guararé produces the finest *polleras* in Panama. Once the daily attire of Spain's lower classes in the 17th and 18th centuries, the *pollera* is today the national costume, distinguished by its stirring beauty and elegance. It is almost entirely handmade, from the attractive embroidery on the blouse and skirt to the delicate filigree ornaments tucked around the gold combs in the hair. The traditional assortment of jewelry worn with a *pollera* can cost upwards of US$10,000.

By convention, the *pollera* consists of two basic pieces: a blouse that rests upon the shoulder tops and a long skirt divided into two fully gathered tiers. Each dress requires no less than 10m of fine white linen or cotton cloth. Elaborate multicolored needlework contrasts with the white background.

Located half way between Guararé and La Enea, **Señora Dilsa Vergara de Saavedra** (☎994-5221, 6529-0445) is a master *pollera* maker and judge known to many queens and for many contests. She's known for giving interesting presentations and offers a nice selection of items to show. If you're interested in purchasing a *pollera,* be advised that every dress is made to order.

Getting There & Away

Buses (US$0.75) link Guararé (2km away) and La Enea about every half-hour. A taxi will cost about US$3.

Las Tablas

POP 8950

Las Tablas is ground zero for the street dancing, booze-soaked celebrations and all-out mayhem associated with the festivals of the Península de Azuero. Home to the country's most famous Carnaval, Las Tablas is the best place in Panama to sample some *seco* (alcoholic drink made from sugarcane) and seriously cut loose.

The capital city of the province of Los Santos, Las Tablas has a fine church and a small museum dedicated to local statesman and three-time president Belisario Porras. The city is also famous for its combined patron saint and *pollera* festival, which is a colorful mix of religious ceremony, medieval merrymaking and a beauty contest.

Sights

Iglesia Santa Librada CHURCH

(Av Belisario Porras) The walls and base of the pulpit in this baroque-style church facing the central plaza are original, as are the painted faces of cherubs on the ornate gold-leaf altar. Consecrated in 1789, the church suffered through an earthquake in 1802 and during a fire in 1958. Cedar wood was used in the construction of the altar, renovated in 2001.

Museo Belisario Porras MUSEUM

(☎994-6326; Av Belisario Porras; adult/child US$0.75/0.25; ⊙8am-4pm Tue-Sat, to noon Sun) South of the main square is the former home of three-time president Belisario Porras, during whose administration the Panama Canal opened. The museum contains artifacts from Porras' life and serves as a monument to the achievements of this widely revered man.

Porras was president for all but two years during the period from 1912 to 1924. He is credited with establishing Panama's network of public hospitals, creating a national registry for land titles and constructing scores of bridges and aqueducts.

Festivals & Events

★**Carnaval** FESTIVAL

Held over the four days preceding Ash Wednesday, Panama's best Carnaval celebration sees floats and musicians parading parallel streets at dusk, and fireworks at night. The queens appear on Saturday night and their coronation is held on Sunday. Monday is masquerade day and on Tuesday townswomen don *polleras.*

The town is divided into two competing groups: *calle arriba* (high street) and *calle abajo* (low street). Each *calle* has its own queen, floats and songs; each day members parade in street clothes and sing songs that poke fun at the rival group. Merrymakers toss tinted water, blue dye and shaving cream at the opposing side. No one is spared, so dress accordingly.

Fiesta de la Pollera FESTIVAL

(⊙22 Jul) This festival features a parade of young women modeling the national costume, while being judged on their grace and on the artisanship, design and authenticity of their costumes.

Fiestas Patronales de Santa Librada FESTIVAL

(⊙Jul) Held for four days from July 19 and incorporating the Fiesta de la Pollera. Church services are accompanied by street celebrations that recall a medieval fair, with gambling, dancing, singing, and excessive eating and drinking.

Sleeping

Hotel Piamonte HOTEL $

(☎923-1603; hotelpiamonte@hotmail.com; Av Belisario Porras; d US$33-57, annex d US$27-50; P ❄ ≋) A clean and well-kept place with frilly bedspreads, friendly Piamonte has 44 rooms; make sure to ask for one with a window. There's a downstairs restaurant in the main building; the rooms in the annex across the street are not as nice, and thus cheaper.

Hotel Don Jesús HOTEL $$

(☎6433-9605, 994-6593; www.hoteldonjesus.com; Calle Ramón Mora; d US$60-100; P ❄ @ ≋) This 21-room hotel in a converted family

Las Tablas

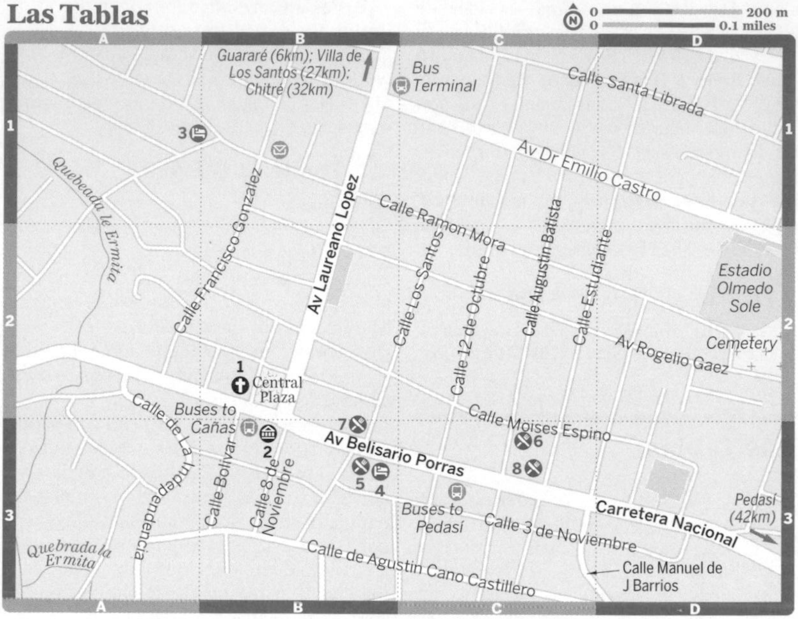

Las Tablas

Sights

1 Iglesia Santa Librada B2
2 Museo Belisario Porras B3

Sleeping

3 Hotel Don Jesús A1
4 Hotel Piamonte B3

Eating

5 Boquitas Caseras B3
6 El Caserón C3
7 Los Portales B3
8 Restaurante Aida C3

home northwest of the main square is the best central place to stay in Las Tablas. The large communal lounge-balcony with book exchange is a plus, as is the large swimming pool.

Hotel La Luna GUESTHOUSE **$$**
(☎6525-9410; www.facebook.com/pages/Hotel-La-Luna/113825222105569; Playa El Uverito; d/tr/q US$75/85/95; P ❄ 📶 🏊) Located about 10km east of Las Tablas on the beach, this modern house has four glass-front rooms, modern art and a kidney-shaped pool. It is run by the charming Lucas from Milan, who can help organize fishing tours, horseback riding and other activities. A taxi from the center of Las Tablas costs US$7.

Eating

El Caserón INTERNATIONAL **$**
(☎994-6066; www.facebook.com/pages/Restaurante-El-Caseron-Las-Tablas/1057814694236037; Calle Moisés Espino; mains US$6-15; ⏲7am-11pm) This pink hacienda-like restaurant has a large covered terrace that is a delight on a warm evening. The emphasis here is on seafood and grills, but the pizzas (from US$4.25 to US$5.50) are also recommended. It's one of the more comfortable places for a sit-down meal in Las Tablas.

Restaurante Aida PANAMANIAN **$**
(Av Belisario Porras; dishes from US$2; ⏲24hr) This very basic *fonda* serves *comida típica* (traditional Panamanian dishes) that won't win any culinary awards; but you can't beat the price or the generous opening hours.

Los Portales PANAMANIAN **$**
(☎994-7908; Paseo Carlos López; mains US$5-7; ⏲6am-3pm) Housed in a handsome colonial building, this low-key spot serves grilled meats and basic Panamanian dishes. Stop by in the morning for a tasty farm-style breakfast to start your day the right way before hitting the road.

Boquitas Caseras
CAFE $

(☑ 923-2377; Av Belisario Porras; mains US$2-4) This snack shop is a perfect hunger fix if you have a few minutes between buses: think marinated meatballs, potato salad and empanadas (turnovers stuffed with meat, cheese or veggie mixes) served in a clean little cafe.

❶ Information

Banco Nacional de Panamá (☑ 994-7262; Av Laureano Lopez; ⊙ 8am-3pm Mon-Fri, 9am-noon Sat) Near Calle 2.

Ministerio de Ambiente (☑ 994-7313; Carretera Nacional; 9am-4pm Mon-Fri) Some 2km south of the center in Santo Domingo en route to Pedasí.

Post Office (Calle 2; ⊙ 7am-5pm Mon-Fri, to 3pm Sat) The post office is northwest of the center.

❶ Getting There & Away

The Carretera Nacional becomes Av Laureano Lopez at the northern edge of town and re-emerges as the road to Santo Domingo on the southeastern side of town. From Las Tablas' bus terminal (cnr Avs Laureano Lopez & Dr Emilio Castro) buses run hourly to Santo Domingo (US$0.35, 10 minutes), Cañas (US$3, 1½ hours), Chitré (US$1.50, 35 minutes), Tonosí (US$3.50, 1½ hours) and Pedasí (US$2.40, one hour). Buses to Cañas (Av Belisario Porras & Calle Bolívar) and Pedasí (Av Belisario Porras) also stop further south along Av Belisario Porras.

There are frequent departures to Panama City (US$9.70, 4½ hours), with additional buses running during festivals.

Pedasí

POP 2410

Unpretentious and picturesque, Pedasí's streets are lined with tiled colonials and leafy spaces. For years this sleepy retreat came to life only at festival times. But outsiders are discovering the big appeal of small-town life and wilderness beaches.

The hometown of former president Mireya Moscoso, Panama's first female chief executive, Pedasí has become the focus of an intensive push to develop the southwestern coastline. It serves as the gateway to the Azuero coastline, and is a convenient base for exploring Refugios de Vida Silvestre Isla Iguana and Isla Cañas.

The Carretera Nacional passes the western part of Pedasí, while the beaches start just a few kilometers to the east. None of the streets in Pedasí are marked with street signs.

🏃 Activities

Snorkeling and diving around nearby islands, which are surrounded by large coral reefs, are major attractions. Sportfishers can land wahoo, tuna, mahimahi, amberjack and Pacific mackerel. For guided trips (from about US$200 for two passengers), ask at Pedasí Sports Club or Pedasí Tours.

Pedasí Tours
ADVENTURE SPORTS

(☑ 995-2466; www.pedasitours.com; Av Central; ⊙ 9am-6pm Mon-Sat) In the dead center of Pedasí, this agency offers everything from Isla Iguana tours and turtle-watching to sportfishing and horseback riding.

Pedasí Sports Club
ADVENTURE SPORTS

(☑ 6749-4308, 995-2894; www.pedasisportsclub. com; Av Central s/n; ⊙ 9am-6pm Mon-Sat) This PADI-certified outfit offers two-tank dives (from US$95) to Isla Frailes and Isla Iguana. Snorkelers (US$75) can join dive trips to Iguana. It also offers sportfishing (US$95), turtle-watching (US$75) and horseback riding (US$75).

🎊 Festivals & Events

Desfile de Carretas
FIESTA

(Wagon Parade; ⊙ Oct) This rather unusual festival in late October sees bullock carts and young women dressed in *polleras* parading up and down Av Central. Lots of merry-making, with the highlight the inevitable coronation of Señorita Pedasí.

**Fiestas Patronales
de Santa Catalina**
FERIA

(⊙ late Nov) The feast day of St Catherine, patron of Pedasí, is celebrated in late November.

🛏 Sleeping

Doña María B&B
B&B $

(☑ 995-2916; www.donamariabnb.com; Av Central s/n; d/tr incl breakfast US$50/65; 🅿 ❄ 🛜) Ideal for couples, this caring family-run lodging has six nice rooms above a family home, featuring tiles, firm queen-sized beds with plush quilted covers and cable TV. The patio has soft sofas that look out onto the main street and a stack of magazines to peruse. An annex features three additional rooms in back, one of which has disabled access.

Dim's Hostal
GUESTHOUSE $

(☑ 6274-4156, 995-2303; reservacionesdimshostal @gmail.com; Av Central s/n; s/d incl breakfast US$33/49; 🅿 ❄ 🛜) Dim's has a family atmosphere and a coveted backyard patio, complete with breakfast tables, hammocks and a mango tree. The nine rooms vary in quality – some are quite cramped and have dull tiled floors – but the owners are delightful and service-oriented. A highlight is the huge breakfast spread served on the patio, where your friendly host cooks up eggs and *tortillas de maíz* made to order.

★Casa de Campo B&B $$
(995-2733, 6780-5280; www.casacampopedasi.com; Av Central s/n; d incl breakfast US$99;) Far and away the nicest place to stay in Pedasí, this hospitable and quite chic B&B screams getaway. The seven rooms are named and themed; our favorite is Marina, which has a king-sized bed and measures a full 380 sq meters. The main street location is deceptive: out back there's a pool and lovely landscaped grounds with thatched *ranchos* and hammocks.

Guests share a family table for big breakfasts with three daily choices, including Panamanian *tortillas de maíz* and eggs, fruit, yogurt, cereal, and fresh bread. Three-course meals (US$20) are available if prebooked by 1pm. Longtime locals, hosts Oividio and Cobi are truly gracious and helpful.

★La Rosa de los Vientos B&B $$
(6530-4939, 6778-0627; www.bedandbreakfastpedasi.com; Via Playa del Toro; d/tr/q incl breakfast US$60/75/85; P) With the feel of a rural hacienda, this lovely red-tile Spanish colonial just up from the beach has three smart rooms with colorful weavings, antique tiles and ocean views. It's designed to be eco-friendly, so there is no air-con, but fans do the trick. Multilingual owners Isabelle and Robert offer warm hospitality.

The 'Rose of the Winds' is 1.5km from town on the road to Playa del Toro (taxis cost US$2.50). The beach is a few minutes away on foot.

Hostal Plaza Pedasí HOTEL $$
(6363-3899, 995-2509; www.plazapedsi.com; s/d US$50/65; P) What was until recently Pedasí's first (and only) hostel has metamorphosed into a charming hotel with eight cool white rooms decorated with wall murals of trees and flowers. It looks out onto the central plaza – thus the name – and behind is a large garden complete with a covered bar.

Pedasito Hotel BOUTIQUE HOTEL $$
(995-2745; http://pedasitohotel.com; Calle Agustín Mocoso No 2; d incl breakfast US$55-90;) Billed both as a boutique hotel and a B&B, this small hotel has a fresh, modern look. A half-dozen rooms feature polished concrete floors, king-sized beds and stenciled walls. Those with pool access (which, mind you, is pea-sized) have private terraces accessed by sliding glass doors. The B&B rooms are smaller but tree murals add a bit of drama. The on-site restaurant has patio seating and worthwhile international fare including seafood.

Casita Margarita B&B $$
(6949-2898, 995-2898; www.pedasihotel.com; Av Central s/n; d incl breakfast US$85-99; P) Stylish and sweet, the Casita Margarita is a reliable choice. Its half-dozen rooms are furnished with king-sized beds, flat-screen TVs, folk art and cool oversized tiles. Local information on offer is quite good, as are the many tours and activities. The hotel offers an honor-system bar.

AZUERO EARTH PROJECT

The most deforested area of Panama, the Península de Azuero has seen generations of cattle ranching degrade what was once tropical dry forest. Gone are the scarlet macaws and spider monkeys. Yet habitat destruction and advancing soil erosion isn't only detrimental to wildlife, it also affects ranchers. Enter the Azuero Earth Project (p128), a nonprofit working to right these wrongs with the help of both volunteers and an elite team of experts collaborating from various fields.

Creating local economic benefits is key to sustainability. Current studies show that locals can win with a greener approach – but it will take time. Ranchers who set aside 10% of their land can double their income by growing hardwoods. The trick is convincing subsistence farmers to wait years for a pay-off when they are used to living day to day.

Currently, the center works closely with the community, promoting organiculture, recycling and conservation education, and working with local elementary schools. Community outreach works with land owners and developers, government agencies and NGOs to make progress toward sustainable solutions.

Casa Loma HOTEL $$
(☎6749-4308, 995-2894; www.casalomapedasi.com; Av Central; s/d/tr/apt incl breakfast US$55/66/72/96; P ❄ @ ☜ ≋) Sister hotel to the Pedasí Sports Club B&B and sharing the same property, pool and restaurant, the Casa Loma counts 10 large and immaculate rooms in a hacienda-like building looking onto a grassy courtyard. There's usually room here when the B&B is full.

Hostal Villa Libera B&B $$
(☎6844-9216, 6791-2387; www.villaliberapedasi.com; d/tr incl breakfast US$60/80; P ❄ ☜) Run by an energetic Italian couple, this pleasant little B&B a short walk from the beach has three simple rooms with marble floors and high ceilings; one room has a bath adapted for guests with disabilities. There's also a simple candlelit restaurant where thin wood-fired pizzas, seafood and steaks cooked on volcanic stones are served. Villa Libera is 600m down a dirt road that branches to the left off the road to Playa Toro.

Pedasí Sports Club B&B $$
(☎6749-4308, 995-2894; www.pedasisportsclub.biz; Av Central s/n; s/d/tr incl breakfast US$50/65/83; P ❄ @ ☜ ≋) Usually booked up for diving packages, the 11 motel-style rooms may lack a certain character but they are impeccably clean and cool, with air-con, wi-fi, satellite TV and hot-water showers. There's a pool that's perfect for dips; equipment checks are offered; and there's a popular restaurant, too.

Eating

Fonda Mama Fefa PANAMANIAN $
(Calle Los Estudiantes s/n; set meals US$2.50-3; ⏲5am-2pm Mon-Sat) Matriarch of creole cooking, Mama Fefa usually runs out of lunch by noon (though you can linger longer). Cheap and cheerful, these *comidas típicas* include meat or fish, rice, salad and a drink. Devotees share the space at a few outdoor tables. Take the side street opposite the landmark supermarket for two blocks. It's on the right.

Smiley's Restaurant NORTH AMERICAN $
(☎995-2863, 6510-9652; www.facebook.com/smileys.restaurante; Av Central s/n; mains US$4-12; ⏲noon-9:30pm Tue-Sun) Catering largely to expats, this friendly bar-restaurant serves up grilled fish, pasta dishes such as lasagna, and deli sandwiches including minced BBQ pork with coleslaw. There's also good live music on Tuesday and Friday nights, sports matches on the tube, and an extensive drinks menu to match. Check the Facebook page for daily specials.

Bakery CAFE $
(☎995-2878; www.thebakerypedasi.com; Av Central s/n; mains US$4-12; ⏲7am-9pm; ✎) Known for exquisite breakfasts with homemade wheat or sourdough breads and organic coffee, this Israeli-run Pedasí institution does a brisk business. In addition to breakfasts, you can order sandwiches, with vegetarian options, and pizza too. The shady porch overlooks the main street.

Pasta e Vino ITALIAN $
(☎6695-2689; mains US$7-11; ⏲6-10pm Wed-Sun) This unadorned Italian-owned restaurant offers pastas, salads and a decent wine list. Food is simple but authentic, such as the pesto with black olives and fresh cheese. It's all about service, expertly executed by hosts Danilo and Elena. Look for a yellow house three blocks past the main plaza on the road to Playa El Toro.

Isla Iguana SEAFOOD $
(☎6620-4073, 995-2867; Av Central s/n; mains US$5-12; ⏲11am-10pm Thu-Tue) For filling seafood that won't break the bank, try this roadside restaurant that somehow manages the atmosphere of a friendly truck stop. Try the *ceviche* (citrus-cured seafood; a specialty) and the sea bass. It's at the southern end of town next to the Eddy gas station.

Dulcería Yely BAKERY $
(☎995-2205; Calle Ofelia Reluz; cakes US$0.50-3; ⏲8am-9pm) This cake shop selling delectable sweets on a side street off Av Central is an institution. The sandwiches are tasty (and cheap) too. While you're here, grab a *chicheme* (a concoction of milk, sweet corn, cinnamon and vanilla).

Pizzeria Tiesto PIZZA $
(☎995-2812; Calle Las Tablas; mains US$2-10; ⏲2-10pm Wed-Mon) With brick-oven pizzas topped with local cheese and tasty US$2 chicken tacos, this plaza-front Panamanian cafe on the southeast corner of the main square proves a magnet for locals and backpackers alike. Sweets include oatmeal cookies and pineapple cake.

Super Centro El Pueblo SUPERMARKET $
(Av Central s/n; ⏲7am-9pm) The town's principal supermarket sits on the corner of Av Central and Calle Los Estudiantes.

★Bienvenidush MIDDLE EASTERN **$$**
(☎6426-3105; www.bienvenidush.com; Calle Agustín Mocoso s/n; mains US$8-12; ⊙11am-4pm & 7-11pm Wed-Mon; ✎) Love, love, love this place serving inventive dishes with Middle Eastern (especially Israeli) accents and lots of vegetarian choices. There are tapas (US$3) and sandwiches (US$6 to US$8) if you're just peckish. You'll find hand-crafted souvenirs for sale, and seating is at the few tables and bar in the tiny front restaurant-cafe or in the back patio. Always a warm welcome.

For tapas try the spicy yogurt dip, the *hamutzim* (pickled vegetables) and the fish carpaccio. 'Big bites' include a great hummus plate.

★Mare Bonita FUSION **$$**
(☎6200-0124; www.facebook.com/pages/Restaurante-Mare-Bonita/372368832954808; Calle Las Tablas; mains US$10-15; ⊙5-10pm) Considered by many to be the best restaurant in Pedasí, it's certainly the most inventive. Chilean chef Luis Morales keeps the menu in a state of flux, offering teriyaki chicken and Thai-style pork one week, and gourmet hamburgers and fired fish *ceviche* the next. The long, narrow dining room done up in sky-blue has an Asian feel to it.

ℹ Information

ATP (☎995-2339; azuero@atp.gob.pa; ⊙8am-4pm Mon-Sat) Helpful but slow, the ATP office lies one block past the main road in the north of town. It has a list of boat contacts for Isla Cañas.

Azuero Earth Project (www.azueroearthproject.org; ⊙8am-5pm Mon-Fri) A volunteer-friendly NGO focuses on behind-the-scenes work in conservation and community education. Visitors can check out the research center library, with naturalist guides and maps for sale. An outdoor information board features a community events calendar. It's on a side street behind the gas station by the town entrance.

Banco Nacional de Panama (☎995-2257; Av Central s/n; ⊙8am-3pm Mon-Fri, 9am-noon Sat) Has an ATM (one of two in town on Av Central) near the entrance to town.

ℹ Getting There & Away

AIR

Air Panama flies from Panama City's domestic Aeropuerto Albrook to Pedasí's Aeropuerto Justiniano Montenegro on Wednesday, Friday and Sunday at 3pm, returning an hour later. The flight takes about 50 minutes. Fares cost from US$70 to US$100 each way. Aeropuerto Justiniano Montenegro is a few kilometers northeast of of Pedasí.

BUS

Buses to Las Tablas leave every hour between 6am and 4pm (US$2.40, one hour) from next to the El Pueblo supermarket. Buses to Playa Venao (US$2, 30 minutes) leave at 7am, noon and 2pm. Buses to Cañas (US$2.40, 45 minutes) depart at 7am and noon.

TAXI

The coastline is easily accessed by private vehicle or taxi (☎6847-7535). The taxi stand sits on Av Central. Standard one-way fares: Playa El Toro US$3.50, Playa La Garita US$5, Playa Los Destiladeros US$7 and Playa Venao US$30.

Around Pedasí

Refugio de Vida Silvestre Isla Iguana

The 55-hectare Refugio de Vida Silvestre Isla Iguana is centered on a deserted island ringed by coral fields. The water is shallow enough for snorkeling and, as elsewhere in the Pacific, the reef fish here are enormous.

Humpback whales also inhabit the waters around Isla Iguana from June to November. These large sea mammals, measuring 15m to 20m long, mate and bear their young here and then teach them to dive. The humpbacks are the famous 'singing whales'; occasionally you can hear their underwater sounds when diving here.

Although the island is supposed to be maintained by the Ministerio de Ambiente, Panama's environmental agency formerly called ANAM, the main beach is often strewn with litter that is washed in with the tide. Also, the US Navy used the island for target practice during WWII and unexploded ordnance is occasionally discovered here. Needless to say, it's unwise to stray off the beaten paths.

ℹ Getting There & Away

Isla Iguana can be reached by boat (US$70) from Playa El Arenal, a beach 3km northeast of the Terpel gas station in Pedasí; the ATP office in Pedasí can help you arrange transport.

Playas El Toro & La Garita

The two closest beaches to Pedasí serve as a popular day trip for local residents, especially since the ocean here is usually safe for swimming. However, the waves can pick up if there's a strong surge coming in. At Playa El Toro you can actually drive onto the beach if you have a vehicle, but Playa La Garita is flanked by a rocky slope, and a hike of about 100m through light scrub and dirt (which turns to mud if there's been any recent rain) is required to reach the beach. Despite their close proximity to Pedasí, both beaches are quite isolated and private. Neither offers much snorkeling – the water is simply too murky.

Eating

There's an open-air restaurant serving seafood and drinks at Playa El Toro and a beach club in a gated community at Playa La Garita.

Getting There & Away

You can reach these beaches by taxi (US$5). Driving from town, turn east off the Carretera Nacional onto Calle Agustín Mocoso and drive about 250m to the Cantina Hermanos Cedeño bar. Then take the road just past the bar for 1km until the road forks. El Toro is 1.5km to the left and La Garita the same distance to the right.

Azuero Coastline

Gorgeous and slightly remote, the rolling green coast of southeast Azuero offers excellent swimming and surfing possibilities as well as some top accommodations. You can surf here year-round but conditions are best between March and November.

Playa Los Destiladeros

About 10km southwest of Pedasí this isolated and protected beach offers excellent surfing, lovely views across the ocean and two wonderful upmarket places to stay.

Sleeping

★ **Posada Los Destiladeros** RESORT **$$**
(☎ 6424-6780; www.panamabambu.net; d incl breakfast US$80-130, beachfront cabins from US$230, ste US$350; P ❄ 📶 🏊) One of the most attractive resorts on the Azuero coast, this 'inn' offers 17 rooms of varying types with lovely views of the pounding surf. Accommodations range from modern rooms to an Africa-inspired thatched hut. The French owner has crafted each space to showcase his own taste and travels; wicker canopy beds sit alongside Polynesian carvings and modern baths.

The themed cabins – Cambodia, Vietnam etc – are made almost entirely of hand-hewn wood, including the baths. A boardwalk links lodgings and public areas across the 2.5-hectare property. The posada's restaurant (mains from US$6 to US$18) is a popular destination also for nonguests. Reserve ahead for a candlelit three-course dinner featuring the catch of the day. There is a good wine list.

Villa Camilla RESORT **$$$**
(☎ 994-3100, 995-9595; www.villacamillapanama.com; d US$230-450, 4-person ocean lofts US$250; P ❄ 📶 🏊) Villa Camilla is a gorgeous adobe compound with sleek lines and chic accents. Privacy is primary – the villa has hosted the likes of Michael Jordan and Shakira. Don't expect TVs; the concept is unplugged. The eight rooms are ample, lit low and coo with Asian-inspired decor. A long footpath of river stones leads though manicured grounds to the beach.

THE TUNA COAST

Home to a large population of yellow-fin tuna, the Azuero coastline serves as a benchmark indicator for the health of global stocks.

Among the most sought-after fish in the world, yellow-fin tuna has spawned a billion-dollar industry. Found in subtropical and tropical waters, tuna reach lengths of more than 2m and can weigh upwards of 200kg. Although typically processed and canned, tuna is increasingly flash frozen and sold in fillets for sushi. Left raw, tuna is blood-red in color, with a smooth texture and a rich buttery taste.

Some 30km southwest of Pedasí, **Laboratorio Achotines** (☎ 995-8166; www.iattc.org; donations requested) tracks the movement and behavior of these fish, tagging them to study migration patterns. This tuna lab is also the only place in the world where tuna are spawned in captivity to be used for study. Affiliated with the Inter-American Tropical Tuna Commission, a global regulatory consortium on tuna fishing, the lab routinely sets quotas for catches along the Pacific coast of the Americas.

Visitors can tour Laboratorio Achotines by appointment and watch an interesting educational video. Another highlight is to show up for the feeding of their prize-sized tunas.

Chef-made meals are available for an extra charge. The property was for sale at the time of writing; check details on the website before making plans.

Getting There & Away

If driving, follow the road from Pedasí south from the Eddy gas station to the village of El Limón for 3km. The road bearing left leads 7km to Playa Los Destiladeros. A taxi will cost about US$10.

La Playita

Popular among Panamanian day-trippers, the **beach** (adult/child US$5/2) at La Playita can get pretty crowded at weekends. It's not the prettiest spot on the coast but the nearby resort and its facilities are an added draw.

Sleeping & Eating

Resort La Playita RESORT **$$**
(996-6727, 6615-3898; www.playitaresort.com; d/q US$120/150 ; P ❄) More rustic retreat than resort, the shady and somewhat dated cabins at Resort La Playita sit surrounded by an informal zoo of guacamayas, macaws, emus and howler monkeys. It also has eight upgraded rooms with air-con and cold-water showers. The best are rooms 6 to 9, which have oversized furnishings made from drift-

SURFING THE AZUERO COAST

Though untapped by the international crowd, the Azuero coast boasts some impressive surf. Panamanians mostly hit the coastline near Pedasí, but there is no shortage of wicked spots (just a shortage of transportation to them).

Playa El Lagarto At Pedasí. Beach bottom. Breaks at all tides. Good rights and lefts. Closes out when the surf is too big. Popular with boogie boarders.

Playa El Toro Near Pedasí. Rock-bottom point break with lefts and rights. Gets big with a strong swell. Best surfed at medium tide, when there's a swell of 1.8m or more.

Playa Los Destiladeros Near Pedasí. Right point over rock bottom, left point over rock bottom, and beach break with pebble bottom. Best at high tide.

Playa Ciruelo Before Venao. Rock-bottom point break that's rarely surfed. Can get really good left tubes when there is a strong swell and no wind.

Playa Venao Sand-bottom beach break popular with local surfers. This spot catches just about any swell. Best surfed at medium to high tide.

Playa Madroño A 30-minute walk from Playa Venao. Surf can get really good, with hollow tubes at low tide. It's necessary to arrive early in the day before the wind picks up.

Playa Guánico South of Tonosí. Two rock-bottom point breaks with rights and lefts. One beach break with rights and lefts.

Playa Raya A secret spot just past Playa Madroño. Waves 4m to 5m on big swells with serious tubes. Many big sharks here as well.

Playa Cambutal Southwest of Tonosí. Perfect beach breaks with rights and lefts. Catches just about every swell. Best at medium to high tide.

Playa Negra West of Playa Cambutal, around the first point. Point break over rocks. Best during medium to high tide.

411 (Quartro Once) East of Playa Cambutal. Locally famous point break with a long right over a rock ledge. Best during medium to high tide.

Dinosaurios Next to 411, east of Playa Cambutal. Rock-bottom break with rights and lefts at medium to high tide. Can get very big with strong swells.

Horcones Beach Break Down the beach west from Dinosaurios. Sand-bottom beach break with rights and lefts. Good most tides.

Dos Rocas Near Horcones Beach Break. Rock-bottom point break beside two jutting boulders. Can get good rights at medium tide.

Corto Circuito At road's end toward Cerro Hoya, Azuero's southwest corner. Rock-bottom point break with powerful peak. Breaks over a rock ledge and throws a huge tube, then peels for about 100m with a great wall.

wood, colorful mosaics, cozy throws and private balconies. The on-site restaurant (mains from US$8 to US$12) serves typical Panamanian fare and seafood.

Getting There & Away

La Playita is about 13km southwest of Pedasí and just east of Playa Venao, about 1.5km down an unsealed road. Buses from Pedasí pass the entrance at 7am, and return to Pedasí at around 3:30pm.

Playa Ciruelo

A pretty half-moon bay, Playa Ciruelo retains its fishing-village atmosphere despite the recent spate of building.

Activities

Agusto López FISHING
(☎6671-9421; pimplisurf@yahoo.com) Fishing tours are easy to book, but keep in mind that you will want a covered boat (for shade) with a decent motor. Captain Agusto López – aka 'Pimply' – is recommended; he owns a 7.5m center-console SeaCraft and is one of the best local fishing tour guides.

Sleeping

Hostal Casa Estrella INN $$
(☎6889-3044, 6471-3090; www.sandpiperdev.com/casadeestrella; d US$77; P ❄ ☎) The excellent value Casa Estrella has four pristine blue rooms with driftwood beds and sea views. Showers have hot water. The house is inviting and immaculate, with hammocks on a shady deck, great views and a comfortable family living area. Fishing trips are available, and the beach is popular with surfers.

Getting There & Away

The bus heading from the village of Cañas to Las Tablas passes by at around 7:30am and stops on its way back to Cañas at 4pm. A taxi from Pedasí costs US$15.

Playa Venao

POP 2500

A long, protected beach, Playa Venao – officially Venado but mispronounced and misspelled as 'Venao' – recently transformed from a wild beach to a 'go to' destination. Surfers lay the first claim to its waters; waves are consistent and break in both directions. Depressingly, this gorgeous stretch of blackish volcanic sand now looks like a building site. Venao will hopefully look lovely again when the construction's finished.

Activities

Cañas Jungle Adventure ADVENTURE SPORTS
(☎6753-4765, 6305-3048; www.zippanama.com; zip line/swing/hiking US$60/20/10, packages US$75; ⏲8am-4pm) In Cañas, 12km west of Venao, this place has eight cable zip lines spanning some 3km above the jungle, as well as two rappels, a scary suspension bridge and a supercool Tarzan swing. Hiking trails lead to waterfalls and natural pools.

Surf Dojo SURFING
(☎848-3070; www.surfdojo.com) On the main road just opposite the landmark Eco Venao lodge, Surf Dojo is a full-scale training facility dedicated to the sport of surfing. It rents boards and other surfing equipment as well as kayaks (US$25 to US$35 per day).

Extreme Surf Shop SURFING
(El Sitio Hotel; ⏲8:30am-7pm) This shop at El Sitio hotel rents surfboards for US$15/25 for a half-/full day. Lessons cost US$40. Rental bikes cost US$10 per day.

Sleeping

★**Eco Venao** LODGE $
(☎832-0530; www.ecovenao.com; campsites per person US$6, dm/d without bathroom US$11/30, 2-person cabins US$40, 6-person houses US$200; P ❄ ☎) On the north side of the main road, North American–owned Eco Venao offers a cool mountain ambience. Perfect for surfers and adventurers, its 20 excellent options range from low to high end, offering something for everyone. The lush 57-hectare property means mini-adventures are close at hand, from howler monkey visits and a playground to a short waterfall hike.

The Surfers Hostel has a rustic (though comfy) dormitory with eight beds, mosquito nets and fans. Privates range from the thatched Cabañas Las Escobas huts on stilts with composting toilets, to air-conditioned colonial-style guesthouses with colorful wovens and wood accents, such as La Casa Mango and the adorable La Casona high up on the hill. Guests can rent horses (US$20) and do yoga. 'Eco' means that trash separation and recycling are practiced, as well as reforestation. It maintains a small footprint, with minimal roads and footpaths leading to the beach.

La Choza HOSTEL $
(☎832-1010; www.facebook.com/La-Choza-de-Playa-Venao-126154604088722; campsites per person US$7, dm US$11-13, d with air-con US$35-45,

without air-con US$25-35; ❄📶) A short hop to the waves, this 17-room option is perfect for shoestringers. Somewhat cramped dorms of up to six beds have polished concrete floors, fans and comfortable mattresses. Some private rooms feature bunks and all rooms have shared bathrooms. There's a communal kitchen and a nearby minimarket open from 9:30am to 10pm for supplies. Reserve through sister property El Sitio Hotel.

★El Sitio Hotel HOTEL **$$**
(☎6246-3648, 832-1010; www.elsitiohotel.com; d US$99-109, ste US$129-195; P❄📶🏊) El Sitio's best feature is its location right on Playa Venao; 'You Are Where You Surf' is its motto. But even if you don't surf, the 15 splendid rooms at this hotel built from recycled shipping containers – how cool is that? – will delight. Choose one of four suites with private balconies and expansive ocean views.

El Sitio boasts what is Veano's best restaurant as well as a surf shop that sells and rents equipment. Massage is available, as are activities such as jungle tours and seasonal whale-watching (from US$35 per person). The welcome here is warm; service is very attentive and professional.

Selina Hostel Playa Venao HOSTEL **$$**
(☎202-5919; www.selinahostels.com; campsites per person US$18, dm US$14-20, d with/without bathroom from US$70/45, d deluxe US$99-119; P📶🏊) This beachside branch of a hostel chain consists of 16 colorful thatched bungalows in rows running down to a pool and the beach. The 38 rooms come in every possible shape and size, from a mixed dorm with 12 beds to a private double with bathroom and balcony.

Our favorite is deluxe double room 204. The hostel's nerve center is the beachside bar and its pool tables, where surfers will regale you with tales of their exploits; escape to the recycled van with the thatched roof opposite. Selina rents boards for US$10/75 per day/week and organizes turtle-watching tours to Isla Cañas (US$90 per person).

Villa Marina Lodge HOTEL **$$$**
(☎832-5044; www.villamarinalodge.com; d incl breakfast US$165-195; P❄📶🏊) At the eastern quieter end of Playa Venao, on the way to La Playita, Villa Marina Lodge is a stunner. Set amid tranquil gardens, this resort exudes charm, from the spurting fountain to the wide, shady veranda. The nine guest rooms are bright and capture ocean breezes, while the larger master bedroom has French doors opening onto a beachfront terrace.

Guests can spend their days swimming in the stone-bottomed pool, lounging around on hammocks, horseback riding on the beach, snorkeling and surfing in the sea, or off on boating and fishing excursions.

Eating

★Coleos Cafe CAFE **$**
(☎6289-2820; www.facebook.com/Coleos-cafe-855109761222106; mains US$8; ⏲9am-10pm) This wonderful little place just up from the beach serves homemade pasta dishes, delicious hummus plates, sandwiches (US$5 to US$7) and a wide range of delectable breads, brownies and cookies. Enjoy breakfast (US$5 to US$9) on the tiny terrace.

Los Sombreros INTERNATIONAL **$**
(☎6634-4550; http://ecovenao.com/restaurant; Eco Venao; mains US$8.50-11; ⏲7am-9pm) The relaxed, thatched-roof loft restaurant at Eco Venao resort is open to the public and caters to beach-goers with an appetite. While surfers usually down the daily special (US$6), you'll find Panamanian specialties on offer as well as huge beef and fish burgers (US$9). There's live music on Saturday nights.

★El Sitio Restaurant INTERNATIONAL **$$$**
(☎832-1010; mains US$9-19; ⏲7:30am-9:30pm) This is far and away the best bet for sunset dining or drinks on Playa Venao. Open-air El Sitio offers sesame-crusted tuna and a host of Asian-inspired dishes such as pad Thai noodles with octopus, Thai crêpes and chicken curry. A pastry chef prepares lovely tropical crème brûlée and coconut macaroons.

Getting There & Away

The Playa Venao turnoff is 33km southwest of Pedasí (2km past the turn for Resort La Playita). The Cañas–Pedasí bus (US$2) passes by between 7am and 9am and makes the round-trip journey between noon and 12:30pm and 2pm and 2:30pm. Confirm exact times with your hotel. You can also take a taxi from Pedasí (from US$18).

Playas Cambutal & Guánico

Playas Cambutal and Guánico, 26km southwest and 22km southeast of Tonosí respectively, are two excellent surf beaches along the Azuero coast.

Tours

Tortuagro TOUR
(☎6264-1936; www.facebook.com/Tortuagro-778435305562796; Cambutal) This community

conservation organization patrols Playa Cambutal with volunteers during turtle season (in July and early September) and also runs tours.

🛏 Sleeping

Hotel Playa Cambutal BOUTIQUE HOTEL $$$
(☑832-0948; www.hotelplayacambutal.net; Playa Cambutal; d incl breakfast US$110-135; ❋ 🛜 ⓧ) This 10-room hotel offers the most comfortable lodgings in the area and takes an ecofriendly approach. It also features a good restaurant and can arrange fishing trips (half-/full day US$550/750), nature walks (US$35), turtle-watching (US$10), horseback riding (US$15 for two hours) and kayaking.

ℹ Getting There & Away

Both Playa Cambutal and Playa Guánico are reachable by dirt road, but access is difficult. First take the Cañas bus from Las Tablas at 7am or 2pm (US$4, 1¼ hours). From Cañas, a bus goes to Tonosí (US$1.50, 30 minutes) and from Tonosí to Playa Cambutal (US$1.50, 20 minutes). From Tonosí's main square infrequent *chivasa* rural buses, often a 28-seat Toyota coaster bus, go to Playa Guánico.

Isla Cañas

From July through early November, thousands of olive ridley sea turtles come ashore at night to lay eggs on the 14km-long beach of Isla Cañas.

Once you reach the island, you will be approached by a guide; as a rule every foreign visitor must be accompanied by one. Paying local guides provides a worthy local alternative to inhabitants selling turtle eggs on the black market.

The turtles arrive late at night, so there's no point in hiring a guide during daylight. Instead, agree on a meeting place and an hour when the guide can walk you across the island to the beach. If you're lucky, you'll arrive at the same time as the expectant mothers. Keep in mind that sea turtles are easily frightened, particularly by bright lights such as flashlights and cameras. Instead of hoping to resist the temptation to use these items, just leave them behind.

👁 Sights

Isla Cañas WILDLIFE RESERVE
(admission US$10) Isla Cañas is one of only a few places that olive ridley sea turtles nest

in high numbers (the others are two Pacific beaches in Costa Rica and two beaches in Orissa on the Bay of Bengal in India). Endangered species including the hawksbill, loggerhead sea, leatherback and green turtle nest here too.

Bring a mosquito net and lots of insect repellent, long pants, a windbreaker or bug jacket and mosquito coils if you have them.

👉 Tours

Frederic Lacoste ECOTOUR
(☑6980-0110; www.islacañasmarina.com) This tour operator offers recommended turtle and general ecotours of the Isla Cañas reserve by boat, paddleboard or sea kayak, the latter two being fun alternatives for exploring the waterways.

Isla Cañas Tours ECOTOUR
(☑6263-4388, 6718-0032; www.facebook.com/infoicturs) Leads turtle-watching tours along the beach and manages the cabins on Isla Cañas.

🛏 Sleeping & Eating

Isla Cañas Tours Cabañas CABIN $
(☑6718-0032; www.facebook.com/infoicturs; dm US$12, d without bathroom US$30) Some four very basic *cabañas* (cabins) are available between the port and the beach should you wish to stay on the island.

Isla Cañas Mariscos SEAFOOD $
(☑6591-6214; mains US$2-10; ⓧnoon-9:30pm) This no-frills little family-run restaurant on the way to the beach offers fresh fish and simple Panamanian dishes. It's very friendly.

ℹ Getting There & Away

The turnoff for Isla Cañas is marked by a blue-and-white sign beside a bus stop on the south side of the Carretera Nacional, just over 6km west of the exit for the town of Cañas. From there it's 2.5km to Isla Cañas.

Buses run from Las Tablas to Puerto de Cañas (US$3.60, two hours) at 7am and 1pm, returning from Puerto de Cañas daily at 7am and 11:30am. From Pedasí buses run to Cañas (US$2.40, 45 minutes) at 7am and noon. From Cañas, take an hourly Tonosí-bound bus, which stops in Puerto de Cañas (US$1.50, 30 minutes).

Once at the *puerto* (port), you'll find a *lancha* (boat) to transport you through the mangrove to the island for US$1. At low tide you'll have to remove your shoes and walk along the very muddy channel to where the water is high enough for the boat to moor.

Veraguas Province

POP 244,415 / AREA 10,590 SQ KM / ELEV TO 3478M

Includes ➡

Best Places to Eat

- Anachoreo Restaurant (p140)
- Chano's Point (p145)
- Hibiscus Garden Restaurant (p144)
- Palati Fini (p144)
- La Moncheria Heladería (p144)

Best Places to Sleep

- Hostal La Qhia (p139)
- Hibiscus Garden (p142)
- La Buena Vida (p143)
- Hotel Heliconia (p151)
- Oasis Surf Camp (p142)

Why Go?

The name of Veraguas province (literally 'see waters') is both descriptive and accurate – it is the only one of Panama's provinces and *comarcas* (indigenous districts) to border both the Pacific Ocean and the Caribbean Sea.

But there's much more here to attract visitors than endless coastline. Unesco World Heritage Site Isla Coiba, the so-called Galápagos of Central America, draws divers, birdwatchers and paradise seekers. Surfing village Santa Catalina is a destination in its own right. Hikes to waterfalls and swimming holes around the highland village of Santa Fé offer an off-the-beaten path retreat.

Veraguas' isolated Caribbean coast will one day be accessible on the Carretera de Caribe, an east-west highway that will link Miguel de la Borda in Colón Province with Rambala in Bocas de Toro, some 230km away. This, and tourism, will help this deforested region of ranchers and subsistence farmers redefine itself and recast its fragile fortunes.

When to Go

➡ **Feb & Mar** The best months to hit the world-class surf breaks in Santa Catalina and elsewhere along the Veraguas coast.

➡ **Aug–Dec** Three species of turtles nest on the beaches of Malena on the Sunset Coast; community volunteers guide these very off-the-beaten-path trips.

➡ **May–Nov** Dry season means the the best weather for the beach, but the rainy season means waterfalls near highland Santa Fé are big – though trails may be muddy.

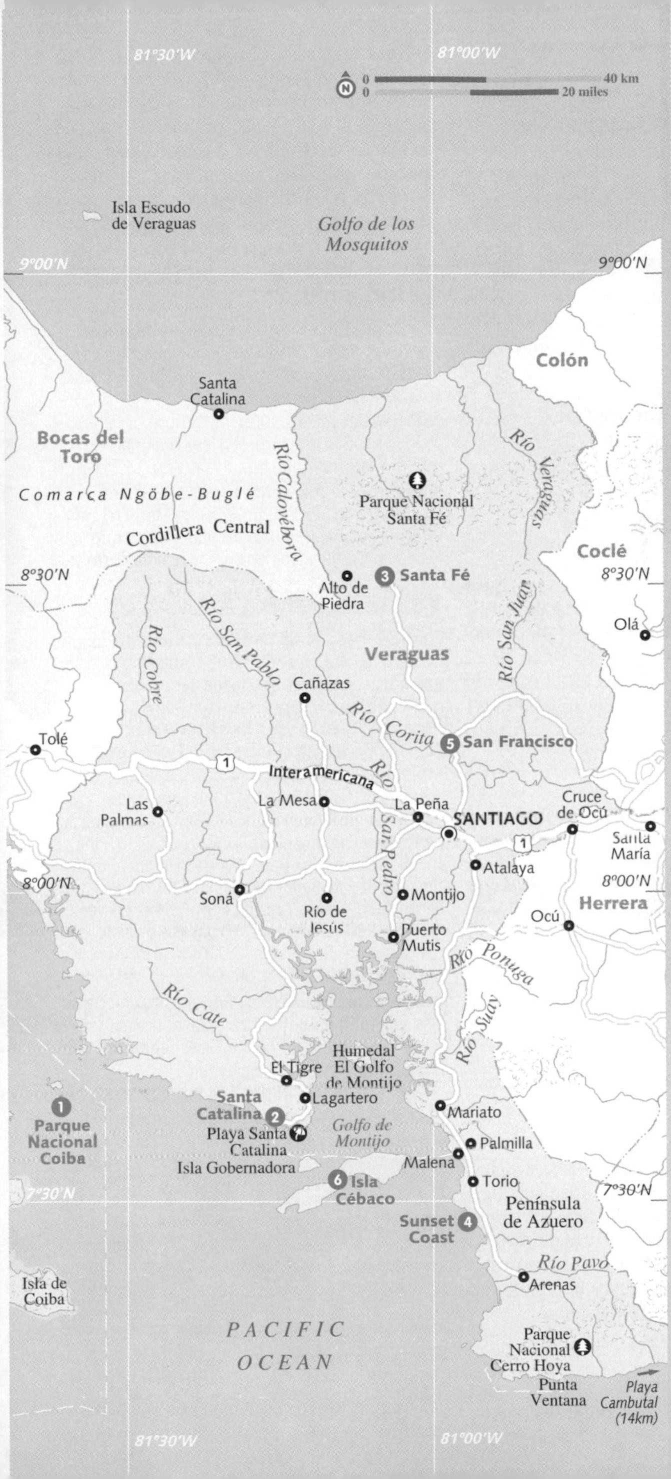

Veraguas Province Highlights

1 Parque Nacional Coiba (p145) Exploring the astounding natural beauty of Parque Nacional Coiba, both above and below the water.

2 Santa Catalina (p140) Surfing some serious waves at Panama's top spot for surfing.

3 Santa Fé (p137) Ascending to this highland village, famous for its waterfalls, steep hills and lush forests.

4 Sunset Coast (p149) Adventuring through the delightfully untrampled Sunset Coast, with remote beaches, great surfing and community turtle tours.

5 San Francisco (p136) Visiting the Iglesia de San Francisco de la Montaña, one of the best examples of baroque religious art and architecture in the Americas.

6 Isla Cébaco (p148) Getting inspired off the beaten path with a retreat to this crowd-free island.

Santiago

POP 41,240

Halfway between Panama City and the Costa Rican border, and just north of the Península de Azuero, Santiago is a bustling hub of rural commercial activity. There's no real reason to stop here, but it's a good place to break up a long drive and recharge for the night. Most of Santiago's commerce and services, including stores, banks, gas stations, restaurants and hotels, are along the Interamericana and Av Central, which runs to the west from the highway.

Sleeping & Eating

Most of Santiago's better hotels are located along the Interamericana. If you're looking to stock up on food, there's a supermarket in front of the bus terminal. Most big hotels also have their own in-house restaurant.

Hotel Plaza HOTEL **$**

(☎6576-5396, 998-3433; hotelplazastgo@gmail.com; d US$33; P ❄ 📶 🏊) Along the Interamericana, but set back, the 34-room Hotel Plaza David is well regarded locally, mainly because of its swimming pool. Rooms are decked in stucco and tile; some of them are drive-up. Choose a room in the back.

Hostal Veraguas HOSTEL **$**

(☎6669-6126, 958-9021; hostalveraguas@yahoo.com; Calle 20C Norte, Barriada San Martín; dm/d US$12/28, outside dm US$10; 📶) Backpackers will appreciate the cheap living at homestay-like Hostal Veraguas. There's a dorm with four beds, two double rooms and a communal kitchen in the main building, and another dorm in a garage-like outbuilding. Host Lidia goes out of her way for guests. The hostel is in a quiet neighbourhood called San Martín, northeast of the town center. Turn right at the Super Carrnes supermarket. Generous discounts are offered for longer stays.

Hotel Galería HOTEL **$$**

(☎958-7950; www.hotelgaleriapanama.com; Interamerica; d US$85; P ❄ 📶 🏊) Uninspiring and hard by the noisy Interamericana, the brick-and-tile Galería nonetheless attracts with its generous-sized pool. It has 69 rooms and a decent restaurant, and is just a hop, skip and a jump from the bus terminal.

Shopping

Ceramica La Peña MARKET

(⊙9am-4:30pm Mon-Fri) A ceramic workshop and artisan market, this place sells wood carvings and baskets made by the Emberá and Wounaan peoples of the Darién, woven purses and soapstone figurines made by local Ngöbe-Buglé people, and masks from the town of Parita. There's also a good selection of pots and sculptures, some of which are made on site. It is on the south side of the Interamericana, 8km west of Santiago, just before the turnoff to the town of La Peña.

Information

There are ATMs at the bus terminal and across the street from it. If you are headed for the islands or smaller towns, make sure you take out sufficient funds here.

ATP Office (☎998-3929; Av Central; ⊙8:30am-3:30pm Mon-Fri) Has regional tourism information.

Ministerio de Ambiente (☎998-4387; Interamericana; ⊙8:30am-3:30pm Mon-Fri) Information on area parks, including Parque Nacional Coiba; also can supply fishing permits.

Getting There & Away

From Santiago's **bus terminal** (☎998-4006; Calle 10 Norte), west of the Interamericana and north of Av Central, buses depart for David (US$9, three hours) hourly from 9am to 3am, Panama City (US$9.50, four hours) hourly from 4am to 9:15pm, and Chitré (US$3, one hour) every 20 minutes.

Buses to Santa Fé (US$2.90, 1½ hours) depart half-hourly from 5am to 7:30pm. To get to Santa Catalina, you must first take a bus to Soná (US$2.10, one hour, half-hourly from 7am to 6pm), then transfer to Santa Catalina (US$4.65, 1½ hours, 5am, 11am, 2pm and 4pm). Buses charge extra for surfboards. Up to 10 buses a day link Santiago with Torio (US$4.25, 1½ hours), via Mariato on the Sunset Coast, between 6am and 5pm.

Express buses to/from Panama City and David also stop at the Centro Piramidal at the eastern end of Av Central on the Interamericana, but at busy times they can often be full.

You can also hire **Radio Taxi** (☎958-8075) to take you to the Iglesia de San Francisco de la Montaña (p137) in San Francisco (US$10 one way) or to the towns of Santa Fé (US$30), Soná (US$30) or Santa Catalina (US$70).

Getting Around

Taxis are easy to hail and they go anywhere in town for around US$2.

San Francisco

POP 2220

The small town of San Francisco, 18km north of Santiago on the way to Santa Fé, can lay claim to one of the best and oldest examples of baroque ecclesiastical art and architecture in the Americas.

Sights & Activities

Iglesia de San Francisco de la Montaña CHURCH

(9.30am-noon & 1-4pm) This simple stone church, built in 1727, contains nine elaborately carved altarpieces, including the ornate main altar of ash and cedar. Although most colonial altars in the Americas were brought over from Europe, this one was carved by local indigenous people. The eight side altars contain images of the crucifixion and the Virgin Mary with saints as well as portraits of the artisans themselves and prominent indigenous people. Their faces are inserted into religious scenes and onto the bodies of cherubs.

The *Retablo de la Pasión de Cristo (Altarpiece of Christ's Passion)* includes both symbols with a religious significance – a chalice, a wine pitcher, a pelican piercing its breast to feed its young, and a skull – as well as items with special meaning for local people (three dice, a Spanish sword, a lantern and an hourglass).

The church's original belfry, used by the Spanish as a lookout to monitor the indigenous people and slaves, survived until 1942, when it collapsed without warning.

Balneario El Salto SWIMMING

Less than a kilometer from the church, these waterfalls have a fine swimming hole for cooling off on hot days. Follow the road behind the old church and then go left just beyond the more modern magenta-coloured one. After a few hundred meters, take the first right; you'll reach the cascades in another several hundred meters or so.

Getting There & Away

To reach the church, head 18km north on the San Francisco turnoff from the Interamericana until you reach the police station near a stop sign. Veer right, proceed 400m and then turn right again at the Supermercado Juan XXIII de San Francisco. Another 100m on, you'll see the church on the left.

A bus leaves the Santiago station for San Francisco (US$1, 30 minutes) every half-hour from 6am to 6pm. An alternative is to hire a taxi in Santiago (about US$18 round-trip).

Santa Fé

POP 3050

This tiny mountain town 53km north of Santiago lies in the shadow of the Continental Divide. At an altitude of 500m, Sante Fé is cooler than the lowlands, and much of the surrounding forest is as it was when the Spanish founded the town in 1557.

Santa Fé

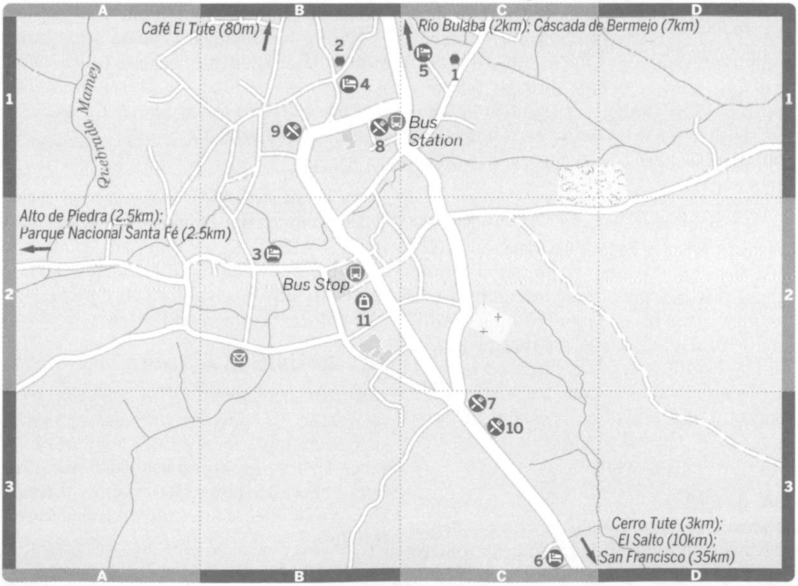

Santa Fé

Activities, Courses & Tours

1 Coffee Mountain Tours C1
2 Fundación Hector Gallego B1

Sleeping

Coffee Mountain Inn .... (see 1)
3 El Caballo Verde B2
4 Hostal La Qhia B1
5 Hotel Anachoreo C1
6 Hotel Santa Fé C3

Eating

Anachoreo Restaurant .... (see 5)
7 Cafe Dorada C3
8 Fonda de la Terminal B1
9 Restaurante Hermanos Pineda B1
10 Super Santa Fe C3

Shopping

11 Mercado B2

Santa Fé has fresh, clean air and bucolic surroundings, yet it sees few foreign visitors. With the lush mountainsides, waterfalls, mountain streams and accessible swimming spots of Santa Fé National Park on the town's doorstep, this is an ideal destination for hikers, birdwatchers and those simply wanting to soak up the beauty of the highlands.

Sights

Cerro Tute MOUNTAIN

With excellent open views of the valley, Cerro Tute is home to the area's famed bird life and features a cliff blasted with up currents that seem to prevent anyone falling off. An extensive trail network winds through primary and secondary rainforest. It's a few kilometers south of town, on the western side of the Santiago–Santa Fé road; count on five hours there and back.

Parque Nacional Santa Fé NATIONAL PARK

(Santa Fé National Park; park admission US$3) This vast, mountainous park covers 726 sq km of pristine wilderness, extending from the northern edge of Santa Fé to the Cordillera Central and includes the rugged area of Alto de Piedra. Part of the northern portion of the province that remained roadless for so long, a dirt road now penetrates the area as far as El Guabal. It's wise to access this sector with an area guide.

Alto de Piedra WATERFALL

There are three waterfalls in Alto de Piedra northwest of town. Though you can do this on your own, access can be difficult and affected by recent weather conditions; we recommend you hire a guide to visit these areas. Aventuras Cesamo (p138) is available for hikes and birdwatching.

El Salto WATERFALL

The impressive waterfall known as El Salto lies about three hours southeast of Santa Fé along a 4WD road that is usually only accessible during the dry season. On foot, it is a full eight-hour excursion including time for bathing.

Cascada de Bermejo WATERFALL

An excellent half-day road and trail walk (five hours round-trip) leads to this tall waterfall with a delightful swimming hole in the dry season. Follow the road past William's inner-tube rentals; after taking the Bulaba bridge, take your first left where the road continues steeply uphill. Continue until the waterfall, following yellow arrow signs into the trail.

You can return looping onto the main road (going right leaving the trail and left at every intersection). In rainy season, you should inquire with locals about conditions before going.

Río Bulaba RIVER

There's a lovely swimming hole on this river about a 20-minute walk from town. Head northeast along the road past the Coffee Mountain Inn on the way to El Pantino. The swimming hole is about 600m from there.

Here a local named William rents **inner tubes** (US$8) and life jackets, which allow you to float idly down the river; it eventually merges with Río Santa Maria. He can also arrange a taxi return.

Café El Tute FACTORY

(tours 1st person US$15, each additional person US$5) Contact the **Fundación Hector Gallego** (954-0737; 8am-8pm Mon-Sat, to 5pm Sun) or Restaurante Hermanos Pineda (p140) to tour this organic coffee-processing plant at the northern end of town.

Activities & Tours

Aventuras Cesamo HORSEBACK RIDING

(6792-0571; www.aventurascesamo.blogspot.com) Reputable local guide Cesar Miranda takes visitors on horseback rides using his own horses. He also guides visitors through the Alto de Piedra area and on walks to waterfalls.

Chon & María Farm Tour TOUR

(☎6525-4832; half-day tour per person US$8;) To see an organic farm up close, visit with Chon and María, hospitable *campesino* (farmer) hosts happy to show you around their small-scale operation. You can also check out their orchids and sample María's homemade cooking (lunch included). Though they only speak Spanish, this lovely couple finds a way to communicate with non-Spanish-speaking visitors that makes the trip worthwhile.

It's excellent for families too, who can take advantage of the country quiet and a nearby swimming hole. Make sure you book ahead.

Coffee Mountain Tours ADVENTURE TOUR

(☎6988-0921; http://coffeemountaininn.com) This very reliable outfit (that also runs a popular B&B in Santa Fé) offers everything from tours of the Parque Nacional Santa Fé by car and on foot (US$42.50 to US$58) to horseback riding (US$25) and tours of lesser-known coffee plantations.

Festivals & Events

Exposición de Orquídeas EVENT

(Orchid Show) Collectors from all over Panama display their finest orchids at the Féria de Santa Fé during the popular orchid exposition each August; the ATP tourist office (p136) in Santiago can provide you with the precise date.

Feria de Agricultura EVENT

(Agricultural Fair) If you're in the area, don't miss this lively event hosted by the small producers of northern Veraguas in early February. The agricultural fair features traditional dancing, horse races, a multitude of food stands and an occasional boxing match or rodeo competition. It's held at the Feria de Santa Fé in the eastern part of town.

Sleeping

★**Hostal La Qhia** GUESTHOUSE $

(☎6592-5589, 954-0903; www.panamamountainhouse.com; dm US$12, d & tr with shared/private bathroom US$39/44; P) Surrounded by lush gardens and hammocks, this original bamboo-and-stone chalet makes a great base camp for mountain adventures around Santa Fé. The three clean, snug rooms all feature crisp bedding; the ones upstairs are complete charmers. Dorms with six beds and a room with private bath occupy a small concrete addition with an outdoor kitchen.

We love the balcony and *rancho* with hammocks. Manager Stephanie provides excellent maps and detailed notes about the area's attractions.

Hotel Anachoreo HOTEL $

(☎6911-4248; www.anachoreo.com; s/d/tr/q incl breakfast US$44/55/66/77; P) Hugging the hillside with panoramic views, this Dutch-Cambodian enterprise is a small hotel boasting four ample rooms with high ceilings and queen-size beds, and tubs in the bathrooms. There's also a new communal kitchen. Fragrant flower, herb and vegetable gardens flank the property on all sides; hammocks abound. The multilingual owner gives local 4WD tours and offers directions for hiking trails.

Hotel Santa Fé HOTEL $

(☎954-0941; www.hotelsantafepanama.com; s/d/tr/q US$22/28/33/39, deluxe d/tr/q US$33/39/47; P) This quiet, motel-style lodging features 16 tidy concrete rooms with cable TV and hot showers; a couple have air-conditioning. They are grouped around a grassy courtyard and shady porch. The attached restaurant serves Panamanian food but isn't always open. The main drawback is that whatever action there is in town is a long walk uphill from here.

Coffee Mountain Inn B&D $$

(☎6988-0921; www.coffeemountaininn.com; d US$65-95, tr incl breakfast US$75-105; P) This welcome addition to the accommodations scene in Santa Fé offers seven rooms in two buildings: the main building has five double rooms while an outbuilding offers two family rooms. All have fine tile floors, queen-sized beds with exceptionally comfortable mattresses and French doors offering direct access to the garden. The main building's long veranda is a delight.

El Caballo Verde GUESTHOUSE $$

(☎6227-3511; www.elcaballoverde.com; d US$85; P) This nifty little guesthouse called the Green Horse – yes, there's a story there – has only two rooms, but they are exceptionally well appointed, with attractive marbled yellow walls, mosquito netting on the beds and very hot showers (no small thing in these sometimes chilly hills). American owner Birch is exceptionally well informed about the area and its attractions.

El Caballo Verde has a cozy in-house restaurant (mains US$15 to US$18) but you must book ahead.

Eating

Restaurante Hermanos Pineda PANAMANIAN $
(☎954-0777; mains US$6-12; ⏰7am-9pm) This welcoming, family-run place just up from the town center serves Panamanian favorites (think beans and lots of fried stuff) and has also branched out to pizza (US$5 to US$12). The large open veranda looking out onto the main road is a plus, as is the large map of the national park in front.

Fonda de la Terminal CAFETERIA $
(mains US$3.50; ⏰7am-7pm) This simple, no-nonsense cafeteria next to the bus station offers some of the best *comida típica* (regional specialties) around. It's friendly and very clean.

Cafe Dorada AMERICAN $
(☎6279-6239; mains US$5.50-8.50; ⏰11am-10pm Wed-Mon) A change in ownership at this sprawling restaurant with a large veranda has seen a change in menu and clientele – neither are 'gringo deluxe' any longer. Expect a fair bit of seafood and Panamanian dishes. We'd to stick with the pseudo (but tasty) Mexican offerings: nachos, tacos and quesadillas.

★ **Anachoreo Restaurant** CAMBODIAN $$
(☎6911-4848; www.anachoreo.com/; mains US$8.50-13.50; ⏰5:30-9pm Wed-Sun) This intimate eatery at the hotel of the same name ranks among the finest eating this side of Panama City. The Cambodian owner-chef is a wonderful cook and delightful presence. Don't miss the Cambodian chicken curry, her famous spring rolls and the exotic 'Fish Amok' wrapped in banana leaves and steamed in ginger and fresh lemongrass.

Enormous organic salads come from produce grown in the backyard. Book ahead.

Super Santa Fe SUPERMARKET
(Av Central; ⏰7:30am-8pm) The town's most complete grocery store is on the right-hand side as you come into town.

Shopping

Mercado MARKET
Just past the entrance to town, this market sells fruits and vegetables, woven handmade bags, a wide range of hats, leather goods and many other interesting items.

Orientation

Spread over hills, Santa Fé's layout is confusing for visitors but pleasant to walk nonetheless. The road from Santiago splits off from the Interamericana via an overpass (the only one in town) and wends its way through lovely valleys, branching out in three directions at the southern edge of town. The middle 'branch' forks yet again after a few more blocks.

Information

None of the streets have names in Sante Fé and directions given by locals can be confusing. It's best to confirm that you're on track before you walk right out of town.

Note that Santa Fé has no ATM. Stock up on cash in Santiago.

Getting There & Away

Buses from Santa Fé to Santiago (US$2.90, 1½ hours) depart from the bus station every 30 minutes from 4am to 6pm, stopping at the more central bus stop en route. Note that if you are trying to reach the surf town of Santa Catalina in one day, you must leave Santa Fé by 9am to make all the bus connections in time.

Las Palmas

POP 3110

There's nothing of special interest in sleepy Las Palmas, a town 7km south of the Interamericana and 33km northwest of the town of Soná. But if you love waterfalls and have your own wheels, this place is for you.

Sights

El Salto de Las Palmas WATERFALL
(Las Palmas Waterfall) This wonderful 45m-high waterfall has a natural pool with refreshing water at its base. The area is surrounded by light forest and you'll probably have this hidden paradise to yourself. Don't forget to take your camera, and be sure to take your valuables with you.

Getting There & Away

To get to the El Salto de Las Palmas from the Interamericana, take the Las Palmas turnoff and drive south for 7km. Bypass the first road into town, but turn left at the second one just before the town's cemetery. Follow this dirt road for 200m and then take the fork to the right. This last 1km to the falls, along a much rougher road, requires a 4WD vehicle. If you're not driving one, it's best to play it safe and walk from here to the falls.

Santa Catalina

POP 300

Santa Catalina is one of Central America's top surf spots. Indeed, the right and left breaks here are comparable to Oahu's Sunset Beach on a good day. The fishing village has a laid-back feel, with limited dining and nonexistent nightlife. Enjoy it while it's still remote, undeveloped and home to some seriously wicked surf.

Santa Catalina is the main springboard for day and overnight trips to Isla de Coiba and its national park. For stunning views of the Golfo de Montijo, hike up the new Sendero de la Cresta (p142) trail on the right as you enter town.

🏃 Activities

Many of the local fisherfolk know a variety of superb snorkeling and spear-fishing spots, as well as some remote surf breaks. Look for guides on the beach or simply ask around. You can also find locals who will lead horseback-riding tours through the nearby forests.

Surfing

The best waves are generally from December to April, though there's surf here year-round. Unlike the Caribbean, the Pacific offers fairly consistent sets, though a good swell will really give a boost to the surfing here. Be advised that many of the breaks in the area are over rocks, and can easily snap your board if you don't know what you're doing. Most of the accommodations in town rent boards and offer surfing lessons.

Surf & Shake SURFING
(☑ 6451-9939; www.surfandshake.com; ⊙ 9am-6pm) On the road to the beach, just 150m in from the main street, Surf and Shake rents boards and sells leashes, boards and surf wear, as well as tasty fruit shakes. Run by German surfers, it's also a good spot for surf info.

Santa Catalina Surf Shop SURFING
(☑ 6780-2104; www.santacatalinasurfshop.com; Calle Estero, Hotel Santa Catalina; ⊙ 9am-noon & 3-8pm) Now in the Hotel Santa Catalina (p144), this surf shop specializes in getting good gear to those who loathe to travel with extra baggage. Sells, rents and buys back quality boards and accessories.

Fishing

The area is famous for big fish, including yellowfin tuna, wahoo, snapper, Spanish mackerel, jacks and rooster fish. Though there's no major sportfishing operator in town, many local fishers rent their boat and services for the day. Prices depend on the number of people in your party and your

destination, since gasoline is very expensive. Cabañas Rolo (p143) arranges half-day trips for US$250 to Isla Cébaco with a knowledgeable local captain.

If you'd prefer to go after reef fish (including snapper and grouper), there are some hidden spots along the coast. Plenty of rocky ledges serve as hideouts for lobster, though be sure to only harvest adults – lobster are in danger of being overfished throughout Panama. **Scuba Coiba** (☑ 6980-7122; www.scubacoiba.com) can set you up with the gear you need, and the local fishers can help you get your feet wet.

If you are sportfishing in Parque Nacional Coiba, you must obtain a fishing permit (US$50) from any mainland Ministerio de Ambiente office; the nearest is Santiago (p136).

Panama Pêche FISHING
(☑ 6852-4798; www.panama-peche.com; half/full day US$330/550) Knowledgeable French angler Jean-Luc Bréant, based at La Gorgona northwest of the center, can organize fishing trips in the waters around Isla de Coiba.

Diving & Snorkeling

Diving and snorkeling are a great way to see some of the spectacular marine life around Isla de Coiba. There is an incredible variety of fauna and even whale sharks have been sighted here. Two-tank dives start at US$130 per person, though diving in the park costs more since the distance is much greater. Snorkelers can join dive trips to Coiba (US$80 including the park fee). A new rule requiring boats to stay overnight with their diver clients has made multiday trips to Coiba very expensive; an overnight with two days in the water is now US$250. Visitors usually check all shops to see which has a trip visiting their preferred destination.

★ Dream Diving DIVING
(☑ 6765-0631; www.dreamdivingpanama.com; ⊙ 8am-4:30pm) 🌿 This excellent dive shop just at the turnoff to the beach is run by a very eco-minded Colombian and offers snorkeling trips to Coiba (US$90) and two-/three-tank dives for US$130/160.

MC Diving Coiba DIVING
(☑ 6421-3008, 6442-6922; www.mcdivingcoiba.com) Among the most professional of dive centers in Santa Catalina, this outfit based at the Hibiscus Garden (p142) on beautiful Playa Lagartero offers a two-tank local dive for US$90 and the usual two-/three-tank

<div style="writing-mode:vertical-rl">VERAGUAS PROVINCE SANTA CATALINA</div>

ones to Coiba (US$175/190). Very ambitious indeed are their three-/five-day diving tours of northern Coiba and Isla Contreras for US$1000/1700.

Panama Dive Center DIVING
(☎6665-7879; www.panamadivecenter.com; ⏲7am-7pm) Friendly and professional, this PADI-certified dive center is a good local resource for information. It offers snorkeling (US$68), all-day two-tank dives (US$150) and courses. It also has longer dive trips to Coiba (two/three nights US$440/660). It's on the main road, opposite the turnoff to the beach.

Coiba Dive Center DIVING
(☎6774-0808, 6780-1141; www.coibadivecenter.com; ⏲8am-6pm) This reputable PADI-certified dive shop is located on the main road and has snorkel gear available for rent. It offers multiday trips to Isla de Coiba (two nights from US$695, with a minimum of three people), which include entry into the national park, lodging at the Ministerio de Ambiente station on Coiba, and meals. Three-day open-water courses start at US$375.

Hiking

Sendero de la Cresta HIKING
(Crest Trail) This new trail just over a kilometer east of the town center leads to a hilltop in about a half-hour, with stunning views of the Golfo de Montijo below.

Tours

Snorkeling Adventure Tours SNORKELING
(☎6705-8450) This simple and very central outfit on the main road in town offers competitively priced trips to Coiba (US$60 including lunch) with four stops, and an in-shore fishing trip for US$50.

Sleeping

★Hibiscus Garden RESORT $
(☎6615-6097; www.hibiscusgarden.com; Playa Lagartero; dm/s/d with shared bathroom US$15/30/35, s/d/q with private bathroom from US$45/55/80; P ❄ 📶) On Playa Lagartero, 11km northeast of Santa Catalina, these relaxed German-owned and Italian-run lodgings fuse modern with rustic, with stylish installations and minimal fuss. There are playful mosaics done by volunteers throughout, while the 14 rooms have recycled driftwood beds and private hammock terraces. An open-air dorm catches the breeze and views. The 6km-long beach is calm, secluded and very swimmable.

For some, the distance from town is a drawback, though a shuttle (round-trip US$6.50) is available. You certainly won't get bored: horseback riding (US$30), surf lessons and fishing trips (US$35) are offered, and there's a professional diving center on site. The Hibiscus Restaurant (p144) is world-class and a destination in itself (though guests also have use of a fully equipped communal kitchen).

Oasis Surf Camp CABIN $
(☎6670-5636, 6671-7049; www.oasissurfcamp.com; camping with/without tent per person US$12/7, dm US$15, d with fan/air-con US$45/55, ste US$135; P ❄ 📶) This Italian-owned surf camp has long been a staple of Santa Catalina, and its beachfront setting is one of the best. Bright, colorful cabins overlooking the black-sand beach have adequate facilities including hot showers and ample hammocks. The suite is a two-bedroom wooden house with wicker furniture, a kitchen and great balcony views. The dorm has five beds.

Panamanian breakfast and authentic Italian dinner with fish, bruschetta and salads are served at the open-air restaurant. You can also rent a variety of surfboards (US$10 to US$15), and surfing lessons cost US$20 to US$30, depending on the number of learners. It's 2km from Santa Catalina's main road, on Playa Estero near the mouth of the river, which you have to wade across to reach the camp.

Rancho Estero CABAÑAS $
(☎6415-6595; www.ranchoestero.com; beach area; dm US$15, 2-person cabaña US$40-45; P) Perched on a hill along the road down to Playa Estero, these exotic *cabañas* made of bamboo and thatch are among the most atmospheric budget places to stay in Santa Catalina. They are surrounded by gardens strewn with hammocks, chaise lounges and deck chairs, and the beach is just in front. We love the simple restaurant and tiki bar.

El Mundo Pequeño GUESTHOUSE $
(☎6355-7367, 6497-7659; http://hostalelmundopequeno.com/; d/tr from US$35/50; P ❄ 📶) With just three guestrooms, the Swiss-owned 'Small World' is just that. It's the first lodgings on the right as you enter town, a bit out of whatever action there is in Santa Catalina, but the rooms are comfortable (with Dr Dream mattresses), colorful (a blast of turquoise, a splash of coral) and certainly not costly.

El Mundo's restaurant has developed quite a reputation in a very short time.

Boarder's Haven GUESTHOUSE $
(☎6572-0664; www.labuenavidahotel.com; s/d/tr US$25/30/35; ❄📶) The ideal choice for those on a shoestring budget, this tiny guesthouse has just seven single beds in three rooms with real mattresses, shared bathrooms and a petite kitchen that's fully equipped. The brightly coloured (and named) rooms have air-con and a ceiling fan. It sits on the main road in the center of town.

Cabañas Rolo CABIN $
(☎6598-9926, 6494-3916; www.rolocabins.net; dm US$12, d/tr with shared bathroom US$20/40, with private bathroom US$55/66; P❄📶) One of Santa Catalina's only locally owned hotels, these rustic cabins are a favorite of surfers on a budget. Each has one to three good beds, a fan and a shared cold-water bathroom. Newer cabins feature ample, more upscale rooms with air-conditioning and bathrooms with hot-water showers. There are 11 rooms in all.

Rooms 10 and 11 have views of the beach. Truck stop–quality coffee comes free in the morning and guests get use of an open-air kitchen. The owner, Rolo Ortega, speaks Spanish and English, offers surf lessons (US$30, 1½ hours), rents surfboards (US$10 per day) and kayaks (US$15), and can arrange surf trips to Isla Cébaco (from US$250 per group).

Hostal Surfers Paradise HOSTEL $
(☎6709-1037; www.facebook.com/surfersparadise.hostal; beach area; dm US$18, s/d/tr/q US$38/48/66/80, with air-con US$44/55/72/88; P❄) You could watch the tubes roll in all day at this hilltop hotel and hostel with a box seat to the waves. The eight rooms in a thatched block spread over two floors include two dorms with up to five beds. There is also a restaurant with views, as well as a large outdoor kitchen for self-caterers.

Rooms on the 2nd floor catch the ocean breeze. Guests can take surf classes and rent boards (US$15 to $25).

Aguas Verdes CABIN $
(☎6954-2626, 6793-8549; www.facebook.com/aguas.verdes.94/about; beach area; s/d US$20/30; ❄📶) These brightly coloured cabins lined up on a hill directly above the beach offer very conveniently located lodgings for surfers on a budget. Rooms have air-conditioning and wi-fi and there's a kitchen too.

Hostel Villa Vento Surf HOTEL $
(☎6659-2900; http://villaventosurfhostels.com; dm/d/tr US$10/40/60; P❄📶🏊) This basic branch of a more established hostel on the Sunset Coast is in a two-story wooden house on the main road above a minimarket. It features six rooms set around a 1st-floor veranda. Two are dorms with five and six beds; the rest are doubles and triples with air-con and en suite bathrooms. There's a very big kitchen and a pool.

Santa Catalina Inn HOTEL $
(☎6559-5981, 6752-4516; www.santacatalinainn.com; d US$45; ❄) While the roadside location won't grab you, the Sunkist-orange color will. The hotel has five good, clean doubles that offer excellent value and the air-con provides needed respite from the heat. Hot water and private room balconies are a perk. It's about 200m from the bus stop on the way to the beach.

Hostal Oasis HOSTEL $
(☎6670-5636; http://hostaloasispma.com; dm/d US$15/30; 📶) A very rustic four-room hostel on the main road into town, this two-story wood house has a wraparound porch and murals. Oasis features male and female dorms and four budget rooms. Concrete stall showers have hot water. Guests get small lockers and free coffee. There's a free beach shuttle at 9:30am daily. It's in the same stable as Oasis Surf Camp. There's also a kitchen that guests can use.

★**La Buena Vida** CABIN $$
(☎6635-1895, 6572-0664; www.labuenavidahotel.com; 2-person villas US$66-88, 4-person studio $110; P❄📶) 🍃 These lovely villas spilling down a leafy hillside along the main road in the center of Santa Catalina will whisk you away from it all. Each is themed and decorated with colourful mosaics and tiles crafted by the American owners. 'Gecko' is the most deluxe, while 'Butterfly' offers the delicious option of showering outdoors. 'Bird' has two floors.

Cabins include a fridge, screened windows and air-conditioning, while one larger group villa (Casa del Mar) with a kitchen and BBQ patio is a steal. Yoga and professional massages are available on site. The owners have ironed out every little detail here, from local tips and recommendations to quality lunch boxes for tours. La Buena Vida composts, recycles and sells local artisan goods.

Cabañas Time Out CABIN $$
(☎6617-1692; www.cabanastimeout.com; beach area; d US$120; P❄📶🏊) Geared towards upscale surf bums, American-owned Time

Out is Santa Catalina's most luxurious hotel and is located right in front of the coveted La Punta break. The eight cabins are tasteful and well equipped, with LCD TV, air-con and full kitchens. In addition to the central restaurant-bar, there's a hammock hut with views and a sparkling pool with magnificent sunset views.

Hotel Santa Catalina HOTEL **$$**
(Kenny's; ☎6571-4387, 6871-4847; www.hotelsantacatalinapanama.com; beach area; d/tr/q US$75/80/85; P ❄ 📶 🏊) With manicured grounds strewn with hammocks and Spanish-tile roofs, this 11-room hotel is an excellent midrange option. Tile rooms somewhat crowded with beds feature electric hot-water showers and individual lockers for gear. A big draw is the surf break of La Punta out front. Guests get free use of kayaks, bicycles and foam boards.

There's an on-site restaurant, though the suites have their own kitchenettes. The mix of natural materials – stone, wood, thatch – is commendable and harmonious.

Sol y Mar CABIN **$$**
(☎6920-2631; www.solymarpanama.com; 2-/3-/4-person cabin incl breakfast US$88/104/121; P ❄ 📶 🏊) Surrounded by greenery, these hilltop cabins with a total of nine rooms have hammock porches, lovely wooden furniture, electric hot-water showers, satellite TV and air-con. Guests rave about the special attention that owner, Luis, showers upon them. About 100 steep stairs lead to cabins, with sea views at the highest level. It's 650m to the town center.

There's a thatched *rancho* with pool table and a lovely pool with views of Coiba and Cébaco islands.

Eating

La Moncheria Heladería ICE CREAM **$**
(☎6849-1796; www.facebook.com/pages/La-Moncheria-Santa-Catalina/864661973552320; ⏰3-10pm) This *gelateria* on a narrow dirt road on the way to La Punta surfing beach serves just about the best ice cream in Panama.

La Vieja Panaderia BAKERY **$**
(The Old Bakery; ☎6900-5776; sandwiches & salads US$5-7.50, pizza US$6.50-8.50; ⏰6:30am-3pm & 6-10pm Thu-Tue) This Italian-run local institution is a bakery by day and a pizzeria after dark. Come before 9:30am as bread (US$1.50 to US$2) sells out and breakfasts (think omelets and pancakes) are slow to get served. There's also great coffee, lunch boxes to go, cakes and delectable muffins. The eight pizzas on offer are tasty and authentic.

La Buena Vida NORTH AMERICAN **$**
(☎6635-1895, 6572-0664; www.labuenavida.biz; mains from US$7; ⏰6am-2pm) If you're hitting the water early, this will be the first spot open for a bite. Great options include breakfast burritos and Greek scrambles with feta, olives, tomatoes and eggs. This funky tiled cafe perched above the main street also sells fresh fruit drinks and a lunchtime selection of salads, tacos and sandwiches on homemade bread.

Pizzeria Jammin PIZZA **$**
(☎6604-3910; pizzas US$6.50-11; ⏰from 6:30pm) A Santa Catalina mainstay, this open-air *rancho* offers delicious thin-crust pizzas baked in a stone oven. Nightlife tends to concentrate here – perhaps it's the cheap beer, though there's also good wine and picnic tables conducive to sharing. It gets crowded, so arrive early in the evening. You'll find it on the road to the hotels facing the beach.

★**Hibiscus Restaurant** FUSION **$$**
(☎6641-2034; www.hibiscusgarden.com; mains US$8.50-15; ⏰7:30am-8:30pm) This fantastic restaurant under the command of German chef Sven Holst serves up award-winning seafood dishes such as local clams with saffron and tomato. Holst's years in Asia are evident in the delightful shrimp *nems* (soft spring rolls) and Thai curries. Less adventurous diners can choose from burgers, fajitas, pasta and a huge range of salads.

Restaurante Iguanito TAPAS **$$**
(☎6549-7464; http://hoteliguanito.com; mains US$11-18; ⏰6:30-9pm Thu-Tue) This cozy restaurant in the hotel of the same name specializes in seafood but also has a wide selection of tapas (US$4.50 to US$12), including such delights as calamari croquettes, clams, *patatas bravas* in a spicy tomato sauce and Serrano ham. It's a short distance up the road to Estero Beach.

El Encuentro SEAFOOD **$$**
(☎6795-8191, 6735-5457; mains US$10-15; ⏰6:30-11pm) This popular watering hole moonlights as a seafood restaurant and the results are superb. *Ceviche peruano* (Peruvian-style citrus-cured seafood) comes in various guises, but the squid version is to die for. Follow that up with grilled fish – the

grouper on coconut with shrimp butter was memorable. Sit indoors or at the outdoor bar.

Chano's Point SEAFOOD **$$**
(6736-1652; mains US$10-17; 6-9pm) This thatched restaurant offers lovely seafood meals and frozen fruit drinks. Start with fresh local clams or salad with tart passion-fruit dressing. The fish in coconut curry and the lobster are divine. And bring your patience because the wait for food is long and they often run out. It's off the first right-hand turn en route to Playa Estero.

Pingüino Cafe ITALIAN **$$**
(mains US$8-17; 11am-10pm) This thatched Italian-owned restaurant on the public beach is the undisputed spot for a sunset beer. Pasta dishes are a tad pricey given their somewhat reckless preparation. We recommended the whole fried fish with *patacones* (fried plantains). Always a warm welcome.

Los Pibes ARGENTINE **$$**
(6599-3632, 6585-1046; www.facebook.com/Restaurante-Los-Pibes-267800839912108/; mains US$6-12; 6-10:30pm Thu-Tue) This good-vibe Argentine eatery is an original – from its menu of nachos, steak and small Argentine-style empanadas (turnovers stuffed with meat, cheese or veggie mixes) to its margaritas and mojitos. They will even cook the fish you catch. Surfers can gorge on mammoth burgers topped with bacon or eggs, or choose healthy salads with basil and gouda. It's 1km from town on the Estero road.

Information

Be advised that there are no ATMs in Santa Catalina and very few places take credit cards. Make sure you arrive with cash.

Getting There & Away

To reach Santa Catalina from Panama City, take a bus to Santiago, then another to Soná where buses leave for Santa Catalina (US$4.65, 1½ hours) at 5:30am, 8:40am, 11:20am, 1:35pm, 2:40pm and 4:45pm. If you miss the bus, hire a taxi from Soná to Santa Catalina from US$45. Direct Panama City–Soná buses run every two hours.

From Santa Catalina, seven buses serve Soná daily, leaving at 6:15am, 7am, 8am, 10:20am, 1:15pm, 3pm and 6pm. In Santa Catalina, the bus stops at the intersection with the beach road. If you're staying outside the town center, most lodgings are a 1km walk on mostly flat but unshaded terrain. Note that there are never taxis in town, unless, of course, someone is arriving from Soná.

Parque Nacional Coiba

With the exception of Ecuador's Galápagos Islands and Isla de Coco in Costa Rica, few destinations off the Pacific coast of the Americas are as exotic as this **national park** (Coiba National Park; www.coibanationalpark.com; park admission US$20) covering the 503-sq-km Isla de Coiba. Although just 20km offshore in the Golfo de Chiriquí, Coiba is a veritable lost world of pristine ecosystems and unique fauna. Isolated for the past century due to its status as a notorious penal colony, Coiba offers travelers the chance to hike through primary rainforest and snorkel and dive in a marine park with increasingly rare wildlife. However, with virtually no tourist infrastructure in place, you're going to have to plan hard (and pay top dollar) to really see it up close.

Coiba was declared a national park in 1992, and in 2005 Unesco made it a World Heritage Site.

Activities

Wildlife-Watching

More than 167 bird species have been identified in Parque Nacional Coiba. While birdwatchers covet sighting the Coiba spinetail, a reddish-brown little bird found only on Coiba, most are awed by the scarlet macaws limited in Panama to Parque Nacional Coiba. The birds nest at Barco Quebrado on the southern tip of Isla Coiba, but are frequently sighted in flight, with distinctive calls that are easy to recognize.

Although a plant survey has been carried out (there are eight ecosystems on the island), Coiba has not had a proper wildlife survey, though it is believed to be home to about 40 different species of mammal. Two rare mammals are endemic to the island – the Coiba agouti and the Coiba howler monkey. While these are difficult to spot, it's common to watch white-faced capuchin monkeys playing on the beach.

Seventeen species of crocodile, turtle and lizard, as well as 15 species of snake – including the dangerous fer-de-lance, coral snakes and boa constrictors – are found here. Enormous crocodiles might inhibit your swim plans at night. Although snakes tend to be extremely shy, you should always walk slowly and carefully through the jungles, stomping occasionally.

The waters surrounding Coiba are home to many large sharks. White-tip reef and bull sharks are the most sighted, though black-tip

Parque Nacional Coiba

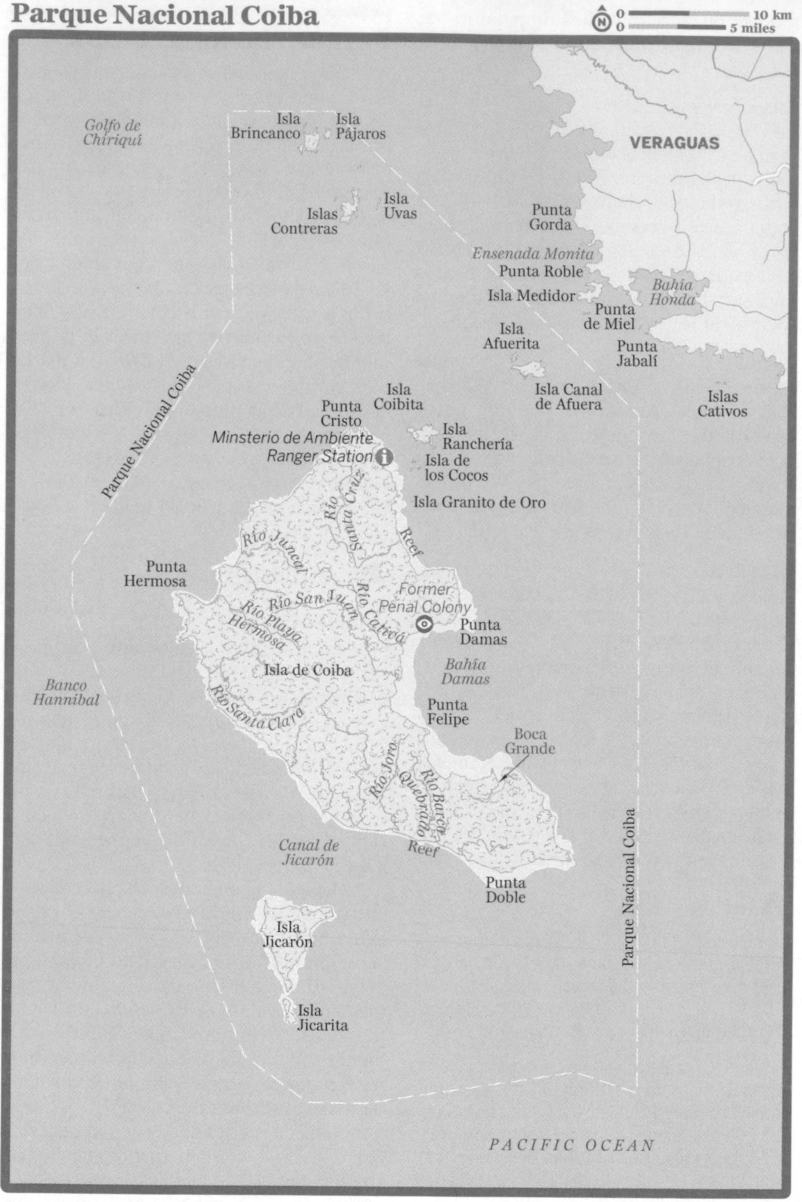

sharks can also be spotted and hammerheads school in large numbers here as well. Lucky divers may see the occasional tiger and whale shark, especially from December to February.

The marine life in the park is simply astounding. The warm Indo-Pacific current through the Gulf of Chiriquí creates a unique underwater ecosystem atypical of this region, attracting large populations of pelagics and enormous schools of fish. Some two dozen species of dolphins and whales have been identified, and humpback whales and spotted dolphins are frequently seen. Sperm and killer whales are also present, but in much lower numbers. The whale-watching season runs from July to October.

The waters around Coiba are also home to sea turtles (olive ridley, hawksbill and the increasingly rare green). In addition to seriously large fish, you're almost guaranteed to spot schools of snapper and jacks as well as large grouper and barracuda.

Hiking

Coiba boasts a half-dozen trails, four of which are easily accessible from the ranger station. These include a trail up to Cerro Gambute, which takes about a half-hour all up, and the short walk to Playa Tito. The 5km-long Sendero de Santa Cruz to the west takes about four hours there and back. Farther afield is Sendero de los Pozos, some 45 minutes away by boat. It leads to themal baths built in an old tiled installation. Since there are no markers, you must do longer trails with a guide.

Sendero de Los Monos HIKING
(Monkey Trail) More or less opposite an islet called Granito de Oro, this trail is only accessible by boat. Though it's less than 2km long, it accesses some beaches and is home to several species of monkey. You're most likely to spot howlers and capuchins in the dry season when the foliage isn't as dense.

Scuba Diving, Snorkeling & Swimming

The cove near the ranger station shelters a small island that you can snorkel around during high tide. Be aware that the current on the island's far side is sometimes very strong. If you're a poor swimmer, do not venture outside the cove.

Two other popular spots for swimming and snorkeling are Isla Granito de Oro and the mangrove forest close to Punta Hermosa in the west. Both can be reached only by boat.

The majority of visitors to Coiba arrange their diving through tour operators or dive centers based in Santa Catalina (p141).

Sportfishing

The seas around Coiba are home to some seriously large fish, and lucky anglers can hook everything from marlin and sailfish to roosters and tarpon. To fish here, you must obtain a sportfishing permit (US$50) for the park, through your outfitter or Ministerio de Ambiente (p136).

One option is to use the local boats around Santa Catalina. Professional outfitters run from about US$2500 per person for all-inclusive three-night/four-day packages; some include private charter flights and group minimums of four passengers.

Pesca Panama FISHING
(☎in USA 844-264-2246; www.pescapanama.com) This New York–based outfitter runs trips to Coiba for fly-fishing and sportfishing aboard a barge. The weeklong trip includes meals, four days' fishing and five nights on board.

Coiba Adventure Sportfishing FISHING
(☎998-1338, in USA 800-800-0907; www.coibadventure.com) This recommended sportfishing operation is run by Tom Yust, widely regarded as Panama's top sportfishing captain. Custom-tailored tours take the hassle out of navigating local logistics. Rates vary depending on the time of year, the boat used and the size of the party, and include transportation from Panama City, meals, accommodations and fishing charters.

Tours

Even if you're normally an independent traveler, Coiba is one destination where it's worth joining up with an organized tour. Although you may be able to save a few dollars organizing your own transport to Coiba from Santa Catalina, that's all you'll get; with an operator you'll get to see and experience a whole lot more, especially the interior. Being part of an expedition also means that you can explore more of the marine park, which is more convenient and ultimately may be cheaper than arranging activities on your own.

★ **Tanager Ecotours** ADVENTURE TOUR
(☎6370-2857, 6676-0220; www.tanagertourism.com; 3-day all-inclusive per person US$500-600) Run by a couple of keen Dutch biologists, these superb guided tours use local fishing boats and include meals, accommodation for three nights at their B&B and on Coiba, and park entry. Package trips include snorkeling at four to five reefs, hiking on two trails, a boat ride through mangroves, birding and wildlife-watching. More tailored visits are possible in the low season.

Tours depart from Palo Seco, north of Malena, on the Sunset Coast and require a two-guest minimum. Rates vary depending on group size.

Bird Coiba BIRDWATCHING
(☎6544-1806; www.birdcoiba.com; full day per person US$75-320) Responsible local guide Javier Elizondo offers tours of Parque Nacional Coiba, both all-inclusive day trips and

several overnight options (two days/one night US$190 to US$410). Prices decrease with the number of participants, so it's worth getting a group together with other travelers. Options include birding, snorkeling, surfing, hiking and visiting the former penal colony.

Javier is a native English speaker with two decades of local knowledge.

Fluid Adventures KAYAKING
(☎6560-6558, in Canada 647-282-8167; www.fluidadventurespanama.com; overnight/3 days & 2 nights per person US$309/499) Run by a team of enthusiastic North Americans, this Santa Catalina–based outfitter offers kayaking trips around Isla de Coiba. Day trips (US$115) reach Coiba by motorboat for a head start. Camping, guides, all meals and transportation are included (but not the park entry fee) and equipment is top-notch.

Coiba Dive Expeditions DIVING
(☎6617-9002, 314-9350; www.coibadiveexpeditions.com; 8-day all-inclusive per person from US$2450) Recommended by reputable guides, this conservation-oriented live-aboard dive tour is run on a 16-guest, 35m dive boat staffed by eight crew. Seven- to 12-day dive expeditions to Coiba include nature tours, a half-day penal colony visit and use of one- and two-person kayaks. Tours depart from Puerto Mutis, a small port about 30km southwest of Santiago.

ARTURIS Coiba ECOTOUR
(Asociación Rural de Turismo Sostenible de la Zona de Amortiguamiento del Parque Nacional Coiba; ☎933-0325, 6529-5802; www.arturiscoiba.com; ⏲2 days & 1 night per person US$210) Arturis is a network of local service providers offering transportation, camping and guides to Coiba for single and multiday trips. Only Spanish is spoken. Boats leave from Puerto Mutis or Santa Catalina; students get discounted rates. For information, contact Faustino Sánchez.

Sleeping & Eating

If traveling as part of a tour, you will not have to worry about meals as everything will be arranged for you. Independent travelers must purchase supplies in advance on the mainland as there is no food available on the island. There is a kitchen but no fuel is provided and utensils are nonexistent.

Ranger Station Cabins CABIN $
(☎333-4570, 500-0855 ext 6418; in Santiago 998-4387; campsite/dm per person US$10/20; ❄) At present the only accommodation on the island is at the Ministerio de Ambiente ranger station. There are four cabins (with a total of 40 beds), each with its own common cold shower and toilet. They are clean but spartan; given Coiba's isolation, you shouldn't expect too much. You can also use a tent or a jungle hammock in the dry season.

Electricity is produced by a diesel generator that runs from dusk to dawn; use of the air-conditioning may be restricted. Be sure to pack insect repellent and toilet paper.

Information

Visitors to the island, day-trippers included, register upon arrival at the ranger station run by the Ministry of the Environment. It is very difficult to arrive on the island as an independent traveler, since you must confirm that there is space for lodging and pay in advance at the Ministerio de Ambiente Office (p136) in Santiago.

The majority of the island is a restricted area, though there is a large distance between the ranger station and the now defunct main prison complex (open to tours).

On the northern end of the island, the **ranger station** (☎333-4570, 500-0855 ext 6418, in Santiago 998-4387; park fee US$20) consists of several basic cabins, a camping pitch, showers and toilets. It is located beside an attractive beach alongside a scenic cove. One former prisoner did not want to leave the island and still works at the Ministerio de Ambiente station, often interacting with Spanish-speaking visitors.

Getting There & Away

The most common departure point for boats heading to Isla de Coiba is Santa Catalina, though boats also arrive from the Sunset Coast on the Península de Azuero and from Puerto Mutis, a small port about 30km southwest of Santiago. Santa Catalina is about an hour and a half away; it takes about two to three hours from the other two ports. There is an airstrip on Coiba Island reserved for private charter flights.

Keep in mind that the open sea can get extremely rough, especially in the dry season and in the afternoon; many fishers have been lost at sea over the years. Boats are required to have as many life jackets as passengers. Make sure you wear one.

Isla Cébaco

POP 650

Panama's third-largest island at 80 sq km (after Isla de Coiba and Isla del Rey), Isla Cébaco in the Gulf of Montijo is very much off the beaten track due to the difficulty of access. No commercial ferries operate there

WORTH A TRIP

ART ISLAND: ISLA GOBERNADORA

If you have ever wanted to watch the moon rise from your thatched hut **Art Lodge** (☎6636-5180, 203-4744; www.artlodgepanama.com; 3-night bungalow incl breakfast s/d/q US$225/285/400, 6-night cottage d/q US$300/400) run by two hospitable French artists on this small island in the Golfo de Montijo, will satisfy that urge...and get the creative juices flowing. Isla Gobernadora, home to a quiet fishing village, has forested trails and a few white-sand beaches. Try to schedule a visit at the end of January when the Feria de Artesanías (Handicrafts Festival) takes place or on July 16, when the Fiesta de la Virgen del Carmen is marked by the fisherfolk.

Accommodation is in one of four *ranchos*, open-air bungalows boasting double beds with mosquito nets and showers half-walled with thatch. The more remote *casita* (cottage) has two guest rooms. While the hillside lodge has a beach, there is also a stream perfect for dips and a lovely lounge area with art, games and futons.

To create income for island women, hosts Valerie and Yves have put together community art cooperatives that use natural materials to make gorgeous quality belts, handbags and decorations crafted with design sense. Guests can tour the village and workshops, talk with locals, snorkel, practice yoga and beachcomb. Set meals – breakfast (US$7), lunch (US$12) and dinner (US$17) – incorporate fresh local seafood, fruit and vegetables. Due to its remoteness, the Art Lodge requires a three-night stay (six nights in the cottage). Discounted rates (US$200) are available for resident artists and there are workshops (US$20) in ceramics, weaving and woodcarving.

Getting There & Away

The only way to reach Isla Gobernadora is by private charter. The Art Lodge charges US$60 for two for a round-trip from Santa Catalina. There's also the possibility of traveling to/from Puerto Mutis (US$140 round-trip for up to six). A taxi from Santiago to Puerto Mutis costs US$20.

and transportation is by private charter only. As a result there is almost no tourism development and the small population, mostly based around the main settlement of El Jobo to the north, is engaged in agriculture, raising livestock and fishing.

Despite all this, Cébaco's beautiful beaches and breathtaking coastline offer the intrepid traveler a variety of activities: hiking trails of varying degrees of difficultly, fishing, diving, snorkeling and surfing. Indeed, Playa Grande on the island's south side is one of the region's new surfing hot spots.

Sleeping

Cébaco Sunrise CABIN $$
(☎6658-6202; www.cebacosunrise.com; per person incl 3 meals & activities tent/cabin US$90/166, extra night US$60/70) This new property on the east coast of Isla Cébaco, facing the Sunset Coast, is simplicity itself. In the main house up from the beach are four double rooms with bathrooms and huge windows. 'Glamping' comes in the form of three tents, each with a double mattress and enclosed by a larger netted tent, creating outside and inside 'rooms'.

The all-inclusive price includes three meals a day taken family-style in a *rancho* by the sea. Should you want to get away from it all and still return to your own bed by nightfall, Cébaco Sunrise offers a day tour (US$80) to the island, including transport, lunch, a snack and use of all facilities. Four new cabins are on the way.

Getting There & Away

You can charter boats to ferry you to Isla Cébaco from Santa Catalina or from Puerto Mutis, 30km southwest of Santiago, but the closest embarkation point (and the one used by Cébaco Sunrise) is Playa Reina. This is about 5km down a paved road west of Mariato, which can be reached by one of 10 daily buses from Santiago (US$4.25, 1¼ hours). Board the boat at the Puerto de los Valientes located at the mouth of the Río Negro. The journey to Cébaco Sunrise takes a half-hour.

The Sunset Coast

The Sunset Coast is the name given to the west side of Península de Azuero facing the Gulfo de Montijo and Pacific Ocean. The sobriquet is accurate for it is the only place in

Panama from which you can watch the sun go down from a beach.

Stretching for about 50km from Mariato in the north to Parque Nacional Cerro Hoya in the south, the Sunset Coast is *terra incognita* for most travelers, which ia a shame as it offers some amazing off-the-beaten-path attractions.

Here you'll find long, sandy beaches virtually empty of holiday makers, excellent surfing and the chance to see three species of turtles hatching. There are nature walks in the mangroves and Parque Nacional Cerro Hoya is just down the road.

The gateway to the Sunset Coast is Santiago, about 60km north of Mariato. Other important settlements include Malena and Torio, 11km and 15km south of Mariato respectively.

Activities

Surfing

Two of the best surfing beaches in Veraguas can be found on the Sunset Coast: Playa Reina near Mariato, and Playa Morillo, the latest hot spot south of Torio.

Wildlife-Watching

Local organizations involved in the protection of turtle nests can help you see these endangered creatures up close.

Malena Beach Conservation Association WILDLIFE WATCHING
(Asociación Conservacionista de Playa Malena; ☎6676-0220, 6685-8908; Playa Malena; donation US$15) Between late June and into January, you can find three species of turtles on the beaches of Malena and volunteers of the Malena Beach Conservation Association work toward their preservation. Chairperson Ana González and her community volunteers take visitors on turtle watches; peak season for laying and hatching is October.

The organization also offers accommodation, horseback riding (US$10 per hour), boat tours and nature walks.

To volunteer, contact Tanager Ecotours (p147). Basic Spanish is necessary.

Centro AAPEQ WILDLIFE WATCHING
(☎6389-5249, 6491-9365; tortugas.aapeq@gmail.com; Rusia de Quebra) This association based near Morillo focuses its attention on the conservation of turtles and reforestation of the Mata Oscura mangrove. The affable couple in charge can take you on a tour (US$10) through the mangroves or through the forest up to a waterfall, where you can you see strawberry poison dart frogs. Kayaks are available as well.

AAPEQ also accepts volunteers for turtle conservation and path maintenance. Contact them directly or Tanager Ecotours (p147).

Fishing

Although the best months for fishing along the Sunset Coast are from January to April, many species (including yellowfin tuna, marlin and sailfish) are caught off-season as the waters support an active and plentiful fish habitat all year.

Torio Tours FISHING
(☎6585-6053; www.facebook.com/pages/Torio-Tours-Fun/340404402833046; Torio; from US$300) This small outfitter based in Torio can organise fishing trips for US$300 a day, including all gear and beer. They can also take you snorkeling and kayaking.

Fishing Machine Charter FISHING
(☎6866-9392, 6477-8196; http://tuckspanamablog.com/tag/jerry-higdon; per day from US$400) Owned and operated by veteran angler Jerry Higdon, this is considered to be one of the best fishing charters on the Sunset Coast.

Sport Fishing Panama FISHING
(☎6206-0721, in USA 562-295-7175; all-inclusive 3-day/4-night packages from US$2300) This conservation-minded charter company run by Panamanian-American Alex Livingston for more than two decades has its own fishing lodge on the Sunset Coast and arranges tailor-made fishing packages to Coiba, as well as to Isla Cébaco, the Tuna Coast, along the southern Península de Azuero and the tuna-rich Banco Hannibal.

Sleeping

Hospedaje Centro AAPEQ HOSTEL $
(☎6491-9365, 6389-5249; tortugas.aapeq@gmail.com; Rusia de Quebro; dm/d/q US$10/30/45; P ❄) This conservation association near Morillo offers basic accommodations in three dormitory rooms with eight beds each. Newer and more comfortable are the two private, air-conditioned rooms accommodating up to four people. Book directly or contact Tanager Ecotours (p147).

Hostal Iguana Verde HOSTEL $
(☎6676-0220, 6685-8908; r US$20) The chairperson of the Malena Beach Conservation Association (p150) rents out a handful of

fan-cooled rooms on the main road in Malena. They are simple but clean, and are a short distance from the beach.

Heliconia Bed & Breakfast B&B $$
(☎6676-0220, 6370-2857; http://hotelheliconiapanama.com; Palmilla; s/d incl breakfast US$50/89; P❄🛜≋) The Sunset Coast's anchor tenant, Heliconia Bed & Breakfast in Palmilla, just north of Malena, is an excellent retreat thoughtfully crafted by two extremely knowledgeable Dutch biologists, who also offer recommended area tours. Heliconia counts four smart rooms set within 8 hectares of botanical gardens, a lovely lounge and terrace, and an above-ground pool.

Kees and Loes also work with the local community in sustainable tourism projects and in the reforestation of their own property.

El Nido del Tucán CABAÑAS $$
(The Toucan's Nest; ☎6430-0987, 6430-0912; www.elnidodeltucan.com; Playas Duarte & Morillo; s/d US$50/80; P❄🛜≋) This handsome property about 2km down a track from the main road to Morillo has a guesthouse with large bedroom and sitting room, fully equipped kitchen and a good sized terrace. Below it are two smaller *cabañas* with kitchenettes and balcony. All have views looking across the water out to Isla Cébaco.

There's a long, narrow pool on site and two beaches – Playas Duarte and Morillo – are within easy walking distance, just down the hill. The lovely Swiss owners couldn't be more welcoming.

Camino del Sol Ecolodge LODGE $$$
(☎6810-7122; www.caminodelsol.com.pa; Punta Duarte; d US$160, bungalow US$240; P❄🛜≋) This stunner of a property south of Torio has three rooms painstakingly created with different types of wood. Each has a king-sized four-post bed, futuristic Italian-designed furnishings, an enormous bathroom and stunning views of the sea and infinity pool. Two bungalows – one all glass –on either side of the main building have their own access and terrace. A three-course set lobster dinner (US$35) is available with advance notice.

Eating

Restaurante Julio José PANAMANIAN $
(Mariato; mains US$5; ⏲11am-6pm Wed-Mon) This little restaurant on the main road just north of Mariato is the best place for a basic Panamanian lunch or (very) early dinner. It's a simple place with just a handful of wooden tables on a covered patio, but you can't beat the location – or the price.

Palati Fini ITALIAN $$
(☎6853-7064, 6423-7880; https://www.facebook.com/Palati-Fini-Torio-Panama-1036029896449089/?hc_location=ufi; Torio; mains US$9.50-15; ⏲noon-9:30pm Wed-Mon) Italian-owned 'Gourmets' may not truly live up to its name, but this is one of the better restaurants on the Sunset Coast. The pasta dishes are tasty and substantial – enough for a main course really – and the mains are overwhelmingly seafood-based. They grow their own basil for pesto sauce.

Shaka Bar INTERNATIONAL $$
(☎6627-9787; mains US$8-15; ⏲5:30pm-midnight Thu-Sun) Entertainment central on the Sunset Coast and the watering hole of choice for both local expats and visiting surfers, Shaka is also a restaurant (food available till 9:30pm) serving cheeseburgers and fish and chips. Visit at least once when in the area.

Cabañas Torio SEAFOOD $$
(☎6939-1436; www.torioresort.com; mains US$5-15; ⏲noon-9pm) Hidden within a somewhat faceless concrete resort of cramped *cabañas* is this rather attractive little *rancho*-style restaurant serving a multitude of seafood dishes. The arrival of a new chef from El Salvador has upped the game and locals can't seem to get enough. Try the lobster or the fried calamari.

Information

Banco Nacional de Panamá (☎999-8657; Av Central, Mariato; ⏲8am-3pm Mon-Fri, 9am-noon Sat)

Getting There & Around

Up to 10 buses a day link Santiago with Torio (US$4.25, 1½ hours), via Mariato, between 6am and 5pm. The buses at noon and 2pm carry on as far as Rusia de Quebra, where Centro AAPEQ (p150) is located.

Once you've arrived on the Sunset Coast, having your own transport is incredibly useful.

Chiriquí Province

POP 451,230 / AREA 6491 SQ KM / ELEV SEA LEVEL TO 3474M

Includes ➜

Best Places to Eat

- Rock (p171)
- Cerro Brujo (p175)
- Boquete Fish House (p171)
- Cuatro (p158)
- Mike's Global Grill (p170)

Best Places to Sleep

- Lost & Found Hostel (p179)
- Los Quetzales Cabins (p177)
- Coffee Estate Inn (p169)
- Bocas del Mar (p160)
- Haven (p169)

Why Go?

Chiriquí claims to have it all: Panama's tallest mountains, longest rivers and most fertile valleys. The province is also home to spectacular highland rainforests and the most productive agricultural and cattle-ranching regions in the country. As a result, *los chiricanos* (natives of Chiriquí) take a particular pride in their province and wave the provincial flag – in every sense – at the slightest opportunity.

It's also a land of immense beauty. On the coast, the pristine Golfo de Chiriquí boasts long sandy beaches and a rich diversity of marine life. The mist-covered mountains near the town of Boquete, a favorite of North American and European retirees, is a good base for adventures such as white-water rafting and hiking the flanks of Panama's highest point, Volcán Barú (3474m). Boquete is also the center of Panama's coffee industry, which means that a potent cup of shade-grown arabica is never more than a cafe away.

When to Go

- **Apr–May** The best months to spot the resplendent quetzal nesting in highland destinations such as Parque Nacional Volcán Barú and Parque Internacional La Amistad. The annual Orchid Fair lights up Boquete in April.
- **Dec–Apr** High season on the Pacific coast has little precipitation, making it the best time to hit highland trails that get muddy and damaged during the rainy season.
- **Jan–Mar** Boquete's Feria de las Flores y del Café draws the crowds in January. La Concepción celebrates its patron's feast day in early February, and David holds the huge Feria Internacional de San José de David over 10 days in early March.

HISTORY

When the Spaniards arrived in what is now Panama in the early 16th century, they encountered a large number of tribes living in relative isolation. Often separated by only a few kilometers, each group maintained a distinct language, culture and religion.

Spanish missionaries arrived and began their conversions. In the early 17th century, a group led by Padre Cristóbal Cacho Santillana rounded up more than 600 indigenous people from across the region and began recording a glossary of the most common words. He was able to identify six distinct languages.

Sadly, measles brought by the colonists swept through the towns and killed half of the study population. The survivors, having had enough of the Spaniards, their linguistic studies and their religion, took to the hills. Unfortunately, their fate was already sealed. Of the 10 distinct tribes, only the Ngöbe-Buglé survived. Today they are the most populous of Panama's seven indigenous groups, though their numbers are but a fraction of what they once were.

During the 17th century and into the 18th century, Chiriquí Province was the target of pirate attacks, much like the rest of Panama. It was just outside Remedios in 1680 that English buccaneer Richard Sawkins, attempting to lead an assault against the well-defended city, was fatally wounded. Six years later, English privateers from Honduras sacked the towns of Alanje and San Lorenzo.

In the 19th century, the climate and slopes of the Chiriquí highlands attracted farmers from North America and Europe who planted coffee and other crops as well as exploiting the forests for timber. The wave of immigration hasn't subsided. Recent arrivals are mainly foreign retirees and real-estate speculators, which has led many *chiricanos* to question who it is that actually owns the land they love so much.

LOWLANDS

Chiriquí has much to offer beyond its famed highland rainforests. The region's lowlands are home to Panama's second-largest city, David, as well as large stretches of striking Pacific coastline, a marine park and some lovely islands.

David

POP 144,860

Although it feels more like an overgrown country town, David is Panama's second-largest city and the capital of Chiriquí Province. It's more a center of agricultural industry than a cultural hub; you will be disappointed if you have museums, clubs and fine dining in mind. Yet with foreign capital flowing into Chiriquí, David is rapidly gaining wealth and importance, and is poised to boom.

For most travelers David is a pit stop on the way to surrounding destinations. Halfway between Panama City and San José (Costa

THE GEISHA COFFEE BEAN

During the 19th century, farmers from North America and Europe discovered that the cool climate and rich volcanic soil of Chiriquí were perfectly suited for the cultivation of coffee. Since dried beans are relatively nonperishable and thus easy to ship, coffee quickly surpassed other cash crops and became an important source of revenue for the area. Although less well known than the Costa Rican competition, Panamanian coffee is praised for its high caffeine content and acidic, multidimensional flavor.

In the early 1990s the collapse in the world quota cartel system dealt the industry a severe blow. Growers could no longer rely on a stable price for their harvest. In turn, a few growers switched tactics, planting quality varieties in smaller amounts, aiming at the gourmet market instead of the usual high-yield crops.

Selectivity paid off. The biggest coup was the emergence of geisha coffee on the world scene. After winning first place in multiple international competitions, geisha became a rock-star bean. Originally from Ethiopia (the birthplace of coffee), geisha is coveted for its light body, citrus and honey notes and jasmine-like aroma.

Geisha has been auctioned for up to US$260/kg and sold at Starbucks for US$7 a cup. You can also find it for sale online, but because it is grown in small quantities, it often sells out. While Boquete's Finca Esmerálda was the first to make good on geisha, it's now found at Café Ruiz (p172), Finca Lérida (p170) and a growing number of local estates.

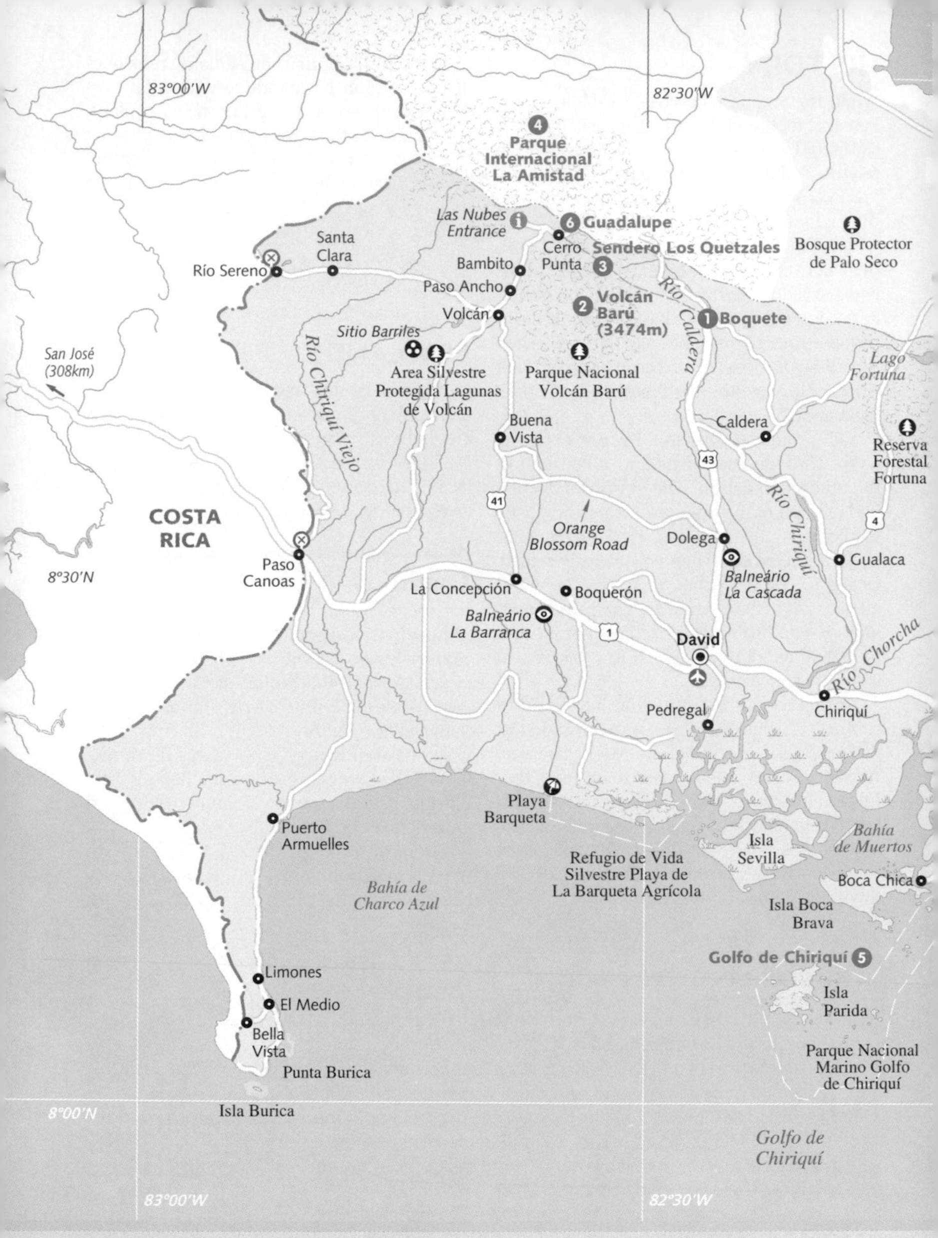

Chiriqui Province Highlights

1. **Boquete** (p163) Fueling up for highland adventures with local mountain-grown coffee in the town of eternal spring.

2. **Volcán Barú** (p172) Ascending for views of both the Pacific and Atlantic coastlines – provided the weather is clear.

3. **Sendero Los Quetzales** (p172) Hiking through cloud forests in search of the elusive quetzal.

4 Parque Internacional La Amistad (p178)
Wondering at why you're the only one around in this pristine and bio-rich park.

5 Golfo de Chiriquí (p160) Island-hopping and exploring the clear blue seas of the national marine park in the 'other side' of Chiriquí.

6 Guadalupe (p177)
Waking up surrounded by wilderness while staying in the cool jungle lodges near Cerro Punta.

Rica), David is an important transportation hub. If the road has you weary, slip into the slow pace, grab a *jugo de caña* (sugarcane juice) in downtown's Parque de Cervantes, the heart of the city, or day-trip to the beach or highlands.

Sights & Activities

Iglesia de la Sagrada Familia CATHEDRAL
The Church of the Sacred Heart, facing downtown's central Parque de Cervantes, has a bell tower and dates largely from the 19th century.

Balneário La Barranca SWIMMING
(11am-6pm) Swim with *chiricanos* at this natural swimming pool with a bar-restaurant about 20km west of David. Hop on a La Concepción-bound bus.

Tours

Carta Vieja Rum Factory TOUR
(772-7073; http://roncartavieja.com) FREE Learn to appreciate rum before you down a tumbler or two. This distillery near Alanje, 10km west of David, has free tours on weekdays. Contact rum master William de Gracia for information. A taxi there and back will cost US$20.

Festivals & Events

Feria Internacional de San José de David FAIR
(www.feriadedavid.com) This big international fair is held for 10 days each March; contact the ATP tourist office for exact dates as they vary from year to year.

Fiesta de La Concepción FERIA
A half-hour drive west of David, the town of La Concepción celebrates the feast day of its patron saint, la Virgen de la Candelaria, on February 2 or the following Saturday if it lands on a weekday.

Sleeping

★ **Bambu Hostel** HOSTEL $
(730-2961; www.bambuhostel.com; Calle de la Virgencita; dm US$11-14, d with/without bathroom US$35/30; P ❄ ✈ ≋) This chilled-out house run by friendly New York City musician Greg has a regular air-conditioned dorm with six beds and a thatched 'jungle house' on stilts out back, with 10 beds and mosquito nets. The seven doubles have air-con and include electric hot-water showers. The sprawling garden has a swimming pool, a cheap beer bar and the requisite hammocks. Wonderful.

There's a large communal kitchen in a central *rancho* and a washing machine for laundry.

Hotel Puerta del Sol HOTEL $
(775-1662, 774-8422; www.hotelpuertadelsol.com.pa; Av 3 Este; d/tr US$45/54; P ❄ ✈) A very secure budget choice, this central hotel offers 86 tasteful tiled rooms with wood furnishings. Rooms are on the small side, but the setting is pleasant. Amenities include hot-water showers, cable TV and a full-service restaurant open daily till 10pm (Sunday lunch only, till 3pm).

Purple House HOSTEL $
(774-4059; www.purplehousehostel.com; cnr Calle C Sur & Av 6 Oeste; dm US$9, d with/without bathroom US$27/25, all incl breakfast; P ❄ ✈) Peace Corp veteran Andrea pioneered David's first hostel and has served as able den mother of this five-room place ever since. Guests have use of a communal kitchen, cable TV and a vertical fountain for cooling off. Tiled dorm rooms with six and 10 beds are clean (and purple) without air-con. Doubles offer optional add-ons such as air-con (US$5).

Purple House is in a residential area but close to restaurants and shops. It's sometimes closed in October; call or email first. The house recycles and has a community partnership selling a few Ngöbe-Buglé crafts.

Hotel Ciudad de David BUSINESS HOTEL $$
(774-3333; www.hotelciudaddedavid.com; Calle D Norte & Av 2 Este; d/ste from US$95/145; P ❄ ✈ ≋) David's flashiest hotel, the sleek 'City of David' has 103 tastefully furnished rooms with wooden floors, minibars and fully wired desks. Rooms 303 and 304 look onto the fabulous amoeba-shaped swimming pool; suite 305 has a balcony as well. There's a sauna, a fully equipped gym and a stylish bar-restaurant called – what else? – Stylo.

Gran Hotel Nacional HOTEL $$
(775-2222; www.hotelnacionalpanama.com; Calle Central & Av 1 Este; d/ste US$95/110, d deluxe US$165; P ❄ ✈ ≋) David's largest hotel offers 119 modern yet fairly sterile rooms that are more suited to domestic businesspeople than travelers. But the hotel isn't short on amenities, and the on-site bar-restaurant, pizzeria, casino and a six-screen cinema sweeten the deal. Some rooms, such as deluxe double room 140, look onto a leafy courtyard and large swimming pool – a plus in Panama's hottest city.

David

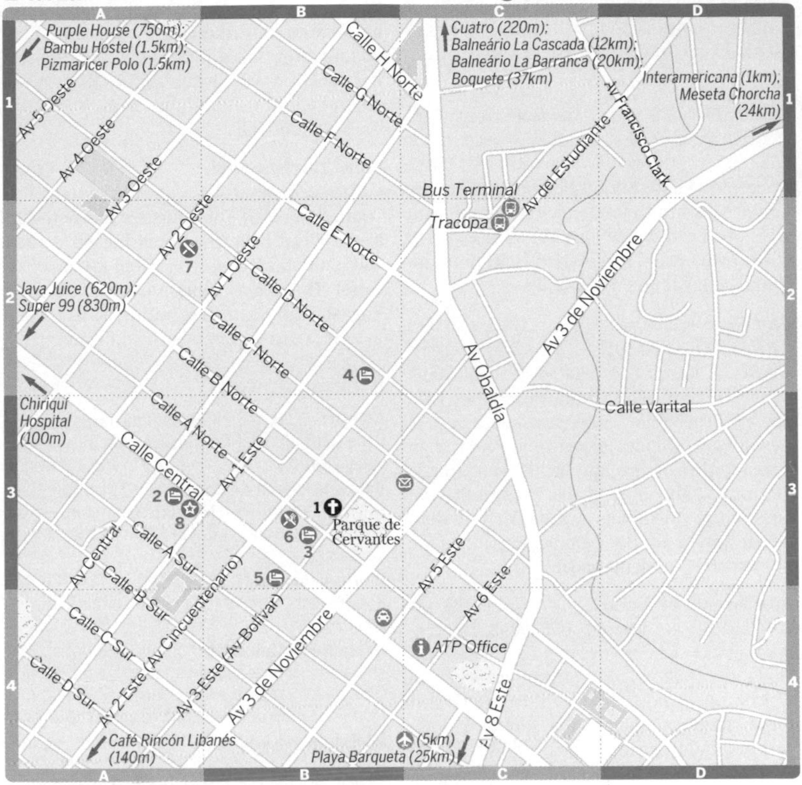

Hotel Castilla HOTEL $$
(☎774-5236, 774-5260; www.hotelcastilladavid.com; Calle A Norte & Av 3 Este; s/d/ste US$49/66/88; P❄📶) Professional and superclean, this hotel offers 69 cheerful tiled rooms with matching beds and desk sets in a vaguely art deco style. Each is equipped with hot-water shower, air-con and cable TV. There's an underground parking garage.

✕ Eating

Pizmaricer Polo PANAMANIAN $
(☎6406-9088; www.facebook.com/pages/Marisqueria-Pizmaricer-polo/298511190316835; Calle de la Virgencita; mains US$4.25-8) A very basic restaurant – a *fonda* almost – in the hostel district, Pizmaricer Polo almost exclusively serves seafood, with a few pork dishes thrown in to keep ichthyophobes happy. The *ceviche* (citrus-cured seafood) is a cut above and the whole fried fish is the best (and probably cheapest) in town.

David

Sights
1 Iglesia de la Sagrada Familia..............B3

Sleeping
2 Gran Hotel Nacional..............A3
3 Hotel Castilla..............B3
4 Hotel Ciudad de David..............B2
5 Hotel Puerta del Sol..............B3

Eating
6 MultiCafe..............B3
7 Restaurante El Fogón..............A2

Entertainment
8 Cine Gran Nacional..............A3

MultiCafe CAFETERIA $
(☎774-6180; www.facebook.com/pages/Multi-Café/317029381703197; cnr Calle A Norte & Av 2 Este; dishes US$2.50-5; ⏱7am-9pm Mon-Sat, to 3pm Sun) An excellent choice if you're looking for something cheap and filling while you're on

the hoof downtown. This colorful cafeteria south of the landmark cathedral has trays of local beef, chicken and pasta dishes as well as salads. Good for a local breakfast too.

Java Juice HEALTH FOOD **$**
(☎730-3794, 730-3461; www.facebook.com/javajuice.com.pa; cnr Calle E Sur & Av 3 Oeste; mains US$2.50-5; ⏰10am-7pm Mon-Sat; 🌿) Fruit smoothies, salads and grilled burgers are the fare at this health-food cafe-restaurant with a US owner in a new location to the west of downtown. Good vegetarian selection, including a great green smoothie.

Café Rincón Libanés MIDDLE EASTERN **$$**
(☎774-2700, 730-3911; www.facebook.com/CafeRinconLibanes; Calle F Sur; mains US$8.50-18; ⏰11am-11:30pm) This fairly authentic 'Lebanese Corner Cafe' restaurant southwest of downtown provides a welcome relief from a steady diet of rice and beans. Homemade hummus, tabbouleh, baba ghanoush and lamb *kofta* (meatballs) will make you wonder if you're in the Middle East. Try the homemade pink lemonade.

Restaurante El Fogón INTERNATIONAL **$$**
(☎775-7091; Av 2 Oeste; US$7.50-18; ⏰noon-midnight Mon-Sat, 5pm-midnight Sun) This spacious red, yellow and orange eatery is a welcome oasis northwest of the center. Grilled meats and seafood are the standard main courses, and there are burgers and sandwiches for the less-than-ravenous. Checkered tablecloths and fake foliage throughout. 'The Stove' is favorite with locals.

★**Cuatro** PANAMANIAN **$$$**
(☎730-5638; www.restaurantecuatro.com; cnr Av Obaldía & Calle Estudiante; mains US$12-20; ⏰noon-3pm & 6:30-10:30pm Mon-Sat) This sleek eatery turns out sophisticated, modern takes on *cocina local* (local cuisine). Classic Panamanian basics such as cassava, tamales and new corn get gourmet treatment; be prepared for some happy surprises. Start with hot corn blinis with shrimp salad and red-onion marmalade. Honey-glazed pork ribs are tender and the stuffed Boquete trout exquisite. Young chef-owner Luis Mendizábal honed his craft in top European and North American restaurants before returning to his native province.

Super 99 SUPERMARKET
(Calle F Sur & Av 4 Oeste; ⏰24hr) Self-caterers can head to the Super 99, a large supermarket open 24 hours a day and convenient to the city's hostels.

☆ Entertainment

Chiricanos are not big on bars and clubs, but they go wild when it's festival time. A certain amount of nightlife centers on the casinos, and you will always find livelier crowds around the 15th and 30th of each month – the local pay days.

Cine Gran Nacional CINEMA
(☎775-2222; www.hotelnacionalpanama.com; Calle Central & Av 1 Este) This old-style movie theater at the Gran Hotel Nacional has six screens and is the perfect spot to catch up on all the 'latest' Hollywood films; the majority are in English with Spanish subtitles. It's also a way to beat David's oppressive heat in summer.

ℹ Information

ATP Office (☎775-2839; chiriqui@atp.gob.pa; Calle Central; ⏰8:30am-4:30pm Mon-Fri) Provides information on David and Chiriquí Province.

Banco Nacional de Panamá (☎774-6400; Calle B Norte; ⏰8am-3pm Mon-Fri, 9am-noon Sat) This central branch with an ATM faces Parque de Cervantes.

Chiriquí Hospital (☎777-8814; cnr Calle Central & Av 3 Oeste) One of the best hospitals in the country.

Costa Rican Consulate (☎774-1923; www.embajadacostaricaenpanama.com; 3rd fl, Edificio Omega, Av Samuel Lewis, Obarrio; ⏰8am-3pm Mon-Fri) South of downtown, towards the airport.

Ministerio de Ambiente (fax 774-6671; ⏰8am-4pm Mon-Fri) Provides tourist information and advice, and camping permits for national parks. It's 4.5km south of David's center.

Post Office (Calle C Norte; ⏰7am-6pm Mon-Fri, 8am-4:30pm Sat)

ℹ Getting There & Away

AIR

David's airport, **Aeropuerto Enrique Malek** (☎721-1072), is about 5km south of the center. There are no buses to the airport; take a taxi (US$5).

Air Panama (☎721-0841; www.flyairpanama.com) and **Copa Airlines** (☎217-2672; www.copaair.com) have daily 45-minute flights to/from Panama City, some as low-priced as US$60 one way. Air Panama also now flies between David and Bocas del Toro town.

BUS

The Interamericana does not go through David but skirts around its western and northern sides. The David bus terminal (Av del Estudiante) is about 500m northeast of Parque de Cervantes. Most buses begin service around 6am.

Tracopa (☎775-0585; www.tracopacr.com) has direct buses between David and San

José, Costa Rica (US$21, seven hours), daily at 8:30am, noon and 4pm from the David bus terminal.

DESTINATION	FARE (US$)	DURATION (HR)	FREQUENCY
Boquete	1.75	1	every 20min to 9:30pm
Caldera	2.40	45min	hourly until 7:30pm
Cerro Punta	3.50	2¼	every 20min to 6pm
Changuinola	9.70	4½	half-hourly to 6:30pm
Guadalupe	3.50	2½	every 20min to 6pm
Horconcitos	2	45min	11am & 5pm
Las Lajas	5	1½	4 daily
Panama City	18	7-8	every 45min, 6:45am to 8pm
Paso Canoas	2.10	50min	every 15min to 9:30pm
Puerto Armuelles	4	2½	every 15min to 9pm
Río Sereno	5.10	2½	every 30min to 5pm
Santiago	9	3	hourly until 9pm
Volcán	3	1½	every 20min to 8pm

Getting Around

David has a complex network of local buses, but the easiest way to get around is by taxi; fares within the city are generally about US$2.

All of the major car-rental companies have booths at the airport.

You can hire a taxi to Pedregal (US$3.50), Boquete (US$20), Volcán (US$30) and Playa Barqueta (US$35).

Playa Barqueta

This long black-sand beach 25km southwest of David is a popular weekend escape, though it remains quiet during the week. Be warned though: as inviting as the ocean seems, riptides are strong, and there are some steep underwater drops as you wade in. This is a great place to break out your surfboard if you've got one.

Some 14km of the eastern beach falls under the jurisdiction of the nature reserve **Refugio de Vida Silvestre Playa Barqueta Agricola** (admission US$5; ⏲6am-3pm), whose mangrove and scrub offer protection to four species of turtles. It's hatching season here from September to December. Contact the Ministerio de Ambiente office in David for information about visits. Purple House, also in David, has information about volunteering.

Capping the western end of Playa Barqueta is **Las Olas Resort** (☎772-3000; http://lasolasresort.com; Playa Barqueta; d/ste US$78/116; P ❄ 📶 🏊), a sprawling yellow hacienda-style resort. Its 48 terraced rooms and suites are decorated with soft, natural colors and feature sweeping ocean views. Facilities include bars and restaurants, an ocean-view pool, a spa and gym, and an equestrian center (note the decorative saddles in the lobby). Room rates drop from April to November.

Renovated room 109, with two double beds and a terrace facing the ocean, is sublime.

Getting There & Away

Two morning buses leave David for the 40-minute trip to Playa Barqueta, but it's easier to catch one

GETTING TO COSTA RICA

The most heavily trafficked border crossing between Panama and Costa Rica is at **Paso Canoas** (⏲7am-7pm), 53.6km northwest of David on the Interamericana. Allow one to 1.5 hours to get through the formalities on both sides. Buses from David depart frequently for the border (US$2.10, 50 minutes, every 15 minutes) from 4:30am. On the Costa Rican side of the border, you can catch regular buses to San José or other parts of the country.

The least trafficked crossing into Costa Rica is the border post at **Río Sereno** (⏲9am-5pm Mon-Sat, to 3pm Sun), located 35km northwest of Volcán. Buses to the border depart from David and travel via La Concepción, Volcán and Santa Clara. On the Costa Rican side of the border, you can take a 15-minute bus or taxi ride to San Vito, where you can catch buses to regional destinations. From David, you can also taxi to Paso Canoas (US$35) or Río Sereno (US$70). Note that you will be asked for an onward ticket if you are entering Costa Rica. If you do not possess one, you can buy a round-trip bus ticket back to Panama. Also note that Costa Rica is one hour behind Panama.

of the frequent departures to Guarumal and then a taxi (US$6) from there. A taxi all the way from David will cost US$35. You should be able to negotiate a reasonable price if you need a ride back to David.

Golfo de Chiriquí

The gem of the Chiriquí lowlands is the Golfo de Chiriquí, home to the **Parque Nacional Marino Golfo de Chiriquí**, a national marine park with an area of just over 147 sq km, protecting 25 islands, 19 coral reefs and abundant wildlife. The marine park also protects the 30-sq-km Isla Boca Brava, a lovely little island with hiking trails and beautiful outer beaches. It's home to howler monkeys, several types of nesting sea turtles and 280 recorded bird species. It is reached from the mainland village of Boca Chica. Resorts in the area offer a range of tours.

Visitors can surf, kayak the calm interior waters, snorkel, watch wildlife under the rainforest canopy or fish for big game.

Sleeping & Eating

Hotel Boca Brava HOTEL **$**
(☎851-0017, 6929-2996; http://hotelbocabrava.com; Isla Boca Brava, Boca Chica; s/d without bathroom US$35/40, d/ste with bathroom from US$50/75; ❄) An unexpected budget option on Isla Boca Brava, this hotel with 15 rooms, ranging from rustic to deluxe, is ideal for mingling with fellow travelers, though we have received some complaints from readers about the quality of the accommodation. Doubles are snug; the cheapest fan-cooled 'economy' doubles have shared bathroom.

At the other end of the spectrum are the delightful bay-view cottage (US$60) and two-bedroom suite (US$75) with air-con. The aerie-like bar and restaurant (mains US$5 to US$8) occupies a cool space on an overhanging deck with expansive water views. It's the perfect setting for a sundowner. The hotel can arrange excursions such as snorkeling, whale-watching and birdwatching.

Seagullcove Lodge RESORT **$$**
(☎851-0036, 6365-3093; www.seagullcovelodge.com; Boca Chica; d US$100-180; P❄📶≋) This small, intimate resort counts just five bungalows, four of them looking to the ocean. Rooms have chunky wooden furniture, huge bathrooms and walk-in closets. We love the pool with a view and the lovely tiki bar at the end of a long pier. It shares a small cove beach with a neighboring resort. Full range of excursions available. Access is to the left from the main road to Boca Chica village, about 500m down a rough, unmade track.

★**Bocas del Mar** RESORT **$$$**
(☎6395-8757; www.bocasdelmar.com; Boca Chica; ste/superior incl breakfast US$189/249; P❄📶≋) This elegant Belgian-owned resort on the mainland has 20 brilliant-white ultramodern bungalows that offer the ultimate in comfort. Amenities range from two infinity pools and massage services to suites with private hot tubs. Rooms have handmade furniture, lovely artwork and windows with smoky glass. A full menu of excursions includes horse riding, kayaking, and fishing and snorkeling tours. Excellent restaurant and service.

The resort has a small private beach and a dock with two boats. To reach the resort follows the the signs from Horconcitos, and take the left-hand turn before Boca Chica.

Cala Mia Boutique Resort RESORT **$$$**
(☎851-0025, 6972-6954, in US 1-210-390-4259; www.boutiquehotelcalamia.com; ste incl breakfast US$260-360; ❄📶≋) Cala Mia on Isla Boca Brava offers luxurious ocean-front tranquility. Some 11 thatched bungalows have ample living spaces, handcrafted local furniture and their own deck with hammock. Two beaches, one with a bar, are just a stroll away, and a massage spa occupies its own islet, reached via suspension bridge. Organic three-course meals (US$40) are served around a big community table. Kayaks and snorkeling are included; other activities use the resort's own boats and guides. Marked trails offer some good hiking trips. A water taxi from the Boca Chica dock to the resort costs US$35.

Getting There & Away

To reach Boca Chica from David, take any of the frequent Interamericana buses heading east to the Horconcitos turnoff (US$2, one hour). From there a van (US$3, 50 minutes) leaves four to five times daily for Boca Chica. At the Boca Chica dock, hire a water taxi (per person US$3) to take you 200m to the Isla Boca Brava dock at Hotel Boca Brava. If you drive your own vehicle, you can safely leave it near the village dock.

Playa Las Lajas

POP 1520

With one of the longest beaches in Panama, 12km-long palm-fringed Playa Las Lajas seems to stretch forever. The beach gathers serious crowds at weekends, but during the week it often lies empty, so you can savor the glorious expanse all by yourself.

Ngöbe-Buglé people sell handicrafts in a wooden-walled structure 500m west of the turnoff to Playa Las Lajas, 76km east of David.

Sleeping & Eating

Naturalmente B&B $
(☎727-0656, 6211-1787; www.naturalmentepanama.com; d incl breakfast US$45-65; P) The three fan-cooled thatched cabins with little terraces at this delightful B&B accommodate between two and four people. It's at the northern end of Las Lajas town – not at the beach – but there's a small above-ground pool in the gardens. The Mediterranean restaurant (mains US$9.50 to US$13) is one of the best eateries on the gulf.

Nahual Eco Hostel HOSTEL $
(Hospedaje Ecológico Nahual; ☎6620-6431; www.nahualpanama.com; dm US$10, s/d with bathroom US$30/40, without bathroom US$15/25; P) With *ranchos* (small house-like buildings) and attractive cabins, this fun, Italian-run place is the best bargain lodging in Las Lajas. It sits across the road from the beach in a leafy garden and is 100% chemical free. There are six rooms, four with bathrooms and two (one a six-bed dorm) with shared facilities. The excellent vegan cafe-restaurant, open daily to 10pm, serves homemade pasta. There's also an open-air kitchen for self-caterers.

According to indigenous folklore a *nahual* is a person who has the power to transform either spiritually or physically into an animal, most commonly a jaguar or puma.

Nelly's Beach Bar & Cabins CABIN $
(☎6706-1191; www.facebook.com/NellysBeachBar; d cabins US$30-40; P) About as bare-bones as you'll find, the five cabins at this popular beach bar with a US owner are seconds from the sand. Surfing tides can reach 6m here. A rough track leads west from the main access road to reach the property, so it has a nice isolated feel to it.

Las Lajas Beach Resort RESORT $$
(☎6790-1972; www.laslajasbeachresort.com; d US$85-110, ste US$132-162; P) A lovely destination on the beach, with 14 impeccable, ample and cheery rooms and great service. We love the indigenous designs on the bedspreads and murals on the walls; room 12 features portraits of Panamanian greats. Guests can float in the pool or ocean, rent body boards (US$6), ride horses (US$25) or visit a Ngöbe community (US$40 per person).

The breezy, open-air restaurant facing the beach serves US-style breakfasts, big cheeseburgers and international fare (mains US$8 to US$14) daily till 9pm.

Finca Buena Vista B&B $$
(☎6814-8693; www.finca-buenavista-laslajas.com; d incl breakfast US$80; P) On the outskirts of Las Lajas town, about 500m to the east, this German-run B&B has sweeping views and warm hospitality. Four spacious and well-appointed rooms feature private patios, small fridges and hot water. Those with lofts are ideal for families. Hosts are happy to arrange fishing, mangrove boat trips and excursions to the local indigenous community.

SURFING IN CHIRIQUÍ PROVINCE

Surfing in Chiriquí is less popular than in other provinces, due to the greater difficulty of access, but there is still great surf to be had. To go beyond the following suggestions, hire a local guide or tour operator.

Isla Silva de Afuera Remote island southeast of Playa Las Lajas, with a right and left break. The right: a big peak breaking over a shallow rock ledge at medium tide. Occasionally throws a big tube with steep drops and no wall. The left: breaks over a rock reef at medium tide. This spot catches almost every swell.

Morro Negrito Near the town of Morro Negrito, southeast of Isla Silva de Afuera near the Veraguas border. About five breaks, including a variety of lefts and rights with occasional tubes.

Playa Barqueta (p159) Southeast of David. Beach-bottom break with rights and lefts. Breaks at all tides, but medium to high tide is best.

Playa Las Lajas Southeast of David. Beach-bottom break with rights and lefts but infrequent waves.

Punta Burica Peninsula shared with Costa Rica. Four left points that break along the point for long, tubing rides. Catches any swell.

Casa Laguna B&B B&B $$
(☎6896-0882; www.casalagunapanama.com; d incl breakfast US$85-100; P❄📶🏊) This Italian-run B&B with just three rooms is a popular option for couples. There are open-air *ranchos* for relaxing in the main garden and facing a lagoon with mangrove in back; the beach is just 100m away. Immense breakfasts include yogurt, fruit and pancakes, and other meals are available upon request. The pool is above ground.

The only drawback is access. It's 2km from the main access road down a track strewn with potholes.

Getting There & Away

To reach Las Lajas, take any bus from David (US$2.75, 90 minutes) that travels to the Las Lajas turnoff, 76km east on the Interamericana. The town of Las Lajas is 3km south of the Interamericana and the beach a further 9km south. At the turnoff, a taxi (US$7) will take you to where the road meets the sea. Turn right and proceed 1.5km until you reach the resort.

The Road to Veraguas Province

Heading to Veraguas Province there are a number of interesting attractions to check out along the way, particularly if you have your own wheels.

Sights & Activities

Parque Arqueológico Petroglifo El Nancito ARCHAEOLOGICAL SITE
(El Nancito Petroglyph Archaeological Park; adult/child US$1/0.25; ⏲9am-5pm Tue-Sun) About 20km east of Las Lajas, El Nancito is a small community known for its underwhelming rock carvings. Locals say that the carved boulders were made more than 1000 years ago, though no one really knows for sure.

From the Interamericana, turn north onto the road to El Nancito. After 3.5km, when you reach the 'Museo' sign, turn left (west) and drive 100m until you come to rather large fenced-in boulders and the park's museum entrance. If taking public transportation, jump off any Interamericana bus at El Nancito, and then hike the 3.5km uphill to the boulders.

Meseta Chorcha LANDMARK
About 25km east of David, on the northern side of the Interamericana, the enormous Meseta Chorcha (Chorcha Plateau) beguiles photographers. From the west, you'll see a white streak running down its glistening granite face – it's actually an extremely tall but inaccessible waterfall. Awesome stuff.

Pozos de Galique HOT SPRING
Soak your travel-weary bones at three no-frills hot springs. The easy-to-miss turnoff for the road to the springs – which requires a 4WD vehicle to access – is 4km east of the turnoff for Playa Las Lajas. The 3.8km-long turnoff leading to the springs is 30m west of a small bridge with a sign that reads 'Galique.' Bring cold drinks and try to visit early morning before the day heats up and, at weekends, crowds descend.

Getting There & Away

Buses running along the Interamericana highway can drop you off at the turnoff to Parque Arqueológico Petroglifo El Nancito and Pozos de Galique, but you'll have to make the rest of the journey on foot (or, if lucky, hitch a ride with a passing vehicle).

David to Boquete

Interesting attractions line the way between David and Boquete, including hot springs, places to cool off in the summer heat and an archaeological site with some excellent petroglyphs.

Sights & Activities

Parque Arqueológico de Piedra Pintada ARCHAEOLOGICAL SITE
(Painted Rock Archaeological Park) FREE Some of the best examples of petroglyphs found in Panama can be seen in this park at Caldera, about 23km southeast of Boquete. It's located 400m down a marked trail about 1km past the police station on the right.

Los Pozos de Caldera HOT SPRINGS
(admission US$2; ⏲dawn-dusk) The area's most famous attraction, Los Pozos de Caldera are natural hot springs renowned for health-giving properties. The springs are located on private land near the town of Caldera, southeast of Boquete. Further on are newer springs called Los Pozos de Abuela (Grandmother's Hot Springs). You may have to make room at both for local indigenous women doing their laundry.

To get to the springs, take a bus or drive to the town of Caldera, which is 8km east of the David–Boquete road. From where the bus drops you off, continue to the end of town; here you'll see a sign indicating the turnoff to the springs. Turn right along this rugged dirt road, accessible by 4WD only. If you're walking it's about one hour from here. Continue along the road until you reach a suspension bridge. Cross it, and take the first left leading up the hill. After 100m you'll see a gate that marks the entrance to the property. Turning right after crossing the bridge will lead you to Los Pozos de Abuela. If you get overheated in the springs, the pleasant Río Caldera is just a stone's throw away, and is a pleasant spot to cool off. Tour agencies in Boquete offer day trips to the hot springs for US$12.

Balneário La Cascada SWIMMING
(admission US$2) Popular swimming spots take the edge off the heat. Balneario La Cascada, about 12km north of David, has two waterfall-side swimming pools and a small bar. Take the bus on Calle F Sur in David to get here. It can get fairly crowded on weekends, though the atmosphere is always upbeat.

Sleeping

El Río Encantado Nature Resort RESORT **$$**
(☎6090-4951; www.rioencantado.com; Caldera; d US$85-95, q US$110-140; P❄📶≋) This remote resort idyllically located on 40 hectares of garden right by the Río Caldera offers four comfortable self-catering cottages, as well as a wonderful treehouse reached by a winding set of steps (not for those with a fear of heights). There's fishing and swimming in the river and the Los Pozos de Caldera (hot springs) are 15 minutes away.

Shopping

Bookmark BOOKS
(☎6635-8604, 776-1688; Dolega; ⏰10am-5pm Tue-Sat) About halfway between David and Boquete, the small town of Dolega is home to Bookmark, a fine bookstore with new and secondhand English-language titles and obscure works. Any Boquete-bound bus can drop you off here.

Getting There & Away

Having your own wheels is best for really exploring this area, though most places can be accessed (at least partially) via public transportation.

HIGHLANDS

The highland rainforests are the heart of Chiriquí Province. From the rugged mountains of Parque Internacional La Amistad and the misty hills of Boquete to the continental divide traversing the *cordillera* (mountain range) this is probably the only spot in Panama where you might need a sweater. While Panamanians relish the chill, you'll appreciate locals' laid-back hospitality and the astounding natural beauty throughout the region.

Boquete

POP 19,000

Boquete is known for its cool, fresh climate and pristine natural surroundings. Flowers, coffee, vegetables and citrus fruits flourish in its rich soil, and the friendliness of the locals seems to rub off on everyone who passes through.

Boquete gained a deluge of expats after the American Association for Retired Persons (AARP) named it a top retirement spot. Until you see the gated communities and sprawling estates dotting the hillsides up close though, you'd be hard-pressed to see what the fuss is about. Downtown Boquete, with its broken pavements, dirty sidewalks and single span across the Río Caldera is not the idyllic mountain town many expect.

The surrounds, however, are another matter. Boquete is one of the country's top destinations for outdoor-lovers. It's a hub for hiking, climbing, rafting, visiting coffee farms, soaking in hot springs, studying Spanish or canopy touring. And, of course, there's nothing quite like a cup of locally grown coffee.

Sights

El Explorador GARDENS
(☎720-1989; www.facebook.com/ElExploradorBQT; Calle Jaramillo Alto; adult/child US$5/2; ⏰10am-6pm) This private garden is located in a hilly area 3km northeast of the town center; you can walk to it in about 45 minutes. The 2 hectares of gardens are designed to look like something out of *Alice in Wonderland,* with no shortage of quirky eye-catching displays, including fanciful suspension bridges, koi ponds and playful sculptures.

Parque José Domingo Médica PARK
Boquete's central plaza has flowers, a fountain and a children's playground.

Activities

Adventure-hub Boquete has the lion's share of outfitters in the region, so it's not a stretch to book coastal trips such as sea kayaking or sportfishing here. Hostels and various

Boquete

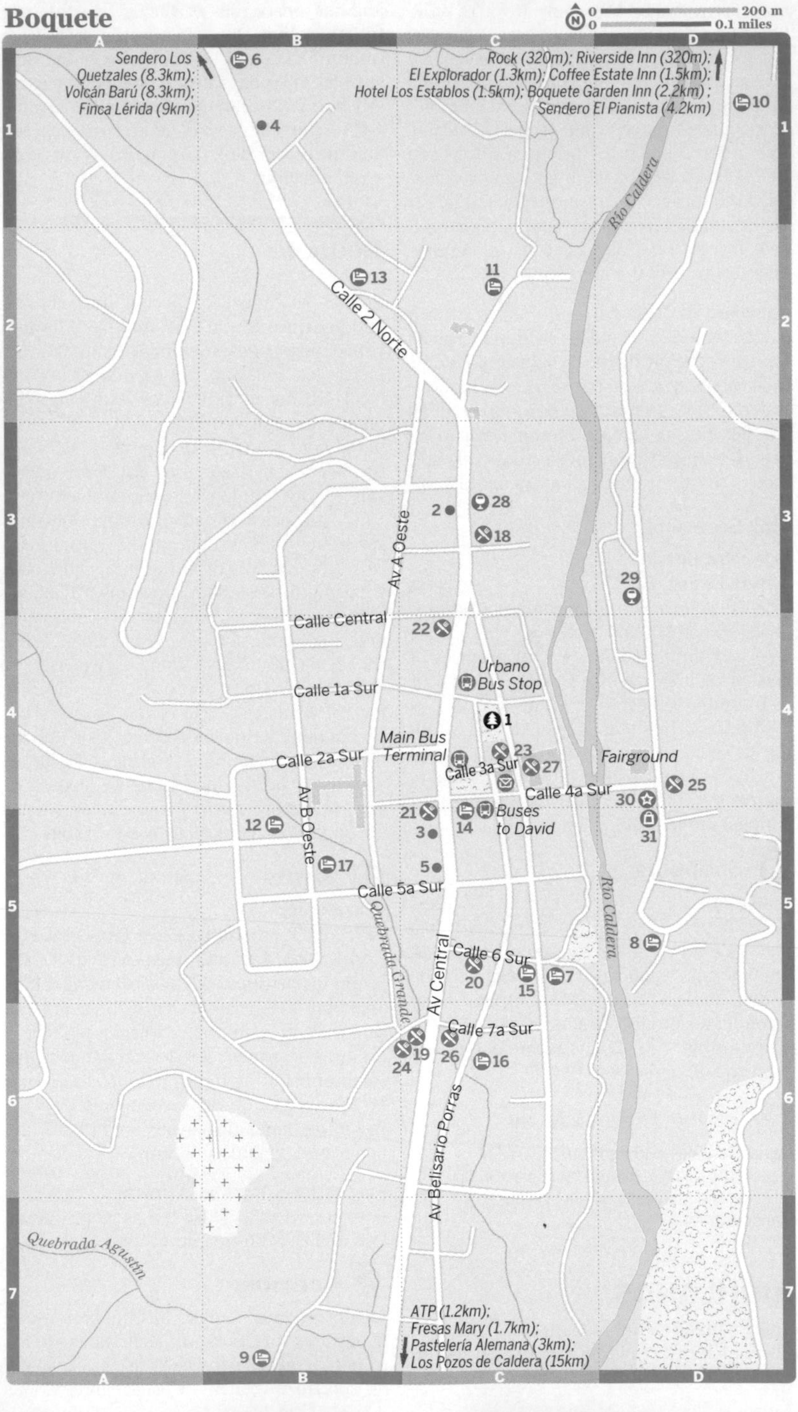
0
200 m
0
0.1 miles
Sendero Los Quetzales (8.3km); Volcán Barú (8.3km); Finca Lérida (9km)
Rock (320m); Riverside Inn (320m); El Explorador (1.3km); Coffee Estate Inn (1.5km); Hotel Los Establos (1.5km); Boquete Garden Inn (2.2km); Sendero El Pianista (4.2km)
Río Caldera
Calle 2 Norte
Av A Oeste
Calle Central
Urbano Bus Stop
Calle 1a Sur
Main Bus Terminal
Calle 2a Sur
Calle 3a Sur
Calle 4a Sur
Fairground
Buses to David
Av B Oeste
Calle 5a Sur
Quebrada Grande
Av Central
Calle 6 Sur
Calle 7a Sur
Av Belisario Porras
Quebrada Agustín
ATP (1.2km); Fresas Mary (1.7km); Pastelería Alemana (3km); Los Pozos de Caldera (15km)

agencies rent bicycles, scooters and ATVs (quad bikes), which are a good way to explore the charms of the surrounding hillsides.

Hiking

With its breathtaking vistas of mist-covered hills and nearby forests, Boquete is one of the most idyllic regions for hiking and walking. Several good paved roads lead out of town into the surrounding hills, passing coffee farms, fields, gardens and virgin forest.

Although many visitors will be content with picturesque strolls along the river, the more ambitious can climb Volcán Barú (p173). There are several entrances to the Parque Nacional Volcán Barú, but the most accessible trail starts near Boquete.

It's possible to access the Sendero Los Quetzales (p172) from Boquete, though the trail is uphill from here; you'll have an easier time if you start hiking from Cerro Punta above Volcán. Landslides have affected the trail in the past. Ask locals about conditions before heading out.

Sendero El Pianista HIKING

(Pianist Trail) This day-hike wends its way through dairy land and into humid cloud forest. You need to wade across a small river after 200m, but then it's a steady, leisurely incline for 2km before you start to climb a steeper, narrow path. Using a guide is highly recommended and should cost US$35/60 for a half-/full day.

The path leads deep into the forest, but you can turn back at any time. To access the trailhead from Boquete, head north on the right bank of the river and cross over two bridges. Immediately before the third bridge, about 4km out of town, a track leads off to the left between a couple of buildings. The trail is not especially difficult but it isn't always well maintained. In April 2014 two Dutch nationals died while hiking here, though the cause of their deaths remains a mystery. Don't go alone and always let the people at your hostel or hotel know your plans.

Rafting

Adventure seekers shouldn't miss the excellent white-water rafting that's within a 1½-hour drive of Boquete. Ríos Chiriquí and Chiriquí Viejo both flow from the fertile hills of Volcán Barú, and are flanked by forest for much of their lengths. In some places, waterfalls can be seen at the edges of the rivers, and both rivers pass through narrow canyons with awesome, sheer rock walls.

The Río Chiriquí is most often run from May to December, while the Chiriquí Viejo is run the rest of the year. Rapids are III and III-plus, and tours last four to five hours.

When booking a trip, inquire if the outfitter uses a safety kayak for descents and

Boquete

Sights

1 Parque José Domingo Médica C4

Activities, Courses & Tours

2 ATV Adventures Boquete C3
3 Boquete Mountain Safari C5
Boquete Outdoor Adventures .... (see 5)
Boquete Tree Trek .... (see 5)
4 Café Ruíz Coffee Tours B1
5 Habla Ya Language Center C5

Sleeping

6 Casa de Montaña B1
7 Downtown Suites C5
8 El Oasis D5
9 Haven B7
10 Hotel Ladera D1
11 Hotel Panamonte C2
12 Isla Verde Hotel B5
13 La Casa de La Abuela B2
14 Mamallena Boquete Hostel C5
15 Pensión Marilós C5
16 Pensión Topas C6
17 Refugio del Río B5

Eating

18 Art Café C3
Big Daddy's Grill .... (see 3)
19 Boquete Fish House C6
20 Café de Punto Encuentro (Olga's) C5
21 El Sabrosón #3 .... C5
22 Gelatería La Ghiotta C4
Greenhouse Cafe .... (see 12)
Hotel Panamonte Restaurant .... (see 11)
23 Mercado Municipal C4
24 Mike's Global Grill C6
25 Pizzeria Ricos Little Italy D4
26 Sugar & Spice C6
27 Supermercado Romero C4

Drinking & Nightlife

28 Boquete Brewing Company C3
Café Ruiz .... (see 4)
29 La Cabaña Boquete D3

Entertainment

30 Boquete Community Playhouse D4

Shopping

31 Tuesday Market D5

if guides are certified in swift-water rescue. These should be minimum requirements for a safe trip.

Tours

Coffee Adventures Tours BIRDWATCHING
(720-3852, 6634-4698; www.coffeeadventures.net; half-day tours per 2 people US$65) Dutch naturalist guides Terry and Hans are locally renowned as great birding and nature guides. They also offer hiking in the cloud forest, including Sendero Los Quetzales, visits to indigenous communities and informative coffee tours (US$35). They have lodgings in three lovely cottages in dense forest 3km southwest of the town center.

Boquete Outdoor Adventures ADVENTURE SPORTS
(6630-1453, 720-2284; www.boqueteoutdooradventures.com; Plaza Los Establos, Av Central; 8am-7:30pm) This highly recommended outfitter run by veteran outdoorsman Jim Omer offers quality rafting trips (US$65 to US$75) and tailored vacations that are ideal for families. The sportfishing adventures on the Golfo de Chiriquí are value-priced (from US$600/1200 inshore/offshore for four passengers). Guides are bilingual and the company uses local service providers. Excellent source of information.

Also offers birdwatching (half-/full day US$40/80) and, from July to October, whale-watching (US$75) tours.

Kotowa Coffee Estate Tour TOUR
(6634-4698, 720-3852; http://coffeeadventures.net; tours US$35; 2pm Mon-Sat) The 3½-hour tours of this gourmet coffee-grower's are said to be the most comprehensive in the area. Guests learn about the estate's history (beginning with a Canadian's arrival in 1918), get a full tour of the production facilities and processing mill, and have a tasting session. Reservations required.

ATV Adventures Boquete ADVENTURE TOUR
(6678-5666; www.facebook.com/atv4x4boquete; Av Central; 9am-7pm) Offers tours of Boquete and surrounds on 4WD ATVs (quad bikes) and side-by-side UTVs. Prices start at US$70 for ATVs and US$100 for UTVs per two people for the 1½-hour Scenic Tour. Longer trips include the 3½-hour Coffee Tour (adult/child US$120/200) and a five-hour Hot Springs Tour (adult/child US$160/375).

Cafes de la Luna Coffee Tour TOUR
(6677-7748; www.boquetecoffeetour.com; tours US$30) If you are looking to learn about small-scale organic coffee production, check out this extended tour of Finca Dos Jefes in the highlands above Boquete that includes roasting and tasting. In addition to guiding the tour, Californian coffee aficionado Richard Lipner is the brains behind the beans. The tour takes about 3½ hours.

Finca Lérida Birdwatching Tour BIRDWATCHING
(720-1111, 720-2816; www.fincalerida.com; tours US$80; 7:30am) Finca Lérida (p170), located 9km northwest of Boquete, is a stunning coffee farm dating back to 1924. It's also considered one of the premier birdwatching spots in Panama, with hundreds of species spotted regularly. A 4½-hour birdwatching trip includes a knowledgeable guide, lunch and transportation. The extensive grounds and forested trails here are prime habitat for the quetzal, a Central American symbol and the national bird of Guatemala. Nearly extinct there, it has found refuge in Chiriquí Province. The quetzals are most likely to be seen here between February and May.

Finca Lérida Coffee Tour TOUR
(720-1111, 720-2816; www.fincalerida.com; 2hr tours US$37.50; 9:30am & 1:30pm) Tours of the Finca Lérida estate are quite thorough, showing both the business side of a small farm and the process of production from coffee cherry to cup. Part of the tour focuses on the farm's transition to organic and sustainable practices, such as through composting and reduced water consumption.

Boquete Mountain Safari DRIVING TOUR
(6627-8829, 730-9353; http://boquetesafaritours.typepad.com; Av Central; half-day 4WD tours US$25; 8am-7:30pm) This agency offers scenic back-country tours in open 4WDs. Highlights of the cloud-forest safari include stops to check out coffee estates, basalt formations and waterfalls, or you can make a beeline for the Caldera hot springs (p162). Also runs rafting tours (US$65), guided horseback riding ($35) in the Caldera hills, and rents scooters (US$25 per hour) and ATVs (US$50 per hour).

Boquete Tree Trek ADVENTURE TOUR
(720-1635; www.boquetetreetrek.com; Plaza Los Establos, Av Central; canopy tours US$65; 8am & 1pm) Travelers love this four-hour canopy tour with 12 zip lines, 14 platforms, a rappel and a Tarzan-swing in secondary forest.

Tours depart daily at 8am and 1pm. The lines pick up some serious speed, so you might want to consider going heavy on the handbrake. Also sells other tours, and includes transportation from the center.

Café Ruíz Coffee Tours TOUR
(☎6672-3786, 730-9575; www.caferuiz-boquete.com; tours US$30; ⏰9am & 1:30pm Mon-Sat) Located on the main road about 600m north of the town center, Café Ruíz is Panama's most famous coffee-grower, and now produces the award-winning geisha varietal. The three-hour tour includes transportation to a nearby coffee farm, a presentation on the history of coffee in Boquete, a tour of a roasting facility and a tasting session. Reservations required.

Courses

Spanish by the River LANGUAGE COURSE
(☎720-3456; www.spanishatlocations.com) The sister school to the popular Spanish school in Bocas del Toro is located 5km south of Boquete near the turnoff to Palmira. Standard/intensive lessons cost US$225/300 for a one-week course. Discounts come with comprehensive packages and longer stays. Also offers homestays (nightly US$18), simple dorms (US$12) and private rooms (US$20).

Habla Ya Language Center LANGUAGE COURSE
(☎730-8344; www.hablayapanama.com; Plaza Los Establos, Av Central; ⏰8am-5:30pm Mon-Fri, 9am-1pm Sat, 1-5pm Sun) Habla Ya offers both group and private Spanish lessons. A week of group lessons (20 hours) starts at US$195. The language school is also well connected to local businesses, so students can take advantage of discounts on everything from accommodations to tours and participate in volunteer projects.

Festivals & Events

Feria de las Flores y del Café FERIA
(http://feriadeboquete.com) The town's annual Flower & Coffee Fair is held for 10 days each January. While there's coffee in the name, it's strangely missing from exhibits, though you will find plenty of rum and children's carnival rides. Book accommodations well ahead.

Boquete Jazz & Blues Festival JAZZ
Local and international talent converge on Boquete for four days in February for the biggest annual music event in Chiriquí Province.

Feria de las Orquídeas FERIA
Showing more than 150 varieties, the orchid fair is held for 10 days every April. It's not all flowers: sundown brings rock concerts and dancing.

Sleeping

Mamallena Boquete Hostel HOSTEL $
(☎6723-2014, 730-8342; www.mamallenaboquete.com; Av Central; dm US$14, d/tr/q with bathroom US$38/55/65, r without bathroom US$33; P 🛜) Facing the central plaza, this turquoise ex-boardinghouse is backpacker central, complete with kitchen, laundry and free pancake breakfasts. For its huge capacity, it feels rather cozy. Three eight-bed dorms boast orthopedic mattresses while 13 of the 16 private rooms have their own bathrooms. There's a sheltered patio area with grill. Service-oriented, it runs tours and shuttles to Bocas and Santa Catalina.

Refugio del Río HOSTEL $
(☎6676-5786, 720-2088; www.facebook.com/hostalrefugiodelrio; Av B Oeste; dm US$13-15, d with/without bathroom US$40/31, cabins US$42; P @ 🛜) With the comfy feel of a large home, this budget stop features a huge guest kitchen and a good location. Some 13 sprawling rooms are pleasant and well furnished, but could be tidier. The dormitory features a row of a dozen single beds with snug covers but saggy mattresses. Reserve ahead for the cool three-person treehouse cabin overlooking the stream.

Pensión Topas GUESTHOUSE $
(☎720-1005; www.facebook.com/pages/Pension-Topas-Boquete-Panama/877290745620094; Av Belisario Porras; s/d with bathroom US$29/42, without bathroom US$16/26; P 🛜 🏊) Built around a small organic garden, this blue-and-orange lodging run by an eccentric German features Tintin murals, a collection of a half-dozen motorbikes and eight tidy rooms. A shady outdoor patio provides ample shared space, and perks include a swimming pool and cable TV. Best rooms are the two on the 2nd floor of the outbuilding, which has a balcony.

Pensión Marilós GUESTHOUSE $
(☎720-1380; marilos66@hotmail.com; cnr Av A Este & Calle 6 Sur; s/d with bathroom US$15/20, without bathroom US$10/15; P) With the feel of a well-worn family home, Marilós offers a central location at bargain rates. Its six rooms are decorated with assorted knick-knacks and doodads reminiscent of the guest bedroom at grandma's house. There's a parrot that's in and out of its cage, ready to greet you at the entrance.

Tinamou Cottage Jungle Lodge COTTAGE **$$**
(☎6634-4698, 720-3852; http://coffeeadventures.net; d incl breakfast US$110-165) If you'd like to get away from it all but still be within striking distance of the town and its amenities, choose these lovely cottages on 9 hectares of dense forest, 3km southwest of Boquete. It's owned by Dutch naturalists who are well-known birding guides. Cottages are quite luxurious, with one or two bedrooms and kitchens, and breakfast comes in a basket.

Boquete Garden Inn INN **$$**
(☎720-2376; www.boquetegardeninn.com; Palo Alto; d incl breakfast US$79-119; P) On the edge of the Río Palo Alto, this garden inn with a dozen rooms in six red-mud cottages is run by a welcoming Briton. The grounds overflow with blossoming tropical flowerbeds, and birds abound (95 species spotted). Rooms – there are five types – with canopy beds are lovely and modern. Service stands out.

Lounging around the patio bar decorated with traditional Panamanian masks proves a fine cap on the day, especially from 6pm to 7pm when drinks are complimentary.

Casa de Montaña B&B **$$**
(☎730-9472; www.casademontana.com; Calle 2 Norte; d US$119-165; P @) A lovely addition to the Boquete accommodations scene, this B&B features six large, fan-cooled rooms with terrace or balcony. Special features include memory-foam mattresses, a fridge, a microwave oven and a dehumidifier in each. Two of the rooms are adapted for guests with disabilities. Breakfasts are a different cuisine every day of the week.

One of the North American owners offers Indian and Pakistani cooking classes (US$25) on Thursday afternoons. The 'Mountain House' is just over 1km northwest of the center – a US$2 taxi ride.

Hotel Ladera HOTEL **$$**
(☎730-9000; www.hotel-ladera.com; Av Buenos Aires, Jaramilla Arriba; s US$99-120, d US$120-142, all incl breakfast; P) This upscale hotel along the the road leading to the Boquete hills features an appealing ultramodern style and attentive staff at the front desk. The 22 rooms have mock-wood tiles and either an outdoor terrace or a small balcony; some larger rooms (eg room 17) feature two king-

THE NGÖBE-BUGLÉ

The Ngöbe-Buglé comprise of two separate ethnolinguistic groups, the Ngöbe and the Buglé, though the distinction is minor, and both are commonly referred to in conjunction with one another. As Panama's largest indigenous community, the Ngöbe-Buglé number close to 200,000. Like the Guna indigenous people, the Ngöbe-Buglé retain their own *comarca* (autonomous region) with its own system of governance and economy while maintaining their language, representation in the Panamanian legislature and full voting rights.

The Ngöbe-Buglé are largely confined to the Chiriquí highlands, and predominantly survive on subsistence agriculture, much like their precolonial ancestors. Their social structure is based on a system of small villages comprised of *chozas* (thatched huts) with dirt floors. In the villages, men practice slash-and-burn agriculture in order to produce staple crops such as plantain, banana, corn, cassava and rice. During the coffee-harvest season, many of the younger men work as migrant laborers in the fields around Boquete, which generates a significant amount of income for the village.

In the villages, women are primarily responsible for raising the children; many also work as skilled artisans, and their crafts can fetch a high price. The two most common items produced by Ngöbe-Buglé women are the *chacara* (a woven bag of plant fibers that is meant to mimic the landscapes of the rainforest) and the *naguas* (a traditional dress of hand-sown appliqué, worn by women and girls). Throughout Chiriquí Province, you can find both items for sale in traditional markets and shops.

As with other indigenous groups in Panama, the Ngöbe-Buglé struggle to maintain their cultural identity, especially as outside pressures continue to descend on the *comarca*. However, although the Ngöbe-Buglé are not as politically organized as the Guna, they are far greater in number, and they control large tracts of undeveloped land. As a result, the Ngöbe-Buglé have been more successful than other indigenous groups, such as the Emberá and Wounaan, in maintaining their cultural identity and resisting the drive to modernize.

sized beds with wicker headboards. There's on-site dining as well as room service.

El Oasis HOTEL $$
(☎720-1586; www.oasisboquete.com; Av Buenos Aires; d incl breakfast US$88; P@🛜) Although it's within walking distance, El Oasis is across the Río Caldera from Boquete proper and is a good deal quieter than staying in town; the river's just meters away. The 18 rooms and suites are immaculate and cozy; at times the place feels more like a B&B than a hotel. The garden restaurant serves good soups.

Downtown Suites HOTEL $$
(☎6461-9134, 790-9302; http://downtownsuites boquete.com; Av A Este; d/tr US$75/99; P🛜) This design-oriented hotel features seven modern suites with living rooms and kitchenettes. It's all spick and span and incredibly good value but a bit, well, austere. Perks include down duvets, flat-screen TVs and safe boxes. Rooms look out on a small grass courtyard with an iron *rancho* (small house).

La Casa de La Abuela HOTEL $$
(☎730-9484; www.lacasadeabuela.com; Calle 2 Norte; s/d incl breakfast from US$70/102; P🛜) Grandmother's House is a modern brick hotel said to be built on the grounds where the family matriarch once tended her chickens. It has 18 comfortable rooms decorated in earth tones and boasting tile floors, flat-screen TVs, hot showers and modern installations. A few also have balconies. There's nice outdoor patio seating, but the roadside location can be noisy at times.

★ **Coffee Estate Inn** B&B $$$
(☎720-2211; www.coffeeestateinn.com; Calle Jaramillo Arriba; 1-/2-bedroom bungalows US$195/250, ste US$165, all incl breakfast; P@🛜) In the lap of coffee-estate luxury, this stunning property is surrounded by orange groves and a 1.5km network of private trails that wind through gardens and forest. The three original bungalows are spacious and smart, with kitchenettes, heated floors and private terraces with valley views. The new owners from the USA have just added four new bungalows and two suites in the main building.

The 2.3-hectare estate is also home to a working coffee farm, the source of your morning brew. Guests get a complimentary coffee tour (three-night minimum stay required). The inn has a small shop, promotes energy conservation and recycling, and offers reusable containers for restaurant take-out.

★ **Haven** BOUTIQUE HOTEL $$$
(☎6491-5578, 730-9345; www.boquetespa.com; Av A Oeste; d standard US$85-140, d deluxe US$125-185, ste US$155-225; P❄🛜≋) This sleekly designed hotel and spa provides a very chic retreat. British-owned, it has eight rooms with cool space-saving designs, set amid verdant gardens. Throughout the property water features, river stones and palms set the scene for relaxation. A full gym and spa with infra-red sauna, steam room, an indoor pool, yoga facilities and a Jacuzzi seal the deal. Professional and service-oriented.

It's 2km south of the town center; watch for signs for the left-hand turn as you approach Boquete.

★ **Isla Verde Hotel** CABIN $$$
(☎720-2751, 720-2533; www.islaverdepanama.com; Av B Oeste; ste US$130-160, d cabins US$110-160; P@🛜) Set in a large, lush garden with a small stream running through it, this delicious property offers different types of lodgings in 14 units – from *casitas* (cottages) to suites and two-story round cabins, all featuring luxuriant mattresses, vaulted ceilings, complete kitchens and roomy bathrooms. It's probably the best in-town retreat, with prompt service and even massages available (from US$55).

Accommodation is for two; each additional person is charged US$20 (kids US$10).

Hotel Panamonte HISTORIC HOTEL $$$
(☎720-1324; www.panamonte.com; Calle 11 de Abril; d/ste incl breakfast US$200/310; P❄🛜) This historic 21-room hotel dating from 1914 wins you over with its sprawling flower gardens, serene spaces, and handsome rooms and public areas. Choose between the original rooms, bursting with character, or new, larger terrace rooms outfitted as modern deluxe. Service is impeccable, and the restaurant (p171) is among Panama's best. The day spa is the perfect complement to a mountain getaway.

You can relax here, knowing that John Wayne, Ingrid Bergman and Richard Nixon did so too. It's located on a quiet road at the northern end of town just west of where the bridge washed away in 2008.

Riverside Inn INN $$$
(☎720-1076; www.riversideinnboquete.com; Av Buenos Aires, Palo Alto; d incl breakfast US$110-145; P🛜) A casual stunner, this exclusive inn with six suites has a relaxed and intimate setting and an excellent restaurant called

the Rock (p171). Living areas feature original artwork and a grand stone fireplace. Suites are expansive, with vaulted ceilings, soft cotton bedding and Jacuzzi baths. Though the setting is lovely, the flat riverside location lacks the mountain panoramas of other inns. It's about 2km north of the town center on the way to the hills.

Hotel Los Establos
BOUTIQUE HOTEL $$$

(☑720-2685; www.losestablos.net; d/ste incl breakfast US$215/330; P@☎) These lavish quarters surrounded by manicured grounds and a coffee farm northeast of the center bear no trace of their past as erstwhile stables. Decor is elegant but a little fussy – heavy on brocade, carved mirrors, candelabras and gold highlights. The dozen rooms and suites have elegant furnishings and private terraces with views, some of Volcán Barú. There's a restaurant and a spa.

Finca Lérida
HISTORIC HOTEL $$$

(☑720-1111; www.fincalerida.com; Alto Quielk; d/ste incl breakfast from US$175/270; P@☎) Famous for its birdwatching opportunities – it's one of the best places in the country to see quetzals – and a working coffee farm (see p166), Finca Lérida is also a somewhat erratically run hotel with 17 rooms and suites plus four cabins. Standard rooms are tastefully decorated with countryside motifs, and each has a deck and outdoor seating for watching the hummingbirds. Suites feature Jacuzzis.

Guests and day-trippers (which are legion) can dine at the on-site restaurant, which features excellent salads made with local produce, well-prepared sandwiches and Panamanian favorites.

✗ Eating

Mike's Global Grill
INTERNATIONAL $

(☑730-9360, 6865-8873; www.mikesglobalgrill.com; Av Central Oeste; mains US$7-12; ☺8am-10pm Mon-Thu, 8am-11pm Fri & Sat, 9am-10pm Sun) This homesick restaurant is the love child of Mike and Heidi who met – where else? – at the South Pole. To further the wanderlust theme, dishes range from Asian fusion to American chili and British fish and chips. The ambience is chilled, with a long bar and sofas. Breakfast daily, and live music on Thursday, Friday and Saturday nights.

Pizzeria Ricos Little Italy
PIZZA $

(☑720-1291, 6390-2415; opposite Calle 4a Sur; pizzas small US$7-10, large US$13-20; ☺11am-9pm Tue-Sun) Enjoy the real McCoy at this hole-in-the-wall pizzeria with six tables. It's just across the bridge and facing the fairgrounds.

Sugar & Spice
BAKERY, DELI $

(Av Central & Calle 7a Sur; breakfast & sandwiches US$4-7.50; ☺8am-6pm Thu-Sat, Mon & Tue, to 4pm Sun) Throngs gather at this artisan bakery, a modest storefront with a couple of patio tables, for US-style sandwiches, organic salads and oh-so-good brownies. You can also take away fresh bread, including whole-grain and ciabatta, and cinnamon buns.

Café de Punto Encuentro (Olga's)
CAFE $

(☑720-2123; Calle 6 Sur; mains US$3.25-8.50; ☺7am-1pm) In a converted carport and garden, this family-run eatery is a find. All guests are *mi amor* (my love) to the affectionate Olga, who cooks breakfast like nobody's business. The menu ranges from pancakes and bacon to Panamanian breakfasts (US$7). Expect to wait, but for this quality of home-cooked food, you won't mind.

Gelateria La Ghiotta
ICE CREAM $

(☑6107-1465; cnr Av Central & Calle Central; 1/2/3 scoops US$1.75/2.75/3.75; ☺11am-8pm Thu-Tue) Great selection of Italian ice cream at this central and very friendly little *gelateria*. Choose from 10 flavors, including *guanabana* (soursop), pineapple and coffee.

Pastelería Alemana
BAKERY $

(Via Boquete; pastries from US$3; ☺8am-noon Thu-Mon) On the main road 3km south of town, this German patisserie serves up decadent apple strudel and tortes, as well as authentic German breads.

Big Daddy's Grill
SEAFOOD $

(☑6675-9887; Av Central; mains US$3-14; ☺noon-9pm Tue-Sat, 9am-8pm Sun) A stalwart choice of gringo *boqueteños,* this friendly eatery serves the most enormous and satisfying fish tacos. The menu also includes chicken wings, lovely salads, margaritas rimmed with chili salt and (if you must) corn dogs. The backyard patio offers privacy and a better atmosphere (in both senses).

Fresas Mary
DESSERT $

(www.facebook.com/pages/Fresa-Mary/3469318 38689243; Calle Volcancito; snacks US$2.75-3.50; ☺10am-7pm Tue-Sun) With strawberry and other fruit *batidos* (fruit shakes) that will make you quake with pleasure, this cute cafe on the road to Volcán Barú makes a worthy stop.

El Sabrosón #3 CAFETERIA $
(☎720-2147; Av Central; mains US$3-6; ⊙6:30am-10pm Mon-Fri, to 11pm Sat & Sun) Our favorite of the three branches of this much-loved local institution cooks up cheap and filling Panamanian cuisine served cafeteria-style, and has tables on a terrace overlooking the main drag. Although Boquete is rapidly being colonized by gringo-friendly boutique eateries, this is one local institution that remains true to its local roots.

Mercado Municipal MARKET $
Fresh produce is sold at this new enclosed market on the northeastern corner of the central plaza.

Supermercado Romero SUPERMARKET $
(Av A Este; ⊙24hr Nov-Feb, 7am-10pm Mar-Oct) One block east of the central plaza, this has Boquete's best selection of groceries. It's open round the clock in high season from November to February.

★ **Boquete Fish House** SEAFOOD $$
(☎6521-2120, 6918-7111; www.facebook.com/BoqueteFishHouseRestaurant; Av Central; mains US$10-14; ⊙noon-8pm Mon-Sat) One of our favorite places in Boquete for a tasty, inexpensive meal is this fish house along the Quebrada Grande. It offers sea bass prepared in eight different ways – from the delightful version that's steamed and wrapped in lettuce leaves to the pedestrian-but-tasty fish and chips. There are meat and vegetarian choices as well.

★ **Il Pianista** ITALIAN $$
(☎720-2728; Palo Alto; mains US$12-17.50; ⊙noon-10pm Tue-Sun) This Italian restaurant and pizzeria has riverstone walls and just a few tables along one of Boquete's hillside roads. Sicilian Giovanni cooks while his Panamanian wife, Doris, serves. A bottle of wine and pizza or calzone make the perfect leisurely lunch, but don't come in a rush: service can be slow. Local buses go past, or follow signs for Boquete Garden Inn; it's just above it.

Il Barolo ITALIAN $$
(☎6558-6616, 6509-7559; www.facebook.com/Ilbaroloboquete; Alto Lino; mains US$6-14; ⊙11am-11pm) This delightful find up in the hills offers some of the best Italian food in Panama. The young chef specializes in a risotto that is legendary in these parts. Panamanians do not live by pasta alone, and 10 *platos mexicanos*, including pork fajitas, fish tacos and veggie burritos, have also found their way onto the menu.

Greenhouse Cafe CAFE $$
(☎720-2751, 720-2533; www.islaverdepanama.com; Av B Oeste; ⊙7am-3pm) This lovely new arrival in a glass-and-steel pavilion on the grounds of the Isla Verde Hotel (p169) is a great place for breakfast or lunch. Salad plates (US$1.50 to US$3) and other dishes lean toward the Middle East (there is a Turkish connection). Best (perhaps only) baklava in town and live guitar music at lunch on Wednesdays.

Art Café FRENCH $$
(☎720-1821; www.boqueteartcafe.com; Av Central; mains US$11-15; ⊙noon-3pm & 5-9pm Tue-Sun) Fresh and festive, this oh-so-French cafe-restaurant serves authentic *cuisine française* in a rainbow setting of primary colors and French doodads. Francophiles will embrace menu options that include duck, rabbit and tenderloin with blue cheese. For lunch there is a daily special (US$15) with dessert and appetizer.

Rock INTERNATIONAL $$$
(☎6982-8876, 720-2516; www.therockboquete.com; Av Buenos Aires, Palo Alto; mains US$10-20; ⊙noon-9:30pm Wed-Mon) This is cosmopolitan dining at its best, at least in the highlands of Panama. Attached to the Riverside Inn (p169), the Rock takes itself very seriously. The pork ribs with papaya sugarcane sauce come widely recommended, as does the herbed octopus with coconut rice. Lovely pasta and seafood also served. Excellent, well-informed service.

The restaurant can be a lively spot for a drink; it has an extensive wine list and a full bar. Two-for-one cocktails are served from 6pm to 7pm. Live jazz on Monday nights.

Hotel Panamonte Restaurant INTERNATIONAL $$$
(☎720-1327; www.panamonte.com; Calle 11 de Abril; mains US$15-22; ⊙noon-11pm) This sophisticated restaurant has a longstanding reputation. Chef Charlie Collins takes a modern approach, exquisitely preparing everything from grilled fillets to mushroom-stuffed ravioli. Local staple *arroz con pollo* (rice with chicken) is transformed into a delectable risotto. While the powder-blue dining room rings romantic, you may prefer a tiny table near the cracking hearth in the bar-lounge. Ideal for cocktails and wine, too.

Drinking & Nightlife

Boquete Brewing Company MICROBREWERY
(☎6494-4992; www.boquetebrewingcompany.com; Av Central; ⊙4-10pm) US-style craft-beer

bars and pubs are all the rage in Panama these days; there are five in the capital, so why should Boquete be left out? This place has eight beers and two hard ciders on tap at any given time, and they range from the sublime (hard lemonade) to the ridiculous (watermelon ale). Cheers!

La Cabaña Boquete CLUB
(Calle de la Feria; cover US$2; ⌚7pm-2am Fri & Sat) Boquete's only dance club has DJs, reggaetón, a young crowd and a steady stream of rum and cola to keep it all flowing. It's by the river, north of the fairground.

Café Ruiz CAFE
(☎6672-3786, 730-9575; www.caferuiz-boquete.com; Calle 2 Norte; cakes US$3; ⌚8am-4pm Mon-Sat) The outdoor patio at Ruiz makes a good spot to sip a cappuccino and watch the mist move across the mountains. It's also the epicenter of Panama's famous coffee industry, so you can be sure that your brew has its origin in the surrounding hillsides.

☆ Entertainment

Boquete Community Playhouse THEATER
(☎6533-0967, 6030-7706; http://bcpeventscenter.org; Calle de la Feria; admission US$15) Hosts local theater and special events. Check with your hotel or tourist office about current offerings.

Shopping

Tuesday Market MARKET
(http://bcpeventscenter.org; Boquete Community Playhouse, Calle de la Feria; ⌚9am-noon Tue) A weekly market at the local theater features arts and crafts, jewelry, organic produce and prepared foods.

ℹ Information

ATP (☎720-4060; chiriqui@atp.gob.pa; Hwy 43; ⌚8am-4pm) About 1.5km south of Boquete on the road to David, the large ATP office sits atop a bluff overlooking town. Here you can pick up maps and obtain information on area attractions. There's a coffee shop on the ground floor and an exhibition upstairs detailing the history of the region (in Spanish only).

Banco Nacional de Panama (☎720-1328; Av Central; ⌚8am-3pm Mon-Fri, 9am-noon Sat) Has an ATM.

Centro Medico San Juan Bautista (☎720-1881; Calle 2 Norte) For medical care.

Global Bank (☎720-2329; Av Central; ⌚8am-3pm Mon-Fri, 9am-noon Sat) Bank with ATM.

Post Office (⌚7am-6pm Mon-Fri, to 5pm Sat) In the former train station on the central plaza.

ℹ Getting There & Away

The main bus terminal is on the main road near the main plaza. Buses to David (US$1.75, one hour, every 30 minutes) depart from the south side of Boquete's main plaza every 30 minutes from 5am to 6:30pm. From David they run from from 6am to 9:30pm. Hourly buses run to the town of Caldera (US$2, 45 minutes).

Shuttle vans departing from in front of the Mamallena Boquete Hostel (p167) link Boquete with Bocas del Toro (US$30 including boat, four hours) and Santa Catalina (US$35, five hours).

Boquete's small size lends itself to easy exploration. The urbano (local) buses that wind through the hills cost US$0.50. They depart on the main road one block north of the plaza. Taxis charge US$2 to US$3 for most places around town.

For scooter (US$25 per hour) or bike rentals (about US$3), check out local travel agencies and hostels. Cars can be rented at **Dollar** (☎721-1103; Plaza Los Establos, Av Central; ⌚8am-5pm), and are a great option to explore more of the local area.

Parque Nacional Volcán Barú

Volcán Barú is Panama's only volcano and the dominant geographical feature of western Panama. It is no longer active but has seven craters and its summit, at 3474m, is the highest point in Panama. On clear days it affords views of both the Pacific and Caribbean coasts. The 143-sq-km **national park** (admission US$5) provides ample opportunities for hiking, mountain climbing and camping. It's home to abundant wildlife, including pumas and the resplendent quetzal, most commonly seen here between February and May.

The fertile soil and the temperate climate of Volcán Barú's mid-altitude slopes support some of Panama's most productive agriculture, especially in the areas around Boquete and Cerro Punta, which is effectively Panama's vegetable garden. Large trees dominate the volcano's lower slopes, giving way on the upper slopes to smaller plants, bushes, scrub and alpine wildflowers.

Activities

★**Sendero Los Quetzales** HIKING
One of Panama's most beautiful trails runs between Cerro Punta and Boquete, crisscrossing Río Caldera. You can hike from either direction, but west to east offers more downhill: the town of Cerro Punta is almost 1000m higher than Boquete. The 8km route takes between four and six hours. Getting to and from the trailhead takes another couple

THE RESPLENDENT QUETZAL

The lore of the resplendent quetzal originated during the era of the Maya and the Aztecs, who worshipped a deity known as Quetzalcoatl (Plumed Serpent). This mythical figure was often depicted wearing a crown of male quetzal tail feathers and was believed to be responsible for bestowing corn upon humans.

A popular legend regarding the scarlet-red breast of the quetzal originated during the colonial period. In 1524 in the highlands of Guatemala, the Spanish conquistador Pedro de Alvarado defeated Tecun Uman, the last ruler of the Quiché people. As Uman lay dying, his spiritual guide, the quetzal, stained its breast with Uman's blood and then died of remorse. From then on, male quetzals bore a scarlet breast, and their song hasn't been heard since.

Today quetzals are regarded in Central America as a symbol of freedom, and it's commonly believed that they cannot survive if held in captivity. Birdwatchers from far and wide continue to brave the elements in Panama for the chance to see the most famous bird in Central America.

The best time to spot a quetzal is in April and May when they nest in the highlands and wait for their young to hatch. Look for their nests in rotted tree trunks that they carve out with their beaks.

of hours either side (about 23km in total). A guide is recommended.

A 4WD taxi can take you to the trailhead on the Cerro Punta side for about US$25 per person; a *collectivo* (shared taxi) will cost US$6. Taxi drivers know the area as Respingo. Road conditions may be very poor due to landslides. The trail is 5km uphill from the main road and 2km from the last paved road. When you exit the trail, it's another 8km along the road to Boquete, though you may be able to catch a taxi along the road. In total, the hike is about 23km, so plan accordingly if you intend to walk the length of the trail.

Buses run from David to Cerro Punta (US$3.50, 2¼ hours); last departure is 6pm. Consider leaving your luggage at one of the hotels in David to save yourself the hassle of backtracking. Take only the bare essentials with you on the walk, and a little cash for a good meal and/or lodging when you arrive in Boquete.

Be aware that conditions can change any time, especially after heavy rain. We recommend that you hike the trail with a guide; there's talk that this may become a requirement. In recent times many travelers have gotten lost on this stretch and resources for rescue are practically nonexistent.

Volcán Barú HIKING

For views from the summit of both the Pacific and the Caribbean coasts, climbing Volcán Barú is a goal of many visitors. It might not be worth it in poor weather, as the going is strenuous and rough, and there is little to see in cloud cover. You can enter the national park on the eastern (Boquete) and western (Volcán) sides of the volcano.

The eastern summit access from Boquete is the easier, but it involves a strenuous uphill hike along a 13.5km road that goes from the park entrance – about 8km northwest of the center of town – to the summit. The road is paved to the ranger station and several kilometers beyond. If you drive or taxi as far up as possible and then walk the rest of the way, it takes about five or six hours to reach the summit from the park gate; walking from town would take another two or three hours each way.

We recommended you hike at night, starting at 11pm or midnight and arriving at dawn to see the sunrise. But for this you'll need to hire a guide and be prepared for the cold. Another option is to spend the night. Camping will also allow you to be at the top during the morning, when the views are best.

The western access is just outside the town of Volcán, on the road to Cerro Punta. The rugged 16.5km-long road into the park (requiring a 4WD vehicle) goes only a short way off the main road to the foot of the volcano. The view of the summit and the nearby peaks from this entrance are impressive, and there's a lovely loop trail that winds through secondary and virgin forest. The ascent takes eight to 10 hours.

Sleeping

Parque Nacional Volcán Barú Camping CAMPGROUND $

(campsites US$5) Camping is possible in the park and on the trail to the summit from the Boquete side, along the Sendero Los Quetzales at a picnic spot called Mirador La Roca or at the ranger station at the entrance to the Sendero Los Quetzales on the Cerro Punta side.

Information

Admission to the park is paid at either of the trailheads leading to the summit or at the ranger station on the Cerro Punto side of the Sendero Los Quetzales. The best time to visit is during the dry season, especially early in the morning when wildlife is most active. Be advised that overnight temperatures can drop below freezing, and it may be windy and cold during the day, particularly in the morning. Dress accordingly and bring a flashlight (torch).

Getting There & Away

The trailhead leading to the summit of Volcán Barú is best accessed from the town of Boquete, while the Sendero Los Quetzales is best approached from Cerro Punta. A taxi will cost US$30 and US$25 respectively.

Volcán

POP 12,720

Volcán is the first sizable town that you pass heading north along the route to Parque Internacional La Amistad. Clinging to the southwest flank of towering Volcán Barú, Volcán has a pleasant feel and serves as a good base for eating and sleeping and as a springboard for excursions. If you want to see what Boquete was like back when it was just another town in the Chiriquí highlands, this may be the perfect stop for you.

Sights

★Arte Cruz WORKSHOP

(☎6622-1502, 6503-1128; www.artecruzpanama.com/artevolcan; ⏰8:30am-noon & 1:30-5:30pm Tue-Fri, from 9am Sat & Sun) FREE On the west (left) side of Hwy 41, some 3.5km south of Volcán, you'll spot this workshop where master carver and artist José de la Cruz González makes and sells exquisite signs, sculptures and furniture in mahogany and other woods, as well as impressive etchings on crystal and glass. José trained in fine arts in Italy and Honduras, and his work has been commissioned by buyers worldwide. Visitors are treated to his entertaining demonstrations.

Área Silvestre Protegida Lagunas de Volcán NATIONAL PARK

Some 4km west of Volcán, this protected area encompasses the highest lake system (1240m) in Panama. The two picturesque lakes swell in the rainy season, with lush, virgin forest at their edges and Volcán Barú in the background. Surrounding woodlands are excellent sites for birdwatching.

To get to the lakes from downtown Volcán, turn west onto Calle El Valle and follow the signs. Buses don't run here, but take a taxi from Volcán for about US$6.

Sitio Barriles ARCHAEOLOGICAL SITE

(☎6575-1828; Barriles; donation US$5; ⏰8am-4pm) The pre-Columbian ruins at this site 6km southwest of Volcán along the Río Gariche date from between AD 300 and 900, when the settlement had as many as 1000 residents. The site is on the private Finca Campestre; the owners have a variety of artifacts on display in their yard and in a small, underwhelming museum. Not all of the artifacts were found on site. Guided tours of the collection and gardens are in both Spanish and English.

Barriles is named after several small stone 'barrels' found in the area. It is one of the few archaeological sites accessible to the public in Panama.

Tours

Janson Coffee Farm TOUR

(☎6867-3884, 6569-7494; www.jansoncoffeefarm.com) Tours of this very productive coffee farm, located about 3km west of Volcán on the way to the lakes, range from a one-hour overview (US$10) to a 3½-hour all-in tour (US$65) that includes tasting expensive geisha coffee and touring the estate. Other activities include birdwatching and fishing tours (US$35 each) and horseback riding (from US$45 for two hours).

Highland Adventures ADVENTURE TOUR

(☎6531-0420, 6685-1682; hlaaizpurua@hotmail.com; Av Central) Activities run by local guide Gonzalo Aizpurua include rainforest mountain-biking, birding or hiking in Parque Internacional La Amistad (US$140 for two people, including transportation) and guided climbs to the top of Volcán Barú (US$170 for two people, from 10 to 12 hours). His shop is 1.5km after the police station on the road to Cerro Punta.

Sleeping

★Mount Totumas Cloud Forest CABIN $$
(☎6963-5069; www.mounttotumas.com; d/tr US$70/110, d/ste lodge US$130/165, 2-bedroom cabins US$175; @☎) This 162-hectare ecolodge lies 20km northwest of Volcán. At 1900m it's among the highest in Panama, and the cloud-forest setting on the southern border of Parque Internacional La Amistad is a nature-lover's dream. Choose from among a dozen rooms in three separate buildings, including a brand-new five-bedroom lodge. Some rooms have fully equipped kitchens and all have hammock decks with views.

The cabins are off the grid, so hot water, electricity and internet comes via a micro-hydroplant. Nine trails covering more than 50km lead to waterfalls and hot springs. Guests can sign up for guided hikes to the top of Mt Totumas (2630m) and into La Amistad park. Transportation is available from Volcán (US$60 one way) or from Boquete and David (US$100). Otherwise guests will need a high-clearance 4WD.

Volcán Lodge GUESTHOUSE $$
(☎6461-2970, 771-4709; www.volcanlodge.webs.com; d/tr/ste US$65/75/120, all incl breakfast; P@☎) This beautifully restored russet-red lodge 100m north of the main thoroughfare has five wood-paneled guestrooms reminiscent of a log cabin on the prairie. The wide veranda and balcony are great on a warm evening, and the 1st-floor restaurant is recommended. Bilingual hosts Jorge and Vicky could not be more welcoming.

Hotel Dos Ríos HOTEL $$
(☎771-4271, 771-5555; www.dosrios.com.pa; d/ste incl breakfast US$79/99; P@☎) On Volcán's main road 500m northwest of the center, this friendly midrange hotel has 20 adequate rooms built around lush gardens and a gurgling stream with a little arched footbridge. We love the antique cash register in the lobby, and there's a decent restaurant, too. Choose room 108 for the views.

Las Plumas VILLA $$
(☎6527-3848, 771-5541; www.las-plumas.com; 2-/3-bedroom bungalows US$60/130; P☎) About 10km northeast of Volcán en route to Cerro Punta, this friendly Dutch-owned property sits on 2.4 hectares of land on the edge of Paso Ancho village. The five fully equipped bungalows sleep two to six people and are beautifully furnished with solid wooden furniture, leather couche and orthopedic mattresses, and fitted with tiled bathrooms. A massive hedge keeps it all secluded.

The main attractions here are the beauty of the surrounding forest, the gushing Río Chiriquí Viejo and the breathtaking mountain views. Minimum stay of three nights, with discounted weekly and monthly rates.

Eating

Cafe Volcán INTERNATIONAL $
(☎6637-4503; Av Central; mains US$6-11; ⏲9am-9pm) This popular eatery with a long breezy terrace overlooking Volcán's main thoroughfare has a menu with Panamanian specialties, and also choices such as Romanian steak that may seem odd until you learn that owner Morena hails from that part of the world. Fish – particularly local trout (US$9) – is good and very fresh. 'No cans here,' said the waiter. Retro-style decor – an antique stove in one corner, and an old sewing machine in another – adds a light touch.

Mana Restaurante PANAMANIAN $
(☎6461-2970, 771-4709; www.volcanlodge.webs.com; mains US$5-12; ⏲11am-8pm) Not heavenly but certainly good, Mana at the Volcán Lodge guesthouse offers an interesting menu that combines Panamanian favorites such as *tostadas* (toasted corn) and *gallo pinto* (blended rice and beans) with North American staples including hamburgers and chili, reflecting the owners' long-term residence there. A favorite with local expats.

La Carbonera ITALIAN $$
(☎6449-7117, 6590-5639; www.facebook.com/pages/Rest-La-Carbonera-Volcan/825098610880136; mains US$7.50-14; ⏲noon-9pm Tue-Sun) Quite a surprising find some 3km along the road heading northeast to Cerro Punta, this authentic Italian eatery serves excellent pasta and pizza (US$7.50 to US$10) as well as more complicated main courses such as chicken breast in white wine and pork fillet with tomato relish. It's a relaxed place with rather relaxed service too.

Cerro Brujo MEDITERRANEAN $$
(☎6669-9196; Brisas del Norte; mains US$14-18; ⏲noon-3pm & 6-10pm Tue-Sun) This unexpected gourmet restaurant is in a funky country house with garden seating. A simple chalkboard menu offers just three or four daily options. Gregarious owner-chef Patti Miranda's mouth-watering creations, using organic and local ingredients only, include squash-blossom soup, coq au vin, a lamb stew to die

for, mahimahi coated in sesame seeds and, for dessert, banana flambé.

It's in the Brisas del Norte district 1km north of Av Central. Grab a taxi there or take the signed turnoff on the main road.

Getting There & Away

Hwy 41, linking Volcán with La Concepción to the south, forks in the center of town: one arrow points left toward Río Sereno, on the Costa Rican border (35km); the other points right toward Cerro Punta (16km), the western entrance to the Sendero Los Quetzales.

Buses to David (US$3, 1½ hours) depart every 15 minutes from 5am to 7:30pm from the station next to the municipal market, 100m northeast of the police station on the road to Cerro Punta. There are also pickup-truck taxis parked by the Delta gasoline station near the Río Sereno–Cerro Punta fork in the road.

Santa Clara

POP 2640

Just over 30km from Volcán, on the highway to Río Sereno and the Costa Rican border, the tiny village of Santa Clara at first appears to offer little more than a grocery store and a gas station. But it's home to **Finca Hartmann** (☎6450-1853; www.fincahartmann.com), a working shade-grown coffee farm situated in highland rainforest (tours per person US$15). The coffee harvest season runs roughly from October to January.

Here you'll also find a rich variety of wildlife – the birdwatching (tours per person US$15) is superb, with more than 280 unique species in the area, and the estate's five hiking trails pass through a variety of habitats between 1300m and 2000m.

It also rents out basic but handsomely constructed **cabins** (2-/4-person cabins US$90/140). The smaller one has a bedroom, bathroom and kitchen, while the bigger lodge counts six guestrooms over two stories, with a veranda running round the top floor. There's hot water but no electricity. Cabins have clean potable spring water and flush toilets. Ardent conservationists, the Hartmanns have hosted a number of scientists affiliated with the Smithsonian over the years.

Getting There & Away

To reach here by public transportation, take the Río Sereno bus (US$5.10, 2½ hours) from David, via La Concepción and Volcán, and ask to be let out at the entrance to Finca Hartmann. It is located a few hundred meters past the gas station, on the right-hand side – look for the small sign. The estate is another 1km up a dirt track.

Bambito

POP 700

There's no shortage of tiny mountain towns and villages along the road to Cerro Punta and Parque Internacional La Amistad, but Bambito is a good place to stop if you want to spend the night or visit a working trout farm.

Activities

Truchas de Bambito FISHING

(admission US$5; ⏲8am-5pm Mon-Fri, 9am-5pm Sat & Sun) This rainbow-trout farm, where thousands of fish are raised in three pools fed by spring water, belongs to the Hotel Bambito opposite and is really all about catching your own lunch or dinner. Pay the admission, throw in your line (included) and within minutes (perhaps even seconds) you'll be reeling in a fish. It costs another US$4.50 to take your fish away with you.

Sleeping & Eating

★**Cielito Sur B&B** B&B $$

(☎771-2038, 6602-3008; www.cielitosur.com; Nueva Suiza; d incl breakfast US$105-115; P@🛜) Just under 3.5km north of Bambito is this sweet highland retreat set in a garden of anthuriums and hummingbirds. Owned by a friendly Panamanian-American couple, it offers four spacious guest rooms named (and decorated) after indigenous tribes; some have kitchenettes. There's also a new two-bedroom house with a large fireplace and a full kitchen.

From here a trail leads to a coffee plantation, whose produce is served daily at the property. Lounge spaces abound both inside and out; the common lounge with fireplaces and a library is an oasis. You can also arrange canoeing, birdwatching and quetzal trail transfers here.

Casa Grande Bambito Highlands RESORT $$

(☎771-5127; www.casagrandebambito.com; d/ste from US$95/125; P@🛜🏊) Just north of Bambito along the Río Chiriquí Viejo, this 20-room resort set in the forest is ideal for families as it offers health-spa facilities, a pool and a list of outdoor activities as long as your arm. Rooms are in small individual cabins or a central low-level building; the wood-paneled restaurant with stained glass is a delight. The friendly staff at the front desk can organize everything from horseback riding (US$17.50 for one hour) and tubing on the river (US$29) to rock climbing (US$50 per two people for one hour).

Hotel Bambito Resort HOTEL **$$**
(☎771-4373, 771-4265; www.hotelbambito.com; d incl breakfast US$90-110; P@ⓦ) This sprawling roadside hotel (a pool does not a resort make) has 45 rooms in both a main building and a stone-and-wood cabin. The grounds are quite attractive, the Truchas restaurant serves trout from the farm across the street, and it's a hop, skip and a jump to Parque Internacional La Amistad. Room 3222 has a king-size bed and a lovely balcony.

Dulces Caseros Alina ICE CREAM
(☎6758-4705; www.facebook.com/DulcesCaseros Alina; ⊙10am-6pm Wed-Mon) This small shop sells fruit jam, candy, milkshakes and ice cream using the region's famous strawberries, which thrive at this altitude. Stock up on some goodies – especially if you're on your way to the Parque Internacional La Amistad. You'll find it about 1.5km north of the landmark Hotel Bambito.

Getting There & Away

Buses from David to Cerro Punta (US$3.50, 2¼ hours, every 20 minutes) pass through Bambito and can drop you off in the center.

Cerro Punta

POP 7750

Lying at 800m, this tranquil highland town is reminiscent of an alpine village. As you near Cerro Punta, the region takes on an almost European look, with meticulously tended vegetable plots and chalet-like houses with steep-pitched roofs. It's unsurprising to learn that a Swiss colony was founded here many decades ago and the hamlet just south is called Nueva Suiza (New Switzerland).

Visitors come to Cerro Punta primarily during the dry season (from mid-December to April) to access the two nearby national parks: Volcán Barú and La Amistad. The town itself makes a charming stop, however, especially since the area is known for its succulent strawberries, available much of the year at roadside stands.

Hotel Cerro Punta (☎6546-7334, 771-2020; www.hotelcerropunta.com; s/d US$24/36; Pⓦ) is a friendly hotel located on the main road offering a row of 10 concrete rooms that are a bit tired and beaten up. But they overlook a grassy backyard, and the private hot-water bathroom will be the last you'll see for a while if you're on your way to Volcán Barú or La Amistad national parks. There's also a decent and good value in-house restaurant.

Getting There & Away

Buses run from David to Cerro Punta (US$3.50, 2¼ hours, every 20 minutes), stopping at Volcán and Bambito along the way, and carrying on to Guadalupe. If you're coming from Costa Rica, catch this bus at the turnoff from the Interamericana at La Concepción.

If you're driving, the main road continues through Cerro Punta and ends at Guadalupe, 3km further. Another road takes off to the left heading for the Las Nubes entrance to Parque Internacional La Amistad, just under 7km to the northwest.

Guadalupe

POP 8400

Situated about 3km north of Cerro Punta and at an elevation of 2200m, Guadalupe is the end of the road. It's a glorious area where you can walk among meticulously tended farms and gardens. This little community is full of flowers, and the agricultural plots curling up on steep hillsides are straight out of a picture book. Wildlife abounds up in the hills.

Sights & Activities

The folks at the Los Quetzales Ecolodge & Spa (p178) can organize any number of activities and excursions, including horseback riding (US$13/8 per hour with/without guide), birdwatching tours (US$60/90 half-/full day) and bicycle rentals (US$5/20 per hour/day).

Just beyond the Los Quetzales Ecolodge & Spa, **Finca Dracula** (☎771-2070; www.facebook.com/fincadracula; adult/student US$10/3.50; ⊙8am-4pm) displays one of Latin America's finest orchid collections, with some 2600 species cultivated here. The extremely knowledgeable staff take great pride in showing off this impressive sanctuary to interested guests on an included 45-minute tour. Have a drink or a cuppa and a snack in the new cafe.

Sleeping & Eating

★**Los Quetzales Cabins** CABIN **$$**
(☎6671-2131, 771-2182; www.losquetzales.com; dm US$30, 4-person cabins US$140-180; ⓦ) Have we died and gone to heaven? Sleep in one of six rustic retreats, or dormitories sleeping between two and 10, tucked into the rainforest; your nose is practically in the canopy. The forested setting, with its darting

hummingbirds, lookout balconies and trout ponds, is among the most spectacular in Panama. All cabins have electricity, hot showers and fireplaces (with wood supplied).

Bring your own food, make arrangements for a cook or groceries to be delivered, or eat in the ecolodge restaurant (open to 9:30pm). The cabins are between 1.5km and 2km from the ecolodge up a 4WD track; transportation is provided.

Los Quetzales Ecolodge & Spa RESORT **$$**
(☎6671-2131, 771-2182; www.losquetzales.com; camping with/without tent US$10/15, dm/d/ste incl breakfast from US$18/85/135; Wi-Fi) Located in town, this large resort complex run by tourism pioneer Carlos Alfaro is a favorite among birdwatchers and hikers. Among the 21 rooms are dorms for men, for women and families, and doubles and suites with vaulted ceilings, wood furnishings and private hot-water bathrooms. Most guests tend to congregate in the excellent restaurant, featuring a bar and cozy fireplace lounge.

Couples might want to splurge on one of the five cedar-walled suites with a romantic hewn-stone fireplace, private bathtub and balcony facing the forest; families can ask about the new farmhouse with up to six bedrooms (US$300) in Bajo Grande, 3km to the southeast. All guests have access to a full-service spa and three hot tubs by the Río Chiriquí Viejo (all water on the premises is piped-in spring water). Also on the premises is an equestrian center with 10 horses and a private network of trails adjoining Parque Nacional Volcán Barú, which is less than an hour's walk away (transportation available).

Getting There & Away

Buses run from David to Guadalupe (US$3.50, 2½ hours, every 20 minutes) via Volcán, Bambito and Cerro Punta.

Parque Internacional La Amistad (Las Nubes)

The 4000-sq-km **Parque Internacional La Amistad** (International Friendship Park; entry US$5, campsites US$10; ⏰8am-4pm), a favorite of hikers and naturalists alike, covers portions of both Chiriquí and Bocas del Toro (p207).Provinces. Although the lion's share of the park lies in the latter, the Chiriquí side, with its entrance at Las Nubes, is more accessible.

Most of the park is inaccessible terrain high up in the Talamanca mountains. It's worth making the trek, though, as the park is home to a recorded 90 mammal species and all six cat species. More than 450 bird species have also been recorded here, including quetzals and harpy eagles.

It was established jointly by Panama and Costa Rica in 1988; two years later it was added to Unesco's World Heritage List. The park contains seven of the 12 classified life zones, and serves as a refuge for a great number of endangered flora and fauna.

Activities & Tours

Sendero La Cascada HIKING
(Waterfall Trail) Starting at the Las Nubes ranger station, this 3.7km round-trip hike takes in three *miradores* (lookouts) as well as a 45m-high waterfall. At the time of research the stairs to the bathing pool were closed due to flood damage.

Sendero Panamá Verde HIKING
This is an easy and well-marked trail of less than a kilometer focusing on local flora. It's just beyond the Las Nubes park entrance.

Sendero El Retoño HIKING
(Shoot Trail) From the Las Nubes ranger station this moderately difficult trail loops a couple of kilometers through secondary forest, crosses a number of rustic bridges and winds through bamboo groves.

Lost World Tours ADVENTURE TOUR
(☎6432-8182, 6920-3036; www.thelostandfoundhostel.com; 2-/4-person hikes per person US$500/400) The La Amistad Trek goes from Guadalupe through the rainforest of the continental divide and across the lowlands to Norteño in Bocas del Toro Province. The trek lasts from three to four days, depending on the group, and is led by a bilingual former Peace Corps volunteer and a local indigenous guide. Accommodation is in Ngöbe villages and food is local.

The terrain is very steep and rugged and the weather can be unpredictable; tours are only recommended for those with considerable hiking experience.

Sleeping

Las Nubes Ranger Station CABIN **$**
(☎775-3163, 774-6671; dm US$15) The basic ranger station at Las Nubes has a dormitory cabin with bunk beds. Due to its popularity among international school groups,

reservations are advisable. Guests have kitchen access; stock up on provisions in Cerro Punta. Bring your own bedding; a mosquito net is a good idea. To reserve, call Ministerio de Ambiente in David or the Co-op Restaurant at the park entrance.

Information

Admission to the park (US$5) is paid at the Las Nubes park office, 6km northwest of Cerro Punta. Camping permits (US$10 per person) are payable at the Las Nubes ranger station.

If you plan to spend much time at Las Nubes, be sure to bring a jacket or sweater. At 2280m above sea level, this area of the park has a cool climate; temperatures are usually around 24°C (75°F) in the daytime but can drop as low as 3°C (38°F) at night.

Getting There & Away

The Las Nubes entrance is about 6km northwest from Cerro Punta; a sign on the main road in Cerro Punta marks the turnoff. A taxi should cost US$7.

The Fortuna Road

Hwy 4, also know as Fortuna Rd after the large artificial lake (Lago Fortuna) supplying much of Panama's hydroelectric power, crosses the continental divide as it wends its way over the Cordillera Central. Not only is it the only way to get from Chiriquí Province to Bocas del Toro Province (short of flying), but it is also where you'll find two of the most interesting places to stay in the province.

Sleeping & Eating

Lost & Found Hostel HOSTEL $
(☎6432-8182; www.thelostandfoundhostel.com; Valle de la Mina; dm/d/tr without bathroom US$15/35/50, breakfast US$4-$6, lunch US$5-6, dinner US$6-8; @📶) The only cloud-forest lodge in Panama, the Lost & Found is a backpacker community perched on a steep hill reached on foot and facing a gaping mountain panorama. There are two dorms (with another on the way) of between 10 and 15 bunk beds, and four basic but clean private rooms. Shared bathrooms are stall-style and well maintained.

The new kitchen is stocked with basic provisions for sale, and you can also order meals. There's a mini-pub, lounge and movie room loft, set well away from sleepers.

The Canadian owners have plotted every detail, from two tricked-out treasure hunts that take visitors mucking through rivers and labyrinths, to an eight-hour maze of trails through La Fortuna Forest Reserve that go as high as 2200m. Activities are varied and well priced, and as many as three excursions depart each day. A highlight is the Lost World Tour (US$40), which takes hikers to an impressive waterfall and visits an indigenous community. You can also tour the trails on horseback (US$40) and visit a local coffee producer (US$25). The hostel's mascot is Rocky, a resident kinkajou who lives in and out of his cage and cannot be released into the wild. We love the viewing tower and the new mini-zip line that's free for guests.

Given the isolation, it's necessary to call or email reservations 24 hours in advance. To reach here take the bus from David (US$3.50, one hour) and ask to be dropped off at Km 42 near the large Lost & Found billboard. Follow the trail to the right of the provisions shop upward for about 20 minutes. You can also take a bus from Bocas del Toro Province, starting in Changuinola or Almirante (around US$7). Special shuttle buses link the Mamallena Hostel in Boquete (US$15) with Lost & Found.

El Refugio La Brisa del Diablo B&B $$
(☎6852-3600, 6597-0296; www.facebook.com/RefugioLaBrisaDelDiablo; Valle Hornito; d US$110-120, tr US$145-155, all incl breakfast; P📶❄) Overlooking a coffee plantation with views of Boquete, Volcán Barú and the Pacific, this tiny B&B punches way above its weight. The main building is built of riverstones and has two guestrooms. Both rooms are gorgeously decorated, boast firm mattresses and internet TV, and have a private terrace. Next door is a self-catering house that sleeps six.

The in-house restaurant (three-course dinners US$25) is a gourmet treat; order in advance. The French-Canadian owners could not be more welcoming and will help organize excursions (US$25) to local hot springs and a coffee plantation. Ask for a map showing hikes in the area.

Getting There & Away

Buses from both David and from Changuinola or Almirante in Bocas del Toro Province run along Hwy 4 (Fortuna Road) and stop at or near accommodations.

Bocas del Toro Province

POP 156,480 / AREA 4657 SQ KM / ELEV SEA LEVEL TO 3336M

Includes ➜

Best Places to Eat

- ➜ El Último Refugio (p192)
- ➜ Up in the Hill (p202)
- ➜ Om Café (p192)
- ➜ Taco Surf (p191)
- ➜ Bibi's on the Beach (p198)

Best Places to Sleep

- ➜ Tranquilo Bay (p203)
- ➜ Hotel Bocas del Toro (p191)
- ➜ Dolphin Bay Hideaway (p200)
- ➜ Hotel Lula's (p190)
- ➜ Casa Cayuko (p204)

Why Go?

With its Caribbean islands dotting a shock of blue waters, Bocas del Toro is all that's tropical. This is Panama's principal tourist draw and it will no doubt provide some of your most memorable experiences. The archipelago consists of six densely forested islands, scores of uninhabited islets and the Parque Nacional Marino Isla Bastimentos, Panama's oldest marine park.

The longtime base of Chiquita Banana, the mainland boasts the Parque Internacional La Amistad, shared with Costa Rica. It's also home to diverse wildlife such as the elusive jaguar, traditional Ngöbe-Buglé settlements, and the Naso, one of few remaining American tribes with its own monarch.

Most visitors come for a hefty dose of sun and surf. Few are disappointed with the Bocas cocktail of water fun and thatched luxury, but there's a lot, lot more to what might be Panama's most beautiful corner.

When to Go

➜ **Dec–Mar, Jul & Aug** The biggest swells for surfers to ride are from December to March, while green turtles can be found nesting on Isla Bastimentos in July and August.

➜ **Feb–Apr, Aug** Dry conditions and calm seas mean the best visibility for snorkeling and diving, with better access to ocean caves from February to April and then again in August.

➜ **Feb–Jul** Turtle nesting is monitored for six months starting in February at Humedal San San Pond Sak.

➜ **Nov** Bocas breaks into mayhem for its anniversary celebration in mid-November, along with a plethora of feast days and public holidays. It's also a boom month for national tourism.

HISTORY

Christopher Columbus visited Bocas del Toro in 1502, during his fourth and final voyage to the New World. Taken by its beauty, he affixed his name to many sites.

During the 17th century the archipelago became a haven for pirates repairing and building ships; they felled the forests and fed upon nesting sea turtles. Despite rumors of buried treasure, their loot has ever been found (or at least reported).

When Huguenots (Protestants) fleeing the religious wars in France settled along the coast in the late 17th and early 18th centuries, a Spanish militia was sent to Bocas to dislodge them. The arrival of diseases and destruction virtually wiped out the indigenous populations.

In the early 19th century, wealthy aristocrat settlers arrived in Bocas, bringing with them many black slaves from the USA and Colombia. When slavery was abolished in 1850, the former slaves became fishers and subsistence farmers. Towards the end of the 19th century, Jamaican blacks joined them to work in the burgeoning banana industry.

In 1899, however, United Fruit Company overtook the small American-owned banana company. As it established vast plantations across the entire peninsula it also constructed elaborate networks of roads, bridges and canals. Entire towns and cities rose up around where its workers settled.

Now called Chiquita Brands International, the multinational company grows and exports 750,000 tons of bananas annually. The largest workforce in the province, Chiquita is also the most diverse nationwide, with West Indians, Latinos, Chinese and indigenous people in its employ.

Getting There & Away

Bocas del Toro is linked with neighboring provinces and the capital by bus, but to reach the archipelago you must board a ferry in Almirante. An international airport at Bocas town links the archipelago with Panama City, David and Changuinola, as well as San José in Costa Rica.

ARCHIPIÉLAGO DE BOCAS DEL TORO

For most travelers, the archipelago *is* Bocas del Toro. Caribbean clichés aside, there's no shortage of postcard-pretty beaches, emerald waters and swaying palms, and scads of things to see and do.

Isla Colón

POP 9000

The archipelago's most developed island is home to the provincial capital of Bocas del Toro. From the mid-1990s, foreign investors flooded the island, creating hotels, restaurants and condos while infrastructure for water, trash and sewage lagged far behind. Today, the island, which runs on diesel, struggles to find a balance between satisfying development and serving community needs.

Note that the town, the archipelago and the province all share the name Bocas del Toro. To avoid confusion, we refer to the provincial capital as 'Bocas town' or simply 'Bocas.'

Activities

Cycling

Whether you're heading along the paved road to Boca del Drago or taking a dirt track to Playa Bluff, a bike can seriously increase your mobility. Note that the bike ride to Boca del Drago from Boca town is taxing; if you're unsure of your fitness level, head for Punta Bluff instead. Bikes are available from some hostels as well as from Ixa's Bike World (p187) and Bocas Bicis (p187) in Boca town. Flying Pirates (p186) rents ATVs/quad bikes.

Fishing

The best option for aspiring anglers on a budget is to go surf casting with the local water-taxi drivers. The hand lines can be a bit tricky at first, but you'll get the hang of it. It's best to go early in the morning.

Hiking

If you're looking to seriously get off the beaten path, there is a network of undeveloped hiking trails that fan out across Isla Colón. One of the more popular hikes starts at the end of the coastal road in Mimbi Timbi to the northeast and carries on west along the coast to Boca del Drago. You will need about six hours of daylight to complete the hike, and you must carry in all your water. The trail winds past caves, caverns and plenty of vine-entangled jungle. A bike will help speed things up a bit, though you'll be carrying it part of the way, especially if it's been raining recently.

Bocas del Toro Province Highlights

1 Archipiélago de Bocas del Toro (p181) Whiling away the days, sipping coconut juice and snorkeling at laid-back resorts.

2 Isla Bastimentos (p200) Swimming through a bat cave or soaking up the sunny rays while lazing on pristine beaches.

3 Bocas del Toro Town (p184) Taking the party from boat bars to cocktail lounges in this lively town.

4 Surfing the Caribbean (p194) Surfing some of the best breaks you'll find in the Caribbean – just watch those shallow reefs!

5 Parque Internacional La Amistad (p207) Exploring where the Naso people live under one of the world's last tribal monarchies.

6 Humedal de San San Pond Sak (p207) Spotting manatees and river otters while boating through the wetlands.

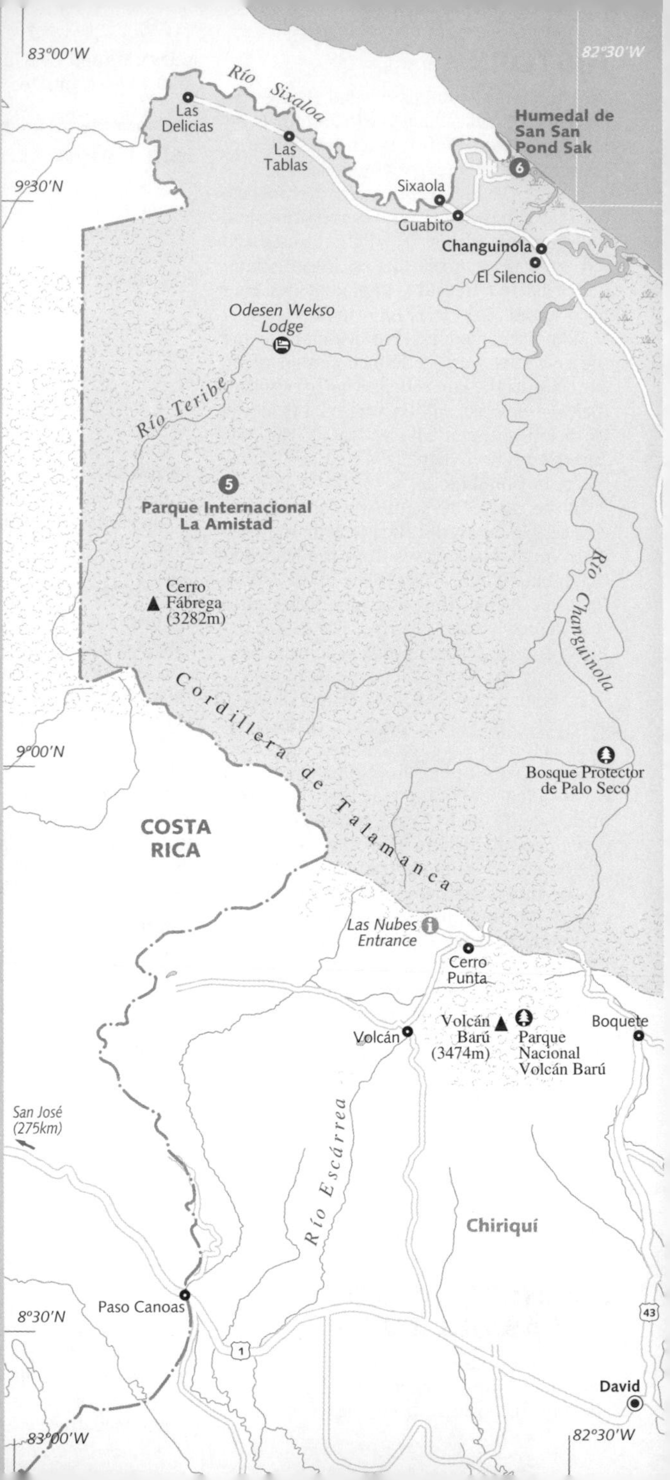

82°00'W
0 20 km
0 12 miles
9°30'N
Snyder (Changuinola) Canal
CARIBBEAN SEA
Isla Colón
Bastimentos
Bocas del Toro Town
3
Isla Solarte
Isla Bastimentos
2
Almirante
Quebrada Sal (Salt Creek)
Isla San Cristóbal
1
Archipiélago de Bocas del Toro
Bahía Azul
Península Valiente
11
Laguna de Chiriquí
Punta Róbalo
Boca de Río Caña
9°00'N
Río Róbalo
Chiriquí Grande
Río Guarumo
Fortuna Rd
Río Guariviara
Río Mananti
Río Cricamola
Altos del Valle
Lago Fortuna
Reserva Forestal Fortuna
Bocas del Toro
Comarca Ngöbe-Buglé
Cordillera Central
4
Río Chiriquí
Río Chorcha
Río Fonseca
Cerro Santiago (2121m)
Gualaca
Chiriquí
82°00'W

Archipiélago de Bocas del Toro

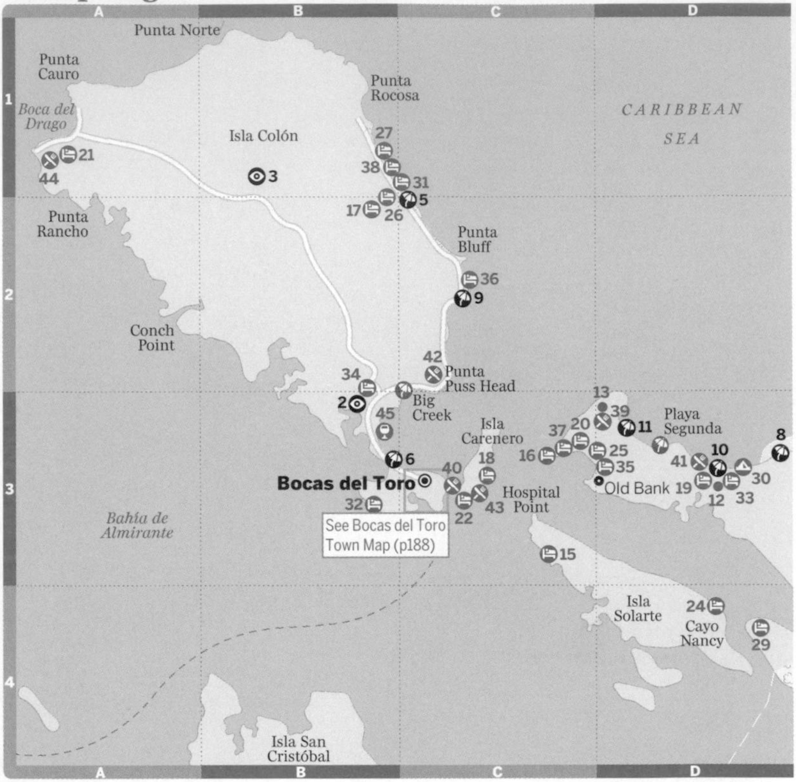

Kayaking

Sea kayaking is a great way to travel between islands. You will need to be wary of boat traffic, though, and the occasional swell. Some dive shops and hostels rent kayaks.

Birdwatching

While birdwatching on the islands isn't as good as that on the mainland, it can still be rewarding. Particularly rare birds, or at least those poorly known to Panama, have been recorded on the islands in recent years, including the red-fronted parrotlet, the chestnut-colored woodpecker, the purple martin and the black-cowled oriole.

Bocas del Toro Town

POP 7400

Colorful and full of Caribbean-style clapboard houses, Bocas del Toro (better known simply as Bocas town) was built by the United Fruit Company in the early 20th century. Today it is a relaxed community of West Indians, Latinos and resident gringos, with a friendly atmosphere that is contagious. It's an easy place to get stuck into and an even easier one in which to linger.

Bocas serves as a convenient base for exploring the archipelago; *taxis marinos* (water taxis) can whisk you away to remote beaches and snorkeling sites for just a few dollars. The real allure here, though, is simply to be able to slow down and soak up the Caribbean vibes.

Sights

Finca Los Monos Botanical Garden GARDENS

(Map p184; ☎6729-9943, 757-9461; www.bocasdeltorobotanicalgarden.com; garden/birdwatching tours US$15/25; ⏰garden tours 1pm Mon & 8:30am Fri, birdwatching tours 6:30am & 5pm upon request) One of the joys of visiting Bocas is touring the 'Monkey Farm' botanical gar-

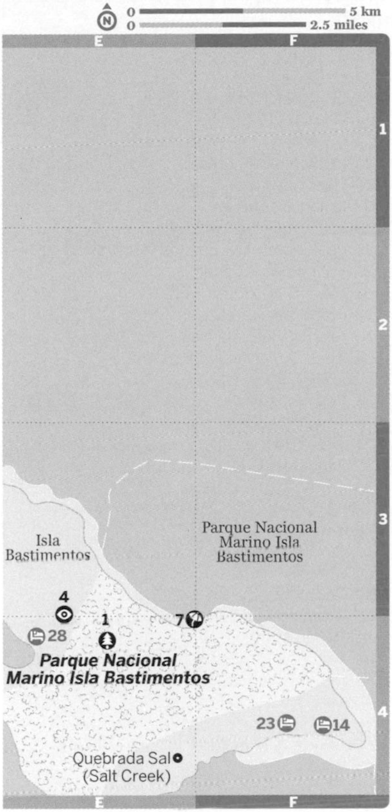

den a couple of kilometers northwest of the center. Painstakingly carved out of 10 hectares of secondary rainforest over almost two decades, it contains hundreds of species of local and imported trees and ornamental plants, and is teeming with wildlife.

Co-owner and guide Lin Gillingham will point out howler and white-faced capuchin monkeys, sloths and various bird species. Tours must be booked in advance; garden tours depart regularly while birding tours are on demand.

La Gruta CAVE

(The Grotto; Map p184; Colonia Santeña; admission US$2; ⏲8am-6pm) If sun, sand and surf isn't your thing then consider a trip to this cave in Colonia Santeña, a small village of cattle farmers 7km northwest of Bocas town. Here you'll wade through waist-high water while trying not to disturb thousands of sleeping bats overhead. It's all over in about five minutes. The cave entrance, marked by a small shrine to the Virgin Mary, is along a short trail on the right along the road to Boca del Drago.

A round-trip taxi should cost about US$20 or you can take the Boca del Drago bus (US$2.50).

Activities

Lil' Spa Shop SPA

(Map p188; ☎6591-3814; www.spashopbythesea.com; cnr Av H & Calle 7; ⏲10am-6pm) Should you need a bit of pampering after a hard day on the waves, head for this lovely oceanfront spa run by a gregarious New Yorker. Massage costs US$45/85 for 35/90 minutes; reflexology (30 minutes) is US$35.

Bocas Yoga YOGA

(Map p188; www.bocasyoga.com; Calle 4; classes US$6) Geared to both locals and travelers, this hatha yoga studio run by the effervescent Laura makes a good break from the party scene. Offers daily classes in English.

Surfing

Mono Loco Surf School SURFING

(Map p188; ☎760-9877; http://monolocosurfschool.com; Calle 2; 3hr lessons US$50; ⏲9am-6pm) Recommended surf shop and school run by a group of serious surfing dudes. Also rents boards (half/full day US$15/20).

Bocas Surf School SURFING

(Map p188; ☎6852-5291, 757-9057; http://bocassurfschool.com; cnr Av H & Calle 5; half-/full-day courses US$54/89) This well-regarded school, conveniently located next to an excellent hostel, has classes daily at 8:30am and 2:30pm. It also rents boards for US$15 per day.

Diving & Snorkeling

Although experienced divers accustomed to crystal-clear Caribbean diving may be disappointed with the archipelago – nearly 40 rivers discharging silt into the seas around the archipelago reduce visibility dramatically – it still has much to offer. The islands' emerald-green waters are home to the usual assortment of tropical species and with a little luck you might see barracuda, stingrays, dolphins and nurse sharks. The better sites include Dark Wood Reef, northwest of Bastimentos; Hospital Point, a 15m wall off Cayo Nancy; and the base of the buoy near Punta Juan, north of Isla Cristóbal.

A two-tank dive will cost between US$70 and US$75. Certification courses start at US$250. A number of reliable suppliers

Archipiélago de Bocas del Toro

Top Sights
1 Parque Nacional Marino Isla Bastimentos E4

Sights
2 Finca Los Monos Botanical Garden B3
3 La Gruta B1
4 Nivida Bat Cave E3
5 Playa Bluff C2
6 Playa El Istmito B3
7 Playa Larga E4
8 Playa Polo D3
9 Playa Punch C2
10 Red Frog Beach D3
11 Wizard Beach D3

Activities, Courses & Tours
Bastimentos Alive .... (see 25)
12 Bastimentos Sky Zipline Canopy Tour D3
Escuela de Mar Surf School .... (see 18)
Institute for Tropical Ecology & Conservation .... (see 21)
13 Up in the Hill D3

Sleeping
14 Al Natural Resort F4
Aqua Lounge .... (see 22)
15 Bambuda Lodge C3
16 Beverly's Hill C3
17 Bluff Beach Retreat B2
18 Bocas Buccaneer Resort C3
19 Bocas Island Lodge D3
20 Bubba's House C3
21 Cabañas Estefany A1
22 Casa Acuario C3
23 Casa Cayuco F4
El Faro del Colibri .... (see 22)
24 Garden of Eden D4
Gran Kahuna Beach Hostel .... (see 22)
25 Hostal Bastimentos D3
26 Hummingbird B2
27 Island Plantation B1
28 La Loma E4
29 Los Secretos Guesthouse D4
30 Palmar Tent Lodge D3
31 Playa Bluff Hotel C1
32 Punta Caracol Acqua Lodge B3
33 Red Frog Bungalows D3
34 Sand Dollar Beach Bed & Breakfast B2
35 Sea Monkey D3
36 Tesoro Escondido C2
Tierra Verde .... (see 22)
37 Tío Tom's Guesthouse C3
38 Turtle Beach House B1

Eating
Bibi's on the Beach .... (see 18)
Chavela .... (see 25)
39 Coco Hill D3
40 Leaf Eaters Cafe C3
41 Nacho Mama's D3
42 Paki Point C2
43 Receta Michilá C3
44 Yarisnori Restaurant A1

Drinking & Nightlife
45 Bocas Brewery B3

offer good-value snorkeling and diving trips out of Bocas.

La Buga DIVING
(Map p188; ☎6781-0755, 757-9534; www.labugapanama.com; Calle 3; ⊙8am-8pm) A very well regarded dive shop, La Buga leads two to three dive trips a day. Highlights include night dives and visits to the caves off Bastimentos (US$90). It also offers surfboard rentals and surf lessons, stand-up paddles (US$15 per hour) and kayak rentals. While you explore your options, grab a bite at the cute cafe attached.

Bocas Dive Center DIVING
(Map p188; ☎757-9737, 6429-5150; www.bocasdivecenter.com; Calle 6 Sur; 1-/2-tank dives US$45/80) Diving trips in many languages are offered by this PADI center at the southern end of town.

Starfleet Scuba DIVING
(Map p188; ☎757-9630; www.starfleetscuba.com; Calle 3) PADI open-water and advanced-diver courses are available. Starfleet offers instruction in English and enjoys a strong reputation among locals and travelers.

Bicycles and ATVs

Flying Pirates ADVENTURE SPORTS
(Map p188; ☎6689-5050; http://flyingpiratesbocas.com; cnr Calle 3 & Av B; half-day US$90-110, full day US$117-140; ⊙9am-7pm) One of the best ways to explore Isla Colón is by ATV/quad bike, and the people at Flying Pirates, based on their own 600-hecatre *finca* (farm) on the way to Playa Bluff, can oblige. They rent out more than 30 of the fat-tired vehicles for use on or off-road, including 15km of trails on private land. The beach is off-limits.

You'll be transported to and from downtown Bocas. There's an information and booking truck in the center. Free beers and hot showers included after your day out.

Ixa's Bike World BICYCLE RENTAL
(Map p188; Av H; per hour US$1, per half-/full day US$7/10; ⏲8am-6pm) Repairs and rents a wide selection of bicycles from a hole-in-the-wall workshop at the northern end of town.

Bocas Bicis BICYCLE RENTAL
(Map p188; Av E; per hour/day low season US$1.50/5, high season US$2/10; ⏲9am-7pm) This little stand between Calles 2 and 3 rents two-wheelers year-round.

Courses

Spanish by the Sea LANGUAGE COURSE
(Map p188; ☎6592-0775, 757-9518; www.spanishbythesea.com; Calle 4) A language school in a relaxed setting. Group lessons are US$225/300 per week for 20/30 hours. The school also offers a popular six-hour survival Spanish course (US$45) to kick-start your travels. Has a branch in Boquete.

Homestays can be arranged (US$25 per night), or you can bunk down in clean and comfy dorms (US$12) or private rooms (US$30). Also organizes parties, dance classes and open lectures.

Habla Ya LANGUAGE COURSE
(Map p188; ☎730-8344, 757-7352; www.hablayapanama.com; cnr Av G & Calle 9 Sur; ⏲8am-5:30pm) This Spanish-language school, with branches in Boquete and Panama City, has a solid reputation. It offers a Spanish for Travelers course that lasts four hours and costs US$55. Classrooms are air-conditioned. Special rates available on lodging in its own dorms and in private rooms with host families.

Tours

Oreba Chocolate Tour TOUR
(☎6649-1457; www.oreba.bocasdeltoro.org; per person US$35) This guided tour leaves Bocas and takes you around an organic chocolate farm, run by the indigenous Ngöbe community, on the mainland near Almirante. Tour the farm, see tree sloths, sample chocolate – classified as some of the highest grade cacao in the world – and enjoy a traditional lunch. Book direct or through Super Gourmet (p192).

The trip (two-person minimum) is guided in Spanish and English. The price does not include the boat trip from Bocas to Almirante (US$12 round trip).

Boat Tours

The most popular tours in the area are all-day snorkeling trips, which are perfect for nondivers who want a taste of the area's rich marine life. A typical tour costs US$25 per person, and goes to Dolphin Bay, Cayo Crawl, Red Frog Beach (US$3 entry) and Hospital Point.

A trip to the distant Cayos Zapatillas costs US$30 (plus an additional US$5 for admission to the marine park), and includes lunch, beach time and a jungle hike on Cayo Zapatilla Sur.

Many 'tours' are really little more than boat transportation to a pretty spot. If you have your own snorkel gear (or if you rent it), you can also charter motor boats. Agree on a price before you go.

Transparente Tours BOAT TOUR
(Map p188; ☎757-7326, 6700-2453; www.transparentetours.bocas.com; Calle 3; per person US$20 25 plus marine park entrance US$10; ⏲8am-10pm) This recommended tour operator provides guides, gear and drinks on boat excursions around the archipelago from 10am to 4:30pm.

Dragon Tours BOAT TOUR
(Map p188; ☎6499-6317, 757-7010; www.dragon-tours.net; cnr Calle 3 & Av C; per person incl lunch US$39-48) This perennially popular charter company sails its purpose-built 19m catamaran complete with water slide to various islands on day trips, which always include lunch (barbecue, pizza etc).

Bocas Sailing BOAT TOUR
(Map p188; ☎6464-4242, 757-7048; www.bocassailing.com; Calle 3; per person US$48; ⏲9:30am-4:30pm) Including affordable overnight adventures and options for snorkeling, fishing and dolphin-watching, Bocas Sailing has popular tours on a 13m catamaran that are kid-friendly, too.

Festivals & Events

Feria del Mar FERIA
The 'Sea Fair' is held on Playa El Istmito (p196), a few kilometers northwest of downtown Bocas, for a week in September.

Día de la Virgen del Carmen RELIGIOUS
Bocatoreños make a pilgrimage to the cave at La Gruta in the middle of the Isla Colón for Mass in honor of the Virgen del Carmen on the third Sunday in July.

Bocas del Toro Town

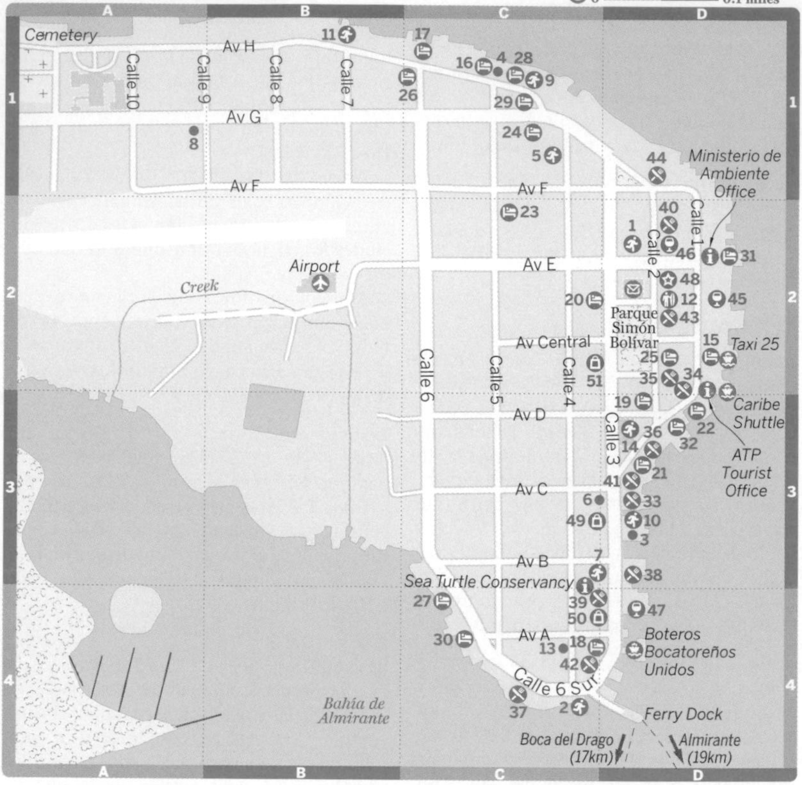

Sleeping

Bocas town is a major tourist draw, though many people don't realize there is no town beach. Water shortage can be a problem, so it's recommended that you take short showers. Reservations are a good idea between December and April, and during national holidays (especially in November) and local festivals. Discounts can be considerable in low season.

Hotel del Parque HOTEL $

(Map p188; ☎757-9008; www.hdelparque.webs.com; Calle 2; s/d/tr/q US$45/50/55/60; ❄ 📶) A classic clapboard Caribbean house fronting the leafy main square, this tranquil place has lots of style but remains within budget reach. Eight ample rooms on two floors have big windows, cool concrete floors, hot showers and firm beds with crisp linens. The terraces provide views of the plaza and hammocks for naps. There is a compact guest kitchen.

Hostel Heike HOSTEL $

(Map p188; ☎757-9708; www.hostelheike.com; Calle 3; dm with/without air-con US$13/11, d/tr incl breakfast US$24/36; ❄ @ 📶) Aglow with colorful murals and natural woods, Heike is the perfect spot for chilling in an old Caribbean-style house right in the center of town. The nine rooms include dorms with up to 10 beds; a sprawling roof deck with hammocks is the perfect spot for a cold beer and a good book. Free purified water and hot drinks.

Complimentary beginner Spanish classes are held three times a week at 2pm. Friendly, well-informed management.

Hotel Olas HOTEL $

(Map p188; ☎6914-4556, 757-9930; www.hotelolas.com; Calle 6 Sur; s/d/tr/q incl breakfast US$55/60/80/100; ❄ @ 📶) Shining like a beacon from the southwestern tip of Bocas town, the three-story, very yellow 'Waves' has 25 clean polished-wood rooms with electric hot-water showers, though rooms are

Bocas del Toro Town

Activities, Courses & Tours

1 Bocas Bicis D2
2 Bocas Dive Center C4
3 Bocas Sailing D3
4 Bocas Surf School C1
5 Bocas Yoga C1
6 Dragon Tours C3
7 Flying Pirates C3
8 Habla Ya A1
9 Ixa's Bike World C1
10 La Buga D3
11 Lil' Spa Shop B1
12 Mono Loco Surf School D2
13 Spanish by the Sea C4
14 Starfleet Scuba D3
Transparente Tours .... (see 3)

Sleeping

15 Bocas Paradise Hotel D2
16 Bocas Surf School & Hostel C1
17 Cocomo C1
18 Gran Hotel Bahía C4
19 Hostal Hansi D3
20 Hostel Heike C2
21 Hotel Bocas del Toro D3
22 Hotel Bocas Town D3
23 Hotel Cala Luna C2
24 Hotel Casa Max C1
25 Hotel del Parque D2
26 Hotel Lula's C1
27 Hotel Olas C4
28 Hotel Vista Mar C1
29 Mondo Taitú C1
30 Residencial Dos Palmas C4
31 Selina Hostel Bocas del Toro D2
32 Tropical Suites D3

Eating

Bocas Barna Q .... (see 18)
33 Buena Vista Bar & Grill D3
34 Cafe del Mar D2
35 El Chitré D2
36 El Limbo on the Sea D3
37 El Último Refugio C4
38 Maracuya D3
39 Om Café C4
40 Panadería & Dulcería Alemana D2
Pizzeria Alberto .... (see 23)
41 Raw Fusion D3
42 Super Gourmet C4
43 Taco Surf D2
44 Tom's D1

Drinking & Nightlife

45 Barco Hundido D2
46 Bookstore Bar D2
47 La Iguana Surf Bar D4
Mondo Taitú Bar .... (see 29)
Selina Bar .... (see 31)

Entertainment

48 Cine Cafe D2

Shopping

49 Artesanía Bribrí C3
50 Lido Isle C4
51 Tropix Surfboards C2

rather small and pretty basic. The biggest draw here is the exceptional ocean-front lounge and restaurant. Offers tours (US$25 to US$35) and bicycle rentals through its travel agency, Olas Tours.

Residencial Dos Palmas HOTEL $

(Map p188; ☎757-9906; www.facebook.com/Residencial-Dos-Palmas 1619749634947555; Calle 6 Sur; d/tr US$30/35; ❄) Boasting as being '100% *bocatoreño*,' Dos Palmas offers eight basic wooden rooms with old-fashioned furnishings and bright turquoise walls. Run by a friendly matriarch, it's not some cookie-cutter lodging, though some might find it a little stuffy. It sits above the water and boasts exceptional views of the bay from the back terrace. Don't miss sunset!

Hotel Casa Max HOTEL $

(Map p188; ☎757-9120; casa1max@hotmail.com; Av G; d/tr US$45/60, with air-con US$60/75; ❄ 📶) This sprawling pea-green Caribbean-style house has 15 brightly painted rooms, with wooden floors and somewhat dated bathrooms. The service isn't much to speak of, but dreamy balconies overlook the town and ocean. There's a large on-site restaurant serving international cuisine (separately run); and the location is very good, just up from the center and on the way to the beaches.

Hostal Hansi GUESTHOUSE $

(Map p188; ☎757-9085; http://hostalhansi.bocas.com; cnr Av D & Calle 2; s with shared bathroom US$13, s/d/tr US$18/33/39; 📶) This cat-mad German-owned guesthouse prides itself on having a quiet interior, hot showers and some strict rules. The 15 rooms have fans and are spotless and comfortable. Doubles sport their own balcony. Guests can cook in an ample kitchen, where fridge space is organized by room number. The Teutonic regimentation may not be to everyone's taste. Strictly no bookings.

Mondo Taitú
HOSTEL $

(Map p188; ☑760-8136; www.mondotaitu.com; Av G; dm/d with shared bathroom US$10/24; @ 🛜) Though it's a shadow of its former self, the original surfer backpacker hostel in Bocas soldiers on, with a chilled social atmosphere and decent nightlife right at home. It's definitely not the choice for those who mind (real) grunge. The 13 rooms include dorms with up to eight beds.

★Hotel Lula's
B&B $$

(Map p188; ☑6629-0836, 757-9057; www.lulabb.com; cnr Av H & Calle 6; d/tr/q incl breakfast US$77/88/99; ✳ @ 🛜) A place of porches and rocking chairs, this lovely B&B is a stylish and welcoming addition to the Bocas accommodations scene. Its eight rooms are immaculate, with air-con, fans, wooden ceilings and floors, and a snug design. The hosts, two affable guys from Atlanta, Georgia, give first-rate service, in addition to big southern breakfasts.

Selina Hostel Bocas del Toro
HOSTEL $$

(Map p188; ☑202-7966; www.selinahostels.com; Calle 1; dm US$14-18, d with/without bathroom from US$60/45, d deluxe US$75-108; @ 🛜) This ever-expanding hostel chain, which has properties in Panama City's Casco Viejo and on Playa Venao in Península de Azuero, has opened a mammoth turquoise 196-bed property on the waterfront, and it has something for everybody. Choose from a rock-bottom bunk in a dorm with 12 beds to a deluxe double with balcony on the top floor (room 312 or 313).

You can swim in azure waters directly from the two-level waterfront deck, watch films in the video room, enjoy a drink at the open-air bar or order the meal of the day (US$7) at the restaurant. There's also a common kitchen for guests' use. An in-house travel agency rents equipment and organizes excursions.

Hotel Bocas Town
HOTEL $$

(Map p188; ☑6750-5174, 757-7381; www.hotelbocastown.com; Calle 1; d incl breakfast US$88-132; ✳ 🛜) This new pink-and-blue hotel on the water next to the police station features 18 rooms with views to the street, the side or the sea. Among the latter, rooms 105 and 106 are choicest, with balconies and views across to Isla Carenero. There's a super restaurant with a huge waterfront deck and a bar with a large mural of rock musicians.

Cocomo
B&B $$

(Map p188; ☑757-9259; www.cocomoonthesea.com; cnr Av H & Calle 6; s/d/tr incl breakfast US$65/85/95; ✳ 🛜) A colorful clapboard house with a tropical garden and waterfront hammock deck, Cocomo wants for nothing. Run by North American tourism pioneer Doug, this four-room B&B knows service. If the weather's bad, this is a snug spot to hole up. All-you-can-eat breakfast includes pastries, cereal, fruit and omelets. There's a laundry service, free use of kayaks and you can swim right off the dock.

Sand Dollar Beach Bed & Breakfast
B&B $$

(Map p184; ☑6627-5906, 757-9671; www.sanddollarbeachbb.com; Sand Dollar Beach; d incl breakfast US$99-132, ste US$149-200; ✳ 🛜) Vaguely reminiscent of a US antebellum plantation, this B&B in a yellow clapboard manor about 3km west of Bocas town counts four lovely rooms, a suite named after flowers and a separate apartment for families. The wraparound verandas on two floors give views of the beach across the road and are the ultimate in relaxation. The surrounding gardens harbor monkeys, sloths and trails. Bicycles and snorkeling gear are available to guests, and cooking classes are run in the huge kitchen (from US$30 per person, minimum four people).

Hotel Vista Mar
B&B $$

(Map p188; ☑757-9198; www.hotelvistamar.net; cnr Av H & Calle 5; r US$66-110; 🛜) This pretty 14-room inn right on the water at the northern end of Bocas town offers rather good value, depending on whether you choose a standard room with a town view or something a bit more extravagant with a balcony facing the sea. The turquoise interiors and fish murals are cheery, and the terrace hammocks are begging to be swung. There's an attractive bar-restaurant.

Bocas Surf School & Hostel
HOSTEL $$

(Map p188; ☑6852-5291, 757-9057; http://bocassurfschool.com; cnr Av H & Calle 5; dm/d with shared bathroom US$20/60, d US$99; ✳ 🛜) It's not every day that your hostel has it's own swim-off dock. This super-cute mint-green cottage set at a celebrated surf school (p185) is a great addition to the local hostel scene. It offers 10 solid bunks in two rooms, and two doubles – the one on the 1st floor is quite posh. There's a communal kitchen. Nonsurfers can rent kayaks (US$10 per half-day).

Bocas Paradise Hotel INN $$
(Map p188; ☎6780-0063, 757-9546; www.bocasparadisehotel.com; Calle 1; d/ste from US$70/115; ❄📶) On the waterfront, this up-market inn has 27 rooms with brocade beds, carved hardwood furniture and little balconies with wooden loungers. Installations are shiny, new and up to date; the bathrooms are quite spacious. Perks include kitchenettes with fridges and microwaves. An on-site restaurant stays open till 10pm.

Gran Hotel Bahía HISTORIC HOTEL $$
(Map p188; ☎757-9626; www.ghbahia.com; cnr Av A & Calle 3; r incl breakfast US$77-115; ❄📶) This landmark was built in 1905 by the United Fruit Company to cater for visitors to its local headquarters. Though it isn't a standout, some careful restorations have revived its 18 rooms and original splendor. Second-floor deluxe rooms (eg room 208) with wicker furniture, safe boxes and original oak floors are considerably bigger and brighter than their ground-floor standard counterparts.

Hotel Cala Luna HOTEL $$
(Map p188; ☎757-9066; www.calalunabocas.com; Calle 5; s/d/tr/q US$60/70/90/100; ❄@📶) Attached to the excellent Pizzeria Alberto (p192), the Italian-owned Cala Luna was built with fine attention to detail. The hotel features cathedral windows, tasteful wood details and eight crisp, functional rooms. There's a lovely lounge with tropical plants, and guests can watch planes coming in for a landing 30m above their heads from the rooftop lookouts.

★**Hotel Bocas del Toro** INN $$$
(Map p188; ☎6673-9018, 757-9018; www.hotelbocasdeltoro.com; Calle 2; d incl breakfast from US$129; ❄@📶) Our favorite place to stay in Bocas town, this three-story waterfront inn has 11 spacious all-hardwood rooms that feature firm beds with luxuriant linens and a warm decor; some have seafront balconies. Perks include concierge service and amenities such as Silico Creek coffee produced by a Ngöbe-Buglé community. There's a fun street-side bar and an excellent deck-side restaurant overlooking the harbor.

Owned and run by Carla from the USA, Hotel Bocas del Toro is a member of APTSO, Panama's sustainable tourism alliance.

★**Punta Caracol Acqua Lodge** CABIN $$$
(Map p184; ☎6612-1088, 757-9410; www.puntacaracol.com; r incl 2 meals US$450-540; @📶) A poster child for Caribbean luxury, Punta Caracol has nine exquisite cabins perched on a long pier over crystal waters. Two-story thatched cabins feature king-sized canopy beds, big skylight windows and soft lighting. There are solar panels and local renewable materials used in construction, and the long boardwalk leads over a reef to a 2km-long mangrove coast. About 3km northwest of Bocas town and accessed only by boat, Punta Caracol is the ultimate in tranquil luxury. Nonguests can dine at the deck-side restaurant (mains from US$10 to US$25), which serves fresh seafood, tasty oversized cocktails and tropical style.

Tropical Suites HOTEL $$$
(Map p188; ☎757-9880; www.bocastropical.com; Calle 1; ste incl breakfast US$150-200; ❄📶) Boasting the island's only elevator, this all-suites hotel has modern comforts including Jacuzzi tubs, flat-screen TVs, hairdryers and room safes. Ample rooms easily fit three, and kitchens have range-tops and refrigerators. For the ultimate in seaside luxury, choose the Starfish suite, which has a balcony plus a porthole in the floor with a direct view into the briny deep.

Eating

★**Taco Surf** MEXICAN $
(Map p188; ☎6951-5739; www.tacosurfbocas.com; Calle 2; mains US$3.50-8.50; ⏲noon-9pm Thu-Tue; 🌱) Just opposite the main plaza, this small garden eatery owned by an affable couple from San Diego serves Baja California–style Mexican food, with fish tacos, California burritos, nachos and specialty fries seasoned with herbs. There are at least six vegetarian choices on the menu. The margaritas – especially the passion fruit and sweet basil – are to die for.

Cafe del Mar CAFE $
(Map p188; ☎6212-8712; www.facebook.com/Cafe-del-Mar-822286594497665; Calle 1; dishes US$5-9; ⏲8am-4pm Tue-Sun; 🌱) This eatery the size of a large closet serves excellent all-natural wraps, sandwiches and burgers. Preservatives of all sorts are banned, and there are plenty of choices for vegetarians. Eat in or take-out. Great coffee (US$1.50 to US$3), too.

Raw Fusion ASIAN $

(Map p188; ☎6938-8473; www.facebook.com/RawFusionBocas; Calle 3; mains US$7-10; ⏰3-10pm Tue-Sun) It's just a little plank restaurant on the water, but the Asian-fusion offerings are spot on. Sake accompanies fresh tofu spring rolls and amazing tuna tapas. The salads are wonderful, and service is friendly and attentive. At night candles are lit and the full bar, specializing in original martinis (from US$7), starts humming.

Super Gourmet SUPERMARKET $

(Map p188; ☎757-9357; www.supergourmetbocas.com; Calle 3; ⏰9am-7pm Mon-Sat) This treasure trove of a grocery store stocks special treats such as rotisserie chicken, Mexican food, wine and frozen bagels. It also has a section of sustainable local gifts, which include handmade soaps and outstanding local Bocas chocolate, as well as kosher foodstuffs.

Pizzeria Alberto PIZZA $

(Map p188; ☎757-9066; Calle 5; pizzas US$8.50-14; ⏰5-10pm Fri-Wed) Sardinian-run Alberto's is a favorite local haunt, where pizza with toppings such as artichokes, olives and Gorgonzola satisfies big appetites.

Tom's PANAMANIAN $

(Map p188; ☎6776-9280, 760-0290; Av G; mains US$5-10; ⏰10:30am-5pm Mon-Sat) Locals of every stripe agree that Tom's is the spot for a tasty lunch (fixed menu US$6) that doesn't break the bank. Head upstairs in a concrete market building and you'll find it on a shaded 2nd-floor terrace overlooking the water. Great views! Seafood or chicken paired with rice or fries.

El Chitré PANAMANIAN $

(Map p188; Calle 2; dishes US$3-5; ⏰6:30am-8pm Mon-Sat) Patronized by locals and travelers alike, this no-frills cafeteria is the best spot in town for cheap but tasty grub. Soups are especially good.

Panadería & Dulcería Alemana BAKERY $

(Map p188; ☎757-9436; www.facebook.com/panaderia.dulceria.alemana; Calle 2; sandwiches US$3-5, dishes US$5-10; ⏰7am-8pm Mon-Sat, 8am-4pm Sun) In addition to moist slabs of carrot cake and freshly baked whole-grain bread, this German bakery and patisserie also sells sandwiches, salads and pasta.

★ **El Último Refugio** CARIBBEAN $$

(Map p188; ☎6726-9851; www.ultimorefugio.com; Calle 6 Sur; mains US$11-16; ⏰6-10pm) One of the best restaurants in Bocas town, this mellow North American–run place on the edge of the sea specializes in Caribbean and seafood dishes, with fare such as red curry calamari and miso-crusted grouper on the chalkboard. Service is friendly and the tranquil location makes it a great spot for a quiet, romantic dinner.

Om Café INDIAN $$

(Map p188; ☎6127-0671; http://omcafebocas.com; Calle 3; mains US$8-15; ⏰4-10pm Mon-Fri year-round, 4-10pm Sat Dec-Apr; 🖉) Guaranteed to make you sweat, this welcoming and very attractive upstairs Indian cafe cooks up classic curries, korma and thalis. Service can be slow, so order up one of the original cocktails to keep you company, such as the Tipsy Turban (US$6), a dizzy mix of passion fruit or lime juice, rum and sugar. Good selection of vegetarian dishes.

Maracuya FUSION $$

(Map p188; ☎6127-0671; www.maracuyabocas.com; Calle 3; mains US$10-13.50; ⏰8am-noon & 5-10pm Mon-Fri) An odd one this, with lots of Thai dishes such as pad Thai noodles, spicy fish cakes and seafood red curry, and almost as many Middle Eastern and Greek choices, including *fattoush* (a salad with lemon, mint, garlic, sumac and fried pita) and pork souvlaki. Lovely location with deck right on the waterfront. Great for breakfast (US$6 to US$8), too.

El Limbo on the Sea SEAFOOD $$

(Map p188; ☎757-9229; Calle 2; mains US$9-18) This rambling seafood restaurant with a back deck that projects like a stage into the water serves fresh seafood dishes. Choose among three classic sauces: Caribbean curry, mango-pineapple chutney or butter and garlic. Decor is a bit hippie. Look to the sea, tuck in and all will be right with the world.

Buena Vista Bar & Grill NORTH AMERICAN $$

(Map p188; ☎757-9035; www.buenavistabocas.com; Calle 3; mains US$8.50-18; ⏰noon-10pm Wed-Mon) This long-established but peripatetic establishment serves some of the best burgers, tacos and wraps in town, and dinner ups the ante with a surf-and-turf menu. Run by a welcoming Panamanian-American couple, it's a good bet for a decent bite and may be the only spot around for swift service. Haven/heaven for hungry expats.

Bocas Barna Q BARBECUE **$$$**
(Map p188; ☎6452-5270; Calle 3; grill for 2 people US$40; ⏲5-10pm) This high-end 'grill and soul food' (we don't get that part) restaurant at the Gran Hotel Bahía is aimed at (but not exclusively for) carnivores, with a meat-fest grill for two priced at US$40 and a meat fondue for US$30. For herbivores there's a vegetarian set meal for two (US$20) and cheese fondue (US$30).

Drinking & Nightlife

Selina Bar CLUB
(Map p188; ☎202-7966; www.selinahostels.com; Calle 1) The bar at this new landmark hostel is open daily, with happy hour between 7pm and 8pm, but most people make it here between 10pm and 2am on a Friday, when all the stops are pulled put and it's party time.

La Iguana Surf Bar CLUB
(Map p188; www.facebook.com/La-Iguana-Surf-Bar-593201014052636; Calle 3; ⏲9:30pm-3am Sun-Wed, to 4am Thu-Sat) Kick off your crazy Bocas night at this popular surfer and skate bar on the waterfront. Start with a US$2 beer-tequila combo. You probably won't be in the mood for the dancing pole yet, though. Saturday is zoo night.

Bookstore Bar BAR
(Map p188; ☎6452-5905; www.facebook.com/pages/Bocas-BookstoreBar-aka-Loco-Daves/1396790643908649; Calle 2; ⏲2pm-2am Mon-Fri, 6pm-2am Sat & Sun) Just what its name suggests: this cavernous spot is both a place selling books and one selling drinks, though most punters seem more interested in the latter. Run by a couple of affable North Americans, it's mecca for gringos at the start (and sometimes at the end) of an evening. Live music on Tuesdays from 9pm.

Mondo Taitú Bar BAR
(Map p188; ☎760-8136; www.facebook.com/MondoTaitu; Av G; ⏲7pm-late) The party-loving US owners at this hostel entertain their guests with a variety of themed events (usually on Tuesdays and Fridays). The creative cocktail list and hookahs make Mondo a good choice any night of the week, with tunes cranked up and gratis jungle juice (alcohol and Kool-Aid, of course).

Barco Hundido BAR
(Map p188; Calle 1; ⏲8pm-midnight) At some point you'll probably find yourself at this open-air bar, affectionately known as the 'Wreck Deck' after the sunken banana boat that rests in the clear Caribbean waters in front. A short boardwalk extends from the bar to an island seating area – including swings; perfect for stargazing.

Bocas Brewery BREWERY
(Map p184; ☎6347-5279; http://bocasbrewery.com; Calle Carreterra, Las Cabañas; ⏲noon-8pm) This in-house brewery-pub a couple of kilometers northwest of downtown in Las Cabañas keeps bankers' hours but has eight types of shop-brewed draught available at any one time and various types of snacks to soak it up: soft pretzels, nachos, fried pickles and burgers (US$5 to US$9)

Entertainment

Cine Cafe CAFE
(Map p188; ☎6549-4158; Calle 2; US$7-8; ⏲3-11pm) Great on a rainy afternoon or evening, Cine Cafe is a chilled (quite literally) spot that offers a wide-ranging selection of movies, comfortable bean bag seating and drinks with popcorn (natch) and some sweets.

Shopping

Artesanía Bribrí HANDICRAFTS
(Map p188; ☎757-9020; Calle 3; ⏲8am-7pm) This centrally located and heavily stocked shop sells hammocks, clothing and local handicrafts, such as jute bags made by indigenous Ngöbe people, *molas* by Guna people and mats from the Darién.

Lido Isle CLOTHING
(Map p188; ☎6789-6337, 760-9981; www.facebook.com/Lido-Isle-Boutique-612090192140000; Calle 3; ⏲10am-7pm Mon-Sat) This upbeat boutique sells women's clothing designed by the Californian owner as well as original jewelry, bags and wallets.

Tropix Surfboards SPORTS
(Map p188; ☎757-9727; http://tropixsurf.tripod.com; Calle 3; ⏲9am-7pm Mon-Sat) Sells custom-made surfboards and a few used ones as well. Also has a large selection of swimwear and other island apparel.

Information

DANGERS & ANNOYANCES

The surf can be dangerous and there are frequent riptides – use caution when going out into the waves.

Unlike in most other places in Panama, tap water is not safe to drink in the archipelago unless it is filtered. Bocas town has a water-treatment plant, but locals say the tap water is

SURFING IN BOCAS

With beginner-friendly beach swells, ripping reef breaks and some seriously suicidal barrels, Bocas del Toro is emerging as an international surf destination. The following is a rundown of the major surfing spots in the archipelago.

If you don't have your own board, you can rent from Tropix Surfshop (p193) or Mondo Taitú (p190) in Bocas town or from various accommodations on the outer islands, including Red Frog Bungalows (p204) on Isla Bastimentos.

Isla Colón

Beginner surfers looking for a bit of reef experience should check out Playa Punch (p196), which offers a good mix of lefts and rights. Although it can get heavy when big, Punch generally offers some of the kindest waves around.

Just past Punch en route to Playa Bluff is a popular reef break known as Dumpers. This left break can get up to 3m and should only by ridden by experienced surfers; wiping out on the reef here dangerous. There is also an inner break known as Inner Dumps, which also breaks left but is more forgiving than its outer mate.

Be careful walking out on the reefs as they are sharp and full of sea urchins – don't go barefoot. If you wipe out and get cut up, be sure to properly disinfect your wounds. Be aware that seawater in the Caribbean does not help the healing process; the warm water temperature means the ocean is full of live bacteria.

The island's most infamous surf spot is Playa Bluff (p196), which throws out powerful barreling waves that break in shallow water along the beach and have a reputation for snapping boards (and occasionally bones). The waves close quickly, but the tubes here are truly awesome, especially when the swells are strong.

Isla Bastimentos

If you're looking for a solid beach break, both Wizard Beach (p201) and Red Frog Beach (p201) offer fairly constant sets of lefts and rights, perfect for beginners and intermediates. When the swells are in, however, Wizard occasionally throws out some huge barrels, though they tend to close up pretty quickly. Silverbacks is a fierce wave break between Isla Bastimentos and Isla Carenero that can reach peak heights of more than 5m during winter months.

Isla Carenero

Very experienced surfers may want to tackle Silverbacks, an enormous barreling right that breaks over a reef and can reach heights of more than 5m. On a good day, Silverbacks is a world-class break that wouldn't look out of place on Hawaii's North Shore. Silverbacks breaks off the coast, so you're going to need to hire a water taxi (from US$3) to get out there.

Two places suitable for beginners are Old Man's, which has an A-frame that breaks in the middle of a channel, and Black Rock, with a right suitable for beginners that also breaks in the middle of the channel with a sandy reef bottom.

not to be trusted. It's certainly fine for brushing your teeth, but for drinking purchase bottled water or purify your own.

The archipelago is generally a conservative place and local law bans men (and women) from walking the streets shirtless. Even if you are on your way to the beach, wear a shirt or you might be sent back to your hotel by the police.

No matter what age you are, you will almost certainly be offered drugs for sale while walking the streets of downtown Bocas. Do not even think about it: Panama takes its drug laws very seriously indeed.

INTERNET RESOURCES

Bocas.com (www.bocas.com) The official tourism website.

Lonely Planet (www.lonelyplanet.com/panama) Destination information, hotel bookings, traveler forum and more.

National Geographic (www.gobluecentralamerica.org) A National Geographic–produced geotourism map guide to Bocas del Toro.

MEDICAL SERVICES

Bocas del Toro Hospital (☎757-9201; Av G; ⌚24hr) The island's only hospital has a 24-

hour emergency room. New Taiwan-funded facility is under construction to the northwest.

MONEY

Banco Nacional de Panamá (☎758-3850; cnr Calle 4 & Av E; ⏰8am-3pm Mon-Fri, 9am-2pm Sat) Exchanges traveler's checks and has a 24-hour ATM.

POST

Post Office (Map p188; Calle 3; ⏰8am-3pm Mon-Fri, to 1pm Sat) In the town hall, overlooking Parque Simón Bolívar from the north.

TOURIST INFORMATION

ATP Tourist Office (Map p188; ☎757-9642; bocasdeltoro@atp.gob.pa; Calle 1; ⏰8:30am-3:30pm Mon-Fri) In a large green government building next to the police station on the eastern waterfront.

Bocas Sustainable Tourism Alliance (☎6956-9520; www.discoverbocasdeltoro.com) This English-speaking organization offers good online reference information for travelers. Arranges tours and visits to a Ngöbe crafts workshop on Isla San Cristóbal.

Ministerio de Ambiente Office (Map p188; ☎757-9442, 758-6822; Calle 1; ⏰9am-5pm Mon-Fri) Can answer questions about national parks or other protected areas.

Sea Turtle Conservancy (Map p188; ☎757-9186; www.conserveturtles.org; Calle 3; ⏰9am-5pm Mon-Fri) World's oldest sea-turtle research and conservation organization has an information office in Bocas town.

Getting There & Away

AIR

Air Panama (☎757-9841; www.flyairpanama.com) flies to Panama City (from US$123, one hour) twice daily sometimes via Changuinola (US$63) as well as to David (US$63). Office at the airport (Map p188). **Nature Air** (☎ in US 800-235-9272; www.natureair.com) flies from San José, Costa Rica (from US$130, 1½ hours), on Monday, Wednesday and Thursday.

BOAT

If you don't fly into Bocas you'll have to take a water taxi (US$6) from Almirante on the mainland. On the waterfront, Taxi 25 (Map p188) makes the half-hour trip between 6am and 6:30pm every 30 minutes.

Caribe Shuttle (Map p188; ☎757-7048; www.caribeshuttle.com) runs a combination boat-bus trip (US$39) to Puerto Viejo in Costa Rica twice daily. There's also an option to go on to Cahuita (US$38) or San Jose (US$75). It provides a hotel pickup but you must reserve one day in advance.

Getting Around

BUS

A cross-island bus goes to Boca del Drago (US$2.50, one hour) from Parque Simón Bolívar, with six departures between 5:30am and 8:30pm. It doubles up as a school bus, so afternoon trips may be delayed.

WATER TAXIS

To reach nearby islands, you can hire boaters operating motorized boats and canoes along the waterfront. As a general rule, you should always sort out the rate beforehand, and clarify if it is for one way or round-trip. Always pay on the return leg – this guarantees a pickup – though most boaters will want some money upfront to buy petrol. Though rates vary, you will get a better deal if you speak Spanish, are with a group and arrange for a pickup.

Boteros Bocatoreños Unidos (Map p188; ☎757-9760; Calle 3; ⏰6:30am-11pm) runs to destinations including Isla Carenero (US$1), Isla Bastimentos and Isla Solarte (US$5) and Red Frog Beach (US$8). Scheduled boats leave for Almirante (20 minutes, US$6) every half-hour. Staff is trained in safe boating and sustainable tourism practices.

Boca del Drago

Located on Isla Colón's northwest coast, this sleepy beach is known for its huge number of starfish along Starfish Beach, a 15-minute walk around the bend. The recent addition of commercial stands and cabins as well as increased water-taxi traffic have taken their toll on the beach, however. There has been a lot of erosion and the starfish have moved much further offshore. Still, the calm and relaxed atmosphere here will draw beach bums. The swimming and snorkeling here are good, and the lack of surge makes this one of the safest spots for swimming in the archipelago.

Courses

Institute for Tropical Ecology & Conservation COURSE

(ITEC; Map p184; ☎6624-9246, 6853-2134; www.itec-edu.org; Boca del Drago) Boca del Drago is home to a branch of the Institute for Tropical Ecology & Conservation, a non-profit education, research and conservation organization. The field station here offers field ecology courses to undergraduate and graduate students, provides facilities for tropical researchers, operates marine conservation programs and engages in community development. A water taxi from the beach will cost US$5. For more information on research, employment and volunteer opportunities at the station, contact ITEC via the website.

Sleeping & Eating

Cabañas Estefany CABIN $
(Map p184; 6582-9912, 6956-4525; www.cabanasturisticasestefany.com; dm US$12, d with kitchen US$35, 6-person cabin US$80-100; @) Though it's a far cry from luxury, 11-room Cabañas Estefany is one of the few budget beach lodgings on Isla Colón. Its wooden *cabañas* (cabins) are bare-bones and bathrooms have cold-water showers. Secure a room with a fan as it can get quite buggy. The rooms on the 1st floor have balconies and ocean views.

Yarisnori Restaurant PANAMANIAN $$
(Map p184; 6615-5580; www.yarisnori.com; Boca del Drago; mains US$8-25; 9am-6pm Wed-Mon) Overlooking the water and with hammocks strung between the palms on the beach, this open-air restaurant is a local favorite, due in large part to the warm hospitality of owners Juany and Willy. Grab a table on the sand and feast on the catch of the day, served with beans and coconut rice. Breakfast is good, too. Yarisnori now offers accommodation in three cramped rooms (doubles US$45) out the back looking out on some pretty gardens.

Getting There & Away

To get here from Bocas town, take a local bus (US$2.50) from Calle 3 near Parque Simón Bolívar, a water taxi (US$25 round-trip) or a taxi (US$15 to US$20 one way).

Playa Bluff & Around

A string of beaches on Isla Colón's east coast can be reached by a road that skirts along the shore up from Bocas town. This has traditionally been the terrain of surfers (and turtles), but as more lodgings pop up, travelers are discovering this once-secluded option. Playa Bluff stretches for 5km all the way to Punta Rocosa. September through to March are sure months to enjoy the beach without worrying about the hatching turtles.

Sights

Playa Bluff BEACH
(Map p184) This lovely beach is pounded by intense waves. Though you wouldn't want to get into the water here without a board, the soft, yellow sand and palm-fringed shores are pristine. The beach is 8km from Bocas town, alongside the road after you round Punta Bluff. It serves as a nesting area for sea turtles from May to September.

Playa Punch BEACH
(Playa Paunch; Map p184) Further up the coast from Playa El Istmito and Sand Dollar Beach is Playa Punch (or Paunch), which is dangerous for swimming but good for surfing. It's about 5km from Bocas town.

Playa El Istmito BEACH
(Isthmus Beach; Map p184) Playa El Istmito, also called Playa La Cabaña, is the closest beach to Bocas town (2.5km away), but as it's on the Bahía Sand Fly the *chitras* (sand flies) here have an itchy bite. This is not the most attractive beach and, unless you're walking, it's worth heading further north to **Sand Dollar Beach** or beyond.

Tours

Anaboca TOUR
(La Asociación Natural Bocas Carey; 6553-6566, 6996-0608; www.anaboca.org; per person US$20) This nonprofit run by the local community addresses marine-turtle conservation. In season (April to August), certified guides offer nighttime tours to view turtle hatching on Playa Bluff. You can also arrange overnight community stays, a good idea if you are there to watch hatching in the wee hours.

Sleeping

★**Tesoro Escondido** CABIN $
(Map p184; 6711-9594; www.bocastesoroescondido.com; d/tr from US$45/55, 2-/3-/4-person cabins US$85/100/115) Exuding a very homespun charm, this colorful seafront lodge with eight rooms, three thatched cottages and a suite works its magic. Mosaic tables and recycled-bottle construction in the showers lend a bohemian air; the hammock-strewn upstairs balcony is a treat; and rooms 7 and 8, accessed by a stepped tree trunk, are awesome.

Guests dine on fixed menus (lunch US$7.50, dinner US$11 to US$14.50) with fab desserts (best chocolate ever?). Snorkel gear is free to borrow; bicycles cost US$10 a day. It's located on the right just before Playa Bluff and has its own tiny private beach.

Turtle Beach House B&B $$
(Map p184; 6673-0383, 202-0857; www.turtlebeachhouse.com; d incl breakfast US$135;) This bright and airy B&B with four suites

over two floors is a stylish midrange choice. Furnishings are of handcrafted wood; the bathrooms are all stone and glass brick; and the large veranda looks over gardens to the sea. There's a great communal kitchen and a rainwater-catchment system in place.

Playa Bluff Hotel LODGE **$$**
(Map p184; ☎6798-8507; www.playablufflodge.com; d incl breakfast US$100-120;) What was until recently the anchor tenant of Playa Bluff has changed direction under a new name and new owners, and the casual on-site bar-restaurant is no longer a local magnet. The nine existing rooms (there are nine more coming) are modern and Mediterranean in style, nestled into a rainforest location that includes lily ponds with caiman and huge trees with sloths.

There's also a pool, and jungle treks (US$15) are available within the 23-hectare property.

★**Hummingbird** B&B **$$$**
(Map p184; ☎6949-3694; www.thehummingbirdpanama; d incl breakfast US$150;) This lovely new B&B on Playa Bluff boasts six rooms in a house and two bungalows constructed entirely of beautifully hued tropical hardwood, including sensational balconies and louvered windows and doors that let in cool breezes. Open-plan bathrooms behind the bedrooms are tastefully designed. Grounds are planted as a botanical garden to attract butterflies and hummingbirds.

Transfers from the airport are included with a three-night stay.

Island Plantation BOUTIQUE HOTEL **$$$**
(Map p184; ☎6612-7798; www.islandplantationbocas.com; d US$159-179, ste US$239; @) Reminiscent of an intimate pint-sized resort in Bali, this boutique property has seven lovely rooms with king-size four-poster beds, mosquito nets and hardwood balconies. The absolute stunner is the two-bedroom suite, featuring an enormous hardwood veranda overlooking the landscaped gardens. Guests have the attractive option of dining by candlelight on the beach. Warm welcome, excellent service.

Bluff Beach Retreat B&B **$$$**
(Map p184; ☎6677-8867; www.bluffbeachretreat.com; Playa Bluff; 2-/4-person cabins US$250/325; 9-person houses US$795, all incl breakfast;) This lush property facing Playa Bluff makes the perfect honeymoon getaway. One large home with a lap pool and two smaller cabins feature open-floor plans, lovely hardwood details, and slatted windows that keep out the sun and prevent the need for air-conditioning. Guests get the use of bicycles; it's also the site of yoga retreats. Three-night minimum stay.

You've also the option to ride horses at the Canadian owners' nearby citrus-fruit farm.

Eating

Paki Point CAFE **$$**
(Map p184; ☎6948-6562; www.facebook.com/pages/Paki-Point/137043396386998; mains US$7-15; ⏲10:30am-7:30pm) This outdoor open-deck restaurant with graffiti art and full views of the beach serves pizzas (US$7 to US$9) and seafood with cold beers and margaritas. For cyclists making the arduous trip to Playa Bluff, it's a godsend. You can also rent surf boards (US$15 per day).

Getting There & Away

There's no public transportation to the beaches. Expect to pay US$15 one way for a taxi to Playa Bluff. Prices fluctuate since the road is sometimes in a ruinous condition. A water taxi will cost US$7 per person.

Many people cycle this route. With a steady effort, it's about an hour one way from Bocas town to Playa Bluff, but be warned that the sun is unrelenting and it isn't a flat route. Take plenty of water and sunscreen. And there's the ATV/quad bike option...

Isla Carenero

POP 350

A few hundred meters southeast from Isla Colón lies the often-overlooked Isla Carenero. This tiny island takes its name from 'careening,' which in nautical talk means to lean a ship on one side for cleaning or repairing. In October 1502, Columbus' ships were careened and cleaned on this cay while the admiral recovered from a bellyache.

In recent times many hotels have been added, and nature isn't as wild here as it is on the more remote islands. Yet Carenero remains a nice alternative if you're seeking peace and quiet. It's also a good place for an easily accessible, leisurely lunch.

Activities

Escuela de Mar Surf School SURFING
(Map p184; ☎6981-2749, 757-9137; www.surfschoolpanama.com; ⏲9am-6pm) For quality

surf classes (US$45 for three hours) or kayak rentals ($10 for three hours), stand-up paddles (US$30 for four hours) and boards (US$15 per day), check out this surf school run by Argentine Luis.

Sleeping

Gran Kahuna Beach Hostel HOSTEL $
(Map p184; ☎757-9551; www.grankahunabocas.com; dm/d US$14/55; ❄@📶) Wildly popular, this waterfront surfer inn is adorable, with yellow concrete cabins, six bright rooms and six-bed dorms, and even a picket fence. It offers a huge flat-screen TV, a communal kitchen and an on-site bar. Cleanliness is impressive; not so the cavalier service – you might have to urge the desk person away from their nails to check in.

Aqua Lounge HOSTEL $
(Map p184; www.bocasaqualounge.info; dm/d/tr incl breakfast US$12/28/42; 📶🏊) Rough, rustic and grungy, this 12-room backpacker palace is a matchstick construction on the dock facing Bocas town. And guests just can't get enough – from the hugely popular US$1-a-bottle bar (open late; party night is Wednesday) to the wraparound dock with swimming platform and swings.

Fan-cooled dorms have up to a dozen beds; choose the one with four on the upper floor. Wi-fi at the bar.

★**Tierra Verde** HOTEL $$
(Map p184; ☎757-9903; www.hoteltierraverde.com; s/d/tr incl breakfast US$65/75/85, ste US$150-175; ❄@📶) This family-run three-story hotel sits back from the beach amid shady palms and flowers. Designed in a contemporary island style, the six spacious all-wood rooms on two floors and the suite at the top feature large windows that allow in ample light. There's hot water and the option of airport pickups (US$10). Go for rooms 4 or 5 for their ocean views.

Casa Acuario INN $$
(Map p184; ☎757-9565; www.casaacuario.com; d US$88-98; ❄📶) This dreamy sky-blue inn sits above crystal-clear blue waters teeming with tropical fish. Its four all-wood rooms on two floors are impeccably outfitted with smart fixtures and rustic, crafty touches, though the art on the walls is pretty awful. The big draws are the private decks and the large open terrace with kitchen.

Bocas Buccaneer Resort CABIN $$
(Map p184; ☎6902-8976, 757-9042; www.bocasbuccaneerresort.com; d/tr/ste incl breakfast US$90/95/105; ❄📶) Located on a lovely strip of sand, this low-key resort is really just a humble clutch of romantic cabins, a bungalow and a phenomenal all-wood suite. Elevated units have polished hardwood floors and walls, a thatched roof, a screened porch and a modern tiled bathroom with composting toilets. Guests get breakfast vouchers for nearby Bibi's restaurant.

El Faro del Colibri CABIN $$
(Hummingbird Lighthouse; Map p184; ☎757-7315, 6791-0840; www.farodelcolibri.com; d incl breakfast from US$98; ❄📶) Six canary-yellow cabins plus a 69-sq-meter mock lighthouse line a wooden dock. With individual swim-up decks and wood floors, they are lovely and considerably private. There are another four apartments in the main building. The buffet breakfast is sumptuous.

Eating

★**Leaf Eaters Cafe** VEGETARIAN $
(Map p184; ☎757-9543; www.facebook.com/bocasleafeaters; dishes US$6-10; ⏲10am-4pm Mon-Sat; 🌶) This vegetarian and vegan lunch place has moved from its old location and settled almost opposite above the water on Isla Carenero. It serves quirky and remarkably flavorful vegetarian dishes such as 'hippie bowls' (brown rice with vegetables and dressing) along with cheese paninis, bean tacos, scrumptious shiitake burgers and chocolate-banana smoothies. Bright and cheery decor and friendly atmosphere

Bibi's on the Beach SEAFOOD $$
(Map p184; ☎757-9137, 6981-2749; http://bocasbuccaneerresort.com/surfside-restaurant-and-bar; mains US$8-18; ⏲8am-10pm) In front of the landmark Bocas Buccaneer resort, this over-the-water restaurant and outfitter makes tasty soups, killer *ceviche* (citrus-cured seafood) and lightly fried fish. The service couldn't be friendlier and the sea views (and cocktails) will keep you lingering.

Receta Michilá CARIBBEAN $$
(Map p184; ☎6368-5251, 757-9551; www.facebook.com/Receta-Michilá-1495699930711817; Gran Kahuna Beach Hostel; tapas US$8-12; ⏲8-11pm Tue-Sat) The French-trained chef at this tiny outdoor restaurant next to the landmark Gran Kahuna Beach Hostel prepares 'contemporary Caribbean' dishes such as

breadfruit croquettes with red-pepper mayonnaise and octopus with pickled tree cucumber. The tasting menu (US$30) of four to five courses is a blowout. Almost 90% of the ingredients used (mostly fish and vegetables) are locally sourced.

Getting There & Away

Isla Carenero is a quick and easy US$1 boat ride from the waterfront in Bocas town. Oddly, there is no public pier. Water taxis dock at the small marina on the tip of the island. From here, there is a track that leads to the little town and continues across the island.

Isla Solarte & Around

Isla Solarte (aka Cayo Nancy) is distinguished by Hospital Point, named after the United Fruit Company hospital built here in 1900 to isolate victims of yellow fever and malaria. At the time, it was not known that these diseases were transmitted by mosquitoes. Although the hospital complex eventually included 16 buildings, it was abandoned after two decades of operation following the blight that killed all of United Fruit's banana trees here.

Today Hospital Point is renowned among snorkelers for its 20m underwater wall.

Sleeping & Eating

★Bambuda Lodge RESORT **$**

(Map p184; ☎6962-4644, 6765-4755; http://bambuda.net; dm US$16, d US$69-99, d with shared bathroom US$59, incl breakfast;) Beg, borrow and/or steal to stay in what is the archipelago's most attractive budget resort. It's a carefully crafted all-wood complex with 11 rooms set up in lush rainforest, with trails and overlooking a coral reef. There's a lovely pool on the slope and a new 60m-long water slide from reception straight down into the ocean. A chilled, welcoming retreat.

Owned and operated by two friends from Toronto who can't do enough for you, Bambuda counts two fan-cooled dorms with 10 beds each and nine private rooms, four of them quite luxurious and with their own bathrooms. The open-sided bar and dining room serves set meals (US$8 to US$12) and the grounds, set on 6 hectares with 40 different tropical fruit trees (mango, star fruit, custard apple etc), are breathtaking with 10km of trails fanning out in several directions. There's snorkeling equipment as well kayaks and canoes available.

Garden of Eden RESORT **$$$**

(Map p184; ☎6967-0187; www.gardenofedenbocas.com; d cabaña/suite incl breakfast US$158/188;) Fenced in by mangroves, this secluded resort sits high on an islet connected to Solarte's southeast. Two snug bungalows and a suite have balconies with sea views. There is no air-con but there are fans and a decent breeze. Guests get free rein to paddle the kayaks, self-serve drinks and lounge at the pool or on the tiny white-sand beach.

The in-house restaurant has an excellent local chef and serves three meals a day (dinner from US$16 to US$28). Guests staying three nights get free transfers to Bocas town. Otherwise the cost to get out here (US$20 round-trip) is steep.

Getting There & Away

Isla Solarte is a quick and easy boat ride (US$3) from the waterfront in Bocas town, but lodgings on the far end are considerably more expensive to reach. If you want to snorkel at Hospital Point, either join an excursion or negotiate a price with a water taxi.

Isla San Cristóbal

POP 450

A half-hour away from Bocas town and you're in another world among the Ngöbe indigenous community on Isla San Cristóbal. These subsistence farmers and fishers have a strong sense of Ngöbe identity, though they live mostly in difficult circumstances.

On a day trip to the main village of San Cristóbal on the northeast coast, you can see how the Ngöbe prepare and dye fibers to make *chacara* bags, tour medicinal gardens and enjoy a traditional meal cooked over the wood fire. For a visitor, it's an opportunity to see life as it's lived without much gloss. Visitor fees (day tours US$20 per person with lunch) benefit the local community. Boat taxis (US$60 round-trip) charge by boat, not per person. For arrangements, you can also contact Bocas Sustainable Tourism Alliance (p195) in Bocos town.

To the south, Dolphin Bay is famous for sightings of dolphin pods.

Tours

★Green Acres Chocolate Farm TOUR

(☎6716-4422; www.greenacreschocolatefarm.com; per person US$15; ⏲10am & 2pm Thu-Tue) Facing Dolphin Bay but actually on the

OFF THE BEATEN TRACK

THE OTHER BOCAS

Tired of the crowds? Find adventure by hiring a boat to try out these excursions:

Cayo Crawl Get lost in these mangrove-dotted channels – also called Coral Cay – near Isla Bastimentos.

Cayos Zapatillas Set out for the pristine white-sand beaches and virgin forests on these two uninhabited islands southeast of Isla Bastimentos.

Dolphin Bay Spot dolphins frolicking at this densely populated breeding ground south of Isla San Cristóbal.

Cayo Swan Spot red-billed tropic birds and white-crowned pigeons in this cay near Isla de Los Pájaros, north of Isla Colón.

mainland's Cerro Bruja peninsula, this chocolate farm sitting within 12 hectares of forested slopes is one of the largest in the archipelago that's open to the public. A two-hour tour led by North American owner Robert will take you seamlessly from cocoa pod to candy bar and leave no question unanswered.

The grounds are stunning and teeming with flora and fauna: hundreds of orchid species, green and black poison dart frogs, and golden silk orb-weaver spiders, whose high tensile-strength webs may one day replace Kevlar.

Sleeping & Eating

★**Dolphin Bay Hideaway** LODGE **$$**
(☎6886-4502; www.dolphinbayhideaway.com; d incl 2 meals US$150-200; 📶) Located amid mangroves and gorgeous gardens, this ecolodge has five rooms on two levels, with a big wooden deck, docks with hammocks and both a lily pond and a pool. Rooms are colorful and well appointed, with canopy beds, mosquito nets and large fans. Two new cabins complete the picture. North Americans Brian and Amy are delightful hosts and offer tours.

There is snorkeling equipment available as well as kayaks, canoes and SUP boards. Meals are eaten communally in the lovely dining room on the top level. Transfer from Bocas town costs US$30 one way.

Dolphin Bay Cabañas CABIN **$$**
(☎6549-6405; http://dolphinbaycabanas.com; d US$65-85, 3-bedroom cottages US$155-185; @) This property on Dolphin Bay, with three simple thatched cabins and a cottage for up to five people, is comfortable enough. It features beautifully landscaped grounds, and a well-and-rainwater catchment system in places. But the emphasis here is on sailing: Hobie Cat, Laser and Optimists are for rent (from US$60) and lessons and guided sailing tours are available.

Table d'hôte meals (breakfast US$7, dinner US$12) are eaten at the wonderful bar-restaurant perched at the end of a dock. Great spot for a sundowner.

Rana Azul PIZZA **$$**
(☎6710-0395; www.facebook.com/pages/Pizzeria-Rana-Azul/260376173999411; pizza US$8-16; ⏰3-8pm Fri, noon-5pm Sun) A real only-when-traveling experience, Rana Azul is a remote restaurant-pizzeria facing Dolphin Bay from the Bocas mainland. It's hosted by Joseph and Maria, who arrived here some years back on their boat from Austria. There are other mains on the menu (eg gargantuan meat plates to share from US$22) but most come here for pizzas cooked in the wood-burning oven.

Getting There & Away

Getting to Isla San Cristóbal from Bocas town is not cheap. A water taxi will cost upwards of US$30.

Isla Bastimentos

POP 1950

Although it's just a 10-minute boat ride from the town of Bocas del Toro, Isla Bastimentos is like a different world. Some travelers say this is their favorite island in their favorite part of Panama. The northwest coast of the island is home to palm-fringed beaches that serve as nesting grounds for sea turtles, while most of the northern and southern coasts consists of mangrove islands and coral reefs that lie within the boundaries of the Parque Nacional Marino Isla Bastimentos.

The main settlement on Bastimentos is Old Bank. It has a prominent West Indian population whose origins are in the banana industry. The island is also home to the Ngöbe-Buglé village of Quebrada Sal (Salt Creek).

Sights

Old Bank

Located on the western tip of the island, Old Bank (also called Bastimentos town) is a small enclave of 1500 residents of West Indian descent. Until the 1990s most of the adults in Old Bank traveled daily to Changuinola to work in banana fields; today, residents have taken to fishing or farming small plots. Some work in the burgeoning tourism industry.

Although Old Bank is very poor and devoid of any real sights, it has a pronounced Caribbean vibe, and it's a relaxing place to stroll around and soak up the atmosphere. It's also the best place in Bocas del Toro to hear Gali-Gali, a hybrid language of Jamaican English and Spanish with elements of the Guaymí language spoken by the Ngöbe-Buglé.

There are no roads, just a wide, concrete footpath lined on both sides with colorfully painted wooden houses.

Parque Nacional Marino Isla Bastimentos

★Parque Nacional Marino Isla Bastimentos PARK
(Map p184; admission US$10) Established in 1988, this 132-sq-km marine park was Panama's first. Protecting 130 islands of the Bocas del Toro archipelago, including the coral-fringed Cayos Zapatillas, and the wetlands in the center of Isla Bastimentos, the marine park is an important nature reserve for mangroves, monkeys, sloths, caiman, crocodile and 28 species of amphibians and reptiles.

Get up-to-date park information from the **ATP** (Autoridad de Turismo Panama; Map p188; ☎757-9642; bocasdeltoro@atp.gob.pa; Calle 1; ⊙8:30am-3:30pm Mon-Fri) or **Ministerio de Ambiente** (Map p188; ☎757-9442, 758-6822; Calle 1; ⊙9am-5pm Mon-Fri) offices in Bocas del Toro town. To camp out anywhere in the park, you are required to first obtain a permit (US$10) from the latter.

Nivida Bat Cave CAVE
(Bahía Honda; Map p184; admission US$5) One of Bastimentos' most fascinating natural wonders, Nivida is a massive cavern with swarms of nectar bats and a subterranean lake. The cave lies within the borders of the Parque Nacional Marino Isla Bastimentos and half the fun is getting here. But it's next to impossible to do it on your own. An organized tour from Old Bank costs US$35 per person.

The tour involves a 25-minute boat ride from Old Bank to the channel entrance. You'll then spend a similar amount of time gliding though mangroves and lush vegetation. From the dock it's then a half-hour hike to the cave. Wear sturdy shoes or boots; you will be provided with headlamps at the cave entrance.

Around the Island

Playa Larga BEACH
(Long Beach; Map p184) This 6km-long beach on the southeast side of the island falls under the protection of the marine park. Hawksbill, leatherback and green sea turtles nest here from March to September. It's also good for surfing. To get here, you can follow the path past Red Frog Beach, but the best access is the one-hour walk with a guide from Salt Creek.

Red Frog Beach BEACH
(Map p184; admission US$3) Small but perfectly formed, Red Frog Beach is named after the *rana rojo* (strawberry poison-dart frog), an amphibian you're most unlikely to encounter here due to development, local kids trapping them to impress tourists, and a tidal wave of day-trippers in season. From Bocas town, water taxis (US$4) head to the public dock next to a small marina on the south side of the island, from where the beach is an easy 15-minute walk.

Playa Polo BEACH
(Map p184) Polo Beach wraps around a sheltered cove and is protected by a reef. It has good snorkeling. Can be reached by short hike from Red Frog Beach.

Wizard Beach BEACH
(Playa Primera; Map p184) The most beautiful beach on Isla Bastimentos is awash in powdery yellow sand and backed by thick vine-strewn jungle. It's connected to Old Bank via a wilderness path, which normally takes 20 minutes or so but can be virtually impassable after heavy rains. The path continues along the coast to Playa Segunda (Second Beach) and Red Frog Beach.

Quebrada Sal (Salt Creek)

The Ngöbe-Buglé village of Quebrada Sal (Salt Creek) is on the southeastern side of the island. Reached via a long canal cut through the mangrove forest, it is home to 750 people, 60-odd houses, an elementary school, a handicrafts store, a general store and a soccer field. The community largely depends on fishing and subsistence farming, travels mostly by canoe, and resides in wooden, thatched-roof huts without electricity or running water.

The Quebrada Sal is slowly modernizing and villagers are friendly and open to visitors, especially if you can speak Spanish. Water taxis can drop you off at the concrete dock near the entrance to the village where you'll need to pay a US$2 entry fee and sign the visitors' book.

If you have the time, it's worth hiring a local guide to walk with you along the roughly one-hour cross-island trail to Playa Larga (US$20 per person); shorter pelican- and caiman-spotting tours are also available, costing US$12 and US$7 respectively.

Tours

★Up in the Hill TOUR
(Map p184; ☎6607-8962, 6570-8277; www.upinthehill.com; Old Bank; drinks & snacks US$2.50-4) It's worth the hot 20-minute haul up to this organic farm at the highest point on Isla Bastimentos for the views, and to see cacao being grown and turned into one of the world's favorite comestibles. There's a cafe serving chocolate drinks, coffee from Boquete and homemade hibiscus tea, and a shop with its own line of coconut-based natural body products.

If you can't bring yourself to leave, there are two basic cabins (US$70) sleeping two or three, with kitchens. To reach Up in the Hill, head right from the dock in Old Bank and follow the signs, turning right at the Methodist church.

Bastimentos Alive ADVENTURE TOUR
(Map p184; ☎6514-7961, 6945-6167; www.bastimentosalive.com; Old Bank; trek with/without BBQ US$45/35; ⏱11am) This new but already well-regarded tour operator leads daily treks through the jungle, with stops at Red Frog Beach and the organic Up in the Hill farm at the highest point on the island. Lunch and a Caribbean-style barbecue at the end of the tour are included. It's a 7½-hour day (six without the BBQ). Add US$10 for transfer from Bocas town.

Tours depart from the Bastimentos Alice office, which is in a small wooden house behind the landmark Hostel Bastimentos. Tours to Nivida bat cave and Laguna de Bastimentos are also planned.

Bastimentos Sky Zipline Canopy Tour ADVENTURE SPORTS
(Map p184; ☎6987-8661, 836-5501; www.redfrogbeach.com/bocas-del-toro-zipline.html; per person US$55; ⏱10am, 1pm & 3:30pm) Seven zip lines, a swaying sky bridge and a vertical rappel are highlights of this attraction, brought to you by a well-known Costa Rican zip-line designer, in the hills just south of Red Frog Beach. Tours last two hours.

Festivals & Events

Día de Bastimentos FIESTA
(Bastimentos Day; ⏱23 Nov) Bastimentos Day is celebrated with a huge parade and drumming demonstrations on the island.

Sleeping

Though most of the action is in Bocas del Toro town, the largely rustic digs in Old Bank offer a laid-back, Caribbean atmosphere. Lodgings outside of town, especially to the south, are mostly resorts, some quite high-end, and usually include transfers from Bocas town in their rates.

Bubba's House GUESTHOUSE $
(Map p184; ☎6403-9447, 6589-8872; www.bubbashouse.com; Old Bank; dm US$16, d US$38-45; ❄📶) This attractive wooden guesthouse on the waterfront is the best place to stay in Old Bank, and it attracts a lively and interesting crowd. The 11 colorful rooms with painted floors include privates as well as en suite dorms for up to six guests. The back-deck bar and restaurant has a great collection of musical instruments. The welcoming hosts are Argentinian.

Bocas Island Lodge HOSTEL $
(Map p184; ☎6533-1615; www.bocasislandlodge.com; Red Frog Beach; dm US$15, d with bathroom US$60, d without bathroom US$30-55; ❄📶) From the public dock serving Red Frog Beach it's a 10-minute walk to this popular 32-room concrete hostel-lodge, part of the original plans for a high-end resort. Dorms have up to a dozen metal bunk beds, a few doubles have private bathrooms and there's a tidy open-air kitchen. While short on charm, it's clean and functional.

The popular on-site restaurant has main meals for US$6 and US$12, including vegetarian options. A movie room shows more than 300 films, there are yoga sessions (US$7) daily at 9am and Red Frog Beach is a short walk downhill on foot.

Tío Tom's Guesthouse GUESTHOUSE **$**
(Map p184; ☎757-9831; www.tiotomsguesthouse.com; Old Bank; d US$38, 2-person bungalow US$48; 📶) This rickety wooden guesthouse perched over the sea has been offering cheap, clean and unfussy rooms for years. A highlight is the waterfront deck strewn with hammocks. There are five rooms for two or three people and a separate bungalow; all have private bathrooms. The German owner offers hearty meals (dinner US$8), organizes diving tours and rents kayaks.

Hostal Bastimentos HOSTEL **$**
(Map p184; ☎6795-8093, 757-9053; www.hostalbastimento.com; Old Bank; dm US$8-10, d US$15-20, d/tr with air-con US$45/50; ❄@📶) On a hill off the main path, this sprawling yellow clapboard house has a bright selection of 28 rooms and hammock decks. Spaces are creaky but serviceable; private rooms with air-con also have fridges and balconies with great views. Backpacker-ready, it includes two kitchens, and a common room with a bar, TV and dartboard.

★**Palmar Tent Lodge** CAMPGROUND **$$**
(Map p184; ☎838-8552; www.palmartentlodge.com; Red Frog Beach; dm tents US$15, d/tr tents from US$50/60, 2-person bungalows US$85) On the edge of the jungle and facing celebrated Red Frog Beach, Palmar has introduced glamping to Bocas del Toro and the archipelago will never be the same. Accommodations are in solar-powered circular tents for two to three, with all the comforts (including large lock boxes for valuables); in an eight-bed dorm; and in a luxurious two-story thatched 'jungalow' for two.

The huge open-sided restaurant-bar is the place to be most nights (and days, come to think of it). The fun and well-informed owners, two mates from Washington, DC, offer a laundry list of tours and excursions and there are yoga classes (US$6) twice daily on site. Water-taxi shuttles (US$4 one way) link the lodge with Bocas town twice a day. No internet.

Los Secretos Guesthouse GUESTHOUSE **$$**
(Map p184; ☎6795-6355; https://lossecretosguesthouse.wordpress.com; western Isla Bastimentos; d US$100-120; ❄📶🏊) This pretty pink-and-green Caribbean-style home sits high on a forested hill. It's a hike up the stairs from the dock, but you'll find five rooms with hardwood floors, balconies and modern comforts. Run by Frenchman Xavier and his mother, you'd assume the hotel has an excellent restaurant – and this one is a winner. Half-board costs US$30 per person extra.

The lovely swimming pool and *rancho* are located by the dock. There's snorkeling equipment and kayaks to use, and a complimentary half-hour guided tour of the surrounding forest, which is full of sloths, monkeys and birds. Transport to Red Frog Beach is free; otherwise a water taxi costs US$10 one way.

Beverly's Hill CABIN **$$**
(Map p184; ☎757-9923; www.beverlyshill.blogspot.com; Old Bank; s/d without bathroom US$17/35, d with bathroom US$60-70; 📶) 🍃 These thatched cabins occupy a lush green garden replete with red frogs – incongruous in the center of Old Bank. The seven immaculate rooms feature fans, firm mattresses and hot-water showers; hammocks abound. The on-site composting and water filtration system makes this one of the most environmentally friendly hotels on the island.

★**Tranquilo Bay** RESORT **$$$**
(☎838-0021; www.tranquilobay.com; southern Isla Bastimentos; per person incl 3 meals & activities US$175-275; ❄@📶) 🍃 The oldest, most remote and arguably the best resort on Isla Bastimentos, this North American–run, family-friendly lodge creates a fantastic environment for play and relaxation. At present the grounds feature six comfortable cabins with orthopedic beds, fine linens and locally crafted hardwood furnishings. Tailored excursions run by biologist guides include wildlife-watching (there's a 25m-tall birdwatching tower). Also perfect for just beaching it.

Four of the cabins face the water and two are in the jungle (and another three-bedroom jungle cabin is on the way). Guests dine at the main lodge (alcohol included), which offers a wraparound porch and ocean views. The lodge composts, captures rainwater, uses a minimum of plastics and educates staff on water usage. Created on around 80 hectares of conservation land, Tranquilo Bay also works with local scientists and conservation agencies and does not print marketing material. Transportation is US$100 per person, round-trip, with travel days on Wednesday and Saturday. Three-night minimum stay.

★Casa Cayuco RESORT **$$$**
(Map p184; www.casacayuco.com; southern Isla Bastimentos; s/d incl 3 meals & wine from US$235/305) This hushed beachfront retreat counts two lofty suites with sweeping views in a post-and-beam hardwood lodge, and four named jungle cabins, some thatched and one (Tortuga) almost in the water. *Table d'hote* meals (wine included) eaten on the dock are a big deal to the foodie owners from Detroit; David brings in lobsters and octopus from just in front.

Kayaks and snorkel gear are included to explore the nearby reefs, mangroves and rivers. Guided excursions run extra but include unique offerings such as in-depth tours of the nearby indigenous village of Quebrada Sal (Salt Creek). The resort runs on solar power and collected rainwater. Located on the white-sand beach of Punta Vieja, it's 30 minutes by boat to Bocas town; transfers are included There's no phone. Minimum stay three nights.

La Loma LODGE **$$$**
(Map p184; 6592-5162, 6619-5364; www.thejunglelodge.com; western Isla Bastimentos; r per person incl 3 meals & activities US$136) Integrated into a 23-hectare rainforest and its community, this 'jungle lodge and chocolate farm' offers tasteful stays to consistently rave reviews. The location is hidden in mangroves, accessed by boat. A steep hill leads past a rushing creek to four sedate, ultra-private cabins with hand-carved beds. Each has a propane-fuelled, rainwater-fed bathroom, a mosquito net and solar-powered energy system.

One cabin is by a rock pool; two are in the tree tops (we love No 2 and its views). Meals include fresh-baked bread and organic vegetables grown on the farm. Two-hour tours are included in the price. Guests can also join a chocolate tour for US$15 (US$25 including lunch) and the Anglo-American owners will soon offer cooking courses in the chocolate house. La Loma distributes a number of beautifully illustrated pamphlets to guide guests through the jungle and to help you appreciate its wildlife and medicinal plants.

Sea Monkey LODGE **$$$**
(Map p184; 6738-5586; www.seamonkeybocasdeltoro.com; Old Bank; d incl breakfast US$150-175;) The two bungalows at this new luxury B&B hover cheekily over the gin-clear water at the far end of Old Bank harbor. Enormous fan-cooled rooms accommodating between three and four people sit 30m from shore, and include hand-hewn wooden king-sized beds, high-quality mattresses and fridges. Glass walls in front afford endless uninterrupted sea views. Private decks with hammocks are great.

The Sea Monkey's breezy bar-restaurant, a destination in itself, serves Asian-fusion dishes (mains US$13 to US$16); one of the American owners lived in China. It's also the perfect spot for a sundowner (cocktails from US$5).

Red Frog Bungalows CABIN **$$$**
(Map p184; 6539-5151; www.redfrogbungalows.com; Red Frog Beach; per person incl 3 meals US$160-250; @) Set in the sheltering jungle, the original Red Frog Beach resort has accommodation in a three-bedroom stilted house meters from the beach; two fabulous bungalows under palms imported from Bali; and a bizarre 'tentalow' – a colorful canvas safari tent with thatched roof. The happening clubhouse has a games room, wide-screen TV, a library and a hot tub.

The owner is a serious surfing dude and leads surf tours (US$120 for four). On the clubhouse walls are broken boards owned (and broken) by visiting word-title holders Kelly Slater and Dusty Payne, among others. On the beach are *palalapas* – open-sided thatched lounging huts for guest use. Price includes transfers to/from Bocas del Toro airport.

Al Natural Resort RESORT **$$$**
(Map p184; 6576-8605, 757-9004; www.alnaturalresort.com; southern Isla Bastimentos; d incl 3 meals from US$220-270) So laid-back it's almost comatose, this desert-island hideaway lends a bohemian twist to all-inclusive. Based on traditional Ngöbe-Buglé architecture, the seven driftwood-and-palm bungalows have an open design that delivers sea views – even from some toilets – as in house 3. The most remote bungalow is house 4. The hosts are uncommonly gracious, and the meals (including wine) well prepared.

Center of the action is the two-story restaurant with cool chill-out room and a bird observatory on the roof. There's a dive shop onsite and the resort loans kayaks to paddle out to choice snorkel spots. The fourth night is half-price and the seventh free. Closed in June and July. Militantly internet-free.

Eating

Chavela SEAFOOD $

(Map p184; ☎6502-0024; www.facebook.com/barrestaurantechavela; Old Bank; mains US$4-12; ⏲6-10pm) An attractive little eatery in a lime-green shack at the bottom of the landmark Hostel Bastimentos, Chavela serves cheap-as-chips burgers but emphasizes seafood in all its guises, from *ceviche de pulpo* (raw octopus cured in lime juice) and fish tacos to barracuda steak.

Nacho Mama's TEX-MEX $

(Map p184; ☎6539-5151; Red Frog Beach; tacos US$5-6, with drink US$12; ⏲11am-5pm Tue-Sun) Pitched on the shifting sands of Red Frog Beach, this one-hit wonder does a thriving business dispensing tacos with fish, shrimp, *ceviche* (citrus-cured seafood) and chicken throughout the day. But never on a Monday. And never nachos.

Coco Hill VEGETARIAN $$

(Map p184; Old Bank; dishes US$7.50-16; ⏲10am-10pm Wed-Mon) Close to the island's highest point, Australian Michelle concocts some pretty exotic meatless dishes at her vegetarian, vegan and gluten-free restaurant and bar. It might seem a bit of a hike, but who can resist red-pepper soup, mixed mezze plates, and Kahlua and rum brownies? The blackboard menu changes daily. Cocktails are made with fresh fruit juices.

If you can't tear yourself away, there are three beautifully bedecked 'jungalows' (doubles US$110 to US$165) on stilts in the forest to stay in.

MAINLAND

The mainland jungles of Bocas del Toro Province teem with wildlife and are pocketed with remote indigenous villages – the contrast with the archipelago could not be greater. Here you'll also find the province's biggest towns and cities.

Almirante

POP 12,730

A clutch of stilted homes on the water, this unkempt village has seen better days, but it remains the springboard for the Archipiélago de Bocas del Toro so is always busy.

About 20km south of Almirante down a steep dirt track from the coastal highway, **La Escapada** (☎6618-6106; www.laescapada.net; Highway 11, Km 48.5; d incl breakfast US$110; P ❄) is a lodge with four comfortable though sparse rooms with large screened porches. A deteriorating boardwalk though the mangroves leads to decks over the water and a restaurant with lovely views to Isla San Cristóbal. The welcoming owners from Florida, USA, can organize fishing and boating trips.

Getting There & Away

Taxi 25 runs a water shuttle to Bocas town (US$6, 30 minutes); a taxi between the bus terminal and the dock should cost no more than US$1.

An air-conditioned bus to Changuinola (US$1.45) leaves every 15 minutes between 6am and 8pm and takes 45 minutes. Taxis to Changuinola (from US$20) can be bargained, particularly if you start your walk from the dock to the bus terminal.

Changuinola

POP 42,000

Headquarters of the Chiriquí Land Company, the company that produces Chiquita bananas, Changuinola is a hot and rather dusty town surrounded by a sea of banana plantations. Although there is little reason to spend any time here, overland travelers linking to Costa Rica will have to pass through. Changuinola also serves as the access point for the Humedal de San San Pond Sak and the Parque Internacional La Amistad. Av 17 de Abril (also called Av Central) runs north to south and serves as the town's main artery.

Sights

Snyder (Changuinola) Canal CANAL

In 1903 a 12km-long canal connecting the Río Changuinola and Almirante Bay was dug parallel to the Caribbean shoreline to facilitate the barging of bananas from the fields of the Bocas del Toro archipelago to ships. Abandoned years ago, the 30m-wide channel is now an amazing spot to view wildlife. It's about 5km east of Changuinola (taxi one way US$2).

Sleeping

Hotel Golden Sahara HOTEL $
(☎758-7908; hotelgolden_sahara@hotmail.com; Av 17 de Abril; s/d US$32/42; ❄@) This big family-run place has 28 rooms, but make sure to choose one in the back as those on the main street near the central bus station are noisy. There are more than a half-dozen PCs in the lobby for guest use. Friendly place.

Hotel Alhambra HOTEL $
(☎758-9819; Av 17 de Abril; s/d/tr US$25/28/36; ❄@) This 33-room place above a shopping center offers some of the best value in town, and is right at the southern end of the main drag leading out of town. Reception is on the 1st floor.

Hotel Semiramis HOTEL $
(☎758-6006; Av 17 de Abril; d/tr US$33/35; ❄wi-fi) This shiny tiled hotel at the southern end of the main street is the best in town. There's air-con, hot water and 20 proper rooms – but not all have windows.

Eating

La Fortuna CHINESE $
(☎758-9395; www.facebook.com/pages/Restaurante-La-Fortuna-Changuinola/365195563543260; Av 17 de Abril; mains US$10-12; ⏰11:30am-10:30pm) It's nothing to write home about (especially if you hail from Beijing) but should you need a fix of rice and noodles La Fortuna, diagonally opposite from the Urraca bus terminal, can oblige.

Cotty's PANAMANIAN $
(☎760-0161; Av 17 de Abril; meals US$2.50; ⏰24hr) On the main road, this clean cafeteria-style restaurant with folkloric murals on the walls prepares unfussy Panamanian fare. A plate of curried chicken and rice (US$2) is gratifying and quick.

Restaurante Ebony CARIBBEAN $$
(☎6506-8402; www.facebook.com/pages/Restaurante-Ebony/175159159345781; Av 17 de Abril; mains US$10-18; ⏰noon-11pm) More expensive than most eateries in Changuinola but loaded with atmosphere, this Afro-Caribbean restaurant at the southern end of the main street serves up creole dishes (shrimp with coconut, rice and peas, achee and salt fish). Carved birds and portraits of black icons Malcolm X, Bob Marley and US president Barack Obama adorn the walls.

Information

Banco Nacional de Panamá (☎758-8136; Av 17 de Abri; ⏰8am-3pm Mon-Fri, 9am-noon Sat) Bank with ATM.

Ministerio de Ambiente Office (Ministerio de Ambiente de Panamá; ☎758-6603; Calle hacia Aeropuerto; ⏰8am-4pm Mon-Fri) Association formerly known as ANAM (Autoridad Nacional del Ambiente); several blocks west of the main drag, Av 17 de Abril.

Post Office (Calle Media Mia; ⏰7am-6pm Mon-Fri, to 5pm Sat) Near the airport, north of the center.

Getting There & Away

AIR

From Panama City, **Air Panama** (☎316-9088; www.airpanamaonline.com) flies to Changuinola (US$127 one way) up to twice a day on weekdays and once daily on weekends. The flight carries on to Bocas town (US$36). Taxis between the Changuinola airport and the center should cost about US$3.

BUS

Buses for Costa Rica leave from the terminal just south of the Delta gas station. Other buses depart from **Terminal Urraca** (☎758-8115) between 6am and 7pm.

DESTINATION	COST (US$)	DURATION (HR)	FREQUENCY
Almirante (with boat connections to Isla Colón)	145	45min	every 30min
Altos del Valle (Bosque Protector de Palo Seco)	7.25	2¼	every 30min
David	9.70	4¾	every 30min
El Silencio (Parque Internacional La Amistad)	1.25	30min	every 20min
Guabito–Sixaola	1	30min	every 30min
Las Tablas (Las Delicias)	2	1½	hourly
Panama City	29	12	daily 7am
San José (Costa Rica)	16	6	daily 10am

TAXI

A taxi seating five people from Changuinola to the Costa Rican border at Guabito costs US$7.50 and takes about a half-hour.

GETTING TO COSTA RICA

The border post at **Guabito–Sixaola** (8am to 5pm), 16km northwest of Changuinola, is a less-frequented crossing than others to/from Chiriquí Province, and most travelers find it hassle-free. Buses from Changuinola depart frequently for the border (US$1, 20 minutes, every half-hour) from 6am to 7pm. On the Costa Rican side of the border, you can catch regular buses on to Puerto Limón and San José, as well as regional destinations.

Note that you can be asked for an onward ticket if you are entering Costa Rica. If you do not possess one, it is acceptable to buy a round-trip bus ticket back to Panama. Also note that Costa Rica is one hour behind Panama.

Humedal de San San Pond Sak

These relatively unknown wetlands covering 160 sq km just 5km north of Changuinola harbor an incredible variety of tropical fauna. In addition to sloths, river otters, white-faced monkeys, caimans, iguanas, sea turtles and poison-dart frogs, the fresh waters of San San are also one of the few known Central American habitats for the manatee.

Tours of the wetlands arranged by **Aamvecona** (Association of Friends & Neighbors of the Coast & its Environment; 6679-7238, 6547 7214; www.aamvecona.com), a conservation organization consisting mainly of volunteers who administer the wetlands in conjunction with the Ministry of the Environment, leave from the road bridge over the Río San San 6km north of Changuinola. Get here on the bus bound for Guabito-Sixaola on the Costa Rican border.

There's a visitors center at the beach at the mouth of the Río San San that has displays on wildlife as well as a manatee-viewing area.

Although it's possible to visit the wetlands in a day trip from Changuinola, the best way to appreciate the area is to stay overnight. Located inside the park on a stunning wilderness beach is a rustic **house** (r per person US$10) on stilts, which has three simple rooms, cold-water showers, a flush toilet (fed by rainwater) and a cooking area.

Bring your own food and drink, as well as a sleeping bag or blanket – bedding is not provided. You will also want to bring a mosquito net and bug spray, as the sand fleas and mosquitoes show no mercy.

Getting There & Away

Reach the Humedal de San San Pond Sak on the Guabito–Sixaola bus (US$1), which leaves every 30 minutes from Changuinola.

Parque Internacional La Amistad (Wekso)

The 4000-sq-km Parque Internacional La Amistad was established jointly in 1988 by Panama and Costa Rica – hence its name of 'Friendship Park.' In 1990 it was declared a

TURTLE PATROL IN SAN SAN POND SAK

There are only eight sea-turtle species in the world and half of those can be found nesting in the Archipiélago de Bocas del Toro, primarily on the long beaches of the northern coast of Isla Bastimentos. The loggerheads appear from April or May, the leatherbacks in March and the hawksbills and greens from July to September.

Sea turtles leave the water only to lay their eggs. Two months after the eggs are laid, the hatchlings break loose from their shells, leave their sandy nests and enter the sea – if they are not stolen or first eaten by raccoons, birds or dogs.

Human predators and the encroachment of development may be their greatest obstacle. Throughout Panama, many communities still eat turtles and their eggs, greatly contributing to turtles' dwindling populations.

The community-based organization Aamvecona, based in the Humedal de San San Pond Sak, is working toward turtle preservation, with projects active between February and July. It accepts volunteers on turtle-nesting and hatching projects, and also offers nature tours.

Unesco World Heritage Site and later became part of the greater Mesoamerican Biological corridor. In Panama the park covers a portion of Chiriquí (p178) and Bocas del Toro Provinces, contains seven of the 12 classified life zones, and serves as a refuge for a great number of endangered flora and fauna.

La Amistad is also home to members of three indigenous groups: the Naso (or Teribe), the Bribrí and the Ngöbe-Buglé. Although these groups are still holding to their traditional ways of life, their numbers are dwindling fast, especially as outside influences continue to invade their culture. However, in an effort to preserve their identity while simultaneously providing a means of income, the Naso created an ecological center at Wekso, the former site of the infamous US-run Pana-Jungla survival school. Today, this and two other Naso ecotourism projects are thriving as more and more travelers discover the beauty of both the rugged wilderness of La Amistad and the Naso's ancestral culture.

History

According to Spanish colonial records, the Naso were present in mainland Bocas del Toro when the first explorers arrived in the region in the early 16th century. The Spaniards referred to the Naso as the Teribe, or the Tjër Di (Grandmother Water) in Naso, which is the guiding spirit that forms the backbone of their religious beliefs. The Spaniards gradually pushed the Naso off their lands, driving the population into exile in the highlands near the Costa Rican border.

Although the establishment of the modern Panamanian state has enabled the Naso to return to their ancestral home, their survival is threatened by the lack of their own *comarca* (autonomous region). This scenario contrasts greatly with other Panamanian indigenous population groups such as the Guna, the Emberá, the Wounaan and the neighboring Ngöbe-Buglé. The plight of the Naso is further amplified by the fact that the tremendous ecotourism potential in Parque Internacional La Amistad is at odds with a massive hydroelectric project planned in the region. Although proposals for establishing a *comarca* are on the table, in true Panamanian form, progress is being held up by bureaucracy.

The Naso population today is estimated at 3500, the majority of whom live in 11 communities along the Río Teribe and survive as subsistence farmers. Although they remained virtually autonomous for generations, the Naso have recently started losing their cultural self-sufficiency due to missionary activity, land encroachment and youth migration. Today, most Naso are bilingual (Naso and Spanish), wear Western-style clothing and practice some form of Christianity. However, strong elements of ancestral Naso culture remain, especially considering that they are one of the few remaining indigenous groups in the Americas to retain their traditional monarchy.

Sights

Before the US invasion of Panama in 1989, Wekso was named Pana-Jungla, and served as a US-run survival school that trained Panamanian and international troops in jungle warfare. Although it was disbanded in 1990 following the ousting of General Noriega, the ruins of the old structures remain scattered around the Wekso grounds. Highlights include the barracks, mess hall, chapel, armory and serpentarium.

Activities

Although most of Parque Internacional La Amistad is inaccessible, the park is home to a recorded 90 mammal species (including six cat species) and more than 450 bird species (including resplendent quetzals and harpy eagles).

Visitors can hire local guides for about US$30. A 3.5km loop trail at Wekso, for example, cuts through secondary and virgin rainforest, with good opportunities for wildlife-watching. You can also take a dip in the river, though be careful of the current. A network of trails links various Naso communities together, though it's best to tackle these with a guide.

For the more ambitious, from Wekso it's a five-hour hike into the Parque Internacional La Amistad. The Caribbean side of La Amistad is much less developed than the Pacific side. You will need to hire the services of local boaters and guides, and you must be completely self-sufficient. The terrain is extremely rugged; it's without hiking trails, and the river rages during the rainy season. If you're prepared for a serious trek, you're almost certain to have an adventure.

Sleeping & Eating

Permits to camp in the park are payable at the ranger station.

Posada Media Luna HOSTEL $
(☎6343-5496, 6874-4530; www.ocen.bocasdeltoro.org/ingles/ocen-lodge-ing.htm; per person US$15, 3 meals extra US$13) This hostel in the village of Bonyic on the Río Teribe has basic accommodation, traditional food (bring your own water) and tours of the area, including a walk to neighboring villages with a round-trip by raft and a hike through the Pana-Jungla past the Wekso entrance of La Amistad park.

The hostel is run by run by OMUB (Organización de Mujeres Unidades de Bonyic), an association of indigenous women.

Odesen Wekso Lodge CABIN $
(☎6574-9874, 6569-2844; http://odesen.bocasdeltoro.org; per person US$20, 3 meals extra US$14) Run by Odesen (Organization for the Sustainable Development of Naso Ecotourism) the first Naso community organization based at Wekso, this guest lodge has a handful of very basic rooms, with a secure water supply, flush toilets and an outdoor shower. It's staffed by community members who prepare meals, lead guided jungle tours and can explain about Naso culture and history.

Information

Admission to the park (US$5) is usually collected at the Wekso entrance near Changuinola.

Bocas del Toro Community Tourism Network (www.redtucombo.bocasdeltoro.org) can help organize visits to Naso communities.

Getting There & Away

The Naso communities at Wekso and Bonyik are upriver from the hamlet of El Silencio, which is easily accessible by bus from Changuinola (US$1.25, 30 minutes, every 20 minutes). It's then another 45-minute boat ride up the Río Teribe. In El Silencio you can hire a six-person boat for around US$70.

Once on the river you'll pass hills blanketed with rainforest and intermittent waterfalls. The backdrop is the glorious Talamanca range and the jungle comes all the way down to the river water. After about 45 minutes on the river, a sign on the right bank announces your arrival at Wekso. Bonyic is on the other side of the river and can also reached by a new road.

Las Delicias

Set in rainforest hills, the small indigenous community of Las Delicias lies along the Río Sixaola, 20km from the Costa Rican border crossing at Guabito. The community has shifted its income source from harvesting and logging to preservation and ecotourism. Visiting is one way you can make a positive contribution.

Attractions include waterfalls, abundant wildlife and impressive viewpoints over the Sixaola river valley and the Talamanca mountains. On a day trip, you can boat the Ríos Sixaola and Yorkín, hike through rainforest or go horseback riding.

Sleeping & Eating

Accommodation is undeveloped in these areas – there's no electricity – so bring your own supplies, especially a water purifier, flashlight (torch), mosquito net and bug repellent. Lunch prepared by villagers is usually fresh fish. Prices are quite reasonable (from US$20 to US$30 per person).

El Guabo Cabins CABIN $
(☎6211-9856; per person US$20) These rustic cabins in El Guabo on the Río Yorkin are run by indigenous women who form a group called Alakolpa (Association of Women Protecting the Forest). There's a shower and toilet but no electricity. Hardy travelers can string up a hammock or pitch a tent at one of the *ranchos*.

Information

Make arrangements to visit Las Delicias through Changuinola's Ministerio de Ambiente (p206) office or by phoning the **community tourism management** at Las Delicias (☎6600-4042) directly.

Getting There & Away

To reach the community, take a bus from Changuinola to Las Tablas (US$2, 1½ hours, hourly) and then a taxi to Las Delicias (US$10). You can also negotiate a price with one of the 4WD taxis in Changuinola. From here, boats ply the Ríos Sixaoloa and Yorkin.

Bosque Protector de Palo Seco

Set high in the Talamanca range, the 1675-sq-km **Bosque Protector de Palo Seco** (Palo

WORTH A TRIP

ADVENTURE IN NASO COUNTRY

On the border of Parque Internacional La Amistad and a proposed Naso *comarca* (autonomous region), **Soposo Rainforest Adventures** (☎6631-2222, 6875-8125; www.soposo.com; day tour per person US$90, 2-/3-day package incl lodging, meals & tours US$140/275) is a unique jungle lodging and sustainable tour operator, and a recommended step off the well-worn trail. Guests stay in stilted thatched huts, eat traditional foods and immerse themselves in Naso culture.

The project, spearheaded by an ex–Peace Corps volunteer and her Naso husband, has been lauded by travelers. It was created to offer the Naso people an alternative income, bolster cultural self-esteem and protect natural resources in the face of a massive hydroelectric project, which is changing the nature of the area. A highlight is a three-day trip up the Río Teribe to the village of the Naso monarch.

From Changuinola, it's a 30-minute taxi ride to the village of El Silencio, from where there's river access to the lodging.

Seco Forest Reserve; US$5) is a lush cloud forest home to monkeys, sloths, armadillos, butterflies, tarantulas and eyelash vipers. Birdwatching is superb – keep an eye out for rarities such as the lanceolated monklet, rufous-tailed jacamar, dull-mantled antbird and speckled tanager. The ashy-throated bush tanager is unique to this area.

The reserve was created in 1983 to serve as a conservation corridor linking La Fortuna Forest Reserve and Parque Internacional La Amistad.

Pay the park admission fee and obtain information about current hiking conditions at the Ministerio de Ambiente station at the entrance. There are three trails in the park, each about 45 minutes in duration, allowing visitors the chance to get a taste of the region's natural wonders.

Ministerio de Ambiente has two-story sleeping facilities with a **dorm** (dm US$7); bring your own food and bedding. Guests have access to the kitchen as well as bathrooms. To ensure there is availability, contact the Ministerio de Ambiente (p206) office in Changuinola.

ℹ Getting There & Away

The entrance to the reserve and the Ministerio de Ambiente station is about 30km south of Chiriquí Grande on Hwy 4, the road over the Continental Divide to David (also called the Fortuna Rd).

From David, take any bus heading toward Changuinola. Ask to stop just before Altos del Valle and disembark at Km 68.5, which is right by the Ministerio de Ambiente station. From Bosque Protector de Palo Seco, buses pass every 30 minutes heading north to Changuinola (US$7.25, 2¼ hours) or south to David (US$5, 2½ hours)

Colón Province

POP 242,000 / AREA 4890 SQ KM / ELEV SEA LEVEL TO 979M

Includes ➡

Best Surf Spots

- Isla Grande (p224)
- Isla Mamei (p224)
- Playa Grande (p211)
- Turtles Beach (p224)
- V-Land Beach (p224)

Best Places to Sleep

- La Morada de La Bruja (p221)
- El Otro Lado (p221)
- Sister Moon Eco Lodge (p225)
- Casa Congo (p221)
- Macondo (p225)

Why Go?

With an edgy reputation more true crime than travel, Colón rarely makes travel wish lists, but there is more to this Caribbean province than its downtrodden capital. Think pristine beaches and lowland rainforests, colonial splendors and modern engineering marvels. Portobelo, with its growing music and art scene, shows the best of vibrant Congo culture, while the luxury train between Panama City and Colón remains one of the greatest rail journeys in the Americas.

The region's incredible history encompasses the earliest European explorers. Black roots also run deep, and Colón was the birthplace of today's ultra-popular *punta* music (better known abroad as reggaetón).

During the colonial era, these coastal cities ranked among the world's richest; their gold and silver stores enticed pirates from English privateer Sir Francis Drake to Admiral Edward Vernon. Today the fallen fortresses and cannons embedded in the coral reefs recall the fallen Spanish empire.

When to Go

- **Dec–Apr** The dry season is a great time for snorkeling or diving for Caribbean treasure, as visibility is at its best. It's high season for lodging and beaches fill up.
- **Oct** Pilgrims from all over Panama set out walking weeks ahead to attend the Black Christ Festival, an enormous event with masses and street celebrations held in October in Portobelo.
- **May–Jul** The summer months of May through July are a relatively good time to visit, with some rain showers and off-season prices.

Colón Province Highlights

1 Panama Railroad (p214) Riding through lush vistas in a 1st-class luxury car heading from Panama City to Colón along this historical railway.

2 Portobelo (p218) Exploring hallowed colonial ruins or finding festival frenzy in Portobelo, once the Caribbean's greatest port.

3 Fuerte San Lorenzo (p217) Living out your *Pirates of the Caribbean* fantasy at this historic Spanish fort that once stood guard over the Caribbean.

4 Isla Grande (p224) Soaking up the natural beauty and laid-back vibe on a picture-perfect gem of a Caribbean island.

5 Caribbean Sea (p219) Finding sharks, cargo ships and military planes while scuba diving the Caribbean Sea around Portobelo.

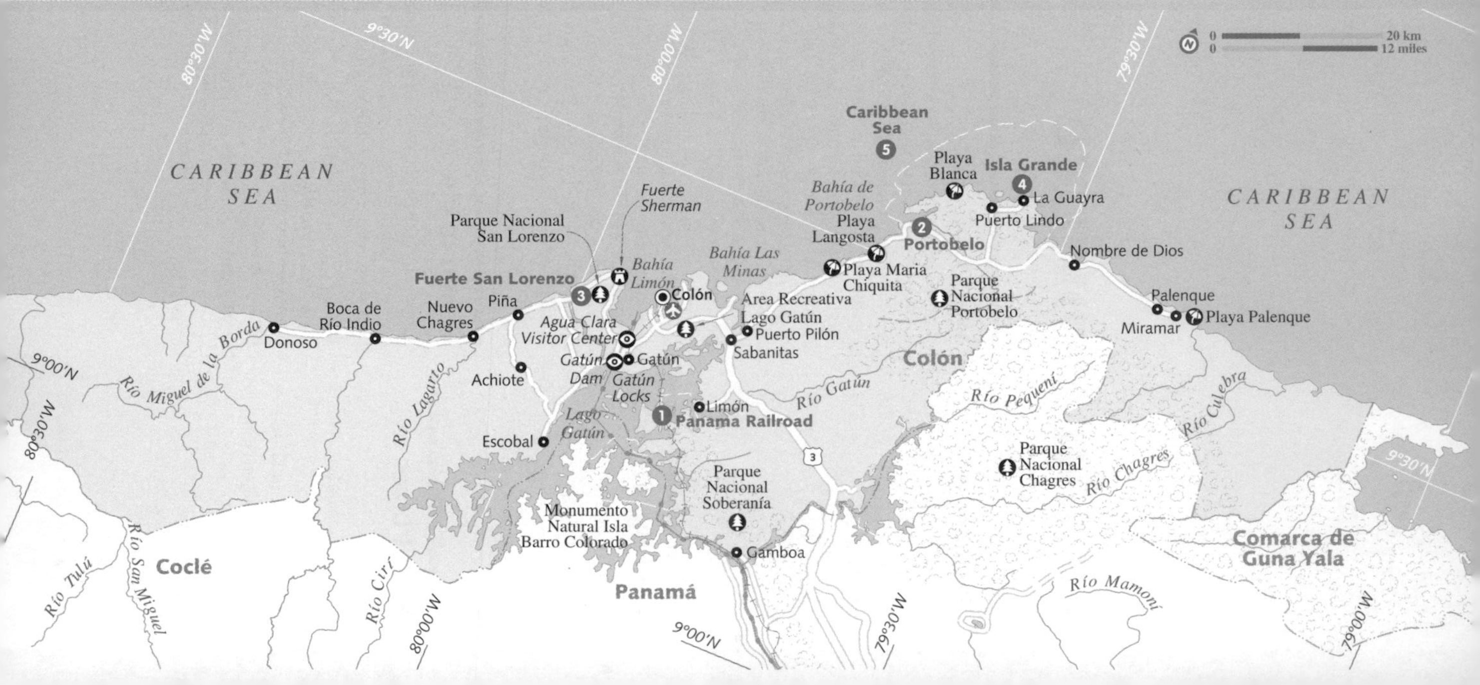

Colón

POP 35,000

With its colonial grandeur crumbling and its neighborhoods marginalized, Colón is the city that Panama forgot, in spite of vigorous development meant to court Caribbean cruise ships. Prior to 1869, the railroad connecting Panama City and Colón was the only rapid transit across the continental Western Hemisphere. A last whiff of prosperity was seen during the construction of the Panama Canal.

On the city's edge, the Zona Libre (Free Zone) was created in 1948. Generating some US$5 billion in annual commerce, little benefit seems to trickle down to locals. From close up, it's an island of materialism floating in a sea of unemployment and poverty.

Recent improvements in city safety are attributed to tighter gang control and an arms for food program that got many guns off the streets. The improved Ruta 3 between Panama City and Colón is now a four-lane highway, resulting in much quicker travel times.

History

In 1850 the city of Colón (originally called Aspinwall for a Panama railroad founder) was established as the Caribbean terminus of the Panama Railroad. It became a boom town attracting east-coast Americans who favored this 'shortcut' to California at the height of gold-rush fever. Even with boating the Atlantic and Pacific oceans and crossing the isthmus, it was considered a faster and less dangerous journey than crossing the US heartland and facing hostile indigenous groups.

Following the completion of the US transcontinental railroad in 1869, Colón faded into obscurity less than 20 years after its founding.

At the peak of Colón's economic depression in 1881, the French arrived to build an inter-oceanic canal, but the city was burnt to the ground four years later by a Colombian hoping to spark a revolution. In the years to follow, the city blossomed, entirely rebuilt in French colonial architectural style. Rivaling Panama City in beauty and wealth, life in the Canal Zone was pleasurable and highly profitable.

The French abandoned their efforts eight years later after huge monetary losses and the death of 22,000 workers from yellow fever and malaria. The USA seized the opportunity, reinventing the vibrant provincial capital as workers from around the world arrived by the shipload.

After the completion of the canal in 1914, unemployment caused Colón's economy to disintegrate and the city spiraled into the depths of depravity. Today most of the colonial city is still intact, though the buildings are on the verge of collapse.

🛏 Sleeping

Meryland Hotel HOTEL $
(☑ 441-7055; www.hotelmeryland.com; cnr Calle 7 & Av Santa Isabel; s/d US$45/60; P ❄ @ 🛜) A massive stone building, this business hotel fronts an attractive city park in a comparatively safe part of Colón. Small tiled rooms with gold tones and wrought-iron furniture have air-con, cable TV and hot-water bathrooms, though you're paying for security, not luxury. The restaurant saves you the trouble of having to leave the hotel at night.

Radisson HOTEL $$
(☑ 446-2000; www.radisson.com; Colón 2000; d/ste US$119/169; P ❄ @ 🛜 ⊠) Really you could be anywhere, but this luxury chain hotel has the friendliest staff and the best digs in Colón. Rooms are comfortable and sufficiently stylish, with minibar and flat-screen TVs, and you can always let off steam with some laps in the pool. Big off-season discounts are available.

✕ Eating

Arrecifes SEAFOOD $$
(☑ info 441-9308; Calle 3 at Paseo Gorgas; mains US$10-15; ☉ noon-8pm Mon-Sat) Local business owners lunch at this nondescript port building cooking up great Caribbean seafood in the gated port area. Expect no frills and no water views, just generous portions of *Criollo*-style seafood, stewed in onions, peppers and tomatoes, and whole fried snapper.

🛍 Shopping

Zona Libre SHOPPING CENTER
(Duty-Free Zone; southeast Colón; ☉ 8am-5pm Mon-Fri, weekend hrs vary) Second in size only to Hong Kong's free-trade zone, Colón's Zona Libre is a huge fortresslike area of giant international stores selling items duty free. Most stores only deal in bulk merchandise and aren't set up to sell to individual

tourists. To enter the Zona Libre, present your passport at the security office.

Individual purchases are sent to Tocumen International Airport in Panama City, where they may be retrieved upon a visitor's departure. Hours vary depending on each store, with some open on weekends.

Colon 2000 SHOPPING CENTER
(Paseo Gorgas; ⌚8am-5pm) Only a decade old, this sterile shopping and entertainment sector geared toward cruise-ship travelers sits on the east side of Colón. Though lacking in any Panamanian flavor, it is safe to peruse and features a good selection of restaurants and souvenir shops, as well as a casino.

Hours vary with each shop or restaurant.

Getting There & Away

BUS

From Panama City, express and regular buses for Colón leave every 30 minutes from the Albrook Bus Terminal.

Colón's terminal de buses (bus terminal; cnr Calle Terminal & Av Bolívar) serves towns throughout Colón Province with hourly departures.

If you are headed east of Colón from Panama City, these buses can be boarded at Sabanitas, the turnoff for Portobelo, thus avoiding a trip into Colón. Be aware that buses may be standing room only, particularly on weekends.

DESTINATION	COST (US$)	DURATION (HR)
Escobal (near Parque Nacional San Lorenzo)	1.25	35min
La Guayra	3	2
Nombre de Dios	3.80	2½
Panama City	3.50	1-1½
Portobelo	1.60	1½

TRAIN

Panama Railroad (☎317-6070; www.panarail.com; one way adult/child US$25/15; ⌚daily departures from Panama City at 7:15am, Colón

RIDE THE PANAMA RAILROAD

One of the best ways to fully appreciate the extent of the canal is to travel from Panama City to Colón along the historic Panama Railroad. The rails fell into disrepair during the Noriega regime, but in 1998 the Panama government partnered with Kansas City Southern, an American-based railway holding company, to create the Panama Canal Railway Company (PCRC). The joint venture sought to re-establish the Atlantic–Pacific rail link and create a profitable alternative to the Panama Canal trade route. In 2001 PCRC also introduced a passenger service with a fully operational vintage train.

If you're looking to relive the golden age of railway travel, the vintage train features exotic wood paneling and blinds, carpeted interiors, glass-domed cars and open-air viewing decks. The hour-long ride parallels the canal, sometimes traversing thick rainforest.

While you're sipping a hot cup of coffee and admiring Panama's scenic interior, consider for a moment this cool train trivia:

- Peaking at US$295 a share, the Panama Railroad was the highest-priced stock on the New York Stock Exchange (NYSE) in the mid-1800s.
- With a total construction bill of US$8 million, the Panama Railroad was, at the time, the most expensive railroad per kilometer ever built.
- Despite being only 76km long, the Panama Railroad required 304 bridges and culverts.
- During the first 12 years of its operations, the Panama Railroad carried over US$750 million in gold and silver, and collected a quarter of 1% on each shipment.
- In 1913 the Panama Railroad hauled 2,916,657 passengers and transported 2,026,852 tons of freight across the isthmus, which was the heaviest per-kilometer traffic of any railroad in the world.
- An estimated 12,000 laborers died during the construction of the Panama Railroad, mainly from malaria and yellow fever.
- Disposing of the dead was such a problem that the Panama Railroad administration started pickling the bodies in barrels and selling them to medical schools, the proceeds of which were used to build a hospital in the Panama Canal Zone.

at 5:15pm) This glass-domed luxury passenger train takes a lovely ride from Panama City to Colón every weekday leaving at 7:15am and returning at 5:15pm. The train follows the canal, at times surrounded by nothing but thick, vine-strewn jungle. If you want to relive the heyday of luxury train travel for an hour or two, this is definitely the way to do it.

Note that the Panama City terminus is actually located in the town of Corazal, which is a 15-minute drive from the capital.

Getting Around

While in Colón, it's not a good idea to walk around unknown neighborhoods. Fortunately, taxis congregate at the bus terminal, train station and the Zona Libre, and fares across the city are usually under US$2.

A round-trip taxi for three to four passengers runs around US$60 to Fuerte San Lorenzo and US$30 to Gatun Locks, fewer passengers should negotiate a better fare. From the terminal you can also take a bus to Gatun Locks (US$1).

Around Colón

Agua Clara Visitor Center VIEWPOINT
(☎276-8325; www.micanaldepanama.com; adult/child US$15/10; ⏰8am-3:15pm) This new observation center offers an exclusive panoramic view of the Panama Canal expansion. Visits take slightly over an hour. Covered decks view Lago Gatún and the locks; there is also a theater with videos in English, exhibits, a cafe and gift shop. With no on-site museum, the focus here is really about getting a good look at the expansion. A short rainforest trail has sloths and monkeys. Exhibits close at 4pm but visitors must enter by 3:15pm.

The turnoff is just past the railroad tracks, to the left; for the locks, continue straight at the turnoff. The center is accessible to travelers with disabilities.

Gatún Locks CANAL
(admission US$5; ⏰8am-4pm) The Gatún Locks, 10km south of Colón, raise southbound ships 29.5m from Caribbean waters to Lago Gatún. Just the size of them is mind-boggling. In *The Path Between the Seas,* David McCullough notes that if stood on its end, a single lock would have been the tallest structure on earth at the time it was built, taller by several meters than even the Eiffel Tower. Each chamber could have accommodated the *Titanic* with room to spare.

Workers poured a record-setting 1,820,000 cubic meters of concrete to construct the Gatún Locks. The concrete was brought from a giant mixing plant to the construction site by railroad cars that ran on a circular track. Huge buckets maneuvered by cranes carried the wet concrete from the railroad cars and poured it into enormous steel forms. Locomotives moved the forms into place. This protracted process continued virtually uninterrupted for four years until the Gatún Locks were completed.

A viewing stand opposite the control tower offers a prime view of the locks in action. The two-hour process is the most interesting stage of the canal transit and the English brochure clearly describes what you're watching.

Once the ships pass through the locks, they travel 37km to the Pedro Miguel Locks, which lower southbound ships 9.3m to Lago Miraflores, a small body of water between two sets of Pacific locks. Ships are then lowered to sea level at the Miraflores Locks.

Buses to the Gatún Locks leave the Colón bus terminal hourly (US$1.25, 20 minutes). If you arrive by taxi you can stop here before heading on to Gatún Dam – another 2km away. A taxi ride from Colón to the locks and dam and back should cost US$60 per party, but agree on a price before leaving.

Gatún Dam LAKE
Constructed in 1908 to shore up the Río Chagres and to create Lago Gatún, the Gatún Dam was once the world's largest earthen dam, while Lago Gatún was also the world's largest artificial body of water (before Lake Mead, USA). Its creation submerged 262 sq km of jungle, entire villages (then relocated) and large sections of the Panama Railroad. Today, power generated by the dam drives all the electrical equipment operating the canal, including the locomotives that tow ships through the locks.

While the sight of the dam is impressive enough, if the spillway is open you can watch millions of gallons of water rushing out. Before going, ask the guard at the entrance to the Gatún Locks if the spillway is open.

If you arrive at the Gatún Locks by bus, it's a leisurely 30-minute walk to the dam. To get there, cross over the bridge spanning the Gatún Locks, turn left and follow the road for approximately 2km.

Parque Nacional San Lorenzo

Centered on the ruins of the crumbling Spanish colonial fortress of Fuerte San Lorenzo, the 9.6-sq-km Parque Nacional San Lorenzo includes the former US military base of Fuerte Sherman, as well as 12 different ecosystems including mangroves, marshlands, semi-deciduous forests and humid rainforests. Since the departure of the US military in 1999, native fauna has slowly recolonized the area, though the future of the San Lorenzo protected area remains uncertain.

As part of the Mesoamerican Biological Corridor, San Lorenzo protects and fosters species migration between the continents. Unfortunately, poachers, loggers and slash-and-burn farmers are threatening the reserve. Yet conservation and tourism may win out, due in part to the massive quantities of unexploded ordnance (UXOs) left in the area by the US military after their hasty exit from Panama. For decades, they used the jungles surrounding Fuerte Sherman for target practice and survival training.

History

Following the destruction of Nombre de Dios by Sir Francis Drake in 1573, the Spanish moved to fortify the Caribbean coast. Of principal concern was the Río Chagres, which flowed inland to the town of Venta de Cruces (near the modern town of Gamboa), and then linked up with the trade route leading to the city of Panamá. In 1595, by order of Phillip II of Spain, Fuerte San Lorenzo was built into the side of a steep cliff near the river mouth. Fuerte San Lorenzo, Portobelo and Panamá, the 'three keys' of the Americas, became known as the strategic hearts of the Spanish trade empire.

Once established, Fuerte San Lorenzo was under constant pirate attack. In 1596, only one year after its completion, Drake seized San Lorenzo. Although later recovered and rebuilt with greater fortifications, San Lorenzo was again assaulted, this time by Sir Henry Morgan in 1671. Captain Morgan (of the spiced-rum fame) succeeded in overpowering its guns and sailing up the Río Chagres. A few months later, Morgan burnt Panamá to the ground, pilfered its riches and sailed back to England with galleons laden with Spanish treasure.

In 1680 a new fortification was built on the highest part of the cliff, but this was no match for British Admiral Vernon, who destroyed San Lorenzo yet again in 1740. In 1761 the Spanish once again rebuilt San Lorenzo, though the decision to abandon the overland trade route in favor of sailing around the Cape Horn meant that the fort didn't suffer further attacks. As a result, Fuerte San Lorenzo was abandoned by Spain in 1821 when Panama became independent. The fort was subsequently used as a Colombian prison, a post office for inbound English mail and a campsite for gold miners en route to California.

In order to defend the Panama Canal Zone, the US military built Fuerte Sherman in 1911 with the purpose of defending the Atlantic side of the canal. Although post-WWII changes in war technology meant that the fortifications were rendered obsolete, the area surrounding the fort became an important jungle warfare training center. In 1963 these operations came under the responsibility of the US-army-run 'School of the Americas' in nearby Fuerte Gullick, but five years later the 'Jungle Operations Training Center' became an independent entity. Fuerte Sherman subsequently became the main jungle operations school for the US army and was used as a training center for Vietnam-bound Special Forces.

On June 30, 1999, under the Torrijos–Carter treaties, Fuerte Sherman, nearby Fuertes Davis and Gullick, and the Parque Nacional San Lorenzo were handed back to the Panamanian Government.

Sights & Activities

Most travelers set their sights on the ruins of Fuerte San Lorenzo, but there are plenty of opportunities here for jungle exploration. The secondary forests of the protected area are rich in bird life and there's no shortage of mountainous trails and waterfall-fed ponds to discover. You can also visit organic shade-grown coffee farms and hike to splendid lookouts with views of the protected area and the Río Chagres.

Centro El Tucán OUTDOORS
(☎6991-3055; ⏰8am-4pm) The protected area at San Lorenzo is best explored with a guide, easily arranged at the Centro El Tucán, a community learning and visitors center that lies on the edge of the reserve. Guides generally charge US$60 per group

for a two-hour hike, though longer and more difficult treks can also be arranged. El Tucán also has an excellent documentation center on the flora and fauna of the reserve, human ecology and history.

The visitors center is located in the village of Achiote, 13km north of Escobal. Since there is no public transportation to the town and few taxis in the area, Achiote is best accessed by private vehicle.

Fuerte San Lorenzo FORT
(www.sanlorenzo.org.pa; ⊘8am-4pm) FREE
Declared a Unesco World Heritage Site in 1980, Fuerte San Lorenzo is perched at the mouth of the Río Chagres on a promontory west of the canal. Despite its violent history, much of San Lorenzo is well preserved, including the moat, the cannons and the arched rooms. The fort also commands a wide view of the river and bay far below, which was one of the reasons the Spanish chose to fortify the site.

San Lorenzo was constructed of blocks of cut coral and armed with row upon row of cannons. If you inspect the cannons closely, you'll notice that some of them are actually British-made, which bespeaks the time in the 17th century when Sir Francis Drake and his pirate brethren occupied the fort.

🛏 Sleeping

Meliá Panamá Canal RESORT $$
(☑470-1100; www.solmelia.com; d US$70; P✳@⊚✖) Building 400 of the notorious School of the Americas is now a giant re-

sort. The US$30 million hotel features comfortable but somewhat dated guest rooms, a cluster of outdoor and indoor pools complete with swim-up bars, and a formal restaurant overlooking Lago Gatún. Service can be slow.

A range of tours operated by Aventuras 2000 include an on-site canopy zipline and fishing, as well as canal, Embera village and Fuerte San Lorenzo visits.

ℹ Orientation

Fuerte San Lorenzo and the Parque Nacional San Lorenzo are located west of the city of Colón and northwest of Lago Gatún. The ruins of San Lorenzo are 9km southwest of Fuerte Sherman on the Caribbean coastal highway and lie along the northwestern boundary of the protected area. Although there is no official entrance to the reserve, there is a visitors center in the village of Achiote, along the northeastern edge of the reserve between the villages of Piña and Escobal.

ℹ Getting There & Away

As there is no public transportation to either Fuerte San Lorenzo or Parque Nacional San Lorenzo, this area is best explored by private vehicle or tour from Panama City. It is, however, possible to take a taxi to Fuerte San Lorenzo from Colón (around US$60 round-trip). Taxis are uncommon closer to the reserve.

If driving, go to the Gatún Locks, continue past the stoplight near the northern entrance to the locks and follow the signs to the dam, 2km away. Drive over the dam and follow the 'Fuerte San Lorenzo' signs. These lead to the entrance of

SWEET DREAMS IN THE DEN OF DICTATORS

The borders of the San Lorenzo protected area are home to Fuerte Espinar, which was known as Fuerte Gullick prior to the US handover. Within this compound is the infamous Building 400, which was the former home of the School of the Americas.

Established in 1949, the School of the Americas trained more than 34,000 Latin American soldiers before moving to Fuerte Benning, Georgia, in 1984. The school was created to keep communism out of Latin America, which quickly translated into teaching Latin American soldiers how to thwart armed communist insurgencies.

The school graduated some of the worst human-rights violators of our time, including former Argentine dictator Leopoldo Galtieri, who 'disappeared' thousands during Argentina's Dirty War of the 1970s, and El Salvador's Roberto D'Aubuisson, who led death squads that killed Archbishop Oscar Romero and thousands of other Salvadorans during the 1980s.

In a bizarre twist, Building 400 is now a giant resort, Meliá Panamá Canal. Not too surprisingly, all evidence that the hotel has ever been anything but an upscale fun center is missing.

In the past, overnight guests at Building 400 arrived via convoy or Blackhawk chopper. Today, it's recommended that you arrive via private vehicle; take the Quatro Altos turnoff on the Transisthmian Hwy and follow signs for the hotel.

Fuerte Sherman, where you'll be asked to show identification. Once you've done this, you will be allowed to proceed the remaining 9km to Fuerte San Lorenzo.

Portobelo

POP 4600

This Caribbean fishing village is so laid-back and languorous, it is incredible to ponder that it was once the greatest Spanish port in Central America. Mules once carried Peruvian gold and Oriental treasures to Panama City via the fortresses at Portobelo. Though English privateers destroyed them several times throughout their history, many of these atmospheric colonial fortresses still stand. Throughout the village, homes are situated among these atmospheric ruins.

Today, Portobelo's residents scratch out a living fishing, tending crops or raising livestock. Though economically depressed, Portobelo is experiencing something of a cultural revival, with interest surging in Congo art and dancing. The town bursts to life every October 21 for the Festival de Cristo Negro (Black Christ Festival), one of the country's most vibrant and spiritual celebrations.

There are also nice beaches, accessed by boat, and worthwhile diving and snorkeling.

History

Colombus named Puerto Bello (Beautiful Port) in 1502, when he stopped here on his fourth New World voyage. Over time, the name shortened to 'Portobelo.'

Portobelo consisted of no more than 10 houses when the celebrated Italian engineer Juan Bautista Antonelli arrived in 1586 on a mission to examine the defensibility of the Caribbean. After noting how well Portobelo's bay lent itself to defensive works, King Félipe II ordered that Nombre de Dios be abandoned and Portobelo colonized. However, it wasn't until after Nombre de Dios was completely destroyed by Sir Francis Drake in 1596 that the transfer took place.

The city of San Felipe de Portobelo was founded in 1597 and its 200-year history was riddled with numerous invasions at the hands of English privateers and the Royal Navy. Portobelo was first attacked in 1602 by the English pirate William Parker, but it was the infamous Sir Henry Morgan who sacked the city in 1671.

However, not all of the invasions were the product of superior tactics or numbers. In 1679 the crews of two English ships and one French vessel united in an attack on Portobelo. They landed 200 men at such a distance from the town that it took them three nights of marching to reach it. As they neared Portobelo, they were seen by a farmer, who ran ahead to sound the alarm, but the pirates followed so closely behind that the town had no time to prepare. Unaware of how small the buccaneer force was, all the inhabitants fled.

The pirates spent two days and nights in Portobelo, collecting plunder in constant apprehension that the Spaniards would return in great numbers and attack them. However, the buccaneers got back to their ships unmolested and then distributed 160 pieces of eight to each man. At the time, one piece of eight would pay for a night's stay at the best inn in Seville.

Attacks on Portobelo continued unabated until the city was destroyed in 1739 during an attack led by Admiral Edward Vernon. Portobelo was rebuilt in 1751, but it never attained its former prominence and, in time, became a virtual ruin. Later, much of the outermost fortress was dismantled to build the Panama Canal and many of the larger stones were used in the construction of the Gatún Locks. There are, however, still considerable parts of the town and fortresses left, and today Portobelo is protected as a national park and as a Unesco World Heritage Site.

Sights

Playa Blanca BEACH

A 20-minute boat ride from Portobelo will bring you to this lovely white-sand beach without road access, on a tranquil cove surrounded by dense wilderness. It boasts some of the least disturbed reefs between Colón and the Archipiélago de San Blás, and its sheltered waters offer better visibility than in nearby Portobelo. There's a colorful reef in the center of the cove near the beach, as well as a second reef that sits in deeper waters about 100m offshore.

San Juan de Dios Chapel CHURCH

Ruins of a Catholic church from 1589.

Real Aduana de Portobelo HISTORIC BUILDING

(admission US$5; 8am-4pm) The handsome, two-story Royal Customs House of Portobelo was originally built in 1630 to serve as the *contaduría* (counting house) for the king's gold. Now the two main rooms house

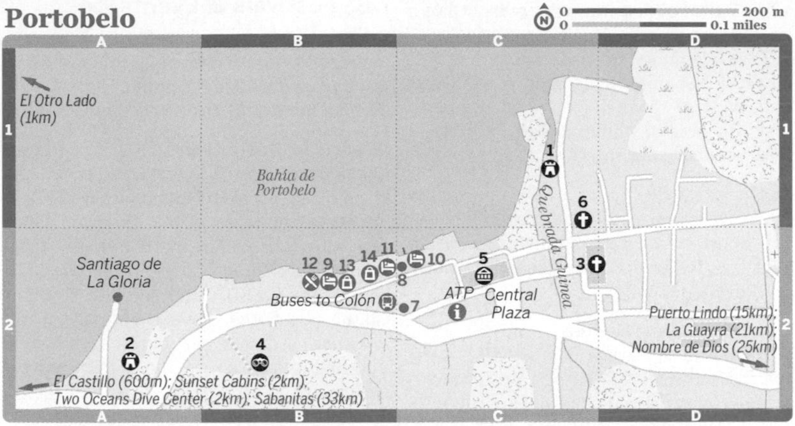

Portobelo

Sights

1 Fuerte San Jerónimo ... C1
2 Fuerte Santiago ... A2
3 Iglesia de San Félipe ... C2
4 Mirador Perú ... B2
5 Real Aduana de Portobelo ... C2
6 San Juan de Dios Chapel ... C1

Activities, Courses & Tours

7 Agrupaciones de Congo ... C2
8 Las Delicias de Sole ... C2

Sleeping

9 Casa Congo ... B2
10 Casa Rayo Verde ... C2
11 La Morada de la Bruja Portobelo ... B2

Eating

12 El Palenque ... B2

Shopping

13 Galería Casa Congo ... B2
14 Taller Portobelo ... B2

permanent exhibitions, including replicas of Spanish-colonial rifles, sketches of Portobelo's forts, 20th-century black-and-white photos of the town and a few dozen rusty cannonballs. There's also an informative video (in English too).

Treasure brought across the isthmus was recorded and stored here until it could be placed on galleons and sailed to Spain. According to early records, no fewer than 233 soldiers were garrisoned in this building alone.

Check out the bronze cannon at the entrance – it was recovered from a sunken galleon and bears a Spanish coat of arms and the date of manufacture (1617).

Iglesia de San Félipe CHURCH

This 1814 Catholic church is the home of Portobelo's famed Black Christ (p221). Believers attribute miracles to the 1.5m statue that was found floating in the bay, and it's celebrated every October with the popular Festival de Christo Negro (p220). The church was the last structure built by the Spanish before they withdrew from Panama.

Activities

Diving & Snorkeling

It's not Belize or the Bay Islands, but if you're an avid scuba diver, you'll have a good time here with no fewer than 16 major dive sites in the nearby waters. Though the visibility can't compare to more traditional Caribbean diving destinations, the variety of underwater attractions include a 34m cargo ship and a C-45 twin-engine plane. In addition to these, the waters around Portobelo are also home to soft coral–laden walls, offshore reefs and rock gardens, some of which are also good for snorkeling. Dive centers have snorkel gear and information.

The good news is that you'll probably see several pelagic animals including nurse sharks, black-tip reef sharks and eagle rays. The bad news is that you probably won't see them very well, especially if it has been raining. Generally speaking, you can expect about 10m of underwater visibility, but don't be surprised if it gets as low as 3m. Fortunately, scuba diving along this stretch of the Caribbean is fairly cheap and a bad day of diving is always better than a good day of work.

Dive operators in Portobelo are located along Sabanitas–Portobelo road, about 2km west of town. If you're planning to dive, it's best to phone ahead or make a reservation via the internet.

Scubaportobelo DIVING
(☎261-3841; www.scubapanama.com) Outfitter Scubaportobelo offers all-inclusive scuba packages. It's located on the road into town, on the left.

Two Oceans Dive Center DIVING
(☎6678-8018, in Panama City 399-4781; www.2oceansdivers.com) A PADI dive center mostly active on weekends and during the high season, located at Coco Plum Lodge. Excursions are made from a comfortable catamaran.

Swimming

If you're looking for a day of fun in the sun, nearby Playa Blanca is a great day trip from Portobelo. Closer, you'll find the small cove beach La Huerta and Puerto Francés, which has a covered hammock hut and bathroom (arrange ahead of time for a key; local boat drivers know the caretakers).

Courses

Las Delicias de Sole COOKING COURSE
(☎6322-6215; per person US$50) Wonderful home cook Soledad prepares Afro-Caribbean cuisine like nobody's business. Join her at La Morada de la Bruja (opposite) to learn some local techniques while preparing a meal to enjoy on-site. The menu varies according to what's fresh and available, but might include specialties *such as fufu* (fish soup) or *tortillas changa* (grilled with maize and coconut).

Though the class is given in Spanish, guests can take home a recipe booklet in English. There's a three-person minimum.

Agrupaciones de Congo DANCE
(☎6693-5690; Calle Principal, Casa Artesanal; per person US$20; ⏲10am-2pm Fri-Sun) This established local group preserves the long-standing tradition of Congo dancing. Aristela Blandon gives tailored dance classes and provides a fascinating background on the slave history behind this unique tradition (in Spanish). Participants can also purchase a CD of original music. The base is a crafts store open only on weekends, but you can call to arrange classes.

Festivals & Events

On the last Sunday of each month there is an Afro Mass with a town fair displaying local food and traditional crafts. Holy Week is also an interesting time to be here.

Festival de Cristo Negro FESTIVAL
(Black Christ Festival) Every October 21, pilgrims from all over Panama arrive in Portobelo to partake in this festival, which honors a miracle-giving 1.5m-high statue of the Black Christ housed in the Iglesia de San Félipe (p219). After the sun sets, the statue is paraded down the streets, while pilgrims bedecked in purple robes and thorned crowns dance and drink until the wee hours.

Festival de Diablos y Congos FESTIVAL
(Devils and Congos Festival; ⏲Feb/Mar) The most intriguing local tradition is Festival de Diablos y Congos, a festival of rebellion and ridicule that mocks the colonial Spaniards. During the festivity, participants assume the role of escaped slaves and take 'captives.' It is held two weeks after Carnaval, sometimes coinciding with March 20, Portobelo's patron saint day. The tradition of Los Congos (named for its participants) dates from the slave-trading days when blacks escaped into the jungle and formed communities of exiles.

In satire, a prisoner is taken and a huge ransom demanded, though the prisoner is freed upon paying a token ransom. The Congos perform before audiences dressed in outlandish outfits that include tattered clothes, hats that resemble crowns and wooden swords.

Beware that a wild group may descend upon an innocent pedestrian and demand thousands of dollars. If you ever find yourself an innocent 'victim' of this tradition, try not to freak out – they'll settle for a few coins.

Sleeping

Particularly during festivals, local families may rent out spare rooms – ask at **ATP** (☎448-2200, 6485-7028; ⏲8am-4pm).

El Castillo HOSTEL $
(☎6738-1561; eponango@hotmail.com; dm/d with shared bathroom US$10/18) This worn seafront restaurant and hostel indeed resembles a castle – one drawn by Miyazaki. Still, its French-speaking Vietnamese host, Richard, is welcoming and it has that tumble-down charm. Rooms are basic, with mosquito

THE LEGEND OF THE BLACK CHRIST

Festival de Cristo Negro honors the statue of the same name, which has many miracles attributed to it. Normally housed in the Iglesia de San Félipe (p219), the Black Christ statue's exact origins are a matter of speculation. All definitive church records were lost in the fire that followed Henry Morgan's sacking of Panamá in 1671. However, there's no shortage of fanciful stories surrounding the origins of the statue.

One story has it that a ship bound for Cartagena, Colombia, tried to leave Portobelo five times, but on each occasion a storm blew the ship back to the town's edge, nearly sinking it. The crew lightened their vessel by tossing a heavy box overboard. On their sixth attempt to sail out, the weather calmed and they were able to go on their way. Several days later, local fishers found the discarded box floating off Portobelo and discovered the Black Christ inside.

A second story claims that the box was instead found floating at sea during a cholera epidemic. After being retrieved by local fishermen, the statue was placed inside the Iglesia de San Félipe. Almost immediately, as the story goes, the epidemic passed and the infected were cured.

nets and fans. The restaurant (mains US$12 to US$25) is open from 9am to 11pm and offers some appealing options for vegetarians, including Thai curry. It's 900m before Portobelo on the ocean side.

Sunset Cabins CABIN **$**

(☎448-2147; www.panamaportobelocabins.com; d/cabin US$48/68; P ❄) Nondivers are welcome at this seafront lodging run by Scubapanama. In a very reduced space, a bright structure has motel-style doubles with balconies, electric showers and air-con. The cabins offer pocket-sized charm – best for a couple or a family with small children. For all-inclusive scuba packages, see the website.

★La Morada de la Bruja Portobelo BOUTIQUE HOTEL **$$**

(☎6759-6987, 6528-0679; www.lamoradadelabrujaportobelo.com; r US$60-75, 4-person loft US$100, 2-bedroom house US$225; P ❄ 📶) This chill photographer's home has been adapted for guests but maintains a very personal touch. A small apartment and two ample waterfront houses sport modern, artful decor and a grassy seafront perfect for lounging. The bright, open interiors showcase photography and local Congo art. There are also kayaks for rent and boat services for excursions to remote beaches.

It is fine to cook here. You can pay extra for prepared meals or take a Caribbean cooking workshop (p220). They also arrange transport to Panama City.

Casa Congo INN **$$**

(☎6672-6620; www.fundacionbp.org.pa; d US$80-90; 📶) Part of a foundation that supports local arts and culture, this attractive waterfront inn features pleasant, bright rooms decorated with Congo art. They also offer workshops with artists. It's mostly doubles with one apartment that accommodates four (US$30 per extra person).

Casa Rayo Verde GUESTHOUSE **$$**

(☎202-0111; info.rayoverde@gmail.com; d/apt US$60/130; ❄ 📶) Run by the resort across the bay, this attractive four-room home is recommended by guests. The property faces the water, with quaint rooms boasting minifridges, private bathrooms and a shared terrace. Attention is lax – you're on your own here. The guesthouse helps fund culture and arts in the local community.

Coco Plum HOTEL **$$**

(☎448-2102; www.cocoplum-panama.com; s/d/tr US$55/65/75; P ❄) An attractive, motel-style lodging, the friendly Coco Plum has been around for years. On the waterfront, the feel of the place is ocean kitsch, replete with nets, shells and pastels, but the effect is cozy. The attached bar-restaurant (mains US$8 to US$16) is popular with travelers – check out the octopus in coconut milk or seafood stew.

It's on the road into town on the left. Two Oceans Dive Center (p220) is attached and there's a salon with games and TV. Can provide boat service.

★El Otro Lado RESORT **$$$**

(☎202-0111; www.elotrolado.com.pa; Bahia Portobelo; cabins incl breakfast US$590, houses US$730-980; ❄ 📶 🏊) 🍃 Awash in Caribbean style under a hush mountainside, this

PORTOBELO'S TOP FIVE ESCAPES

- Taking a water taxi to Puerto Francés (p220) for private swims and jungle hikes.
- Snorkeling (p219) around Spanish cannons encrusted in the coral landscape.
- Kayaking up the tranquil Río Claro.
- Watching a sunset from Fuerte San Fernando (opposite).
- Joining a Congo dance workshop (p220) and sweat to cool African rhythms.

luxury resort provides a laid-back, restful retreat – don't expect beach parties. Set across the bay from Portobelo, that short distance keeps the Congo drumming at bay. Set around an infinity pool, a handful of pastel cabins display exquisite, playful taste. Large, art-filled homes sit tucked in the rainforest.

The grounds are enormous and interesting – the resort borders some of the Spanish ruins and was once the site of an American community brought to work on the Panama Canal. The housing has since been torn down, but some remnants of that time, including a dammed jungle reservoir, are fascinating. The dining room is an elaborate gazebo with glass walls and high-style Caribbean cooking (meals US$52 to US$58). Boats can taxi guests to remote beaches and fishing spots. The resort supports Fundación Bahía Portobelo, a community nonprofit promoting local art and culture.

Eating

Portobelo has several bakeries and *fondas* (cheap eateries) clustered around the main road and plaza.

El Palenque PANAMANIAN **$$**
(☎202-0111; mains US$8-16; ⏲9am-9pm) Located at the Casa Congo (p221), the best feature of this restaurant is its location. There's ample open-air seating right on the beautiful bay of Portobelo. Whole fried fish, *patacones* (fried plantain) and coconut rice are prepared nicely, but the service is woefully slow.

Shopping

★Galería Casa Congo ARTS
(☎6672-6620; www.fundacionbp.org; Casa Congo; ⏲9am-5pm) A wonderful gallery with museum-quality pieces made by Panamanian photographers, crafts people and artists. Helpful displays explain the cultural background of the groups represented, including Afro-Caribbean and indigenous cultures. It's not all high end – you will also find reasonably priced jewelry and souvenirs.

Taller Portobelo ARTS
(☎6777-5022; ⏲9am-noon & 2-5pm) This artist-run studio is fascinating for art and culture buffs. Resident artist Gustavo can explain the historical and cultural significance of Congo art. There may also be works for sale. It's located behind La Morada de la Bruja (p221).

Information

Just off the main road through town, ATP (p220) has good information. Ask Mirsa Jimenez for information about dance classes, volunteering or working on community projects; only Spanish is spoken.

Portobelo consists of about 15 square blocks beside a paved, two-lane road that intersects with the Panama City–Colón road at the town of Sabanitas, 33km to the west. East of Portobelo, the road forks after 9km. The right branch of the road extends 14km further east to Nombre de Dios; the left branch extends 11km to the hamlet of La Guayra, where you can hire boats to Isla Grande.

Getting There & Away

Buses to Portobelo (US$1.60, 1½ hours, every 30 minutes) depart from Colón's Terminal de Buses from 6:30am to 6pm. Buses to Colón leave from a bus stop on the main road through town.

From Panama City you can avoid Colón. Take the Colón bus and get off at El Rey supermarket in Sabanitas, 10km before Colón. Next, catch the bus coming from Colón to Portobelo when it passes through Sabanitas (US$1.40, 1¼ hours). Since it's often full, take as little luggage as possible.

Getting Around

Taxis exist but can be scarce. Along the Sabanitas–Portobelo road you can flag down any bus headed in your direction. After dark, there is no public transportation.

Leaving from Fuerte Santiago, co-op **Santiago de La Gloria** (☎448-2266) water taxi charges a two-person minimum to Playa La Huerta (US$30), Playa Blanca (US$45) and the beach at Puerto Francés (US$35); all fees are round-trip. **Water Taxi Juan** (☎6008-6867) may offer better rates.

Parque Nacional Portobelo

Located in and around Portobelo, this 34,846-hectare park and Unesco World Heritage Site protects islands and coastal communities of coral reefs, mangroves and tropical forest. Ruined forts hail from colonial times when treasures of gold and silver from throughout the Americas were brought here in order to be transported to Europe in Spanish galleons. At one time, all the pirates of the Caribbean lusted after the treasures of Portobelo.

There is no information center, but you can stop by the tourism office (p220) in Portobelo for assistance.

Sights

There are plans to introduce fees for visiting the forts.

Mirador Perú VIEWPOINT

On a hill overlooking Santiago and much of the bay is a small but well-preserved watchtower called Mirador Perú, which was built at the same time as Fuerte Santiago. There are steps carved into the hillside to reach the lookout, and the views of the coastline from here are expansive.

Fuerte San Jerónimo FORT

Fuerte San Jerónimo, close to Portobelo center, was the largest fortress ever built to protect the bay. Eighteen cannon embrasures face the mouth of the bay, some exactly where the Spanish troops left them in 1821, the year Panama declared independence. Beyond the impressive gateway, there's the remains of the officers' quarters, barracks and a guardroom.

If you're short on time, San Jerónimo is the most complete of Portobelo's accessible forts and makes for the best visit.

Fuerte San Fernando FORT

In 1601 Fuerte San Félipe and Fuerte San Diego were built near the mouth of the bay, but were subsequently destroyed by Admiral Vernon in 1739. Fuerte San Fernando was later built over the ruins. American engineers later dismantled much of the fort later, using its walls to create the breakwater protecting the northern end of the Panama Canal.

Boats can be hired from the water's edge (US$5 per person round-trip) to bring you across the bay to the fort.

Fuerte Santiago FORT

Approaching from the west, Portobelo's first fort is Fuerte Santiago. Built after Vernon's attack, some walls were 3m thick, made entirely of cut coral. Known to the Spaniards as 'reef rock,' coral was a popular building material since it's easily shaped, tough as granite yet light as pumice. Ruins include officers' quarters, artillery sheds, a sentry box, barracks and watchtowers.

After mudslides, some coral walls had to be replaced with concrete reinforcements.

Puerto Lindo

Located a few kilometers before La Guayra, this snoozy village has a protected bay increasingly favored by sailboats voyaging to the San Blás or Cartagena, Colombia. Excursions to the nearby Isla Mamey visit a beautiful beach and surrounding mangroves. If you are deciding between Mamey and Isla Grande, this may be a better choice, particularly on crowded high-season weekends.

Sleeping & Eating

Visitors can eat at a basic cafe or cook at their lodgings.

Hostel Wunderbar HOSTEL $

(☎6700-7790, 448-2426; www.hostelwunderbar.com; d US$35-55, house US$150; ❄) Run by a German-Austrian couple who traded their sailboat for a hostel, this breezy retreat has a relaxed setting. Mosaic tiles adorn the shady outdoor kitchen and rooms have attractive, colorful decor. The more expensive rooms have air-conditioning. There are also bike rentals, sailing and canoe trips to the mangroves. Wi-fi is available at a cafe next door.

Hostel Puerto Lindo HOSTEL $

(☎6221-8061; http://hostelpuertolindo.blogspot.cl; dm/d/q US$10/26/56; ❄) With a waterfront location, this Panamanian-run hostel offers affordable rates and a good vibe. Doubles have air-con. Outings can be made to nearby islands for snorkeling or paddling

SURFING IN COLÓN PROVINCE

One of Panama's least surfed provinces will make you a believer with its great unknown breaks.

Playa Maria Chiquita In front of Maria Chiquita. Beach break with lefts and rights, but limited to big swell.

Isla Grande In front of La Guayra, it's best reached by water taxi. Reef bottom break with three peaks, rights and lefts.

Isla Mamei Next to Isla Grande, it's reached by boat or paddling from Isla Grande. Left-hand point break over shallow reef.

Playa Palenque/Cuango In front of Cuango village. Beach break with rights and lefts. Surfers are seldom seen here.

Playa Grande Mainland East of Isla Grande. Beach break with some reef. Waves break left and right.

Turtles Paddling distance from Playa Grande. Waves are great; unreal tubes if it is glassy with a big swell.

V-Land Near Devils Beach in Sherman. Unbelievable right-point reef break with great tubes when there's big swell and it's glassy.

by kayak. The hostel can also recommend sailboats to Colombia.

Getting There & Away

Buses headed to La Guayra from Colón stop in Puerto Lindo (US$3, 1¾ hrs).

Isla Grande

POP 1000

Palm trees and white-sand beaches form the backdrop to this lovely little island, just 15km from Portobelo. A popular getaway for Panama City folk fleeing the urban grind, Isla Grande is an ideal setting for snorkeling, scuba diving or simply soaking up the island's relaxed vibe. There are no roads, just a path along the eastern island perimeter. A few hundred people of African descent live on Grande, most of whom eke out a living from fishing and coconuts – you'll get a taste of both when you sample the fine island cuisine.

Owing to its location on Panama's northern Caribbean coast, Isla Grande gets a lot of rain year-round. Terms like 'rainy' and 'dry' seasons don't apply here, though torrential showers are usually intense and short-lived.

Activities

This 5km-long, 1.5km-wide island has two trails, one that loops the shoreline and another slippery cross-island trail. The lovely beaches on the northern side of the island can be reached by boat or on foot.

Some fine snorkeling and dive sites are within a 10-minute boat ride of the island. For diving, contact a Portobelo-based operator (p219). Diving is limited to between April and December, when seas are calmer.

Boat taxis can also take you further afield to explore the mangroves east of Isla Grande or snorkeling off the coast of the nearby islets.

Festivals & Events

Isla Grande Carnaval FESTIVAL

(Feb-Mar) Isla Grande celebrates Carnaval in rare form: women wear traditional *polleras* (festive dresses), while men wear ragged pants tied at the waist with old sea rope, and everyone dances to African-influenced Conga drums and song. There are also satirical songs about current events and a lot of joking in the Caribbean calypso tradition.

Festival de San Juan Bautista FESTIVAL

(June 24) Isla Grande celebrates the Festival of San Juan Bautista with swimming and canoe races.

La Virgen del Carmen FESTIVAL

(July 16) The Virgen del Carmen is honored with a land and sea procession, baptisms and masses.

Sleeping

Macondo Hostel HOSTEL $

(☎6102-6262; dm/d US$15/35;) Follow the signposted path a block inland to this agreeable, breezy two-story hostel set under the rainforest canopy. Bunks occupy dark and ample rooms with fans. It's good value for budget travelers, with shady, pleasant shared spaces and hammocks. And if you want to party during the day, you'll probably find company.

There's no website but they do have a Facebook page.

Sister Moon CABAÑAS $$

(☎6948-1990; www.hotelsistermoon.com; d/tr/q with fan US$77/116/153, d with air-con US$140, day pass US$20;) Your best bet for island lodging is this lovely clutch of hillside cabins surrounded by swaying palms and crashing waves. With no beach, guests sunbathe on attractive waterfront decks, though the surf can be rough. Perks include private balconies with porch hammocks. Showers are tiny. They also rent attractive houses at Brother Sun next door.

Day passes are US$20. It's at the far end of the island.

Hotel Isla Grande CABAÑAS $$

(☎225-2798, in Colon 448-2019; 4-person cabin US$110, d with/without view US$198/165, day pass US$10) On the closest point to the mainland, this hotel boasts the only decent beach within reach of services. This explains its popularity, as rooms – while decent and clean – are wildly overpriced. Without a website or email, phone reservations are necessary. Cabins lack kitchens but there's an on-site restaurant that's open from 8am to 5pm on weekdays and to 7pm on weekends.

Eating

Many visitors bring a picnic lunch, though there is a handful of expensive seaside restaurants.

Hotel Congo Restaurante SEAFOOD $$

(☎6296-8624; mains US$15) Set at the end of a pier, this shady, open-air restaurant and bar serves some great fare. Spanish-run, a welcome Mediterranean influence employs olive oil and caramelized onions in fragrant seafood dishes. Meanwhile, the on-site budget hotel is undergoing some serious renovations, though some rooms are open to the public. Located mid-island.

El Nido del Postre CARIBBEAN $$$

(☎448-2061; mains US$12-25; 8am-5pm Mon-Fri, to 8pm Sat & Sun) Located next to Hotel Isla Grande, this tiny thatched restaurant serves some of the best food on the island, though portions are a little too modest. Try the local shrimp sauteed in garlic and served with coconut rice. There's also fresh fish and cocktails, in addition to a breakfast menu.

Sister Moon Restaurant RESTAURANT $$$

(www.hotelsistermoon.com; mains US$15-25) Sister Moon hotel's bar-restaurant is built right over the water. The menu features the island's famous coconut-infused seafood alongside high-end cocktails.

Getting There & Away

Isla Grande is a 10-minute boat ride from La Guayra, a tiny coastal hamlet that is connected to Colón via frequent bus connections. Boats arrive at Isla Grande dock in front of Hotel Isla Grande.

Buses to La Guayra leave from the Colón bus terminal (US$3, 1½ hours). From Panama City, take a Colón-bound bus to Sabanitas and change buses next to El Rey supermarket for La Guayra. Buses return from La Guayra at 8am, 9am and 1pm. Panama City tour operators bring day-trippers from Panama City.

In La Guayra, boats at the dock go to the island (or beyond). Each leaves when full. The 10-minute boat ride costs US$3 to US$5 per person; secure parking costs US$5 per day.

Comarca de Guna Yala

POP 31,600 / AREA 2360 SQ KM / ELEV SEA LEVEL TO 748M

Includes ➡

Best Off-the-Beaten-Path Spots

- Cayos Holandeses (p237)
- East Lemon & Chichime Cays (p235)
- Cayos Los Grullos (p237)

Best Places to Sleep

- Dolphin Lodge (p238)
- De Mar Achu (p234)
- Camping Salardup (p235)
- Akwadup Lodge (p239)
- Yandup Lodge (p238)

Why Go?

Imagine a turquoise tropical archipelago with one island for every day of the year. With white sand and waving palms, these Caribbean islands cheat no one's version of paradise. The Comarca is home to the Guna, the first group in Latin America to gain indigenous autonomy. Though they have had contact with Europeans since Columbus sailed these waters in 1502, clan identity is paramount, and many make tenacious efforts to preserve a traditional way of life.

In 2009 the road to Cartí was completed, making the region more accessible than ever and opening up options for day trips. Still off the beaten track, this narrow, 226km-long strip on the Caribbean coast stretches from the Golfo de San Blás to the Colombian border.

Community islands are acre-sized cays packed with bamboo huts, livestock and people. Visitors often prefer the more remote outer islands with fewer inhabitants. Most areas require landing fees.

When to Go

- **Dec–Apr** During trade-wind season there's little rain. It can get hot in the thatched huts, but conditions are ideal for sailing, with winds from the north and northeast.
- **Oct** Isla Tigre celebrates traditional dance at the Nogagope, which brings communities together for a week of dancing as well as canoe races and an art fair.
- **May–Aug** There's good visibility for snorkeling, though rainstorms are around and so are annoying *chitras* (sand flies). Thunderstorms mean it's not a preferable time to sail.

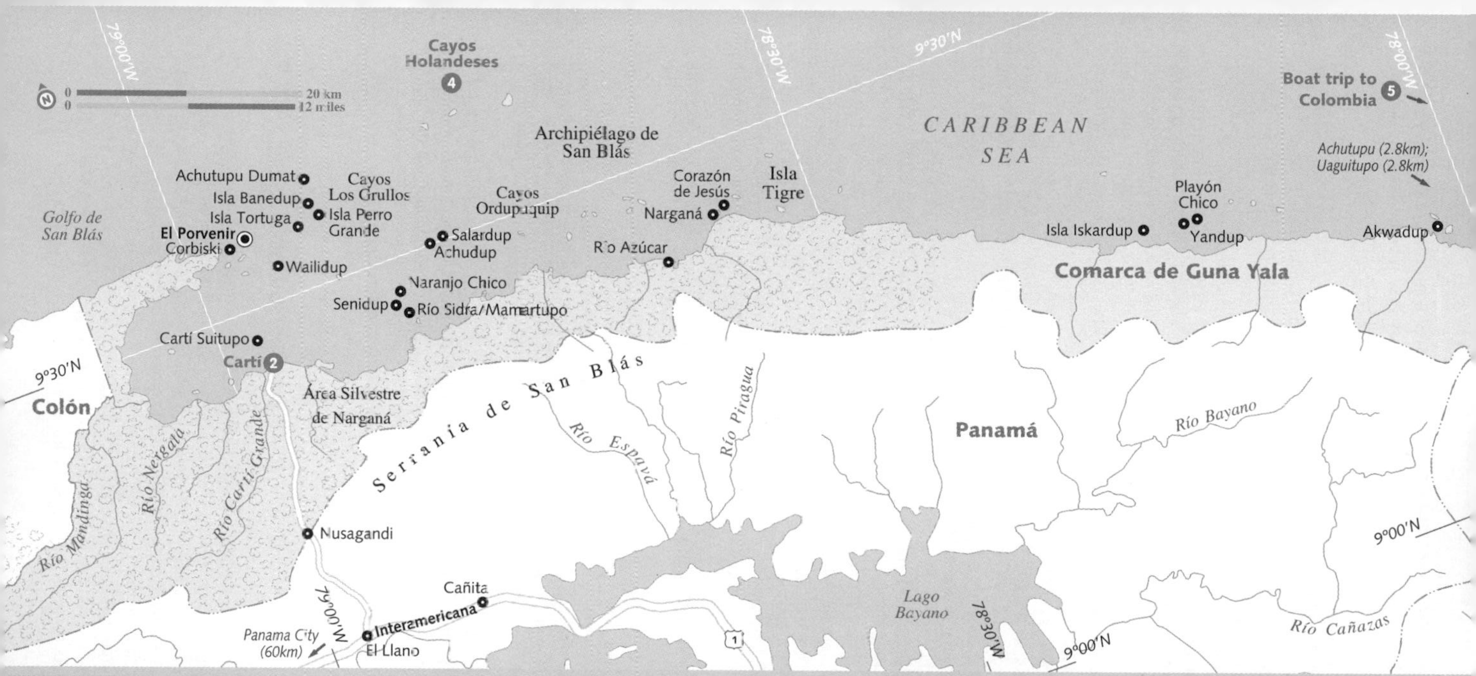

Comarca de Guna Yala Highlights

1 Guna (p228) Interacting with the Guna, a fiercely independent people who maintain their traditions in a changing world.

2 Sailing (p234) Cruising white-sand cays, swimming in clear waters and soaking up sunrise on a sailboat – most trips depart from **Cartí**.

3 Molas (p231) Shopping the community islands for *molas*, traditional Guna textiles that have become the national handicraft of Panama.

4 Cayos Holandeses (p237) Snorkeling aquamarine waters through reefs and wrecks in the magical Cayos Holandeses.

5 Colombia (p234) Camping on sandy beaches and living the adventure of a three-day **motorboat trip to Colombia**.

The Guna

History

Although the Guna have lived in eastern Panama for at least two centuries, scholars fiercely debate their origins. Language similarities with people who once lived several hundred kilometers to the west would indicate that the Guna migrated eastward. However, oral tradition has it that the Guna migrated to San Blás from Colombia after the 16th century, following a series of devastating encounters with other tribes armed with poison-dart blowguns.

Regardless of the Guna's origins, scholars agree that life on the islands is relatively new for them. Historians at the end of the 18th century wrote that the only people who used the San Blás islands at that time were pirates, Spaniards and the odd explorer. However, the Guna flourished on the archipelago due to the abundance of seafood. They supplemented this with food crops, including rice, yams, yucca, bananas and pineapples, grown on the nearby mainland.

Today, there are an estimated 50,000 Guna; almost 32,000 live on the district's islands, 8000 live on tribal land along the coast and many live outside the district. So communal are the island-dwelling Guna that they inhabit only 49 of the nearly 400 keys; the rest are mostly left to coconut trees, sea turtles and iguanas.

Culture

The traditional Guna belief structure is based on three principal concepts: God, nature and the cosmos.

According to the Guna religion, the world was created by God, Paba Tummat, and the Great Mother, Nan Tummat, who continue to keep watch over everyone's daily actions. Although Guna shamans often look into the future and make minor divinations, everything in life is believed to be preordained by God and the Great Mother. In fact, the Guna make great efforts in their daily lives to ensure that their actions follow the will of Paba and Nan Tummat, even though they do not know their fate.

The Guna identify strongly with nature, and their rich oral traditions are full of songs, hymns and prayers that recount the beauty and majesty of the wind, the land and the sea. To the Guna, people and nature are considered parts of the same entity and thus the rules of nature follow human life from birth to death. The Guna love and admire nature, and they believe that true happiness is only experienced within its presence.

Guna cosmology is based on the doctrine that the knowledge of a concept allows the

RESPONSIBLE TRAVEL IN GUNA YALA

When visiting the Comarca de Guna Yala, consider how your visit may affect the community. Tourism revenue can play a vital role in the development of the region, particularly if you are buying locally produced crafts or contracting the services of a Guna guide. However, Western interests have already caused irreversible damage to the region. Be aware of your surroundings and remain sensitive about your impact.

One look at the paradisiacal setting, the rainbow flag and the distinctive Guna dress and you might feel transported into the pages of *National Geographic*. Don't snap that shutter just yet, though. If the Guna appear unfriendly, consider their predicament. When cruise ships visit, the number of people on an already congested island can triple. Then, nearly two-thirds of the populace (the tourists) turn paparazzi on the other third (the Guna). It's an unsavory scene repeated again and again. To rein in the situation, the Guna charge fees for photographs taken of them as well as visitation fees for each island. If you can't afford the photo fee, tuck away your camera and strike up a conversation instead.

Remain mindful of the way you dress. Guna men never go shirtless and Guna women dress conservatively, with their cleavage, their belly and most of their legs covered. Arriving in Guna villages in a bikini or shirtless is interpreted as a sign of disrespect.

Trash is a problem on the islands, and there is no effective plan for its management. For the Guna, the cost of removal to the mainland is too high, and there is no designated site or 'culture' of waste management, since all refuse was relatively innocuous until outside influence prevailed. You may see litter and burning piles of plastics. With no current solution to the issue, do what you can to pack out your own garbage, if necessary, and try to consume fresh products with minimal packaging – ie choose coconut water over cola.

knower to manipulate the power of the concept. As a result, Guna myths and legends have both a literal and a symbolic meaning. For example, the story of the Ibeorkun, who descended to Earth to teach the Guna how to have chiefs, is often associated with most of the moral and ethical teachings of the Guna.

Lifestyle

Not surprisingly, the cornerstone of the Guna political organization is the Ibeorkun (community gathering house). Here, men gather nightly for heated discussions about local events, to make decisions about important problems and to listen to the advice of chiefs. Generally, each island has at least three chiefs and their authority is officially recognized by the Panamanian government. Every year, there are two general assemblies for the representatives from all of the islands in the Comarca at which major issues affecting the Guna are discussed.

Historically the Guna were matrilocal, meaning that when a man marries, he moves into the household of his wife's parents and comes under the control of his father-in-law. Today, this pattern is yielding to neolocality, in that newlyweds will establish a residence away from both parents. As recently as a generation ago, Guna households had an average size of seven to 12 people, but today households often comprise as few as five people.

The distinctive dress of the Guna is immediately recognizable no matter where you are in Panama. Most Guna women continue to dress as their ancestors did. Older women may be adorned with a black line painted from the forehead to the tip of the nose, with a gold ring worn through the septum. Colorful fabric is wrapped around the waist as a skirt, topped by a short-sleeved blouse covered in brilliantly colored *molas*. The women wrap their legs, from ankle to knee, in long strands of tiny beads, forming colorful geometric patterns. A printed headscarf and many necklaces, rings and bracelets complete the wardrobe. In sharp contrast to the elaborate women's wear, Guna men have adopted Western dress, such as shorts and sleeveless shirts.

In recent years, Guna culture has come under growing threat of Westernization, particularly as young Guna are drawn to Panama City in search of employment and increased opportunities. However, Guna culture has survived countless generations of foreign encroachment, and communities are just as committed to preserving their identity today as they were when the Spanish first arrived.

Economy

Until the late 1990s, the district's principal currency was the coconut. (In recent years, the sale of *molas* replaced the sale of coconuts as the Guna's number-one revenue source.) The Guna are coconut barons: a good year's harvest reaches more than 30 million. Coconuts are bartered to Colombians, whose old wooden schooners can hold 50,000 to 80,000 coconuts. In return, the Colombians provide clothing, jars of coffee, vinegar, rice, sunglasses, canned milk, batteries, soups and other goods.

In Colombia the coconuts are exported or used in the production of candy, gelatin capsules, cookies, shampoos and other products. Colombia has many processing plants for coconuts, but Panama, oddly, has none.

Shrewd businesspeople, the Guna regulate the price of coconuts on a yearly basis to prevent buyers from bargaining down individual sellers. Every year, Guna chiefs agree on one price for coconuts. A Guna found selling coconuts below or above price is severely punished by the community. By stabilizing the sale of coconuts and enforcing trade restrictions, the chiefs prevent price wars among the Guna.

In another protectionist move, Guna law prohibits outsiders from owning property in the district. A conscious move to ensure limitations on tourism in the region, the law also prevents foreigners from speculating in real estate and driving up living costs. Today, lodgings are 100% owned and managed by local Guna families and are fairly uniform in offerings and quality.

Sleeping & Eating

Carefully selecting your accommodations on the islands is key, since their remoteness makes it difficult to change your mind. Camping on an uninhabited island isn't wise, because you run the risk of encountering drug traffickers in the night. The Guna do not allow the Panamanian coast guard or US antidrug vessels to operate in the archipelago, so the uninhabited islands are occasionally used by Colombian traffickers running cocaine up the coast.

There is only a handful of lodgings on the islands and none on the mainland. Most of these are basic but comfortable. Most densely populated islands in the district have a store selling basic items, as well as pay phones for

GUNA LIVING 101

Lodging considerations in the Comarca are vastly different from those on the mainland. Here, a spot in a thatched hut with a sand floor can cost anywhere between US$50 and US$150 per night. So what's the difference?

Often it has more to do with access, ambience and organization than anything else. Densely populated community islands are more likely to have budget options, but they will not live up to your image of a remote tropical paradise. Resort islands generally have a bigger price tag, but they may not offer many opportunities to interact with locals. When planning, consider why you're going and the following:

- **Space** Does the island have shade? Privacy? Are there pleasant areas to swim or do you have to take a boat to reach swimming and snorkeling sites?
- **Access** Is the island too remote, requiring expensive transfers to do anything?
- **Hospitality** Ask other travelers about their experience.
- **Water** Is it potable? Consider bringing a filter.
- **Bathrooms** Are there modern installations or does the toilet sit at the end of a dock?
- **Safety** Do excursion boats have life vests and good motors?

Lodgings generally include three meals (but not drinks), one outing per day (snorkeling or a community visit, for example) and transportation to or from the airport or Cartí, but do confirm ahead. Fees for drinking water and visits to Guna islands may be separate. It is always wise to bring snacks, insect repellent, a first-aid kit and a flashlight. Rates are generally lower from April to November.

When booking, remember that internet access is not prevalent and any cell-phone number is only good until that phone accidentally falls into the ocean. But approach your hosts with good humor and patience, and they will probably reciprocate in spades.

domestic and international calls. The phones are public, but there's usually a Guna standing nearby charging a telephone tax of US$1 per call or more. Cell phones work in some areas.

Since there are almost no restaurants, each lodging provides meals for guests. They are usually seafood based, with lobster available at an extra cost. Quality varies, as some of the fishing stocks have been depleted, but there is always rice and a healthy supply of fresh coconuts. Always ask before taking a coconut – they are among the region's main sources of income.

Activities

Most lodgings offer complete packages, where a fixed price gets you a room, three meals a day and boat rides to neighboring islands for swimming, snorkeling and lounging on the beach. If you seek community life, you can also arrange visits to more populated islands. Before swimming off the shores of a heavily populated island, consider that all waste goes here, unfiltered in most cases.

Snorkeling is good in places, but many coral reefs are badly damaged. You can often rent snorkeling equipment from your hotel; serious snorkelers should bring their own gear. Jaunts to hike the mainland jungles are arranged with a guide. Most travelers are content with soaking up the Caribbean sun.

Pantalasa SAILING
(www.pantalasa.com) Charter sailing trips with an experienced and warm Spanish couple offering personalized attention.

Blue Sky Sailing SAILING
(☎6009-9042; www.sailingbluesky.com) Charter sailing trips with a friendly and experienced American couple. Includes kayaks, fishing gear and snorkel gear.

San Blas Sailing SAILING
(☎314-1288; www.sanblassailing.com) A small agency exclusively focused on San Blás charters (not Colombia trips), working with a handful of responsible sailboats and multilingual captains. Sustainable practices include using filtered, not bottled, water, employing Guna services and purchasing most provisions from the local community.

Tours

Panama Travel Unlimited TOUR
(Map p46; ☎6676-5583, 6993-9919; http://panamatravelunlimited.com; Calle Primera, Perejil

Casa 7-62, Panama City; ⌚9am-6pm Mon-Sat) Specializing in travel to Guna Yala, this small English-speaking Panama City agency focuses on services for backpackers, including transportation, day tours, overnight packages and boats to Colombia. It's a good resource for comparing products. It also coordinates community volunteering through a nonprofit. Located in Mamallena hostel in Panama City.

Cacique Cruiser BOAT TOUR
(Map p54; ☎6111-4241; www.caciquecruiser.com; Luna's Castle; day trips US$150) A licensed tour agency specializing in backpacker trips to San Blàs, from day trips to three-day packages. Also coordinates boat trips to Colombia and can help travelers compare services on different boats. The agency is involved in community recycling efforts on the islands.

Kuna Yala Expeditions BOAT TOUR
(☎6708-5254; eliasperezmartinez@yahoo.com) Local entrepreneur Elías Perez speaks English and offers day tours in covered *pangas* (small motorboats) with fast, two-stroke motors. Excursions include kayaking mangroves, a visit to the mainland cemetery and a hike, and snorkeling Cayos Holandeses. Though service is good, the boating can be a bit fast. Bottled water is included. The outfit also offers camping on more remote islands, with tent and boat transfer included.

Germain Perez TOUR
(☎6734-3454; www.cartihomestaykunayala.blogspot.com) Offering tours and activities, as well as transfers from Panama City to Cartí (per person US$25).

Festivals & Events

Nogagope CULTURAL
(⌚Oct 10-16) The Nogagope celebrates a traditional dance and takes place on Isla Tigre. The event is marked by communities from outlying islands converging on the island and dancing for three days straight. The event is followed by a huge four-day festival that includes more dancing as well as art expositions and various games and canoe races.

Guna Revolution of 1925 CULTURAL
(⌚Feb 25) One of the biggest holidays in Guna Yala is the commemoration of the anniversary of the Guna Revolution of 1925. It marks the day when the Guna rebelled against the Panamanian police occupying the islands, and expelled them from the Comarca. On Isla Tigre this event is remembered through an emotional reenactment of the rebellion.

Shopping

Molas are the most famous of Panamanian traditional handicrafts. Made of brightly colored squares of cotton fabric sewn together, the finished product reveals landscape scenes, birds, sea turtles, fish and beasts – often surrounded by a mazelike geometric pattern. Traditional geometric designs are usually valued more than modern ones. Craftsmanship varies considerably. The simplest are sold for upwards of $10; elaborate designs are works of art valued at several hundred dollars. You can find *molas* on the islands (or, rather, the *mola* sellers will find you).

Mola work originated from the transfer of body-painting designs to cloth, particularly blouses. When the Panamanian government tried to modernize the Guna by prohibiting traditional dress, the *mola* emerged as a symbol of independence. Even when Guna schools were administered by Panamanian officials, girls wore special *molas* in school colors as a silent protest.

Today there is a wonderful sense of pride among Guna women regarding *molas*. In addition to being an integral part of the Guna culture, *molas* are unique to the Comarca.

Molas are classified by differences in the technical process:

➡ **Abiniguat** One color; refers to a single layer of color sewn onto a base layer.

➡ **Obagalet** Two colors; refers to two layers sewn onto a base layer.

➡ **Mor-Maralet** A few colors; refers to two or more layers sewn onto a base layer.

➡ **Morgonikat** Many colors; refers to two or more layers sewn onto a base layer with additional filler layers, embroidery and/or appliqué.

Information

Flights are limited, so book as far in advance as possible. You should also reserve your hotels in advance, especially since package deals are the norm in the Comarca. There's no cash machine, so visit an ATM *before* reaching the islands.

From May through November temperatures are generally lower. When there's no breeze and the mercury rises, humidity sets in and life on the San Blás islands can cease to be paradisical. During January and February the trade winds arrive.

In the Comarca it helps to have a good command of Spanish as few Guna outside the tourist centers speak English. In fact, many older Guna do not speak Spanish. In more remote areas your guide or boat operator may have to do the talking

A GUIDE TO THE GUNA LANGUAGE

Feeling a little tongue-tied? The following glossary will help you break the ice with the Guna. Note: the second entry in all listings is Spanish, and the third is Guna.

Getting Started

Yes.	Sí.	Elle.
No.	No.	Suli.
Thanks.	Gracias.	Dot nuet.
Please.	Por favor.	Uis anga saet.
OK.	Esta bien.	Nued gudii o.
Good.	Bueno.	Nabir, nuedi.
Welcome.	Bienvenidos.	Nuegambi uese be noniki.

Greetings

Hello.	Hola.	Na.
How are you?	¿Como esta usted?	Bede nued guddi?
Fine, thank you. And you?	Bien, gracias. ¿Y usted?	An nuedi. Bedina?
Fine.	Bien.	Nuedi.
What is your name?	¿Cual es su nombre?	Igi be nuga?
My name is...	Mi nombre es...	An nuga...
Nice to meet you.	Encantado.	An yeel itoe.
Where are you from?	¿De dónde es usted?	Be bia lidi?
I am from...	Soy de...	An... ginedi.

Feelings

I'm hungry.	Tengo hambre.	An ukur itoe.
I'm thirsty.	Tengo sed.	An gobie.
I'm cold.	Tengo frío.	An dambe itoe.
I'm warm.	Tengo calor.	An uerba itoe.
I'm sleepy.	Estoy cansado.	An nue gapie.

for you. A few words of Guna will win you friends and favors wherever you go.

The Guna are very particular about what foreigners do on their islands. As a result, tourists must register and pay a visitation fee, between US$3 and US$12 per person, on nearly every island. You're expected to pay regardless of whether you stay for a week or only half an hour. On smaller, privately owned islands, you must seek out the owner, obtain permission to stay and pay a fee of around US$7 per person.

Visitors are expected to pay to take photographs of the Guna people (around US$1 per subject or photo). If you want to take someone's photo, ask his or her permission first. You may not be required to pay for a photograph taken of an artisan from whom you buy crafts, but it depends on the person. Some islands may charge you US$50 just for possessing a video camera.

You must carry your passport to enter the region.

Getting There & Away

Previously, the only way to visit the Comarca de Guna Yala was by plane or private sailboat. In 2009 a 4WD road linking the Cartí coast to the Interamericana was finished. Hired 4WDs now make the trip. Visitors must show their passports and pay an entry fee (US$20) on entering the Comarca.

From Cartí, boat transportation can be arranged from the docks (US$2 usage fee) to the islands. Those staying on one of the far-flung islands have the option of flying into one of several remote landing strips scattered throughout the Comarca.

AIR

Air Panama (☎316-9000; www.airpanama.com) has daily flights to Playón Chico, Ogobsucum and Achutupu. Flights depart from Albrook airport in Panama City and take 30 minutes to an hour. Ticket prices vary according to season and availability. Book as far in advance

I'm happy.	Estoy contento.	An yee ito dii.

Useful Expressions

Let's go.	Vamos.	Anmar nae.
How much does this cost?	¿Cuánto cuesta?	Qui mani?
I want to buy it.	Quiero comprarlo.	An bag-bie.
Do you speak English?	¿Habla inglés?	Be sumake merki galla?
Come here.	Venga aquí.	Uesik dage.
Look at that.	Miralo.	Dake.
Speak slowly, please.	Hable despacio por favor.	Uis binna sunmake.
I don't understand.	No entiendo.	Aku ittoe.
I'm sorry.	Lo siento.	An oakue.
Foreigner	Extranjero	Uaga

Food & Drink

Rice	Arroz	Oros
Bread	Pan	Madu
Fish	Pescado	Ua
Lobster	Langosta	Dulup
Coconut	Coco	Koibir
Coffee	Café	Cabi

Saying Goodbye

Goodbye.	Adiós.	Degi malo.
Good luck.	Buena suerte.	Nuedgine, nuegan bi.
I'll see you tomorrow.	Hasta manãna.	An banedse be dakoe.
I had a good time.	Me divertí.	An yer ittosa.

as possible, as demand far exceeds supply. Note that planes may stop at several islands in the archipelago, loading and unloading passengers or cargo before continuing on.

CAR

The El Llano–Cartí road is the only road that leads into the district. It connects the town of El Llano, on the Interamericana 70km east of Panama City, to the San Blás coastal hamlet of Cartí. The road begins near El Llano at the turnoff for Nusagandi.

It's best to take a shared 4WD with a powerful engine, a winch and good tires. Ask your Panama City hostel to arrange transportation. **Tito** (☎ 6151-8827), Kuna Yala Expeditions (p231) and driver Germain Perez (p231) also provide transfers.

BOAT

Sailboats travel to Colombia via the archipelago, but most board in Colón Province. Lodgings in Panama City have more information about these privately run trips.

More a tour than just transport, the popular new **San Blas Adventures** (www.sanblas adventures.com; per person all-inclusive US$375) four-day service takes backpackers between Cartí and La Miel (the Colombian border), visiting Guna communities, camping on beaches and snorkeling along the way. Fiberglass boats have outboard engines. It's a good alternative to the sailboat crossing, avoiding cramped overnight quarters and rough seas. See the website for useful planning details.

ℹ Getting Around

Few islands in the archipelago are more than 10km from the district's mainland. All of the heavily inhabited islands are very close to the coast to permit access to agricultural areas and vital natural resources, such as water, firewood and construction materials. Also on the mainland are the giant trees from which the Guna make their chief mode of transportation – the *cayuco* (a dugout canoe made from a burned and hollowed-out trunk). There are nine towns on the mainland, all within 100m of the sea, though there are no restaurants or hotels in these towns.

BOAT

Boats await the arrival of planes to shuttle people to their island destination (US$2 to US$80). If you want to travel by boat between island groups or explore some of the far-flung islets, you can either hire local guides at the docks or have your hotel make the arrangements. Inquire about your ride in advance if you don't like small craft (some go quite slowly).

It is becoming more common to see pleasure yachts and sailboats in the region, though it is not without controversy. Some perceive these 'floating hotels' as competition, but individual Gunas who live in remote areas are often supportive, since the boats support locals by buying their produce and *molas* (embroidered designs). At present, the Guna Congress is in the process of regulating commercial sailing trips, but it has become more open to them than it was in the past.

Sailboats charge between US$150 and US$350 per person per day, including meals and some drinks, and they usually provide snorkeling gear. Costs like Guna island-visitation fees and boat transfers are not included.

Cartí & Around

Cartí

POP 400

Cartí is the collective name for a group of islands and a small strip of coast near the road. If you've arrived in the Comarca by 4WD, the coastal hamlet of Cartí will be your first port of call. The nearby islands are minutes away by boat.

Most places here are all in Cartí Suitupo or 'Crab Island,' a mere 100m from the mainland and one of the most densely populated islands in the Comarca: crowded as Manhattan at rush hour and terribly polluted. Be warned that if there's a cruise ship docked here, your cultural experience will take on a whole new definition.

The small **museum** (☎6085-9592; admission US$3; ⏲8am-4pm) offers a better cultural and historical understanding of the Guna. For general tours, contact English-speaking Guna guide **Hernan Martinez** (☎6517-7417).

Cartí Suitupo also serves as a base for exploring nearby Isla Aguja (Needle Island),

SAILING THE GUNA YALA TO COLOMBIA

If you're a backpacker or don't mind living like one in the name of adventure, consider this. Small sailboats can take passengers to Colombia via the scenic Archipiélago de San Blás for the same price as a flight. But the trip may not be for everyone.

Potential guests should know that these boats are not official charters: passengers help out in exchange for cheap passage. But in exchange you usually get a few days of sun and sand in the San Blás, often with a snorkeling trip or two. The rough open-sea passage to Cartagena accounts for half the duration of the trip. Before you book, find out the following:

- Are accommodations a cabin or floor space?
- What is the size of the boat and the number of passengers?
- Is the boat equipped with adequate lifeboats and life vests for all passengers?
- Does it have adequate safety equipment and a functioning radio?
- Does the captain have a charter license?
- What are the meals like? (Some boats serve beans and rice three times a day.)

We have heard happy reports, but travelers have also complained about boats skimping on meals, overcrowding passengers or traveling despite bad weather in order to fit in more trips. Bring snacks and ask ahead whether the boat needs fresh groceries (hard to stock when boats spend extended periods in the islands). Do your research and check a boat or captain's references with hostels and other travelers before committing. If you are only traveling for the novelty of sailing, consider a trip that sticks to the Guna Yala.

The best place to inquire about scheduled departures is at any of the youth hostels in Panama City. A typical five-day backpacker sailing trip, including food and activities (but not island fees), costs around US$550. Another alternative is the motorboat trip offered by San Blas Adventures (p233), which stops to camp on beaches.

a picture-perfect retreat with lazy palms, golden sands and gentle surf.

Catering to backpackers, **Cartí Homestay** (☎6734-3454, 6517-9850; www.cartihomestaykunayala.blogspot.com; Carti Suitupo; r per person incl 3 meals & tour US$50; @) is the best place to meet young Gunas and strike up a conversation, though the inflatable Jägermeister bottle in the corner is a good indicator of the kind of cultural interactions you might expect. The English-speaking hosts also offer cabin lodgings on a more remote island and coordinate speedboats to Puerto Obaldia for Colombia-bound travelers. Internet, via stick modem, is US$1 per hour.

Getting There & Away

With the only road access, Cartí is the gateway to the archipelago. Most visitors come here by 4WD contracted via their lodgings. You can also call Tito (p233) for reliable shuttle service from Panama City.

At the pier or on the river, motorboats transfer visitors to islands near and far. Most trips are included with lodgings. Visitors must pay a port fee (US$2).

Corbiski

Corbiski (aka Pelican Island) is a populated community island with plenty of opportunities to interact with locals. While it's a convenient launching point, Corbiski is crowded and does not have great swimming or snorkeling off the island itself.

The new sky-blue cabins at **Bungalows Corbiski** (☎6708-5254; eliasperezmartinez@yahoo.com; per person incl tour, meals & transfer US$85), each with its own bathroom, sit right over the water. Snorkeling tours are included in the price. The owner, Elías Perez, provides boat services so you can get around the islands easily.

East Lemon & Chichime Cays

A lovely island chain popular with yachts (there's a mooring close to a good scuba site), the cays are likely to draw visitors who are traveling by sailboat.

Isla Banedup

Sailboats moor alongside this tiny private isle, where you can stop by for seafood meals (US$10 to US$15).

DON'T MISS

MOLAS TO GO

Visitors to the East Lemon Cays may be approached by a motorized dugout canoe carrying traveling master *mola* maker **Venancio Restrepo** (☎6061-7415, 6500-7302). He carries buckets of beautiful *molas* (US$20 to US$80) made by himself or others.

You can also stay on this family-run island in one of its thatched **huts** (☎6119-4743; cabins per person incl meals US$50) reinforced with tarps. For information contact manager Mayron Morris. Tours are extra but could include snorkeling at Isla Perra and Isla Pelicano.

Located near Isla Banedup is **Isla Perro Grande** (☎6137-1441; per person US$7), a tiny island with zero infrastructure offering wild camping for adventurous souls with their own gear. To preserve the site, guests must pack out all trash and practice leave no trace ethics. Host Daniel can provide simple meals of fish and rice (US$10) and transfers to Cartí (US$35 to US$40 per person for a group of 10).

Achutupu Dumat

Most refer to this area as 'Chichime,' but this island has two other names: Achutupu Dumat (Big Dog Island) and Wissudub (after the tropical icaco fruit). A popular anchorage point for boats arriving from Colombia, it's a meeting place for sailors in the region.

Host **Argelio Morales** offers shady camping and six thatched cabins with electricity, plus one tour per day (☎6846-5217; argeliomorales2347@gmail.com; per person camping/dm/private r incl 3 meals & transfer to Carti US$70/80/90). As at other island destinations, trash is building up here – guests are required to pack out their own. Campers are supplied with tents and camping equipment. If you have your own, ask for a discount.

Isla Tortuga (Morodup)

Hardly bigger than a postage stamp, this idyllic island, run by a single family, is kept immaculate with a raked white-sand beach and limited visitation.

Only 10 guests at a time are allowed to camp under the palms at **Isla Tortuga Camping** (☎6006-7020; www.sanblastourspanama.com; camping per person incl meals & transfer from Cartí US$86). Tents and cushions are provided, and **meals** (dishes US$5-15; ⏲7-11am & 3-8pm) including lobster, fish and fried patacones (plantains), by Blas Preciado who earned his whites as a Panama City chef, are well prepared.

Be aware that more than one island in the region is known as Isla Tortuga.

Wailidup

In the Lemon Cays, this picturesque island, also labelled on nautical charts as Tiadup, has a sprawling beach and dense forest. With ample mooring, it's a popular stop for sailboats. Come during the trade-wind season to avoid *chitras* (sand flies).

On a beautiful spit of white sand, **Kuna Niskua Lodge** (☎6043-6327, 6715-2335; cabins per person incl meals & tour US$150, r with shared/private bathroom US$75/85) has five lovely high-ceilinged cabins on stilts that sit over the water, with shady decks and breezes. The cabins are considerably better than the lodge rooms, where the shared bathroom could use a scrubbing. An attached restaurant and bar offers dishes (mains US$10-15) of fresh octopus, fish, crab and lobster. It's connected to the island via a long wooden dock. Contact Ceraldo for reservations. Transfers to Cartí (US$40) are charged separately.

Río Sidra & Nearby Islands

Río Sidra

Located 15km east of Cartí Suitupo, Río Sidra is a major settlement in the **Archipiélago de San Blás**. From here it's a quick and easy boat ride to Naranjo Chico, Salardup and De Mar Achu; it's also relatively close to the far-flung Cayos Los Grullos, Holandeses and Ordupuquip.

Río Sidra is extremely congested and the effects of Westernization are more prevalent here than on other islands (50 Cent isn't exactly traditional Guna music).

Local historian and expert *mola* maker **Lisa Harris** (☎6695-7081, 6158-8590) offers a recommended walking tour (US$20 per person, minimum four people) on the mainland to a waterfall, with a focus on birds, medicinal plants and Guna legends. Her *molas* receive wide acclaim, and some are quite affordable. Any local can point you to her house, but try to make contact in advance.

Río Sidra's small dock isn't too far from the airport, though it currently only receives charter flights. Most visitors access the area from Cartí, 15km west.

Achudup (De Mar Achu)

Located in the area of Río Sidra, this beautiful palm-forest island offers good value accommodations at **De Mar Achu** (☎6513-6597, 6595-6806; camping/cabins US$55/80 per person incl transfer, tour & 3 meals), with prices cut in half for stays longer than one night.

Cabins are well spaced for privacy, with options for families or couples. There are spacious new concrete bathhouses, volleyball and hammocks, while the shady campsites are also all-inclusive and well priced. There's electricity thanks to solar panels, and grounds are raked for debris and kept immaculate.

Excursions and snorkeling to nearby Isla Pelicano and Isla Estrella, where there is a natural pool, and community visits to Río Sidra, can be arranged.

Contact Lisette or caretaker Alfaro for stays.

Salardup (Isla Estrella)

Lovely in the extreme, this island begs for exploration, with long forested stretches and beaches facing both the mainland and open water. Huge starfish are not uncommon in these waters (have a look, but avoid handling them). Swimming here is great. Cultural excursions visit the mainland traditional Guna cemetery, a nearby river and a waterfall.

Camping Salardup (☎6152-6269, 6152-5564) is the only accommodation on this beautiful island – visitors must bring their own camping equipment. The contact is Lalo Gonzalez. To arrange transfers from Cartí (charged separately from camping fees), contact **Leon Marino** (☎6659-2581; idelonsosa@gmail.com; per person round-trip to Cartí US$30).

Meals are available from the family caretakers of the islands (three meals US$25).

Isla Senidup

A tiny islet divided by chain-link fence, this is a popular destination for backpackers. **Cabañas Senidup** (☎6945-4301; cabanas_senidub@hotmail.com; dm/private cabins per person incl 3 meals US$26/31) is a thatched village of tourist cabins run by Sr Sugu. It's a popular spot, even though the dorms

WRECK REEF

Approximately 100m north of Cayos Holandeses is a spot known as Wreck Reef, which earned its name by snaring all kinds of vessels over the years. The reef's notoriety stems from the fact that it's fairly far offshore from the closest island, though the water south of the reef is barely 1m deep – the ocean floor north of the reef plunges 100m in half that distance. From a captain's perspective, this means that the ocean floor very quickly rises 100m to a dangerously shallow depth.

Over the years, many experienced sailors have died here, though these days it's mostly smugglers who meet their doom. In 1995 a smugglers' boat filled with TV sets slammed into the reef at night. Although the smugglers had hoped to skip out on import taxes by sailing from Colón's Zona Libre to Cartagena, Colombia, they instead helped local Guna communities catch up on their favorite Venezuelan soap operas without paying a cent.

are a little crowded. There's usually one English-speaking host on site. Guests have access to beach games and volleyball, and free use of snorkel gear. Transfers to Cartí are US$20 round-trip.

Naranjo Chico

Three kilometers northwest of Río Sidra is the island of Naranjo Chico, Little Orange or Narascandub Pipi, depending on who you ask. Naranjo Chico is somewhere between a community and a resort island – it is populated, but it's also possible to find solitude.

Sleeping & Eating

There are several lodging options on the island with similar amenities.

Cabañas Naranjo Chico CADAÑAS $$
(☎6686-7437, 6086-7716; www.sanblaskunayala.com; r per person with/without bathroom incl 3 meals, transfer & tours US$110/85) Six cabins offer quiet and a lovely swimming beach. Those with shared bathrooms have sand floors, newer cabins with private bathrooms are set on stilts over the water. All have solar power. The del Valle family are prompt with response times for reservations, which is rare in these parts. Transfers leave the river port near Carti.

Cabañas Miro CABAÑAS $
(☎6769-5801; r per person incl 3 meals US$25) For shoestringers who want nothing more than some thatch over their head and sand beneath their toes, this is it. However, it's about to get a bit more crowded, with seven new cabins under construction. There is little to do here, but dining outdoors around the picnic table provides the perfect opportunity to mix with fellow travelers. Transfers to Cartí are charged separately.

Cayos Los Grullos, Holandeses and Ordupuquip (The Cays)

The undisputed gems of the Archipiélago de San Blás are the Cayos Los Grullos, Holandeses and Ordupuquip, a triangle of three virtually uninhabited island chains that are separated by calm blue-green waters and surrounded by shallow reefs.

At the lower western corner of the triangle are the Cayos Los Grullos, a mere 10km northwest of Río Sidra. Heading clockwise, the tip of the triangle is formed by the Cayos Holandeses (Dutchmen Keys), while the Cayos Ordupuquip are located in the southeastern corner. Despite the lack of tourist facilities in the cays, yachties love to anchor near these islands, though it takes skill behind the wheel to keep your boat afloat here. Needless to say, the snorkeling in the Cayos Holandeses is astounding, though you'll see plenty of tropical fish and colorful reefs anywhere in the cays.

Getting There & Away

Most visitors come by sailboat on multiday tours. Depending on the distance between your hotel and the Cays, motorboat transfers charge around US$150 round-trip from Cartí. The sea can get very rough out here, so make sure you have confidence in your captain and vessel, and make sure there are enough life jackets on board for everyone. Don't forget your snorkeling gear!

Corazón de Jesús & Narganá

The densely populated islands of Corazón de Jesús and Narganá, which are linked by an arcing wooden footbridge, are of little interest to travelers, especially since they're the most Westernized Guna communities in

CHOCOSANOS

Historically, most of the boats claimed by Wreck Reef were the victims of *chocosanos* ('storms that come from the east', in Guna). *Chocosanos* are ghastly tempests that whip up monstrous waves that can overrun entire islands. Such waves have swept many Guna and their homes out to sea, though there are early warning signs, such as a purple-black easterly sky and a lack of breeze and birdsong.

When a *chocosano* is approaching, Guna elders traditionally combat the storm by blowing into conch shells. The sound alerts their benevolent god, Paba Tummat, who tries to intervene and disperse the *chocosano*.

At the southern end of Wreck Reef, a freighter lies with its hull fully exposed and its deck flat against the ocean floor – the hulking vessel was flipped like a pancake by a mighty *chocosano*.

the Comarca. Here Guna families inhabit concrete cinderblock houses, wear Western clothing and hold all-island baseball tournaments. The people are friendly and the visit makes an interesting contrast to some of the less Westernized islands. The islands are a service center for nearby Isla Tigre, one of the most traditional islands in the Comarca.

Narganá is at the southwestern end of the bridge. It's home to the district's only courthouse and jail, so there are a lot of policemen on the island. If any ask for your passport, politely present it – jotting down tourists' names in little books gives them something to do.

Information

Banco Nacional de Panamá (Narganá; 8am-3pm Mon-Fri, 9am-noon Sat) Will change large bills at a poor rate and Amex traveler's checks for a nominal fee. No ATM.

Getting There & Away

Charter flights from Panama City arrive at the coastal airstrip in Corazón de Jesús. There is currently no commercial service. Travel here by boat from Cartí.

Isla Waidup

This tiny private isle is a stone's throw from Corazón de Jesús and Narganá. **Waidup Lodge** (6040-8914, 6103-0436, 225-7619; cabins per person incl 3 meals & tours US$75) has simple cabins on stilts, with good mattresses, woven fiber walls and waterfront balconies. There are modern bathrooms in the rooms, but the water is unheated. Still, it's more private than other spots. A small bar-restaurant is at your service and the water is swimmable. Tours go to nearby Isla Tigre.

Isla Tigre

Just a short boat ride from Corazón de Jesús and Narganá, Isla Tigre ranks among the most traditional islands in the Comarca – though the whole island is lit up by solar energy. With wide walkways separating homes, the island is tidy and uncrowded, which makes it easy to interact with local Guna. However, an island guide must accompany visitors.

Stay at **Cabañas Tigre** (6099-2738; cabins with/without bathroom US$25/15). The best feature here is its relaxed reception – guests have their own ample space but also get to see a fair amount of typical village life, with locals who are more open and relaxed toward travelers than they are elsewhere. They also recycle. Pleasant bamboo-and-thatch *cabañas* have concrete floors, colorful hammocks and shared facilities, and are near the beach.

The ocean here is crystal clear and fairly placid, so perfect for kayaking (from December to June) or snorkeling. Snorkel gear, meals (US$3 to US$7) and transfers to Cartí (US$30) are extra.

Isla Tigre is also home to some of the biggest festivals and events in the Comarca. Traditional dances are performed free of charge, but visitors should offer a tip.

Playón Chico & Nearby Islands

Playón Chico

With regular air connections to Panama City, Playón Chico serves as a popular gateway to San Blás, especially since it's located near the archipelago's most expensive hotel, on neighboring Isla Iskardup. If you're looking for more modestly priced accommodations, Playón Chico also serves as a convenient jumping-off point for nearby Yandup.

While much of the island is still covered by traditional dwellings, the main drag in Playón Chico is home to everything from missionaries and concrete churches to video shops and liquor stores. Although Playón Chico isn't set up to receive tourists, a quick stroll from the airstrip to the docks reveals the conflicting pressures shaping modern Guna life.

Getting There & Away

Air Panama (p69) has regular flights to Playón Chico (US$73). From here, lodges on islands further out transport their guests via motorboat.

Yandup

Just five minutes by boat from Playón Chico, the islet of Yandup is home to a recommended lodge **Yandup Lodge** (261-7229; www.yandupisland.com; per person incl 3 meals & tour US$172) run by a very attentive Spanish-Guna family. Accommodations are simple but comprise lovely octagonal thatched-roof cabins with private bathrooms. Light comes from solar panels and water from the mainland. The island's grassy grounds, palm shade and powder-fine beach might be reason enough to just stay put.

Guests can be catered to with vegetarian meals and tailored excursions, which include cultural visits as well as the usual snorkeling and hiking.

Achutupu & Nearby Islands

Achutupu

With daily flights to Panama City, Achutupu (like Playón Chico to the west) serves as a popular gateway to San Blás, especially since it's located near the archipelago's second most expensive hotel (on Uaguitupo).

Although the densely populated island of Achutupu isn't set up to receive overnight visitors, it's a popular day trip for visitors from Uaguitupo who are interested in seeing Guna village life. Of particular interest is the community gathering house at the center of the island, which often hosts important meetings, rituals and celebrations.

Getting There & Away

Air Panama (p69) flies here from Panama City (US$74) daily.

Uaguitupo

Although it's a mere 100m from Achutupu, the grassy isle of Uaguitupo is a private and pristine place aimed at high-rolling travelers.

More relaxed and traditional than its upmarket brethren, **Dolphin Lodge** (Uaguinega Lodge; 6090-8990, 396-4805; www.dolphinlodgesanblas.com; s/d incl 3 meals & tours US$140/200; @) has known repeat visitors, though its current state is a little run-down. Taking up virtually all of Uaguitupo, it features a clutch of thatched cabins with wooden floors and wicker furniture. Rooms feature cold-water showers, 24-hour solar electricity and environmentally friendly flush toilets.

A great spot to kick back, the breezy restaurant faces the breakers. The English-speaking staff is extremely attentive to guests, and can help you hire a boat to explore the surrounding area. Another big plus is that the island doesn't have *chitras* (sand flies). Air Panama (p69) services the nearby island of Achutupu (US$74), and Dolphin Lodge can provide boat transfers from there.

Akwadup

Pretty and petite, this palm-frond isle is well removed from the usual tourist route. The draw here is **Akwadup Lodge** (832-5144; www.sanblaslodge.com; s/d/tr incl 3 meals & tours US$165/240/330; @), the most upscale lodge (in relative terms) of the archipelago, providing breezy mint-green octagonal cabins over the waterfront. Dining is fresh and simple, featuring local lobster, fish, yucca and coconut. These so-secluded lodgings represent fine Guna hospitality and details including vaulted thatched ceilings, private bathrooms, screened doors and 24-hour electricity.

The private decks suggest that you might like to laze away the sunset with beer in hand, although romance might be your agenda if you've come all the way to the middle of a secluded nowhere. Excursions – including cultural visits, snorkeling and fishing – are handily nearby. Prices include airport transfers but not snorkeling equipment. Air Panama (p69) has flights to nearby Achutupu (US$74). The lodge provides boat transfers.

Darién Province

POP 48,400 / AREA 8653 SQ KM / ELEV SEA LEVEL TO 3478M

Includes ➡

Best Off-the Beaten-Path Spots

- Parque Nacional Darién (p247)
- Piji Basal (p248)
- Pacific Coast (p253)
- Jaqué (p253)
- Reserva Natural Punta Patiño (p250)

Best Places to Sleep

- Filo de Tallo (p246)
- Canopy Camp (p245)
- Punta Patiño Lodge (p250)
- Piji Basal (p248)
- Tropic Star Lodge (p253)

Why Go?

One of world's richest biomes is the 5760-sq-km Parque Nacional Darién, where the primeval meets the present with scenery nearly unaltered from one million years ago. Even today in the Darién, the Emberá and Wounaan people maintain many of their traditional practices and retain generations-old knowledge of the rainforest. In a stroke of irony, much of the Darién has remained untouched because of its volatile reputation.

The road to Yaviza – the most accessible part of the province – has scenes of habitat destruction. Cruising the waterways and hiking trails are the only ways to explore the slow-paced interior Darién and the Pacific coast, where Emberá, Wounaan and African-Darienita cultures coexist.

The region's issues are complex. Police checkpoints are frequent because of narcotrafficking. The Darién is not for everyone, but with careful planning and the right destinations, it offers opportunities for intrepid travelers to discover something truly wild.

When to Go

- **Dec–Mar** The premium months for sportfishing in the Pacific.
- **Dec–mid-Apr** The best time to visit, with drier trails and easier and more reliable transport connections.
- **Oct–Feb** Marine turtle hatching on the Pacific coast.

Darién Province Highlights

1 Reserva Natural Punta Patiño (p250) Searching for capybara while exploring the lush jungle reserve of Reserva Natural Punta Patiño on the edge of Golfo de San Miguel.

2 Rancho Frío (p249) Hiking along the spectacular jungle trails surrounding Rancho Frío, a ranger station on the edge of Parque Nacional Darién.

3 Mogué (p251) or **Piji Basal** (p248) Looking for harpy eagles and interacting with the Emberá around these traditional villages.

4 Filo de Tallo (p246) Enjoying excursions into indigenous communities and the dreamy savanna-like setting of this ecolodge.

5 Jaqué (p253) Helping to rescue marine turtles in this Pacific Ocean community.

History

Living within the boundaries of the Darién, the group commonly known as the Chocóes emigrated from Colombia's Chocó region long ago. Anthropologists use two linguistic groups – the Emberá and the Wounaan – though with the exception of language, the groups' cultural features are virtually identical. Both groups prefer to be thought of as two separate peoples.

Before the introduction of guns, the Emberá and Wounaan were experts with the *boroquera* (blowgun), using envenomed darts with lethal toxins from poisonous frogs and bullet ants. Many scholars believe that they forced the Guna out of the Darién and into the Caribbean coastal area they now inhabit.

The Emberá and Wounaan are known for their incredibly fine dugout canoes. Known as *piraguas*, they have shallow bottoms that are ideal for the dry season, when rivers run low. The Panama Canal Authority has long employed Emberá and Wounaan craftsmen to make the *piraguas* that are used by officials to reach the upper parts of the canal's watershed. Until the late 1990s, the US Air Force solicited Emberá and Wounaan help with jungle living. Many of them trained US astronauts and air-force pilots at Fuerte Sherman, near Colón, in tropical-wilderness survival.

Today the majority of the nearly 10,000 Emberá and Wounaan in Panama live deep in the rainforests of the Darién, particularly along the Ríos Sambú, Jaqué, Chico, Tuquesa, Membrillo, Tuira, Yapé and Tucutí.

Culture

The Emberá and Wounaan survive on subsistence agriculture supplemented by limited fishing and poultry raising. Historically both groups were more reliant on slash-and-burn agriculture and hunting, which are practices now restricted in the national park. Increased commercial rice and maize plantations offer work for seasonal migrant laborers.

The Emberá and Wounaan are also exceptional woodcarvers and basket weavers. Boas, frogs and birds were traditionally carved from dark cocobolo hardwood, and now tiny animal figurines are also made from tagua nuts. The women produce some of the finest baskets in Latin America. Woven from palm fibers, each requires months of intensive labor. These products fetch a high market price and provide a much-needed secondary income for most communities.

Built on stilts 3m to 4m off the ground, Emberá and Wounaan homes are well suited to the rainforest. Flooring uses thin, strong strips of plentiful palm bark, and the vaulted design protects occupants and food from ground pests and swollen rivers. Beneath, medicinal plants and edible vegetables and roots are grown. Many homes are thatched and open-sided for breezes, with mud ovens.

Western clothing is replacing traditional attire, except for older individuals. Women, who traditionally wore only a skirt, increasingly don bras and shirts. Many wear traditional jewelry, especially wide silver bracelets and elaborate silver-coin necklaces. They also stain their bodies with purplish-black designs made with juice from the *jagua* fruit. The dye is believed to have health-giving properties and wards off insects.

Like the Guna, the Emberá and Wounaan have a strong measure of political autonomy, though this is under threat by increasing external pressures. These include encroachment by Latino settlers and habitat destruction by loggers, accelerated in recent years due to the paving of the Interamericana. Missionaries, particularly evangelicals, have

RESPONSIBLE TRAVEL IN THE DARIÉN

Travelers should carefully consider the impact they might have if they visit Emberá and Wounaan communities in the Darién. Unlike Guna Yala, the Darién sees few foreign visitors. Yet the Emberá and Wounaan are very hospitable.

Make an effort to respect the sensibilities of your hosts. Although some women still go topless, these are fairly conservative societies. Most villagers are happy to pose for a photo, but you should always ask first. Photos of communities sent back in thanks (via a guide) are treasured.

Instead of giving out candy or coins to village children, consider buying dictionaries, Spanish-language books and much-needed supplies to donate to local schools.

Tourism has a long way to go in the region, which is one reason that a visit to an Emberá or Wounaan village is so refreshing. Visitors must work together with locals to promote cultural preservation.

GETTING TO COLOMBIA

The Interamericana stops at the town of Yaviza and reappears 150km further on, far beyond the Colombian border. Overland crossings through the Darién Gap (p246) on foot are not recommended.

The Caribbean crossing between Puerto Obaldía (Panama) and Capurganá (Colombia) has become a better option than in the past. Air Panama flies to Puerto Obaldía. From here, there are no buses. You must boat or walk to the Colombian village of Sapzurro. On foot, this takes about 2½ hours, but the track is indistinct in places, and sporadic regional insecurity makes boating the better option. Just on the border, the Panamanian village of La Miel is building a hostel and features a gorgeous beach (it's 20 minutes on foot from Sapzurro).

From Sapzurro, ferries go to Capurganá; alternatively, it's a two-hour walk. As the security situation constantly changes, it's best to get an update with solid information about the route beforehand.

Sailing or boating to Colombia is by far the safest option after flying.

More of a tour than just transport, the popular **San Blas Adventures** (☎6696-1554, 6731-2530; http://sanblasadventures.com; 4-day trip US$375) takes backpackers from Panama to Colombia, passing through the San Blás Islands and coastal Darién, camping and snorkeling on the way. On the Panamanian side, the trip starts in Cartí and ends in Sapzurro (Colombia). Travel is on a covered boat with outboard motors. There are regular set departures and the website features useful details for planning.

almost entirely eliminated the core religious values of both groups. Youth flee to the cities for their employment prospects, or work for drug traffickers as mules, both of which have prompted fears that the Emberá and Wounaan cultures are under serious threat.

Tours

The Darién is the only major part of Panama where a guide is necessary, and one is required in the national park. You can hire Spanish-speaking guides locally for about US$25 to US$35 per day. However, transportation costs can be very expensive. Tour operators can take care of all arrangements without a language barrier, teach you about the incredible local ecology, cook for you and humor you when you have blisters. Another option is to go with an independent naturalist guide.

★ **Jungle Treks** ADVENTURE TOUR
(☎6438-3130; www.jungletreks.com) Run by a veteran naturalist guide, this recommended outfitter specializes in boutique, expedition-style travel for groups of six or more. Destinations include the interior and Pacific coast. Check the website for set dates. Custom trips have a three-day minimum. Fluent in English.

Panama Exotic Adventures TOUR
(☎in Panama City 223-9283; www.panamaexoticadventures.com) With an ecolodge in Metetí and long experience in the region, this dedicated French-run operator offers three- to eight-day trips with hands-on visits to indigenous communities, kayaking and outings. Ask about tailor-made trips.

Ancon Expeditions TOUR
(☎269-9415; www.anconexpeditions.com) Ancon travels to its own private lodge in Punta Patiño on the Pacific coast and further afield. Special programs for birdwatchers and hikers are excellent.

Ecocircuitos ECOTOUR
(☎315-1488; www.ecocircuitos.com; Albrook Plaza, 2nd fl, No 31, Ancón, Panama City) A great outfitter offering four-day trips to Parque Nacional Darién with visits to an Emberá community. It's a member of APTSO (Asociación Panameño de Turismo Sostenible), Panama's sustainable-tourism alliance. English spoken.

Information

Information on the Darién rapidly becomes outdated. Always seek updates, ideally from a guide who leads frequent trips to the area.

Note that in order to travel in the area you must write to **SENAFRONT** (Servicio Nacional de Fronteras; ☎527-1000; www.senafront.gob.pa) in Panama City ahead of time, in Spanish, with details of your itinerary and carry photocopies of the letter with them as it may be examined at checkpoints. The office can also suggest local guides.

DEFORESTATION IN THE DARIÉN

As little as 50 years ago, more than 70% of Panama was covered by forest. Now, deforestation is the country's gravest environmental problem. Trees continue to be felled at a rapid pace, with the Darién serving as the ecological ground zero.

Logging trucks and river barges move the trunks to mills. Floated lumber is sprayed with a chemical that prevents rot but also wreaks havoc on the environment, particularly agricultural plots and fish stocks.

At stake are not only local animal populations but also migratory animals seeking seasonal food supplies. Rainforest destruction also threatens the traditional cultures of the Emberá and the Wounaan. Deforestation results in regional water shortages during the dry season, as well as a number of other environmental problems, ranging from pollution to erosion.

For much of the rural population, hunting and logging have been a way of life for generations. Many communities feel that their economic welfare is dependent on these practices. In 2011 Panama's national environmental agency sought the protection of the UN-backed convention governing trade in illegal species (CITES) to help regulate trade in its rare hardwoods because of rampant illegal logging, which continues today.

Fighting the problem isn't easy. Panama's national parks are sparsely staffed, but their territory is colossal. In the Parque Nacional Darién, only 20 rangers protect 5760 sq km, an area more expansive than some countries.

For more information on the environmental situation in Panama, visit the home page of **ANCON** (☎314-0060; www.ancon.org).

In Yaviza, the Sede Administrativa Parque Nacional Darién (p247) can provide some information on the park and potentially help you find guides (usually rangers with days off). Travelers must register here to visit the park and check in with the police before heading out into the jungle. There are also police checkpoints along the road to Yaviza and at ports.

Panama City's Instituto Geográfico Nacional (p69) sells topographical maps for some regions of the Darién.

DANGERS & ANNOYANCES

The greatest hazard in the Darién is the difficult environment. Trails, when they exist at all, are often poorly defined and are never marked. Many large rivers that form the backbone of the Darién transportation network create their own hazards. Any help at all, let alone medical help, is very far away. If you get lost, you are done for. To minimize these risks, it's recommended that you explore the Darién either as part of an organized tour or with the help of a qualified guide.

Dengue and malaria are serious risks. Consult your doctor before you go about necessary medication, and cover up as much as possible, especially at dawn and dusk. Areas of the Parque Nacional Darién are prime territory for the deadly fer-de-lance snake. The chances of getting a snakebite are remote, but do be careful and always wear boots on treks. Although they don't carry Lyme disease, ticks are widespread. Bring tweezers and a few books of matches to ensure you're able to remove the entire tick if it's burrowed well into your skin.

The US State Department warns travelers against visiting remote areas of the Darién off the Interamericana. This blanket advisory includes the entirety of Parque Nacional Darién, although certain destinations may be OK to visit. Particularly treacherous, however, are the areas between Boca de Cupe and Colombia, the traditional path through the Darién Gap. As there's only minimal police presence, you're on your own if trouble arises.

Although the no-go zones in the Darién are well removed from the traditional tourist destinations, their dangers cannot be underestimated. Narcotraffickers who utilize these jungle routes don't appreciate encountering travelers. In the past, former Colombian guerrillas or runaways took refuge here. Missionaries and travelers alike have been kidnapped and killed in the southern area of the Darién.

Despite all this, parts of the Darién can be visited safely.

Getting There & Away

The Interamericana terminates 266km from Panama City in the frontier town of Yaviza, and the vast wilderness region of the Darién lies beyond. The highway starts again 150km further on in Colombia. This break between Central and South America is known as the Darién Gap (p246) – literally the end of the road.

There are buses on Sunday, Tuesday and Thursday from Panama City to Yaviza between 3:30am and 7am (US$16, 4½ hours). Be sure to tell the bus driver your destination.

With irregular frequency, **Air Panama** (☎316-9000; www.airpanama.com) has flights to Jaqué and Puerto Obaldía.

Getting Around

In the vast jungles of Darién Province, rivers are often the only means of travel, with *piraguas* (long canoes; mostly motorized) providing the transport.

Transport to interior destinations like El Real and La Palma leaves from Puerto Quimba, near the Interamericana city of Metetí, and Yaviza. In La Palma, you can hire motorized boats to the Río Mogué and the Río Sambú. From El Real, travelers can access Piji Basal or Parque Nacional Darién.

THE ROAD TO YAVIZA

The Interamericana runs from Panamá Province along the spine of Darién Province, with Yaviza the end of the road (for now). Police checkpoints are frequent on this road, so have your passport ready and be prepared to discuss your travel plans. Occasionally, a soldier will lecture you about the dangers near the border – that's because it's their job to go there if something happens.

Forty-five kilometers east of Lago Bayano is the town (or towns) of **Ipetí**: Ipetí Emberá, Ipetí Guna and Ipetí Colono. Each is occupied by a different cultural group (Guna, Emberá and Latino). A small handicrafts store sells Emberá woven baskets and you can receive a traditional tagua body painting for a few dollars. This henna-like plant extract leaves a temporary tattoo for up to two weeks.

Twelve kilometers past Ipetí is the village of Tortí, a useful stop with a restaurant, police station and health clinic.

Tours

Panama Travel Unlimited CULTURAL TOUR
(☎6738-1708; http://ecotourspanama.net) Offers day tours from Panama City to an Emberà village in Ipetí. The tour operator works with the community on sanitation, recycling, education and organic food production.

Igua Jimenez TOUR
(☎6791-6499, 6700-3512; iguat28@yahoo.com) A recommended English-speaking Guna naturalist guide, Igua leads boat tours to nearby Lago Bayano and can lead hikes into the rainforest. Note, though, that it helps to have a decent command of Spanish.

Sleeping & Eating

Hospedaje Tortí HOTEL $
(☎6743-3697; d with shared/private bathroom US$30/18; P ❄) Hospedaje Tortí has squat cinderblock rooms, each with a decent mattress and clean towels for cold-water showers. Rooms with bathrooms have air-con.

Avicar PANAMANIAN $
(☎6746-0051; Interamericana s/n, Tortí; dishes US$3-5; ⏲6am-9pm) Roadside restaurant Avicar serves traditional country-style Panamanian dishes. You're likely to share a table with some pretty interesting characters.

Getting There & Away

From Panama City to Yaviza it's 264km. The last stop with decent services before Darién Province is Tortí, 136km from Panama City. Police checkpoints start shortly afterwards. Always stop at the checkpoints; note that your papers – ID, letter to SENAFRONT (p243) and driver's license if driving – may be reviewed.

Metetí

Located 1km southeast of a police checkpoint, Metetí is the Darién's fastest-growing locality, with the best infrastructure in the region. The surroundings are being quickly deforested, though interesting ecolodges are found on the outskirts. Travelers come to link to La Palma and interior Darién via a scenic boat ride.

Sleeping

Hotel Felicidad HOTEL $
(☎299-6544; www.hotelfelicidad.com; d US$25; ❄) Bleach-scented with clean concrete rooms, friendly service and flowery gardens. Avoid rooms without an outside window as they tend to be musty.

Canopy Camp LODGE $$$
(☎in Panama City 264-5720; 7-night package high/low season US$2799/1799; 📶) 🌿 Catering to serious birdwatchers, this eco-camp sits in verdant secondary rainforest. Spacious, multi-room tents with wooden decks are outfitted with comfortable beds, screens, electricity and fans. Each lodging is extremely private, with freestanding bathrooms equipped with open-air showers that bring the forest and its wildlife that much closer. Guiding is top notch, with dedicated naturalists and on-site trails.

For birdwatchers, a trip to the Darién is a chance to glimpse a harpy eagle or a crested

THE LAST ROADLESS PLACE: DARIÉN GAP

Since the first Interamericana Congress met in Buenos Aires in 1925, the nations of the Americas have been dedicated to the completion of a great hemispheric road system. Today only 150km of unfinished business prevents that system from being realized – the Darién Gap. This defiant stretch of wilderness, which separates the continents of North and South America, is the sole barrier in the way of an otherwise unbroken 30,600km highway winding from Circle in Alaska to Puerto Montt in Chile.

Constructing this missing bit of pavement would increase trade and travel options. Colombia's civil war got in the way for years, and during that time the Darién Gap was both buffer zone and safe haven for rogue factors. Today narcotrafficking in the region has become the greater issue. But there is still a lobby for a unified Panamerican highway (Interamericana).

Detractors, many of them Panamanians, cite the cost of excavating rugged terrain, the threat of foot-and-mouth disease spreading to North America and the still-delicate issue of security. Every year, SENAFRONT (the national border service; p243) seizes hundreds of kilos of drugs making their way through the region from Colombia. Human traffickers also transport migrants heading to North America via this ungovernable expanse.

Road building provides a quick conduit for resource extraction, and thus a road through the Darién Gap would likely spur the deforestation of one of the world's finest remaining tropical rainforests, precipitating devastating habitat loss for its unique flora and fauna. A cultural shift in remote communities would inevitably follow.

Currently Panama's mostly paved Interamericana highway traverses deforested cattle country to end at the sweaty, ramshackle town of Yaviza in Darién Province. The road, marked by many police checkpoints, frequently deteriorates due to weather and heavy use by trucks. Yaviza is 264km from Panama City.

eagle, in addition to poison-dart frogs, golden-headed manakins and barred puffbirds. Sitting on 40 hectares of forest with orange, papaya, banana and soursop trees, the lodge is made sustainable by such initiatives as solar panels and wastewater treatment. In low season, lodging may be open to passers-by. Visitors mostly come on four- to seven-day packages that include meals, guiding and transfers from Panama City.

Filo de Tallo LODGE **$$$**
(☎6673-5381; www.panamadarien.com; 4-day package per person from US$1050) Perched upon a grassy knoll on the outskirts of Metetí, this handsome ecolodge is run by Panama Exotic Adventures. Thatched bamboo huts feature firm beds draped in mosquito netting and attached bathrooms with pastel river stones and handcarved basins. Enjoy wine and good international-Panamanian meals in the open-air living and dining area with a stunning panorama of the region.

Once a shooting range for the Noriega camp, the transformation of this space to ethno-adventure tourism couldn't be stranger. Activities include kayaking and visiting a Wounaan village. While the lodge occupies a deforested sector just on the tip of the Darién, it is one of the best lodgings in the region and provides a good dose of indigenous culture. It is also certified as carbon-neutral by Forest Finance. Packages include all meals and activities and transportation to/from Panama City.

Eating

For last-minute purchases there is a good-sized grocery store.

Restaurante Doña Lala PANAMANIAN **$**
(☎6722-8022; cam a Puerto Quimba; mains US$3.50-5; ⏲6am-10pm) Cheap and cheerful, this spotless cafeteria-style restaurant is usually packed with locals. Breakfasts such as shredded beef and eggs are popular. Lunch options include stewed chicken, grilled meat, rice and plantains. It's 800m inland from the Interamericana on the way to Puerto Quimba.

Information

BNP (Banco Nacional de Panama; ☎299-6094; Interamericana s/n; ⏲8am-3pm Mon-Fri, 9am-noon Sat) Has an ATM.

Getting There & Away

From Panama City, buses to Yaviza stop in Metetí (US$15, four hours) on Sunday, Tuesday and Thursday.

For boats to La Palma or Sambú, take the turnoff for Puerto Quimba, a port on the Río Iglesias. A passenger pickup shuttles between Metetí and Puerto Quimba every 30 minutes from 6am until 9pm (US$2), or take a taxi (US$10). The paved road between Metetí and Puerto Quimba is about 20km long.

From Puerto Quimba, unscheduled boats to La Palma (20 minutes) leave when full between 7:30am and 6:30pm (US$4). A one-way charter may also be an option. Passengers must register at the police checkpoint next to the ticket counter.

Boats also go to Sambú on Monday, Wednesday and Friday (US$24, 2½ hours).

Yaviza

POP 4500

Part bazaar and part bizarre, this concrete village is the end of the road. Here the Interamericana grinds to a halt and beyond lies the famous Darién Gap. Rough edged and misshapen, it's hardly a destination in its own right unless you have cockfighting in mind. For travelers, it is an essential check-in stop for entry to Parque Nacional Darién. If you need to stay somewhere, try **Hospedaje Sobia Kiru** (☎299-4409; d US$25; ❄), a two-story turquoise house with clean rooms and blessed air-conditioning. It's on a side street across from the port, next to the Cable Onda office. Ask for Leticia. Or the **Ya Darien** (☎6653-0074; d US$25; ❄), which has tidy rooms with cold-water showers; the help may be slow as molasses, but it works.

For cheap eateries (*fondas)* and a small supermarkets head to the port area.

Getting There & Away

Buses from Panama City go to Yaviza (US$16, 4½ hours) on Sunday, Tuesday and Thursday.

Public boats to El Real go sporadically when full (US$5). The cost of a private boat charter to El Real (US$60 to US$90 one way) depends on motor size and fuel costs.

PARQUE NACIONAL DARIÉN

Parque Nacional Darién is the most ecologically diverse land-based national park in all of Central America. Although it's often overshadowed by the security situation in the province, there is no doubt that it is the crown jewel of Panama's national parks, mostly sought after by specialists like biologists and botanists.

El Real

POP 1200

Riverside El Real, also known as El Real de Santa María, dates from the conquistador days when it was merely a fort beside Río Tuira. The settlement prevented pirates from sailing upriver to plunder Santa María, where gold from the Cana mines was stored. Today El Real is one of the largest towns in the Darién, though it's still very much a backwater settlement.

El Real is the last sizable settlement before the national park. Those heading up to Rancho Frío should either hire a local guide or be part of a tour – the Ministerio de Ambiente will not let you proceed unescorted. Before your arrival, send a letter of intent to SENAFRONT (p243) and contact the Panama City office of the Ministerio de Ambiente to pay the park entry fee (foreigners US$15) and lodging fees.

If you arrive in town too late to start the trek to Rancho Frío, you can spend the night at a rustic *pensión*. The best option is to arrive early to continue on to Piji Basal or Parque Nacional Darién. **Fonda Doña Lola** (meals US$3-5) is a cheap eatery serving rice and meat dishes with fried plantains.

KNOW BEFORE YOU GO

To visit the Parque Nacional Darién you must pay the entry fee and all lodging costs before you go. Call or visit the **Ministerio de Ambiente** (☎299-6430; www.miambiente.gob.pa; Calle Broberg 804, Cerro Ancón, Albrook; ⏲8am-4pm Mon-Fri) in Panama City for the direct-deposit account number for the 'Cuenta de Vida Silvestre' at Banco Nacional de Panama (BNP). Visit any branch, but be sure to keep your bank receipt to show at the **Sede Administrativa Parque Nacional Darién** (☎299-4495; Interamericana, Ministerio de Ambiente bldg; park entry US$15; ⏲8am-4pm Mon-Fri) in Yaviza, where you must stop to register. If you somehow forget, the closest BNP outlet to Yaviza is in Metetí (see opposite). At present, there is no way to make the payment online, but this is in the works.

The park also requires visitors to be accompanied by a guide. If you don't have one once you have reached Yaviza, the office can recommend community guides.

SURVIVING THE DARIÉN

Parque Nacional Darién is the most ecologically diverse land-based national park in all Central America, yet it is also one of the least-visited parks. Chalk it up to its reputation: with its serious risks and poisonous snakes, the Darién isn't for all. Yet as a destination it is fascinating and fulfilling – provided you take the necessary precautions and are prepared.

Security

In the past, this rugged and roadless expanse proved to be the perfect hideout for armed groups resting from military action in Colombia. Today the jungle remains an ideal hideout for rogue elements and a transit point for illegal migrants. The Panamanian police take defending this area very seriously and it is unwise to go against their recommendations for the sport of it.

Established routes are recommended both for your safety and for legal reasons. The police have been known to detain those on unauthorized routes and suspect them of illegal activity – even if they are with a guide.

Safety

Even if you have crossed Central America on your own by bus, solo travel here is not recommended. Since trails are unmarked, it is easy to get lost. No one is likely to come to your aid, but you might come across poisonous snakes and scorpions – who could end your trip (or your time on Earth) unexpectedly.

Preparations

Though it's remote, the Darién is not cheap. Travelers should make a careful budget, noting that even those who loathe taking tours generally do so here. Decide whether going with an independent guide and paying all the fuel and food costs separately will really work out to your advantage – especially since the cost of fuel can be astronomical. Those who contract a local guide should speak Spanish, otherwise the whole endeavor is prone to frustrating misunderstandings. If problems arise, speaking Spanish will help you find a solution.

Keep your baggage to a minimum on any jungle trek. Insect repellent, sunblock, a hat and rain gear are essential. Food can only be found in the few towns; it's not available at the ranger stations. Bring some drinking water and a means of purifying water.

Visit during the dry season (mid-December through mid-April); otherwise, you'll be slogging your way through thick mud and swatting at moth-size mosquitoes.

Getting There & Away

Veteran boatman **Chicho Bristan** (☎6913-0321, 299-6566; round-trip for 3 passengers US$60) offers charter trips between El Real and Yaviza or Puerto Quimba. When your boat arrives to El Real, register with SENAFRONT at the stand in front of the boat landing.

Pickup trucks transfer passengers to Piji Basal (US$25) and Pirre 1 (US$30), a 1½-hour hike from Rancho Frío, the entry point to Parque Nacional Darién.

Piji Basal

Tourism is new to this welcoming Emberá indigenous village adjacent to Parque Nacional Darién, but it is worth visiting if you are in the vicinity. On the banks of the Río Pirre, the village consists of a handful of thatched huts raised on stilts around a large grassy plaza. Come with insect repellent and boots.

Villagers sell crafts, such as baskets and masks, and may be willing to paint you with tagua juice (these traditional 'tattoos' are considered a form of insect repellent and wash off after a few weeks). As part of a visit you can participate in activities (US$5 to US$40) such as birdwatching or trips to the national park with a local Emberá guide.

Visitors can stay in the village in an open-air thatched **hut** (Community Tourism; ☎6907-3716; pijibasal@gmail.com; per person US$15) equipped with tents and air mattresses. There's a concrete bathroom with unheated showers and electricity courtesy of solar panels. Meals (US$5) such as fish with rice and fruit are taken in a community hut.

Getting There & Away

Piji Basal is 11km from El Real, where you can arrange a transfer in the back of a pickup (US$25

Engines break, flights are postponed; in short, travel delays are about as common as raindrops in the Darién. Go with extra food and cash, a flashlight, matches, good personal equipment and flexibility in your schedule.

Guides

Guides are now required for the Parque Nacional Darién. Paying more usually means getting more. A naturalist guide will have a different skill set from that of a *guía local* (local or community guide). Consider your needs and criteria.

The following are essential attributes in a guide:

- Experience in the area
- Extensive local contacts and problem-solving skills
- A planned itinerary with realistic travel times and contracted transportation
- Good equipment (tents etc) if you do not have your own
- Any necessary permits

The following are desirable attributes:

- Skill at spotting animals
- Knowledge of local history, animals and plants
- Knowledge of English (or another language)
- First aid kit and skills
- Handheld radio and/or cell phone for areas with coverage

Fellow travelers can provide guide references, but it is important to meet your guide beforehand – particularly if you're traveling solo.

Find out ahead of time if gas, transportation, food and fees are included. Perhaps the most important factor for a local guide is that they have extensive contacts in the region: people who can help arrange logistics and know the actual terrain. Don't assume that a local guide is experienced – some have sold trips despite never having set foot in the national park. The Sede Administrativa Parque Nacional Darién (p247) keeps a list of community guides.

one way). In the rainy season (April to November) it may be possible to transfer via the Río Pirre.

Rancho Frío

Thirteen kilometers south of El Real, as the lemon-spectacled tanager flies, is the Rancho Frío sector of Parque Nacional Darién. It's home to Pirre Station (Pirre 2), not be confused with the station at the top of Mt Pirre near Cana. Rare bird species represented here include the crimson-bellied woodpecker, the white-fronted nunbird and the striped woodhaunter. It's a riveting spot for birdwatchers.

The excellent trail network includes a two-day trek to Mt Pirre ridge and a one-hour walk through thick jungle to a series of cascades. Neither should be attempted without a guide as they are unmarked, and if you get lost out here you're finished.

Visitors must write SENAFRONT (p243) in Panama City in Spanish of their travel intentions in the Darién and carry photocopies of the letter with them. It may be examined at checkpoints. Depending on the security situation, SENAFRONT may require visitors to go with a guide.

Sleeping & Eating

Visitors must bring their own food and purified water. Cooking fuel is scarce, so let the rangers do the cooking (US$10 to US$15 a day for the service is most appreciated). Try the zapote fruit growing at the station – its fleshy orange meat has the taste and texture of mango.

Barracks CABIN **$**

(per person US$15) At Pirre Station, these barracks have fold-out cots for visitors, a small outdoor dining area beside a very basic kitchen, a *palapa* (open-sided shelter) with a few chairs and a number of flush toilets and cold-water showers. Pay the Ministerio del Medio Ambiente directly in Panama City, if possible.

Campsite CAMPGROUND $
(per person US$6) At this shady camp site you can either pitch a tent or string up a jungle hammock. Pay the Ministerio del Medio Ambiente directly in Panama City, if possible.

Getting There & Away

Pirre Station can only be reached by hiking (four hours), or a combination of boating and hiking or 4WD transportation (from US$30) and hiking from El Real or Piji Basal. Transport only goes as far as in Pirre 1, a 1½-hour hike from Rancho Frío. For those hiking, the road offers minimal indications. It is best to go with a guide.

INTERIOR DARIÉN

La Palma

POP 4200

The provincial capital of Darién Province, La Palma is a one-street town located where the wide Río Tuira meets the Golfo de San Miguel. Pastel stilt houses lord over the muddy waterfront, a scene abuzz with commerce, bars and evangelist messages.

Most travelers pass through La Palma to take a boat ride to somewhere else, like the Ancon nature reserve and lodge at Reserva Natural Punta Patiño or the Emberá villages lining the banks of the Río Sambú. If you have time, check out the ruins of 17th-century Spanish forts, five minutes away by boat (US$30).

Every facility of interest to the traveler is located on the main street, which is within 300m of the airstrip. There's a bank, a hospital and a police station as well as three hotels, three bars and several food stands. Those who intend to go further inland should talk to the police here first.

There are several basic lodging options on the main road. Simple and sweet, **Hotel Biaquira Bagara** (☎299-6224; d with/without bathroom US$25/17; ❄📶) has hardwood decks, wicker furniture and firm beds. While on the waterfront **La Paila del Pueblo** (☎299-6490; Calle Central Abajo; s/d US$10/15; 📶) has thin walls and mattresses but good sea views. Ask to arrange visits to the Emberá community of Mogué.

There's no shortage of cheap and somewhat cheerful eateries in town. The clean **Restaurante Lola** (☎6721-8632; mains US$5-15; ⏰7am-7pm Mon-Sat) serves shrimp or fish *criollo*-style (with a flavorful sauce) in addition to grilled meats, while if you avoid the bathrooms, **La Paila del Pueblo Restaurante** (mains US$3-5; ⏰7am-10pm) offers inexpensive meals (think soup or meat with rice) in a waterfront setting.

Stock up on groceries here if you are going upriver.

Getting There & Away

Boats to Puerto Quimba (US$4, 20 minutes) leave when full, running between 5:30am and 5pm. Puerto Quimba has buses to Metetí, where other buses go to Panama City or Yaviza.

To charter a private boat and a guide, look in the vicinity of the dock for a responsible captain with a seaworthy motorboat (US$120 to US$300 per day, gas included).

Reserva Natural Punta Patiño

On the southern shore of the Golfo de San Miguel, 25km from La Palma, is this private 263-sq-km wildlife preserve owned by ANCON and managed by the organization's for-profit arm, Ancon Expeditions (p243). It contains species-rich primary and secondary forest, and is one of the best places in Panama to spot harpy eagles. Even if the big bird doesn't show, there's a good chance of seeing everything from three-toed sloths to capybaras, the world's largest rodent.

The only way to reach the preserve is by boat or plane. Landing on the tiny strip of ocean-side grass that's called a runway in these parts is definitely part of the experience.

In a gorgeous nature reserve, the wooden cabins of **Punta Patiño Lodge** (☎in Panama City 269-9415; www.anconexpeditions.com; 3-night package incl guide, meals & lodging per person US$895; ❄) have air-con, comfortable mattresses and private cold-water showers – you won't miss hot water in these climes. Staff are extremely attentive and meals are fresh and well prepared. The lodge itself is perched atop a ridge with arresting gulf panoramas. Activities include guided nature hikes, night tours and boating the mangroves.

Ancon Expeditions' (p243). three-night Coastal Darien Explorer tour includes the round-trip airfare between Panama City and

THE MOTHER OF ALL EAGLES

The harpy eagle, Central America's most striking raptor, is considered by many to be the world's most powerful bird of prey. Unfortunately, opportunities to see it in the wild are limited as they are rare throughout most of their range and hard to spot in the canopy. Fortunately, you're in the Darién, and the area surrounding Reserva Natural Punta Patiño is home to a healthy nesting population. Although your chances of spotting one are still low, they're better here than anywhere else in Central America.

Harpy eagles are enormous birds with a wingspan of 2m and a height of 1.5m – they are immediately recognizable. Adults tend to have white breasts with a broad black chest band and faint leg barring as well as grey upper parts. They also have piercing yellow eyes that can be seen from the forest floor, as well as powerful yellow talons and a hooked bill.

Harpies rarely soar above the treetops, and usually hunt by rapidly attacking prey through the canopy. Monkeys are plucked from the foliage, unwary birds are taken from tree limbs and snakes are swept off the forest floor. However, the majority of the harpy's diet consists of sloths, which are extremely vulnerable basking in the morning sun. A harpy will sit nearby – sometimes for days – until it is hungry, and then snatch the sloth at its leisure.

Anyone who has had the privilege to watch a harpy eagle hunt will tell you that it is simply awesome. A harpy can hunt a large male howler, crush the monkey's skull with her talons and carry it back to the nest unhindered. With massive claws as big as a grizzly bear's, and legs as thick as a man's wrist, the harpy is nature's Terminator.

With females weighing up to 9kg, such a large predator obviously has high energy requirements. As a result, harpies hunt all but the largest forest mammals. As an apex predator (like the jaguar), the harpy eagle probably never occurred in high densities, though deforestation has removed much of its prey base and its habitat. Furthermore, its habit of perching for long spells, even when people approach, makes it vulnerable to poachers.

Punta Patiño, lodging, food and activities. This can also be combined with a trip up the Río Mogué to the Emberá village of Mogué and a guided hike to a harpy eagle's nest. Punta Patiño is also a destination on Ancon's highly recommended two-week Darién Explorer Trek.

Mogué

Mogué is an Emberá village on the banks of the Río Mogué, roughly between Punta Patiño and La Palma. Villagers here are keen to show off their culture and lifestyles, and extremely adept at finding harpy-eagle nests in the surrounding jungle. Though Mogué is set up for tourism, it remains a traditional village, seeing fewer visitors than Emberá villages in Panamá Province and Guna villages in the Comarca. Everything done for the benefit of tourists certainly has a price tag, but the atmosphere is extremely relaxed and there is no pressure to buy crafts, give gifts or spend money.

Visitors can watch traditional dances, purchase crafts or get body painted with jagua juice. Like henna, the tattoo lasts for up to two weeks. Although just a faint design will appear immediately on your skin, the next morning you'll be about as blue as a Smurf.

Visitors may sleep in a tent underneath the communal gathering hall, or string up a jungle hammock (bring your own). A private outhouse and cold shower are unlocked when tour groups arrive. Although the village sounds are part of the whole experience, light sleepers may want to bring earplugs.

Getting There & Away

Several outfitters and guides offer overnight excursions to Mogué. In the future, there may be access via paved road.

Río Sambú

The mouth of the wide, brown Río Sambú is 1½ hours by boat south of Punta Patiño (usually accessed via La Palma). Fortitude is a must, but a trip up the Sambú offers true adventure while you glide past spectacular jungle and traditional Emberá and Wounaan villages.

Be warned, though, that it's not everyone's cup of tea. If riding in a boat laden with leaking gasoline cans bothers you, you should probably pass on the Sambú – you'll need to bring several large containers of gas from La Palma (where you'll arrange boats and guides for this section of the trip) to fuel the canoe you hire upriver.

Getting There & Away

If you speak Spanish, boats and guides can be hired in La Palma, but once you reach the Río Sambú, you will need to hire another guide and a separate, smaller *piragua* (long canoe) to navigate the narrow, shallow sections upriver. In rainy season, the river is navigable by *piragua* all the way to Pavarandó, the most inland of the eight indigenous communities on the Sambú.

Sambú

Riverside Sambú is an interesting stop, populated by Emberá and *cimarrón* people (the ancestors of the latter escaped the slave trade by living in the jungle). Urban by Darién standards, it has an airstrip, a hospital and a pay phone. Given the ease of flying in here, it makes a good launching point for visiting riverside Emberá and Wounaan communities and absorbing the slow jungle pace.

From Sambú, visitors can plan enjoyable trips to Puerto Indio (with permission from the Emberá and Wounaan) and visit petroglyphs or mangrove forests. Bocaca Verano is a lagoon with crocodiles and prolific birdlife. Local guide Lupicinio, found in front of Sambú Hause hotel, guides hiking excursions to see harpy eagles and tours to Bocaca Verano in dry season.

For boat tours, **Juan Murillo** (☎6940-7765; gulf fishing US$90) takes visitors fishing in the Golfo de San Miguel in his 75-horsepower boat.

Sleeping & Eating

The simple lodging options here can be difficult to arrange in advance.

Mi Lindo Sueño HOTEL **$**
(☎333-2512; r without bathroom US$15) A perfectly acceptable option, sitting alongside the airstrip. Rooms have fans. Note that the phone number is that of a public phone outside the hotel.

Sambú Hause GUESTHOUSE **$$**
(☎6672-9452, 268-6905; www.sambuhausedarienpanama.com; s/d incl meals US$75/125) The only jungle B&B around, Sambú House is an American-owned, attractive yellow clapboard run by friendly Mabel. Cozy but simple, this might be the only place to get pancake breakfasts in the Darién. You can also arrange cultural tours here.

Comidas Benedicta PANAMANIAN **$**
(meals US$4) You can get cheap and tasty meals at Comidas Benedicta, where US celebrity chef Anthony Bourdain dined when in Sambú.

Getting There & Away

At the time of writing, there were only charter flights to Sambú. A *panga* (small motorboat) from Puerto Quimba (US$24) goes to Sambú in the early morning on Monday, Wednesday and Friday, with one stop in La Palma.

Round-trips are not scheduled far in advance; ask around to confirm a date. From Puerto Quimba there is a bus service to Metetí (US$2) and on to Panama City.

TURTLE VOLUNTEERING

From mid-July through December, throngs of marine turtles make a pilgrimage to this wild coast to lay eggs where they were born. The presence of avid predators – including humans – is threatening this natural cycle and turtle populations have been dwindling.

Grupo de Conservación de Tortugas de Jaqué (opposite) has spent the past decade patrolling beaches and releasing hatchlings, a daily task that takes place both late at night and in the dawn hours. Now it is looking for help.

The five species found along this coast are the olive ridley, the endangered greenback, the endangered hawksbill, the endangered leatherback and the critically endangered Kemp's ridley. Volunteers patrol the beach, transfer eggs to a safe nursery until their hatching and help in their release. From October to February hundreds of turtles are released in the dawn hours. It's a magnificent experience to take part in.

October marks the height of the season. In low season, volunteers can assist with community outreach or work with mangrove reforestation along the Río Jaqué.

WORTH A TRIP

DEEP SEA FISHING DELUXE

Overlooking Bahía Piña near the southern tip of the Darién, legendary fishing lodge **Tropic Star Lodge** (☎in USA 800-682-3424; www.tropicstar.com; Bahía Piña; 3-day & 4-night non-fishing/fishing package per person from US$2280/3550; ❄@≋), boasts the most International Game Fish Association (IGFA) world records. No expense has been spared in creating this remote luxury lodge with first-class facilities. With everything done right, there's a sense of camaraderie among guests, many of whom are professional sportfishers and celebrities.

Standalone cabins have modern conveniences and satellite TV. Immaculate grounds with dramatic ocean views invite guests to lounge in manicured gardens, wade in the palm-shaded pool and dine on the catch of the day in the sophisticated bar-restaurant. There's even a 'palace' built by a Texas oil tycoon as his home away from home in 1961.

Of course, all of this shouldn't distract you from why you're really here – to fish. The lodge's fleet of 31ft Bertrams, the Ferraris of sportfishing boats, is outfitted with top-notch gear and staffed by some of the best captains in the world.

Packages include the use of a boat with captain and mate, all meals, and fishing tackle and leaders. Rates vary according to the number of people on the boat. Costs increase in winter (December to March). Tropic Star arranges charter flights (for an extra fee) to and from Panama City.

PACIFIC COAST

With rough surf, jungle rivers and deep wilderness, the Pacific coast of the Darién is barely a destination, save for hard-core deep-sea fishers and the odd adventurer. There is little here in terms of infrastructure, but it is a fascinating area that merits preservation.

Jaqué

POP 2400

On a pretty coastline pounded by waves, Jaqué is a sleepy village with no road access. Concrete sidewalks run down the middle of streets and there's a diverse population of Afro-Darienitas, Emberá and Wounaan. Marine turtles come to nest here seasonally and volunteers can get involved (see box opposite) during the seasonal *arribadas* (arrivals).

A large SENAFRONT (border control) presence flags the town's proximity to the Colombian border, though there is no official border crossing here. Check in with SENAFRONT upon arrival and departure; it's a large concrete building near the river port.

There are small markets (only some sell alcohol) and cheap, informal restaurants around town. On the beach, the cute cabins with kitchenette at **Marie Village** (☎6003-8468; per person incl breakfast US$20) are the best digs in town, though they're a good 10-minute walk to the center. Mariela is a great host, but guests should be comfortable with dogs. Dinner is available with advance notice.

Activities & Tours

Grupo de Conservación de Tortugas de Jaqué VOLUNTEERING
(Colegio de la Tierra; ☎6047-2373; www.colegiodelatierra.org) This grassroots organization made up of concerned Jaqué residents was able to save over 14,000 marine-turtle hatchlings in 2015. From October to February hundreds of hatchlings are released back into the wild. The rest of the year, volunteers can assist with community outreach, or mangrove reforestation along the Río Jaqué. Dorm accommodation including three meals is available for US$35.

Ovedio Cardenas BOAT TOUR
(☎6124-8123; 1hr boat ride US$45) Boat driver Ovedio speaks Spanish and can take visitors upstream to see Bioquera, a Wounaan village where you can purchase tagua carvings and handmade baskets. Available mostly weekends.

Getting There & Away

From Panama City, Air Panama (p245) flies to and from Jaqué (US$84) on Friday and Monday.

Understand Panama

Panama Today

As Panama cuts the ribbon on one of the world's most ambitious transportation projects, the mood is mixed. Will the Panama Canal expansion turn out to be a sound investment? The country is already in the hole for its recent spending spree. Though modernity rules, dig a little and you will find that challenges persist for the underserved population of indigenous groups and the rural poor. Also working through conflicting ambitions of conservation and growth, this is a country at the crossroads.

Best on Film

Hands of Stone (2016; dir. Jonathan Jakubowicz) The anticipated biopic of boxing legend Roberto Durán, with Robert De Niro.

Quantum of Solace (2008; dir. Marc Forster) Agent 007 is out for revenge, with scenes filmed in Casco Viejo.

The Tailor of Panama (2001; dir. John Boorman) A reluctant spy lets loose.

Best in Print

Getting to Know the General (Graham Greene; 1984) A portrait of General Omar Torrijos by his longtime friend.

Empire of Blue Water (Stephen Talty; 2008) An intriguing pirate history; a *New York Times* bestseller.

Panama (Carlos Ledson Miller; 2007) Explores the turmoil of the Noriega years with snapshots of history.

Confessions of an Economic Hitman (John Perkins; 2005) Investigates the shadowy world of overseas business.

Best Food Websites

www.degustapanama.com
www.panamarestaurantweek.com
www.andresmadrigal.com
http://ecofarmspanama.org

The Expanding Canal

The fastest-growing economy in Latin America, Panama owes much of its prosperity to the Panama Canal. The 80km belt of locks links the Atlantic to the Pacific, and east with west. In the last century, the canal has cast the isthmus as the western hub of global commerce. Each year, more than four million containers traverse it, their hulls filled with everything from bananas and grains to oil, lumber and shiny new cars. You may have never visited Panama, but it is quite likely that both the fruit in your juice and the accessories in your pocket once did.

One of the world's largest transportation projects, the Panama Canal's US$17 billion expansion will double the capacity and triple the traffic in the canal by digging deeper to accommodate bigger vessels and adding a third lane. The canal already hauls in US$2 billion annually.

A financial boon for Panama, the expanded Panama Canal is expected to be completed on the heels of the canal's 100-year anniversary – slightly behind schedule. The canal is also expected to shift trade patterns, upsetting the prosperity of North American west-coast ports. As the project nears completion – though way over budget – Panamanian hopes are high.

Detractors fear that the project – along with the tab for the new US$1.2 billion Panama City subway system, the US$200 billion beltway in Bahía de Panamá, a new international airport and other projects – will shackle Panama with serious debt. Or is the infrastructure upgrade a savvy investment? With the supersizing of merchant ships worldwide, and Nicaragua starting its own big dig, the gamble is necessary if Panama is to remain a key shipping hub.

Sitting on Green Riches

Although the canal has defined Panama for the last century, it's what lies just beyond this engineering marvel that could define the next 100 years. A third of the country is set aside as protected areas and national parks, and the culture and customs of Panama's indigenous populations remain largely intact. Yet visitor numbers are nowhere near those of neighboring Costa Rica. Many outsiders assume that Panama is all about its capital and commerce. But while Panama races toward rapid-fire development, the resources it has always had (and often neglected) have started to attract attention.

Panama's intriguing history, which includes the voyages of Columbus and the plunders of 17th-century pirates, may be its main intact treasure. One of the most biodiverse places in the world, the country is a refuge for an incredible array of species. Its first-rate nature destinations range from lush, untapped rainforests to solitary beaches and uninhabited isles. Is it packaged and tourist ready? Not exactly. Yet many travelers will find that that's precisely its charm.

Dividing the Pie

There is a sharp contrast between Panama's urban and rural counterparts. Panama City is all sparkling skyscrapers, cement mixers and scaffolds, yet an hour outside of the capital, indigenous Emberá paddle dugout canoes. The modern and ancient somehow coexist, but each year there is friction at their boundaries.

While poverty has reduced by 10% in the last decade, Panama still has the second-worst income distribution in Latin America. Many provincial residents have relocated to Panama City in search of opportunity. City dwellers blame the most recent influx for increasing traffic, pollution and crime. Yet, with record low unemployment and robust foreign investment, Panama has remained dogged in its attempts to unlock its potential. It's also very good at putting its best foot forward. Stroll through the renovated historic Castro Viejo, ride the new subway or drive the ultra-modern coastal beltway and you might think all is right with the world.

There is hope that the country's investments in infrastructure will pay off. But with US$23 billion of national debt, many Panamanians are weary of the national 'spend now, pay later' approach. More and more, disgruntled citizens have been protesting about the privatization of public resources, high-level corruption and unchecked development. For Panama, it's time to put the people first.

POPULATION: **3.7 MILLION**

AREA: **75,420 SQ KM**

GDP GROWTH: **6.2%**

INFLATION: **2.6%**

UNEMPLOYMENT: **4.5%**

if Panama were 100 people

65 would be Mestizo
12 would be Indigenous
9 would be African descent
7 would be European descent
7 would be of mixed African and Spanish descent

belief systems

(% of population)

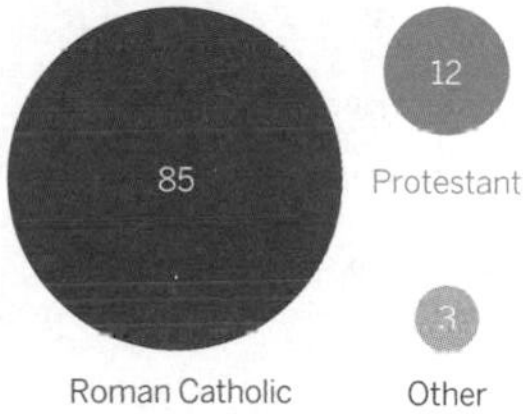

population per sq km

History

The waistline of the Americas, Panama has played a strategic role in the history of the western hemisphere, from hosting the biological exchange of species to witnessing clashes between cultures. Once an overland trade route linking ancient Peru and Mexico, post–Colombian conquest Panama became the conduit for exported Inca treasures. Set amid two oceans, transit is a longtime theme here. As the Panama Railroad once brought prospectors to the California gold rush, the Panama Canal has become the roaring engine of global commerce.

Lost Panama

The coastlines and rainforests of Panama have been inhabited by humans for at least 10,000 years, and it's estimated that several dozen indigenous groups, including the Guna, the Ngöbe-Buglé, the Emberá, the Wounaan and the Naso were living on the isthmus prior to the Spanish arrival. However, the tragedy of Panama is that, despite its rich cultural history, there are virtually no physical remains of these great civilizations.

Unlike the massive pyramid complexes found throughout Latin America, the ancient towns and cities of Panama vanished in the jungles, never to be seen by the eyes of the modern world. However, tales of lost cities still survive in the oral histories of Panama's indigenous communities, and there is hope among Panamanian archaeologists that a great discovery may yet be made. Considering that much of Panama consists of inaccessible mountains and rainforests, perhaps these dreams aren't so fanciful.

Panama: Four Hundred Years of Dreams and Cruelty by David A Howarth chronicles the history of the isthmus from Balboa's 1513 exploration through to 1964, with scintillating tales of conquistadors and buccaneers.

What is known about pre-Columbian Panama is that early inhabitants were part of an extensive trading zone that extended as far south as Peru and as far north as Mexico. Archaeologists have uncovered exquisite gold ornaments and unusual life-size stone statues of human figures as well as distinctive types of pottery and *metates* (stone platforms that were used for grinding corn).

Panama's first peoples also lived beside both oceans, and fished in mangrove swamps, estuaries and coral reefs. Given the impact that fishing has had on the lives of isthmians, it seems only fitting that the country's name is derived from an indigenous word meaning 'abundance of fish.'

TIMELINE

11,000 BC

The first humans occupy what is now Panama, and their populations quickly flourish thanks to the rich resources found along both the Pacific and Atlantic coastlines.

2500 BC

Panama is home to some of the first pottery-making villages in the Americas, including those of the Monagrillo culture, dating from 2500 to 1700 BC.

100 BC

Panama becomes part of an extensive trade network of gold and other goods that involves many disparate civilizations and extends from Mesoamerica to the Andes.

New World Order

In 1501 the discovery of Panama by Spanish explorer Rodrigo de Bastidas marked the beginning of the age of conquest and colonization in the isthmus. However, it was his first mate, Vasco Núñez de Balboa, who was to be immortalized in the history books, following his discovery of the Pacific Ocean 12 years later.

On his fourth and final voyage to the New World in 1502, Christopher Columbus went ashore in present-day Costa Rica and returned from the encounter claiming to have seen 'more gold in two days than in four years in Spain.' Although his attempts to establish a colony at the mouth of the Río Belén failed due to fierce local resistance, Columbus petitioned the Spanish Crown to have himself appointed governor of Veraguas, the stretch of shoreline from Honduras to Panama.

The Sack of Panamá: Sir Henry Morgan's Adventures on the Spanish Main by Peter Earle details the Welsh pirate's looting of Panamá in 1671.

Following Columbus' death in 1506, King Ferdinand appointed Diego de Nicuesa to settle the newly claimed land. In 1510 Nicuesa followed Columbus' lead and once again tried to establish a Spanish colony at Río Belén. However, local resistance was once again enough to beat back Spanish occupation, and Nicuesa was forced to flee the area. Leading a small fleet with 280 starving men aboard, the weary explorer looked upon a protected bay 23km east of present-day Portobelo and exclaimed: *'¡Paremos aquí, en nombre de Dios!'* ('Let us stop here, in the name of God!'). Thus was named the town of Nombre de Dios, one of the first Spanish settlements in the continental New World.

The famous crossing of the isthmus included 1000 indigenous slaves and 190 Spaniards, including Francisco Pizarro, who would later conquer Peru.

Much to the disappointment of Columbus' conquistador heirs, gold was not abundant in Panama. Add tropical diseases, inhospitable terrain and less than welcoming natives to the mix, and it's easy to see why Nombre de Dios failed several times during its early years. However, a bright moment in Spanish exploration came in 1513 when Balboa heard rumors about a large sea and a wealthy, gold-producing civilization across the mountains of the isthmus – almost certainly, these rumors referred to the Inca empire of Peru. Driven by equal parts ambition and greed, Balboa scaled the Continental Divide, and on September 26, 1513, he became the first European to set eyes on the Pacific Ocean. Keeping up with the European fashion of the day, Balboa immediately claimed the ocean and all the lands it touched for the king of Spain.

The Empire Expands

In 1519 a cruel and vindictive Spaniard named Pedro Arias de Ávila (or Pedrarias, as many of his contemporaries called him) founded the city of Panamá on the Pacific side, near where Panama City stands today. The governor is best remembered for such acts as ordering the beheading of Balboa in 1517 on a trumped-up charge of treason, as well as ordering

At one time the Panama Railroad was the highest-priced stock on the New York Stock Exchange, at US$295 a share.

1501

Spaniard Rodrigo de Bastidas becomes the first European to see Panama; Christopher Columbus arrives a year later and explores Bocas, coastal Veraguas and Portobelo.

1506

Christopher Colombus dies and Diego de Nicuesa is appointed to settle the territory known as Veraguas.

1513

Searching for a city of gold, Vasco Núñez de Balboa leads a grueling overland expedition and is the first European explorer to see the Pacific Ocean.

1519

Pedro Arias de Ávila (Pedrarias) founds the city of Panamá, which becomes a major transit point for gold plundered from Peru, packed overland to the Pacific coast and transferred by galleon to Spain.

Heat, starvation and botfly infestations were just some of the challenges troops faced in the US Army's disastrous 1854 Darién expedition, chronicled by Todd Balf in *The Darkest Jungle*.

murderous attacks against the indigenous population, whom he roasted alive or fed to dogs when the opportunity arose.

Despite his less than admirable humanitarian record, Pedrarias established Panamá as an important Spanish settlement, a commercial center and a base for further exploration, including the conquest of Peru. From Panamá, vast riches including Peruvian gold and Oriental spices were transported across the isthmus by foot to the town of Venta de Cruces, and then by boat to Nombre de Dios via the Río Chagres. Vestiges of this famous trade route, which was known as the Sendero Las Cruces (Las Cruces Trail), can still be found throughout Panama.

As the Spaniards profited from the wealth of plundered civilizations, the world began to notice the prospering colony, especially the English privateers lurking in coastal waters. In 1572 Sir Francis Drake destroyed Nombre de Dios and set sail for England with a galleon laden with Spanish gold. It was during this expedition that Drake climbed a high tree in the mountains, thus becoming the first Englishman to set eyes on the Pacific.

Hoping to stave off further ransacking and pillaging, the Spanish built large stone fortresses at Portobelo and Fuerte San Lorenzo. However, these fortifications weren't enough to stop the Welsh buccaneer Sir Henry Morgan from overpowering Fuerte San Lorenzo and sailing up the Río Chagres in 1671. After crossing the length of the isthmus, Morgan destroyed the city of Panamá, made off with its entire treasure and arrived back on the Caribbean coast with 200 mules loaded with loot.

After Panamá burnt to the ground, the Spanish rebuilt the city a few years later on a cape several kilometers west of its original site. The ruins of the old settlement, now known as Panamá Viejo, as well as the colonial city of Casco Viejo, are both located within the city limits of present-day Panama City.

SALVAGING SUNKEN GALLEONS

During the period of colonization between the 16th and 18th centuries, Spanish galleons left home carrying goods to the colonies and returned laden with gold and silver mined in Colombia, Peru and Mexico. During these years, literally thousands of ships – not only Spanish but also English, French, Dutch and pirate, and those carrying African slaves – foundered, overcome by pirates or hurricanes, in the green-blue waters of the Caribbean.

Often great storms wiped out entire fleets, resulting in a tremendous loss of lives and cargo. The frequency of shipwrecks spurred the Spaniards to organize operations to recover sunken cargo. By the 17th century, Spain maintained salvage flotillas in the ports of Portobelo, Havana and Veracruz. These fleets awaited news of shipwrecks and then proceeded immediately to the wreck sites, where the Spaniards used Caribbean and Bahamian divers, and later African slaves, to scour sunken vessels and the sea floor around them.

1671

Henry Morgan overpowers Fuerte San Lorenzo, sails up the Chagres and sacks the city of Panamá. After a crushing defeat, a new walled city is built in present-day Casco Viejo.

1698

A Scottish trading colony established in the Darién fails and plunges Scotland into economic depression. The financial losses heavily influence the union of Scotland with England in 1707.

1739

Following numerous pirate attacks, Spain finally abandons the short but perilous trans-isthmian trade route in favor of sailing all the way around Cape Horn in South America.

1821

Liberator Simón Bolívar leads the northern swath of South America to independence from Spain, and Panama joins the newly formed union of Gran Colombia.

British privateering didn't cease with the destruction of Panamá. In 1739 the final nail was hammered into the Spanish coffin when Admiral Edward Vernon destroyed the fortress of Portobelo. Humiliated by their defeat and robbed of one of their greatest defenses, the Spanish abandoned the Panamanian crossing in favor of sailing the long way around Cape Horn to the western coast of South America.

Spanish readers and history buffs should pick up *El Caballo de Oro* by Juan David Morgan, a novel about the building of the Panama Railroad in the quest for California gold.

The Empire Ends

Spain's costly Peninsular War with France from 1808 to 1814 – and the political turmoil, unrest and power vacuums that the conflict caused – led Spain to lose all its colonial possessions in the first third of the 19th century.

Panama gained independence from Spanish rule in 1821 and immediately joined Gran Colombia, a confederation of Colombia, Bolivia, Ecuador, Peru and Venezuela – a united Latin American nation that had long been the dream of Simón Bolívar. However, internal disputes led to the formal abolition of Gran Colombia in 1831, though fledgling Panama retained its status as a province of Colombia.

Birth of a Nation

Panama's future forever changed from the moment that the world's major powers learned that the isthmus of Panama was the narrowest point between the Atlantic and Pacific Oceans. In 1846 Colombia signed a treaty permitting the USA to construct a railway across the isthmus; it also granted it free transit and the right to protect the railway with military force. At the height of the California gold rush in 1849, tens of thousands of people traveled from the east coast of the USA to the west coast via Panama in order to avoid hostile Native Americans living in the central states. Colombia and Panama grew wealthy from the railway, and talks of an inter-oceanic canal across Central America began.

The idea of a canal across the isthmus was first raised in 1524 when Charles V of Spain ordered that a survey be undertaken to determine the feasibility of constructing such a waterway. In 1878, however, it was the French who received a contract from Colombia to build a canal. Still basking in the warm glory of the recently constructed Suez Canal in Egypt, French builder Ferdinand Marie de Lesseps brought his crew to Panama in 1881. Much like Napoleon before him, de Lesseps severely underestimated the task at hand, and over 22,000 workers died from yellow fever and malaria in less than a decade. By 1889, insurmountable construction problems and financial mismanagement had driven the company bankrupt.

The USA saw the French failure as a lucrative business opportunity that was ripe for the taking. Although it had been scouting locations for a canal in Nicaragua, the USA pressured the French to sell them their concessions.

The Panama Railroad website (www.panamarailroad.org) contains photographs, historical information and fascinating travelogues, including one written by Mark Twain in 1868.

1855

An estimated 12,000 laborers die, particularly from malaria and yellow fever, while building the Panama Railroad. Despite being only 76km long, the railroad requires 304 bridges and culverts.

1856

The Watermelon War becomes the first US intervention in Panama. Large-scale race riots result from white US soldiers mistreating locals. Marines eventually put down the conflict.

1878

The French are granted the right to build a canal though Panama. After malaria and yellow fever claim over 22,000 lives, the French declare bankruptcy and abandon the project.

1887

French post-impressionist painter Paul Gauguin moves to Isla Taboga after working with a French crew on the first Panama Canal attempt.

In 1903 de Lesseps' chief engineer, Philippe Bunau-Varilla, agreed to the sale, though the Colombian government promptly refused to accede to it.

In what would be the first of a series of American interventions in Panama, Bunau-Varilla approached the US government to back Panama if it declared its independence from Colombia. On November 3, 1903, a revolutionary junta declared Panama independent, and the US government immediately recognized the sovereignty of the country. Although Colombia sent troops by sea to try to regain control of the province, US battleships prevented them from reaching land. Colombia did not recognize Panama as a legitimately separate nation until 1921, when the USA paid Colombia US$25 million in 'compensation.'

Growing Pains

Following independence, Bunau-Varilla was appointed Panamanian ambassador to the USA and his first act in office paved the way for future American interventions in the region. Hoping to profit from the sale of the canal concessions to the USA, Bunau-Varilla arrived in Washington, DC, before Panama could assemble a delegation. On November 18, Bunau-Varilla and US Secretary of State John Hay signed the Hay–Bunau-Varilla Treaty, which gave the USA far more than had been offered in the original treaty. In addition to owning concessions to the canal, the USA was also granted 'sovereign rights in perpetuity over the Canal Zone,' an area extending 8km on either side of the canal, and a broad right of intervention in Panamanian affairs.

Despite opposition from the tardy Panamanian delegation as well as lingering questions about the treaty's legality, the treaty was ratified, ushering in an era of friction between the USA and Panama. Construction began again on the canal in 1904, and despite disease, landslides and harsh weather, the world's greatest engineering marvel was completed in only a decade. The first ship sailed through the canal on August 15, 1914.

Mountains were moved and 25,000 perished in the process. *Panama Fever* by Matthew Parker, makes real the magnitude of building the Panama Canal, documenting the imperial vision and the back-breaking work of the laborers from the West Indies.

In the years following the completion of the canal, the US military repeatedly intervened in the country's political affairs. In response to growing Panamanian disenchantment with frequent US interventions, the Hay–Bunau-Varilla Treaty was replaced in 1936 by the Hull–Alfaro Treaty. The USA relinquished its rights to use its troops outside the Canal Zone and to seize land for canal purposes, and the annual sum paid to Panama for use of the Canal Zone was raised. However, increased sovereignty was not enough to stem the growing tide of Panamanian opposition to US occupation. Anti-US sentiments reached boiling point in 1964 during a student protest that left 27 Panamanians dead and 500 injured. Today the event is commemorated as Día de Los Mártires (National Martyrs' Day).

As US influence waned, the Panamanian army grew more powerful. In 1968 the Guardia Nacional deposed the elected president and took control

1902
US President Theodore Roosevelt convinces the US Congress to take control of the abandoned French project. At the time, Colombia was in the midst of the Thousand Days' War.

1912
Isla de Coiba becomes a penal colony infamous for its brutality. It is closed in 2004 and now operates as a national park renowned for its biodiversity.

1914
The Panama Canal is finally completed after a decade of monumental effort, thanks to the work of 75,000 laborers, many thousands of whom perish during the construction.

1964
The riots of January 9 (Martyrs' Day) escalate tensions between Panama and the USA over occupation rights of the Canal Zone. Twenty Panamanian rioters are killed and more than 500 are wounded.

of the government. Soon after, the constitution was suspended, the national assembly was dissolved and the press was censored, while the Guardia's General Omar Torrijos emerged as the new leader. Torrijos' record is spotty. Though he plunged the country into debt as a result of a massive public-works program, Torrijos was successful in pressuring US President Jimmy Carter into ceding control of the canal to Panama. The Torrijos–Carter Treaty guaranteed full Panamanian control of the canal as of December 31, 1999, as well as a complete withdrawal of US military forces.

The US Army's School of the Americas, previously based in Panama, trained some of the worst human-rights abusers in Latin America – including Manuel Noriega. For information on the school's history visit www.soaw.org.

The Rise & Fall of Noriega

Still feeling triumphant from the recently signed treaty, Panama was unprepared for the sudden death of Torrijos in a plane crash in 1981. Two years later, Colonel Manuel Antonio Noriega seized the Guardia Nacional, promoted himself to general and made himself the de facto ruler of Panama. Noriega, a former head of Panama's secret police, a former CIA operative and a graduate of the School of the Americas, quickly began to consolidate his power. He enlarged the Guardia Nacional, significantly expanded its authority and renamed it the Panama Defense Forces. He also created a paramilitary 'Dignity Battalion' in every city, town and village, its members armed and ready to inform on any of their neighbors if they showed less than complete loyalty to the Noriega regime.

Things went from bad to worse in early 1987 when Noriega became the center of an international scandal. He was publicly accused of involvement in drug trafficking with Colombian cartels, murdering his opponents and rigging elections. Many Panamanians demanded Noriega's dismissal, protesting with general strikes and street demonstrations that resulted in violent clashes with the Panama Defense Forces. In February 1988 Panamanian President Eric Arturo Delvalle attempted to dismiss Noriega, though the general held on to the reins of power, deposing Delvalle and forcing him to flee Panama. Noriega subsequently appointed a substitute president who was more sympathetic to his cause.

Noriega's regime became an international embarrassment. In March 1988 the USA imposed economic sanctions against Panama, ending a preferential trade agreement, freezing Panamanian assets in US banks and refusing to pay canal fees. A few days after the sanctions were imposed, an unsuccessful military coup prompted Noriega to step up violent repression of his critics. After Noriega's candidate failed to win the presidential election in May 1989, the general declared the election null and void. Meanwhile, Guillermo Endara, the winning candidate, and his two vice-presidential running mates were badly beaten by some of Noriega's paramilitary Dignity Battalions, and the entire bloody scene was captured by a TV crew and broadcast internationally. A second failed coup in October 1989 was followed by even more repressive measures.

1968

The Panamanian army overthrows president-elect Arnulfo Arias after just 11 days in office. Exploiting the power gap, General Omar Torrijos becomes Panama's leader.

1977

The Torrijos–Carter Treaty is signed, allowing for the complete transfer of the canal and 14 US army bases from the USA to Panama by 1999.

1980

Panamanian boxer Roberto Durán beats Sugar Ray Leonard for the world welterweight championship.

1983

Following General Torrijos' death in a plane crash in 1981, former CIA operative Manuel Noriega rises to power and ushers in an era of repression.

On December 15, 1989, Noriega's legislature declared him president and his first official act of office was to declare war on the USA. The following day, an unarmed US marine dressed in civilian clothes was killed by Panamanian soldiers while exiting a restaurant in Panama City.

The US reaction was swift and unrelenting. In the first hour of December 20, 1989, Panama City was attacked by aircraft, tanks and 26,000 US troops in 'Operation Just Cause,' though the US media often labeled it 'Operation "Just 'cuz."' Although the intention of the invasion was to bring Noriega to justice and create a democracy, it left more than 2000 civilians dead and tens of thousands homeless, and destroyed entire tracts of Panama City.

On Christmas Day, the fifth day of the invasion, Noriega claimed asylum in the Vatican embassy. US forces surrounded the embassy and pressured the Vatican to release him, as entering the embassy would be considered an act of war against the tiny country. However, the USA memorably used that psychological tactic beloved of disgruntled teenagers, namely bombarding the embassy with blaring rock music (Van Halen and Metallica were among the selections). The embassy was also surrounded by mobs of angry Panamanians calling for the ousting of Noriega.

After 10 days of psychological warfare, the chief of the Vatican embassy persuaded Noriega to give himself up by threatening to cancel his asylum. Noriega surrendered to US forces on January 3 and was flown immediately to Miami, where he was convicted of conspiracy to manufacture and distribute cocaine. After his US prison sentence ended in 2007, he was extradited to Paris in April 2010. A retrial found Noriega guilty and sentenced him to seven years in prison, but he was conditionally released in order to serve 20 years in Panama, starting in December 2011, where he is incarcerated today.

Modern Woes

After Noriega's forced removal, Guillermo Endara, the legitimate winner of the 1989 election, was sworn in as president, and Panama attempted to put itself back together. The country's image and economy were in a shambles, and its capital had suffered damage not only from the invasion itself but also from the widespread looting that followed. Corruption scandals and internal fighting were rampant during the Endara administration. There was 19% unemployment and a lack of connection with the country's significant poor population, as the administration was peopled by wealthy businessmen. By the time Endara was voted out of office in 1994, his approval ratings were in single digits.

In the 1994 election, the fairest in recent Panamanian history, Ernesto Pérez Balladares became president. Under his direction, the Panamani-

Learn how one company's tropical meddling created a model for capiltalism in *Bananas: How the United Fruit Company Shaped the World* by Peter Chapman.

1988
US President Ronald Reagan invokes the International Emergency Economic Powers Act, freezing Panamanian government assets in US banks and prohibiting payments by American businesses to the Noriega regime.

1989
The US invades Panama and extradites Noriega to Miami, where he is later convicted on charges of conspiracy and drug trafficking. He is incarcerated until September 2007.

1994
Ernesto Pérez Balladares is sworn in as president after an internationally monitored election campaign. Balladares emphasizes his party's populist Torrijos roots rather than its former association with Noriega.

1999
Mireya Moscoso is elected Panama's first female president. The USA ends nearly a century of occupation by closing all of its military bases and turning over control of the canal.

an government implemented a program of privatization that focused on infrastructure improvements, health care and education. Although Pérez Balladares allocated unprecedented levels of funding, he was viewed as corrupt. In the spring of 1999, voters rejected his attempt to change constitutional limits barring a president from serving two consecutive terms.

In 1999 Mireya Moscoso – the widow of popular former president Arnulfo Arias, head of the conservative Arnulfista Party (PA) – took office and became Panama's first female leader. Moscoso's ambitious plans for reform were not realized. As Panama celebrated its centenary in 2003, unemployment rose to 18%. Moscoso was accused of wasteful spending – as parts of the country went without food, she paid US$10 million to bring the Miss Universe pageant to Panama. She was also accused of looking the other way during Colombian military incursions into the Darién. She left office in 2004 failing to fulfill even a single campaign promise.

Moscoso was followed by Martín Torrijos, a member of the Revolutionary Democratic Party (PRD) and the son of former leader Omar Torrijos. Although there has been much debate regarding the successes and failures of his administration, he did implement a number of fiscal reforms, including an overhaul of the nation's social-security system. His proposal to expand the Panama Canal was overwhelmingly approved in a national referendum on October 22, 2006.

Old Panama and Castilla Del Oro by CLG Anderson, is a narrative history of the Spanish discovery, conquest and settlement of Panama as well as the early efforts to build a canal.

Current Panama

On May 3, 2009, Panama bucked the Latin American leftist trend by electing conservative supermarket magnate Ricardo Martinelli president. Part of the conservative Democratic Change (CD) party, Martinelli was a pro-business choice who created an investment boom by slashing trade barriers and red tape. During his tenure, ambitious public projects like Central America's first subway system became the order of the day and Panama's 8% growth rate sparkled as the best in Latin America.

Eventually the honeymoon ended and the success story turned part pulp fiction, part political thriller. Martinell's former vice president and dark-horse opposition leader Juan Carlos Varela was elected president in 2014 on promises to play by the book and implement constitutional checks and balances. Martinelli faces charges of corruption in a US$45 million program to feed poor schoolchildren. There was also a wire-tapping scandal involving political foes. Remember those colossal infrastructure projects? Now US$1.2 billion of contracts have come under scrutiny and some project directors with government contracts have been arrested. Martinelli maintains his innocence from Miami, where he fled via private jet to a luxury condo that was made famous in the film *Scarface*.

In Panama, the future remains uncertain, but it is very unlikely to be dull.

For all things canal related visit www.pancanal.com, the official site, with historical information, photographs and even webcams of the canal in action.

2006

Seventy-eight per cent of Panamanian voters cast a 'yes' ballot in support of an expanded canal that could double its present capacity; expansion is under way.

2010

After Noriega finishes his US prison sentence, France indicts him on charges of money laundering, but before he can serve his seven-year term, he is extradited by Panama to serve a 20-year sentence there.

2014

Opposition leader Juan Carlos Varela is elected president on the back of promises to tame corruption; previous president Ricardo Martinelli flees to Miami while he is investigated in relation to various charges.

2016

Panama anticipates the inauguration of the US$17 billion canal expansion, which will triple container traffic to meet the growing needs of international shipping.

Panamanian Way of Life

At the crossroads of the Americas, the narrow isthmus of Panama bridges not only two continents but also two vastly different paradigms of Panamanian culture and society. Roughly one hour from the gleaming skyscrapers of Panama City, you can find an indigenous family paddling a dugout canoe. Sharp contradictions simply coexist in Panama. But when they clash it raises the question: what exactly is the Panamanian national character?

The National Psyche

Panamanian identity is in many ways elusive. Perhaps it's only natural given the many years that Panama has been the object of another country's meddling. From the US-backed independence of 1903 to the strong-armed removal of Noriega in 1989 – with half-a-dozen other interventions in between – the USA has left a strong legacy in the country.

Nearly every Panamanian has a relative or at least an acquaintance living in the USA, and parts of the country seem swept up in mall fever, with architectural inspiration straight out of North America. Panamanians (or at least the ones who can afford to) deck themselves out in US clothes, buy US-made cars and take their fashion tips straight from Madison Ave.

Others are quite reticent to embrace the culture from the north. Indigenous groups like the Emberá and Guna struggle to keep their traditions alive as more and more of their youth are lured into the Western lifestyles of the city. On the Península de Azuero, where there is a rich Spanish cultural heritage exemplified by traditional festivals, dress and customs, villagers raise the same concerns about the future of their youth.

Given the clash between old and new, it's surprising the country isn't suffering from a serious case of cognitive dissonance. However, the exceptionally tolerant Panamanian character weathers many contradictions – the old and the new, the grave disparity between rich and poor, and the stunning natural environment and its rapid destruction.

Much of the famous Panamanian tolerance begins in the family, which is the cornerstone of society and plays a role in nearly every aspect of a person's life. Whether among Guna sisters or Panama City's elite, everyone looks after each other. Favors are graciously accepted, promptly returned and never forgotten.

This mutual concern extends from the family into the community, and at times the whole country can seem like one giant extended community.

RESPONSIBLE TRAVEL

Traveling sensitively in Panama means being mindful of the environment around you. Try to patronize locally owned businesses and small businesses, and spend your money where it will go directly to the people working for it.

Don't support businesses that keep exotic pets. It's an offense to keep a parrot, toucan or macaw in a cage. In some restaurants you may see endangered species on the menu; avoid *tortuga* (sea turtle), *huevos de tortuga* (turtle eggs), *cazón* (shark), *conejo pintado* (paca), *ñeque* (agouti) and *venado* (deer).

In the political arena, the same names appear time and again, as nepotism is the norm rather than the exception. Unfortunately, this goes hand-in-hand with Panama's most persistent problem: corruption.

Panamanians view their leaders' fiscal and moral transgressions with disgust, and they are far from being in the dark about issues. Yet they accept things with patience and an almost fatalistic attitude. Outsiders sometimes view this as a kind of passivity, but it's all just another aspect of the complicated Panamanian psyche.

Lifestyle

In spite of the skyscrapers and gleaming restaurants lining the wealthier districts of Panama City, 26% of the country's population lives in poverty. It's a grim figure, though it actually represents an improvement from just five years ago, when a third of the population lived below the poverty line. Panama is chipping away at the problem, but improvement might not be fast enough for its residents. Indigenous people make up a growing proportion of Panama's poor, while other rural populations have improved their income with urban migration. Almost 67% of the population is now urban. Those hardest hit by poverty tend to be in the least-populated provinces: Darién, Bocas del Toro, Veraguas, Los Santos and Colón.

In the Emberá and Wounaan villages of the Darién, traditional living patterns persist much as they have for hundreds of years. The communities are typically made up of 30 to 40 *bohíos* (thatched-roof, stilted, open-sided dwellings), and they survive by means of subsistence agriculture, hunting, fishing and pastoralism. However, existence can be extremely difficult in these frontier villages – life expectancy is about 10 years below the national average and the majority of Emberá and Wounaan communities lack access to clean water and basic sanitation.

Today Panamanians who earn minimum wage make an average of US$2.50 per hour. A proposal in the national assembly would raise that amount by almost 9%. For the *campesinos* (farmers), life is hard. A subsistence farmer in the interior earns far below the national average of US$12,000 per year. Rural dwellings might consist of a simple cinder-block building, with a roof and four walls and perhaps a porch. Families have few possessions and every member assists with working the land or contributing to the household.

The middle and upper classes largely reside in Panama City environs, enjoying a level of comfort similar to their economic brethren in Europe and the USA. They live in large homes or apartments, have a maid, a car or two and, for the lucky few, a second home on the beach or in the mountains. Cell phones are *de rigueur*. Vacations are often enjoyed outside of the country in Europe or the USA. Most middle-class adults can speak some English and their children usually attend English-speaking schools.

Celebrations, weddings and family gatherings are a social outlet for rich and poor alike, and those with relatives in positions of power – nominal or otherwise – don't hesitate to turn to them for support.

Population

The majority of Panamanians (65%) are *mestizo*, which is generally a mix of indigenous and Spanish descent. Many non-black immigrants are also thrown into this category, including a sizable Chinese population – some people estimate that as much as 10% of the population is of Chinese ancestry. There are several other large groups: about 9% of Panamanians are of African descent, 7% of European descent, 7% of mixed African and Spanish descent, and 12% are indigenous. Generally, black Panamanians are mostly descendants of English-speaking West Indians, such as Jamaicans and Trinidadians, who were originally brought to Panama as laborers.

Formal marriage is rare outside the middle and upper classes. Some estimate that 60% of children are born to short-term unions.

A People Who Would Not Kneel: Panama, the United States and the San Blás Kuna by James Howe describes the struggles the Guna underwent in order to gain the independence they enjoy today.

Indigenous Groups

Of the several dozen native tribes that inhabited Panama when the Spanish arrived, only seven now remain. While indigenous culture is much more vibrant and present than in neighboring countries, an inordinately high percentage of the indigenous population lives in poverty. In the *comarcas* (autonomous regions), illiteracy runs between 10% and 30%. Access to health care and education is a serious issue.

Smaller indigenous populations include the Bokotá, who inhabit Bocas del Toro Province, and the Bribrí, found in Costa Rica and in Panama along the Talamanca reserve. Both of these groups maintain their own language and culture, but their numbers and political influence are less than for the larger groups.

Ngöbe-Buglé

Panama's largest indigenous group is the Ngöbe-Buglé (pronounced Nobay Boo-glAY), who number around 156,000 and occupy a *comarca* that spans the Chiriquí, Veraguas and Bocas del Toro Provinces. Similarly to the Guna, the Ngöbe-Buglé enjoy a high degree of political autonomy and have been successful in managing their lands and protecting their cultural identity. Unlike the Emberá and the Wounaan, the highland Ngöbe-Buglé have largely resisted outside cultural interventions, primarily because their communities are scattered among huge tracts of undeveloped land. In recent years, their youth has been increasingly heading to the cities for work, and missionaries have made numerous inroads in their attempt to convert the indigenous population to Christianity. Religion aside, the Ngöbe-Buglé continue to live much as they have always done by relying almost exclusively on subsistence agriculture.

The Guna

Perhaps the most well-known group in the West, due to their distinctive dress, is the Guna, who inhabit the Archipiélago de San Blás and run their native lands as a *comarca*. Regarded as having one of the largest degrees of autonomy in Latin America, the Guna are fiercely protective of their independence and routinely introduce new legislation to protect their lands from foreign cultural invasion. In recent years, this has resulted in barring foreigners from owning property in the *comarca*, imposing restrictions on tourism in San Blás and introducing standard fees for visitation, photography and video throughout the region. This tenacity has proved successful, as one of the highlights of visiting San Blás is witnessing firsthand the vibrancy of the Guna's unique culture.

In 2011 the Panamanian government recognized the Guna wish to change the official spelling of their name from Kuna to Guna, and also changed the spelling of Kuna Yala to Guna Yala, as the hard 'k' sound does not exist in the Guna language.

Emberá and Wounaan

The Emberá and Wounaan inhabit the jungle of the eastern Panamá Province and the Darién, and although the groups distinguish themselves from one another, the difference is more linguistic than cultural. Historically, both groups have eked out a living on the edges of the jungles through hunting, fishing, subsistence farming and rearing livestock, though rapid deforestation has reduced the extent of their traditional lands. Today the majority of Emberá and Wounaan inhabit the edges of the Darién and live on the fringes of the destruction wrought by loggers, farmers and ranchers. Narcotrafficking through the region from Colombia has further compromised their situation. An increasing number of communities are turning to tourism for survival, particularly in the Canal Zone, where traditional lifestyles are no longer feasible. There are also Emberá refugees from Colombia, who fled heavy fighting in the Chaco region by the thousands in early 2004.

The Naso

The Naso (Teribe) inhabit mainland Bocas del Toro and are largely confined to the Panamanian side of the binational Parque Internacional La Amistad. Unlike other indigenous population groups, the Naso do not have an independent *comarca* of their own, which has resulted in the rapid destruction of their cultural sovereignty in recent years. Another blow for them is the tremendous tourism potential of the international park, which has prevented the Panamanian government from coming to their aid. Today traditional villages are rapidly disappearing throughout the region and only a few thousand Naso remain. However, in an effort to ensure their cultural survival, a few villages have banded together to create an ecological center near the Wekso entrance to the park, which aims to draw more visitors to the region and employ more Naso as tourist guides.

Sports

Owing to the legacy of US occupation, baseball is the preferred pastime in Panama. This is indeed a rarity in Latin America, where *fútbol* (soccer) is normally the national craze. Panama has sent more players to the US big-league baseball teams than any other Central American country.

Although there are no professional teams in Panama, the amateur leagues host games in stadiums throughout the country. Panamanians have their preferred teams but are usually more interested in their favorite players in the US major leagues. A dozen Panamanian players currently play pro ball in the USA. (Try counting the Yankees caps you see around Panama City.) Mariano Rivera is a former record-setting Panamanian pitcher for the New York Yankees. Carlos Lee from Aguadulce was an outfielder for the Miami Marlins. Carlos Ruiz from Chiriquí is a catcher for the Philadelphia Phillies. Batting champ Rod Carew, another Panamanian star, was inducted into the Hall of Fame in 1991. Roberto Kelly, who played for the Yankees for many years, is also fondly remembered.

Boxing is another popular spectator sport and a source of pride to Panamanians (and Latin Americans) ever since Roberto Durán, a Panama City native and boxing legend, won the world championship lightweight title in 1972. He went on to become the world champion in the welterweight (1980), light middleweight (1983) and super middleweight (1989) categories. There are four Panamanians in the International Boxing Hall of Fame: Roberto Durán, Eusebio Pedroza, Ismael Laguna and Panama Al Brown. Currently, Panama also has three reigning world boxing champions.

Panama's first Olympic gold came in 2008 when Irving Saladino won the long jump in Beijing.

Multiculturalism

Panama has a rich mix of cultures, with immigrants from around the globe as well as a diverse indigenous population. Shortly after the Spanish arrived, slaves were brought from Africa to work in Panama's mines and perform grunt labor in the colony. Slaves that escaped set up communities in the Darién jungle, where their *cimarrones* (descendents) still live today. Subsequent waves of immigration coincided with the construction of both the Panama Railroad in 1850 and the Panama Canal – the French effort in the late 1800s and the American completion in the early 1900s. During these times, thousands of workers were brought to Panama from the West Indies, particularly Jamaica and Trinidad.

Molas are beautiful, elaborate patches of embroidery. To learn about the culture, history and sewing of world-famous Guna *molas*, visit www.molasfrompanama.com.

Just outside Panama City, the City of Knowledge (Ciudad del Saber; http://ciudaddelsaber.org) is a sustainable city and a campus for international nonprofits. Learn more about this unique spot on its website.

Workers also came from the East Indies and from China to labor – and many to die – on these massive projects. The majority of the Chinese settled in Panama City, and today you can see two Chinatowns (one is near Casco Viejo, the other is in El Dorado). There are two daily Chinese newspapers and even a private school for Chinese. The term for Chinese Panamanians is 'Once' (pronounced '*awn*-say').

Mixed-race offspring – and mixed marriages – are increasingly common. Among the East Indian community, Hindus complain that their culture is disappearing: where once it was common for young men to return to India to find a bride, this is no longer the case. This intermixing of races happens across the nation, although indigenous groups and whites – representing each end of the economic scale – are least likely to marry outside of their group.

Although Panama is a much more racially tolerant society than many other Latin American countries, there is distrust among groups, particularly between indigenous groups and *mestizos*. This stems largely from *mestizo* land grabs – by loggers, ranchers and settlers – that have pushed indigenous communities off their lands. Indigenous communities also view the government as corrupt and largely indifferent to their plight – and to some extent, they are correct.

Class distinctions also persist. While politicians from the president on down take pride in mingling with the public and maintaining some semblance of a classless society, the *rabiblancos* (whites) control the majority of the wealth and have nearly all the power.

Class divisions and racism exist in Panama. Generally, members of a certain class marry only members of that same class. And at the Union Club (*the* social club of Panama City), memberships are rarely given to people with dark skin.

Racism is abhorrent no matter where it's found, but racism in Panama is mild compared to the brand found in many other countries. For all its inequities, Panama is closer to the ideal in this respect than most developed nations.

Media

Panama has a number of daily newspapers, ranging from sensationalist rags to astute independents. However, in Panama City, the most popular form of mass media is television. Mainstream broadcast views tend to represent business and the oligarchy, which is for the most part what urban viewers want to hear.

Outside the capital, however, radio is the most important medium. There are approximately 90 radio stations on the dial, though most Panamanians have two or three favorites – morning talk shows are particularly popular and represent a wide range of viewpoints.

The Martinelli government took media criticism hard, even pursuing imprisonment and fines for journalists for 'offending the honor' of a public figure. This is a legacy of Noriega, who used such laws to suppress the voices of critics. International human-rights and press-advocacy organizations have decried Panama as supporting one of the most repressive regimes in the Americas because of the various 'gag laws' that bureaucrats can use to stifle opposition.

Check out the *Panama Digest* (www.thepanamadigest.com) for 'unfiltered' lifestyle, tourism, crime, development and environment news in English.

In the current media environment, underfunding is an issue. There's a lamentable lack of investigative reporting and broad-spectrum coverage on controversial issues. Still, many young Panamanians in particular have turned to the web to inform and be informed. For an alternative, Spanish-language view on national issues, interesting sites include www.kaosenlared.net and the environment-focused www.ciampanama.org. For perspectives in English, check out www.thepanamanews.com and www.latinpost.com.

Religion

Religion in Panama can best be observed by walking the streets of the capital. Among the scores of Catholic churches, you'll find breezy Anglican churches filled with worshippers from the West Indies, synagogues, mosques, a shiny Greek Orthodox church, an impressive Hindu temple and a surreal Baha'i House of Worship (the headquarters for Latin America).

Freedom of religion is constitutionally guaranteed in Panama, although the preeminence of Roman Catholicism is also officially recognized, with 85% of the population describing themselves as Catholic. Schoolchildren have the option to study theology, though it is not compulsory. Protestant denominations account for the remaining 15% of the population; although a recognizable population of Muslims and Baha'i also exists, and approximately 3000 Jews (many of them recent immigrants from Israel), 24,000 Buddhists and 9000 Hindus also live in Panama.

The various indigenous tribes of Panama have their own belief systems, although these are fading quickly due to the influence of Christian missionaries. As in other parts of Latin America, the evangelical movement is spreading like wildfire.

Although Catholics are the majority, only about 20% of them attend church regularly. The religious orders aren't particularly strong in Panama either – only about 25% of Catholic clergy are Panamanian, while the rest are foreign missionaries.

Most visitors go to Guna Yala, and they might see an Emberá or Wounaan village outside the capital, but what about Panama's other indigenous groups? Learn more about the Ngöbe-Buglé at http://comarcangobebugle.com.

Women in Panama

Women enjoy more opportunities in Panama than they do in most other Latin American countries. Panama even had a female president, Mireya Moscoso, whose term ended in 2004. At the forefront of the country's political arena is the PNF (Feminist National Party), which was founded in 1923 and is one of the oldest feminist parties in Latin America. Historically, the PNF has been strongly critical of the male-dominated government and has secured numerous social reforms for women and children. In 1941 the PNF helped women secure the right to vote, while in 1981 it helped ratify the law that eliminated all forms of discrimination against women. The Family Code, adopted in 1995, upholds the equal rights of women and abolished discriminatory clauses in the code of 1917.

In spite of these advances, women still face many obstacles in Panamanian society. Machismo and gross stereotypes are more prevalent in rural areas than in urban ones, but even in the cities women have to face lower wages and sexual harassment, and they are nearly twice as likely to be unemployed. Although women make up nearly half the workforce, they remain underrepresented in positions of power and in public service, with 19% representation in parliament.

Overall, women are having fewer children and are having them later in life. Many postpone motherhood to enter the workplace – a pattern that also exists in Europe and the USA. Panama has a growing number of single mothers, particularly in the lower income bracket. This problem is compounded by the facts that women have no right to an abortion (it's illegal in Panama) and that the teenage-pregnancy rate is high. As the legal age for marriage for girls is 14 (for boys it's 16), teenage marriage is still prevalent. The average age for women to marry in Panama is 22; at the same time, they are expected to work and help support the household.

In indigenous communities, women face many hardships, including poor access to health care and a low level of prenatal care. Prevailing stereotypes also mean that girls are less likely to attend school – among indigenous populations, more than half of women are illiterate, compared to one-third of men. Women also enter motherhood much earlier than their *mestizo* counterparts and bear more children.

Move over, Brooklyn: coworking stations, where creative professionals convene with wi-fi and a comfortable shared space, are popping up in Panama City (http://cascostation.com).

Music

While Panamanians may have an inordinate degree of affection for '80s rock, there is far more diversity at work in this small country – it helps to have a population of many cultures. From West Indian calypso to jazz, salsa, electronica, reggaeton and rock 'n' roll, music is always drifting out of taxis and apartment windows and into your experience.

Salsa

With blaring brass horns, the swish of skirts and pulsing rhythms, salsa music is the very air one breathes in the Latin Caribbean. And Panama is home to the biggest icon of them all: renowned salsa singer Rubén Blades. Raised in Panama City, Blades has had several international hits, has appeared in a few motion pictures and once even ran for president – he finished third.

Salsa has traditionally been the most popular music in Panama, but live salsa has become harder to come by, given the current popularity of reggaetón (known here as *plena*).

El Salsero: Rubén Blades

Salsa singer, songwriter, lawyer, actor and politician Rubén Blades was born on July 16, 1948, and raised in a middle-class neighborhood in Panama City. As a songwriter, Blades is revered for bringing lyrical sophistication to salsa and creating intelligent dance music. His 1978 hit 'Pedro Navaja' still remains the biggest-selling single in salsa history. Today his music continues to be incredibly popular in Panama, throughout Latin America and in the West. After a failed attempt at the Panamanian presidency in 1994, Blades served as the minister for tourism under President Martín Torrijos.

A case study in Panamanian versatility, Blades also personifies the love-hate relationship between Panama and the USA. Blades inherited musical talent from his mother, a Cuban immigrant who played the piano and sang on the radio, and his father, a police detective who played the bongos. Inspired by doo-wop singing, Blades began singing North American music in his early teens. However, the political upheaval in Panama during the mid-1960s made Blades increasingly patriotic. For a brief period he refused to sing in any language other than Spanish.

Blades has not shied away from politically charged lyrics. In 1980 he became embroiled in controversy over his song 'Tiburon,' which used a shark metaphor to describe American political and military intervention in the Caribbean. It was eventually banned on Miami radio. In the '80s Blades experimented with a fusion of Latin, rock, reggae and Caribbean music while simultaneously completing a masters degree in international law at Harvard University and breaking into Hollywood.

The same year he formed Los Seis de Solar, Blades got his first acting role in the film *The Last Fight* (1983). Blades' character, a singer-turned-boxer, seeks to win a championship against a fighter portrayed by real-life world-champion boxer Salvador Sánchez. In the years to follow, Blades appeared in a string of movies, including *The Milagro Beanfield War* (1988), *The Two Jakes* (1990), *Mo' Better Blues* (1990), *The Devil's Own* (1997) and *Cradle Will Rock* (1999). However, his most memorable performances were in Paul Simon's Broadway musical *The Capeman* (1997) and in the cult movie *Once Upon a Time in Mexico* (2003).

After a mediocre stint in national politics as minister for tourism, Blades returned to the music scene, rapping with Puerto Rican sensation Calle 13 in 'La Perla,' just to keep it real. But perhaps he hasn't quite recovered from the political bug. Last we heard, he was considering running for president of Panama in 2019.

For a heads-up on new Latin music beyond the mainstream, including Panamanian artists, check out the weekly US-based radio program *Alt. Latino* www.npr.org/sections/altlatino.

Jazz

Jazz came to Panama from the USA and found a welcoming home: it can be heard in several Panamanian clubs. Composer Danilo Pérez is widely acclaimed by American and European jazz critics. He has recorded with many greats from around the world and now serves on the faculty of the Berklee College of Music in Boston (USA).

Reggaetón & Beyond

These days reggaetón permeates all social levels in Panama. Like rap, reggaetón spread from the urban poor to conquer all social strata, though at its heart it's a youth trend. Key artists include Danger Man, who died in gang violence; balladeer Eddie Lover; and the artist known as Flex, who has also been very successful in Mexico. Alt-cool Los Rakas is popular – check out their addictive version of Rubén Blades' 'Camaleon.' From Colón, Kafu Banton is a popular reggae star.

Rock 'n' roll, in both English and Spanish, is played on most Panamanian FM radio stations, and some decent bands play it in Panama City clubs. For classic rock, Los Rabanes is considered Panama's most well-known sound.

Panamanian Folk

Attend any Azuero festival and you will see Panamanian *típico* (folkloric music) alive and thriving. In *típico* the accordion is dominant. The style is well represented by Dorindo Cárdenas, the late Victorio Vergara (whose band lives on as Nenito Vargas y los Plumas Negras) and the popular brother-sister pair of Samy and Sandra Sandoval.

Arts

Panamanian art reflects the country's stunning ethnic mix, with indigenous, African and Latin influences informing a diversity ranging from delicate carvings of wood and tagua nut to flamboyant costumes and extraordinary lace dresses. These treasures are found in the depths of the Darién or in dusty villages of the Península de Azuero, where artisans pursue traditions that have been handed down over many generations. Panama's talented photographers, painters and writers are also reinventing understandings of this tropical crossroads.

The Written Word

Often inward-looking, Panamanian literature has not carved much of a presence in international circles.

Several of the country's best novelists wrote around the mid-19th century. *El Ahogado* (The Drowned Man), a 1937 novel by Tristán Solarte (the pen name of Guillermo Sánchez Borbón, a well-known poet, novelist and journalist), ingeniously blends elements of the detective, gothic and psychological genres, along with a famous local myth. *El Desván* (In the Garret), a 1954 novel by Ramón H Jurado, explores the emotional limits of the human condition. *Gamboa Road Gang*, by Joaquín Beleño, is the best work of fiction about the political and social events surrounding the Panama Canal.

Fiction writer (and half-Panamanian) Cristina Henríquez offers insight into Panamanian identity from a sometimes displaced point of view. Her 2010 novel *The World in Half* was followed in 2014 by *The Book of Unknown Americans*, a love story that weaves in the experiences of diverse Latin immigrants to the USA.

American RM Koster has written about Panama as his adopted home for decades. Reissued in 2013, his cult classic *The Prince* portrays an imaginary Central American country; it's the first in a still-unfolding magical-realism trilogy.

Current authors to look for include poet and novelist Giovanna Benedetti, historical novelist Gloria Guardia and folk novelist Rosa María Britton.

Panama in Film

Though Panama has served as the backdrop for several Hollywood films (for example, *The Tailor of Panama* and *Quantum of Solace*), the country is just beginning to produce its own commercial features. The first released in Panama was 2009's *Chance,* a tropical comedy about class shenanigans, told through the adventures of two maids and the upper-class family they work for.

Burwa dii Ebo (The Wind and the Water), directed by Vero Bollow and the Igar Yala Collective, was an official Sundance Film Festival selection in 2008. A narrative drama with social undercurrents, the story follows an indigenous Guna teenager who moves to Panama City from the Caribbean islands of his homeland. The movie has yet to be commercially distributed but has won numerous international awards.

Michel Perrin's *Magnificent Molas: The Art of the Kuna Indian* contains photographs of 300 fabric works of art. Perrin describes the vivid relationship between Guna art and culture.

The 1992 documentary *The Panama Deception* recounts the events that led up to the US removal of Noriega, including his previous collaboration with the CIA. Seeing this movie is a must to understand the complications and nuances of US–Panama relations. Also worthwhile, *Curundú* is a 2011 documentary by Ana Endara Mislov that shows the artistic vision of a charming photographer hoodlum trying to chronicle neighborhood life in this tough Panama City slum.

The first Panamanian film submitted for the Best Foreign Language Oscar, *Invasión* is a 2014 documentary written and directed by Abner Benaim about the 1989 US invasion. It was followed by *Caja 25* (Box 25), a 2015 Panamanian documentary directed by Mercedes Arias and Delfina Vidal about letters written by the men building the Panama Canal.

Action thriller *Contraband* is a 2012 film directed by Baltasar Kormákur, starring Mark Wahlberg and Kate Beckinsale. The 2016 *Hands of Stone* is a biopic about boxer Roberto Durán, starring Édgar Ramírez and Robert De Niro. Much of the film was shot in Panama.

Made by Hand

Panama's indigenous groups produce high-quality woodcarvings, textiles, ceramics, masks and other handicrafts. The Latin folk tradition from the Penínusula de Azuero – *polleras* (elaborate traditional outfits of Spanish origin; p122), masks and leather sandals – is also worth noting.

The Wounaan and Emberá people in the Darién create carvings of jungle wildlife from cocobolo, a handsome tropical hardwood, and tiny figurines from the ivory-colored tagua nut.

However, the Emberá and Wounaan are most renowned for producing beautiful woven baskets of incredibly high quality. There are two types: the utilitarian and the decorative. The utilitarian baskets are made primarily from the chunga palm but can contain bits of other plants, vines, bark and leaves. They are usually woven, using various plaiting techniques, from single plant strips of coarse texture and great strength, and are rarely dyed. These baskets are often used for carrying seeds or harvesting crops.

The decorative baskets are much more refined, usually featuring many colors, and are created from materials of the nahuala bush and the

For the beat on current cultural events and contemporary Panamanian authors, check out the Spanish-language website www.escritores panama.com.

HOW TO BUY A MOLA

Molas are as ubiquitous as soccer shirts in Panama. A traditional Guna handicraft, a *mola* is made of brightly colored squares of cotton fabric laid atop one another. Cuts are made through the layers, forming basic designs. The layers are then sewn together with tiny, evenly spaced stitches to hold the design in place.

Mola means 'blouse' in Guna, and Guna women make *molas* in thematically matching but never identical pairs. A pair will comprise the front and back of a blouse. The most traditional colors are black, maroon and orange, while the most traditional designs are abstract and geometric. These days *molas* can feature anything from cartoonish animals to Christmas themes, but the most valued ones are classically designed.

Regardless of the design, the very best *molas* should always have the following characteristics:

- Stitches closely match the color of the cloth they are set against.
- Stitches are very fine and neatly spaced.
- Stitches are pulled evenly and with enough tension to be barely visible.
- Curves are cut smoothly and the sewing follows the curves of the cut.
- Outline strips are uniform in width, with no frayed edges.

chunga palm. The dyes are 100% natural and are extracted from fruits, leaves, roots and bark. Typical motifs are of butterflies, frogs, toucans, trees and parrots. The baskets are similar in quality to the renowned early-20th-century Chemehuevi Indian baskets of California. You can buy baskets at any of the markets.

The Guna of the Comarca de Guna Yala are known worldwide for their *molas* (the blouse panels used by women in their traditional dress). Also sold as crafts, *molas* symbolize the identity of the Guna people to outsiders, and their colorful and elaborate designs often depict sea turtles, birds and fish.

Ocú and Penonomé people produce superior Panama hats.

Polleras are handmade in Guararé and other villages in Las Tablas and Los Santos Provinces. Also available on the Península de Azuero are handcrafted festival masks from Villa de Los Santos and Parita.

Huacas are golden objects made on the isthmus centuries before the Spanish conquest. They were placed with indigenous leaders at the time of burial, intended to accompany and protect their souls on the voyage to the other world. Most took the form of a warrior, crocodile, jaguar, frog or condor. You can also purchase exact (solid gold) and near-exact (gold plated) reproductions of these palm-sized objects.

Because of their proximity to mineral-rich Colombia and Brazil, the jewelry stores here often have high-quality gems at excellent prices. Buyers beware: there are many fake gems on the world market, as well as many flawed gems that have been altered to appear more valuable than they really are.

Painting

Panama has internationally recognized artists, even though it is all-too-difficult for them to establish a public presence in their own country. There is promise in endeavors like the MAC (Museo de Arte Contemporáneo), but there is almost no government support for museums or training. Yet art is far from dead: graffiti murals, small-scale expositions and cooperatives work hard to close the gap.

CONGO RENAISSANCE

Started by the descendants of escaped slaves, Congo art tells the story of contemporary Portobelo by recounting their self-liberation. The movement started after the US invasion of Panama. Arturo Lindsay, a native Panamanian, artist and professor at Spelman College, says, 'My adopted country had invaded my homeland. Crime and drugs were rampant. There was poverty. The workshop grew out of seeing how I could help.'

Lindsay and photographer Sandra Eleta created Taller Portobelo, an artists' workshop for a community in the throes of hardship. It was art as salvation, and it worked. Lindsay describes Congo as contemporary art with folk elements. Extremely expressive, with color and textures such as beads or broken mirror shards, Congo paintings are often self-portraits. Painted *bastones* (walking sticks) represent those used by slaves to escape to freedom into the mountains and ward off pursuing Spaniards and forest predators.

Congo art has evolved and matured since its initial period, and artists have found the stability that is so hard to come by through commissions and gallery showings. In annual exchanges with visiting US artists, the groups collaborate on earthworks, sustainable architecture and biodegradable installations in addition to painting. Lindsay describes Spelman's Summer Art Colony as a cultural bridge. 'It is not just about work, but creating new friendships and a new network that will bring others into the fold.'

Portobelo is the best place to buy paintings direct, but you can also find Congo art in Panama City at Karavan. Look for work by Yaneca Esquina, the movement's best-known artist.

Trained in France, Roberto Lewis (1874–1949) became the first prominent figure in Panama's art scene. He painted portraits of the nation's leaders and allegorical images to decorate public buildings. Among his most notable works are those in the Palacio de las Garzas in Panama City. In 1913 Lewis became the director of Panama's first art academy, where he and his successor, Humberto Ivaldi (1909–47), educated a generation of artists.

Among the school's students were Juan Manuel Cedeño and Isaac Benítez, as well as the painters who would come to the fore in the 1950s and '60s. This group includes Alfredo Sinclair, Guillermo Trujillo, Eudoro Silvera and others. More recent artists include Olga Sinclair and Brooke Alfaro. Most of these artists are still active, with occasional shows at local galleries.

The largest Panamanian art exposition – the Bienal de Arte – is held every two years at the MAC in Panama City.

Photography

Panama has several gifted photographers, including Iraida Icaza, Stuart Warner and Sandra Eleta. Icaza's abstract art is bold and innovative, made with photographic equipment. After living in Tokyo for many years, she now resides in New York.

Warner, who has spent much of his life in Asia, the Middle East, Europe and the USA, captures the human spirit in beautiful landscapes and portraits.

Producing stunning and thought-provoking work, Sandra Eleta is among the most important photographers in Latin America. Particularly lauded are her portraits of the black inhabitants of Panama's Caribbean coast (particularly those of Portobelo, where she resides part of the year). She also founded the Panama City gallery Karavan, featuring Guna and Congo art.

Inauguración de La Fe (Inauguration of La Fe) by Consuelo Tomás is a collection of tales depicting the idiosyncrasies of the popular neighborhoods of Panama City.

Land & Wildlife

Imagine a country slightly bigger than Ireland yet so diverse that it boasts 21 times more plant species per square kilometer than Brazil. Panama is gaining fame for its vast tropical forests, hundreds of pristine islands and astounding biodiversity. Though only slightly bigger than Ireland or Austria, Panama is home to an incredible variety of landscapes. In the span of a week, you can hike through highland cloud forests and verdant jungles and take a dip in both the Caribbean Sea and the Pacific Ocean.

The Land

Panama is both the narrowest and the southernmost country in Central America. The long S-shaped isthmus borders Costa Rica in the west and Colombia in the east. Its northern Caribbean coastline measures 1160km, compared to a 1690km Pacific coastline in the south, and its total land area is 78,056 sq km.

A Neotropical Companion by John Kricher, is an excellent book for learning about ecology, evolutionary theory and biodiversity in the New World tropics.

Panama is just 50km wide at its leanest point, yet it separates two great oceans. The Panama Canal, which is about 80km long, effectively divides the country into eastern and western regions. Panama's two mountain ranges run along its spine in both the east and the west. Volcán Barú is the country's highest point and only volcano.

Like all of the Central American countries, Panama has large, flat coastal lowlands with huge banana plantations. There are about 480 rivers in Panama and 1518 islands near its shores. The two main island groups are the San Blás and Bocas del Toro archipelagos on the Caribbean side, but most of the islands are on the Pacific side. Even the Panama Canal has islands, including Isla Barro Colorado, which has a world-famous tropical-rainforest research station.

Wildlife

Although Panama is still largely undiscovered, more and more visitors are drawn to its remarkable wildlife. Panama's rainforests are home to countless creatures, from agoutis scurrying across the canopy floor to jaguars prowling the forests. In the sea, shallow coral-reef beds support countless varieties of tropical fish, while hammerheads and manta rays roam deeper waters. In the air, nearly a thousand avian species make Panama one of the top birdwatching destinations in the world.

The country's rich biodiversity owes a great deal to its geological history. Around 65 million years ago, North and South America were joined by a land bridge not unlike what exists today. Around 50 million years ago, the continents split apart and remained separate for millions of years.

Find out about upcoming seminars and recent publications about tropical ecology and biodiversity topics on the Smithsonian Tropical Research Institute website (www.stri.org).

During this time, unique evolutionary landscapes were created on both continents. South America experienced an astonishing diversification of many species. The land soon gave rise to many bird families (toucans and hummingbirds included), unique Neotropical rodents (agoutis and capybaras) and groups such as iguanas, poison-dart frogs and basilisks. In North America, which collided repeatedly with Eurasia, animal species that had no relatives in South America (horses, deer, raccoons, squirrels and mice) flourished.

SEA TURTLE NESTING

TURTLE	NESTING SEASON	PEAK	HOT SPOTS
green	May–Oct (Caribbean)	Aug–Oct (Caribbean)	Isla Bastimentos
	Jun–Dec (Pacific)	no peak	Humedal de San San Pond Sak
hawksbill	Apr–Oct (Caribbean)	Jun & Jul (Caribbean)	Isla Bastimentos
	Apr–Nov (Pacific)	Jun & Jul (Pacific)	Humedal de San San Pond Sak
leatherback	Mar–Jul (Caribbean)	Apr & May (Caribbean)	Isla Bastimentos
	Oct–Mar (Pacific)	Nov–Jan (Pacific)	Humedal de San San Pond Sak
loggerhead	May–Sep (Caribbean)	no peak	Isla Bastimentos
	Apr–Sep (Pacific)		Humedal de San San Pond Sak
olive ridley	year-round (Pacific)	Jun–Nov (Pacific)	Isla de Cañas

The momentous event that would change natural history for both continents occurred around three million years ago when the land bridge of Panama arose. Species from both continents mingled: northern animals went south and southern animals went north. In the lush forests and wetlands along the isthmus, the great variety of plant species created ideal conditions for nourishing wildlife.

Today, the interchange of species between North and South America is limited to winged migrations, though this annual event can be breathtaking to behold.

Animals

Panama's biodiversity is staggering: the country is home to 220 mammal species, 226 species of reptile, 164 amphibian species and 125 animal species found nowhere else in the world. Panama also boasts 978 avian species, which is the largest number in Central America.

Land & Marine Mammals

Panama's many species of primate include white-faced capuchins, squirrel monkeys, spider monkeys and howler monkeys. Some fascinating varieties, like the Geoffroy's tamarin, are found nowhere else in Central America. These tiny, gregarious monkeys can live in groups of up to 40 in lowland forest, and many weigh less than 600g. They're identified by their whistles and chirps, mottled black-and-brown fur, white chests and diminutive stature. Spot them in Parque Natural Metropolitano, Monumento Nacional Isla Barro Colorado and the Darién.

Big cats prowl the jungles of Panama. Although you'd be extremely fortunate to catch even a glimpse of one, their prints are easy to come across. Jaguars, pumas, ocelots, jaguarundis and margays are all found on the isthmus. The jaguar is the largest cat in the Americas, needing large tracts of land in order to survive. Without sufficient space, the big cats gradually exhaust their food supply (which numbers 85 hunted species) and perish. They are excellent swimmers and climbers and at times are spotted resting on sunny riverbanks.

Panama's offshore waters host a fascinating assortment of creatures. Reefs found off both coasts support a plethora of tropical fish, and visitors to the national marine parks might spot humpback whales, reef sharks, bottlenose dolphins, and killer or sperm whales. Underwater, hammerheads, whale sharks, black- and whitetip sharks and occasionally tiger sharks also visit.

One of Panama's biggest coastal draws is the sea turtle. Of the world's seven species, five can be seen in Panama at various times throughout the year. All sea turtles evolved from terrestrial species and the most

The passage of a ship through the entire Panama Canal requires approximately 52 million gallons of water.

Monkey's Bridge: Mysteries of Evolution in Central America by David Rains Wallace tells of the colorful evolutionary unfolding of fauna and flora on the isthmus, beginning three million years ago and ending in the present.

important stage of their survival happens on land when they come to nest. Although you'll need a bit of luck and a lot of patience, the experience of seeing hatchlings emerge is unparalleled.

Arribadas (arrivals) are rare events that occur when thousands of female sea turtles flood the beach to lay their eggs. This happens occasionally on Isla Cañas when 40,000 to 50,000 olive ridleys come to nest at a single time (p133). It mostly happens in the wet season (usually September to October) during the first and last quarter of the moon.

Birds

Birdwatchers consider Panama to be one of the world's best birdwatching sites. Quetzals, macaws, amazons, parrots and toucans all have sizable populations here, as do many species of tanager and raptor. Right outside Panama City hundreds of species have been spotted along the famous 17km-long Pipeline Rd in Parque Nacional Soberanía.

One of the most sought-after birds is the harpy eagle, the national bird of Panama. With a 2m wingspan and a weight of up to 12kg, this raptor is the world's most powerful bird of prey and a truly awesome sight. It's recognizable by its huge size, its broad, black chest band with white underneath, its piercing yellow eyes and its prominent, regal crest. The harpy's powerful claws can carry off howler monkeys and capuchins, and it also hunts sloths, coatis, anteaters and just about anything that moves. It's best spotted in the Parque Nacional Darién around Reserva Natural Punta Patiño.

The elusive, emerald-green quetzal lives in habitats throughout Central America, but Panama is one of the best places to see it. The male has an elongated wing covert (train) and a scarlet breast and belly, while females have duller plumage. Parque Nacional Volcán Barú is a top spot for sightings, as is Parque Internacional La Amistad. Quetzals are best spotted in the breeding season, from March to June, when males grow their spectacular trains and start calling for mates.

Panama's geographical position also makes it a crossroads for migratory birds. Out of the country's 950 bird species, 122 occur only as long-distance migrants (ie they don't breed in Panama). From August to December, North American raptors migrate south into Central America by the millions – at times, there are so many birds that they make a black streak across the sky. The canopy tower in Panama's Parque Nacional Soberanía is a particularly good vantage point for watching this migration.

FINDING NEW SPECIES

In a country known for its biodiversity, the disappearance of species is unsettling on many levels. But there may be even greater concern over species not yet identified, particularly in light of rapid habitat destruction. We may never understand their roles in local ecosystems or potential contributions toward scientific research. In just the past few years, scientists have made these findings:

Bush dog *(Speothos venaticus)* Rare and nocturnal. A foot tall, it resembles a small pig and keeps company in aggressive packs in the tropical forests of Central and South America. Its habitat, near the borders, is threatened by clear cutting.

Poison-dart frog *(Andinobates geminisae)* Found in Colón Province. Tiny and orange, it's no bigger than a fingernail. Habitat loss is a serious concern as it only exists in a very reduced area.

River dolphin *(Isthminia panamensis)* Now extinct it lived some six million years ago. As whales and dolphins evolved from terrestrial to marine mammals, these river dolphins represent a reversal, showing when the species turned inland to freshwater ecosystems.

In Bocas del Toro, keep an eye out for kettling hawk migrations – October is the best month to see them in large numbers. The migration of turkey vultures over the islands in early March and again in October is another striking sight. These big, black-bodied, red-necked birds can streak the sky and are able to soar for long periods without a single flap as they migrate between southern Canada and Tierra del Fuego.

Endangered Species

According to UN data, there are 347 threatened species in Panama. Among the animals appearing on its 'red list' for Panama are the jaguar, the spectacled bear, the Central American tapir, the American crocodile, all five species of sea turtle that nest on Panamanian beaches and dozens of birds, including several eagle species and the military and scarlet macaw.

Laws meant to curb illegal hunting are widely ignored due to lack of enforcement. For example, keeping a parrot, toucan or macaw in a cage is a fineable offense in Panama. Nonetheless, it's common to see them in cages, even in some public venues.

You can help reduce the threat to Panama's endangered species. If you see caged animals at a hotel, complain to the manager, take your business elsewhere and report the crime to APPC (www.appcpanama.org), a conservation nonprofit organization with experience in wild-animal rescue.

Plants

Humid, tropical rainforest is the dominant vegetation in the canal area, along the Caribbean coast and in most of the eastern half of the country – Parque Nacional Darién protects much of Panama's largest tropical rainforest. Other vegetation zones include dry tropical rainforest and grassland on the Pacific coast, cloud forest in the highlands, alpine vegetation on the highest peaks and mangrove forest on both coasts and around many islands. Among the flora, Panama has over 10,000 species of plant, including approximately 1200 orchid species, 675 fern species and 1500 species of tree.

National Parks

Today Panama has around 40 national parks and officially protected areas, and about 33% of the country's total land is set aside for conservation. In many of the national parks and protected areas there are *mestizo* and indigenous villages. In some scenarios these communities help protect and maintain the park.

Headquartered in Panama City, the Ministerio de Ambiente (Autoridad Nacional del Ambiente; Panama's national environmental authority; www.miambiente.gob.pa) runs Panama's parks. To enter a national park, travelers must pay US$5 (US$20 if it's a national marine park) at a regional office or ranger station in the park being visited. Permits to camp or stay at a ranger station can generally be obtained in these places as well.

In Panama City, the 265-hectare Parque Natural Metropolitano protects vast expanses of tropical semideciduous forest within the city limits.

A short distance from the capital in Panamá Province, Parque Nacional Soberanía is a birdwatcher's paradise where, in a single day, you can see hundreds of species. Lush rainforest also abounds on the nearby biological reserve of Monumento Natural Isla Barro Colorado, where scientists study the area's rich biodiversity. Also close to Panama City is the historical Fuerte San Lorenzo.

The lovely Parque Nacional Omar Torrijos is in Coclé Province. It remains largely overlooked since access is difficult, requiring a good 4WD

Emergent Ecologies by Eben Kirksey (2015) examines how chance encounters, historical gaffes and parasitic invasions have shaped ecological communities, with examples from Panama.

THE VALUE OF RAINFORESTS

Why get serious about saving the rainforest? Even though they may be far from our daily experience, rainforests and their survival affect every one of us in more ways than we realize.

Carbon Sink Effect

As developing nations modernize, global carbon emissions are on the rise, and evidence of the greenhouse effect can already be seen across the planet.

One of the best defenses humans have against rising carbon-dioxide levels is the tropical rainforest. Rainforests limit the greenhouse effect of global warming by storing carbon, which reduces the amount of carbon dioxide in the atmosphere. With fewer densely wooded sub-canopy trees, the ability of tropical rainforests to act as a carbon sink is in jeopardy. The deforestation of Latin America can impact desertification as far away as the Sahel in Africa. This reality eventually affects us all.

Bioprospecting

Scientific research in Panama could have long-lasting implications for rainforest conservation around the globe. With cooperation from universities and pharmaceutical companies, Smithsonian Tropical Research Institute scientists are scouring the rainforest for compounds that may one day become new treatments for disease or useful in agriculture. The results place a great deal of importance on the rainforest's biodiversity. With important findings already established, bioprospecting could help unlock the mysteries of the rainforest and consequently preserve them through funding. Ultimately, this would make conservation both the end and the means.

Intrinsic Value

Panama's vegetation was originally almost all forest, though much of this has been cleared in recent generations to create pastures and agricultural land. Countless flora and fauna species have been wiped out. Beyond the plants and animals that actually inhabit the forests, deforestation also threatens the traditional cultures of the Emberá and Wounaan, who have lived in the rainforest for generations. But the effects do not stop there. Migratory animals also pass through the forests annually, such as bats, butterflies and birds. A simple argument for saving the rainforest is simply that its intrinsic value is enough to warrant increased conservation efforts.

or at least an hour's walk to reach the entrance. It offers prime birdwatching and the possibility of viewing both the Atlantic and the Pacific Oceans.

In Azuero, the Refugio de Vida Silvestre Cenegón del Mangle is a mangrove forest and wildlife refuge that's a prime nesting ground for herons and other birdlife. It also contains a series of pools said to have therapeutic properties.

Although the province of Los Santos has no national parks, there is an attractive wildlife refuge and a protected area frequented by nesting sea turtles. The Refugio de Vida Silvestre Isla Iguana near Pedasí offers snorkeling, and occasional sightings of humpback whales. Nearby, Isla de Cañas is a major nesting site for olive ridley sea turtles.

In Veraguas, Parque Nacional Coiba is one of the largest marine parks in the world. It contains Panama's largest island, the 493-sq-km Isla de Coiba, which is regarded by scientists as a biodiversity hot spot. Also in Veraguas, the 32,577-hectare Parque Nacional Cerro Hoya protects some of the last remaining patches of dry tropical forest on the Península de Azuero. The newest national park is Parque Nacional Santa Fé, around Santa Fé.

In Chiriquí Province, Parque Nacional Marino Golfo de Chiriquí is an impressive 14,740-hectare marine park with 25 islands and numerous coral reefs. The aquatic life here is astounding. In the highlands, Parque Nacional Volcán Barú surrounds Panama's only volcano, a fine destination for hikers and birdwatchers. Volcán Barú (3474m) is Panama's highest peak. Chiriquí also has part of the binational Parque Internacional La Amistad. Although largely unexplored, La Amistad offers several excellent day hikes, and local indigenous guides lead overnight excursions.

In the Archipiélago de Bocas del Toro, Parque Nacional Marino Isla Bastimentos protects various areas of the archipelago and is an important nature reserve for many species of Caribbean wildlife. Turtles nest on its beaches and its abundant marine life makes for great snorkeling and diving. On the mainland is the other sector of Panama's share of the binational Parque Internacional La Amistad. Wekso, as this sector of the park is called, is home to several indigenous groups, pristine rainforest and abundant wildlife. Near the border with Chiriquí Province, the Bosque Protector de Palo Seco contains several hiking trails through lush cloud forest high in the Talamanca range.

Panama's crown jewel is the Parque Nacional Darién, which boasts 576,000 hectares of wildlife-rich rainforest. The heart of this Unesco World Heritage Site is Cana, a former mining valley that is now regarded as one of the best birdwatching spots in the world. Unfortunately, at the time of writing, authorization was closed for visits to this area. The Darién is also home to the Reserva Natural Punta Patiño, a 26,315-hectare wildlife reserve on the southern shore of the Golfo de San Miguel. This private reserve is one of the best places in the country to see the harpy eagle.

Environmental Issues

Panama faces grave environmental threats at the hands of loggers, miners, developers and indifferent or corrupt government agencies, who apparently don't understand that the country's finest gem – its natural beauty – is rapidly disappearing.

According to the Centro de Incidencia Ambiental, 33% of Panama's land is set aside for conservation – more than any other Central American country. Panama's forests also contain the greatest number of species of all the New World countries north of Colombia.

The principal threat to Panama's ecology is deforestation, which is picking up momentum throughout the country, most notably in the Darién. In addition, the balance between conservation and development is tipping in favor of the latter, particularly in tourist hot spots like the Península de Azuero and Bocas del Toro.

Panama's national parks are staffed by few rangers. Although their areas of coverage are colossal, many rangers aren't given patrol vehicles or radios. In Parque Nacional Darién, for instance, there are usually no more than 20 rangers (generally unarmed and poorly paid) assigned to protect 576,000 hectares – an area larger than some countries. Meanwhile, illegal hunting, settling and logging take place inside parks. Unless drastic measures are taken, it may not be long before the country's protected areas are nothing more than national parks on paper.

In recent years, increased foreign investment, coupled with the desire to improve tourist infrastructure, has threatened several of Panama's most pristine ecosystems. Development projects such as dams and mines are allowed to proceed without environmental-impact assessments. This green-light approach to divvying up environmental resources has stirred the utmost concern in conservation circles.

Tropical rainforests cover just 7% of the Earth's surface but account for 50% of the world's biodiversity.

Deforestation

Panama's forests have decreased by 15% in the past 20 years. Illegal logging now accounts for nearly half of Panama's timber industry,

ENVIRONMENTAL ORGANIZATIONS

Though there is little public sensitivity about environmental issues in Panama, a number of organizations strive to protect the environment and biodiversity.

ANCON (☎314-0060; www.ancon.org) Founded in 1985 by academic and business leaders, it has played a major role in the creation of national parks and on many occasions has spurred the government into action.

Audubon Society (☎232-5977; www.audubonpanama.org; Casa No 2006-B, Llanos de Curundú, Curundú) Promoting birds in Panama for more than 35 years, with more than 20 birdwatching field trips every year. Find upcoming events online.

Centro de Incidencia Ambiental (CIAM; ☎262-8831; www.ciampanama.org) Promotes environmental advocacy through grass-roots campaigns.

Fundación Albatros Media (☎317-3450; www.albatrosmedia.com) Creates quality environmental documentaries on Panama.

Fundación Avifauna Eugene Eisenmann (☎306-3133; www.avifauna.org.pa) Promotes the preservation of tropical forest to support Panama's astounding diversity of birdlife. Created the Panama Rainforest Discovery Center on Pipeline Rd.

Fundación Mar Viva (☎317-4350; www.marviva.net) Patrols protected marine areas in Costa Rica and Panama with the goal of ending illegal fishing and replenishing marine life. Also promotes conservation and the sustainable use of marine resources.

Nature Conservancy (☎317-0328; www.nature.org) Prominent international conservation agency working extensively in the areas of Bocas del Toro, the Península de Azuero, the upper Chagres and the Darién Biosphere Reserve.

according to a 2015 report by the Ministerio de Ambiente. Most of this wood is sourced in the Darién, one of the richest biomes on the planet. Just over three decades ago, the region north of Yaviza – the town where the Interamericana ends – was covered with virgin forest. Unfortunately, everything changed when the highway was extended from Chepo to Yaviza.

The loggers initially sought big trees within easy reach, felling all the giants near the highway and trampling young trees with their machinery. Once the giant trees were gone, the loggers cut roads perpendicular to the highway, which led into tall stands of hardwoods. After those stands were removed, more roads were cut and yet more stands were leveled.

Right behind the loggers were thousands of settlers looking to eke out a living by turning the trampled vegetation left by the loggers into cropland. With the mature trees gone, all that was required to create cropland was an ax and a match. After some crackling, sizzling and a lot of smoke, subsistence farmers had fields for planting. All of this is not only legal but actively encouraged by Panamanian law.

However, the story doesn't end here. In a healthy rainforest ecosystem, huge, exposed tree roots prevent heavy rains from washing away the thin layer of nutrient-rich topsoil. But a big storm over a denuded area will quickly carry the topsoil into rivers and out to sea, leaving only the nutrient-deficient lower soil where the vibrant jungle once stood. In the space of only two to three years, the soil in the Darién could no longer support a decent harvest and little more than grass grew on it. Since cattle eat grass, the ranchers stepped in and bought fields that frustrated farmers could no longer use.

Today, with the Interamericana paved to Yaviza, the succession of loggers, farmers and ranchers keeps growing, although now loggers must further explore secondary roads to find trees. The farmers are still a step behind the loggers, unintentional nomads employing the slash-and-burn method so widespread in the developing world. And everywhere the settler-farmers go, ranchers move in behind them.

Mining

Today roughly 26% of Panama is mined or under mining concessions, prompting concerns of contaminated water sources, and the destruction of forest and human habitats. In 2013 mining activity rose by a quarter, and that's just the beginning, according to CAMIPA (Cámara Minera de Panamá), which estimates that Panama is sitting on some US$200 billion in mineral reserves.

In spite of objections by prominent environmental groups, the government has approved and expedited large-scale mining projects, most notably a US$6.2-billion project – an investment greater than the initial Panama Canal expansion – to extract gold and copper.

A major victory for community interests was the 2012 passing of law 415, which prohibits extraction in indigenous territories and requires their approval for hydroelectric projects. The change came after a shutdown of Ngöbe-Bugle community protests in February 2012 left two protesters dead.

Yet protests persist, as most of the gold and copper reserves lie within indigenous lands. Panama is currently looking at reforming the mining industry in order to keep the peace, but environmentalists and rural residents worry that reform will not provide sufficient protection for the community and the environment.

For more information on mining issues, contact the Centro de Incidencia Ambiental (see box opposite for contact details).

Dams

Dams may become an epidemic in Panama, where proposals have been submitted for almost every river in the country. One of the most alarming is the US$50 million hydroelectric-dam project on Naso tribal territory. The Río Bonyic project threatens the settlement, the water supply and nearby Unesco World Heritage Site Parque Internacional La Amistad. In addition to drawing international opposition, the dam has divided the tribe and deposed its king, who acted in favor of the dam without the approval of his assembly. These controversies resulted in the Inter-American Development Bank removing its funding, though construction on the dam went through, impeded by indigenous protests that periodically cut off the access road.

In 2015, the Ministerio de Ambiente imposed a US$1.2 million fine on hydroelectric companies building a controversial dam in Chiriquí Province known as the Barro Blanco project. The companies had failed to provide compensation to relocate people displaced by the dam and were charged with illegally discharging material into the river, affecting a nearby Ngöbe-Buglé community.

Development

As Panama City grows, even conservation sites are coming under threat.

After a long tussle with developers, Bahía de Panamá was finally returned to being a wildlife-refuge site in 2015. The bay came under threat in 2012 when the government removed its protected status to make way for urban and resort development, including hotels and golf courses. As a Ramsar wetland site, it's crucial to the hemisphere as it hosts up to two million shorebirds in their annual migrations. The Audubon Society (see box opposite for contact details) led campaigns crucial in its recuperation. The bay is also key for mangroves that provide a vital nursery for fish and shellfish, a natural filter for sewage, and a buffer zone protecting the city from storms.

In 2004 Panama, Costa Rica, Colombia and Ecuador created the Eastern Pacific Marine Biological Corridor to preserve the area's ecosystems.

TRADING DEBT FOR FOREST

Conservationists are rethinking how to keep valuable resources in countries whose national debt represents a more pressing public concern. Nonprofits are purchasing national debts and using later payments toward forest-protection programs. The USA, with the involvement of the Nature Conservancy (www.nature.org), has forgiven US$21 million in debt-for-nature swaps in Panama. This is good news, though a downturn in the trend has been attributed to the high cost of commercial debt in secondary markets.

The Martinelli administration expanded the coastal highway known as Cinta Costera into the sea to wrap around the historic neighborhood of Casco Viejo, a Unesco World Heritage Site. With a price tag of US$189 million, the completed project has done little to mitigate the traffic problems it sought to address, as entry and entrance points miss the bottleneck traffic areas.

Isla de Coiba

One of the hottest environmental topics in Panama is the future of Isla de Coiba. This rainforest-covered island and Unesco World Heritage Site is set in one of the largest marine parks on the planet – scientists often compare Coiba to the Galápagos Islands. Yet, with paltry funding, it is far from the Galápagos standard. A lack of funding also hinders patrols in combating illegal fishing activity.

Owing to the presence of a penal colony, this island and its surrounding waters remained long untouched, but now that the prison has been phased out, developers and members of the government see glorious tourism possibilities for this ecological gem. There are concerns that big development plans would destroy the fragile ecosystem.

A Field Guide to the Orchids of Costa Rica and Panama by Robert Dressler has 240 photos, and almost as many drawings, of orchids within its 274 pages.

The unregulated presence of cruise ships has caused disturbing situations, with sometimes as many as 200 tourists visiting the tiny snorkeling island of Granito de Oro – a number that is outrageously unsustainable. In 2015 a 200-passenger cruise ship ran aground in Coiba. Little is being done to preserve the penal colony as a historic site; unfortunately, it is deteriorating rapidly.

Survival Guide

Directory A–Z

Accommodations

B&Bs

Relatively new to Panama, B&Bs are opening across the country. Rates are usually midrange. You'll find them at major tourist destinations including Panama City, Boquete and Bocas del Toro. B&Bs offer personalized service and a comfortable room with private bathroom; breakfast is included in the price.

Camping

Camping facilities are usually limited to beach areas and national parks.

Homestays

Informal homestays, sometimes with meals included, are most common in small towns and indigenous villages in Guna Yala and Darién Province. Find lodgings by asking around.

Hostels

As Panama becomes more popular with backpackers, hostels are springing up across the country. At the time of writing, none were part of international youth-hostel federations, though facilities are mostly good.

Hotels

Advance reservations are generally possible and recommended for midrange to high-end accommodations and, in general, in Bocas del Toro town on Isla Colón. Online bookings are most common. Doubles generally have private bathrooms.

Before accepting a room, ask to see several options. The same prices are often charged for rooms of widely differing quality. Even at budget lodgings it's worth comparing. If you're on a tight budget, ask if economical rooms are available. Some Panamanian hotels have smaller, less expensive rooms but don't post their lowest prices.

Lodges

A handful of high-end lodges are scattered about the country. Although these places aren't cheap, they provide an excellent opportunity to be surrounded by nature with access to some spectacular hiking and wildlife-watching nearby.

Resorts

Resort prices often include meals, activities, private beach access and all amenities. Resorts can be a good option for travelers with children, as most offer plenty of family-oriented diversions.

SLEEPING PRICE RANGES

The following price ranges refer to a double room with bathroom in high season or a hostel dorm bed. Unless otherwise stated, tax is included in the price.

$ less than US$60

$$ US$60 to $130

$$$ more than US$130

BOOK YOUR STAY ONLINE

For more accommodations reviews by Lonely Planet authors, check out http://lonelyplanet.com/hotels/. You'll find independent reviews, as well as recommendations on the best places to stay. Best of all, you can book online.

Activities

Panama has scores of ways to spend a sun-drenched afternoon, from hiking through lush rainforest to snorkeling coral reefs. Diving, surfing, birdwatching and fishing are just a few of Panama's star attractions. See p32 for more information.

Children

Panamanians have a family-oriented culture, and will generally be very accommodating to travelers with children. The same can't be said of many businesses owned by expats, who very clearly state the age requirements of their guests.

Most of Panama is quite safe to travel with children, though dengue fever and malaria are present in some limited areas. Bring good insect repellent and light long-sleeved tops and long pants.

A number of tours, some low intensity, are an enjoyable way for you and your children to see Panama's lush environment. Look for agencies with tailored family outings.

For more ideas about making the most of your family travels, look for Lonely Planet's *Travel with Children*.

Practicalities

High chairs in restaurants are a rarity in Panama, but safety seats in rental cars can be provided upon request. For diapers, creams and other supplies, stock up in Panama City and David. Generally speaking, the supermarkets are excellent in Panama, and you can find just about any product you'd find in the USA.

Customs Regulations

You may bring up to 10 cartons of cigarettes and five bottles of liquor into Panama tax free. If you try to leave Panama with products made from endangered species – such as jaguar teeth, ocelot skin and turtle shell – you'll face a steep fine and jail time.

Electricity

The electrical current is 120V in Panama City and 110V, 60Hz elsewhere. Plugs are two pronged, as in the US and Canada.

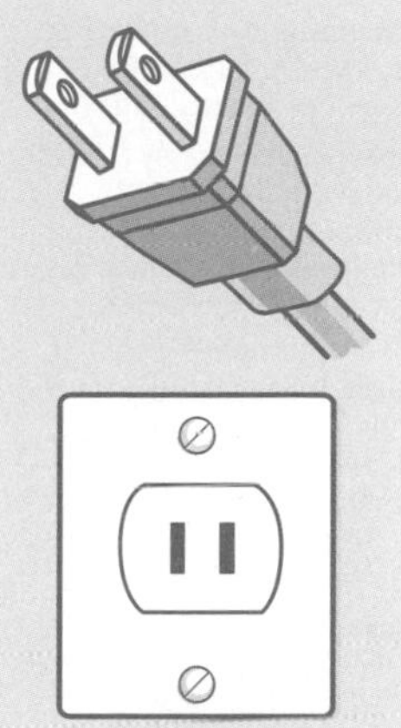

110V/60Hz

110V/60Hz

Climate

Bocas Del Toro

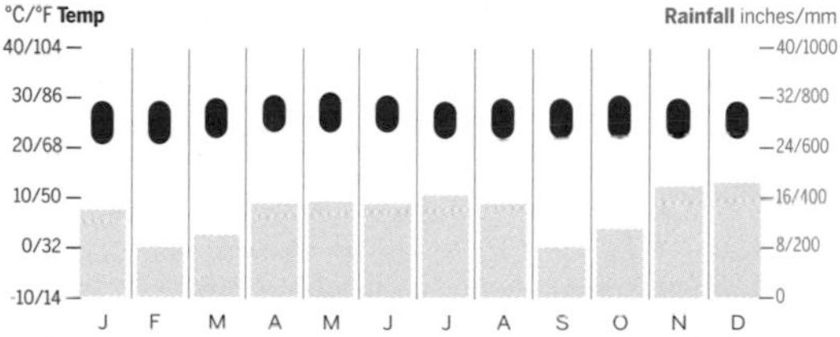

David

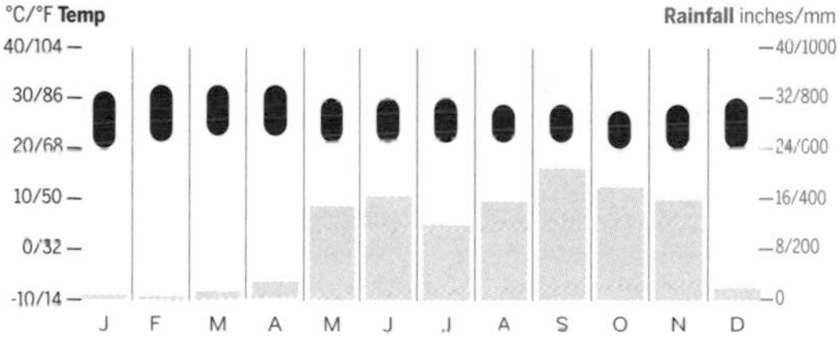

Panama City

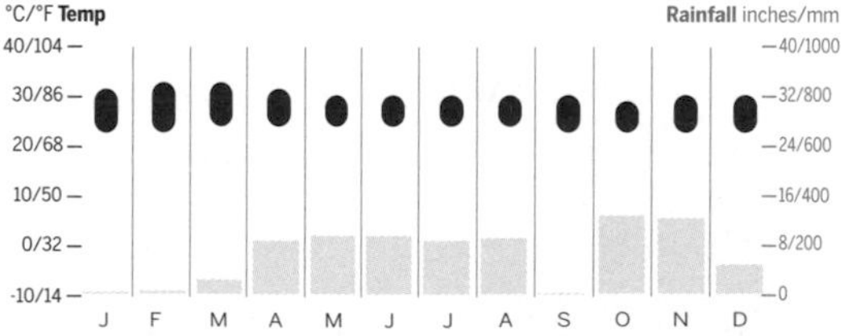

Embassies & Consulates

More than 50 countries have *embajadas* (embassies) or *consulados* (consulates) in Panama City. With the exception of those of the USA and France, most embassies are located in the Marbella district of Panama City.

Ireland, Australia and New Zealand have no consulates or embassies in Panama.

Canadian Embassy (☎294-2500; www.canadainternational.gc.ca/panama; Piso 11, Tower A, Torre de las Americas, Punta Pacifica)

Colombian Embassy (☎392-5586; http://panama.consulado.gov.co; 1st fl, Condominio Posada del Rey, Vía Italia, Punta Paitilla; ⏰7:30am-1:30pm Mon-Fri)

Costa Rican Embassy (☎264-2980; www.embajadacostaricaenpanama.com; 30th fl, Edificio Bisca, cnr Aquilino de la Guardia & Av Balboa, Bella Vista)

Costa Rican Consulate (☎774-1923; www.embajadacostaricaenpanama.com; 3rd fl, Edificio Omega, Av Samuel Lewis, Obarrio; ⏰8am-3pm Mon-Fri)

French Embassy (☎211-6200; www.ambafrance-pa.org; Plaza de Francia, Las Bóvedas, Casco Viejo)

German Embassy (☎263-7733; www.panama.diplo.de; Piso PH, World Trade Center, Calle 53 Este, Marbella; ⏰9am-noon Mon-Fri)

Netherlands Consulate (☎280-6650; http://panama.nlambassade.org; No 23, 23rd fl, Tower 1000, Calle Hanono Missri, Punta Paitilla; ⏰9am-3pm Mon-Fri)

UK Embassy (☎297-6550; www.gov.uk/government/world/panama; 4th fl, Humbolt Tower, Calle 53 Este, Marbella; ⏰7:30am-4:30pm Mon-Thu, to 12:30pm Fri)

US Embassy (☎317-5000; www.panama.usembassy.gov; Av Demetrio Basillo Lakas 783, Clayton; ⏰8am-5:30pm Mon-Thu, to noon Fri)

Food

In Panama City there is an excellent range of restaurants serving everything from cheap set meals to gourmet cuisine. Outside the capital and major tourist attractions, there is much less variety.

Panama's national dish is *sancocho* (chicken and vegetable stew). *Ropa vieja* (literally 'old clothes'), a spicy shredded-beef combination served over rice, is another common and tasty dish. Rice – grown on dry land – is the staple of Panama. Green salads are hard to come by outside the capital, but tropical fruit is abundant.

Meat figures prominently in the Panamanian diet. In addition to staples such as *bistec* (steak) and *carne asado* (roast meat), you'll encounter specialties such as *carimañola* (a yucca roll filled with chopped meat and then deep-fried). Common snacks include the *empanada* (a fried turnover filled with ground meat) and the *tamale* (ground corn filled with spices and chicken or pork, wrapped in banana leaves and boiled).

One breakfast staple is *tortillas de maíz*. Unlike those found in Mexico and Guatemala, Panamanian tortillas are much thicker – essentially deep-fried cornmeal cakes. They go quite nicely with eggs or roast meat. *Hojaldras* (similar to doughnuts; deep-fried masses of dough served hot and covered with sugar) are served at breakfast and available at snack bars.

At *almuerzo* (lunch), many Panamanians opt for simple *comida corriente*, the meal of the working class. This is an inexpensive set meal of beef, chicken or fish served alongside *arroz* (rice), *frijoles* (black beans), *plátano* (fried plantain), chopped cabbage and maybe an egg or an avocado.

Seafood is abundant. On the Caribbean coast and islands, everyday foods include shrimp, Caribbean king crab, octopus, lobster and fish such as *corvina* (sea bass). Along the Caribbean coast, dishes have a West Indian influence. Seafood is often mixed with coconut milk; coconut rice and coconut bread are also Caribbean treats.

You may see people pushing carts and selling *raspados* (cones filled with shaved ice topped with fruit syrup and sweetened condensed milk).

LGBT Travelers

Panamanians are more out than ever, though this openness is much more prevalent in the capital than anywhere else. More than in other parts of Central America, you will probably meet openly gay locals, though the culture is generally discreet. Gay unions are still not legal here, but many think this may change relatively soon. Perhaps it's a legacy of *machismo*, but, according to locals, discrimination is more prevalent against lesbians.

Panama City has a bathhouse and a few gay and lesbian clubs and bars. Outside the capital, gay bars are hard to come by and discrimination is more widespread.

EATING PRICE RANGES

The following price ranges refer to a main dish.

$ less than US$12

$$ US$12 to $18

$$$ more than US$18

In most instances, gays and lesbians just blend in with the straight crowd at the hipper places and avoid village beer halls and other conventional lairs of homophobia.

Gay Pride is held annually in downtown Panama City, usually in June. The parade is sponsored by Asociación Hombres y Mujeres Nuevos de Panamá, Panama's first and only lesbian and gay association.

Health

There are no required vaccinations for Panama, but among those recommended are yellow fever, typhoid, rabies, and hepatitis A and B. See your doctor well ahead, since most vaccines don't produce immunity until at least two weeks after being given. Request an International Certificate of Vaccination (aka the yellow booklet); it's mandatory for countries that require proof of yellow-fever vaccination.

Tap water is generally drinkable in Panama, except for in Bocas del Toro and the Comarca de Guna Yala. Visitors who have recently arrived may want to start with bottled water and minimal amounts of tap water.

A superb book called *International Travel and Health,* revised annually and available online at no cost, is published by the World Health Organization (www.who.int/ith). Another website of general interest is MD Travel Health (www.mdtravelhealth.com), with complete travel-health recommendations for every country, updated daily, also accessible at no cost.

Before You Go

HEALTH INSURANCE

- Prior to your trip, sign up for a travel-insurance policy to cover theft, loss and medical problems.
- Read the fine print. Some policies specifically exclude dangerous activities, which can include scuba diving, motorcycling and even trekking.
- Look into policies that pay doctors or hospitals directly instead of requiring a payment on the spot and a subsequent claim.
- If you have to claim later, ensure you keep all documentation.
- Check that the policy covers ambulances or an emergency flight home.

MEDICAL CHECKLIST

- Acetaminophen (Tylenol) or aspirin
- Adhesive or paper tape
- Antibacterial ointment (eg Bactroban) for cuts and abrasions
- Antibiotics
- Antidiarrheal drugs (eg loperamide)
- Antihistamines (for hay fever and allergic reactions)
- Anti-inflammatory drugs (eg ibuprofen)
- Bandages, gauze, gauze rolls
- DEET-containing insect repellent for the skin
- Malaria pills – recommended for the Darién
- Oral rehydration salts
- Permethrin-containing insect spray for clothing, tents and bed nets
- Pocket knife
- Scissors, safety pins, tweezers
- Steroid cream or cortisone (for poison ivy and other allergic rashes)
- Sunblock
- Syringes and sterile needles
- Thermometer

In Panama

AVAILABILITY & COST OF HEALTH CARE

Good medical care is widely available in Panama City and also David – it's even sought after, with the cities doing brisk business in medical tourism – though it's limited elsewhere. Most doctors and hospitals expect cash payment, regardless of whether you have travel health insurance.

INFECTIOUS DISEASES

Chikungunya

Chikungunya is a virus transmitted by mosquitoes. Common symptoms include fever and joint pain, though sufferers may experience headache, muscle pain, joint swelling or rash. Since there is no vaccine or treatment, travelers should prevent mosquito bites by using insect repellent, wearing long sleeves and pants, and staying indoors. Consult www.cdc.gov for up-to-date information.

Dengue Fever

A viral infection, dengue fever (breakbone fever) is transmitted by mosquitoes breeding in standing water. It is especially common in densely populated, urban environments. Flu-like symptoms include fever, muscle aches, joint pains, headaches, nausea and vomiting, often followed by a rash. Most cases resolve in a few days. Take analgesics such as acetaminophen/paracetamol (Tylenol) and drink plenty of fluids. Severe cases may require hospitalization. In recent times, Panama has reported cases nationally.

> **PRACTICALITIES**
>
> - Panama uses the metric system, but occasionally weights and measures are given in pounds and miles.
> - Gasoline is measured by the *galón* (gallon).

Hepatitis A

The vaccine for hepatitis A is extremely safe and highly effective. The second most common travel-related infection (after traveler's diarrhea), it's a viral infection of the liver that is usually acquired by ingestion of contaminated water, food or ice. Symptoms include fever, malaise, jaundice, nausea, vomiting and abdominal pain. Most cases resolve without complications, though hepatitis A occasionally causes severe liver damage. There is no treatment.

Hepatitis B

Hepatitis B is a liver infection usually acquired by sexual contact or by exposure to infected blood, generally through blood transfusions or contaminated needles. The hepatitis B vaccine is safe and highly effective. A total of three injections is necessary to establish full immunity.

Leishmaniasis

Leishmaniasis occurs in rural and forested areas throughout Panama, especially the eastern and south-central regions. The disease causes slow-growing ulcers on the body, but the infection may become generalized, especially in those with HIV. Leishmaniasis is transmitted by sand flies. To protect yourself, follow the same precautions as for mosquitoes, with finer-size mesh on mosquito netting (at least 18 holes to the linear inch).

Leptospirosis

Leptospirosis is acquired by exposure to water contaminated by the urine of infected animals. The greatest risk occurs at times of flooding, when sewage overflow may contaminate water sources. Initial symptoms resemble a mild flu and usually subside in a few days, but a minority of cases are complicated by jaundice or meningitis. Minimize your risk by staying out of bodies of fresh water that may be contaminated by animal urine.

Malaria

Malaria is transmitted by mosquito bites, usually between dusk and dawn. High-spiking fevers may be accompanied by chills, sweats, headache, body aches, weakness, vomiting or diarrhea. Severe cases may lead to seizures, confusion, coma and death.

Malaria pills are recommended for rural areas in the provinces east of the Panama Canal and Ngöbe-Buglé Comarca. There have been rare cases in the provinces of Bocas del Toro, Colón and Veraguas.

Protecting yourself against mosquito bites is the best prevention. If you develop a fever after returning home, see a physician, as malaria symptoms may not occur for months.

Rabies

In Panama, rabies is transmitted mainly by vampire bats. If you are bitten by any animal, thoroughly wash the wound and visit a doctor to determine whether further treatment is necessary. A vaccine is recommended if you will be in wild areas, since Panama does not carry the immunoglobulin that bite victims without the vaccine need right away (getting it involves an urgent flight out).

Traveler's Diarrhea

To prevent traveler's diarrhea, avoid untreated tap water, eat fresh fruits or vegetables that are cooked or peeled, and be highly selective when eating food from street vendors.

If you develop diarrhea, drink plenty of fluids, preferably an oral rehydration solution containing lots of salt and sugar. A few loose stools don't require treatment, but if you start having more than four or five stools a day, you should start taking an antibiotic (usually a quinolone drug) and an antidiarrheal agent (such as loperamide). If diarrhea is bloody or persists for more than 72 hours, or is accompanied by fever, shaking chills or severe abdominal pain, seek medical attention.

Typhoid

Typhoid is caused by ingestion of food or water contaminated by *Salmonella typhi;* fever occurs in virtually all cases. Other symptoms may include headache, malaise, muscle aches, dizziness, loss of appetite, nausea and abdominal pain. Either diarrhea or constipation may occur. Possible complications include intestinal perforation or bleeding, confusion, delirium and, rarely, coma.

The vaccine is usually given orally but is also available as an injection. The treatment drug is usually a quinolone antibiotic such

TAP WATER

Tap water in Panama City *is* safe to drink, as is the water in most other parts of the country. However, you're better off buying bottled water or purifying your own water in the provinces of Bocas del Toro and Guna Yala.

If you have the means, vigorous boiling for one minute is the most effective method of water purification. Another option is to disinfect water with iodine pills; add 2% tincture of iodine to one quart or liter of water (five drops to clear water, 10 drops to cloudy water) and let stand for 30 minutes. If the water is cold, longer times may be required.

VACCINATIONS

VACCINE	RECOMMENDED FOR	DOSAGE	SIDE EFFECTS
hepatitis A	all travelers	1 dose before trip; booster 6-12 months later	soreness at injection site, headaches, body aches
typhoid	all travelers	4 capsules by mouth, 1 taken every other day	abdominal pain, nausea, rash
yellow fever	all travelers	1 dose lasts 10 years	headaches, body aches; severe reactions are rare
hepatitis B	long-term travelers in close contact with the local population	3 doses over 6-month period	soreness at injection site, low-grade fever
rabies	travelers who may have contact with animals and may not have access to medical care	3 doses over 3- to 4-week period	soreness at injection site, headaches, body aches
tetanus-diphtheria	all travelers who haven't had a booster within 10 years	1 dose lasts 10 years	soreness at injection site
measles	travelers born after 1956 who have only had one measles vaccination	1 dose	fever, rash, joint pains, allergic reaction
chickenpox	travelers who've never had chickenpox	2 doses 1 month apart	fever, mild case of chickenpox

asciprofloxacin (Cipro) or levofloxacin (Levaquin).

Yellow Fever

A life-threatening viral infection, yellow fever is transmitted by mosquitoes in forested areas. Flu-like symptoms include fever, chills, headache, muscle aches, backache, loss of appetite, nausea and vomiting. Some patients enter a second, toxic phase, which can lead to death.

Vaccination is recommended for travelers visiting Chepo, Darién and continental Guna Yala.

Zika

Zika virus spreads through the bite of an infected *Aedes* species mosquito. Common symptoms include fever, rash, joint pain and conjunctivitis. Most victims experience mild illness with symptoms that last for several days to a week. Since Zika may cause brain damage in to infants in utero, pregnant women should avoid visiting a Zika hot spot. The virus may also be sexually transmitted by an infected partner. Since there is no vaccine or treatment, travelers should prevent mosquito bites by using insect repellent, wearing long sleeves and pants, and staying indoors. Consult www.cdc.gov for up-to-date information.

Internet Access

Most cities and towns in Panama have inexpensive internet cafes. Public wi-fi access is increasingly common in bus terminals, plazas, libraries and restaurants. Hotels and hostels in more tourist-oriented areas have wi-fi and some computer terminals for use; the Guna Yala and Darién regions are exceptions.

In listings, the internet symbol indicates a computer available for public use; the wi-fi symbol indicates free wi-fi for guests or patrons.

Legal Matters

The legal drinking age in Panama is 18, which is strictly enforced in Panama City and generally ignored elsewhere.

Remember that you are legally required to carry identification at all times. This should be a photographic ID, preferably a passport. Although this may seem like an inconvenience, police officers reserve the right to request documentation from tourists at all times, and several readers have been forced to spend the night in prison for failure to produce proper ID.

It is illegal for men and women to walk around topless, even if you are on your way to the beach. This rule is strictly enforced in Bocas del Toro town on Isla Colón, and you can expect to be stopped on the streets by police officers if you don't cover up.

In Panama you are presumed guilty until found innocent. If you are accused of a serious crime, you will be taken to jail, where you will likely spend several months before your case goes before a judge. Some simple but valuable advice: stay away from people who commit crimes. For example, you can expect to go to jail if discovered in a car found to contain illegal drugs, even if they aren't yours.

In Panama penalties for possession of even small amounts of illegal drugs are much stricter than in the USA, Europe, Australia and almost everywhere else. Defendants often spend years in prison before they are brought to trial and, if convicted (as is usually the case), can expect sentences of several more years. Most lawyers won't accept drug cases because the outcome is certain: conviction.

If you are jailed, your embassy will offer only limited assistance. This may include a visit from an embassy staff member to make sure your human rights have not been violated, letting your family know where you are and putting you in contact with a lawyer (whom you must pay yourself). Embassy officials will not bail you out.

Maps

International Travel Maps (☎in Canada 604-273-1400; www.itmb.com) publishes an excellent 1:800,000 color map showing the geographical features, cities, towns, national parks, airports and roads of Panama. Maps are available for purchase online.

At **Instituto Geográfico Nacional** (Tommy Guardia; Map p46; ☎236-2444; La Cresta; ⌚8am-4pm Mon-Fri) in Panama City, you can buy topographical maps of selected cities and regions. Various free tourist publications distributed in Panama also have maps, though hiking maps are rarely available at national-park ranger stations.

Money

ATMs

Throughout Panama, ATMs are readily available, except in the Darién, on Isla Contadora and in the Archipiélago de San Blás. Look for the red 'sistema clave' sign. Generally speaking, ATMs accept cards on most networks (Plus, Cirrus, Mastercard, Visa, Amex), though a charge is usually levied depending on your issuing bank. The amount that can be withdrawn at one time varies from bank to bank, though it is usually around US$500.

There are several places where it's essential to show up with cash. Among tourist destinations, the following places have no banks, and it's a long way to the nearest ATM: Santa Catalina, Santa Fé, Boca Brava, Isla Contadora, Isla Grande (Archipiélago de Bocas del Toro), Portobelo, Isla de Coiba and the Darién.

Credit & Debit Cards

Although they are widely accepted at travel agencies, upscale hotels and many restaurants, credit cards can present difficulties elsewhere. In short, carry enough cash to get you to the next bank or ATM.

Always find out if your hotel or restaurant accepts credit in advance to avoid unpleasant surprises.

If charging a big-ticket item, it's best to check in with your bank in advance. Most cards charge a fee (between 3% and 10%) for international use.

Currency

Panama uses the US dollar as its currency. The official name for it is the Balboa, but it's exactly the same bill. People use the terms *dólar* and Balboa interchangeably.

Panamanian coins are of the same value, size and metal as US coins, though both are frequently used. Coins include one, five, 10, 25 and 50 *centavos* (or *centésimos*) – 100 *centavos* equal one Balboa (dollar). Most businesses won't break US$50 and US$100 bills, and those that do may require you to present your passport.

Moneychangers

The only bank that exchanges foreign currency is the Banco Nacional de Panamá counter at Tocumen International Airport. Outside the airport, only a *casa de cambio* (exchange house) can change foreign currency for dollars. They are rare outside Panama City.

Taxes & Refunds

A tax of 10% is added to the price of hotel rooms. When you inquire about a hotel, ask whether the quoted price includes the tax.

A 5% sales tax is levied on all nonfood products.

Traveler's Checks

Although they can be cashed at a few banks, traveler's checks are rarely accepted by businesses, and traveler's checks in currencies other than US dollars are not accepted anywhere in Panama. In addition, some banks will only accept American Express traveler's checks. The banks that do accept traveler's checks typically charge an exchange fee equal to 1% of the amount of the check.

Opening Hours

Opening hours vary throughout the year. The following are high-season hours.

Banks 8:30am to 1pm or 3pm; some open Saturday morning

Bars and clubs Bars from 9pm; clubs from 11pm to 3am or 4am

Government offices 8am to 4pm Monday to Friday

Malls and shops 10am to 9pm or 10pm

Offices 8am to noon and 1:30pm to 5pm Monday to Friday

Restaurants 7am to 10am, noon to 3pm and 6pm to 10pm; later in Panama City; often closed Sunday

Supermarkets 8am to 9pm; some open 24 hours

Photography

Panamanians may be low-key about having their photo taken, but it is always best to ask before doing so. General landscape scenes that include locals are usually fine. Flash equipment is forbidden in Panama's churches and museums.

In general, indigenous people should not be photographed without their permission. In addition, it may ruin any chance of interaction you have with locals. In the Comarca de Guna Yala, photographing locals is considered rude. Those who will pose may attach a price tag – usually US$1 per photo.

Those honing their skills should consult Lonely Planet's *Travel Photography*.

Post

Correos de Panama (www.correospanama.gob.pa) operates Panama's mail service; check the website for locations. Airmail to the USA takes five to 10 days; to Europe and Australia it takes 10 days. Panama has neither vending machines for stamps nor drop-off boxes for mail. You may be able to buy stamps and send mail from an upscale hotel to avoid going to the post office and standing in line. To mail packages, bring all packing materials yourself.

Public Holidays

Días feriados (national holidays) are taken seriously in Panama, and banks, public offices and many stores close. Public transportation tends to be tight on all holidays and the days immediately preceding or following them – book tickets ahead.

There is no bus service at all on the Thursday afternoon and Friday before Easter, and many businesses are closed for the entire Semana Santa (Holy Week; the week before Easter). From Thursday to Easter Sunday, all bars are closed and alcohol sales are prohibited. Beach hotels are usually booked several weeks in advance for Semana Santa, though a limited choice of rooms is often available.

The week between Christmas and New Year, along with the first week of the year, tends to be an unofficial holiday. In addition, various towns have celebrations for their own particular days throughout the year. These other holidays and special events are not official holidays, and businesses remain open.

Most national holidays are celebrated on Monday to create long weekends. When holidays fall on a Thursday or Friday, they are celebrated on the following Monday; holidays that happen to fall on Tuesday or Wednesday are usually celebrated the prior Monday.

New Year's Day January 1

Martyrs' Day January 9

Good Friday, Easter March/April

Workers' Day May 1

Founding of Old Panama (Panama City only) August 15

Hispanic Day October 12

National Anthem Day November 1

All Souls' Day November 2

Independence Day November 3

First Call for Independence November 10

Independence from Spain November 28

Mothers' Day December 8

Christmas Day December 25

Safe Travel

Crime is a problem in parts of Panama City, though the city's better districts are safer than in many other capitals. The city of Colón has street crime, so consult hotel staff on areas to avoid.

Parts of Darién Province bordering Colombia are still a staging ground for narco-traffickers and human traffickers. Always register with **SENAFRONT** (Servicio Nacional de Fronteras; ☎ in Panama City 527-1000; www.senafront.gob.pa) in Panama City before traveling and preferably go with a guide See p243 for more information.

There have been cases of drug trafficking on boats traveling the Caribbean from Colombia north to Panama, and to a lesser extent on the Pacific side.

Hiking Safety

Though it's tropical, Panama runs the gamut from hot to cold and hiking is not easy here. Always ask local outfitters or rangers about trail conditions before heading out, and ensure you go adequately prepared. Carry plenty of water, even on short journeys, and always bring food, matches and adequate clothing – jungles *do* get quite a bit colder at night, particularly at higher elevations.

Hikers have been known to get lost in rainforests, even seemingly user-friendly ones such as Parque Nacional Volcán Barú and the Sendero Los Quetzales. Landslides, storms and vegetation growth can make trails difficult to follow. In some cases, even access roads can deteriorate enough for transport to leave you a few miles before your intended drop-off point. This is just the reality of the jungle, and there is no official rescue organization to help. If you are heading out without a guide, let your plans be known at your hotel and tell them the number of days you will be gone.

Never walk in unmarked rainforest; if there's no trail going in, you can assume that there won't be one when you decide to turn around and come back out. Always plan your transportation in advance – know where and when the last bus will pass your terminus, or arrange for a taxi pickup with a responsible, recommended transporter.

Police

Police corruption is not as big a problem in Panama as it is in some other Latin American countries. However, it's not unheard of for a police officer to stop a motorist for no obvious reason, invent a violation, and levy a fine to be paid on the spot. Showing confusion will sometimes fluster the officer into letting you go. If there has been a violation, offer to go to the police station to pay.

Some cities in Panama have tourist police – a division created to deal specifically with travelers. Identifiable by armbands on their uniform, officers in this division may be more helpful.

Swimming Safety

Unfortunately, drownings occur every year in Panamanian waters, about 80% of them caused by rip currents. A rip is a strong current that pulls the swimmer out to sea. It occurs when two currents that move parallel to the shore meet, causing the opposing waters to choose the path of least resistance, which is the path out to sea.

Some tips:

- If you are caught in a rip, stay calm and swim parallel to the shore to get out of it – rip currents dissipate quickly.
- It is most important to remember that rip currents will pull you out but not under.
- When the current dissipates, swim back in at a 45-degree angle to the shore to avoid being caught by the current again.
- Do not try to swim directly back in, as you would be swimming against the rip and would only exhaust yourself.
- If you feel a rip while you are wading, try to come back in sideways, thus offering less body surface to the current. If you cannot make headway, walk parallel to the beach until you get out of the rip.

Thefts & Muggings

Tourist-oriented crime is uncommon in Panama, but it does happen.

- Be smart – avoid carrying all your money in one place and avoid entering areas that appear unsafe. If you look like you don't have anything of value on you, you're less likely to interest a mugger.
- Ask your hotel about spots to avoid and stay where it's well lit and well populated.
- Victims of any crime should get a police report as soon as possible. This is a requirement for any insurance claim, although it is unlikely that the police will be able to recover the property. Non-Spanish speakers can ask their embassy for help.
- Panama has a long history of business-related crime, particularly with regard to real estate. If you want to make local investments, make sure you check them out *thoroughly*. If a deal seems too good to be true, it probably is.

GOVERNMENT TRAVEL ADVICE

Government websites have information on potential danger areas and general safety tips. They sometimes err on the side of excessive caution:

Australia (www.smartraveller.gov.au)

Canada (www.voyage.gc.ca)

Germany (www.auswaertiges-amt.de)

Japan (www.mofa.go.jp)

Netherlands (www.minbuza.nl)

New Zealand (www.safetravel.govt.nz)

UK (www.fco.gov.uk)

USA (https://step.state.gov/step)

Telephone

Panama's country code is ☎507. To call Panama from abroad, use the country code before the seven-digit Panamanian telephone number. There are no local area codes in Panama.

Pay phones have been replaced with internet calling services. If you are traveling for an extended period, it may be useful to get a SIM card (US$5) if you have an unlocked cell phone. Otherwise, kiosks in malls sell pay-per-use phones for as little as US$20, and many come with minutes loaded. Having a phone can be invaluable for last-minute reservations or directions, especially since some lodgings are unresponsive to emails.

Cell Phones

Local SIM cards can be used in unlocked phones. Choose your carrier carefully, as only certain operators have coverage in the San Blás Islands and Darién Province.

International Calls

Travelers wishing to make international calls can do so via an internet cafe or a public wi-fi connection. Some cafes provide headphones for internet calls.

Connecting to an international operator from a landline is easy. To connect with a local international operator, simply dial ☎106. For an international operator in the USA, dial ☎109 (AT&T). To reach a Costa Rican operator, dial ☎107; for a Colombian operator, dial ☎116.

Time

From late October to early April, Panama coincides with Eastern Standard Time, which is one hour ahead of the rest of Central America. The country does not observe daylight-saving time.

Toilets

Most bathrooms have signs requesting users to place used toilet paper in trash bins instead of flushing it because the narrow piping may clog up.

Be advised that in parts of Guna Yala and Bocas del Toro, whatever you flush goes straight out to sea. While you certainly can't stop nature from calling, be sure not to flush anything else that doesn't belong in the sea.

Public toilets are found mainly in bus terminals, airports and restaurants. In Spanish, restrooms are called *baños* and are often marked *caballeros* (gentlemen) and *damas* (ladies). Outside the cities, toilet paper is not always provided, so consider carrying a personal supply.

Tourist Information

Autoridad de Turismo Panamá (ATP; Panama Tourism Authority; Map p50; ☎526-7000; www.visitpanama.com; 29th fl, Edificio Bisca, cnr Av Balboa & Aquilino de la Guardia, Bella Vista; ⏰8:30am-3pm Mon-Fri) is the national tourism agency. Outside the flagship Panama City office, ATP runs offices in Bocas del Toro, Boquete, Colón, David, Paso Canoas, Penonomé, Portobelo, Santiago, Villa de Los Santos, Las Tablas, El Valle and Pedasí. There are smaller information counters in Casco Viejo, and in both Tocumen International Airport and Albrook domestic airport.

ATP has a few useful maps and brochures but often has a problem keeping enough in stock for distribution to tourists. Most offices are staffed with people who speak only Spanish. Some employees really try to help, but others are just passing the time. As a general rule, you will get more useful information if you have specific questions.

Travelers with Disabilities

Panama is generally not wheelchair friendly, though high-end hotels provide wheelchair-accessible rooms. There are parking spaces for people with disabilities and some oversized bathroom stalls. Outside the capital, adequate infrastructure is lacking.

Download Lonely Planet's free *Accessible Travel guide* from http://lptravel.to/AccessibleTravel.

Visas

Onward Tickets

Travelers officially need onward tickets before they are allowed to enter Panama. This requirement is not often checked at Tocumen International Airport, but travelers arriving by land should anticipate a need to show an onward ticket.

If you're heading to Colombia, Venezuela or another South American country from Panama, you may need an onward or round-trip ticket before you will be allowed entry into that country or even allowed to board the plane if you're flying. A quick check with the appropriate embassy – easy to do via the internet – will tell you whether the country that you're heading to has an onward-ticket requirement.

Passports, Tourist Cards & Visas

Every visitor needs a valid passport and an onward ticket to enter Panama, but further requirements vary by nationality and change occasionally. Anyone planning a trip to Panama is well advised to check online to obtain the latest information on entry requirements. Ticketing agents of airlines that fly to Panama and tour operators can often provide this information. Some tips:

- Tourist-card fees are included in the price of your air ticket.
- Visitors generally get a 90-day stamp in their passport upon entering Panama.
- After 90 days, visas and tourist cards can be extended at *migración* (immigration) offices.
- Travelers entering Panama overland will probably be asked to show an onward ticket and potentially proof of sufficient funds (US$500) or a credit card.

At the time of research, people holding passports from the following countries needed to show only their passports to enter Panama: Argentina, Austria, Belgium, Chile, Colombia, Costa Rica, Czech Republic, Denmark, El Salvador, Finland, France, Germany, Greece, Guatemala, Holland, Honduras, Hungary, Ireland, Israel, Italy, Luxembourg, Paraguay, Poland, Portugal, Singapore, South Korea, Spain, Sweden, Switzerland, the UK and Uruguay.

People from the following countries need a passport and a tourist card: Antigua, Australia, Bahamas, Barbados, Belize, Canada, China, Dominican Republic, Granada, Guyana, Jamaica, Japan, New Zealand, Taiwan, Thailand, Tobago, Trinidad, the USA and Venezuela.

Citizens from countries not on this list will need to

obtain a visa, available at Panamanian embassies or consulates. Contact the one nearest you or call **Migración y Naturalización** (Immigration Office; ☎507-1051, 507-1800; www.migracion.gob.pa; cnr Av Cuba & Calle 28 Este, Calidonia; ⏰7:30am-3:30pm Mon-Fri) in Panama City.

In the event that you lose your passport while in Panama, you'll need proof of when you entered the country to be able to leave. That proof, strangely enough, does not come from an immigration office but from the airline you flew in on. You need to go to the airline's main office in Panama City and request a certification of your entry date *(certificación de vuelo)*. There's no charge, but you'll likely be asked to come back the next day to pick it up. When you leave the country, along with your new passport (obtained from your embassy in Panama City), you'll present your *certificación de vuelo* to an immigration agent.

Extensions

Visas and tourist cards are both good for 90 days. To extend your stay, you'll have to go to an Migración y Naturalización office in Panama City, David or Chitré. You must bring your passport and photocopies of the page with your personal information and of the stamp of your most recent entry to Panama. You must also bring two passport-size photos, an onward air or bus ticket and a letter to the director stating your reasons for wishing to extend your visit. You must have proof of funds (US$500) for the remainder of your stay. You will have to fill out a *prórroga de turista* (tourist extension) and pay a fee. You will then be issued a plastic photo-ID card. Go early in the day as the whole process takes about two hours.

If you have extended your time, you will also need to obtain a *permiso de salida* (exit permit) to leave the country. For this, bring your passport and a *paz y salvo* (a certificate stating you don't owe any back taxes) to the immigration office. *Paz y salvos* are issued at Ministerios de Economia y Finanzas, found in towns with immigration offices; obtaining one simply requires that you bring in your passport, fill out a form and pay US$1.

These documents can be obtained in Panama City at the **Migración y Naturalización** and the **Ministerio de Economia y Finanzas, Dirección de Ingresos** (☎800-4636; www.dgi.gob.pa; cnr Via España & Calle 52 Este, Campo Alegre).

Volunteering

Volunteer opportunities are few in Panama, so potential volunteers should look for programs run by reputable, well-known NGOs.

Women Travelers

Female travelers usually find Panama safe. A minority of Panamanian men may make flirtatious comments, hiss, honk their horn or stare, even if you're accompanied. Don't take it as a challenge. A kind of hormonal babble, this behavior is as much about male bonding as the female passerby. The best response is to follow the lead of Panamanian women: give these men a wide berth, ignore their comments and look away.

While locals might get away with skimpy, stretchy clothing, travelers will naturally attract less attention with a more conservative approach. In the interior, dress is more formal, with skirts and nice sandals the norm. It is not legal to go topless, even in beach towns, and even for men.

Women traveling solo will get more attention than those traveling in pairs or groups. Although assault and rape of foreign travelers is rare, avoid placing yourself in risky scenarios. In bars, do not take drinks from strangers. In general, don't walk alone in isolated places, don't hitchhike and always pay particular attention to your surroundings.

If you are taking a long-distance bus, sit next to a woman or a family if you are nervous about come-ons. Be picky about your taxis: though shared taxis (between unknown parties) are common, avoid those with more than one man. If the driver tries to pick up another fare, you can offer to pay more to travel alone.

Work

It's difficult for foreigners to find work in Panama. The government prefers to give jobs to Panamanians, and labor laws reflect this sentiment. Foreigners legally employed in Panama generally have their own businesses, possess skills not found in Panama, or work for companies that have special agreements with the Panamanian government.

Transportation

GETTING THERE & AWAY

Entering the Country

Passengers entering Panama by air are less scrutinized than those crossing by land. Upon arrival, travelers may have to fill out a tourist card depending on their nationality.

The most popular overland crossing is from Costa Rica at Paso Canoas. You may be asked to show an onward ticket – a return bus ticket to Costa Rica will suffice. Other crossings include the low-key border at Sixaola & Guabito and the seldom-used Río Sereno.

Air

Airports

Panama has four international airports, but you're likely to arrive at one of the following two:

- **Tocumen International Airport** (238-2700; www.tocumenpanama.aero; Av Domingo Díaz; Panama City)
- **Aeropuerto Enrique Malek** (721-1072; David)

Viva Colombia airline uses Panamá Pacífico International Airport, the former US Howard Air Force Base, located 10km from Panama City.

Currently only package charters use the coastal Scarlett Martinez International Airport in Río Hato, Coclé Province. Commercial flights from the capital may soon begin.

Airlines

Airlines with international flights to Panama:

- **Air Panama** (316-9000; www.airpanama.com)
- **American Airlines** (264-8999; www.aa.com)
- **Avianca** (264-5919; www.avianca.com)
- **Copa** (217-5656; www.copaair.com; 8am-5pm Mon-Fri)
- **Delta Airlines** (238-4793; www.delta.com)
- **Iberia** (238-4116; www.taca.com)
- **Taca Airlines** (238-4116; www.taca.com)
- **Viva Colombia** (800-157-1073; www.vivacolombia.co)

Land

Many travelers arrive in Panama by bus from Costa Rica. It's recommended that you get to the border early in order to ensure that you don't miss onward transportation on the other side. There are no roads into Colombia, and travelers are strongly discouraged from crossing overland due to the instability of the border region.

CLIMATE CHANGE & TRAVEL

Every form of transport that relies on carbon-based fuel generates CO_2, the main cause of human-induced climate change. Modern travel is dependent on airplanes, which might use less fuel per kilometer per person than most cars but travel much greater distances. The altitude at which aircraft emit gases (including CO_2) and particles also contributes to their climate change impact. Many websites offer 'carbon calculators' that allow people to estimate the carbon emissions generated by their journey and, for those who wish to do so, to offset the impact of the greenhouse gases emitted with contributions to portfolios of climate-friendly initiatives throughout the world. Lonely Planet offsets the carbon footprint of all staff and writer travel.

Border Crossings

There are three border crossings between Costa Rica and Panama. Most travelers cross at Paso Canoas. Note that Panama is always one hour ahead of Costa Rica. (Opening and closing times below are given in Panama time.)

To enter Panama from Costa Rica, you'll need a passport and an onward ticket. Some nationalities may require a visa (p16).

You can also be asked for an onward ticket if you are entering Costa Rica. If you do not possess one, it is acceptable to buy a return bus ticket back to Panama.

PASO CANOAS

The most heavily trafficked border crossing to/from Costa Rica is at **Paso Canoas** (⊙7am to 7pm), 53.6km northwest of David on the Interamericana.

➡ The best place to sleep before crossing is David.

➡ Ensure that you have both entry and exit stamps put in your passport.

➡ Allow one to 1½ hours for the formalities on both sides. Buses from David depart frequently for the border (US$2.10, 50 minutes, every 15 minutes) from 4:30am.

➡ On the Costa Rican side, you can catch regular buses to San José or other parts of the country.

➡ From David, there are also taxis to Paso Canoas (US$35).

SIXAOLA & GUABITO

The Caribbean border post at **Guabito & Sixaola** (⊙ 8am to 5pm), 16km northwest of Changuinola, sees less traffic than Pacific-side routes, though most travelers find it hassle-free.

➡ Buses from Changuinola depart frequently for the border (US$1, 20 minutes, every half-hour) from 6am to 7pm.

➡ On the Costa Rican side of the border, you can catch regular buses on to Puerto Limón and San José, as well as regional destinations.

RÍO SERENO

The least trafficked crossing into Costa Rica is the border post at **Río Sereno** (⊙9am-5pm Mon-Sat, to 3pm Sun), located 35km northwest of Volcán.

➡ Buses to the border depart from David and travel via La Concepción, Volcán and Santa Clara (US$5.10, 2½ hours, every half-hour).

➡ On the Costa Rican side of the border, you can take a 15-minute bus or taxi ride to San Vito, where you can catch buses to regional destinations.

Sea

It's possible to cross to Colombia by sea, though it can be a rough crossing. Multiday motorboat and sailboat trips depart from Colón Province (p211) or the Comarca de Guna Yala (p226).

Tours

Panama's tourism industry is still young, though the number of tour operators is growing rapidly. While increasingly navigable for the independent traveler, Panama does have special conditions (complex logistics, limited public access and big wilderness) that make contracting a tour operator a good option. Top attractions including the Darién and Coiba are relatively inaccessible without a guide.

Prices vary depending on the services you require and whether you are prepared to join a group. It's increasingly common for hostels to provide their own budget tours for guests.

Ancon Expeditions (Map p50;☑269-9415; www. anconexpeditions.com; Edificio Dorado, No 3, Calle 49 A Este, El Cangrejo) Ancon offers quality service and employs the country's best nature guides, many with decades of experience and speaking multiple languages. Regular departures visit destinations throughout Panama. The company operates the Punta Patiño lodge in the Darién. It's also active in conservation.

Ecocircuitos (☑315-1488; www. ecocircuitos.com; Albrook Plaza, 2nd fl, No 31, Ancón, Panama City) ✔ A great outfitter offering a range of tailored tours throughout the country, including wildlife-watching, adventure tourism, community tourism and beach destinations. It is a member of APTSO (Asociación Panameño de Turismo Sostenible), Panama's sustainable-tourism alliance. English is spoken.

Jungle Treks (☑6438-3130; www.jungletreks.com) Started by a bilingual naturalist guide, Jungle Treks runs a number of unique, recommended expeditions. Destinations include the Darién, the Chiriquí highlands, Veraguas and the canal watershed. Trips can be custom made but require six participants and a three-day minimum.

Scubapanama (☑261-3841; www.scubapanama.com; Calle 52c Oeste, Vista Hermosa) The country's oldest dive operator, offering a variety of trips throughout the country.

Sendero Panama (☑390-5526, 6429-8163; www.sendero panama.com) ✔ A reputable outfitter offering a variety of private tours around Panama, as well as day trips from Panama City. Options include walking, birding, family tours and multisport activities. English is spoken. Also a member of APTSO.

Yala Tours (☑232-0215, 6641-6676; www.yalatourspanama. com) This recommended small outfitter specializes in nature travel and indigenous culture. In the canal area, Rainald offers wildlife observation in Lago Gatún by boat or kayak. Day trips include Parque Nacional Soberanía and Emberá village visits. Swiss-run, with multiple languages spoken. Also has good experience in the Darién for tailored expedition-style trips.

Independent Guides

Skilled independent naturalists and guides are available for trips to locations throughout the country.

Ivan Hoyos (☎6678-2657; migratorio@hotmail.com) A naturalist guide with years of experience, specializing in the Darién, the Chiriquí highlands and Pipeline Rd. Speaks fluent English and German.

Mario Bernal (☎info 6693-8213; mariobernalg@gmail.com) An English- and Spanish-speaking guide from El Valle available for highland tours, birdwatching and trips around Panamá Province.

GETTING AROUND

As most Panamanians use public transportation, it's reasonably priced and connections are frequent.

Bus Most cities have a bus terminal with frequent regional departures and connections to Panama City and Costa Rica.

Car Rentals are not cheap, but roads are generally in good condition. Some areas, including Panama City and many rural parts of the country, are very poorly signposted.

Train Mostly a novelty, a rail service runs between Panama City and Colón.

Air Domestic flights depart Panama City's Albrook Airport to destinations throughout the country.

Air

Airlines in Panama

Panama's domestic destinations are served by **Air Panama** (☎316-9000; www.airpanama.com) and **Copa Airlines** (☎217-5656; www.copaair.com; ⏲8am-5pm Mon-Fri). Domestic flights depart Panama City from Albrook Airport. Located near the Costa Rican border, David's Aeropuerto Enrique Malek frequently handles flights to and from San José.

Book ahead in high season, when demand for flights to destinations such as Bocas overflows. Always confirm bookings.

Bicycle

If you can get over the heat, you can cycle through Panama easily enough, with lodgings within a day's ride. Cycling within larger Panamanian cities – particularly Panama City – is not for the faint of heart. Roads tend to be narrow, and people drive aggressively. Also, frequent rains reduce motorists' visibility and bicycle-tire grip.

The best places for cyclists in Panama City are the coastal routes of the Cinta Costera (a dedicated bike trail from downtown and around Casco Viejo) and the Causeway. Weekend cyclist groups often go out to Gamboa via a shady but narrow road.

Outside the cities, Panama's Interamericana boasts the best quality in Central America, although sections have an extremely narrow shoulder. Roads in many of the provinces (especially in Veraguas and Colón) are in poor shape – plan accordingly and bring lots of spare parts.

Boat

Boats are the chief means of transportation in several areas of Panama, particularly in Darién Province, the Archipiélago de Las Perlas, and the San Blás and Bocas del Toro island chains.

From Panama City, there are regular ferries from the Causeway to Isla Taboga and Isla Contadora. Panama City is also the jumping-off point for partial and full Panama Canal transits.

If you're planning an excursion to Isla de Coiba and the national marine park, the best way to reach the island is through an organized boat tour. Local fishers also ply the waters off the coast of Veraguas, though this is a riskier proposition as the seas can get really rough.

The tourist mecca of Bocas del Toro on Isla Colón is accessible from Almirante by frequent water taxis.

Colombian and Guna merchant boats carry cargo and passengers along the San Blás coast between Colón and Puerto Obaldía, stopping at up to 48 of the islands to load and unload passengers and cargo. However, these boats are often dangerously overloaded. Taking passage on a sailboat, or the four-day motorboat service to Colombia, is a wiser option.

Since there aren't many roads in the eastern part of Darién Province, boat travel is often the most feasible way to get from one town to another, especially during the rainy season. The boat of choice here is the *piragua* (long canoe), carved from the trunk of a giant ceiba tree. The shallow hulls of these boats allow them to ride the many rivers that comprise the traditional transport network of eastern Panama. Many are motorized.

Bus

You can take a bus to just about any community in Panama that is reachable by road. Some of the buses are full-size Mercedes Benzes equipped with air con, movie screens and reclining seats. These top-of-the-line buses generally cruise long stretches of highway.

Most common are small Toyota Coaster buses, affectionately called *chivas*. Use these to visit towns on the Península de Azuero and along the Interamericana.

Panama City is phasing out its converted school buses, known as *diablos rojos* (red devils). Replacing them is the Metrobus system. Riders can obtain swipe cards at **Albrook Bus Terminal** (Gran Terminal; Map p46; ☎303-3030, 303-6255; www.grantnt.com) or main bus stops. Official bus stops are used and the transport is air-conditioned.

Car & Motorcycle

Signs can be confusing or wholly absent. In Panama, there are many poor secondary roads, and even paved roads often resemble a lunar landscape.

- On all primary roads the speed limit is 80km/h; on secondary roads it's 60km/h or less.
- Drivers should carry their passport and driver's license.
- If there's an accident, do not move the vehicles (even if they're blocking traffic) until after the police have arrived and made a report. It's also essential for insurance claims.
- Oncoming cars with flashing headlights often indicate that there is a problem or a police speed trap ahead. Slow down immediately. Piles of branches placed on the road's edge often signal a broken-down vehicle.

Rental

Due to the low cost and ready availability of buses and taxis, it isn't necessary to rent a vehicle in Panama unless you intend to go off the beaten track. Some beach areas have notoriously poor roads. There are car-rental agencies in major cities such as Panama City and David. Several also operate from Tocumen International Airport.

To rent a vehicle in Panama, you must be 25 years of age or older and present a passport and driver's license – if you are over 21 and can present a valid credit card, some agencies will waive the age requirement. Even with an international agency, you are usually renting through their subsidiaries and will not get any support from them outside Panama.

Prices for rentals in Panama run from US$35 per day for an economy car to US$110 per day for a *cuatro por cuatro* (4WD). When you rent, carefully inspect the car for minor dents and scratches, missing radio antennae, hubcaps and the presence of a spare tire. Damage *must* be noted on your rental agreement; otherwise you may be charged for it when you return the car.

There have been many reports of theft from rental cars. You should never leave valuables in an unattended car, and you should remove all luggage from the trunk when you're checking into a hotel overnight – most hotels provide parking areas for cars.

Hitchhiking

Hitchhiking is not as widespread in Panama as elsewhere in Central America; most people travel by bus, and visitors would do best to follow suit. Hitchhiking is never entirely safe in any country and we do not recommend it, but it's not uncommon as you arrive in rural areas.

Local Transport

Bus

Metrobus covers Panama city and its outskirts, but services can be difficult to figure out. Panamanians are usually friendly, including bus drivers; they'll often be able to tell you where to wait for a particular bus if you ask in Spanish (few bus drivers speak English). Panama City's Metro system is easy but has a limited route. In general, taxis are cheap and can save a lot of time and hassle.

Taxi

Taxis are cheap and plentiful, though not all drivers have a good grasp of locations.

- Before even getting into a taxi, state your destination and settle on a rate. Panamanian taxis don't have meters, but there are standard fares between neighborhoods of Panama City.
- Get informed. Ask the staff at your accommodation for typical rates between city sectors; these usually go up after dark.
- Taxis can be scarce late at night and around the holidays. At these times, it's best to call for a radio taxi.
- More expensive 'sedan' taxis operate from upscale hotels. They charge double what you'd pay a hailed cab.

Subway

Panama City's new transportation system is known as **El Metro** (www.elmetrodepanama.com; fare US$0.35-1.35; ⏲5am-10pm). The main line connects Albrook with Vía Transistmica, Vía España and Calidonia. It will eventually extend to Tocumen International Airport and branches will go to the suburbs. The main terminal is across from Albrook Bus Terminal. Fares are paid with the same card used for the Metrobus system.

Train

The country's only rail line is the historic Panama Railroad, which runs from Panama City to Colón. **Panama Canal Railway Company** (PCRC; ☎317-6070; www.panarail.com; Carretera Gaillard, Corozal; one way adult/child US$25/15) offers daily passenger service on a fully operational vintage train. Aimed at tourists looking to relive the heyday of luxury rail travel, the hour-long ride runs parallel to the canal and at times traverses thick jungle and rainforest.

Note that the Panama City terminus is located in Corozal, which is a 15-minute cab ride from the capital.

Language

Spanish is the national language of Panama (see also p232 for the basics of the Guna language, spoken in the Comarca de Guna Yala). Latin American Spanish pronunciation is easy, as there's a clear and consistent relationship between what you see written and how it's pronounced. Also, most sounds have equivalents in English.

Note that kh is a throaty sound (like the 'ch' in the Scottish *loch*), v and b are like a soft English 'v' (between a 'v' and a 'b'), and r is strongly rolled. There are also some variations in spoken Spanish across Latin America, the most notable being the pronunciation of the letters *ll* and *y*. In our pronunciation guides they are represented with y because they are pronounced as the 'y' in 'yes' in most of Latin America. Note, however, that in some parts of the continent they sound like the 'lli' in 'million'. Read our colored pronunciation guides as if they were English, and you'll be understood. The stressed syllables are indicated with italics in our pronunciation guides.

The polite form is used in this chapter; where both polite and informal options are given, they are indicated by the abbreviations 'pol' and 'inf'. Where necessary, both masculine and feminine forms of words are included, separated by a slash and with the masculine form first, eg *perdido/a* (m/f).

BASICS

Hello.	*Hola.*	o·la
Goodbye.	*Adiós.*	a·*dyos*

WANT MORE?

For in-depth language information and handy phrases, check out Lonely Planet's *Latin American Spanish Phrasebook*. You'll find it at **shop.lonelyplanet.com**, or you can buy Lonely Planet's iPhone phrasebooks at the Apple App Store.

How are you?	*¿Qué tal?*	ke tal
Fine, thanks.	*Bien, gracias.*	byen *gra*·syas
Excuse me.	*Perdón.*	per·*don*
Sorry.	*Lo siento.*	lo *syen*·to
Please.	*Por favor.*	por fa·*vor*
Thank you.	*Gracias.*	*gra*·syas
You are welcome.	*De nada.*	de *na*·da
Yes./No.	*Sí./No.*	see/no

My name is ...
Me llamo ... me *ya*·mo ...

What's your name?
¿Cómo se llama Usted? *ko*·mo se *ya*·ma oo·*ste* (pol)
¿Cómo te llamas? *ko*·mo te *ya*·mas (inf)

Do you speak English?
¿Habla inglés? *a*·bla een·*gles* (pol)
¿Hablas inglés? *a*·blas een·*gles* (inf)

I don't understand.
Yo no entiendo. yo no en·*tyen*·do

ACCOMMODATIONS

I'd like a single/double room.
Quisiera una habitación individual/doble. kee·*sye*·ra *oo*·na a·bee·ta·*syon* een·dee·vee·*dwal*/*do*·ble

How much is it per night/person?
¿Cuánto cuesta por noche/persona? *kwan*·to *kwes*·ta por *no*·che/per·*so*·na

Does it include breakfast?
¿Incluye el desayuno? een·*kloo*·ye el de·sa·*yoo*·no

campsite	*terreno de cámping*	te·*re*·no de *kam*·peeng
guesthouse	*pensión*	pen·*syon*
hotel	*hotel*	o·*tel*
youth hostel	*albergue juvenil*	al·*ber*·ge khoo·ve·*neel*

Signs

Abierto	Open
Cerrado	Closed
Entrada	Entrance
Hombres/Varones	Men
Mujeres/Damas	Women
Prohibido	Prohibited
Salida	Exit
Servicios/Baños	Toilets

air-con	*aire acondicionado*	*ai*·re a·kon·dee·syo·*na*·do
bathroom	*baño*	*ba*·nyo
bed	*cama*	*ka*·ma
window	*ventana*	ven·*ta*·na

DIRECTIONS

Where's ...?
¿Dónde está ...? — *don*·de es·*ta* ...

What's the address?
¿Cuál es la dirección? — kwal es la dee·rek·*syon*

Could you please write it down?
¿Puede escribirlo, por favor? — *pwe*·de es·kree·*beer*·lo por fa·*vor*

Can you show me (on the map)?
¿Me lo puede indicar (en el mapa)? — me lo *pwe*·de een·dee·*kar* (en el *ma*·pa)

at the corner	*en la esquina*	en la es·*kee*·na
at the traffic lights	*en el semáforo*	en el se·*ma*·fo·ro
behind ...	*detrás de ...*	de·*tras* de ...
in front of ...	*enfrente de ...*	en·*fren*·te de ...
left	*izquierda*	ees·*kyer*·da
next to ...	*al lado de ...*	al *la*·do de ...
opposite ...	*frente a ...*	*fren*·te a ...
right	*derecha*	de·*re*·cha
straight ahead	*todo recto*	*to*·do *rek*·to

EATING & DRINKING

Can I see the menu, please?
¿Puedo ver el menú, por favor? — *pwe*·do ver el me·*noo* por fa·*vor*

What would you recommend?
¿Qué recomienda? — ke re·ko·*myen*·da

Do you have vegetarian food?
¿Tienen comida vegetariana? — *tye*·nen ko·*mee*·da ve·khe·ta·*rya*·na

I don't eat (red meat).
No como (carne roja). — no *ko*·mo (*kar*·ne *ro*·kha)

That was delicious!
¡Estaba buenísimo! — es·*ta*·ba bwe·*nee*·see·mo

Cheers!
¡Salud! — sa·*loo*

The bill, please.
La cuenta, por favor. — la *kwen*·ta por fa·*vor*

I'd like a table for ...	*Quisiera una mesa para ...*	kee·*sye*·ra *oo*·na *me*·sa *pa*·ra ...
(eight) o'clock	*las (ocho)*	las (*o*·cho)
(two) people	*(dos) personas*	(dos) per·*so*·nas

Key Words

bottle	*botella*	bo·*te*·ya
breakfast	*desayuno*	de·sa·*yoo*·no
(too) cold	*(muy) frío*	(mooy) *free*·o
dinner	*cena*	*se*·na
fork	*tenedor*	te·ne·*dor*
glass	*vaso*	*va*·so
hot (warm)	*caliente*	kal·*yen*·te
knife	*cuchillo*	koo·*chee*·yo
lunch	*comida*	ko·*mee*·da
plate	*plato*	*pla*·to
restaurant	*restaurante*	res·tow·*ran*·te
spoon	*cuchara*	koo·*cha*·ra
with/without	*sin/con*	seen/kon

Meat & Fish

beef	*carne de vaca*	*kar*·ne de *va*·ka
chicken	*pollo*	*po*·yo
duck	*pato*	*pa*·to
lamb	*cordero*	kor·*de*·ro
pork	*cerdo*	*ser*·do
prawn	*langostino*	lan·gos·*tee*·no
salmon	*salmón*	sal·*mon*
seafood	*mariscos*	ma·*rees*·kos
tuna	*atún*	a·*toon*
turkey	*pavo*	*pa*·vo
veal	*ternera*	ter·*ne*·ra

Fruit & Vegetables

apple	*manzana*	man·*sa*·na
apricot	*albaricoque*	al·ba·ree·*ko*·ke
banana	*plátano*	*pla*·ta·no
beans	*judías*	khoo·*dee*·as
cabbage	*col*	kol

capsicum	*pimiento*	pee·*myen*·to
carrot	*zanahoria*	sa·na·o·rya
cherry	*cereza*	se·*re*·sa
corn	*maíz*	ma·ees
cucumber	*pepino*	pe·*pee*·no
grape	*uvas*	*oo*·vas
lemon	*limón*	lee·*mon*
lettuce	*lechuga*	le·*choo*·ga
mushroom	*champiñón*	cham·pee·*nyon*
nuts	*nueces*	*nwe*·ses
onion	*cebolla*	se·*bo*·ya
orange	*naranja*	na·*ran*·kha
peach	*melocotón*	me·lo·ko·*ton*
peas	*guisantes*	gee·*san*·tes
pineapple	*piña*	*pee*·nya
plum	*ciruela*	seer·*we*·la
potato	*patata*	pa·*ta*·ta
spinach	*espinacas*	es·pee·*na*·kas
strawberry	*fresa*	*fre*·sa
tomato	*tomate*	to·*ma*·te
watermelon	*sandía*	san·*dee*·a

Other

bread	*pan*	pan
cheese	*queso*	*ke*·so
egg	*huevo*	*we*·vo
honey	*miel*	myel

SPANISH IN PANAMA

Here's a rundown on some of the local expressions and colorful colloquialisms you may hear while traveling in Panama.

salve – street slang for *propina*, or tip

tongo – street slang for 'cop'

hota – street slang for 'police car'

diablo rojo – literally 'red devil'; refers to public buses

¡Bien cuidado! – 'Well taken care of!'; often used by a street person asking for a tip for taking care of your car (in parking lots at restaurants, cinemas, bars)

una pinta/fría – literally, 'one pint' or 'a cold one'; means 'a beer'

Dame una fría. – Give me a cold one (a beer)

guaro – hard liquor

chupata – an all-out drinking party

vuelve loco con vaca – literally 'makes crazy with cow'; refers to drinking *seco* and milk

buena leche – literally 'good milk'; means 'good luck'

salado/a (m/f) – literally 'salty'; refers to someone who is having bad luck

Me estoy comiendo un cable. – literally 'I'm eating a cable'; means 'I'm down on my luck'

Eso está bien pretty. – refers to something nice

¡Eso está pretty pretty! – refers to something supernice

¡Entonces laopé! – Hey, dude!

¡Juega vivo! – Be alert! (look out for your best interests)

¡Ayala bestia! – Holy cow!

¡Chuleta! – common expression similar to 'Holy cow!'

enantes – just now

Voy por fuera. – I'm leaving right now

Pa' lante. – Let's go now

Nos pillamos. – We'll see each other later

pelao/pelaito – common expression for a child

chombo/a (m/f) – an acceptable reference to a black person of Antillean descent

¡Pifioso! – a show-off, or something that looks cool

Tas buena, mami. – You're looking good, mama

racataca/meña – both terms refer to women who wear lots of gold jewelry and are perceived as lacking class

mangajo/a (m/f) – someone who is filthy

ladilla – literally 'crab louse'; refers to an annoying person

Eres un comemierda. – said to a pretentious person

rabiblanco/a (m/f) – literally 'white-tipped'; pejorative reference to a member of the socio-economic elite; comes from *paloma rabíblano* (white-tipped dove), a bird that walks with its head held high and its chest thrust out in a seemingly pretentious way

yeye – refers to kids and adults who pretend to be rich (eg by wearing fancy clothes and maybe driving a fancy car) but who in reality are living well beyond their means for as long as they can

vaina – common word used for 'thing,' as in *Pásame esa vaina* (Pass me that thing)

nueve letras – literally 'nine letters'; refers to Seco Herrerano, the national drink

jam	*mermelada*	mer·me·*la*·da
pepper	*pimienta*	pee·*myen*·ta
rice	*arroz*	a·*ros*
salad	*ensalada*	en·sa·*la*·da
salt	*sal*	sal
soup	*sopa*	*so*·pa
sugar	*azúcar*	a·*soo*·kar

Drinks

beer	*cerveza*	ser·*ve*·sa
coffee	*café*	ka·*fe*
(orange) juice	*zumo (de naranja)*	*soo*·mo (de na·*ran*·kha)
milk	*leche*	*le*·che
red wine	*vino tinto*	*vee*·no *teen*·to
tea	*té*	te
(mineral) water	*agua (mineral)*	*a*·gwa (mee·ne·*ral*)
white wine	*vino blanco*	*vee*·no *blan*·ko

EMERGENCIES

Help!	*¡Socorro!*	so·*ko*·ro
Go away!	*¡Vete!*	*ve*·te

Call ...!	*¡Llame a ...!*	*ya*·me a ...
a doctor	*un médico*	oon *me*·dee·ko
the police	*la policía*	la po·lee·*see*·a

I'm lost.
Estoy perdido/a. es·*toy* per·*dee*·do/a (m/f)

I'm ill.
Estoy enfermo/a. es·*toy* en·*fer*·mo/a (m/f)

I'm allergic to (antibiotics).
Soy alérgico/a a (los antibióticos). soy a·*ler*·khee·ko/a a (los an·tee·*byo*·tee·kos) (m/f)

Where are the toilets?
¿Dónde están los baños? *don*·de es·*tan* los *ba*·nyos

Question Words

How?	*¿Cómo?*	*ko*·mo
What?	*¿Qué?*	ke
When?	*¿Cuándo?*	*kwan*·do
Where?	*¿Dónde?*	*don*·de
Which?	*¿Cuál?* (sg) *¿Cuáles?* (pl)	kwal *kwa*·les
Who?	*¿Quién?*	kyen
Why?	*¿Por qué?*	por ke

SHOPPING & SERVICES

I'd like to buy ...
Quisiera comprar ... kee·*sye*·ra kom·*prar* ...

I'm just looking.
Sólo estoy mirando. *so*·lo es·*toy* mee·*ran*·do

Can I look at it?
¿Puedo verlo? *pwe*·do *ver*·lo

I don't like it.
No me gusta. no me *goos*·ta

How much is it?
¿Cuánto cuesta? *kwan*·to *kwes*·ta

That's too expensive.
Es muy caro. es mooy *ka*·ro

Can you lower the price?
¿Podría bajar un poco el precio? po·*dree*·a ba·*khar* oon *po*·ko el *pre*·syo

There's a mistake in the bill.
Hay un error en la cuenta. ai oon e·*ror* en la *kwen*·ta

ATM	*cajero automático*	ka·*khe*·ro ow·to·*ma*·tee·ko
credit card	*tarjeta de crédito*	tar·*khe*·ta de *kre*·dee·to
internet cafe	*cibercafé*	see·ber·ka·*fe*
market	*mercado*	mer·*ka*·do
post office	*correos*	ko·*re*·os
tourist office	*oficina de turismo*	o·fee·*see*·na de too·*rees*·mo

TIME & DATES

What time is it?	*¿Qué hora es?*	ke *o*·ra es
It's (10) o'clock.	*Son (las diez).*	son (las dyes)
It's half past (one).	*Es (la una) y media.*	es (la *oo*·na) ee *me*·dya

morning	*mañana*	ma·*nya*·na
afternoon	*tarde*	*tar*·de
evening	*noche*	*no*·che
yesterday	*ayer*	a·*yer*
today	*hoy*	oy
tomorrow	*mañana*	ma·*nya*·na

Monday	*lunes*	*loo*·nes
Tuesday	*martes*	*mar*·tes
Wednesday	*miércoles*	*myer*·ko·les
Thursday	*jueves*	*khwe*·ves
Friday	*viernes*	*vyer*·nes
Saturday	*sábado*	*sa*·ba·do
Sunday	*domingo*	do·*meen*·go

Numbers

1	*uno*	oo·no
2	*dos*	dos
3	*tres*	tres
4	*cuatro*	kwa·tro
5	*cinco*	seen·ko
6	*seis*	seys
7	*siete*	sye·te
8	*ocho*	o·cho
9	*nueve*	nwe·ve
10	*diez*	dyes
20	*veinte*	veyn·te
30	*treinta*	treyn·ta
40	*cuarenta*	kwa·ren·ta
50	*cincuenta*	seen·kwen·ta
60	*sesenta*	se·sen·ta
70	*setenta*	se·ten·ta
80	*ochenta*	o·chen·ta
90	*noventa*	no·ven·ta
100	*cien*	syen
1000	*mil*	meel

January	*enero*	e·ne·ro
February	*febrero*	fe·bre·ro
March	*marzo*	mar·so
April	*abril*	a·breel
May	*mayo*	ma·yo
June	*junio*	khoon·yo
July	*julio*	khool·yo
August	*agosto*	a·gos·to
September	*septiembre*	sep·tyem·bre
October	*octubre*	ok·too·bre
November	*noviembre*	no·vyem·bre
December	*diciembre*	dee·syem·bre

TRANSPORTATION

boat	*barco*	bar·ko
bus	*autobús*	ow·to·boos
plane	*avión*	a·vyon
train	*tren*	tren

... ticket	*billete de ...*	bee·ye·te de ...
1st-class	*primera clase*	pree·me·ra kla·se
2nd-class	*segunda clase*	se·goon·da kla·se
one-way	*ida*	ee·da
return	*ida y vuelta*	ee·da ee vwel·ta

first	*primero*	pree·me·ro
last	*último*	ool·tee·mo
next	*próximo*	prok·see·mo

bus stop	*parada de autobuses*	pa·ra·da de ow·to·boo·ses
cancelled	*cancelado*	kan·se·la·do
delayed	*retrasado*	re·tra·sa·do
ticket office	*taquilla*	ta·kee·ya
timetable	*horario*	o·ra·ryo
train station	*estación de trenes*	es·ta·syon de tre·nes

I want to go to ...
Quisiera ir a ... kee·sye·ra eer a ...

Does it stop at ...?
¿Para en ...? pa·ra en ...

What stop is this?
¿Cuál es esta parada? kwal es es·ta pa·ra·da

What time does it arrive/leave?
¿A qué hora llega/sale? a ke o·ra ye·ga/sa·le

Please tell me when we get to ...
¿Puede avisarme cuando lleguemos a ...? pwe·de a·vee·sar·me kwan·do ye·ge·mos a ...

I want to get off here.
Quiero bajarme aquí. kye·ro ba·khar·me a·kee

I'd like to hire a ...	*Quisiera alquilar ...*	kee·sye·ra al·kee·lar ...
bicycle	*una bicicleta*	oo·na bee·see·kle·ta
car	*un coche*	oon ko·che
motorcycle	*una moto*	oo·na mo·to

helmet	*casco*	kas·ko
mechanic	*mecánico*	me·ka·nee·ko
petrol/gas	*gasolina*	ga·so·lee·na
service station	*gasolinera*	ga·so·lee·ne·ra

Is this the road to ...?
¿Se va a ... por esta carretera? se va a ... por es·ta ka·re·te·ra

(How long) Can I park here?
¿(Cuánto tiempo) Puedo aparcar aquí? (kwan·to tyem·po) pwe·do a·par·kar a·kee

The car has broken down (at ...).
El coche se ha averiado (en ...). el ko·che se a a·ve·rya·do (en ...)

I have a flat tyre.
Tengo un pinchazo. ten·go oon peen·cha·so

I've run out of petrol.
Me he quedado sin gasolina. me e ke·da·do seen ga·so·lee·na

GLOSSARY

For terms for food, drinks and other culinary vocabulary, see p304. For additional terms and information about the Spanish language, see the Language chapter on p303. This glossary contains some words in Guna (G) – for more on their language, see boxed text, p232.

ANAM – Autoridad Nacional de Ambiente; former name for Panama's national environmental agency
ANCON – Asociación Nacional para la Conservación de la Naturaleza; National Association for the Conservation of Nature, Panama's leading private environmental organization
árbol – tree
artesanía – handicrafts

bahía – bay
balboa – the basic unit of Panamanian currency
baño(s) – restroom(s)
biblioteca – library
bocas – savory side dishes or appetizers
bohío – see rancho
boleto – ticket; for bus, museum etc
bolitas de carne – a snack of mildly spicy meatballs
boroquera – blowgun once used by the Emberá and Wounaan Indians
bote – motorized canoe

caballero(s) – gentleman (gentlemen)
cabaña – cabin
cacique – Guna tribal leader
calle – street
campesino/a – rural resident; peasant
carretera – highway
casa de cambio – money-exchange house
cascada – see chorro
catedral – cathedral
cayuco – dugout canoe
centavos – cent(s); 100 centavos equal one US dollar (or one Panamanian balboa)
cerro – hill
certificación de vuelo – certification of entry date into Panama
cerveza – beer
ceviche – marinated raw fish or shellfish
chévere – cool (slang)
chichas – heavily sweetened, fresh fruit drinks
chitra – sand fly
chiva – a rural bus, often a 28-seat Toyota coaster bus
chocosano (G) – storm that comes from the east
chorro – waterfall
cielo – the sky; the heavens
cine – cinema
ciudad – city
cocina – kitchen
cocobolo – a handsome tropical hardwood; used for carving life-sized images of snakes, parrots, toucans and other jungle wildlife
comarca – district
comida corriente – a set meal of rice, beans, plantains and a piece of meat or fish
conejo pintado – raccoon-like animal abundant in Parque Nacional Volcán Barú
cordillera – mountain range
corredor de aduana – customs broker
corvine – a flavorful white fish; Panama's most popular fish dish
cuatro por cuatro – 4WD vehicle
cuidado – caution
Cuna – See Guna

dama(s) – lady (ladies)
directo – direct bus
día feriado (días feriados) – national holiday(s)

edificio – building
Emberá – indigenous group living in Darién Province
empanada – corn turnover filled with ground meat, chicken, cheese or sweet fruit

feria – festival
fiesta – party
finca – farm
floresta – forest
frontera – border
fuerte – fort

Gali-Gali – the distinct Creole language of Bocas del Toro Province; it combines English, Spanish and Guaymí
galón (galones) – gallon(s); fluid measure of 3.79L
gringo/a – tourist; especially a North American tourist
gruta – cave
guacamayo – macaw
Guna – the 70,000-strong indigenous tribe living in the Comarca de Guna Yala

habano – Havana cigar
haras – stable (for horses)
hombre – man
hormiga – ant
hospedaje – guesthouse
huaca(s) – golden object(s); made on the Panamanian isthmus in the pre-Columbian era and buried with Indians
huevo(s) – egg(s)

iglesia – church
Interamericana – the Pan-American Hwy; the nearly continuous highway running from Alaska to Chile (it breaks at the Darién Gap)
invierno – winter
IPAT – Instituto Panameño de Turismo; the national tourism agency
isla – island

kilometraje – mileage
Kuna – see Guna

lago – lake

lancha – motorboat
lavamático/lavandería – laundromat
librería – bookstore
llanta – tire
llantería – tire repair shop
lleno – full
lluvia – rain
loro – parrot

manglar – mangrove
mariposa – butterfly
mercado – market
Merki (G) – American
mestizo/a – person of mixed indigenous and Spanish ancestry
metate – flat stone platform; used by Panama's pre-Columbian Indians to grind corn
migración – immigration
Migración y Naturalización – Immigration and Naturalization office
mirador – lookout point
molas (G) – colorful hand-stitched appliqué textiles made by Guna women
mono – monkey
montaña – mountain
muelle – pier
mujer(es) – woman (women)
museo – museum

Naso – an indigenous group scattered throughout the Bocas del Toro Province; also called the Teribe
Ngöbe Buglé – an indigenous tribe located largely in Chiriquí Province

ola(s) – wave(s)

pájaro – bird
palapa – thatched, palm leaf–roofed shelter with open sides
panadería – bakery
parada (de autobús) – bus stop
Patois – a local dialect on the islands of Boca del Toro; a blend of English, Spanish and Gali-Gali
penca – palm tree leaves
permiso de salida – exit permit
pescador – fisherman
pescar – to fish
pipa – coconut water, served straight from the husk
piragua – canoe carved from a tree trunk
playa – beach
polleras – the intricate, lacy, Spanish-influenced dresses of the Península de Azuero; the national dress of Panama for festive occasions
pozo(s) – spring(s)
preservativo(s) – condom(s)
prohibido – prohibited; forbidden
prórroga de turista – a permit that resembles a driver's license, complete with photo; it allows you to stay in Panama for longer than the 90 days permitted for tourists
propina – tip; gratuity
protector solar – sunscreen lotion
puente – bridge
puerto – port
punta – point
puro – cigar

quebrada – stream

rana – frog
rana dorada – golden frog
rancho – a thatched-roof hut
raspados – shaved ice flavored with fruit juice
regalo – gift; present
río – river

seco – an alcoholic drink made from sugarcane
selva – jungle
Semana Santa – Holy Week; preceding Easter
sendero – trail
serpiente – snake
serranía – mountain range
sol – sun
supermercado – supermarket

tabla – surfboard
tagua – an ivory-colored nut that is carved into tiny figurines
tajadas – ripe plantains sliced lengthwise and fried
taller – workshop
tamales – spiced ground corn with chicken or pork, boiled in banana leaves
tarjeta(s) – plastic phonecard(s)
tarjeta de circulación – vehicle control certificate
tasajo – dried meat cooked with vegetables
taxi marino – water taxi
tigre – jaguar
típico – typical; traditional Panamanian folk music
tortilla de maíz – a thick, fried cornmeal tortilla
tortuga – sea turtle
trucha – trout

urbano – local (as in buses)

valle – valley
verano – summer
viajero – traveler
viento – wind
volcán – volcano

waga (G) – tourist
Wounaan – indigenous group living in Darién Province

Behind the Scenes

SEND US YOUR FEEDBACK

We love to hear from travelers – your comments keep us on our toes and help make our books better. Our well-traveled team reads every word on what you loved or loathed about this book. Although we cannot reply individually to your submissions, we always guarantee that your feedback goes straight to the appropriate authors, in time for the next edition. Each person who sends us information is thanked in the next edition – the most useful submissions are rewarded with a selection of digital PDF chapters.

Visit **lonelyplanet.com/contact** to submit your updates and suggestions or to ask for help. Our award-winning website also features inspirational travel stories, news and discussions.

Note: We may edit, reproduce and incorporate your comments in Lonely Planet products such as guidebooks, websites and digital products, so let us know if you don't want your comments reproduced or your name acknowledged. For a copy of our privacy policy visit lonelyplanet.com/privacy.

OUR READERS

Many thanks to the travelers who used the last edition and wrote to us with helpful hints, useful advice and interesting anecdotes:

Alejandro Del Bosco, Andris Krumins, Anny Ruesink, Åsa Lidmark, Aylin Dincer, Eesha Williams, Elisa Rebella, Erika Scanu, Heikki Kivinen, Heko Köster, Jane Johnson, John Hardwick, Karen Okamoto, Kristin Panke, Kryssandra Heslop, Lee Scott, Lena Wendt, M Turnbull, Maribel Pinilla, Martin Dragt, Melinda Doughty, Renee Brown, Tony Adam, Victoria Budzisch, Will Martin

WRITER THANKS

Carolyn McCarthy

I am very indebted to the many locals, experts and travelers who shared their version of paradise. Ignacio and Judit were Caribbean dream captains. For assistance in the Darién, I'm indebted to Segundo Sugasti, Beatriz Schmidt and Maija Meri. Thanks to Sandra |Eleta for her hospitality. *Abrazos* to the Bethels, Catherine, Dave and Ellen for their exceptional company. Next time, el Camino Real. *Hasta la proxima!*

Steve Fallon

Muchas gracias to those who offered assistance, ideas and/or hospitality along the way, especially to my ATV-cruising partner, Carla Rankin, of Bocas del Toro town. Other helpful folk I met along the way included Juan José Calvache in Panama City; Loes Roos and Kees Groenendijk on Isla de Coiba and the Veraguas Sunset Coast; Alberto Young Lim in El Valle; Jane Walker and Barry Robbins in Boquete; and Brian and Amy Wilcox on Isla San Cristóbal. Thanks to co-writer Carolyn McCarthy for all the right contacts and to editor Bailey Johnson, who got me out of a mess more than once. My great love goes to my partner, Michael Rothschild, who can't believe I'm still alive after my encounter with that green-and-black poison-dart frog.

ACKNOWLEDGEMENTS

Climate map data adapted from Peel MC, Finlayson BL & McMahon TA (2007) 'Updated World Map of the Köppen-Geiger Climate Classification', Hydrology and Earth System Sciences, 11, 163344.

Cover photograph: Woman wearing decorative Guna arm beads, Bruce Yuanyue Bi / Getty Images ©

THIS BOOK

This 7th edition of Lonely Planet's *Panama* guidebook was researched and written by Steve Fallon and Carolyn McCarthy. The previous two editions were also written by Carolyn McCarthy. This guidebook was produced by the following:

Destination Editor Bailey Johnson

Product Editors Kate Chapman, Elizabeth Jones, Amanda Williamson

Senior Cartographers Mark Griffiths, Alison Lyall

Book Designer Cam Ashley

Assisting Editors Sarah Bailey, Peter Cruttenden, Lauren O'Connell, Susan Paterson

Cover Researcher Naomi Parker

Thanks to Melanie Dankel, James Hardy, Liz Heynes, Andi Jones, Anne Mason, Karyn Noble, Kirsten Rawlings, Angela Tinson, Tony Wheeler

Index

Map Pages **000**
Photo Pages **000**

INDEX D-I

Map Pages **000**
Photo Pages **000**

Map Pages **000**
Photo Pages **000**

Map Legend

Sights

- Beach
- Bird Sanctuary
- Buddhist
- Castle/Palace
- Christian
- Confucian
- Hindu
- Islamic
- Jain
- Jewish
- Monument
- Museum/Gallery/Historic Building
- Ruin
- Shinto
- Sikh
- Taoist
- Winery/Vineyard
- Zoo/Wildlife Sanctuary
- Other Sight

Activities, Courses & Tours

- Bodysurfing
- Diving
- Canoeing/Kayaking
- Course/Tour
- Sento Hot Baths/Onsen
- Skiing
- Snorkeling
- Surfing
- Swimming/Pool
- Walking
- Windsurfing
- Other Activity

Sleeping

- Sleeping
- Camping

Eating

- Eating

Drinking & Nightlife

- Drinking & Nightlife
- Cafe

Entertainment

- Entertainment

Shopping

- Shopping

Information

- Bank
- Embassy/Consulate
- Hospital/Medical
- Internet
- Police
- Post Office
- Telephone
- Toilet
- Tourist Information
- Other Information

Geographic

- Beach
- Gate
- Hut/Shelter
- Lighthouse
- Lookout
- Mountain/Volcano
- Oasis
- Park
- Pass
- Picnic Area
- Waterfall

Population

- Capital (National)
- Capital (State/Province)
- City/Large Town
- Town/Village

Transport

- Airport
- Border crossing
- Bus
- Cable car/Funicular
- Cycling
- Ferry
- Metro station
- Monorail
- Parking
- Petrol station
- Subway/Subte station
- Taxi
- Train station/Railway
- Tram
- Underground station
- Other Transport

Note: Not all symbols displayed above appear on the maps in this book

Routes

- Tollway
- Freeway
- Primary
- Secondary
- Tertiary
- Lane
- Unsealed road
- Road under construction
- Plaza/Mall
- Steps
- Tunnel
- Pedestrian overpass
- Walking Tour
- Walking Tour detour
- Path/Walking Trail

Boundaries

- International
- State/Province
- Disputed
- Regional/Suburb
- Marine Park
- Cliff
- Wall

Hydrography

- River, Creek
- Intermittent River
- Canal
- Water
- Dry/Salt/Intermittent Lake
- Reef

Areas

- Airport/Runway
- Beach/Desert
- Cemetery (Christian)
- Cemetery (Other)
- Glacier
- Mudflat
- Park/Forest
- Sight (Building)
- Sportsground
- Swamp/Mangrove

OUR STORY

A beat-up old car, a few dollars in the pocket and a sense of adventure. In 1972 that's all Tony and Maureen Wheeler needed for the trip of a lifetime – across Europe and Asia overland to Australia. It took several months, and at the end – broke but inspired – they sat at their kitchen table writing and stapling together their first travel guide, *Across Asia on the Cheap*. Within a week they'd sold 1500 copies. Lonely Planet was born.

Today, Lonely Planet has offices in Franklin, London, Melbourne, Oakland, Beijing and Delhi, with more than 600 staff and writers. We share Tony's belief that 'a great guidebook should do three things: inform, educate and amuse'.

OUR WRITERS

Carolyn McCarthy

Author of more than 30 travel guides, Carolyn McCarthy has been writing about the Americas since 1998. For this visit she rode dugout canoes in lawn chairs, saw hundreds of marine turtles hatching and spent hours in Panama City traffic. She also drank the water. This is her third time writing the Panama guide. Her work has also appeared in *BBC Magazine*, *National Geographic*, *Boston Globe*, *Outside* and other publications.

Steve Fallon

Born in the USA, Steve traveled to Latin America as a youngster. Somehow the middle bit, especially Panama, remained *terra incognita* to him beyond hats and a canal until Lonely Planet sent him packing. And what discoveries he made: hummingbirds' nests, cobalt-blue and scarlet frogs, a spider that spins a golden web. Then there was the coffee, the chocolate, the orchids, the beaches, the corals... He's said it once and he'll say it again: Panama, who knew?

Published by LP Global Limited
CRN 554153
7th edition – October 2016
ISBN 978 1 78657 117 5

10 9 8 7 6 5 4 3 2 1
Printed in China